T0335883

Intelligent Data Analysis:
Developing New Methodologies Through Pattern Discovery and Recovery

Hsiao-Fan Wang
National Tsing Hua University, Taiwan, ROC

INFORMATION SCIENCE REFERENCE

Hershey · New York

Director of Editorial Content:	Kristin Klinger
Managing Development Editor:	Kristin M. Roth
Senior Managing Editor:	Jennifer Neidig
Managing Editor:	Jamie Snavely
Assistant Managing Editor:	Carole Coulson
Copy Editor:	Jennifer Young
Typesetter:	Chris Hrobak
Cover Design:	Lisa Tosheff
Printed at:	Yurchak Printing Inc.

Published in the United States of America by
Information Science Reference (an imprint of IGI Global)
701 E. Chocolate Avenue, Suite 200
Hershey PA 17033
Tel: 717-533-8845
Fax: 717-533-8661
E-mail: cust@igi-global.com
Web site: http://www.igi-global.com

and in the United Kingdom by
Information Science Reference (an imprint of IGI Global)
3 Henrietta Street
Covent Garden
London WC2E 8LU
Tel: 44 20 7240 0856
Fax: 44 20 7379 0609
Web site: http://www.eurospanbookstore.com

Product or company names used in this set are for identification purposes only. Inclusion of the names of the products or companies does not indicate a claim of ownership by IGI Global of the trademark or registered trademark.

Library of Congress Cataloging-in-Publication Data

Intelligent data analysis : developing new methodologies through pattern discovery and recovery / Hsiao-Fan Wang, Editor.

    p. cm.

  Summary: "This book tackles those data sets and covers a variety of issues in relation to intelligent data analysis so that patterns from frequent or rare events in spatial or temporal spaces can be revealed. This book brings together current research, results, problems, and applications from both theoretical and practical approaches"--Provided by publisher.

  ISBN-13: 978-1-59904-982-3 (hardcover)

  ISBN-13: 978-1-59904-983-0 (e-book)

  1. Pattern perception--Data processing. 2. Artificial intelligence. I. Wang, Hsiao-Fan.

  Q327.I545 2008

  003'.52--dc22

                                    2007046947

British Cataloguing in Publication Data
A Cataloguing in Publication record for this book is available from the British Library.

All work contributed to this book set is original material. The views expressed in this book are those of the authors, but not necessarily of the publisher.

Editorial Advisory Board

Table of Contents

Section I
Introduction

Section II
Pattern Discovery from Huge Data Set: Methodologies

Section III
Pattern Discovery from Huge Data Set: Applications

Section IV
Pattern Recovery from Small Data Set: Methodologies and Applications

Detailed Table of Contents

Section I
Introduction

Chapter I

    Martin Spott, Intelligent Systems Research Centre, UK
    Detlef Nauck, Intelligent Systems Research Centre, UK

Chapter I. provides a software platform for automatic data analysis that uses a fuzzy knowledge base for automatically selecting and executing data analysis methods. The authors show that a system based on a fuzzy pattern base that stores heuristic expert knowledge from data analysis can successfully lead to automatic intelligent data analysis. Therefore, the system is able to support business users in running data analysis projects more efficiently

Chapter II

    Hung T. Nguyen, New Mexico State University, USA
    Vladik Kreinovich, University of Texas at El Paso, USA
    Gang Xiang, University of Texas at El Paso, USA

Chapter II provides a rigorous theory of random fuzzy sets in its most general form. Imprecise data which are both random and fuzzy are focused. Critical issues in relation to such kind of data with hybrid natures are discussed and a framework based on Probability Theory is proposed for analysis.

Chapter III highlights meaningful pattern discovery techniques for gene expression data. The properties of gene expression data themselves are examined and the possible patterns are suggested. The classes of clustering techniques in the context of their application to gene expression data are investigated and a comparative analysis of standard and non-standard methods is given with the suggestion of areas for possible future development.

Chapter IV describes the use of fast, data-mining algorithms such as TreeNet and Random Forests (Salford Systems Ltd) to identify ecologically meaningful patterns and relationships in subsets of data that carry various degrees of outliers and uncertainty. An example of using satellite data from a wintering Golden Eagle shows that the proposed approach has provided a promising tool for wildlife ecology and conservation management.

Chapter V applies Atanassov's theory of intuitionistic fuzzy sets to analyze imbalanced and overlapping classes by defining both the membership and non-membership degrees for each member. Since imbalanced and overlapping classes are a real challenge for the standard classifiers. The method proposed in this chapter is crucial not only in theory but also on many different types of real tasks.

Section II
Pattern Discovery from Huge Data Set: Methodologies

Chapter VI introduces fuzzy neural network models as means for knowledge discovery from databases. It not only describes architectures and learning algorithms for fuzzy neural networks, but also proposes an algorithm for extracting and optimizing classification rules from a trained fuzzy neural network. An example of multispectral satellite images is given and it shows that the presented models and the methodology for generating classification rules from data samples provide a valuable tool for knowledge discovery.

Chapter VII discusses the paradigm of genetic algorithms and their incorporation into machine learning. Special attention is given to 3 issues: (a) The ways of initialization of a population for a genetic algorithm, (b) representation of chromosomes in genetic algorithms, and (c) discretization and fuzzification of numerical attributes for genetic algorithms. Furthermore, this chapter surveys new trends of dealing with the variable-length chromosomes and other issues related to the genetic learners.

Chapter VIII introduces the evolutionary computing as a whole and discusses specifically in details on two sub-areas of nature-inspired computing in Evolutionary Computing, namely, Evolutionary Algorithms and Swarm Intelligence. The theoretical background of these sub-areas are illustrated with demonstration of some real-world applications. The chapter also points out future trends and directions in these areas.

Chapter IX proposes two composite approaches which combine conventional data fitting with peak-matching to cope with 'noise' data in solving an inverse light scattering problem for single, spherical, homogeneous particles using least squares global optimization and show that they lead to a more robust identification procedure.

Chapter X

Chapter X introduces an approach called *Markov chain Monte Carlo* for the *exact* simulation of sample values from complex distributions. The proposed algorithm facilitates the implementation of a Markov chain that has a given distribution as its stationary distribution. The applications of these algorithms in probabilistic data analysis and inference are given.

Section III
Pattern Discovery from Huge Data Set: Applications

Chapter XI

Chapter XI provides suitable knowledge bases (KBs) for carrying out forward and reverse mappings of Tungsten Inert Gas (TIG) welding process. Both the forward as well as reverse mappings are required for an effective on-line control of a process. Although conventional statistical regression analysis is able to carry out the forward mapping efficiently, it may not be always able to solve the problem of reverse mapping. Fuzzy logic (FL)-based approaches are adopted to conduct the forward and reverse mappings of the TIG welding process and they have shown to solve the above problem efficiently.

Chapter XII

Chapter XII concerns a problem of road travel in the US, namely the discernment of the levels of traffic fatalities across the individual states. Based on the cognitive uncertainties evident in the imprecision inherent with the data values, a fuzzy approach to decision tree is adopted for inference. The results show that the inference from the tree structure takes advantage of the ability of humans to distinguish between patterns and observable characteristics.

Chapter XIII provides a method to resolve the major problem of time discontinuity resulting from the transactional character of events in telecom market. By gradually enriching the data information content from the prior lifetime expectancy through standard static events data up to decay-weighted data sequences, the proposed sequential processing of appropriately preprocessed data streams is shown to be able to have better performance of customer churn prediction.

Chapter XIV applies Dempster-Shafer Theory to object classification and ranking. Based on this theory, a method called CaRBS is proposed and an application to cope with uncertain reasoning on Moody's Bank Financial Strength Rating (BFSR) process is demonstrated. The value of this chapter is placed on the measures of ignorance such that during a series of classification and ranking analyses, decision on adopting or abandoning the existing evidence can be determined.

Chapter XV illustrates how to describe the individual's preference structure and utilize its properties to define an individual's risk level for the confronted risk. Then, a response evaluation model was proposed to develop the appropriate response strategy. These two stages of risk analysis and a risk response contribute to a complete individual risk management process (IRM). A case of A-C court was demonstrated and the results showed that the proposed method is able to provide more useful and pertinent information than the traditional method of decision tree which is based on the expected monetary value (EMV).

Section IV
Pattern Recovery from Small Data Set: Methodologies and Applications

Chapter XVI introduces the use of the bootstrap in a nonlinear, nonparametric regression framework with dependent errors. The AR-Sieve bootstrap and the Moving Block bootstrap which are used to generate bootstrap replicates with a proper dependence structure are used to avoid the inconsistent choice inherent in conventional Bootstrap method. In the framework of neural network models which are often used as an accurate nonparametric estimation and prediction tool, both procedures have shown to have satisfactory results.

Chapter XVII

    Lean Yu, Chinese Academy of Sciences, China & City University of Hong Kong, Hong Kong
    Shouyang Wang, Chinese Academy of Sciences, China
    Kin Keung Lai, City University of Hong Kong, Hong Kong

Chapter XVII proposes a methodology based on Hilbert-EMD-based support vector machine (SVM) to predict financial crisis events for early-warning purpose. A typical financial indicator currency exchange rate reflecting economic fluctuation conditions is first chosen. Then the Hilbert-EMD algorithm is applied to the economic indicator series. This chapter also applies the proposed method to two real-world cases of South Korea and Thailand who suffered from the 1997-1998 disastrous financial crisis experience. The results show that the proposed Hilbert-EMD-based SVM methodology is capable of predicting the financial crisis events effectively.

Chapter XVIII

    Chun-Jung Huang, National Tsing Hua University, Taiwan, ROC
    Hsiao-Fan Wang, National Tsing Hua University, Taiwan, ROC

Chapter XVIII proposed an alternative approach named Data Construction Analysis (DCA) to overcome the problem derived from insufficient data, in particular, the defects existent in one commonly used approach called *Intervalized Kernel method of Density Estimation* (IKDE). Comparative studies have shown that the proposed DCA is not only resolve the insufficient data in general; but also improve the prediction accuracy in both degrees and stability of IKDE. From the content described above, it can be noted that this book will be useful for both researchers and practitioners who are interested in receiving comprehensive views and insights from the variety of issues covered in this book in relation to pattern discovery and recovery. In particular, those who have been working on data analysis will have an overall picture of the existing and potential developments on the issues related to intelligent pattern recognition

Foreword

Professor Hsiao-Fan Wang has prepared a technically excellent and timely book on a new, important, and rapidly developing area of research and applications: *Intelligent Data Analysis: Developing New Methodologies through Pattern Discovery and Recovery.*

This book includes two categories of non-classical data analysis of Data Mining and Data Construction. It is perhaps the first book that provides comprehensive methodologies and real case applications towards huge data warehouses and small data nests. In particular, the book takes the viewpoint of pattern recognition and demonstrates that the tools developed can be applied to studies in learning and decision making of general human activities as a whole.

Professor Hsiao-Fan Wang should be congratulated for an outstanding job on this edited version of the book. Her vision on placing the theme on this rapidly developed yet very basic agenda of data analysis is valuable and significant. Professor Wang's balanced approach between theories and applications is a reflection of her own extensive research experience. Her way to tackle small data samples demonstrates very well her deep understanding of the needs and the trends of development in the real engineering world. While data mining has become a matured research area, developing data construction techniques for such rare events will undoubtedly draw more and more research attention in the future.

As we are entering an era in which machine intelligence and artificial intelligence will play significant roles in the design of intelligent and complex systems, the problem of recognizing patterns from either huge or small data set will continue to challenge the researchers and practitioners. And I am sure this book will play an important role in motivating a leading further development and applications in the area of intelligent data analysis.

Chung Laung Liu
Honorary Chair Professor
National Tsing Hua University

C.L. Liu received his advanced degrees from the Massachusetts Institute of Technology. He taught at MIT, the University of Illinois at Urbana Champaign, and the National Tsing Hua University. From 1996 to 1998, he served as associate provost at UIUC. From 1988 to 2002, he was president of National Tsing Hua University (NTHU). Dr. Liu is a member of Academia Sinica, and also, fellow of IEEE and ACM. After his term as president of NTHU, Dr. Liu continues his teaching and research activities. He also serves as consultant to high tech companies, works for a charitable foundation in Hong Kong, and, in the last two years, hosts a weekly radio show on technology and humanities in the radio station IC975 in Hsinchu, Taiwan, ROC.

Preface

Intelligent Data Analysis: Developing New Methodologies Through Pattern Discovery and Recovery provides learning tools of finding data patterns based on artificial intelligence. Pattern Recognition has a long history of applications to data analysis in business, military, and social economic activities. While the aim of pattern recognition is to discover the pattern of a data set, the size of the data set is closely related to the methodology one adopts for analysis. The classic approach is using certain statistical techniques to deal with data sets of more than 30 samples and by dimension reduction to reveal the pattern. With the rapid increase of Internet development and usage, the amount of data has been enormous. The term "Data Warehouse" has been used to describe such quantities of data and the corresponding methodologies for analysis are under the title of "data mining."

In contrast to the huge amount of data sets, there is another type of data set which is small (less than 30), but still is significant in terms of socioeconomic cost. Consider severe earthquakes, random terrorist attacks, and nuclear plant explosions; the occurrences of such events are relatively few that the conventional statistic assumptions cannot be verified and thus the methods fail to apply. The ability to predict such kinds of events remains a challenge for the researchers. This leads to the necessity of recovering a pattern by constructing data.

Apart from these two extreme cases related to the amount of data which affect the method of analysis to be adopted, the types of the data are another major factor needed to be considered. Since in reality, the collected data are never complete, a certain degree of uncertainty is always embedded. The classical approach to coping with uncertainty is based on Probability Theory in random nature. Along with different methodologies and observations being investigated, data types other than randomness are studied and explored. Among these, fuzzy data, grey data, and coarse data with their hybrid forms are studied most extensively. The results pave a way to find data patterns from binary groupings to degree of belongings in more accurate and precise manner.

For all of these data types in quantity and quality, apart from Probability Inference being adopted for analysis, a group of heuristic approaches, namely soft computing (or computational intelligence), has been developed and employed for different areas of applications. Fuzzy logic, evolutionary computing, neural net analysis, and so on have shown their capability in coping with such kinds of data sets. It is an art and science for intelligent data analysis

Since pattern recognition has been a learning process ever since living beings began, classical approaches to classifying data into binary groups have been enormous in the literature. Due to the increasing impact of extreme events on the socio-economic costs, 38 authors from 10 different countries contributed their findings to 18 chapters in this book, each addresses different issues of intelligent pattern discovery and recovery from both theoretical and practical viewpoints. The readers will benefit from the integration of these two extreme cases in a comparative manner.

The book is categorized into four sections. After an introduction of the up-to-date development and research on methodologies and data properties in Section I, issues and resolution of pattern discovery from huge data set are discussed and applied respectively in Sections II and III. Finally, in Section IV, methodology developments and the possible applications of pattern recovery from small data sets are presented. It can be noted from the unbalanced numbers of chapters related to huge data sets and small data sets, methods related to pattern recovery from small data set require the devotion of more researchers. The outline of each chapter is given below.

In **Section I**, five chapters are included, as outlined below:

Chapter I provides a software platform for automatic data analysis that uses a fuzzy knowledge base for automatically selecting and executing data analysis methods. The authors show that a system based on a fuzzy pattern base that stores heuristic expert knowledge from data analysis can successfully lead to automatic intelligent data analysis. Therefore, the system is able to support business users in running data analysis projects more efficiently

Chapter II provides a rigorous theory of random fuzzy sets in its most general form. We focus on imprecise data which are both random and fuzzy. Critical issues in relation to such kinds of data with hybrid natures are discussed and a framework based on Probability Theory is proposed for analysis.

Chapter III highlights meaningful pattern discovery techniques for gene expression data. The properties of gene expression data themselves are examined and the possible patterns are suggested. The classes of clustering techniques in the context of their application to gene expression data are investigated and a comparative analysis of standard and non-standard methods is given with the suggestion of areas for possible future development.

Chapter IV describes the use of fast, data-mining algorithms such as TreeNet and Random Forests (Salford Systems Ltd) to identify ecologically meaningful patterns and relationships in subsets of data that carry various degrees of outliers and uncertainty. An example of using satellite data from a wintering golden eagle shows that the proposed approach has provided a promising tool for wildlife ecology and conservation management.

Chapter V applies Atanassov's theory of intuitionistic fuzzy sets to analyze imbalanced and overlapping classes by defining both the membership and non-membership degrees for each member. Since imbalanced and overlapping classes are a real challenge for the standard classifiers, the method proposed in this chapter is crucial not only in theory but also on many different types of real tasks.

Section II of methodologies regarding pattern discovery from huge data set contains five chapters; each is introduced as below:

Chapter VI introduces fuzzy neural network models as a means for knowledge discovery from databases. It not only describes architectures and learning algorithms for fuzzy neural networks, but also proposes an algorithm for extracting and optimizing classification rules from a trained fuzzy neural network. An example of multispectral satellite images is given and it shows that the presented models and the methodology for generating classification rules from data samples provide a valuable tool for knowledge discovery.

Chapter VII discusses the paradigm of genetic algorithms and their incorporation into machine learning. Special attention is given to three issues: (a) the ways of initialization of a population for a genetic algorithm, (b) representation of chromosomes in genetic algorithms, and (c) discretization and fuzzification of numerical attributes for genetic algorithms. Furthermore, this chapter surveys new trends of dealing with the variable-length chromosomes and other issues related to the genetic learners.

Chapter VIII introduces the evolutionary computing as a whole and discusses specifically in detail two sub-areas of nature-inspired computing in Evolutionary Computing; namely, evolutionary algorithms and swarm intelligence. The theoretical background of these sub-areas is illustrated with demonstration of some real-world applications. The chapter also points out future trends and directions in these areas.

Chapter IX proposes two composite approaches which combine conventional data fitting with peak-matching to cope with "noise" data in solving an inverse light scattering problem for single, spherical, homogeneous particles using least squares global optimization and show that they lead to a more robust identification procedure.

Chapter X introduces an approach called *Markov chain Monte Carlo* for the *exact* simulation of sample values from complex distributions. The proposed algorithm facilitates the implementation of a Markov chain that has a given distribution as its stationary distribution. The applications of these algorithms in probabilistic data analysis and inference are given.

Section III of the applications of pattern discovery from huge data set contains five cases from different industrial sectors of manufactory, transportation, and services:

Chapter XI provides suitable knowledge bases (KBs) for carrying out forward and reverse mappings of the Tungsten Inert Gas (TIG) welding process. Both the forward as well as reverse mappings are required for an effective online control of a process. Although conventional statistical regression analysis is able to carry out the forward mapping efficiently, it may not be always able to solve the problem of reverse mapping. Fuzzy logic (FL)-based approaches are adopted to conduct the forward and reverse mappings of the TIG welding process and they have shown to solve the above problem efficiently.

Chapter XII concerns a problem of road travel in the US, namely the discernment of the levels of traffic fatalities across the individual states. Based on the cognitive uncertainties evident in the imprecision inherent with the data values, a fuzzy approach to decision tree is adopted for inference. The results show that the inference from the tree structure takes advantage of the ability of humans to distinguish between patterns and observable characteristics.

Chapter XIII provides a method to resolve the major problem of time discontinuity resulting from the transactional character of events in telecom market. By gradually enriching the data information content from the prior lifetime expectancy through standard static events data up to decay-weighted data sequences, the proposed sequential processing of appropriately preprocessed data streams is shown to be able to have better performance of customer churn prediction.

Chapter XIV applies Dempster-Shafer Theory to object classification and ranking. Based on this theory, a method called CaRBS is proposed and an application to cope with uncertain reasoning on Moody's Bank Financial Strength Rating (BFSR) process is demonstrated. The value of this chapter is placed on the measures of ignorance such that during a series of classification and ranking analyses, decision on adopting or abandoning the existing evidence can be determined.

Chapter XV illustrates how to describe the individual's preference structure and utilize its properties to define an individual's risk level for the confronted risk. Then, a response evaluation model was proposed to develop the appropriate response strategy. These two stages of risk analysis and a risk response contribute to a complete individual risk management process (IRM). A case of A-C court was demonstrated and the results showed that the proposed method is able to provide more useful and pertinent information than the traditional method of decision tree which is based on the expected monetary value (EMV).

Section IV contains three chapters of current methodologies developed for analyzing small sample sets with illustrations of their applications.

Chapter XVI introduces the use of the bootstrap in a nonlinear, nonparametric regression framework with dependent errors. The AR-Sieve bootstrap and the Moving Block bootstrap which are used to generate bootstrap replicates with a proper dependence structure are used to avoid the inconsistent choice inherent in conventional Bootstrap method. In the framework of neural network models which are often used as an accurate nonparametric estimation and prediction tool, both procedures have shown to have satisfactory results.

Chapter XVII proposes a methodology based on Hilbert-EMD-based support vector machine (SVM) to predict financial crisis events for early-warning purpose. A typical financial indicator currency exchange rate reflecting economic fluctuation conditions is first chosen. Then the Hilbert-EMD algorithm is applied to the economic indicator series. This chapter also applies the proposed method to two real-world cases of South Korea and Thailand, which suffered from the 1997-1998 disastrous financial crisis experience. The results show that the proposed Hilbert-EMD-based SVM methodology is capable of predicting the financial crisis events effectively.

Chapter XVIII proposed an alternative approach named Data Construction Method (DCM) to overcome the problems derived from insufficient data; in particular, the defects existent in one commonly used approach called *Intervalized Kernel method of Density Estimation* (IKDE). Comparative studies have shown that the proposed DCA is not only resolve the insufficient data in general; but also improve the prediction accuracy in both degrees and stability of IKDE.

From the content described above, it can be noted that this book will be useful for both researchers and practitioners who are interested in receiving comprehensive views and insights from the variety of issues covered in this book in relation to pattern discovery and recovery. In particular, those who have been working on data analysis will have an overall picture of the existing and potential developments on the issues related to intelligent pattern recognition.

Hsiao-Fan Wang
National Tsing Hua University

Acknowledgment

The editor would like to acknowledge the help of all involved in the collation and review process of the book, without whose support the project could not have been satisfactorily completed. Deep appreciation and gratitude is due to two organizations of the Department of Management, University of Canterbury, NZ and National Science Council, Taiwan, ROC for their facility and financial support this year as visiting professor.

Deep gratitude first is sent to Dr. Chung Laung Liu, the formal president of National Tsing Hua University, for his Foreword, full of encouragement and kind support. We also would like to thank all authors for their excellent contributions to this volume. In particular, most of the authors of chapters included in this book also served as referees for chapters written by other authors. Thanks go to all those who provided comprehensive reviews and constructive comments. Special thanks also go to the publishing team at IGI Global, in particular to Ross Miller and Jessica Thompson, who continuously prodded via e-mail to keep the project on schedule and to Mehdi Khosrow-Pour, whose enthusiasm motivated me to initially accept his invitation for taking on this project.

Special thanks go to National Tsing Hua University and the colleagues of the Department of Industrial Engineering and Engineering Management in Taiwan, without their understanding and support, this volume won't be possible.

Finally, I wish to thank my boys, I-Fan (Daniel) and Tao-Fan (Ray), for their understanding and immense love during this project.

Editor,
Hsiao-Fan Wang
Tsing Hua Chair Professor
Taiwan, Republic of China
October 2007

Section I
Introduction

Chapter I
Automatic Intelligent Data Analysis

Martin Spott
Intelligent Systems Research Centre, UK

Detlef Nauck
Intelligent Systems Research Centre, UK

ABSTRACT

This chapter introduces a new way of using soft constraints for selecting data analysis methods that match certain user requirements. It presents a software platform for automatic data analysis that uses a fuzzy knowledge base for automatically selecting and executing data analysis methods. In order to support business users in running data analysis projects the analytical process must be automated as much as possible. The authors argue that previous approaches based on the formalisation of analytical processes were less successful because selecting and running analytical methods is very much an experience-led heuristic process. The authors show that a system based on a fuzzy knowledge base that stores heuristic expert knowledge about data analysis can successfully lead to automatic intelligent data analysis.

INTRODUCTION

Data is one of the most valuable assets of today's businesses and timely and accurate analysis of available data is essential for making the right decisions and competing in today's ever-changing business environment. Most businesses today face the *analytics challenge* and build ever-growing data warehouses but face a lack in analytical competence and resources. Data owners typically are domain experts who understand the processes that generated the data and what the data represents. However, data owners typically are not at the same time expert analysts and struggle with the application of advanced analytics. Passing data on to an analyst results in a *communication challenge* that requires the domain expert to explain the data context and generate a problem statement that the analyst can use as the basis for analysing the data. When that has been done the analyst has to present the results in a way that the data owner can relate them to his context and derive valuable information for future decision making.

What then follows is an *application challenge* that requires IT support staff to turn analytical results into software that can be integrated into operational systems. With the introduction of data analysis functionality in databases and a standardised language for model descriptions like PMML (Predictive Model Markup Language) defined by the Data Mining Group (www.dmg. org), the integration may become simpler in the future. Under the assumption that the analysis tool is able to create a PMML description for the model in question and the database implements the underlying analysis algorithm, the PMML description can simply be included in a database script (e.g., PL/SQL for Oracle databases) that will be used to analyse data in the operational system. However, it still will take many years before data analysis is standard in databases and a large variety of models can be transferred in that way.

Commercial data analysis software that is aimed at a business context either is too simplistic and the manufacturer has decided to provide only limited functionality that non-expert users can handle or the software is too complex and provides advanced functionality that is aimed directly at expert analysts. In order to overcome both the analytics challenge and the communication challenge, tools are required that empower domain experts and data owners to run advanced analytics themselves with as little help from analysts as possible. One approach is to hide complex analytics under a layer of automation that provides an interface that allows users to work goal-oriented instead of method-oriented.

In this chapter we describe an approach to automating data analysis based on a fuzzy matching approach between user requirements and features of analytical models. We first discuss some general issues around automating analytics and then we present a software system that implements our approach.

AUTOMATING DATA ANALYSIS

When we talk about data analysis in this chapter we refer to the task of discovering a relationship between a number of attributes and representing this relationship in form of a model. Typically, we are interested in determining the value of some attributes given some other attributes (inference) or in finding groups of attribute-value combinations (segmentation). In this context we will not consider describing parameters of attribute distributions or visualisation.

Models are typically used to support a decision making process by inferring or predicting the (currently unknown) values of some output attributes given some input attributes or by determining a group to which the currently observed data record possibly belongs to. In this scenario we expect a model to be as accurate as possible. Models also can be used to explain a relationship between attributes. In this scenario we want a model to be interpretable.

A model is created in a (machine) learning process, where the parameters of the models are adapted based on set of training data. The learning process can be controlled by a separate validation set to prevent over-generalisation on the training set. The model performance is finally tested on a different test set.

In business environments data and problem owners are typically domain experts, but not data analysis experts. That means they do not have the required knowledge to decide which type of model and learning algorithm to choose, how to set the parameters of the learning procedure, how to adequately test the learned model, and so on. In order to support this group of users, we have developed an approach for automating data analysis to some extent.

Previous approaches towards automating data analysis or knowledge discovery in databases were based on AI techniques. Analysis methods were broken down into formal blocks and user requirements were also represented in a formal language. Then a search algorithm would identify suitable blocks and arrange them in a way to carry out an analysis process (Wirth, Shearer, Grimmer, Reinartz, Schloesser, Breitner, Engels, & Lindner 1997). These approaches had to face the problem of formalising mainly heuristic methods and that it is usually not feasible to formally compute all necessary parameters to execute an analysis method. Other authors discussed mainly architectural features of systems that could automate data analysis or data mining and avoided discussing how to automatically select and execute analysis methods (Botia, Velasco, Garijo, & Skarmeta, 1998; Botia, Skarmeta, Velasco, & Garijo 2000).

A more recent approach and the system closest to our approach regarding the required capabilities is the one described by Bernstein and Provost (2001) and Bernstein, Hill, and Provost (2002). Their system uses an ontology-based approach and simply describes analysis methods and pre-/post-processing methods as input/output blocks with specific interfaces. The system is built on top of the data analysis package Weka (Witten & Frank, 2000). If the interfaces between two blocks match, they can be concatenated in an analysis process. If a user wants to analyse a data set, all possible analysis processes are created and executed. Once a suitable analysis process has been identified, it can be stored, re-used, and shared. The authors suggest a heuristic ranking of analysis processes in order to execute only the best processes. However, they only use speed as a ranking criterion, which can be easily determined as a feature of an algorithm. More useful features about the

quality of the analysis like accuracy obviously are dependent on the analysis process as well as the analysed data and are much more difficult to determine up front. Therefore, the reported results have not been very encouraging so far.

In this chapter we describe a different approach that we have followed. We have used a fuzzy knowledge base that maps user requirements onto properties of analysis methods by using a fuzzy compatibility measure (Spott & Nauck, 2005). Each requirement is represented by a fuzzy variable that assumes weighted combinations of fuzzy words as values (Spott, 2001, 2005). Rather than modelling the weights as probabilities as Spott (2001, 2005) describes, we assume a possibility density function (Gebhard & Kruse, 1993; Spott, 2001) on the fuzzy words, which allows for alternative values which, as an extreme case, could all be possible without restriction. This allows a user to easily specify alternatives he is equally happy to accept as the outcome of a modelling process.

When conducting any kind of data analysis and planning to use the results in an application we can assume to have the following.

1. **A problem definition:** What is the problem we would like to solve? Do we want to predict or classify, find groups (segmentation, clustering), rules or dependencies, and so on?

2. **Preferences regarding the solution:** If the model can be adapted to new data, if it is easy to understand (rule-based, simple functions), its accuracy, execution time, and so on.

Experts in data analysis are well aware of these analysis problems and preferences. In the following, we assume that the data has already been prepared for analysis, that is, it has been compiled from different data sources, if necessary, and formatted in a way that it can be used by standard data analysis tools. This process is mostly done with ETL tools (Extract, Transform, and Load). An expert would then perform the following steps.

1. Choose analysis algorithms which are suited for the problem and the given preferences.
2. If required pre-process the data to make it suitable for the selected algorithms.
3. Configure the training parameters of the algorithms.
4. Run the algorithms, check the performance of the created models and compare against the preferences again.
5. If further improvement seems necessary and possible, go back to Step 3.
6. Implement the model in an executable form.
7. Integrate the executable model into an operational system.

In the following section we introduce the software environment SPIDA and illustrate how it covers Steps 1-5. Then we will describe the theoretical concepts SPIDA uses to match user preferences to attributes of data analysis methods.

The final two steps of the above list are discussed after that.

SPIDA

We have developed a research prototype of an automatic intelligent data analysis platform that uses a fuzzy knowledge base to encode expert knowledge about data analysis algorithms. SPIDA (Soft Computing Platform for Intelligent Data Analysis; Nauck, Spott, & Azvine, 2003) is a Java based client/server application that is capable of:

- Automatically creating a data analysis model based on user requirements,
- Wrapping a learned model into an executable analytical module for integration with operational systems, and
- Monitoring the performance of an operational system and trigger the generation of a new analytical module in case of performance deterioration.

Figure 1. The SPIDA Wizard allows users to specify several high-level preferences for the outcome of the analysis process. Preferences for an explanation facility, for example, are used to select appropriate data analysis algorithms while preferences for accuracy and simplicity can only be used after models have been built.

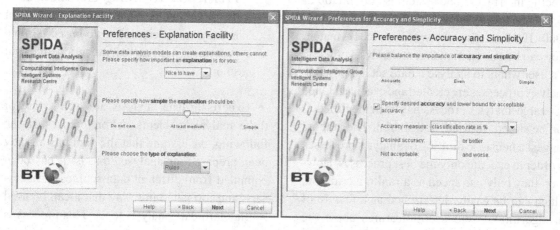

SPIDA provides a wizard interface that guides non-expert users through the data analysis process. The process starts with identifying a data source which can be loaded from an ASCII file, a spreadsheet, or a database connection and completes with an analytical model that can be used to process data in the same format as the initially selected data source.

The user begins with stating the purpose of the analysis. The current version supports prediction (i.e., classification and regression) and finding groups (i.e., clustering). After identifying a data source SPIDA loads the data and automatically identifies the type of variables present in the data. The user can override the type selection and assign any variable as the target of the subsequent analysis. In the next few steps the user can specify some high-level preferences for the outcome of the analysis process (Figure 1). For example, the user can specify if the model should be interpretable, that is, it should be possible to explain how a certain output value was computed. It is possible to specify the simplicity of the explanation and the type of explanation (rules or equations). Simplicity is measured by the number of parameters in the model. For a rule-based model,

for example, a model with, say, 10 rules using two to three variables each would be considered simpler than a model with eight rules using five variables each.

The fact that the user prefers an interpretable model is used in the selection process for analysis methods. A neural network, for example, is considered not to be interpretable, while a decision tree is.

Other preferences like accuracy and simplicity of the model can only be evaluated after models have been built and can only be used in selecting the best model.

After the user has selected the preferences important to him SPIDA can automatically decide which analysis methods can be applied to the data that has been loaded and how well each method matches those user preferences that can be compared against method features. SPIDA uses a fuzzy knowledge base for this purpose. The knowledge base encodes heuristic expert knowledge about the suitability of analysis methods. For each method certain features are defined, for example, what kind of data it can process, if it produces an interpretable model, if it can adapt to new data, and so on. The knowledge base compares these features against the specifications of the loaded data and the selected user preferences and assigns a suitability score to each applicable method (Figure 2). The user can now let SPIDA automatically create models based on all identified methods or intervene and execute only a subset.

All selected methods are then automatically configured, executed and evaluated. This is done for all methods in parallel and possibly iteratively if the model evaluation reveals that the results are not yet satisfactory and do not match the user requirements sufficiently.

In the current version SPIDA supports the following data analysis methods: neural networks (classification and regression), neuro-fuzzy systems (classification and regression), support vector machines (classification and regression), decision trees (classification), linear regression, and fuzzy

Figure 2. Based on the type of data, the required analysis type (here: classification) and the user preferences, SPIDA selects suitable analysis methods and ranks their suitability.

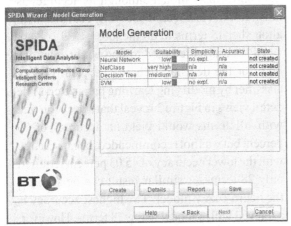

Figure 3. After models have been built, SPIDA re-evaluates their suitability based on the outcome of the learning process. For some algorithms the SPIDA fuzzy knowledge base contains heuristics for re-running the learning process with different parameters in order to find simpler or more accurate solutions. The solution that best matches the requirements is automatically selected.

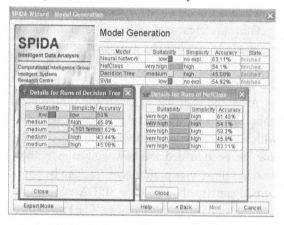

cluster analysis (finding groups). In addition SPIDA provides a large number of data filters for treatment of missing values, re-coding, scaling and normalisation, variables selection, record selection (e.g., for splitting data into training and test sets for cross-validation), and so on.

In order to execute a particular analysis method, SPIDA automatically pre-processes or re-codes the data in order to convert it to a format the analysis method can process. For example, if the method cannot handle missing values those can be imputed automatically based on different strategies. If the method can only handle numeric data, but symbolic data is present this can be re-encoded numerically. This is done, for example, for neural networks. Created models are evaluated automatically against test data that has been withheld from the model training process. The model performance and other features like simplicity are then compared against the user preferences again based on the rules encoded in the SPIDA knowledge base. If SPIDA concludes

that the match with the user preferences is insufficient it uses heuristics from the knowledge base to change the parameters controlling the model creation process. For example, if a neural network is not providing good enough accuracy, SPIDA may decide to repeat the training process using more hidden neurons. A decision tree, for example, could be re-build with stronger pruning parameters if it turns out that it is too complex for the required level of simplicity.

In Figure 3 the outcome of an analytical process on the glass data set is shown. The glass data set is a forensic data set of 214 records about six types of glass described by nine attributes. The data set is available at the UCI Machine Learning Repository (UCI, 2007). By default SPIDA uses 50 percent of the data for model building and 50 percent for testing. For this example, we requested a "simple" model, that is, the balance between accuracy and simplicity was skewed towards simplicity (Figure 1). SPIDA decided to build a neural network, a neuro-fuzzy classifier based on the NEFCLASS algorithm (Nauck, 2003), a decision tree and a support vector machine. The most accurate model found is the neural network with 63.11 percent accuracy on the test data. However, SPIDA ranks its suitability as low, because the specified user requirements in this example requested a simple interpretable model, preferably based on rules. A neural network is not interpretable in terms of rules. The most suitable model in this example is the neuro-fuzzy model although its accuracy is much lower. However, it uses only six rules with altogether 15 terms to do the job.

SPIDA has attempted to find better solutions both for the decision tree and the neuro-fuzzy classifier by modifying learning parameters. The detail views in Figure 3 reveal that a decision tree with 101 terms would yield an accuracy of 50 percent but was not recommended, because a tree with the lower accuracy of 45.03 percent required only 28 terms. A similar result can be seen for the neuro-fuzzy model. The highest accuracy is achieved with a model using 28 terms. However,

Figure 4. For each created model SPIDA provides a detailed report. Here the confusion matrix over the test data set and the fuzzy rules of a NEFCLASS model are shown.

Spida Report ☒

Results for model NefClass

● Overall Accuracy: 54.1%

orig \ pred	building_float	building_non_float	vehicle_float	containers	tableware	headlamps	Sum
building_float	37	3	0	0	0	0	40
building_non_float	33	7	1	1	0	0	42
vehicle_float	7	0	0	0	0	0	7
containers	0	5	1	5	0	0	11
tableware	0	1	0	0	1	2	4
headlamps	0	0	0	1	1	16	18
Sum	77	16	2	7	2	18	122

● The rules generated are:

    ◇ **Class building_non_float**
      R0: IF Na < ≈11.98 AND Mg < ≈0.97 AND Al < ≈0.65 THEN class = building_non_float
    ◇ **Class building_float**
      R1: IF Mg > ≈3.99 THEN class = building_float
    ◇ **Class headlamps**
      R2: IF Na > ≈15.71 AND Mg < ≈0.97 AND Al > ≈2.71 THEN class = headlamps
    ◇ **Class containers**
      R3: IF Na < ≈11.98 AND Mg < ≈0.97 AND Al > ≈2.71 THEN class = containers
    ◇ **Class vehicle_float**
      R4: IF Mg ≈ 2.92 AND Al > ≈2.71 THEN class = vehicle_float
    ◇ **Class tableware**
      R5: IF Na > ≈15.71 AND Mg ≈ 2.92 AND Al < ≈0.65 THEN class = tableware

Figure 5. For each model SPIDA automatically creates and executes a workspace containing graphs of function blocks. Experts can set up and run workspaces manually if they wish.

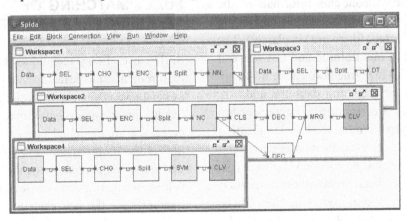

because of the requested simplicity the model with the second lowest accuracy of 54.1 percent and 15 terms is recommended as matching the user requirements best.

Based on this information the user can reconsider his requirements on model simplicity. By returning to the dialog on balancing accuracy and simplicity (Figure 1) and relaxing the simplicity requirement in favour of accuracy, SPIDA re-evaluates the model performances and changes its recommendation accordingly (without building the models again). SPIDA now would recommend the neuro-fuzzy model with 63.11 percent accuracy and 28 terms. The user can easily try different preference combinations and guided by the results report (Figure 4) decide which model to finally select for implementation.

Behind the scenes, SPIDA automatically creates workspaces for each selected data analysis algorithm and executes them in parallel (Figure 5). A workspace encapsulates a program in SPIDA's graphical programming language that connects function blocks into graphs representing the flow of data. Expert users can directly configure and run workspaces if they wish.

Workspace 2 in Figure 5 is the representation of the neuro-fuzzy classifier in our glass data example. We can see that the data is first passed through a selection filter that selects the data columns used in the process. The data is then encoded to turn it into a format the neuro-fuzzy classifier can use. In this example the method requires the column with the symbolic class information to be re-encoded by six numeric columns containing membership degrees (there are six classes). The data then is split into training and test sets and fed into the neuro-fuzzy method. The neuro-fuzzy block outputs the incoming data and adds six prediction columns containing fuzzy membership degrees for each pattern and class. A classification filter defuzzifies the classification columns and decides what the class prediction is for each pattern. Two decode filters combine the classification columns into the original symbolic class labels. One filter decodes the columns containing the information from the training and test sets and one filter decodes the predictions. A merge filter combines the columns with the actual class information with the predicted class information and the final classification visualiser block computes the confusion matrices for training and test data and the overall performance of the model.

The workspaces and the parameters in all blocks are created, configured and executed by SPIDA fully automatically based on the information encoded in SPIDA's fuzzy knowledge base. It is possible to reconfigure the knowledge base to build SPIDA versions for different application areas. In financial services, for example, simplicity may not be a concept of interest, but instead return of investment or profit. In some technical areas ROC (receiver/operator curve) or predictive gain may be preferred over accuracy. Any type of user preference and any features that can be attributed to a method or a model can be encoded in the knowledge base. As long as suitable fuzzy rules have been added to the knowledge base matching preferences to features SPIDA can use them to control the IDA process.

In the following section we explain how SPIDA matches user requirements and method properties—the approach used by the fuzzy knowledge base to decide which analysis methods to execute.

FUZZY MATCHING OF REQUIREMENTS AND PROPERTIES

SPIDA uses fuzzy techniques to describe user requirements and the features and desired properties of data analysis methods and created models. In addition, mappings between requirements and properties are modelled as fuzzy rules. A closer look at the requirements and properties reveals that some of them carry symbolic (categorical) values, whereas others are of numeric nature. Examples for the first category are the type of analysis problem (classification, function approximation, clustering, etc.), while accuracy and simplicity represent the second category. Obviously, fuzzy sets can be defined on numeric as well as symbolic (categorical) domains. However, a more homogeneous approach has been presented by Spott (2001). The main idea is to represent information by two levels of abstraction. The lower level is the level of details like the potentially infinite number of possible values in a continuous numeric domain of discourse. At the higher level of abstraction we only deal with a finite number of symbols by abstracting from details. In other words, the granularity of information can be either fine or coarse (potentially, entire hierarchies of granularity are conceivable). If we measure accuracy of a prediction model we can do so at the level of details as a value in [0,1], for example, or at the symbolic level in terms of symbols like "high accuracy," "medium accuracy," or "low accuracy." What this approach allows us to do is to represent inherently symbolic information like the type of analysis problem mentioned above at the same level as symbols like "high accuracy" which in fact are abstractions from a level of finer granularity.

The advantage of this approach compared to simply defining fuzzy sets on symbolic or numeric domains becomes more obvious when we think of expressing information using a combination of symbols like "I fully accept a model of high accuracy, but to a lower degree I would accept a model of medium accuracy, as well." This expression could be quantified in a requirement as "high accuracy (1.0) + medium accuracy (0.6)." We call such an expression a *weighted combination of symbols* or in short a *combination*. Spott (2005) has shown how to process such expressions at the symbolic level. Therefore, it does not matter, if the terms used are inherently symbolic or if they are actually fuzzy sets themselves. In this way, all symbols can be treated in a coherent way.

Spott (2001, 2005) proposed a probabilistic model for the weights in combinations. That means in particular that the sum of the weights is 1. For SPIDA we extended this model by allowing a sum of weights larger than 1 (Spott & Nauck, 2005). Obviously, such weights can not be interpreted as probabilities; rather, they represent the existence of alternatives.

We assume that the original user requirements have already been mapped onto desired properties and that information about the respective method and model properties is available. Each property is represented by a fuzzy variable that assumes combinations of fuzzy words as values. The desired accuracy, for example, could be "medium (1.0) + high (1.0)" whereas a created analysis model might be accurate to the degree of "low (0.3) + medium (0.7)." In other words, we are looking for a model with medium or high accuracy, and the created model's accuracy is low with degree 0.3 and medium with degree 0.7. In this example, the weights for the desired accuracy sum up to two, whereas the ones for the actual accuracy add up to one. We interpret a combination of fuzzy words with sum of weights greater than one as alternative fuzzy words. Rather than modelling the weights as probabilities, we assume a possibility density function (Gebhardt, 1993; Spott, 2001) on the fuzzy words, which allows for alternative values which, as an extreme case, could all be possible without restriction. This way, we define the degree of possibility of a fuzzy word in conjunction with probabilities of the related method or model property. The degree of possibility stands for the maximum acceptable probability of a property. Degrees of possibility can be any real number in [0,1].

In the example above, we were entirely happy with an analysis model of medium or high accuracy. We therefore assigned the possibilistic weight 1 to both of them, that is, models exhibiting the property "low (0.0) + medium (a) + high (b)" with $a+b=1$ are fully acceptable. In case of the requirement "low (0.0) + medium (0.0) + high (1.0)" and the above property with $a>0$ the weight a exceeds the possibility for "medium" and therefore at least partially violates the requirements.

Building on these ideas we stipulate that *requirements* are represented as a possibilistic combination of fuzzy words, that is, at least one of the fuzzy words carries the weight one, so the sum of weights of the fuzzy words is at least one. This is based on the assumption that at least one of the alternative requirements is fully acceptable.

Properties on the other hand stand for existing properties of a given model, so we assume that they are represented by a combination of fuzzy words, where the sum of weights of fuzzy words equals one.

The following part of the section deals with the question of how a match of requirements and properties can be quantified, that is, we are looking to measure the compatibility of properties with requirements. We will first focus on the compatibility of a single pair of requirement/property and then consider ways of combining several degrees of compatibility in one value.

In order to find an appropriate compatibility measure we stipulate a number of required properties. For reasons of simplicity, we refer to combinations of fuzzy words simply as fuzzy sets (on fuzzy words) $\widetilde{R}$ for requirements and ~P for properties, defined on a finite universe of discourse X. Subsethood of fuzzy sets is defined in the traditional way (Zadeh, 1965) by $\widetilde{A} \subseteq \widetilde{B} \Leftrightarrow \forall x \in X : \mu_{\widetilde{A}}(x) \leq \mu_{\widetilde{B}}(x)$ with $\mu_{\widetilde{A}}$ being the membership function of $\widetilde{A}$. For a compatibility measure $C(\widetilde{P}, \widetilde{R})$ we require

C1 $C(\widetilde{P}, \widetilde{R}) \in [0,1]$

C2 If the fuzzy sets are disjoint, compatibility is 0: $\widetilde{P} \cap \widetilde{R} = \varnothing \Rightarrow C(\widetilde{P}, \widetilde{R}) = 0$

C3 If the requirement fuzzy set is a superset of the property fuzzy set, compatibility is 1: $\widetilde{R} \supseteq \widetilde{P} \Rightarrow C(\widetilde{P}, \widetilde{R}) = 1$.

C4 Monotony in both arguments:
   a) $\widetilde{P}' \subseteq \widetilde{P} \Rightarrow C(\widetilde{P}', \widetilde{R}) \geq C(\widetilde{P}, \widetilde{R})$,
   b) $\widetilde{R}' \supseteq \widetilde{R} \Rightarrow C(\widetilde{P}, \widetilde{R}') \geq C(\widetilde{P}, \widetilde{R})$.

C1 is simply a normalisation, whereby a match value of 1 means full match and a value of 0 stands for no match. If the fuzzy sets are disjoint the property does not meet any requirement and the match is therefore 0 (C2). In C3 we make sure that the degree of match is 1 as long as the requirement covers the property, that is, the property is fully acceptable. Finally, monotony in C4 means that

the more relaxed the spectrum of requirements or the more specific the properties are the higher is the degree of compatibility.

Properties C1 - C4 resemble typical properties of measures for fuzzy set inclusion. Normally, such measures are generalisations of the inclusion of crisp sets based on a number of axioms (Cornelis, Van der Donck, & Kerre, 2003; Sinha & Dougherty, 1993). However, many of these axioms are too strict for our application. Also, the inclusion measure $Inc(\widetilde{A}, \widetilde{B}) = \min_{x \in X} I(\mu_{\widetilde{A}}(x), \mu_{\widetilde{B}}(x))$ with fuzzy implication operator I proposed in the above publications suffers from the serious drawback that it draws its value from a minimum operation, that is, for quite different fuzzy sets $\widetilde{A}$, for instance, *Inc* would return the same degree of inclusion. In mathematical terms, *Inc* is not strictly monotonous. Furthermore, it does not take into account the relation in size of the subset of $\widetilde{A}$ that is included in $\widetilde{B}$ and the one that is not included.

We therefore propose a different measure which meets all our requirements. As already mentioned above, we assume $\sum_{x \in X} \mu_{\widetilde{R}}(x) \geq 1$ and $\sum_{x \in X} \mu_{\widetilde{P}}(x) = 1$.

$$C(\widetilde{P}, \widetilde{R}) := 1 - \frac{1}{2}\left(\sum_{x \in X} \left| \mu_{\widetilde{R}}(x) - \mu_{\widetilde{P}}(x) \right| - \sum_{x \in X} \mu_{\widetilde{R}}(x) + 1 \right)$$

which can be rewritten as

$$C(\widetilde{P}, \widetilde{R}) = 1 - \sum_{\substack{x \in X \\ \mu_{\widetilde{P}}(x) > \mu_{\widetilde{R}}(x)}} \mu_{\widetilde{P}}(x) - \mu_{\widetilde{R}}(x). \qquad (1)$$

Before we prove that the measure C fulfils requirements C1 - C4 let us explain what the measure actually does. Figure 6 shows a fuzzy set $\widetilde{R}$ for requirements on the left hand side (we used a continuous domain for better illustration), the right triangular function is the fuzzy set $\widetilde{P}$ for properties. The right term in (1) measures the size of the grey area, which can be interpreted as a degree to which the properties violate the requirements. The size of the area is bounded by the area underneath the membership function of $\tilde{P}$ which we stipulated to be 1. That means that the right term measures the proportion of properties $\tilde{P}$ that violate the requirements. Determining the grey area is related to determining the size of the fuzzy difference $\tilde{P}$-$\tilde{R}$, but the operator $t(1-\mu_{\tilde{R}}(x),\mu_{\tilde{P}}(x))$ for the fuzzy difference does not match our semantics for properties and requirements.

From (1) immediately follows:

Lemma 1: For the fuzzy set $\tilde{R}'$ with $\mu_{\tilde{R}'}(x)=\min\{\mu_{\tilde{R}}(x),\mu_{\tilde{P}}(x)\}$ holds $C(\tilde{P},\tilde{R}')=C(\tilde{P},\tilde{R})$.

The Lemma shows that the requirements $\tilde{R}$ can be stripped down to the intersection $\tilde{R}'$ of requirements and properties $\tilde{P}$ (using min as t-norm) without changing the compatibility of properties with requirements, see Figure 6.

Lemma 2: The measure C defined above conforms to properties C1 - C4.

Proof:

1. Since the right term in (1) is obviously not negative and the following holds

$$\sum_{\substack{x\in X\\ \mu_{\tilde{P}}(x)>\mu_{\tilde{R}}(x)}}\mu_{\tilde{P}}(x)-\mu_{\tilde{R}}(x)\overset{(*)}{\le}\sum_{x\in X}\mu_{\tilde{P}}(x)=1, \quad (4)$$

C meets requirement C1.

2. In case of $\tilde{P}\cap\tilde{R}=\emptyset$, we have equality at (*) in (4) and therefore C2 is met.
3. If $\tilde{R}\supseteq\tilde{P}$, then the set $x\in X:\mu_{\tilde{P}}(x)>\mu_{\tilde{R}}(x)$ is empty, the right term in (1) is 0 and therefore $C(\tilde{P},\tilde{R})=1$.
4. If $\tilde{R}$ grows or $\tilde{P}$ shrinks the value of the right term in (1) cannot decrease (equivalently the size of the grey area in Figure 6 cannot shrink) therefore the value of C does not decrease.

Furthermore, it turns out that C is a measure of satisfiability as defined by Bouchon-Meunier, Rifqi, and Bothorel (1996) which is not surprising since their notion of satisfiability is very similar to our understanding of compatibility.

Since we deal with a set of requirements and properties, we end up having one match value for each requirement/property pair. Requiring a set of properties can formally be interpreted as a logical conjunction of the individual requirements. Given the assumption that all requirements are equally important, we therefore propose to use a t-norm to aggregate the individual match values. We decided to use multiplication, as it is a strictly monotonous operator. Strict monotony basically means that the overall match value decreases with any of the individual match values. Other operators like minimum do not have this property. In case of minimum, the overall match obviously is the minimum of the individual matches. That means

Figure 6. Fuzzy sets of requirements, properties $\tilde{P}$ and the intersection $\tilde{R}'$ (we used a continuous domain for better illustration). The grey area represents incompatibility of properties with requirements.

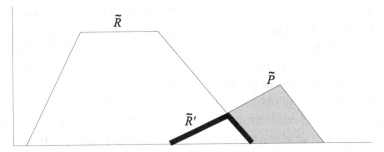

that all the match values apart from the minimum can be increased without changing the overall value. This is not the desired behaviour in our case since many different sets of properties would result in the same overall match value as long as the minimal value is the same. So the proposed measure for a multi-criteria match is

$$C(\widetilde{P}, \widetilde{R}) = \prod_{j=1}^{m} C(\widetilde{P}_j, \widetilde{R}_j)$$

$$= \prod_{j=1}^{m} \left(1 - \sum_{\substack{x \in X_j \\ \mu_{\widetilde{P}_j}(x) > \mu_{\widetilde{R}_j}(x)}} \mu_{\widetilde{P}_j}(x) - \mu_{\widetilde{R}_j}(x) \right)$$

SPIDA AS AN ANALYTICAL SERVICE

A model that has been created by SPIDA only really becomes useful if it can be integrated into an operational process. For example, the customer relationship management system of a business may require a model to classify customers for marketing purposes like cross-selling, a network management system may require a model to monitor traffic patterns and identify potential intrusions or a financial services system may require a model for predicting tomorrow's stock exchange rates to support buy/sell decisions. In order to support these types of operational systems, a model has to be taken out of the analytical software environment and it has to be integrated in order to continuously score new data.

Integration can be done loosely, by running models out of the analytical environment and applying it to database tables that are in turn used by operational systems. In the future, the modern database system will offer analytical services and store models in PMML thus integrating analytical environment and data management. However, sometimes this form of integration is not sufficient, because operational system can be based on proprietary database systems without common interfaces or data must be scored on the fly in real time without first going into a database table.

Integration is made more difficult by the fact that from time to time, models have to be adjusted in order to keep up with changes in the business or the market. Such adaptations are usually done manually by analysts, who produce new models based on new data. Most of the times, the underlying analysis algorithm stays the same, only parameters change. For example, the weights of a neural network or the rules in a fuzzy system might be adapted.

In case of data analysis functionality in the database and a PMML model, even algorithms can be changed without compromising the integrity of operational systems. For example, it might turn out that a decision tree performs better on a new data set than a support vector machine that has been used before. By simply exchanging the PMML description of the model in the database, the new model can be integrated seamlessly. However, such database systems are not standard, yet, and furthermore the decision for the new algorithm and its integration would still require manual interaction.

The SPIDA wizard can automate this process by selecting, configuring, and implementing new algorithms without user interaction. The final decision, if a new algorithm will be uploaded into the operational system probably will remain under human supervision, but the difficult part of creating it can mostly be achieved by SPIDA.

A schema summarising all scenarios in combination with SPIDA is shown in Figure 7. Data is fed into the operational system from a data warehouse. The data analysis module conducts data analysis for the operational system. This way it influences the system's performance or the performance of related business processes, because analysis results are usually used to make business decisions. For example, the data analysis module might be used to predict if a customer is going to churn (i.e., cancel his contract) and performance measures might be the relative number of churners not being flagged up by the system and the resulting loss of revenue. In this example,

Figure 7. Monitoring of system performance and requirements and automatic creation and integration of data analysis modules according to given requirements

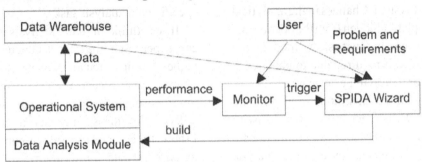

a drop in system performance will be the result of an inferior analytics model. Such a drop in performance will be detected by the monitor and trigger the generation of a new analysis model. The easiest way to detect dropping performance is by comparing against predefined thresholds.

The reasons for deterioration can be manifold. In most cases, the dynamics of the market are responsible, that is, the market has changed in a way that cannot be detected by the analytical model. Other reasons include changes in related business processes and data corruption.

Whenever model generation is triggered by the monitor, the wizard takes the user requirements and the latest data to build a new model. Another reason for building a new model is a change of user requirements. For example, due to a change of company policy or for regulatory reasons, a model may now be required to be comprehensible. If, for instance, a neural network had been used to measure the credit line of a potential borrower, we would be forced to switch to methods like decision trees or fuzzy systems which create a rule base that can be understood by managers and the regulator. This may be required to demonstrate that the model conforms to an equal opportunities act, for example.

When it comes to integrating modules with operational systems, software engineers can nowadays choose from a variety of techniques that both depend on the operational system and

the module. Where some years ago, modules were quite often especially tailored for the operational system, nowadays, much more modular approaches are used that allow for using the same modules in different operational systems on the one hand, and replacing modules in operational systems on the other hand. Apart from the database approach where data analysis can directly be conducted by the database and analysis models are defined using a standard like PMML, other techniques use libraries with standard interfaces (API) and provide a respective interface in the operational system or use even less coupled techniques like Web services. For SPIDA, we decided to build executable Java libraries which can easily be used in either way.

Since we require a variety of different data analysis techniques to cover as many applications as possible, the starting point for the generation of analysis modules are data analysis platforms like SPIDA. The actual analysis model required by an operational system typically uses only a tiny fraction of such a platform's functionality. For reasons of saving space and potentially licensing costs we want to restrict the module to the functions actually needed by the underlying data analysis model or process.

In case of SPIDA, we are looking to create analytical modules, which are pieces of software independent from the SPIDA platform, corresponding to a particular data analysis model.

Once extracted, the independent software module can be used as a library with an exposed API by the operational system. Changes in the analytical model are completely hidden from the operational system by the module, that is, the module can easily be replaced if required due to changes in requirements or a drop in performance.

At the heart of the integration of an analytic module in SPIDA is a general framework with which an operational system can communicate and specify its requirements and obtain an analytic module from SPIDA as a Java library.

First, the definition of the analysis problem and the user requirements are specified in XML. The SPIDA wizard parses the XML description and identifies the corresponding analysis components like data access, filters, and the actual analysis blocks. A mapping is made between the required components and the corresponding Java classes of the platform. SPIDA's software extractor component then finds all the dependent classes for this initial set of classes. The extractor uses application knowledge and a host of other extraction techniques to find all the additional classes required to make it executable and independent from the platform. This complete set of all component classes is turned into a Jar library with suitable properties by SPIDA's Jar creator. This Jar library is passed to the operational system, which can access the API provided in the library to control the execution of the analysis module. It is also possible to instruct SPIDA to deliver the

Jar library in form of a stand-alone package that is able to directly execute the included model for specific data analysis tasks.

If we think of data analysis services, we can expect many different concurrent analysis requests. Since each analysis process will create an executable object, the size of dedicated Jar libraries should be kept as small as possible in order to allow for as many users as possible. Table 1 shows the compression rates for libraries created for different data mining algorithms compared to the whole SPIDA package, which range between 47 percent and 17 percent.

CASE STUDIES

The SPIDA platform discussed in this chapter is a research demonstrator, and its main purpose was to build and test methods for automatically generating predictive models in a data analysis process. Although the platform is constantly used in our team for doing day-to-day data analysis applying it to operational processes requires further work. In this section we briefly mention three successful internal applications that build on SPIDA technology, that is, methods for automatically building models from data. Instead of making the whole platform available in an operational environment we decided to build smaller self-contained applications targeting three business areas: travel management for mobile workforces, customer satisfaction analysis, and customer life cycle modelling.

BT has a large mobile workforce for maintaining its network, providing customers with products and service and repairing faults. A dynamic scheduler is used to plan the working day of each engineer and assign the right job to the right person. In order to provide good schedules it is important to have good estimates for job durations and inter-job travel times. We have built an intelligent travel time estimation system (ITEMS) that estimates inter-job times based on historic

Table 1. Compression rates of dedicated Java libraries for various data analysis algorithms compared to whole SPIDA package

Model	Relative Size
Linear Regression	33%
NEFPROX	48%
Decision Trees	17%
Support Vector Machines	17%
Neural Networks	21%
NEFCLASS	47%

Figure 8. The ITEMS system with automatically derived rules for explaining travel patterns

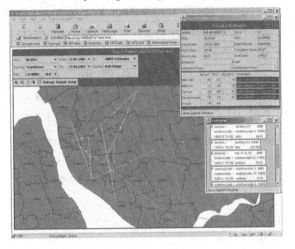

evidence (Azvine, Ho, Kay, Nauck, & Spott, 2003). An important part of ITEMS is a graphical interface where resource managers can study patterns that lead to engineers arriving late for jobs. The purpose of this system is to understand where process issues lead to delays and how the process can be improved. SPIDA technology is used to learn patterns from data.

In order to be useful the rules must be simple and sparse and they must be created automatically in real-time for a specific set of journeys for which the user requires explanations (Nauck, 2003). We had two algorithms available from SPIDA that were suitable for this purpose: decision trees and a neuro-fuzzy classifier (NEFCLASS). These two algorithms and the required SPIDA configurations for creating small interpretable rules based were implemented into ITEMS. Figure 8 displays a screen shot of typical situation while using ITEMS. A user analyzes the travel pattern of some technician and has clicked an arrow in the displayed map. Additional windows display detailed information about the corresponding job. The top right window displays two fuzzy rules matching the travel information of the selected job. The user can see the degree of fulfilment of a rule and decide, if a particular rule is useful for

explaining the selected travel pattern, that is, why the technician was late, early, or on time.

Another application based on SPIDA technology has been built in the area of customer satisfaction analysis. Most service-oriented companies regularly survey their customers to learn about their satisfactions with the company's customer services. Variables in a survey typically display high degrees of interdependences which is important to take into account when modelling survey results. In our application we also had to provide abilities for conducting what-if analyses and target setting, that is, planning how to achieve certain level of customer satisfaction. We identified Bayesian networks as the ideal model for this scenario and used SPIDA technology to implement an application—iCSat—that fully automatically learns a Bayesian network from data (Nauck, Ruta, Spott, & Azvine, 2006). It allows the user to identify drivers of customer satisfaction, to run what-if scenarios for understanding how satisfaction levels might change when certain drivers change, and to simulate desired levels of customer satisfaction for identifying targets for drivers of satisfaction.

The final application based on SPIDA technology is used to model customer life cycles. We have built an intelligent customer analytics platform that can automatically learn hidden Markov models from customer event data (Azvine, Nauck, Ho, Broszat, & Lim, 2006). The models can be used to predict probabilities and timings of relevant future customer events like churn, complaints, purchases, and so on. The predictions are used to control pro-active customer services, like contacting a customer in time before a service problem escalates and could lead to complaints or churn.

CONCLUSION

As a new direction in automating data analysis, we introduced the concept of using soft constraints for the selection of an appropriate data analysis method. These constraints represent the user's requirements regarding the analysis problem (like prediction, clustering, or finding dependencies) and preferences regarding the solution.

Requirements can potentially be defined at any level of abstraction. Expert knowledge in terms of a fuzzy rule base maps high-level requirements onto required properties of data analysis methods which will then be matched to actual properties of analysis methods.

As a result of our work, we introduced a new measure for the compatibility of fuzzy requirements with fuzzy properties that can be applied to other problems in the area of multi-criteria decision making. The methods presented above have been implemented as a wizard for our data analysis tool SPIDA, which has been successfully used to produce solutions to a variety of problems within BT.

SPIDA can serve as a smart data analysis service for operational systems. Where current systems require manual intervention by data analysis experts if a data analysis module needs updating, our architecture automatically detects changes in performance or requirements, builds a new data analysis model, and wraps the model into an executable Java library with standard API that can easily be accessed by operational systems. When building data analysis models, the wizard takes into account high-level user requirements regarding an explanation facility, simplicity of an explanation, adaptability, accuracy, and so on. In this way, we can vary the data analysis solution as much as possible without violating requirements. Before, adaptive solutions only retrained models based on new data, for example, an analysis method like a neural network was selected once and only adapted to new data. Switching automatically—without user interaction—to another method, for example, to a support vector machine was not possible, let alone considering user requirements for the automatic selection of the most suitable analysis method.

REFERENCES

Azvine, B., Ho, C., Kay, S., Nauck, D., & Spott, M. (2003). Estimating travel times of field engineers. *BT Technology Journal, 21*(4), 33-38.

Azvine, B., Nauck, D.D., Ho, C., Broszat, K., & Lim, J. (2006). Intelligent process analytics for CRM. *BT Technology Journal, 24*(1), 60-69.

Bouchon-Meunier, B., Rifqi, M., & Bothorel, S. (1996). Towards general measures of comparison of objects. *Fuzzy Sets & Systems, 84*(2), 143–153.

Bernstein, A., Hill, S., & Provost, F. (2002). *Intelligent assistance for the data mining process: An ontology-based approach* (CeDER Working Paper IS-02-02). New York: Center for Digital Economy Research, Leonard Stern School of Business, New York University.

Bernstein, A. & Provost, F. (2001). *An intelligent assistant for the knowledge discovery process* (CeDER Working Paper IS-01-01). New York: Center for Digital Economy Research, Leonard Stern School of Business, New York University.

Botia, J.A., Velasco, J.R., Garijo, M., & Skarmeta, A.F.G. (1998). A generic datamining system. Basic design and implementation guidelines. In H. Kargupta & P.K. Chan (Eds.), *Workshop in distributed datamining at KDD-98.* New York: AAAI Press.

Botia, J.A., Skarmeta, A.F., Velasco, J.R., & Garijo, M. (2000). A proposal for Meta-Learning through a MAS. In T. Wagner & O. Rana (Eds.), *Infrastructure for agents, multi-agent systems, and scalable multi-agent systems* (pp. 226-233). Lecture notes in artificial intelligence 1887. Berlin: Springer-Verlag.

Cornelis, C., Van der Donck, C., & Kerre, E. (2003). Sinha-Dougherty approach to the fuzzification of set inclusion revisited. *Fuzzy Sets & Systems, 134*, 283–295.

Gebhardt, J. & Kruse R. (1993). The context model – An integrating view of vagueness and uncertainty. *International Journal of Approximate Reasoning, 9,* 283–314.

Nauck, D.D. (2003a). Fuzzy data analysis with NEFCLASS. *International Journal of Approximate Reasoning, 32,* 103-130.

Nauck, D.D. (2003b). Measuring interpretability in rule-based classification systems. *Proceedings of the 2003 IEEE International Conference on Fuzzy Systems (FuzzIEEE2003), 1,* pp. 196-201. Saint Louis, MO: IEEE Press.

Nauck, D.D., Ruta, D., Spott, M., & Azvine, B. (2006) A tool for intelligent customer analytics. *Proceedings of the IEEE International Conference on Intelligent Systems,* pp. 518-521. London: IEEE Press.

Nauck, D.D., Spott, M., & Azvine, B. (2003). Spida – A novel data analysis tool. *BT Technology Journal, 21*(4), 104–112.

Sinha, D. & Dougherty, E. (1993). Fuzzification of set inclusion: theory and applications. *Fuzzy Sets & Systems, 55,* 15–42.

Spott, M. (2001). Combining fuzzy words. *Proceedings of IEEE International Conference on Fuzzy Systems 2001.* Melbourne, Australia: IEEE Press.

Spott, M. (2005). Efficient reasoning with fuzzy words. In S.K. Halgamuge & L.P. Wang (Eds.), *Computational intelligence for modelling and predictions,* pp. 117-128. Studies in Compuational Intelligence 2. Berlin: Springer Verlag.

Spott, M. & Nauck, D.D. (2005). On choosing an appropriate data analysis algorithm. *Proceedings of the IEEE International Conference on Fuzzy Systems 2005,* Reno, NV: IEEE Press.

University of California at Irvine (2007). UCI Machine Learning Repository. Accessed March, 26, 2007 at http://www.ics.uci.edu/~mlearn/ML-Repository.html.

Wirth, R., Shearer, C., Grimmer, U., Reinartz, J., Schloesser, T.P., Breitner, C., Engels, R., & Lindner, G. (1997). Towards process-oriented tool support for knowledge discovery in databases. *Principles of Data Mining and Knowledge Discovery. First European Symposium, PKDD '97,* pp. 243–253. Lecture Notes in Computer Science 1263, Berlin: Springer-Verlag.

Witten, I.H. & Frank, E. (2000). *Data mining: Practical machine learning tools and techniques with JAVA implementations.* San Francisco: Morgan Kaufmann Publishers.

Zadeh, L. A. (1965). Fuzzy sets. *Information and Control,* 8, 338–353.

Chapter II
Random Fuzzy Sets

Hung T. Nguyen
New Mexico State University, USA

Vladik Kreinovich
University of Texas at El Paso, USA

Gang Xiang
University of Texas at El Paso, USA

ABSTRACT

It is well known that in decision making under uncertainty, while we are guided by a general (and abstract) theory of probability and of statistical inference, each specific type of observed data requires its own analysis. Thus, while textbook techniques treat precisely observed data in multivariate analysis, there are many open research problems when data are censored (e.g., in medical or bio-statistics), missing, or partially observed (e.g., in bioinformatics). Data can be imprecise due to various reasons, for example, due to fuzziness of linguistic data. Imprecise observed data are usually called coarse data. In this chapter, we consider coarse data which are both random and fuzzy. Fuzziness is a form of imprecision often encountered in perception-based information. In order to develop statistical reference procedures based on such data, we need to model random fuzzy data as bona fide random elements, that is, we need to place random fuzzy data completely within the rigorous theory of probability. This chapter presents the most general framework for random fuzzy data, namely the framework of random fuzzy sets. We also describe several applications of this framework.

FROM MULTIVARIATE STATISTICAL ANALYSIS TO RANDOM SETS

What is a random set? An intuitive meaning. What is a random set? Crudely speaking, a random number means that we have different numbers with different probabilities; a random vector means that we have different vectors with different probabilities; and similarly, a random set means that we have different sets with different probabilities.

How can we describe this intuitive idea in precise terms? To provide such a formalization, let us recall how probabilities and random vectors are usually defined.

How probabilities are usually defined. To describe probabilities, in general, we must have a set Ω of possible situations $\omega \in \Omega$, and we must be able to describe the probability P of different properties of such situations. In mathematical terms, a *property* can be characterized by the *set* of all the situations ω which satisfy this property. Thus, we must assign to sets $A \subseteq \Omega$, the probability value $P(A)$.

According to the intuitive meaning of probability (e.g., as frequency), if we have two disjoint sets A and A', then we must have $P(A \cup A') = P(A) + P(A')$. Similarly, if we have countably many mutually disjoint sets A_i, we must have:

$$P\left(\bigcup_{i=1}^{n} A_i\right) = \sum_{i=1}^{\infty} P(A_i).$$

A mapping which satisfies this property is called σ-*additive*.

It is known that even in the simplest situations, for example, when we randomly select a number from the interval $\Omega = [0,1]$, it is not possible to have a σ-additive function P which would be defined on *all* subsets of $[0,1]$. Thus, we must restrict ourselves to a class A of subsets of Ω.

Since subsets represent properties, a restriction on subsets means restriction on properties. If we allow two properties F and F', then we should also be able to consider their logical combinations F & F', $F \vee F'$, and $\neg F$ – which in set terms correspond to union, intersection, and complement. Similarly, if we have a sequence of properties F_n, then we should also allow properties $\forall n F_n$ and $\exists n F_n$ which correspond to countable union and intersection. Thus, the desired family A should be closed under (countable) union, (countable) intersection, and complement. Such a family is called a σ-*algebra*.

Thus, we arrive at a standard definition of a *probability space* as a triple $(\Omega, \mathbf{A}, P)$, where Ω is a set, A is a σ-algebra of subsets of Ω, and $P : A \to [0,1]$ is a σ-additive function.

How random objects are usually defined. Once a probability space is fixed, a random object from the set C is defined as mapping $V : \Omega \to \mathbf{C}$. For example, the set of all d-dimensional vectors is the Euclidean space $\mathbf{R}^d$, so a random vector is defined as a map $V : \Omega \to \mathbf{R}^d$.

The map V must enable us to define probabilities of different properties of objects. For that, we need to fix a class of properties; we already know that such a class $\mathbf{B}$ should be a σ-algebra. For each property of objects, that is, for each set $B \in \mathbf{B}$, it is natural to define the probability $P(B)$ as the probability that for a random situation ω, the corresponding object $V(\omega)$ belongs to the set B (i.e., satisfies the desired property). In precise terms, this means that we define this probability as $P(V^{-1}(B))$, where $V^{-1}(B)$ denotes $\{\omega : V(\omega) \in B\}$.

For this definition to be applicable, we must require that for every set B from the desired σ-algebra B, the set $V^{-1}(B)$ must belong to $\mathbf{A}$. Such mappings are called $\mathbf{A}$-$\mathbf{B}$-*measurable*.

How random vectors are usually defined. In particular, for random vectors, it is reasonable to allow properties corresponding to all open sets B

$\subseteq \mathbf{R}^d$ (like $x_1 > 0$) and properties corresponding to all closed sets B (such as $x_1 \geq 0$). So, we must consider the smallest σ-algebra which contains all closed and open sets. Sets from this smallest subalgebra are called *Borel sets*; the class of all Borel sets over $\mathbf{R}^d$ is denoted by $\mathbf{B}(\mathbf{R}^d)$. So, a random vector is usually defined as $\mathbf{A}$-$\mathbf{B}^d$ measurable mapping $V{:}\Omega{\to}\mathbf{R}^d$.

Alternatively, we can consider the vectors themselves as events, that is, consider a probability space $(\mathbf{R}^d, \mathbf{B}(\mathbf{R}^d), P_V)$. In this reformulation, as we have mentioned, for every set B, we get $P_V(B) = P(V^{-1}(B))$, so we can say that P_V is a composition of the two mappings: $P_V = PV^{-1}$. This measure P_V is called a *probability law* of the random vector.

How random vectors are usually described. From the purely mathematical viewpoint, this is a perfect definition of a random vector. However, from the computational viewpoint, the need to describe $P_V(B)$ for all Borel sets B makes this description impractical. Good news is that due to σ-additivity, we do not need to consider all possible Borel sets B, it is sufficient to describe $P_V(B)$ only for the sets of the type $(-\infty, x_1] \times \ldots \times (-\infty, x_d]$, that is, it is sufficient to consider only the probabilities that $\xi_1 \leq x_1 \& \ldots \& \xi_d \leq x_d$.

In the one-dimensional case, the probability $F(x)$ that $\xi \leq x$ is called a (cumulative) distribution function. Similarly, in the general d-dimensional case, the probability $F(x_1,\ldots,x_d)$ that $\xi_1 \leq x_1$, …, and $\xi_d \leq x_d$ is called a distribution function. In these terms, the probability measures on $\mathbf{B}(\mathbf{R}^d)$ are uniquely characterized by their distribution functions. This result was first proved by Lebesgue and Stieltjes and is thus called the *Lebesgue-Stieltjes theorem*.

From random vectors to slightly more general random objects. The above definition of a random vector does not use any specific features of a multi-dimensional vector space $\mathbf{R}^d$ so it can be naturally generalized to the case when the set $\mathbf{C}$ of objects (possible outcomes) is a locally compact Hausdorff second countable topological space. Such spaces will be described as LCHS, for short.

From random vectors to random sets. As we have mentioned, in some real-life situations, the outcome is not a vector by a set of possible vectors. In this case, possible outcomes are subsets of the vector space $\mathbf{R}^d$, so the set $\mathbf{C}$ of possible outcomes can be described as the set of all such subsets—a *power set* $\mathbf{P}(\mathbf{R}^d)$.

Need to consider one-element sets. An important particular case of this general situation is the case when we know the exact vector x. In this case, the set of all possible vectors is the corresponding one-element set $\{x\}$. So, one-element sets must appear as possible sets.

Restriction to closed sets. From the practical viewpoint, it is sufficient to only consider *closed sets*.

Indeed, by definition, a closed set is a set which contains all the limits of its elements. If $x_n \in S$ and $x_n \to x$, then, by definition of a limit, this means that whatever accuracy we choose, we cannot distinguish between x and values x_n for sufficiently large n. Since $x_n \in S$ and x is undistinguishable from x_n, it makes sense to conclude that x also belongs to S–that is, that S is indeed a closed set.

Since one-element sets are closed, this restriction is in accordance with the above-mentioned need to consider one-element sets. (In a more general framework of a LCHS space, the requirement that all one-point sets be closed is one of the reasons why we impose the restriction that the topology must be Hausdorff: for Hausdorff topological spaces, this requirement is satisfied.)

With this restriction, the set $\mathbf{C}$ of possible outcomes is the class of all closed subsets of the space $\mathbf{R}^d$; this class is usually denoted by $\mathbf{F}(\mathbf{R}^d)$, or simply $\mathbf{F}$, for short.

It is worth mentioning that the decision to restrict ourselves to closed sets was made already in the pioneering book (Mathéron, 1975) on random sets.

We need a topology on F. To finalize our definition of closed random sets, we must specify a σ-field on **F**. To specify such a field, we will follow the same idea as with random vectors—namely, we will define a topology on **F** and then consider the σ-field of all the Borel sets in this topology (i.e., the smallest σ-field that contains all sets which are open or closed in the sense of this topology.

In his monograph (Mathéron, 1975), Mathéron described a natural topology that he called a *hit-or-miss* topology. (It is worth mentioning that this topology was first introduced in a completely different problem: the construction of the regularized dual space of a C^*-algebra [Fell, 1961, 1962]).

Mathéron's motivations and definitions work well for random sets. However, they are difficult to directly generalize to random fuzzy sets. Since the main objective of this paper is to describe and analyze random fuzzy sets, we will present a different derivation of this topology, a derivation that can be naturally generalized to random fuzzy sets.

This alternative definition is based on the fact that on the class of closed sets, there is a natural order $A \supseteq B$. The meaning of this order is straightforward. If we have a (closed) set A of possible vectors, this means that we only have partial information about the vector. When we gain additional information, this enables us to reduce the original set A to its subset B. Thus, $A \supseteq B$ means that the set B carries more information about the (unknown) vector than the set A.

It turns out that in many important situations, this order enables us to describe a natural topology on the corresponding ordered set. Specifically, this topology exists when the corresponding order forms a so-called continuous lattice. To describe this topology in precise terms, we thus will need to recall the basic notions of lattice theory and the definition of a continuous lattice.

Basics of lattice theory. Lattices are a particular case of *partially ordered sets* (also knows as *posets*); so, to define the lattice, we must first recall the definition of a poset. A poset is defined as a set X together with a relation $\leq$ which satisfies the following properties:

(i) $\leq$ is *reflexive*, that is, $x \leq x$ for all $x \in X$;

(ii) $\leq$ is *anti-symmetric*, that is, for all $x, y \in X$, $x \leq y$ and $y \leq x$ imply that $x = y$;

(iii) $\leq$ is *transitive*, that is, for all $x, y, z \in X$, if $x \leq y$ and $y \leq z$, then $x \leq z$.

An element $u \in X$ is called an *upper bound* for a pair x, y if $x \leq u$ and $y \leq u$. Dually, an element $v \in X$ is called a *lower bound* for a pair x, y if $v \leq x$ and $v \leq y$. These concepts can be naturally extended to arbitrary collections of elements $A \subseteq X$: an element $u \in X$ is an *upper bound* for A if $x \leq u$ for all $x \in A$; an element $v \in X$ is a *lower bound* for A if $v \leq x$ for all $x \in A$.

The least upper bound is exactly what it sounds like: the least of all the upper bounds. Similarly, the greatest lower bound is the greatest of all the lower bounds. In precise terms, an element $u \in X$ is called the *least upper bound* of the set A if it satisfies the following two conditions:

1. u is an upper bound for the set A (i.e., $x \leq u$ for all $x \in A$); and

2. if w is an upper bound for the set A, then $u \leq w$.

The least upper bound of a set A is also called its *join* or *supremum* and is usually denoted by $\wedge A$ or sup A.

Similarly, an element $v \in X$ is called the *greatest lower bound* of the set A if it satisfies the following two conditions:

1. v is a lower bound for the set A (i.e., $v \leq x$ for all $x \in A$); and

2. if w is an lower bound for the set A, then $w \leq v$.

The greatest lower bound of a set A is also called its *meet* or *infimum* and is usually denoted by $\vee A$ or $\inf A$.

For two-element sets, $\wedge\{a,b\}$ is usually denoted by $a \wedge b$ and $\vee\{a,b\}$ by $a \vee b$.

A poset X is called a *lattice* if $a \wedge b$ and $a \vee b$ exist for all pairs $a,b \in X$. A poset X is called a *complete lattice* if both $\vee A$ and $\wedge A$ exist for any set $A \subseteq X$.

Examples of lattices. The set $\mathbf{R}$ of all real numbers with a standard order is a lattice, with $a \vee b = \max(a,b)$ and $a \wedge b = \min(a,b)$. This set is not a complete lattice, since it does not have a join $\vee \mathbf{R}$: no real number is larger than all the others.

A slight modification of this example makes it a complete lattice: namely, the set of all real numbers from an interval $[\underline{x},\overline{x}]$ is a complete lattice.

The set of all n-dimensional vectors $a = (a_1,\dots,a_n)$ with a component-wise order $a \le b \leftrightarrow a_1 \le b_1 \& \dots \& a_n \le b_n$ is also a lattice, with $(a \vee b)_i = \max(a_i,b_i)$ and $(a \wedge b)_i = \min(a_i,b_i)$. Another example of a lattice is the set of all the functions, with $(f \vee g)(x) = \max(f(x),g(x))$ and $(f \wedge g)(x) = \min(f(x),g(x))$.

Continuous lattices and Lawson topology. In some posets, in addition to the original relation $<$ ("smaller"), we can define a new relation $<$ whose meaning is "much smaller." This relation is called *way below*.

The formal definition of $<$ requires two auxiliary notions: of a directed set and of a dcpo. A set $A \subseteq X$ is called *directed* if every finite subset of A has an upper bound in A. Of course, in a complete lattice, every set is directed.

A poset X is called a *directed complete partial order (dcpo)*, if each of its directed subsets D has a supremum $\vee D$. In particular, every complete lattice is a dcpo.

We say that x is *way below* y ($x < y$) if for every directed subset D for which $y \le D$, there exists an element $d \in D$ such that $x \le d$.

In particular, a one-element set $D = \{y\}$ is always directed, and for this set, we conclude that $x \le y$—that is, that "way below" indeed implies $\le$. Another simple example: for a natural order on the set of real numbers, $x < y$ simply means $x < y$.

From the common sense viewpoint, we expect that if x is way below y and z is even smaller than x, then z should also be way below y. This is indeed true for the above definition: indeed, if $x < y$ and $z \le x$, then $z < y$, then for every D, we have $x \le d$ for some d and hence $z \le x \le d$, that is, $z \le d$ for that same element $d \in D$. Similarly, we can proof all three statements from the following lemma.

Lemma 1. *Let $(L,\le)$ be a dcpo. Then, for any u, x, y, z in L, we have:*

(i) $x < y$ *implies* $x \le y$;
(ii) $u \le x < y \le z$ *implies* $u < z$;
(iii) *if* $x < z$ *and* $y < z$, *then* $x \vee y < z$.

For example, to prove (iii), for every directed set D, we must prove that $z \le \vee D$ implies that $x \vee y \le d$ for some $d \in D$. Indeed, from $x << z$ and $y << z$, we conclude that $x \le d_x$ and $y \le d_y$ for some $d_x, d_y \in D$. Since D is a directed set, there exists an element $d \in D$ which is an upper bound for both d_x and d_y, that is, for which $d_x \le d$ and $d_y \le d$. From $x \le d_x$ and $d_x \le d$, we conclude that $x \le d$ and similarly, that $y \le d$, so d is an upper bound for x and y. By definition of the least upper bound $x \vee y$, it must be smaller than or equal than any other upper bound, hence $x \vee y \le d$. The statement is proven.

We can define a topology if we take, as a subbase, sets $\{y \in X : y << x\}$ and $\{y \in X : x \nleq y\}$ for all $x \in X$. In other words, as open sets for this topology, we take arbitrary unions of finite intersections of these sets. This topology is called a *Lawson topology*.

It is worth mentioning that for the standard order on real numbers, the sets $\{y \in X : y << x\} = \{y : y < x\}$ and $\{y \in X : x \nleq y\} = \{y : y > x\}$ are indeed open, and the corresponding topology coincides with the standard topology on the real line.

There is an important reasonably general case when the Lawson topology has useful properties: the case of a continuous lattice. A complete lattice X is called a *continuous lattice* if every element $x \in X$ is equal to the union of all the elements which are way below it, that is, if $x = \vee\{y \in X : y << x\}$ for all $x \in X$. It is known that on every continuous lattice $(X, \leq)$, the Lawson topology is *compact* and *Hausdorff*; see, for example, Gierz, Hofmann, Keimel, Lawson, Mislove, and Scott (1980).

Final definition of a (closed) random set and the need for further analysis. In our analysis of random sets, we will use the Lawson topology to describe the σ-algebra of subsets of **F**—as the class of all Borel sets in the sense of this topology.

From the purely mathematical viewpoint, this is a (somewhat abstract but) perfect definition. However, since our objective is to make this definition applicable to practical problems, we need to first reformulate this general abstract definition in more understandable closer-to-practice terms.

THE LAWSON TOPOLOGY OF CLOSED SETS

First try. Let us describe what these notions lead to in the case of closed sets. For the class **F** of closed sets, there is a natural ordering relation $\leq$: a set inclusion $F \subseteq F'$. The corresponding poset $(\mathbf{F}, \subseteq)$ is indeed a complete lattice: indeed, for every family $F_i (i \in I)$ of closed sets, there exist both the infimum and the supremum:

$$\wedge \{F_i \in \mathbf{F} : i \in I\} = \bigcap \{F_i : i \in I\};$$

$$\vee \{F_i : i \in I\} = \text{the closure of } \bigcup \{F_i : i \in I\}.$$

The resulting complete lattice is not continuous. Let us show that with $\subseteq$ as the ordering relation $\leq$, **F** is *not* continuous. Specifically, as we will show, that, for example, in the one-dimensional case $\mathbf{R}^d = \mathbf{R}$, the definition $F = \vee\{G \in$

$\mathbf{F} : G << F\}$ of a continuous lattice is violated for $F = \mathbf{R}$.

For that, we will prove that for every two sets F and G, $G << F$ implies that $G = \phi$. We will prove this by reduction to a contradiction. Let us assume that $G \neq \phi$ and $G << F$. Since the set G is not empty, it contains an element $x \in G$. For this element x, the one-point set $S = \{x\}$ is a closed subset of G: $S \subseteq G$. By our first-try definition of $\leq$, this means that $S \leq G$. We have already mentioned that if $S \leq G$ and $G << F$, then $S << F$. By definition of the "way below" relation $<<$, this means that if $F \leq \vee D$, then there exists an element $d \in D$ for which $S \leq d$. In particular, we can take as D the family $\{d_n\}_n$, where for every positive integer n, $d_n \stackrel{\text{def}}{=} (-\infty, x - \frac{1}{n}] \cup [x + \frac{1}{n}, +\infty)$. It is easy to see that $d_{n_1} \vee \ldots \vee d_{n_k} = d_{\max(n_1, \ldots, n_k)}$, so the family D is indeed directed. The union $\bigcup_n d_n$ of these sets is equal to $(-\infty, x) \cup (x, +\infty)$. Thus, the closure $\vee D$ of this union is the entire real line $\mathbf{R}$. Since F is a subset of the real line, we have $F \leq \vee D$. However, for every $d_n \in D$, we have $x \notin d_n$ and thus, $S \nleq d_n$. The contradiction shows that a non-empty set G cannot be way below any other set F. Therefore, the only set G for which $G << \mathbf{R}$ is an empty set, so $\vee \{G \in \mathbf{F} : G < \mathbf{R}\} = \phi \neq \mathbf{R}$.

Correct definition. Fortunately, a small modification of the above definition makes **F** a continuous lattice. Namely, as the desired ordering relation $\leq$ on the class **F** of all closed sets, we can consider the reverse inclusion relation $\supseteq$.

It is easy to show that $(\mathbf{F}, \supseteq)$ is a complete lattice: indeed,

$$\wedge \{F_i \in \mathbf{F} : i \in I\} = \text{the closure of } \bigcup \{F_i : i \in I\};$$

$$\vee \{F_i : i \in I\} = \bigcap \{F_i : i \in I\}.$$

Let us prove that $(\mathbf{F}, \supseteq)$ is a continuous lattice. By definition, a continuous lattice means that for every closed set $F \in \mathbf{F}$, we have $F = \vee \{G \in \mathbf{F} : G << F\}$ for every set $F \in \mathbf{F}$. Since $G << F$ implies $G \leq F$, that is, $G \subseteq F$, we thus have $\vee \{G \in \mathbf{F} : G << F\} \supseteq F$. So, to prove the desired equality, it is sufficient to prove that $F \supseteq \vee\{G \in \mathbf{F} : G << F\}$.

We have already mentioned that in the lattice $(\mathbf{F},\supseteq)$, the union $\vee$ is simply the intersection of the corresponding sets, so the desired property can be rewritten as $F \supseteq \cap\{G \in \mathbf{F} : G << F\}$. It turns out that it is easier to prove the equivalent inclusion of complements, that is, to prove that $F^c \subseteq \cup\{G^c : G \in \mathbf{F}, G << F\}$ (where F^c denotes the complement of the set F).

There is no easy and intuitive way to immediately prove this result, because the notion of "way below" is complex and is therefore not intuitively clear. So, to be able to prove results about this relation $<<$, let us reformulate it in an equivalent more intuitive way.

Lemma 2. *For $X = \mathbf{R}^d$ (and, more generally, for an arbitrary locally compact Hausdorff second countable topological space X), for $F, G \in \mathbf{F}(X)$, $F << G$ if and only if there exists a compact set $K \subseteq X$ such that $F^c \subseteq K \subseteq G^c$.*

Proof

1. **Sufficiency.** Let $F, G \in \mathbf{F}(X)$ and let K be a compact set such that $F^c \subseteq K \subseteq G^c$. Let $G \leq \vee D$ for some directed family D, that is, let $G \supseteq \vee D$. We already know that $\vee$ is simply an intersection, that is, $G \supseteq \cap D$. In terms of complements, we get an equivalent inclusion $G^c \subseteq \cup\{d^c : d \in D\}$. Since $K \subseteq G^c$, we conclude that $K \supseteq \cup\{d^c : d \in D\}$. Complements d^c to closed sets $d \in D$ are open sets. Thus, the compact K is covered by a family of open sets d^c, $d \in D$. By definition of a compact set, this means that we can select a finite subcover, that is, conclude that $K \subseteq F_1^c \cup \ldots \cup F_n^c$ for some closed sets $F_i \in D$. Since $F^c \subseteq K$, we thus have $F^c \subseteq F_1^c \cup \ldots \cup F_n^c$, that is, equivalently, $F \supseteq F_1 \cap \ldots \cap F_n$, that is, $F \leq F_1 \vee \ldots \vee F_n$.

Since sets $F_1, \ldots, F_n$ belong to the directed family D, this family must also contain an upper bound $d \in D$. By definition of the least upper bound, we have $F_1 \vee \ldots \vee F_n \leq d$, hence $F \leq d$. Thus, indeed, $G << F$.

2. **Necessity.** Let $F << G$. Since the underlying topological space X is locally compact, each point $x \in G^c$ has a compact neighborhood $Q_x \subseteq G^c$ such that its interior $\overset{\circ}{Q}_x$ contains x. We thus have $G^c = \cup\{\overset{\circ}{Q}_x : x \in G^c\}$ or, equivalently,

$$G = \cap\{(\overset{\circ}{Q}_x)^c : x \in G^c\} = \vee\{(\overset{\circ}{Q}_x)^c : x \in G^c\}.$$

Finite unions of closed sets $(\overset{\circ}{Q}_x)^c$ form a directed family D, for which the union is the same set G. Since $G \leq \vee D$ and $F << G$, we conclude (by definition of the "way below" relation) that $F \leq \vee\{(\overset{\circ}{Q}_{x_i})^c : i = 1, \ldots, n\}$, $x_i \in G^c$. Thus, $F \supseteq \bigcap_{i=1}^{n}(Q_{x_i})^c$ or, equivalently, $F^c \subseteq \bigcup_{i=1}^{n}(Q_{x_i})$. Therefore, $F^c \subseteq \bigcup_{i=1}^{n} Q_{x_i} \subseteq G^c$. Since each set Q_{x_i} is compact, their union is also compact, so we have the desired inclusion $F^c \subseteq K \subseteq G^c$ with $K = \bigcup_{i=1}^{n} Q_{x_i}$. The lemma is proven.

Proof that $(\mathbf{F}(X), \supseteq)$ is a continuous lattice. Let us now use this Lemma 2 to show that $(\mathbf{F}(X), \supseteq)$ is a continuous lattice. We have already mentioned that to prove this fact, we must prove that $F^c \subseteq \cup\{G^c : G \in \mathbf{F}, G << F\}$ for every closed set $F \in \mathbf{F}(X)$. Indeed, let F be a closed set. Since X is locally compact, for every point x from the open set F^c, there exists a compact neighborhood $K_x \subseteq F^c$ such that its interior $\overset{\circ}{K}_x$ contains x. The complement $A = (\overset{\circ}{K}_x)^c$ to this (open) interior is a closed set $A \in \mathbf{F}(X)$, for which $x \in A^c = \overset{\circ}{K}_x \subseteq K_x \subseteq F^c$. So, due to Lemma 2, $A << F$. In other words, if $x \in F^c$, then there is an $A \in \mathbf{F}$ such that $x \in A^c$ and $A << F$. So, we conclude that $F^c\{ G^c : G \in \mathbf{F}, G << F\}$ that is, that $\mathbf{F}(X) \supseteq)$ is indeed a continuous lattice.

Lawson topology on the class of all closed sets. Since $\mathbf{F}(X) \supseteq)$ is a continuous lattice, we can define Lawson topology for this lattice. For this lattice, let us reformulate the general abstract notion of the Lawson topology in more understandable terms. In the following text, we will denote the class of all compact subsets of the space X by, $\mathbf{K}(X)$ and the class of all open subsets of X by $\mathbf{O}(X)$. When the space X is clear from the context, we will simply write $\mathbf{K}$ and $\mathbf{O}$.

Theorem 1. *For every LCHS X, the Lawson topology on the continuous lattice $(\mathbf{F}(X), \supseteq)$ is generated by the subbase consisting of subsets of $\mathbf{F}$ of the form $\mathbf{F}^K \overset{\mathrm{def}}{=} \{F \in \mathbf{F} : F \cap K = \phi\}$ and $\mathbf{F}_G \overset{\mathrm{def}}{=} \{F \in \mathbf{F} : F \cap G \neq \phi\}$, where $K \in \mathbf{K}$ $K \in \mathbf{K}$ and $G \in \mathbf{O}$.*

Comment. The class $\{F \in \mathbf{F} : F \cap K = \phi\}$ is the class of all random sets F which *miss* the set K, and the class $\{F \in \mathbf{F} : F \cap G \neq \phi\}$ is the class of all random sets F which *hit* the set G. Because of this interpretation, the above topology is called the hit-or-miss topology (Mathéron, 1975). So, the meaning of Theorem 1 is that the Lawson topology on $(\mathbf{F}(X), \supseteq)$ coincides with the hit-or-miss topology.

Proof. By definition, the Lawson topology has a subbase consisting of sets of the form $\{F' \in \mathbf{F} : F << F'\}$ and $\{F' \in \mathbf{F} : F \nleq F'\}$ for all $F \in \mathbf{F}$, where $\leq$ is $\supseteq$. It turns out that to prove the theorem, it is sufficient to reformulate these sets in terms of $\supseteq$.

1. Clearly:

$$\{F' \in \mathbf{F} : F \nleq F'\} = \{F' \in \mathbf{F} : F' \cap F^c \neq \phi\}.$$

2. For $K \in \mathbf{K}$, we have:

$$\{F \in \mathbf{F} : F \cap K = \phi\} = \bigcup_{F' \in \mathbf{F}, F' \subseteq K^c} \{F \in \mathbf{F} : F' << F\}.$$

Indeed, if $F \in \mathbf{F}$ and $F \cap K = \phi$, then K is a subset of the open set F^c. Since the space X is locally compact, there exists an open set B and a compact K' such that $K \subseteq B \subseteq K' \subseteq F^c$. The complement $G = B^c$ to an open set B is a closed set for which $K \subseteq G^c \subseteq K' \subseteq F^c$. By Lemma 2, this means that $G << F$ and, of course, $G \subseteq K^c$.

Conversely, let $f \in \mathbf{F}$ and $F' << F$ with $F' \subseteq K^c$. Then, by the same Lemma 2, there is a compact set K' with $(F')^c \subseteq K \subseteq {}'F^c$. On the other hand, $F' \subseteq F^c$ implies that $K \subseteq (F')^c$, so we have $K \subseteq F^c$ and $K \cap F = \phi$. The theorem is proven.

From topology to metric: need and possibility. We have defined topology on the class of all closed sets. Topology describes the intuitive notion of closeness in *qualitative* terms. From the viewpoint of applications, it is convenient to use *quantitative* measures of closeness such as a *metric*.

Before we start describing a corresponding metric, let us first prove that this metric is indeed possible, that is, that the corresponding topological space is metrizable. It is known that for every continuous lattice, the corresponding Lawson topology is compact and Hausdorff. Let us prove that for LCHS spaces X, the Lawson topology on $(\mathbf{F}(X), \supseteq)$ is not only compact and Hausdorff, it is also second countable—and therefore metrizable.

Theorem 2. *For every LCHS X, the Lawson topology on $(\mathbf{F}(X), \supseteq)$ is second countable.*

Proof. This proof is given in Mathéron (1975) for the hit-or-miss topology. We reproduce it here for completeness.

Since X is locally compact Hausdorff second countable space, there exists a countable basis $\mathbf{B}$ for the topology $\mathbf{O}$ consisting of *relatively compact* sets $B \in \mathbf{B}$ (i.e., sets whose closure $\bar{B}$ is compact). The fact that $\mathbf{B}$ is a basis means that every open set $G \in \mathbf{O}$ can be represented as a union of open sets from this basis, that is, that it can be represented in the form $G = \bigcup_{i \in I} B_i$, where $B_i \in \mathbf{B}$, and $\bar{B}_i \subseteq G$.

By definition of the hit-or-miss topology, its subbase consists of the sets $\mathbf{F}^A = \{F \in \mathbf{F} : F \cap A = \phi\}$ for compact sets A and sets $\mathbf{F}_A = \{F \in \mathbf{F} : F \cap A \neq \phi\}$ for open sets A. Thus, the base of this topology consists of the finite intersections of such sets. The intersection of two sets $\mathbf{F}^A \stackrel{\text{def}}{=} \{F \in \mathbf{F} : F \cap A = \phi\}$ and $\mathbf{F}^{A'} \stackrel{\text{def}}{=} \{F \in \mathbf{F} : F \cap A' = \phi\}$ consists of all the sets F which do not have common points neither with A nor with A'; this is equivalent to saying that F has no common points with the union $A \cup A'$, that is, that $\mathbf{F}^A \cap \mathbf{F}^{A'} = \mathbf{F}^{A \cup A'}$. Thus, finite intersections which form the basis of the hit-or-miss topology (or, equivalently, Lawson topology) have the form $\mathbf{F}^K_{G_1,\ldots,G_n} \stackrel{\text{def}}{=} \{F \in \mathbf{F} : F \cap K = \phi, F \cap G_i \neq \phi, i = 1,2,\ldots,n\}$ for all possible $K \in \mathbf{K}$ and $G_i \in \mathbf{O}$.

Let us consider the following subset of this basis:

$$\mathbf{T} = \left\{ \mathbf{F}^{\overline{D}_1 \cup \ldots \cup \overline{D}_k}_{B_1,\ldots,B_m} ; m, k \geq 0, B_i, D_j \in \mathbf{B} \right\}.$$

Clearly $\mathbf{T}$ is countable. We need to verify that $\mathbf{T}$ is a basis for the Lawson topology. For this, we need to prove that for every element $F \in \mathbf{F}$ in every open neighborhood of F, there is an open set from $\mathbf{T}$ that contains F. It is sufficient to prove this property only for the neighborhood from the known basis.

Indeed, let $F \in \mathbf{F}$ and let the open set $\mathbf{F}^K_{G_1,\ldots,G_n}$ be a neighborhood of F. We need to find a $U \in \mathbf{T}$ such that $F \in U \subseteq \mathbf{F}^K_{G_1,\ldots,G_n}$. We will prove this by considering two possible cases: $F = \phi$ and $F \neq \phi$.

If $F = \phi$, then we cannot have $F \cap G_i \neq \phi$, so n must be 0, and $\mathbf{F}^K_{G_1,\ldots,G_n} = \mathbf{F}^K$. Since B is a basis, the compact set K can be covered by open sets from this basis. Since K is compact, we can extract a finite cover from this cover, that is, conclude that $K \subseteq D_1 \cup \ldots \cup D_k$ for some elements $D_j \in B$. Thus, $K \subseteq \overline{D}_1 \cup \ldots \cup \overline{D}_k$. Clearly, the empty set has no common point with anyone, so $F \in \mathbf{F}^{\overline{D}_1 \cup \ldots \cup \overline{D}_k}$.

If a set has no common points with a larger set, then it will no common points with a subset either; so we conclude that $F \in \mathbf{F}^{\overline{D}_1 \cup \ldots \cup \overline{D}_k} \subseteq \mathbf{F}^k$. So, we can take $U = \mathbf{F}^{\overline{D}_1 \cup \ldots \cup \overline{D}_k}$ as the desired neighborhood.

If $F = \phi$, then the fact that F belongs to the neighborhood $\mathbf{F}^K_{G_1,\ldots,G_n}$ means that $F \cap G \neq \phi$ for every i. This means that for every $i = 1,2,\ldots,n$, we can pick a point $x_i \in F \cap G_i$. Since $\mathbf{B}$ is a basis

for every i, there exists an open set $B_i \in B$ such that $x_i \in B_i \subseteq \overline{B}_i \subseteq G_i \cap K^c$.

This means that our set F not only has no common points with K, it also has no common points with the closed sets $\overline{B}_i$. Since the closed sets K and $F \cup \left(\bigcup_{i=1}^n \overline{B}_i \right)$ are disjoint and the space X is Hausdorff, we can find two disjoint open sets A_1 and A_2 which contain these sets: $K \subseteq A_1$ and $F \cup \left(\bigcup_{i=1}^n \overline{B}_i \right) \subseteq A_2$. Since B is a basis, we can represent the open set A_1 as a union of open sets from B: $K \subseteq A_1 = \bigcup D_j$ for some $D_j \in B$ for which $\overline{D}_j \subseteq A_1$. The set K is compact and thus, from this open cover of K, we can extract a finite sub-cover, that is, we have:

$$K \subseteq \bigcup_{j=1}^k D_j \subseteq \bigcup_{j=1}^k \overline{D}_j \subseteq A_1 \subseteq A_2^c,$$

and

$$\left(\bigcup_{j=1}^k \overline{D}_j \right) \cap A_2 = \phi.$$

Thus, $F \in U \stackrel{\text{def}}{=} \mathbf{F}^{\overline{D}_1 \cup \ldots \cup \overline{D}_k}_{B_1,\ldots,B_n} \subseteq \mathbf{F}^K_{G_1,\ldots,G_n}$.

The theorem is proven.

METRICS ON CLOSED SETS

From theoretical possibility of a metric to a need for an explicit metric. In the previous section, we have shown that for every LCHS X (in particular, for $X = \mathbf{R}^d$), when we define Lawson topology on the set $\mathbf{F}(X)$ of all closed subsets of X, then this set $\mathbf{F}(X)$ becomes metrizable. This means that *in principle*, this topology can be generated by a metric.

However, from the *application* viewpoint, it is not enough to consider a theoretical possibility of a metric, it is desirable to describe a specific explicit example of a metric.

Known metric on the class of all closed sets: Hausdorff metric. Intuitively, the metric describes the notion of a distance between two sets. Before we start describing an explicit metric which is compatible with the Lawson topology, let us first describe natural ways to describe such a distance.

For points $x, y \in \mathbf{R}^d$, the standard distance $\delta(x, y)$ can be described in terms of neighborhoods: the distance is the smallest value $\varepsilon > 0$ such that x belongs to the ε-neighborhood of y and y is in the ε-neighborhood of x.

It is natural to extend the notion of ε-neighborhood from points to sets. Namely, a set A is collection of all its points; thus, an ε-neighborhood $N_\varepsilon(A)$ of a set A is a collection of ε-neighborhoods of all its points. In other words, we can define:

$$N_\varepsilon(A) \overset{\text{def}}{=} \{x \in X : \delta(x, a) \le \varepsilon \text{ for some } a \in A\}.$$

Now, we can define the distance $d_H(A, B)$ between the two sets as the smallest smallest value $\varepsilon > 0$ for which A is contained in the ε-neighborhood of B and B is contained in the ε-neighborhood of A:

$$H_\delta(A, B) \overset{\text{def}}{=} \inf\{\varepsilon > 0 : A \subseteq N_\varepsilon(B) \,\&\, B \subseteq N_\varepsilon(A)\}.$$

This metric is called the *Hausdroff metric* (after the mathematician who proposed this definition).

Examples. Hausdorff distance between a one-point set $\{0.3\}$ and an interval $[0,1]$ is 0.7: indeed, all the elements from the set $\{0.3\}$ are contained in the interval $[0,1]$, and every element of the interval $[0,1]$ is contained in the 0.7-vicinity of the point 0.3.

This example can be viewed as a degenerate case of computing the Hausdorff distance between two intervals $[\underline{a}, \overline{a}]$ and $[\underline{b}, \overline{b}]$—namely, the case when $\underline{a} = \overline{a}$. In general, the Hausdorff distance between the two intervals is equal to $\max(|\underline{a} - \underline{b}|, |\overline{a} - \overline{b}|)$.

Limitations of the known metric. Hausdorff metric works well for bounded sets in $\mathbf{R}^d$ or, more generally, for subsets of a compact set. However, if we use the Haudorff metric to described distances between arbitrary closed sets $A, B \subseteq \mathbf{R}^d$, we often get meaningless infinities: for example, in the plane, the Hausdorff distance between any two non-parallel lines is infinity.

How to overcome these limitations: the notion of compactification. To overcome the above limitation, it is desirable to modify the definition of a Hausdorff metric.

Since Hausdorff metric works well for compact spaces, a natural idea is to somehow embed the original topological spaces into a compact set. Such a procedure is known as *compactification*.

Simplest compactification. In the simplest compactification, known as *Alexandroff* (or *one-point*) *compactification*, we simply add a single point ∞ to the original space X.

The corresponding topology on $X \cup \{\infty\}$ is defined as follows:

- if a set $S \subseteq G$ does not contain the new point ∞, then it is open if and only if it was open in the original topology;
- if a set S contains ∞, then it is called open if and only if its complement S^c is a compact subset of the original space X.

From points to closed sets. This compactification can be extended to an arbitrary closed set F: namely, a set F which was closed in X is not necessarily closed in the new space $X \cup \{\infty\}$ so we have to take the closure $\overline{F}$ of this set.

If we have a matric δ' on the compactification, then we can define a distance between closed sets $F, F' \in \mathbf{F}$ as $H_{\delta'}(\overline{F}, \overline{F'})$.

Compactification of $\mathbf{R}^d$. For $\mathbf{R}^d$, the one-point compactification can be implemented in a very natural way, via a so-called *stereographic pro-*

jection. Specifically, we can interpret a one-point compactification of the space $\mathbf{R}^d$ as a sphere $\mathbf{S}^d \subseteq \mathbf{R}^{d+1}$. The correspondence between the original points of $\mathbf{R}^d$ and $\mathbf{S}^d$ is arranged as follows. We place the space $\mathbf{R}^d$ horizontally, and we place the sphere $\mathbf{S}^d$ on top of this plane, so that its "South pole" is on that plane. Then, to find the image $\pi(x)$ of a point $x \in \mathbf{R}^d$ on the sphere, we connect this point x with the "North pole" of the sphere by a straight line, and take, as $\pi(x)$, the intersection between this line and the sphere. In this manner, we cover all the points on the sphere except for the North pole itself. The North pole corresponds to infinity—in the sense that if $x \to \infty$, then $\pi(x)$ tends to the North pole.

In this sense, $\mathbf{S}^d$ is a one-point compactification of the original space $\mathbf{R}^d$: it is a compact space, and it is obtained by adding a point (North pole) to (the image of) $\mathbf{R}^d$.

From points to closed sets. By using this construction, we can naturally find the projection of an arbitrary closed set $F \in \mathbf{F}(\mathbf{R}^d)$ as the collection of all the projections of all its points, that is, as $\pi(F) = \{\pi(x) : x \in F\}$. The only minor problem is even while we started with a closed set F, this collection $\pi(F)$, by itself, may be not closed. For example, a straight line on a plane is closed, but its projection is not closed—since it has point arbitrary close to the North pole but not the North pole itself.

To resolve this problem, we can then take a closure of this image. Thus, we arrive at the following *stereographic Hausdorff metric* $H_{\delta'}(\pi(F), \pi(F'))$, where δ' is the standard distance on the sphere $\mathbf{S}^d$.

Relation between this metric and the Lawson topology. It turns out that the Lawson topology on $\mathbf{F}(\mathbf{R}^d)$ is compatible with the Hausdorff metric on a one-point compactification.

For the stereographic Hausdorff metric, this equivalence is proven, for example, in Rockafeller and Wets (1984); for the general LCHS space, this is proven in Wei and Wang (in press).

RANDOM CLOSED SETS: FINAL DEFINITION AND CHOQUET THEOREM

Final definition of a random (closed) set. With the material developed in previous sections, we are now ready to formulate rigorously the concept of random closed sets as *bona fide* random elements. These are generalizations of random vectors and serve as mathematical models for observation processes in which observables are sets rather than points.

Again, let $\mathbf{F}(\mathbf{R}^d)$ ($\mathbf{F}(X)$) be the space of closed sets of $\mathbf{R}^d$, or more generally, of a LCHS space X. Let $\sigma(\mathbf{F})$ denote the Borel σ-field of subsets of $\mathbf{F}$ where $\mathbf{F}$ is equipped with the Lawson topology. Let $(\Omega, \mathbf{A}, P)$ be a probability space. A map $V : \Omega \to \mathbf{F}$, which is $\mathbf{A}$-$\sigma(\mathbf{F})$-measurable, is called a *random closed set* (RCS) on $\mathbf{R}^d$. As usual, the probability law governing V is the probability measure $P_V = PV^{-1}$ on $\sigma(\mathbf{F})$.

Application-motivated need to describe a random set. A random set is, in effect, a probability measure on the class of all closed subsets $\mathbf{F}(X)$ of the LCHS X. In principle, we can thus describe the random set by listing, for different subsets $S \subseteq \mathbf{F}$, the corresponding probability $P(S)$.

From the application viewpoint, however, this description is duplicating—for example, since due to additivity, the probability $P_V(S \cup S')$ of a union of two disjoint sets is equal to the sum $P_V(S) + P_V(S')$ of the probabilities $P_V(S)$ and $P_V(S')$ and thus, does not have to be described independently.

For random numbers and for random vectors, the solution was to only give probability of sets from a given subbase. For real numbers, this subbase consisted of sets $(-\infty, x]$—which let to the notion of a probability distribution.

For elements of $\mathbf{R}^d$, we considered sets of the type $(-\infty, x_1] \times \ldots \times (-\infty, x_d]$. For the hit-or-miss topology on the space $\mathbf{F}(X)$, the subbase consists of the sets $\{F : F \cap A = \phi\}$ for compact A and $\{F : F \cap A \neq \phi\}$ for open sets A. It is therefore reasonable to define the probability only on the sets of this type.

The set $\{F : F \cap A = \phi\}$ is a complement to the set $\{F : F \cap A \neq \phi\}$, so we do not have to describe its probability separately: it is sufficient to describe the probability of the sets $\{F : F \cap A \neq \phi\}$.

Resulting description: capacity functionals. As a result, we arrive at the following definition. Once a random closed set X is defined, we can define the mapping $T : \mathbf{K} \to [0,1]$ as $T(K) = P\{\omega : X(\omega) \cap K \neq \phi\} = P_X(\mathbf{F}_K)$. This mapping is called a *capacity functional* of a random closed set.

Is this description sufficient? A natural question is whether from this functional we can uniquely determined the corresponding probability measure. A related question is: what are the conditions under which such a measure is possible?

It can be checked that T satisfies the following properties:

i. $0 \leq T(\cdot) \leq 1, T(\phi) = 0$;
ii. If $K_n \searrow K$ then $TK_n \searrow T(K)$;
iii. T is *alternating of infinite order*, that is, T is monotone (with respect to $\subseteq$) and for $K_1, K_2, \ldots, K_n$, $n \geq 2$,

$$T\left(\bigcap_{i=1}^{n} K_i\right) \leq \sum_{\phi \neq I \subseteq \{1, 2, \ldots, n\}} (-1)^{|I|+1} T\left(\bigcup_{i \in I} K_i\right)$$

where $|I|$ denotes the cardinality of the set I.

It turns out that under these conditions, there is indeed such a measure.

Theorem (Choquet) *Let $T : \mathbf{K} \to \mathbf{R}$. Then the following two statements are equivalent to each other:*

- *there exists a probability measure Q on $\sigma(\mathbf{F})$ for which $Q(\mathbf{F}_K) = T(K)$ for all $K \in \mathbf{K}$;*
- *T satisfies the conditions i, ii and iii.*

If one of these statements is satisfied, then the corresponding probability measure Q is uniquely determined by T.

For a proof, see Mathéron (1975).

This theorem is the counter-part of the Lebesgue-Stieltjes theorem characterizing probability measures on the Borel σ-field of $\mathbf{R}^d$ in terms of multivariate distribution function S of random vectors. For subsequent developments of RCS, see for example Nguyen (2006).

FROM RANDOM SETS TO RANDOM FUZZY SETS

Need for fuzziness. As stated in the Introduction, random set observations are coarse data containing the true, unobservable outcomes of random experiments on phenomena.

A more general type of random and imprecise observations occurs when we have to use *natural language* to describe our perception. For example, the risk is "high" is an "observation" containing also imprecision at at a higher level due to the *fuzziness* in our natural language. Modeling fuzziness in natural language, that is, modeling the meaning of terms is crucial if we wish to process information of this type.

How we can describe fuzziness. Following Zadeh, we use the theory of *fuzzy sets* to model the meaning of a nature language; see, for example, Nguyen and Walker(2006) for fuzzy sets and fuzzy logics.

The theory is in fact valid for any LCHS space X. For concreteness, one can keep in mind an example $X = \mathbf{R}^d$. By a *fuzzy subset* of X we mean a function $f : X \to [0,1]$ where $f(x)$ is the degree to which the element x is compatible with the fuzzy concept represented by f. This function f is also called a *membership function*.

For example, the membership function f of the fuzzy concept $A=$ "small non-negative numbers" of $\mathbf{R}$ could be $f(x)=0$ if $x < 0, e^{-x}$ for $x \geq 0$, where $f(x) = e^{-x}$ is the degree to which x is considered as a "small non-negative number."

Ordinary subsets of X are special cases of fuzzy subsets of X, where for $A \subseteq X$, its indicator function $I_A: \mathbf{R}^d \to \{0,1\} \subseteq [0,1]$, $I_A(X) = 1$ if $x \in A$, and $I_A(X) = 0$ if $x \notin A$, is the membership function of A.

An alternative way to describe fuzzy sets: α-cuts. Informally, the fact that the actual (unknown) value $_{act} \in X$ satisfies the property described by a fully set f means the following:

- with confidence 1, the actual value x_{act} satisfies the condition $f(x_{act}) > 0$;
- with confidence 0.9, the actual value x_{act} satisfies the condition $f(x_{act}) > 1 - 0.9 = 0.1$, that is, belongs to the set $\{x : f(x) \geq 0.1\}$; and so on.

In view of this interpretation, instead of describing the fuzzy set by its membership function $f(x)$, we can alternatively describe it by the corresponding sets $A_\alpha \overset{\text{def}}{=} \{x \in X : f(x) \geq \alpha\}$ for different $\alpha \in [0,1]$. These sets are called *alpha-cuts*.

Alpha-cuts are *nested* in the sense that if $\alpha < \alpha'$, then $A_a \supseteq A_a$. So, a fuzzy set can be viewed as a nested family of sets (corresponding to different degrees of confidence); see, for example, Klir and Yuan (1995), Nguyen and Kreinovich (1996), and Nguyen and Walker (2006).

Fuzzy analog of closed sets. In our description of random sets, we limited ourselves to *closed* sets. Since a fuzzy set can be viewed as a nested family of sets (its alpha-cuts), it is reasonable to consider fuzzy sets in which all alpha-cuts are closed sets.

In other words, it is reasonable to restrict ourselves to fuzzy sets $f : X \to [0,1]$ which have the following property: for every $\alpha \in \mathbf{R}$, the set $A_\alpha = \{x \in X : f(x) \geq \alpha\}$ is a closed subset of X. In mathematics, functions f with this property are called *upper semicontinuous* (*usc*, for short). We will thus call a fuzzy set a *fuzzy closed set* if its membership function is usc.

Closed sets are a particular case of fuzzy closed sets. We have already mentioned that traditional (crisp) sets are a particular case of fuzzy sets. It is easy to check that closed crisp sets are also closed as fuzzy sets.

Moreover, a subset of X is closed if and only if its indicator function is upper semicontinuous.

Towards a definition of a random fuzzy closed set. To formalize the concept of random fuzzy (closed) sets, we will therefore consider the space $USC(X)$ (where X is a LCHS space), of all usc functions on X with values in $[0,1]$.

As we mentioned earlier, a natural way to define a notion of the random fuzzy closed set is to describe a topology on the set $USC(X)$. Similar to the case of closed sets, we will use the Lawson topology generated by a natural order on $USC(X)$.

The space $USC(X)$ has a natural pointwise order: $f \leq g$ if and only if $f(x) \leq g(x)$ for all $x \in X$. We can also consider the dual order $f \geq g$ (which is equivalent to $g \leq f$). We will now look for the corresponding Lawson topology!

THE CONTINUOUS LATTICE OF UPPER SEMICONTINUOUS FUNCTIONS

First try: $USC(X)$, $\leq$. Let X as any LCHS space. By $USC(X)$ we mean the set of all usc functions $f : X \to [0,1]$.

With the order relation $\leq$, $USC(X)$ is complete lattice, where:

$$\left(\underset{j \in J}{\wedge} f_j\right)(x) = \inf\{f_j(x), j \in J\} \text{ and,}$$

$$\left(\underset{j \in J}{\vee} f_j\right)(x) = \sup\{\alpha \in [0,1] : x \in A_\alpha\}$$

where $A_\alpha = \text{closure of} \bigcup_{j \in J}\{y \in X : f_j(y) \geq \alpha\}$.

Remarks

(i)   Clearly

$$f = \inf\{f_j, j \in J, f_j \in USC(X)\} \in USC(X).$$

Indeed, let $\alpha \in [0,1]$, then $\{x \in X : f(x) < \alpha\} = \bigcup_{j \in J}\{x : f_j(x) < \alpha\}$ is an open set.

(ii)   Let us explain why we cannot simply use pointwise supremum to define $\vee$.

Indeed, for $f_n(x) = I_{[\frac{1}{n}, +\infty)}(x), n \geq 1$, we have $fn \in USC(X)$, but the pointwise supremum $\sup_n\{I_{[\frac{1}{n}, +\infty)}(x), n \geq 1\} = I_{(0, +\infty)}(x) \notin USC(X)$.

To define $\vee\{f_j : j \in J\}$, we proceed as follows: For $\alpha \in [0,1]$, let

$$A_\alpha = \text{closure of} \bigcup_{j \in J}\{y \in X : f_j(y) \geq \alpha\},$$

and define $f(x) = \sup\{\alpha \in [0,1] : x \in A_\alpha\}$. We claim that f is the least upper bound of $\{f_j : j \in J, f_j \in USC(X)\}$ in $USC(X)$ with respect to $\leq$.

Clearly each A_a is closed and $\alpha < \beta$ implies $A_b \subseteq A_a$. As such $f \in USC(X)$.

Next, for $x \in X$, we have

$$x \in \text{closure of} \bigcup_{j \in J}\{y : f_j(y) \geq f_i(x)\} = A_{f_i(x)}$$

for any $i \in J$. Thus, for every $i \in J$, we have $f_i(x) \leq f(x)$. Since this is true for every x, we thus conclude that $f \geq f_i$ for all $i \in J$.

Now, for $g \in USC(X)$, we can write $g(x) = \sup\{\alpha \in [0,1] : x \in A_\alpha(g)\}$ where $A_\alpha(g) = \{y \in X : g(y) \geq \alpha\}$.

For any $y \in \bigcup_{j \in J}\{x : f_j(x) \geq \alpha\}$, that is, for any y for which $f_j(y) \geq \alpha$ for some j, we have $g(y) \geq \alpha$ if $g \geq f_j$ for all $i \in I$. Thus, $y \in A_a(g)$, implying that $A_a \subseteq A_a(g)$, since $A_a(g)$ is closed. But then $\sup\{\alpha \in [0,1] : x \in A_\alpha\} \leq \sup\{\alpha \in [0,1] : x \in A_\alpha(g)\}$ and hence $f \leq g$.

(iii)   However, the complete lattice $(USC(X), \leq)$ is not continuous.

The proof of this statement is similar to the proof that the lattice $(\mathbf{F}(X)$ is not continuous. Indeed, let $f : X \to [0,1]$ be a function for which $f(x) = 1$ for all $x \in X$. Let us then show that the zero function, that is a function g for which $g(x) = 0$ for all $x \in X$, is the only function in $USC(X)$ which is way below f.

It suffices to show that for any real number $r > 0$, the function $r \cdot I_{\{y\}}(\cdot)$ (e.g., $\frac{1}{2} \cdot I_{\{0\}}(\cdot)$), is not way below f.

Let:

$$f_n(x) = I_{(-\infty, y-\frac{1}{n}) \cup (y+\frac{1}{n}, +\infty)},$$

then $\underset{n \geq 1}{\vee} f_n = 1$, but for any K, we have

$$\overset{K}{\underset{n=1}{\vee}} f_n(y) = 0,$$

thus $r \cdot I_{\{y\}} \not\leq \overset{K}{\underset{n=1}{\vee}} f_n$, implying that $r \cdot I_{\{y\}}$ is not way below f.

Correct description: $(USC, \geq)$. Thus, as in the case of $\mathbf{F}(X)$, we should consider the reverse order $\geq$.

Box 1.

$$\inf\{g \in USC(X): \ g << f\} \le f = \inf\left\{g_{r,K} \ : \ f(y) < r \text{ for all } y \in K\right\}.$$

Theorem 3. *The complete lattice* $(USC(X),$ $\ge)$, *where* $\vee\{f_j \ : \ j \in J\} = \inf\{f_j : j \in J\}$ *and* $\wedge\{f_j \ : \ j \in J\} = h$ *with:*

$$h(x) = \sup\{\alpha \in [0,1]: \ x \in A_\alpha\} \ and$$

$$A_\alpha = \text{closure of } \bigcup_{j \in J}\{y \in X \ : \ f_j(y) \ge \alpha\},$$

is continuous.

Before proving this theorem, we need a representation for elements of $USC(X)$. For every real number r and for every compact set $K \in \mathbf{K}(X)$, let us define an auxiliary function $g_{r,K}$ as follows:

$g_{r,K}(x) = r$ if $x \in K$ and $g_{r,K}(x) = 1$ otherwise.

Lemma 3. *Any* $f \in USC(X)$ *can be written as* $f(\cdot) = \inf\left\{g_{r,K}(\cdot): \ f(y) < r \text{ for all } y \in K\right\}$, *where infimum is taken over all pairs* $r \in [0,1]$ *and* $K \in \mathbf{K}(X)$ *for which* $f(y) < r$ *for all* $y \in K$.

Comment. In this definition, the infimum of an empty set is assumed to be equal to 1.

Proof. Let $x \in X$. Let us consider two possible cases: $f(x) = 1$ and $f(x) < 1$.

(i)   Let us first consider the case when $f(x) = 1$.

To prove the formula for this case, we will consider two cases: when $x \notin \overset{\circ}{K}$ and when $x \in \overset{\circ}{K}$.

In the first subcase, when $x \notin \overset{\circ}{K}$, we have $g_{r,K}(x) = 1$ by definition of the function $g_{r,K}$. Thus, the infimum is equal to 1, that is, to $f(x)$.

In the second subcase, when $x \notin K$, then there is no r such that $f(y) < r$ for all $y \in K$. Thus, the infimum is also equal to $1 = f(x)$.

(ii)   Let us now consider the case when $f(x) < 1$.

We need to prove that $f(x)$ is the greatest lower bound of the values $g_{r,K}(X)$. Let us first prove that $f(x)$ is a lower bound. For that, we will again consider two subcases: $x \notin \overset{\circ}{K}$ and when $x \in \overset{\circ}{K}$.

When $x \in \overset{\circ}{K}$, we have $f(x) < r = g_{r,K}(x)$. When $x \notin K$, we have $f(x) < 1 = g_{r,K}(x)$. Thus, in both subcases, $f(x)$ is indeed a lower bound of $\{g_{r,K}(x)\}$.

Let us now prove that $f(x)$ is the greatest lower bound. In other words, let us prove that for any $\varepsilon > 0$, the value $f(x) + \varepsilon$ is not a lower bound of $\{g_{r,K}(x)\}$.

Indeed, let $r_0 = f(x) + \frac{\varepsilon}{2}$, then x belongs to the open set $\left\{y \in X \ : \ f(y) < r_0 = f(x) + \frac{\varepsilon}{2}\right\}$. By local compactness of X, we conclude that there is a compact set $K_0 \subseteq \{y : \ f(y) < r_0\}$ such that $x \in \overset{\circ}{K_0}$, implying that $g_{r_0,K_0}(x) = r_0 < f(x) + \varepsilon$, that is, that for every $y \in K_0$, we have $f(y) < r_0$ and $g_{r_0,K_0}(x) < f(x) + \varepsilon$. The Lemma is proven.

Now, we are ready to prove the theorem.

Proof of Theorem 3. Consider $(USC(X),$ $\ge)$. For $f \in USC(X)$, we always have $f \le \inf\{g \in USC(X) : g << f\}$, thus it is sufficient to show that (see Box 1.)

To prove this relation, it is sufficient to show that $g_{r,K} < f$ for any (r, K) such that $f(y) < r$ for all $y \in K$.

Indeed, let $F \subseteq USC(X)$ be a directed set such that $f \ge \vee F$, that is, $\inf F \le f$ (pointwise). To prove the desired "way below'" relation, we need to find $h \in F$ such that $h \le g_{r,K}$.

For (r, K) with $r > f \ge \inf F$ (pointwise on K), we will show that there exists an $h \in F$ such that $h < r$ on K. For any $h \in F$, denote $K_h \overset{\text{def}}{=} \{x \in K : \ r \le h(x)\}$.

Since h is usc, the set K_h is a closed set.

Let us prove that the intersection $\bigcap_{h \in F} K$ of all these sets K_h is the empty set. Indeed, if $x \in \bigcap_{h \in F} K$, then by definition of K_h, it means that $r \le h(x)$ for all $h \in F$. This will imply that $r \le \inf F$ on K, contradicting the fact that $r \le \inf F$ on K.

Since every set K_h is closed, its complement K_h^c is open. From $\bigcap_{h \in F} K_h = \phi$, we conclude that $\bigcup_{h \in F} K_h^c = X$ and thus, $K \subseteq \bigcup_{h \in F} K_h^c$. Since K is a compact set, from this open cover, we can extract a finite subcover, hence $K \subseteq \bigcup_{i=1}^{n} K_{h_i}^c$ for some functions h_i. Thus, we have $\bigcap_{i=1}^{n} K_{h_i} \subseteq K^c$. Since $K_h \subseteq K^c$ for all h, we thus conclude that $\bigcap_{i=1}^{n} K_{h_i} = \phi$.

Since F is directed, we have
$$h \overset{\text{def}}{=} \vee (h_i : i = 1, \ldots, n) = \inf\{h_i : i = 1, \ldots, n\} \in F.$$

For this h, we have $K_h = \bigcap_{i=1}^{n} K_{h_i} = \phi$. This means that for every $x \in K$, we have $h(x) < r$.

Now, for an arbitrary point $x \in X$, we have two possibilities: $x \in X$ and $x \notin K$. If $x \in X$, then $h(x) < r < g_{r,K}(x)$. On the other hand, if $x \notin K$, then $h(x) \le 1$ and $g_{r,K}(x) = 1$, hence also $h(x) \le g_{r,K}(x)$. So, for all $x \in X$, we have $h(x) \le g_{r,K}(x)$. The statement is proven.

Towards an application-oriented description of the corresponding Lawson topology. Since $(USC, \ge)$ is a continuous lattice, we can define the corresponding Lawson topology.

The Lawson topology is defined in very general, very abstract terms. To be able to efficiently apply this abstractly defined topology to random fuzzy closed sets, it is desirable to describe the Lawson topology for such sets in easier-to-understand terms. Such a description is given by the following result.

Theorem 4. *The following sets form a subbase for the Lawson topology on* $(USC(X), \ge)$*: the sets of the form* $\{f : f(y) < r$ *for all* $y \in K\}$ *for all* $r \in (0, 1]$ *and* $K \in \mathbf{K}(X)$*, and the sets* $\{f : g(x) < f(x)$ *for some* $x \in X\}$ *for all* $g \in USC(X)$*.*

Proof. By definition, the Lawson topology on $USC(X)$, $\ge$) is generated by the subbase consisting of the sets $\{f : g \ll f\}$ and $\{f : g \not\ge f\}$. For the ordered set $(USC(X), \ge)$, clearly, $\{f : g \not\ge f\} = \{f : g(x) < f(x)$ for some $x \in X\}$.

Let us now considers sets $\{f : g \ll f\}$. It is known that these sets form a base of a topology which is called *Scott topology*; see, for example, Gierz et al. (1980). A Scott open set is thus an arbitrary union of sets of the type $\{f : g \ll f\}$ with different g. So, to prove our theorem, it is sufficient to prove that the sets $\{f : f(y) <$ for all $y \in K\}$ form a subbase of the Scott topology.

To prove this, we first prove that each such set is indeed a Scott open set; this is proved in the Lemma below. It then remains to verify that the above sets indeed form a subbase for the Scott topology.

Indeed, let A be a Scott open set which contains an element h. Since $A = \bigcup\{f : g \ll f\}$, we have $h \in \{f : g \ll f\}$ for some g, that is, $g \ll h$. It is easy to show that:

$$h = \inf_{r,K}\{g_{r,K} : h(y) < r \text{ for all } y \in K\} =$$

$$\vee\{g_{r,K} : h(y) < r \text{ for all } y \in K\}.$$

Box 2.

$$\{f \in USC(X) : f(y) < r \text{ for all } y \in K\} = \bigcup_{\mathring{K}_i \supseteq K} \{f \in USC(X) : g_{r,K_i} \ll f\}.$$

Box 3.

$$\{f \in USC(X) : f(y) < r \text{ for all } y \in K\} \subseteq \bigcup_{\mathring{K}_i \supseteq K} \{f \in USC(X) : g_{r,K_i} \ll f\}.$$

Thus, by definition of the "way below" relation, $g < f$ implies that

$$g \geq \vee \{g_{r_i,K_i} \ : \ h(y) < r_i \text{ for all } y \in K_i, i = 1,2,\ldots,n\} =$$
$$\inf \{g_{r_i,K_i} \ : \ h(y) < r_i \text{ for all } y \in K_i, i = 1,2,\ldots,n\},$$

and hence, $h \in \bigcap_{i=1}^{n} \{f : f(y) < r_i \text{ for all } y \in K_i\}.$

Let us show that this intersection is indeed a subset of A. Observe that for every $f \in USC(X)$, we have $g_{r_i,K_i} << f$ if $f(y) < r_i$ for all $y \in K_i$. Now let $\hat{f}$ be an arbitrary function from the intersection, that is, $\hat{f} \in \bigcap_{i=1}^{n} \{f \ : \ f(y) < r_i \text{ for all } y \in K_i\}.$

Then:

$$g \overset{\text{def}}{=} \inf \{g_{r_i,K_i} \ : \ h(y) < r_i \text{ for all } y \in K_i, i = 1,\ldots,n\} << \hat{f}$$

and hence, by the representation of A,

$$\bigcap_{i=1}^{n} \{f \ : \ f(y) < r_i \text{ for all } y \in K_i, i = 1,\ldots,n\} \subseteq A.$$

To complete the proof, it is therefore sufficient to prove the following lemma:

Lemma 4. *For every $r \in (0,1]$ and $K \in \boldsymbol{K}(X)$, we have (see Box 2).*

Proof. Let $f \in USC(X)$ be such that $f(y) < r$ for all $y \in K$. Since f is usc, the set $A = \{x \in X : f(x) < r\}$ is an open set of X which contains K. Thus, there exists separating sets: an open set U and a compact set V such that $K \subseteq U \subseteq V \subseteq A$. Since $U \subseteq V$ and U is an open set, we thus conclude that $U \subseteq V$.

By definition of the function $g_{r,K}$, from $V \subseteq A$, we conclude that $g_{r,V} << f$. So (see Box 3).

Conversely, if $g_{r,K_i} << f$, where $\overset{\circ}{K} \supseteq K$, then for every $y \in K$, there exist r_y and K_y such that $y \in K_y$ and $f(z) < r_y \leq g_{r,K_i}(z)$ for all $z \in K_y$. In particular, for $z = y$, we $f(y) < r_y \leq g_{r,K_i}(y) = r$, so that $f(y) < r$ for all $y \in K$. The lemma is proven, and so is the theorem.

METRICS AND CHOQUET THEOREM FOR RANDOM FUZZY SETS

Resulting formal definition of a random fuzzy set. As we have mentioned, in general, a random object on a probability space $(\Omega,\mathbf{A},P)$ is defined a mapping $x : \Omega \to O$ which is $\mathbf{A}$-$\mathbf{B}$-measurable with respect to an appropriate σ-field $\mathbf{B}$ of subsets of the set O of objects.

For closed fuzzy sets, the set $\mathbf{O}$ is the set $USC(X)$ of all semicontinuous functions, and the appropriate σ-algebra is the algebra $\mathbf{L}(X)$ of all Borel sets in Lawson topology.

Thus, we can define a *random fuzzy* (closed) *set S* on a probability space $(\Omega,\mathbf{A},P)$ as a map $S : \Omega \to USC(X)$ which is $\mathbf{A}$-$\mathbf{L}(X)$-measurable.

Properties of the corresponding Lawson topology. From the general theory of continuous lattices, we can conclude that the space $USC(X)$ is a compact and Hausdorff topological space. When X is a LCHS space, then, similarly to the case of the set of all (crisp) closed sets $\mathbf{F}(X)$, we can prove that the set of all fuzzy closed sets $USC(X)$ is also second countable (see the proof below) and thus, metrizable.

Later in this section, we will discuss different metrics on $USC(X)$ which are compatible with this topology, and the corresponding Choquet theorem.

Theorem 5. *The topological space $USC(X)$ with the Lawson topology is second countable.*

Proof. It is known that for every continuous lattice, the Lawson topology is second countable if and only if the Scott topology has a countable base (Gierz et al., 1980). Thus, to prove our result, it is sufficient to prove that the Scott topology has a countable base.

In view of the results described in the previous section, the Scott topology has a base consisting of sets of the form

$$\bigcap_{i=1}^{n}\{f \in USC(X): f(y) < r_i \text{ for all } y \in K_i\},$$

where $r_i \in (0,1]$, $K_i \in \mathbf{K}(X)$, and $n \geq 0$. Let us denote

$$U(r_i, K_i) \stackrel{\text{def}}{=} \{f : f(y) < r_i \text{ for all } y \in K_i\}.$$

In these terms, the base of the Scott topology consists of the finite intersections $\bigcap_{i=1}^{n} U(r_i, K_i)$. Recall that since X is LCHS, X is normal, and there is a countable base $\mathbf{B}$ of the topological space $(X, \mathbf{O})$ such that for every $B \in \mathbf{B}$, the closure B is compact, and for any open set $G \in \mathbf{O}$, we have $G = \bigcup_{j \in J} B_j$ for some $B_j \in B$ with $B_j \subseteq G$.

Our claim is that a countable base of $USC(X)$ consists of sets of the form:

$$\bigcap_{i=1}^{n} U\left(q_i, \bigcup_{j=1}^{m_i} \overline{B}_{ij}\right),$$

where q_i are rational numbers from the interval $(0,1]$, and $B_{ij} \in B$.

It suffices to show that every neighborhood $\bigcap_{i=1}^{n} U(r_i, K_i)$ of a closed fuzzy set $f_n \in USC(X)$ contains a sub-neighborhood

$$\bigcap_{i=1}^{n} U\left(q_i, \bigcup_{j=1}^{m_i} \overline{B}_{ij}\right) \text{ (which still contains } f).$$

Indeed, by definition of the sets $U(r_i, K_i)$, the fact that $f \in \bigcap_{i=1}^{n} U(r_i, K_i)$ means that for every i and for every $y \in K_i$, we have $f(y) < r_i$. Let us denote by A_i the set of all the values $x \in X$ for which $f(x) \geq r_i$: $A_i = \{x \in X : f(x) \geq r_i\}$. Since the function f is upper semicontinuous, the set A_i is closed. The sets A_i and K_i are both closed and clearly $A_i \cap K_i = \phi$. Since the space X is normal, there exists an open set G_i that separates A_i and K_i, that is, for which $K_i \subseteq G_i$ and $A_i \cap G_i = \phi$. Due to the property of the base, we have $G_i = \bigcup_{j \in J} B_{ij}$ with $\overline{B}_{ij} \subseteq G_i$. Thus, $K_i \subseteq \bigcup_{j \in J} B_{ij}$. Since the set K_i is

compact, from this open cover, we can extract a finite sub-cover, that is, conclude that

$$K_i \subseteq \bigcup_{j=1}^{m_i} B_{ij} \subseteq \bigcup_{j=1}^{m_i} \overline{B}_{ij} \subseteq G_i.$$

From $A_i \cap G_i = \phi$, we can now conclude that:

$$A_i \cap \left(\bigcup_{j=1}^{m_i} \overline{B}_{ij}\right) = \phi$$

implying that for every $y \in \bigcup_{j=1}^{m_i} \overline{B}_{ij}$, we have $y \notin A_i$, that is, $f(y) < r_i$. Thus, $f(y) < r_i$ for any $y \in \bigcup_{j=1}^{m_i} \overline{B}_{ij}$.

Since f is usc, it attains its maximum on $\bigcup_{j=1}^{m_i} \overline{B}_{ij}$ at some point $y_{\max}$. For this maximum value, we therefore also have $f(y_{\max}) < r_i$ and therefore, there exists a rational number q_i such that $f(y_{\max}) < q_i < r_i$. Since the value $f(y_{\max})$ is the maximum, we conclude that $f(y) \leq f(y_{\max})$ for all other $y \in \bigcup_{j=1}^{m_i} \overline{B}_{ij}$. Thus, for all such y, we have $f(y) < q_i$. This means that $f \in \bigcap_{i=1}^{n} U\left(q_i, \bigcup_{j=1}^{m_i} \overline{B}_{ij}\right)$.

It is easy to show that:

$$\bigcap_{i=1}^{n} U\left(q_i, \bigcup_{j=1}^{m_i} \overline{B}_{ij}\right) \subseteq \bigcap_{i=1}^{n} U(r_i, K_i).$$

The theorem is proven.

Towards defining metrics on $USC(X)$. We have proven that the Lawson topology on $USC(X)$ $USC(X)$ is metrizable, that is, that there exists a metric with is compatible with this topology. From the viewpoint of possible applications, it is desirable to give an explicit description of such a metric.

In Section 4, we used the point compactification procedure to explicit describe a specific metric compatible with the Lawson topology on the set

$\mathbf{F}(X)$ of all closed (crisp) sets. Let us show that for the class $USC(X)$ of closed fuzzy sets, we can define a similar metric if we identify these closed fuzzy sets with their *hypographs*, that is, informally, areas below their graphs.

Formally, for every function $f : X \to [0,1]$, its *hypograph Hyp* (f) is defined as:

$$Hyp\ (f) = \{(x, \alpha) \in X \times [0,1]: f(x) \geq \alpha$$

Every hypograph is a subset of $X \times [0,1]$. Since we consider usc functions, each hypograph is closed.

Let $HYP(X)$ denote the set of all hypographs of all functions $f \in USC(X)$. Then, $f \to Hyp(f)$ is a bijection from $USC(X)$ to $HYP(X)$; see Nguyen, Wang, and Wei (in press). One can easily check that the set $HYP(X)$ is a closed subset of $\mathbf{F}(X \times [0,1])$. Note that since X is a LCHS space, the set $\mathbf{F}(X \times [0,1])$ is also a LCHS space, so the set $\mathbf{F}(X \times [0,1])$ of all its closed subsets is a topological space with a canonical Lawson topology. Thus, according to Section 4, $\mathbf{F}(X \times [0,1])$ has a compatible metric H. Then the induced metric on $HYP(X)$ is also compatible with the induced Lawson topology (or hit-or-miss topology) on $HYP(X)$. The only things that remains to be proven is that $(HYP(X), H)$ is homeomorphic to $(USC(X), \mathbf{L})$, where $\mathbf{L}$ denotes the Lawson topology on $USC(X)$. This result was proven in Nguyen and Tran (2007).

Finally, a Choquet theorem for $USC(X)$ can be obtained by embedding $USC(X)$ into $\mathbf{F}(X \times [0,1])$ via hypographs and using Choquet theorem for random closed sets on $X \times [0,1]$. For more details, see Nguyen et al. (in press).

TOWARDS PRACTICAL APPLICATIONS

From the general theory to computationally feasible practical applications. In the previous sections, we described a general theory of random fuzzy sets, a theory motivated by (and tailored towards) potential applications. Our main motivation is to prepare the background for as wide a range of applications as possible. Because of this objective, we tried our best to make our theory as general as possible.

Because of this same application objective, we also tried our best to make the resulting techniques as computation-friendly as possible. However, as we will see in this section, the resulting problems are computationally difficult even in the simplest cases. Because of this difficulty, in this chapter, we will mainly concentrate on such simple cases.

Practical need for random sets and random fuzzy sets: reminder. We have started this paper with explaining the practical motivation for random sets and random fuzzy sets.

This motivation is that due to measurement uncertainty (or uncertainty of expert estimates), often, instead of the actual values x_i of the quantities of interest, we only know the intervals $x = [\tilde{x}_i - \Delta_i, \tilde{x}_i + \Delta_i]$, where $\tilde{x}_i$ is the known approximate value and Δ_i is the upper bound on the approximation error (provided, for measurements, by the manufacturer of the measuring instrument).

These intervals can be viewed as *random intervals*, that is, as samples from the interval-valued random variable. In such situations, instead of the exact value of the sample statistics such as covariance $C[x,y]$, we can only have an interval $\mathbf{C}[x,y]$ of possible values of this statistic.

The need for such random intervals is well recognized, and there has already been a lot of related research; see, for example, Moeller and Beer (2004). In this approach, the uncertainty in a vector quantity $x = (x_1,...,x_d) \in \mathbf{R}^d$ is usually described by describing intervals of possible values of each of its components. This is equivalent to describing the set of all possible values of x as a *box* ("multi-dimensional interval") $[\underline{x}_1, \overline{x}_1] \times ... \times [\underline{x}_n, \overline{x}_n]$. However, the resulting data processing problem are often very challenging, and there is still a large room for further development.

One such need comes from the fact that uncertainty is often much more complex than intervals. For example, for the case of several variables, instead of an multi-dimensional interval, we may have a more complex set $S \subseteq \mathbf{R}^d$. In such a situation, we need a more general theory of random sets.

We also have mentioned that to get a more adequate description of expert estimates, we need to supplement the set S of possible values of the quantity (or quantities) of interest with describing the sets S_α which contain values which are possible with a certain degree α. In such situations, we need to consider random fuzzy sets.

What is needed for practical applications: an outline of this section. As we have just recalled, there is a practical need to consider random sets and random fuzzy sets. In order to apply the corresponding theory, we first need to estimate the actual distribution of random sets or random fuzzy sets from the observations.

In other words, we need to develop *statistical* techniques for random sets and random fuzzy sets. In this section, we start with a reminder about traditional number-valued and vector-valued statistical techniques, and the need for extending these techniques to random sets and random fuzzy sets. Then, we overview the main sources of the corresponding data uncertainty and techniques for dealing with the corresponding uncertainty. This will prepare us for the case study described in the following section.

Traditional statistics: brief reminder. In traditional statistics, we assume that the observed values are independent identically distributed (i.i.d.) variables $x_1, \ldots, x_n, \ldots$, and we want to find statistics $C_n(x_1, \ldots, x_n)$ that would approximate the desired parameter C of the corresponding probability distribution.

For example, if we want to estimate the mean E, we can take the arithmetic average $E_n[x] = \frac{x_1 + \ldots + x_n}{n}$. It is known that as $n \to \infty$, this statistic tends (with probability 1) to the desired mean: $E_n[x] \to E$. Similarly, the sample variance $V_n[x] = \frac{1}{n-1} \cdot \sum_{i=1}^{n} (x_i - E_n[x])^2$ tends to the actual variance V, the sample covariance

$$C_n[x,y] = \frac{1}{n-1} \cdot \sum_{i=1}^{n} (x_i - E_n[x]) \cdot (y_i - E_n[y])$$

between two different samples tends to the actual covariance C, and so on.

Coarsening: a source of random sets. In traditional statistics, we implicitly assume that the values x_i are directly observable. In real life, due to (inevitable) measurement uncertainty, often, what we actually observe is a *set* S_i that contains the actual (unknown) value of x_i. This phenomenon is called *coarsening*; see, for example, Heitjan and Rubin (1991). Due to coarsening, instead of the actual values x_i, all we know is the sets $X_1, \ldots, X_n, \ldots$ that are known the contain the actual (un-observable) values $x_i : x_i \in X_i$.

Statistics based on coarsening. The sets $X_1, \ldots, X_n, \ldots$ are i.i.d. *random sets*. We want to find statistics of these random sets that would enable us to approximate the desired parameters of the original distribution x. Here, a statistic $S_n(X_1, \ldots, X_n)$ transform n sets $X_1, \ldots, X_n$ into a new set. We want this statistic $S_n(X_1, \ldots, X_n)$ to tend to a limit set L as $n \to \infty$, and we want this limit set L to contain the value of the desired parameter of the original distribution.

For example, if we are interested in the mean $E[x]$, then we can take $S_n = (X_1 + \ldots + X_n)/n$ (where the sum is the Minkowski—element-wise—sum of the sets). It is possible to show that, under reasonable assumptions, this statistic tends to a limit L, and that $E[x] \in L$. This limit can be viewed, therefore, as a set-based average of the sets $X_1, \ldots, X_n$.

Important issue: computational complexity. There has been a lot of interesting theoretical research on set-valued random variables and corresponding statistics. In many cases, the corresponding statistics have been designed, and their asymptotical properties have been proven; see, for example, Goutsias, Mahler, and Nguyen (1997); Li, Ogura, and Kreinovich (2002); Nguyen (2006); and references therein.

In many such situations, the main obstacle to a practical use of these statistics is that going from random numbers to random sets drastically increases the computational complexity—hence, the running time—of the required computations. It therefore is desirable to come up with new, faster algorithms for computing such set-values heuristics.

Sources of uncertainty: general reminder. Traditional engineering statistical formulas assume that we know the *exact* values x_i of the corresponding quantity. In practice, these values come either from measurements or from expert estimates. In both case, we get only *approximations* $\tilde{x}_i$ to the actual (unknown) values x_i.

When we use these approximate values $\tilde{x}_i \neq x_i$ to compute the desired statistical characteristics such as E and V, we only get approximate valued $\tilde{E}$ and $\tilde{V}$ for these characteristics. It is desirable to estimate the accuracy of these approximations.

Case of measurement uncertainty. Measurements are never 100 percent accurate. As a result, the result $\tilde{x}_i$ of the measurement is, in general, different from the (unknown) actual value x of the desired quantity. The difference $\Delta x \overset{def}{=} \tilde{x} - x$ between the measured and the actual values is usually called a *measurement error*.

The manufacturers of a measuring device usually provide us with an upper bound Δ for the (absolute value of) possible errors, that is, with a bound Δ for which we guarantee that $|\Delta x| \leq \Delta$. The need for such a bound comes from the very nature of a measurement process: if no such bound is provided, this means that the difference between the (unknown) actual value x and the observed value $\tilde{x}$ can be as large as possible.

Since the (absolute value of the) measurement error $\Delta x = \tilde{x} - x$ is bounded by the given bound Δ, we can therefore guarantee that the actual (unknown) value of the desired quantity belongs to the interval $[\tilde{x} - \Delta, \tilde{x} + \Delta]$.

Traditional probabilistic approach to describing measurement uncertainty. In many practical situations, we not only know the interval $[-\Delta, \Delta]$ of possible values of the measurement error; we also know the probability of different values Δx within this interval; see, for example, Rabinovich (2005).

In practice, we can determine the desired probabilities of different values of Δx by comparing the results of measuring with this instrument with the results of measuring the same quantity by a standard (much more accurate) measuring instrument. Since the standard measuring instrument is much more accurate than the one use, the difference between these two measurement results is practically equal to the measurement error; thus, the empirical distribution of this difference is close to the desired probability distribution for measurement error.

Interval approach to measurement uncertainty. As we have mentioned, in many practical situations, we do know the probabilities of different values of the measurement error. There are two cases, however, when this determination is not done:

- First is the case of cutting-edge measurements, for example, measurements in fundamental science. When a Hubble telescope detects the light from a distant galaxy, there is no "standard" (much more accurate) telescope floating nearby that we can use to calibrate the Hubble: the Hubble telescope is the best we have.
- The second case is the case of measurements on the shop floor. In this case, in principle, every sensor can be thoroughly calibrated,

but sensor calibration is so costly—usually costing 10 times more than the sensor itself—that manufacturers rarely do it.

In both cases, we have no information about the probabilities of Δx; the only information we have is the upper bound on the measurement error.

In this case, after performing a measurement and getting a measurement result $\tilde{x}$, the only information that we have about the actual value x of the measured quantity is that it belongs to the interval $\mathbf{x} = [\tilde{x} - \Delta, \tilde{x} + \Delta]$. In this situation, for each i, we know the interval $\mathbf{x}_i$ of possible values of x_i, and we need to find the ranges E and V of the characteristics E and V over all possible tuples $x_i \in \mathbf{x}_i$.

Case of expert uncertainty. An expert usually describes his/her uncertainty by using words from the natural language, like "most probably, the value of the quantity is between 6 and 7, but it is somewhat possible to have values between 5 and 8." To formalize this knowledge, it is natural to use *fuzzy set theory*, a formalism specifically designed for describing this type of informal ("fuzzy") knowledge (Klir & Yuan, 1995; Nguyen & Walker, 2006).

As a result, for every value x_i, we have a fuzzy set $\mu_i(x_i)$ which describes the expert's prior knowledge about x_i: the number $\mu_i(x_i)$ describes the expert's degree of certainty that x_i is a possible value of the i-th quantity.

As we have mentioned earlier, an alternative user-friendly way to represent a fuzzy set is by using its α-cuts $\{x_i : \mu_i(x_i) \geq \alpha\}$. In these terms, a fuzzy set can be viewed as a nested family of intervals $[\underline{x}_i(\alpha), x_i(\alpha)]$ corresponding to different level α.

Estimating statistics under fuzzy uncertainty: precise formulation of the problem. In general, we have fuzzy knowledge $\mu_i(x_i)$ about each value x_i; we want to find the fuzzy set corresponding to a given characteristic $y = C(x_1, \ldots, x_n)$. Intuitively,

the value y is a reasonable value of the characteristic if $y = C(x_1, \ldots, x_n)$ for some reasonable values x_i, that is, if for some values $x_1, \ldots, x_n, x_1$ is reasonable, and x_2 is reasonable, ..., and $y = C(x_1 \ldots, x_n)$. If we interpret "and" as min and "for some" ("or") as max, then we conclude that the corresponding degree of certainty $\mu(y)$ in y is equal to

$$\mu(y) = \max\{\min(\mu_1(x_1), \ldots, \mu_n(x_n)) : C(x_1, \ldots, x_n) = y\}.$$

Reduction to the case of interval uncertainty. It is known that the above formula (called *extension principle*) can be reformulated as follows: for each α, the α-cut $\mathbf{y}(\alpha)$ of y is equal to the range of possible values of $C(x_1, \ldots, x_n)$ when $x_i \in \mathbf{x}_i(\alpha)$ for all i. Thus, from the computational viewpoint, the problem of computing the statistical characteristic under fuzzy uncertainty can be reduced to the problem of computing this characteristic under interval uncertainty; see, for example, Dubois, Fargier, and Fortin (2005).

In view of this reduction, in the following text, we will consider the case of interval (and set) uncertainty.

Estimating statistics under interval uncertainty: a problem. In the case of interval uncertainty, instead of the true values $x_1, \ldots, x_n$, we only know the intervals $\mathbf{x}_1 = [\underline{x}_1, \overline{x}_1], \ldots, \mathbf{x}_n = [\underline{x}_n, \overline{x}_n]$ that contain the (unknown) true values of the measured quantities. For different values $x_i \in \mathbf{x}_i$, we get, in general, different values of the corresponding statistical characteristic $C(x_1, \ldots, x_n)$. Since all values $x_i \in \mathbf{x}_i$ are possible, we conclude that all the values $C(x_1, \ldots, x_n)$ corresponding to $x_i \in \mathbf{x}_i$ are possible estimates for the corresponding statistical characteristic. Therefore, for the interval data $\mathbf{x}_1, \ldots, \mathbf{x}_n$, a reasonable estimate for the corresponding statistical characteristic is the range

$$C(\mathbf{x}_1, \ldots, \mathbf{x}_n) \stackrel{\text{def}}{=} \{C(x_1, \ldots, x_n) : x_1 \in \mathbf{x}_1, \ldots, x_n \in \mathbf{x}_n\}.$$

We must therefore modify the existing statistical algorithms so that they compute, or bound these ranges.

Estimating mean under interval uncertainty. The arithmetic average E is a monotonically increasing function of each of its n variables $x_1, \ldots, x_n$, so its smallest possible value $\underline{E}$ is attained when each value x_i is the smallest possible ($x_i = \underline{x}_i$) and its largest possible value is attained when $x_i = \overline{x}_i$ for all i. In other words, the range $\mathbf{E}$ of E is equal to $[E(\underline{x}_1, \ldots, \underline{x}_n), E(\overline{x}_1, \ldots, \overline{x}_n)]$. In other words, $\underline{E} = \frac{1}{n} \cdot (\underline{x}_1 + \ldots + \underline{x}_n)$ and $\overline{E} = \frac{1}{n} \cdot (\overline{x}_1 + \ldots + \overline{x}_n)$.

Estimating variance under interval uncertainty. It is known that the problem of computing the exact range $\mathbf{V} = [\underline{V}, \overline{V}]$ for the variance V over interval data $x_i \in [\tilde{x}_i - \Delta_i, \tilde{x}_i + \Delta_i]$ is, in general, NP-hard; see, for example, (Kreinovich et al., 2006), (Kreinovich et al., 2007). Specifically, there is a polynomial-time algorithm for computing $\underline{V}$, but computing $\overline{V}$ is, in general, NP-hard.

Comment. NP-hard means, crudely speaking, that no feasible algorithm can compute the exact value of $\overline{V}$ for all possible intervals $\mathbf{x}_1, \ldots, \mathbf{x}_n$; see, for example, (Kreinovich et al., 1997).

In many practical situations, there are efficient algorithms for computing $\overline{V}$: for example, an $O(n \cdot \log(n))$ time algorithm exists when no two narrowed intervals $[x_i^-, x_i^+]$, where $x_i^- \overset{\text{def}}{=} \tilde{x}_i - \frac{\Delta_i}{n}$ and $x_i^+ \overset{\text{def}}{=} \tilde{x}_i + \frac{\Delta_i}{n}$, are proper subsets of one another, that is, when $[x_i^-, x_i^+] \not\subseteq (x_j^-, x_j^+)$ for all i and j (Dantsin et al., 2006).

What can be done if we cannot effectively compute the exact range. As we have just mentioned, the problem of computing statistical characteristics under interval uncertainty is often NP-hard – which means, crudely speaking, that we cannot efficiently compute the exact range for these characteristics.

A natural solution is as follows: since we cannot compute the *exact* range, we should try to find an *enclosure* for this range. Computing the range $C(\mathbf{x}_1, \ldots, \mathbf{x}_n)$ of a function $C(x_1, \ldots, x_n)$ based on the input intervals $\mathbf{x}_i$ is called *interval computations*; see, for example, (Jaulin et al., 2001).

Interval computations techniques: brief reminder. Historically the first method for computing the enclosure for the range is the method which is sometimes called "straightforward" interval computations. This method is based on the fact that inside the computer, every algorithm consists of elementary operations (arithmetic operations, min, max, etc.). For each elementary operation $f(a, b)$ if we know the intervals $\mathbf{a}$ and $\mathbf{b}$ for a and b, we can compute the exact range $f(\mathbf{a}, \mathbf{b})$. The corresponding formulas form the so-called *interval arithmetic*. For example (see Box 4).

In straightforward interval computations, we repeat the computations forming the program C for computing $C(x_1, \ldots, x_n)$ step-by-step, replacing each operation with real numbers by the corresponding operation of interval arithmetic. It is known that, as a result, we get an enclosure $\mathbf{Y} \supseteq C(\mathbf{x}_1, \ldots, \mathbf{x}_n)$ for the desired range.

In some cases, this enclosure is exact. In more complex cases (see examples below), the enclosure has excess width.

There exist more sophisticated techniques for producing a narrower enclosure, for example, a centered form method. However, for each of these techniques, there are cases when we get an excess width. (Reason: as have mentioned, the problem of computing the exact range is known to be NP-hard even for population variance.)

Box 4.

$$[\underline{a}, \overline{a}] + [\underline{b}, \overline{b}] = [\underline{a} + \underline{b}, \overline{a} + \overline{b}]; \quad [\underline{a}, \overline{a}] - [\underline{b}, \overline{b}] = [\underline{a} - \overline{b}, \overline{a} - \underline{b}];$$

$$[\underline{a}, \overline{a}] \cdot [\underline{b}, \overline{b}] = [\min(\underline{a} \cdot \underline{b}, \underline{a} \cdot \overline{b}, \overline{a} \cdot \underline{b}, \overline{a} \cdot \overline{b}), \max(\underline{a} \cdot \underline{b}, \underline{a} \cdot \overline{b}, \overline{a} \cdot \underline{b}, \overline{a} \cdot \overline{b})].$$

CASE STUDY: A BIOINFORMATICS PROBLEM

In this section, we describe an example of a practical applications. This example was first outlined in (Kreinovich et al., 2007) and (Xiang, 2007). For other applications, see (Kreinovich et al., 2006), (Kreinovich et al., 2007) and references therein.

Description of the case study. In cancer research, it is important to find out the genetic difference between the cancer cells and the healthy cells. In the ideal world, we should be able to have a sample of cancer cells, and a sample of healthy cells, and thus directly measure the concentrations c and h of a given gene in cancer and in healthy cells. In reality, it is very difficult to separate the cells, so we have to deal with samples that contain both cancer and normal cells. Let y_i denote the result of measuring the concentration of the gene in i-th sample, and let x_i denote the percentage of cancer cells in i-th sample. Then, we should have $x_i \cdot c + (1 - x_i) \cdot h \approx y_i$ (approximately equal because there are measurement errors in measuring y_i).

Let us first consider an idealized case in which we know the exact percentages x_i. In this case, we can find the desired values c and h by solving a system of linear equations $x_i \cdot c + (1 - x_i) \cdot h \approx y_i$ with two unknowns c and h.

It is worth mentioning that this system can be somewhat simplified if instead of c, we consider a new variable $a \stackrel{\text{def}}{=} c - h$. In terms of the new unknowns a and h, the system takes the following form: $a \cdot x_i + h \approx y_i$.

The errors of measuring y_i are normally i.i.d. random variables, so to estimate a and h, we can use the Least Squares Method (LSM) $\sum_{i=1}^{n} (a \cdot x_i + h - y_i)^2 \to \min_{a,h}$. According to LSM, we have $a = \frac{C[x,y]}{V[x]}$ and $h = E[y] - a \cdot E[x]$, where $E[x] = \frac{1}{n}(x_1 + \ldots + x_n)$, $E[y] = \frac{1}{n}(y_1 + \ldots + y_n)$, and $V[x] = \frac{1}{n-1} \cdot \sum_{i=1} (x_i - E[x])^2$, Once we know $a = c - h$ and h, we can then estimate c as $a + h$.

The problem is that the concentrations x_i come from experts who manually count different cells, and experts can only provide interval bounds on the values x_i such as $x_i \in [0.7, 0.8]$ (or even only fuzzy bounds). Different values of x_i in the corresponding intervals lead to different values of a and h. It is therefore desirable to find the range of a and h corresponding to all possible values $x_i \in [\underline{x}_i, \overline{x}_i]$.

Comment. Our motivation for solving this problem comes from bioinformatics, but similar problems appear in various practical situations where measurements with uncertainties are available and statistical data is to be processed.

Linear approximation. Let $\tilde{x}_i = (\underline{x}_i + \overline{x}_i)/2$ be the midpoint of i-th intervals, and let $\Delta_i = (\overline{x}_i - \underline{x}_i)/2$ be its half-width. For a, we have

$$\frac{\partial a}{\partial x_i} = \frac{1}{(n-1) \cdot V[x]} \cdot (y_i - E[y] - 2a \cdot x_i + 2a \cdot E[x]).$$

We can use the formula $E[y] = a \cdot E[x] + h$ to simplify this expression, resulting in

$$\Delta_a = \frac{1}{(n-1) \cdot V[x]} \sum_{i=1}^{n} |\Delta y_i - a \cdot \Delta x_i| \cdot \Delta_i,$$

where we denoted $\Delta y_i \stackrel{\text{def}}{=} y_i - a \cdot x_i - h$ and $\Delta x_i \stackrel{\text{def}}{=} x_i - E[x]$.

Since $h = E[y] - a \cdot E[x]$, we have:

$$\frac{\partial h}{\partial x_i} = -\frac{\partial a}{\partial x_i} \cdot E[x] - \frac{1}{n} \cdot a, \text{ so } \Delta_h = \sum_{i=1}^{n} \left|\frac{\partial h}{\partial x_i}\right| \cdot \Delta_i.$$

Prior estimation of the resulting accuracy. The above formulas provide us with the accuracy *after* the data has been processed. It is often desirable to have an estimate *prior* to measurements, to make sure that we will get c and h with desired accuracy.

The difference Δy_i is a measurement error, so it is normally distributed with 0 mean and standard deviation $\sigma(y)$ corresponding to the accuracy of measuring y_i. The difference Δx_i is distributed with 0 mean and standard deviation $\sqrt{V[x]}$. For estimation purposes, it is reasonable to assume that the values Δx_i are also normally distributed. It is also reasonable to assume that the errors in x_i and y_i are uncorrelated, so the linear combination $\Delta y_i - a \cdot \Delta x_i$ is also normally distributed, with 0 mean and variance $\sigma_y^2 + a^2 \cdot V[x]$. It is also reasonable to assume that all the values Δ_i are approximately the same: $\Delta_i \approx \Delta$.

For normal distribution ξ with 0 mean and standard deviation σ, the mean value of $|\xi|$ is equal to $\sqrt{2/\pi} \cdot \sigma$. Thus, the absolute value $|\Delta y_i - a \cdot \Delta x_i|$ of the above combination has a mean value $\sqrt{2/\pi} \cdot \sqrt{\sigma_y^2 + a^2 \cdot V[x]}$. Hence, the expected value of Δ_a is equal to $\frac{2}{\pi} \cdot \frac{\sqrt{\sigma_y^2 + a^2 \cdot V[x]} \cdot \Delta}{V[x]}$.

Since measurements are usually more accurate than expert estimates, we have $\sigma_y^2 \ll V[x]$, hence $\Delta_a \approx \frac{2}{\pi} \cdot a \cdot \Delta$.

Similar estimates can be given for Δ_h.

Why not get exact estimates? Because in general, finding the exact range is NP-hard. Let us show that in general, finding the exact range for the ratio $C[x,y]/V[x]$ is an NP-hard problem; this proof was first presented in Kreinovich, Longpre, Starks, Xiang, Beck, Kandathi, Nayak, Ferson, and Hajagos (2007).

The proof is similar to the proof that computing the range for the variance is NP-hard (Ferson, Ginzburg, Kreinovich, Longpre, & Aviles, 2005): namely, we reduce a partition problem (known to be NP-hard) to our problem. In the partition problem, we are given m positive integers $s_1, \ldots, s_m$, and we must check whether there exist values $\varepsilon_i \in \{-1,1\}$ for which $\sum_{i=1}^{m} \varepsilon_i \cdot s_i = 0$. We will reduce this problem to the following problem:

$n = m+2, y_1 = \ldots = y_m = 0, y_{m+1} = 1, y_{m+2} = -1, x_i = [-s_i, s_i]$

for $i \leq m$, $x_{m+1} = 1$, and $x_{m+2} = -1$. In this case:

$E[y] = 0$, so

$$C[x,y] = \frac{1}{n-1} \sum_{i=1}^{n} x_i \cdot y_i - \frac{n}{n-1} \cdot E[x] \cdot E[y] = \frac{2}{m+2}.$$

Therefore, $C[x,y]/V[x] \to \min$ if and only if $V[x] \to \max$.

Here,

$$V[x] = \frac{1}{m+1} \cdot \left(\sum_{i=1}^{m} x_i^2 + 2 \right) - \frac{m+2}{m+1} \cdot \left(\frac{1}{m+2} \cdot \sum_{i=1}^{m} x_i \right)^2.$$

Since $|x_i| \leq s_i$, we always have:

$$V[x] \leq V_0 \overset{\text{def}}{=} \frac{1}{m+1} \cdot \left(\sum_{i=1}^{m} s_i^2 + 2 \right)$$

and the only possibility to have $V[x] = V_0$ is when $x_i = \pm s_i$ for all i and $\sum x_i = 0$. Thus, $V[x] = V_0$ if and only if the original partition problem has a solution. Hence, $C[x,y]/V[x] = \frac{2}{\sum s_i^2 + 2}$ if and only if the original instance of the partition problem has a solution.

The reduction is proven, so our problem is indeed NP-hard.

Comment 1. In this proof, we consider the case when the values x_i can be negative and larger than 1, while in bioinformatics, x_i is always between 0 and 1. However, we can easily modify this proof: First, we can shift all the values x_i by the same constant to make them positive; shift does not change neither $C[x,y]$ nor $V[x]$. Second, to make the positive values ≤ 1, we can then re-scale the values x_i ($x_i \to \lambda \cdot x_i$), thus multiplying $C[x,y]/V[x]$ by a known constant.

As a result, we get new values $x_i' \overset{\text{def}}{=} \frac{1}{2} \cdot (1 + x_i/K)$, where $K \overset{\text{def}}{=} \max s_i$, for which $x_i' \in [0,1]$ and the problem of computing $C[x,y]/V[x]$ is still NP-hard.

Comment 2. Since we cannot compute the exact range, what can we do to compute the more accurate estimates for the range than those provided by linear approximation? One possibility is to use known algorithms to find the ranges for $C[x,y]$ and for $V[x]$ (Kreinovich, Xiang, Starks, Longpre, Ceberio, Araiza, Beck, Kandathi, Nayak, Torres,

& Hajagos, 2006; Kreinovich et al., 2007), and then use the division operation from interval arithmetic to get the interval that is guaranteed to contain $C[x, y] / V[x]$.

ACKNOWLEDGMENT

This work was supported in part by NSF grants HRD-0734825 and EAR-0225670, by Texas Department of Transportation grant No. 0-5453, and by the Japan Advanced Institute of Science and Technology (JAIST) International Joint Research Grant 2006-08. The authors are thankful to the anonymous referees for their valuable suggestions.

REFERENCES

Dantsin, E., Kreinovich, V., Wolpert, A., & Xiang, G. (2006). Population variance under interval uncertainty: A new algorithm. *Reliable Computing, 12*(4), 273-280.

Dubois, D., Fargier, H., & Fortin, J. (2005). The empirical variance of a set of fuzzy intervals. *Proceedings of the 2005 IEEE International Conference on Fuzzy Systems FUZZ-IEEE'2005*, Reno, Nevada, May 22–25, pp. 885-890.

Fell, J. M. G. (1961). The structure of algebras of operator fields. *Acta Mathematics, 101,* 19-38.

Fell, J. M. G. (1962). A Hausdorff topology for the closed sets of a locally compact non-Hausdorff space. *Proceedings of the American Mathematical Society, 13,* 472–476.

Ferson, S., Ginzburg, L., Kreinovich, V., Longpre, L., & Aviles, M. (2005). Exact bounds on finite populations of interval data. *Reliable Computing, 11*(3), 207-233.

Ferson, S., & Hajagos, J. (2007). Interval versions of statistical techniques, with applications to environmental analysis, bioinformatics, and privacy in statistical databases. *Journal of Computational and Applied Mathematics, 199*(2), 418-423.

Gierz, G., Hofmann, K. H., Keimel, K., Lawson, J. D., Mislove, M., & Scott, D. S. (1980). *A compendium of continuous lattices*. Berlin, Heidelberg, New York: Springer-Verlag.

Goutsias, J., Mahler, R. P. S., & Nguyen, H. T. (Eds.) (1997). *Random sets: Theory and applications*. New York: Springer-Verlag.

Heitjan D. F., & Rubin, D. B. (1991). Ignorability and coarse data. *Ann. Stat., 19*(4), 2244-2253.

Jaulin L., Kieffer, M., Didrit, O., & Walter, E. (2001). *Applied interval analysis*. London: Springer-Verlag.

Klir, G., & Yuan, B. (1995). *Fuzzy sets and fuzzy logic: Theory and applications*. Upper Saddle River, NJ: Prentice Hall.

Kreinovich V., Lakeyev, A., Rohn, J., & Kahl, P. (1997). *Computational complexity and feasibility of data processing and interval computations*. Dordrecht: Kluwer.

Kreinovich, V., Longpre, L., Starks, S. A., Xiang, G., Beck, J., Kandathi, R., Nayak, A., Ferson, S., & Hajagos, J. (2007). Interval versions of statistical techniques, with applications to environmental analysis, bioinformatics, and privacy in statistical databases. *Journal of Computational and Applied Mathematics, 199*(2), 418-423.

Kreinovich, V., Xiang, G., Starks, S. A., Longpre, L., Ceberio, M., Araiza, R., Beck, J., Kandathi, R., Nayak, A., Torres, R., & Hajagos, J. (2006). Towards combining probabilistic and interval uncertainty in engineering calculations: Algorithms for computing statistics under interval uncertainty, and their computational complexity. *Reliable Computing, 12*(6), 471-501.

Li, S., Ogura, Y., & Kreinovich, V. (2002). *Limit theorems and applications of set valued and fuzzy valued random variables*. Dordrecht: Kluwer.

Matheron, G. (1975). *Random sets and integral geometry.* J. Wiley.

Moller, & Beer, M. (2004). *Fuzzy randomness: Uncertainty in Civil Engineering and Computational Mechanics.* Springer-Verlag.

Nguyen, H. T. (2006). *An introduction to random sets.* Chapman and Hall/CRC Press.

Nguyen, H. T., & Kreinovich, V. (1996). Nested intervals and sets: Concepts, relations to fuzzy sets, and applications. In R.B. Kearfott & V. Kreinovich (Eds.). *Applications of interval computations*, pp. 245-290. Dordrecht: Kluwer.

Nguyen, H. T. & Tran, H. (2007). On a continuous lattice approach to modeling of coarse data in system analysis. *Journal of Uncertain Systems, 1*(1), 62-73.

Nguyen, H. T., & Walker, E. A. (2006). *A first course in fuzzy logic* (3rd edition). Chapman and Hall/CRC Press.

Nguyen, H. T., Wang, Y., & Wei, G. (in press). On Choquet theorem for random upper semi-continuous functions. *International Journal of Approximate Reasoning.*

Rabinovich, S. (2005). *Measurement errors and uncertainties: Theory and practice.* New York: Springer-Verlag.

Rockafellar, R. T., & West, J. B. (1984). Variational systems an introduction. In *Springer lecture notes in mathematics*, Vol. 1091, 1–54.

Wei, G., & Wang, Y. (in press). On metrization of the hit-or-miss topology using Alexandroff compactification. *International Journal of Approximate Reasoning.*

Xiang, G. (2007). Interval uncertainty in bioinformatics. *Abstracts of the New Mexico Bioinformatics Symposium*, Santa Fe, Mexico, March 8–9, p. 25.

Chapter III
Pattern Discovery in Gene Expression Data

Gráinne Kerr
Dublin City University, Ireland

Heather Ruskin
Dublin City University, Ireland

Martin Crane
Dublin City University, Ireland

ABSTRACT

Microarray technology[1] provides an opportunity to monitor mRNA levels of expression of thousands of genes simultaneously in a single experiment. The enormous amount of data produced by this high throughput approach presents a challenge for data analysis: to extract meaningful patterns, to evaluate its quality, and to interpret the results. The most commonly used method of identifying such patterns is cluster analysis. Common and sufficient approaches to many data-mining problems, for example, Hierarchical, K-means, do not address well the properties of "typical" gene expression data and fail, in significant ways, to account for its profile. This chapter clarifies some of the issues and provides a framework to evaluate clustering in gene expression analysis. Methods are categorised explicitly in the context of application to data of this type, providing a basis for reverse engineering of gene regulation networks. Finally, areas for possible future development are highlighted.

INTRODUCTION

A fundamental factor of function in a living cell is the abundance of proteins present at a molecular level, that is, its *proteome*. The variation between proteomes of different cells is often used to explain differences in phenotype and cell function. Crucially, gene expression is the set of reactions that controls the level of messenger RNA (mRNA) in the *transcriptome*, which in turn maintains the proteome of a given cell. The transcriptome is never synthesized *de novo*; instead, it is maintained by gene expression replacing mRNAs that have been degraded, with changes in composition brought about by switching different sets of genes on and off. To understand the mechanisms of cells, involved in a given biological process, it is necessary to measure and compare gene expression levels in different biological phases, body tissues, clinical conditions, and organisms. Information on the set of genes expressed, in a particular biological process, can be used to characterise unknown gene function, identify targets for drug treatments, determine effects of treatment on cell function, and understand molecular mechanisms involved.

DNA microarray technology has advanced rapidly over the past decade, although the concept itself is not new (Friemert, Erfle, & Strauss, 1989; Gress, Hoheisel, Sehetner, & Leahrach 1992). It is now possible to measure the expression of an entire genome simultaneously, (equivalent to the collection and examination of data from thousands of single gene experiments). Components of the system technology can be divided into: (1) Sample preparation, (2) Array generation and sample analysis, and (3) Data handling and interpretation. The focus of this chapter is on the third of these.

Microarray technology utilises base-pairing hybridisation properties of nucleic acids, whereby one of the four base nucleotides (A, T, G, C) will bind with only one of the four base ribonucleotides (A, U, G, C: pairing = A – U, T – A, C – G, G - C). Thus, a unique sequence of DNA that characterises a gene will bind to a unique mRNA sequence. Synthesized DNA molecules, complementary to known mRNA, are attached to a solid surface, referred to as *probes*. These are used to measure the quantity of specific mRNA of interest that is present in a sample (the *target*). The molecules in the target are labelled, and a specialised scanner is used to measure the amount of hybridisation (intensity) of the target at each probe. Gene intensity values are recorded for a number of microarray experiments typically carried out for targets derived under various experimental conditions (Figure 1). Secondary variables (covariates) that affect the relationship between the dependent variable (experimental condition) and independent variables of primary interest (gene expression) include, for example, age, disease, and geography among others, and can also be measured.

Figure 1. mRNA is extracted from a transcriptome of interest, (derived from cells grown under precise experimental conditions). Each mRNA sample is hybridised to a reference microarray. The gene intensity values for each experiment are then recorded.

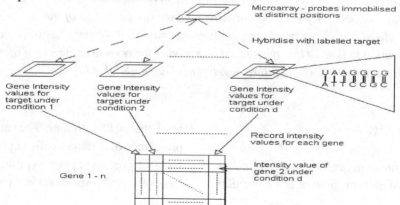

An initial cluster analysis step is applied to gene expression data to search for meaningful informative patterns and dependencies among genes. These provide a basis for hypothesis testing—the basic assumption is that genes, showing similar patterns of expression across experimental conditions, may be involved in the same underlying cellular mechanism. For example, Alizadeh, Eisen, Davis, Ma, Lossos, Rosenwald, Boldrick, Sabet, Tran, Yu, Powell, Yang, Marti, Moore, Hudson Jr, Lu, Lewis, Tibshirani, Sherlock, Chan, Greiner, Weisenburger, Armitage, Warnke, Levy, Wilson, Grever, Byrd, Botstein, Brown, and Staudt (2000) used a hierarchical clustering technique, applied to gene expression data derived from diffuse large B-cell lymphomas (DLBCL), to identify two molecularly distinct subtypes. These had gene expression patterns, indicative of different stages of B-cell differentiation—germinal centre B-like DLBCL and activated B-like DLBCL. Findings suggested that patients, with germinal centre B-like DLBCL, had a significantly better overall survival rate than those with activated B-like DLBCL. This work indicated a significant methodology shift towards characterisation of cancers *based on gene expression*, rather than morphological, clinical and molecular variables.

BACKGROUND

The Gene Expression Dataset

Data are typically presented as a real-valued matrix, with rows representing the expression of a gene over a number of experiments, and columns representing the pattern of expression of all genes for a given microarray experiment. Each entry x_{ij} is the measured expression of a gene i in experiment j, (Figure 1). The following terms and notations are used throughout this chapter:

- A gene/gene profile x is a single data item (feature vector) used by the clustering algorithm. It consists of d measurements, $x = (x_1, x_2, \dots x_d)$.
- A condition y is a single microarray experiment corresponding to a single column in the gene expression matrix, $y = (x_1, x_2, \dots x_n)^T$, where n is the number of genes in the dataset.
- The individual scalar components of each gene vector x_{ij} represent the measured expression of gene i under experimental condition j.

Table 1. Selection of publicly available dataset repositories

Database	Description	URL
ArrayExpress	Gene expression and hybridisation array data repository	http://www.ebi.ac.uk/arrayexpress/#ae-main[0]
CellMiner	Data from 60 cancer cell lines based on Affymetrix and cDNA microarray data	http://discover.nci.nih.gov/cellminer
ExpressDB	Collection of E. Coli and Yeast RNA expression datasets	http://arep.med.harvard.edu/ExpressDB/
GEO	Gene expression and hybridisation array data repository	http://www.ncbi.nlm.gov/geo/
RAD	Gene expression and hybridisation array data repository	http://www.cbil.upenn.edu/RAD/
SMD	Extensive collection of microarray data	http://genome-www.stanford.edu/microarray

There are a number of publicly available dataset repositories, which contain a wealth of microarray datasets[2]: Table 1 provides a sample of these. Typically, these repositories store data using the 'minimum information about microarray experiment' (MIAME) standard (Brazma, Hingamp, Quackenbush, Sherlock, Spellman, Stoeckert, Aach, Ansorge, Ball, Causton, Gaasterland, Glenisson, Holstege, Kim, Markowitz, Matese, Parkinson, Robinson, Sarkans, Schulze-Kremer, Stewart, Taylor, Vilo, & Vingron, 2001), which allow researchers to replicate the experiments. This allows analysts to compare gene expression data from different laboratories effectively, based on information about the microarrays used in experiments, how these were produced, samples obtained and mRNA extracted and labelled. Additional information is also recorded on methods used to hybridise the sample, scan the image and normalise the data.

Characteristics of the Gene Expression Dataset

Choice of the appropriate clustering technique relies on the amount of information on the particular properties of gene expression data available to the analyst, and hence the likely underlying structure. The following data characteristics are typical of the gene expression dataset:

Measurement accuracy of mRNA expression levels depends on the experimental design and rigour. While design of experiments is not a specific focus of this chapter, a good design minimises variation and has a focused objective (Kerr & Churchill, 2001). *Technical variation* between microarray slides depends on numerous factors including experimental technique, instrument accuracy for detecting signals, and observer bias. *Biological variation* may arise due to differences in the internal states of a population of cells, either from predictable processes, such as cell cycle progression, or from random processes such as partitioning of mitochondria during cell division, variation due to subtle environmental differences, or ongoing genetic mutation (Raser & O'Shea, 2005). *Pre-processing techniques* attempt to remove technical variation while maintaining interesting biological variation.

Many variables, both random and fixed, (biological and technical), are associated with microarray measurements. Data is thus **intrinsically noisy** and outliers in the dataset need to be identified and managed effectively. This usually takes one of two forms, (i) outlier accommodation; uses a variety of statistical estimation or testing procedures, which are robust against outliers, (ii) identification and decision on inclusion/exclusion, used when outliers may contain key information (Liu, Cheng, & Wu, 2002). *Normalisation procedures* applied to gene expression data (Bolstad, Irizarry, Astrand, & Speed, 2003), aim at minimising the effect of outliers (assuming these to be due to experimental variation and thus undesirable). Most manufacturers of microarrays, aware of effects of optical noise and non-specific binding, include features in their arrays to measure these directly: these measurements can be used in the normalisation procedures. Note: although pre-processing methods attempt to remove all noise these may be only partially successful.

Missing values are common to microarray data, and can be caused by insufficient resolution in image analysis, image corruption, dust or scratches on the slide, robotic method used to create the slide, and so on, (Troyanskaya, Cantor, Sherlock, Brown, Hastie, Tibshirani, Botstein, & Altman, 2001). In general, the number of missing values increases with the number of genes being measured. Many clustering algorithms, used for gene expression data, require a complete matrix of input values. Consequently, imputation or missing data estimation techniques need to be considered in advance of clustering. The effect of missing data on pattern information can be minimised through *pre-processing*.

Commonly, missing values in the gene expression matrix are replaced by zeroes or by an average expression level of the gene, (or "row average"). Such methods do not, however, take into account the correlation structure of the data and more sophisticated options include K-Nearest Neighbour (KNN) and Support Vector Decomposition type methods. Troyanskaya et al. (2001) note that KNN and SVD-based methods are more effective than traditional methods of replacement, with KNN being more robust as the number of missing values increases.

Clustering algorithms that ***permit overlap (probabilistic or fuzzy clusters)*** are typically more applicable to gene expression data since: (i) the impact of noisy data on clusters obtained is a fundamental consideration in algorithm choice. (The assumption is that "noisy genes" are unlikely to belong to any one cluster, but are equally likely to be members of several clusters): (ii) the underlying principal of clustering gene expression data, is that genes with similar change in expression for a set of conditions are involved, together, in a similar biological function. Typically, gene products (mRNA) are involved in several such biological functions and groups need not be co-active under all conditions. This gives rise to high variability in the gene groups and/or some overlap between them. For these reasons, constraining a gene to a single cluster (*hard clustering*) is counter-intuitive with respect to natural behaviour.

Additionally, methods that aim at a ***partial clustering*** tend to be more suited to expression data, with some genes or conditions not members of any cluster (Maderia & Oliveira, 2000). Clustering the microarray dataset can be viewed in two ways: (i) genes can form a group which show similar expression across conditions, (ii) conditions can form a group which show similar gene expression across all genes. It is this interplay of conditions and genes that gives rise to bi-clusters, whereby conditions and genes are simultaneously grouped. Such partial clusterings, (or *bi-clusters*), are defined over a subset of conditions and a subset of genes, thus capturing local structure in the dataset. Clearly, this allows: (i) "noisy genes"

to be left out, with correspondingly less impact on the final outcome, (ii) genes belonging to no cluster—omitting a large number of irrelevant contributions, (iii) genes not belonging to well-defined groups. (Microarrays measure expression for the entire genome in one experiment, but genes may change expression, independent of the experimental condition, [e.g. due to stage in cell cycle]. *Forced inclusion* of such genes in well-defined but inappropriate groups may impact the final structures found for the data).

Methods of Identifying Groups of Related Genes

Cluster definition is dependent on clearly defined metrics, which must be chosen to reflect the data basis. Metric categories include:

Similarity-Based

The cluster is defined to be the set of objects in which each object is closer, (or more similar), to a prototype that defines that cluster as opposed to any other cluster prototype. A typical gene expression cluster prototype is often the *average* or *centroid* of all gene vectors in the cluster. The *similarity metric* used affects the cluster produced. Common measures include: (i) Euclidean distance, (ii) Manhattan distance, and (iii) Squared Pearson correlation distance (Quakenbush, 2001), with the last being the most popular as it captures gene expression "shape" without regard to the magnitude of the measurements. However, this distance measurement is quite sensitive to outliers, although, correlation, rather than "distance," is inherently more important for gene expression data. Take, for example, two gene vectors $X_1=(1,2,3,4,5)$ and $X_2=(3,6,9,12,15)$. These two profiles result in a Euclidean distance of 14.8323 and a Manhattan distance of 30. The Pearson correlation distance however is 0, reflecting the fact that the two genes are showing the same patterns of expression.

Density-Based

Clusters, in this instance, are based on dense regions of genes, surrounded by less-dense regions. Such methods are often employed when clusters are irregular or intertwined, and when noise and outliers are present (Sander, Ester, Kriegel, & Xu, 1998). However, as each cluster is assumed to have a *uniform* density, the method is not readily applicable to gene expression data, as some biological functions involve more gene products than others. The high dimensionality also means that density thresholds can be difficult to define and expensive to compute.

Model-Based

Despite the convenience of similarity-based measures, it can be biologically meaningless to characterise a cluster through a cluster prototype, such as the mean or centroid, as these may be poorly representative of the cluster elements as a whole. As a typical gene expression dataset is large, noisy distortion of these prototypes may be considerable, resulting in relatively uninformative structures. In contrast, model-based techniques, applied to expression space, consider the "fit" of genes in a given cluster to the "ideal" cluster. Concentrating on the strengths of the bi-clustering approach, and following notation from Maderia and Oliveira (2004), four types of model can be identified:

(i) **Bi-clusters with constant values.** A perfect cluster is a sub-matrix (I,J) of the gene expression matrix (N,D), with all values equal, $x_{i,j} = \mu$. The ideal bi-cluster is, of course, rarely found in noisy gene expression data.

(ii) **Bi-clusters with constant values on rows or columns.** A subset of the "ideal" or constant bi-cluster model, and one which is more realistic for gene expression data is a

sub-matrix with constant rows or columns. For the former, rows have constant value in a sub-matrix (I,J) given by $a_{ij} = \mu + \alpha_i$ or $a_{ij} = \mu \times \alpha_i$, where μ is the "typical" bi-cluster value and α_i is the row offset for $i \in I$. Similarly, perfect bi-clusters with constant columns can be obtained for $a_{ij} = \mu + \beta_j$ or $a_{ij} = \mu \times \beta_j$, where $j \in J$.

(iii) **Bi-clusters with coherent values.** From *ii*, a combined additive model can be derived. In this framework, a bi-cluster is a sub-matrix (I,J), with coherent[3] values, based on the model:

$$a_{ij} = \mu + \alpha_i + \beta_j \qquad \textbf{Eq. 1}$$

(where μ, α_i and β_j are as for *(ii)*). Similarly, the multiplicative model assumes that a perfect bi-cluster could be identified using $a_{ij} = \mu' \times \alpha'_i \times \beta'_j$. Note: the additive form clearly follows for $\mu = log(\mu')$, $\alpha_i = log(\alpha'_i)$ and $\beta_j = log(\beta'_j)$.

The artificial example in Figure 2(a) and (b) illustrates this point. The sub-matrix is an ideal bi-cluster found in a fictional dataset, where $\mu=1$, the offset for row 1 to 3 is $\alpha_1=0$, $\alpha_2=2$, $\alpha_3=4$ respectively, and the offset for columns 1 to 6 is $\beta_1=0$, $\beta_2=1$, $\beta_3=2$, $\beta_4=4$, $\beta_5=1$, $\beta_6=-1$ respectively. The expression levels can be obtained from Eq. 1. Of course, when searching the dataset for a fit to this model, the mean and offset parameters are unknown and must be estimated from the data. The schematic illustrates the coherent expression profile over the six conditions. Similarly for the multiplicative model where $\mu=1$, $\alpha_1=1$, $\alpha_2=2$, $\alpha_3=5$, $\beta_1=1$, $\beta_2=2$, $\beta_3=4$, $\beta_4=6$, $\beta_5=3$, $\beta_6=1.5$.

In reality, these "perfect" bi-clusters are, of course, unlikely to occur, so each entry in the sub-matrix can be regarded as having a *residue component* (Cheng & Church, 2000):

$$r_{ij} = \mu + \alpha_i + \beta_j - \alpha_{ij}. \qquad \textbf{Eq. 2}$$

Figure 2. Models in gene expression datasets. The matrix gives clusters found, where rows are gene expression values across 6 experimental conditions (columns). X-axis indicates experimental condition or time point, y-axis indicates gene expression level. Model forms are (a) Additive for rows and columns, (b) Multiplicative for rows and columns and (c) Coherent evolution.

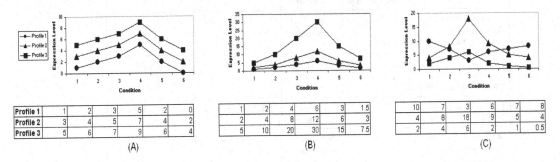

Thus, finding bi-clusters is equivalent to finding sub matrices that minimise the average residue.

(iv) **Bi-clusters with coherent evolution.** Local structures, with *coherent evolution* across a sub-matrix *(I,J)*, can exist in the data regardless of the exact values. This occurs if there is a pattern of co-regulation for a subset of genes and conditions. Expression can occur at different levels, so for example if two genes are up-regulated by different degrees, (e.g. due to a specific condition), these are said to experience coherent evolution.

Taking Figure 2(c) as an example. Gene 1 and gene 2 are regulated, with similar periodicity, while gene 3 shows alternated periodicity. Although the genes are expressed at different levels, each change in expression level is triggered by the same condition. In a simple form, each gene can be said to be exhibiting three states, down-regulated, up-regulated or no change. Additional states can be used, for example strongly up-regulated, weakly up-regulated etc. depending on the detail of the model required. Adding additional states, of course, adds complexity to the model, and cut-off points between states of regulation must be considered carefully. The problem then reduces to finding profiles that show consistent patterns of regulation across all conditions.

CLUSTER ANALYSIS

Current Methods

With extensive choice of metric, structure, completeness etc. in cluster analysis it is useful to consider a framework (Table 2) for performance comparison. The taxonomy used is due to Jains, Murty, and Flynn (1999).

Hierarchical Methods

Ever since the landmark paper of Eisen et al. (1998), numerous clustering algorithms have been applied to gene expression data. Predominantly these have been hierarchical methods, (Higgins, Shinghal, Gill, Reese, Terris, Cohen, Fero, Pollack, van de Rijn, & Brooks, 2003; Khodursky, Peter, Cozzarelli, Botstein, Brown, & Yanofsky, 2000; Makretsov, Huntsman, Nielsen, Yorida, Peacock, Cheang, Dunn, Hayes, van de Rijn, Bajdik, & Gilks, 2004; Wen, Fuhrman, Michaels, Carr, Smith, Barker, & Somogyi, 1998), due mainly to ease of implementation, visualisation capability and general availability.

The basic steps of a hierarchical clustering algorithm include: (i) computation of the proximity matrix of distances between each gene, (initially

Table 2. Popular clustering techniques applied to gene expression data. Partial (overlapping) clusters are more relevant in this context.

Common Clustering techniques				
	Gene Membership	Cluster Structure	Cluster Type	Complete/Partial
Hierarchical (Eisen, Spellman, Brown, & Botstein, 1998)	Hard	Hierarchical (nested)	Similarity-Based	Complete
K-Means (Tavazoie, Hughes, Campbell, Cho, & Church, 1999)	Hard	No structure	Similarity-Based	Complete
FCM (Gasch & Eisen, 1999)	Fuzzy	No structure	Similarity-Based	Complete
SOM (Golub, Slonim, Tamayo, Huard, Gaasenbeek, Mesirov, Coller, Loh, Downing, Caligiuri, Bloomfield, & Lander, 1999)	Hard	Topological Structure	Similarity and Neighbourhood kernal function-based	Complete
Delta clusters (Cheng & Church, 2000)	Shared	Overlap	Based on Coherent Additive Model	Partial
FLOC (Yang, Wang, Wang, & Yu, 2003)	Shared	Overlap	Based on Coherent Additive Model	Partial
SAMBA (Tanay, Sharan, & Shamir, 2002)	Shared	Overlap	Based on Coherent Evolution Model	Partial

each is in a unique cluster of size one), (ii) searching the proximity matrix for the two closest clusters, (iii) merging these two clusters and updating the proximity matrix, and (iv) repeating steps two and three until all genes are in one cluster.

Such *agglomerative* clustering techniques vary with respect to the (i) distance metric used and the decision on cluster merger (that is linkage choice as single, complete, average or centroid; see Quackenbush [2001]). Typically output of a hierarchical clustering algorithm is a dendogram, representing nested patterns in the data and the similarity level at which clusters are merged. The choice of parameters affects both structure of, and relationship between the clusters. Hierarchical cluster structure works well for situations where *membership is crisp*, but, despite their popularity these methods may *not be appropriate to capture natural structures in gene expression data.*

Nevertheless, some successes of clustering *conditions* based on gene expression have been reported. For example, Makrestov et al. (2004) used gene expression profiles, to determine whether sub-types of invasive breast cancer could be identified, with a view to improving patient prognosis. Hierarchical clustering successfully identified three cluster groups with significant differences in clinical outcome. Similarly, a study on renal cell carcinoma, Higgins et al. (2003), found that hierarchical clustering led to segregation of "histologically distinct tumour types solely based on their gene expression patterns" (p. 925). These studies indicate that characterisation of tumours is potentially viable from gene expression profiling.

Hierarchical clustering algorithm properties include location of complete clusters, forced membership and large time-space complexity, but inclusion of "noisy genes" in the cluster can affect the final grouping, (depending to a greater or lesser extent on the linkage method and the distance measure used). As algorithms are prototype-based, further iterations exacerbate noise effects. Given the distance metric basis, hierarchical techniques also tend to produce globular structures.

Partitive Methods

In contrast to hierarchical algorithms, which create clusters in a bottom up fashion resulting in nested levels of clustering, partitive methods optimise a function of given criteria, partitioning the entire dataset and obtaining one cluster structure.

Partitive K-Means clustering (MacQueen, 1967) produces *hard clustering* with no structural relationship between the individual clusters. The main steps of the K-means algorithm are: (i) Identification K prototype vectors for K clusters in the dataset. (ii) Assignment of each gene to a cluster based on its similarity to the cluster prototype, (iii) computation of cluster prototypes based on current genes in the cluster, (iv) repeating steps two and three until *convergence criteria* are satisfied. These may be for example no (or minimal) reassignment of genes to new clusters or for example minimal improvement in optimisation of the criteria function. A typical optimisation approach is to minimise the squared error within a cluster:

$$C = \sum_{j=1}^{k} \sum_{i=1}^{n} y_{ij} d(x_i, q_j) \qquad \textbf{Eq. 3}$$

where q_j is the vector representing the mean of the cluster, x_i is the vector representing the gene, $d(x_i, q_j)$ is a distance measure and y_{ij} is a partition element. Here $y_{ij} \in \{0,1\}$, and $y_{ij}=1$, indicates that gene i is assigned to cluster j.

An example of use of the K-means method is discussed in Tavazoie et al. (1999), and is based on a yeast time-course gene expression dataset, containing profiles for more than 6000 genes,

with 15 time points (at 10 minute intervals—over nearly two cell cycles), (Cho, Campbell, Winzeler, Steinmetz, Conway, Wodicka, Wolfsberg, Gabrielian, Landsman, Lockhart, & Davis,, 1998). (This work succeeded in identifying transcriptional co-regulated genes in yeast). Unfortunately, initial prototype vectors in K-Means usually have a large impact on the data structures found. Prototype vectors are often genes selected at random from the dataset. Alternatively, Principal Component Analysis can be used to project the data to a lower dimensional sub-space and K-means is then applied to the subspace (Zha, Ding, Gu, He, & Simon, 2002). Whichever method is used in practice to select prototype vectors, it is usually the case that different initial prototypes are investigated to assess stability of the results, with the best configuration, (according to the optimisation criteria), used as output clusters.

Fuzzy Methods

As observed, (Section *Characteristics of the Gene Expression Dataset*), multiple cluster membership is more appropriate for gene expression data. The Fuzzy C-Means (FCM) algorithm extends the standard K-means algorithm, to the case where each gene has a membership degree indicating its "fuzzy" or percentage association with the centroid of a given cluster. Typically, each gene has a total membership value of 1, which is divided proportionally between clusters according to its similarity with the cluster means. A *fuzzy partition matrix Y*, (of dimension *NK*, where K is the number of clusters and N is the number of genes), is created, where each element y_{ij} is the membership grade of gene i in cluster j and a weighted version of Eq. 3 applies. At each iteration, the membership value, y_{ij}, and the cluster center, k_j, is updated by:

$$y_{ij} = 1 \Big/ \sum_{c=1}^{k} \left(\frac{d(x_i - k_j)}{d(x_i - k_c)} \right)^{\frac{2}{m-1}} \qquad \textbf{Eq. 4}$$

$$k_j = \left. \sum_{i=1}^{N} y_{ij}^{m} x_i \middle/ \sum_{i=1}^{N} y_{ij}^{m} \right. \qquad \textbf{Eq. 5}$$

where *m*>1 denotes the degree of fuzziness, (everything else is as for Eq. 3). The iterations stop when $max \mid j_{ij}^{k+1} - j_{ij}^{k} \mid < \varepsilon$, where ε is a *termination criterion* with value between 0 and 1, and *k* is the number of iterations.

Given the usual constraint that membership values of a gene must sum to unity, these values should be interpreted with care. A large "membership value" does not indicate "strength of expression" but rather reduced co-membership across several clusters (Krishnapuram & Keller, 1993). Table 3 illustrates this idea for three clusters. FCM was carried out on published yeast genomic expression data (Gasch & Eisen, 2002; results available at http://rana.lbl.gov/FuzzyK/data.html). The membership values for gene B and gene D are very different for cluster 21, although they are approximately equidistant from the centroid of the cluster. Similarly, gene C and gene D have comparable membership values for cluster 4. However, gene C is more "typical" than gene D. With similar centroid distance measures, membership value for gene B in cluster 21 is smaller than membership value of gene A in cluster 46. These values arise from the constraint that membership values must sum to unity across all clusters, forcing a gene to give up some of its membership in one cluster to increase it in another. Listing the genes

of a cluster, based on membership values alone is somewhat non-intuitive as it is not a measure of their compatibility with the cluster. However, if interpretation of the list in terms of degree of sharing between clusters is of value.

The work of Gasch and Eisen (2002) on the use of FCM in analysing microarray data looked at clustered responses of yeast genes to environmental changes. Groups of known functionally co-regulated genes, and novel groups of co-regulated genes, were found by this method, although missed by both hierarchical and K-means methods.

Artificial Neural Networks

Artificial neural networks (ANN) mimic the idea of biological neural networks, where links between various neurons (nodes) can be strengthened or weakened through learning. A number of ANN types have been explored, with Self-Organising Maps (SOM) (Kohonen, 1990) proving popular for the analysis of gene expression, as these provide a fast method of visualising and interpreting high dimensional data. The network *maps the high-dimension input gene vector into a lower dimensional space.* A SOM is formed by an input layer of *D* nodes, (where *D* is the gene vector dimension), and an output layer of neurons arranged in a regular grid (usually of 1 or 2 dimensions). A vector, of the same dimension as the input gene, references each node in the output layer. Briefly, the mechanism involves: (i) initialisation

Table 3. Difficulties interpreting membership values for FCM. GENE1649X (Gene A), GENE6076X (Gene B), GENE5290X (Gene C) and GENE2382X (Gene D). The table highlights distance to cluster centroid, in terms of Euclidean distance, and the associated membership values of the gene.

GID	Cluster 4		Cluster 21		Cluster 46	
	Centroid Dist.	Mem.	Centroid Dist.	Mem.	Centroid Dist.	Mem.
GENE1649X	10.691	0.002575	8.476	0.002002	3.864	0.482479
GENE6076X	6.723	0.009766	3.855	0.009341	6.33	0.007381
GENE5290X	6.719	0.007653	5.29	0.00515	8.024	0.005724
GENE2382X	7.725	0.007609	3.869	0.01782	6.279	0.010249

of the prototype vectors of the output nodes, (ii) training the network to find clusters in the data (Genes are selected at random from the dataset and the closest output neuron is identified by its prototype vector. Once an output neuron is identified, its topological neighbours are updated to reflect this. Training continues until the reference vectors satisfy a stopping criterion), and (iii) Sequential application of all gene vectors to the SOM, where only one output neuron "fires" upon receiving an input gene vector. "Members" of a cluster, represented by output neuron i, are the set of genes, applied to the input neurons, causing output neuron i to fire.

ANN techniques have been used in a number of gene expression studies, including Tamayo, Slonim, Mesirov, Zhu, Kitareewan, Dmitrovsky, Lan-der, and Golub (1999) (to analyse haematopoietic differentiation); Toronen, Kolehmainen, Wong, & Castren (1999) (to analyse yeast gene expression data); and Golub et al. (1999) (to cluster acute lymphoblastic leukaemia [ALL] and acute myeloid leukaemia [AML]). The stopping criterion of the SOM is crucial, since over-fitting to the training dataset is a risk. A further disadvantage is the amount of prior information needed. SOM requires input parameters such as learning rate, neighbourhood size and kernel function, as well as topology of the map, (typically hexagonal or square). The stability of results is also an issue, as a particular gene vector can be found to cause different output nodes to fire at different iterations, (Jains et al. 1999). Furthermore, clusters produced by the SOM are sensitive to choice of initial vectors for the output neurons, and a *sub-optimal structure* may result from a poor selection.

Search Based Methods

While methods considered so far focus on finding *global structures* in the data, local structures are frequently of great interest. Cheng and Church (2000) adapted work of Hartigan (1972) for gene expression data, producing simultaneous clusters of genes and conditions and an *overall partial clustering* of the data. From Eq. 1 each value a_{ij} of a sub-matrix can be defined from the typical value within the bi-cluster a_{IJ}, plus the offsets for the row mean, $a_{iJ}-a_{IJ}$ and column mean $a_{Ij}-a_{IJ}$. Thus, each value in the sub-matrix should (ideally) be:

$$a_{ij} = a_{ij} - a_{iJ} - a_{Ij} + a_{IJ} \qquad \textbf{Eq. 6}$$

The Cheng and Church technique defines the *Mean Residue Score (H)* of a sub-matrix, based on Eq. 2 and Eq. 6, such that:

$$H(I,J) = \frac{1}{|I||J|} \sum_{i \in I, j \in J} (r_{ij})^2 \qquad \textbf{Eq. 7}$$

The algorithm carries out greedy iterative searches for sub-matrices (I,J), which minimise this function (Eq. 7), generating a large time cost, as each row and column of the dataset must be tested for deletion. (A sub-matrix is considered a bi-cluster if its Mean Residue Score falls below a user specified threshold). A further overhead is the *masking of a bi-cluster with random numbers* once it is found, to prevent finding the same clusters repeatedly on successive iterations. There is, nevertheless, high probability that this replacement with random numbers affects the discovery of further bi-clusters. To overcome this random "interference" Yang et al. (2003) developed **flexible overlapped bi-clustering** (FLOC), generalising the model of Cheng and Church to incorporate null values.

For both the Cheng and Church (2000) algorithm and the FLOC generalisation, K can be specified to be much larger than the desired number of groups, without affecting the outcome, as each row and column in the expression matrix can belong to more than one bi-cluster, (Cheng & Church, 2000; Yang et al., 2003). Selecting K then reduces to selecting the percentage of the bi-clusters with the best Mean Residue-score (Eq. 7). The cost is increased computation time—the Cheng and Church algorithm finds one bi-cluster

Figure 3. Bipartite graph representing expression for seven genes under five conditions—edges indicate a change in expression

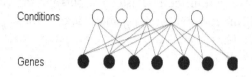

at a time while FLOC finds all simultaneously. However, a major additional strength of the bi-clustering techniques is *the minimal requirement for domain knowledge*. Also, as FLOC accounts for null values in the dataset, the preliminary imputation of missing values is not necessary.

Graph theoretic Methods:

A further approach, which is proving useful in the analysis of large complex biological datasets, is that of graph theory, (Aiello, Chun, & Lu, 2000; Aittokallio & Schwitowski, 2006; Guillaume & Latapy, 2006; Maslov, Sneppen, & Zaliznyak, 2004). A given gene expression dataset can be viewed as a *weighted bipartite graph, G= (V, U, E),* where *V* is the set of gene vertices, *U* is the set of condition vertices, with $V \cap U = \Phi$, and *E* is the set of edges, with $(u, v) \in E$ having a weight a_{uv} proportional to the strength of the expression of gene *v* under condition *u* (Figure 3).

Analysis of the models involved focuses on identification of similarly or densely connected sub graphs of nodes and, of course, relies greatly on the method used to define the *edge weights*. Clustering by graph network leads to similar issues as before; (i) results are highly sensitive to data quality and input parameters, (ii) predicted clusters can vary from one method of graph clustering to another. Clusters that share nodes and edges of a graph networks, clearly "overlap" and as noted in the section titled *Characteristics of the Gene Expression Dataset*, are desirable for gene expression interpretation.

The "Statistical Algorithmic Method for Bi-cluster Analysis" (SAMBA) (Tanay et al., 2000), uses a graphical approach and, unlike previous bi-clustering techniques, finds coherent evolution in the data. An edge is defined to exist between a gene node *u* and a condition node *v* if there is significant change in expression of gene *u* under condition *v*, relative to the genes normal level (a non-edge exists if *u* does not change expression under *v*). Each edge and non-edge is then weighted, based on a log likelihood model, with weights:

$$\log \frac{p_c}{P_{(u,v)}} > 0 \text{ for edges, and } \log \frac{(1 - P_c)}{(1 - P_{(u,v)})} < 0$$

for non-edges. **Eq. 8**

Here, $P_{(u,v)}$ is the fraction of random bipartite graphs, with degree sequence identical to *G*, that contain edge *(u,v),* and P_c is a constant probability assigned by the user. For $P_c > \max_{(u,v) \in U \times V} P_{(u,v)}$, edges are taken to occur in a bi-cluster with equal probability. Weights as determined by Eq. 8 are assigned to the edges and non-edges in the graph. A major strength of this method is that statistical significance of any sub graph is then simply determined by its weight.

Cluster Evaluation and Comparison

Evaluation is not particularly well developed for clustering analyses applied to gene expression data, as very little may be known about the dataset beforehand. Many clustering algorithms are designed to be exploratory; producing different clusters according to given classification criteria and will discover a structure, meaningful in that context, which may yet fail to be optimal or even biologically realistic. For example, for K-Means the "best" structure is one that minimises the sum of squared errors (MacQueen, 1967) while, for the Cheng and Church algorithm (Cheng & Church, 2000), it is that which minimises of the Mean Residue-Score (Eq. 7). The two may not

Figure 4. Gene expression profiles for two equivalent clusters; cluster in (B) has Profile 1 scaled down by one third

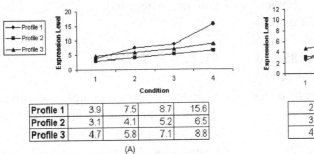

Profile 1	3.9	7.5	8.7	15.6
Profile 2	3.1	4.1	5.2	6.5
Profile 3	4.7	5.8	7.1	8.8

(A)

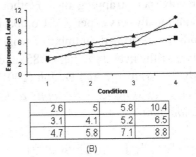

2.6	5	5.8	10.4
3.1	4.1	5.2	6.5
4.7	5.8	7.1	8.8

(B)

be directly comparable, as the former highlights *global patterns* in the data and the latter *local patterns*. While larger deviations from the mean may also correspond to large residue scores this will not always be the case. For example, Figure 4 highlights a simple situation with three genes in a cluster. According to the K-means criterion, the within cluster distance is approximately 11.02, based on Euclidean distance and centroid of the cluster. The Mean Residue Score is 0. Reducing the scale of profile 1 by one third, (Figure 4(b)), decreases the within-cluster distance to 7.91, while increasing the Mean Residue Score slightly to 0.0168. Both (a) and (b) are roughly equivalent. Consequently, interpretation of cluster results relies on some level of subjectivity as well as independent validation and integration of findings. Subjective evaluation, even for low dimensional data, is non-trivial at best, but becomes increasingly difficult for high dimensional gene expression data. Clearly, each technique *will* find patterns even if these are not meaningful in a biological context.

The benefits of the individual techniques, as applied to gene expression data, were highlighted in the last section. This section aims at providing navigational guidelines for some degree of objective evaluation and comparison.

Determining the Correct Number of Clusters

Cluster number, in the absence of prior knowledge, is determined by whether a non-random structure exists in the data. Limiting to a specific number of groups will bias the search, as patterns tend to be well-defined only for the strongest signals. Commonly, statistical tests for spatial randomness test if a non-random structure exists, but identification of small, biologically meaningful clusters remains non-trivial. This is particularly true of standard methods, which find global structure, but lack fine-tuning to distinguish local structures. Selection of the correct *number* of clusters *(K)* thus is inherently iterative. Near optimal *K* should clearly minimise heterogeneity between groups, while maximising homogeneity within groups, but determining the number of significant clusters relies, not only on direct extraction (or assessment) but also on appropriate hypothesis testing. Direct methods are based on various of criteria[4]. Nevertheless, improvement in terms of identification of local clusters is slight. Specific tests include Gap Statistic (Tibshirani, Walther, & Hastie, 2001), Weighted Discrepant Pairs (WADP) (Bittner, Meltzer, Chen, Jiang, Seftor, Hendrix, Radmacher, Simon, Yakhini, Ben-Dor, Sampas, Dougherty, Wang, Marincola, Gooden, Lueders, Glatfelter, Pollock, Carpten, Gillanders, Leja, Dietrich, Beaudry, Berens, Alberts, & Sondak,

2000), and a variety of permutation methods (Bittner et al., 2000; Fridlyand & Dudoit, 2001). Since most involve bootstrapping, these methods can be computationally very expensive. Comparison of methods for selecting the number of groups is discussed by Milligan and Cooper (1985) and, more recently, by Fridlyand and Dudoit (2001), who note that *no existing tests are optimal for gene expression data.*

Comparing Results from Clustering Algorithms

Numerical measures of cluster "goodness" include **cluster cohesion** (compactness or tightness), that is how closely related genes in a cluster are, while measures of **cluster separation** (isolation), determine how distinct each cluster is. The *Group Homogeneity Function*, is often used to measure the association (distinctiveness) of genes within and between groups.

Comparison with Metadata

Including biological function information in the gene list for each cluster inevitably provides a more complete picture of the dataset and of the success of the technique. This information can be used to validate the clusters produced, and a number of functional annotation databases are available. The Gene Ontology database (Ashburner, Ball, Blake, Botstein, Butler, Cherry, Davies, Dolinski, Dwight, Epping, Harris, Hill, Issel-Tarver, Kasarskis, Lewis, Matese, Richardson, Ringwald, Rubin, & Sherlock, 2000) for example, provides a structured vocabulary that describes the role of genes and proteins in all organisms. The database is organised into three ontologies: biological process, molecular function, and cellular component. Several tools[5] have been developed for batch retrieval of GO annotations for a list of genes. Statistically relevant GO terms can be used to investigate the properties shared by a set of genes. Such tools facilitate the transi-

tion from data collection to biological meaning by providing a template of relevant biological patterns in gene lists.

FUTURE TRENDS

Despite the shortcomings, the application of clustering methods to gene expression data has proven to be of immense value, providing insight on cell regulation, as well as on disease characterisation. Nevertheless, not all clustering methods are equally valuable in the context of high dimensional gene expression. Recognition that well-known, simple clustering techniques, such as K-Means and Hierarchical clustering, do not capture more complex local structures in the data, has led to bi-clustering methods, in particular, gaining considerable recent popularity, (Ben-Dor, Chor, Karp, & Yakhini, 2002; Busygin, Jacobsen, & Kramer, 2002; Califano, Stolovitzky, & Tu, 2000; Cheng & Church, 2000; Getz, Levine, & Domany, 2000; Kluger, Basri, Chang, & Gerstein, 2003; Lazzeroni & Owen, 2002; Liu & Wang, 2003; Segal, Taskar, Gasch, Friedman, & Koller, 2003; Sheng, Moreau, & De Moor, 2003; Tanay et al., 2002; Yang et al., 2003;). Indications to date are that these methods provide increased sensitivity at local structure level for discovery of meaningful biological patterns.

Achieving full potential of clustering methods is constrained at present by the lack of robust validation techniques, based on external resources, such as the GO database. *Standardisation of gene annotation methods* across publicly available databases is needed before validation techniques can be successfully integrated with clustering information found from datasets.

The "Central Dogma" that "DNA makes mRNA makes proteins" that comprise the proteome is overly simple. A single gene does not translate into one protein and protein abundance depends not only on transcription rates of genes but also on additional control mechanisms, such as mRNA stability[6], regulation of the translation of mRNA to proteins[7] and protein degradation[8]. Proteins also can be modified by *post-translation activity*[9] (Brown, 2002a). The study of proteomic and transcription data investigates the way in which changes connect gene expression to the physical chemistry of the cell. Integration and merger of proteomic and transcription data sources across platforms is needed, together with development of automated high-throughput comparisons methods if detailed understanding of cell mechanisms is to be achieved. To this end, a standard method of gene and protein annotation across databases is overdue (Waters, 2006). The development of Bioinformatics/data-mining tools that span different levels of *"omics"* is a necessary next step in the investigation of cell function.

CONCLUSION

Clustering gene expression data is non-trivial and selection of appropriate algorithms is vital if meaningful interpretation of the data is to be achieved. Successful analysis has profound implications for knowledge of gene function, diagnosis, and for targeted drug development amongst others. The evidence to date is that *methods, which determine global structure, are insufficiently powerful given the complexity of the data.* Bi-clustering methods offer interpretability of data features and structure to a degree not possible with standard methods. However, even though less sophisticated algorithms such as K-means are achieving some success and while bi-clustering methods seem promising, these are the first steps only to analysing cellular mechanisms and obstacles remain substantial. A significant barrier to the integration of genomic and proteomic platforms and understanding cellular mechanisms is the lack of standardisation. Integration of heterogeneous datasets must be addressed before analysis of gene expression data comes of age.

REFERENCES

Aiello, W, Chun, F., & Lu, L. (2000). A random graph model for massive graphs. *Proceedings of the 32nd Annual ACM symposium on Theory of computing,* Portland, Oregon, USA, 171 – 180, ACM Press.

Aittokallio, T. & Schwikowski, B. (2006). Graph-based methods for analyzing networks in cell biology. *Briefings in Bioinformatics, 7*(3), 243 – 255.

Al-Shahrour, F., Díaz-Uriarte, R., & Dopazo, J. (2003). FatiGO: A Web tool for finding significant associations of Gene Ontology terms with groups of genes. *Bioinformatics, 20*(4), 578 – 580.

Alizadeh, A. A., Eisen, M. B., Davis, R. E., Ma, C., Lossos, I. S., Rosenwald, A., C. Boldrick, J. C., Sabet, J., Tran, T., Yu, X. Powell, J. I. Yang, L., Marti, G. E., Moore, T., Hudson Jr., J. Lu, L., Lewis, D. B., Tibshirani, R., Sherlock, G., Chan, W. C., Greiner, T. C., Weisenburger, D. D., Armitage, J. O., Warnke, R., Levy, R., Wilson, W., Grever, M. R., Byrd, J. C., Botstein, D., Brown, P. O., & Staudt, L. M. (2000). Distinct types of diffuse large b-cell lymphoma identified by gene expression profiling. *Nature, 403*(6769), 503-511.

Ashburner, M., Ball, C.A., Blake, J.A., Botstein, D., Butler, H., Cherry, J. M., Davies, A. P., Dolinski, K., Dwight, S. S., Epping, J. T., Harris, M. A., Hill, D. P. Issel-Tarver, L., Kasarskis, A., Lewis, S., Matese, J.C., Richardson, J. E., Ringwald, M., Rubin, G. M., & Sherlock, G. (2000). Gene ontology: Tool for the unification of biology. The Gene Ontology Consortium. *Nature Genetics, 25*(1), 25-29.

Ben-Dor, A., Chor, B., Karp, R., & Yakhini, Z. (2002). Discovering local structure in gene expression data: The order-preserving submatrix problem. *Proceedings of the 6th International Conference on Computational Biology (RECOMB '02),* Washington DC, USA, 49 – 57, ACM Press.

Bittner, M., Meltzer, P., Chen, Y., Jiang, Y., Seftor, E., Hendrix, M., Radmacher, M., Simon, R., Yakhini, Z., Ben-Dor, A., Sampas, N., Dougherty, E., Wang, E., Marincola, F., Gooden, C., Lueders, J., Glatfelter, A., Pollock, P., Carpten, J., Gillanders, E., Leja, D., Dietrich, K., Beaudry, C., Berens, M., Alberts, D., & Sondak, V. (2000). Molecular classification of cutaneous malignant melanoma by gene expression profiling. *Nature, 406*(6795), 536-540.

Bolstad, B. M., Irizarry, R. A., Astrand, M., & Speed, T. P. (2003). A comparison of normalization methods for high density oligonucleotide array data based on variance and bias. *Bioinformatics, 19*(2), 185-93.

Brazma, A., Hingamp, P., Quackenbush, J., Sherlock, G., Spellman, P., Stoeckert, C., Aach, J., Ansorge, W., Ball, C.A., Causton, H.C., Gaasterland, T., Glenisson, P., Holstege, F.C., Kim, I.F., Markowitz, V., Matese, J.C., Parkinson, H., Robinson, A., Sarkans, U., Schulze-Kremer, S., Stewart, J., Taylor, R., Vilo, J., & Vingron, M. (2001). Minimum information about a microarray experiment (MIAME)-toward standards for microarray data. *Nature Genetics, 29*(4), 365-371.

Brown, T. A. (2002a). Transcriptomes and proteomes. In *Genomes, 2 edition,* pp. 70 – 91. Manchester, UK: Wiley-Liss.

Brown, T. A. (2002b). Synthesis and processing of the proteome. In *Genomes, 2 edition,* pp. 314 – 344. Manchester, UK: Wiley-Liss.

Busygin, S., Jacobsen, G., & Kramer, E. (2002). Double conjugated clustering applied to leukaemia microarray data. *Proceedings of the 2nd SIAM International Conference on Data Mining, Workshop on Clustering High Dimensional data,* Arlington, Virgina, USA, 420 – 436, Soc for Industrial & Applied Math.

Califano, A., Stolovitzky, G., & Tu, Y. (2000). Analysis of gene expression microarrays for phenotype classification. *Proceedings of the International Conference on Computational Molecular Biology,* Tokyo, Japan, 75 – 85, ACM Press.

Cheng, Y. & Church, G. M. (2000). Biclustering of expression data. *Proceedings of the International Conference on Intelligent Systems for Molecular Biology; ISMB. International Conference on Intelligent Systems for Molecular Biology 8, 93-103.*

Cho, R.J., Campbell, M.J., Winzeler, E. A., Steinmetz, L., Conway, A., Wodicka, L., Wolfsberg, T. G., Gabrielian, A. E., Landsman, D., Lockhart, D. J., & Davis, R. W. (1998). A genome-wide transcriptional analysis of mitotic cell cycle. *Molecular Cell 2, 1,* 65-73.

Dennis, G., Sherman, B. T., Hosack, D. A., Yang, J., Gao, W., Lane, H. C., & Lempicki, R. A. (2003). DAVID: Database for Annotation, Visualization and Integrated Discovery. *Genome Biology, 4,* R60.

Draghici, S., Khatri, P., Martins, R. P., Ostermeier, G. C., & Krawetz, S. A. (2003). Global functional profiling of gene expression. *Genomics, 81*(2), 98 – 104.

Eisen, M B., Spellman, P. T., Brown, P. O., & Botstein, D. (1998). Cluster analysis and display of genome wide expression patterns. *PNAS, 95*(25), 14863-14868.

Fridlyand, J. & Dudoit, S. (2001). *Applications of resampling methods to estimate the number of clusters and to improve the accuracy of a clustering method.* (Technical Report 600), Berkeley, California: University of California, Department of Statistics.

Friemert, C., Erfle, V., & Strauss, G. (1989). Preparation of radiolabeled cDNA probes with high specific activity for rapid screening of gene expression. *Methods Molecular Cell Biology, 1,* 143ˉ-153.

Gasch, A. P. & Eisen, M.B. (2002). Exploring the conditional coregulation of yeast in gene expression through fuzzy K-Means clustering.

Genome Biology, 3(11), RESEARCH0059.1 – RESEARCH0059.22.

Golub, T. R., Slonim, D. K., Tamayo, P., Huard, C., Gaasenbeek, M., Mesirov, J. P., Coller, H., Loh, M. L., Downing, J. R., Caligiuri, M. A., Bloomfield, C. D., & Lander, E. S. (1999). Molecular classification of cancer: Class discovery and class prediction by gene expression monitoring. *Science 286*(5439), 531-537.

Getz, G., Levine, E., & Domany, E. (2000). Coupled two-way clustering analysis of gene microarray data. *PNAS, 97*(22), 12079 – 12084.

Gress, T.M., Hoheisel, J.D., Sehetner, G., & Leahrach, H. (1992). Hybridization fingerprinting of high-density cDNA-library arrays with cDNA pools derived from whole tissues. *Mammalian Genome, 3,* 609‾ -619.

Guillaume, J. L. & Latapy, M. (2006). Bipartite graphs as models of complex networks. *Physica A, 317,* 795 – 813.

Hartigan, J.A. (1972). Direct clustering of a data matrix. *Journal of the American Statistical Association, 67*(337), 123-129.

Higgins, J. P., Shinghal, R., Gill, H., Reese, J. H., Terris, M., Cohen, R. J., Fero, M., Pollack, J. R. van de Rijn, M., & Brooks, J. D. (2003). Gene expression patterns in renal cell carcinoma assessed by complementary DNA microarray. *The American Journal of Pathology, 162*(3), 925 – 932.

Hosack, D. A., Dennis, G. Jr., Sherman, B. T., Lane, H. C., & Lempicki, R. A. (2003). Identifying biological themes within lists of genes with EASE. *Genome Biology, 4,* R70.

Jains, A.K., Murty M.N., & Flynn P.J. (1999). Data clustering: A review. *ACM Computing Surveys, 31*(3), 264-323.

Kaufmann, L. & Rousseeuw, P. J. (1990). *Finding groups in data: An introduction to cluster analysis.* New York: John Wiley and Sons Inc., Chinchester, Weinheim.

Kerr, M.K. & Churchill, G.A. (2001). Experimental design for gene expression microarrays, *Biostatistics, 2*(2), 183 – 201.

Khodursky, A. B., Peter, B. J., Cozzarelli, N. R., Botstein, D., Brown, P. O., Yanofsky, C. (2000). DNA microarray analysis of gene expression in response to physiological and genetic changes that affect tryptophan metabolism in Escherichia coli. *PNAS, 97*(22), 12170 - 12175

Kishnapuram R. and Keller J.M. (1993) A possibilistic approach to clustering. *Fuzzy Systems, IEEE Transactions on,* 1(2), 98-110.

Kluger, Y., Basri, R., Chang, J. T., & Gerstein, M. (2003). Spectral biclustering of microarray data: Coclustering genes and conditions. *Genome research, 13*(4), 703-716.

Kohonen, T. (1990). The self-organizing map. *Proceeding of the IEEE, 78*(9), 1464-1480.

Lazzeroni, L. & Owen, A. (2002). Plaid models for gene expression data. *Statistica Sinica, 12,* 61 – 86.

Liu, J. & Wang, W. (2003). Op-cluster: Clustering by tendancy in high dimensional space. *Proceedings of the 3rd IEEE International Conference on Data Mining,* Melbourne, Florida, USA, 187 – 194, IEEE Computer Society Press.

Liu, X., Cheng, G., & Wu, J. X. (2002). Analyzing outliers cautiously. *IEEE Transactions on Knowledge and Data Engineering, 14*(2), 432-437.

MacQueen, J.B. (1967). Some methods for classification and analysis of multivariate observations, *Proceedings of 5-th Berkeley Symposium on Mathematical Statistics and Probability,* Berkeley, 1, 281-297, University of California Press.

Maderia S. C. & Oliveira, A. L. (2004). Biclustering algorithms for biological data analysis: A survey. *IEEE Transactions on Computational Biology and Bioinformatics, 1*(1), 24-45.

Makretsov, N. A., Huntsman, D. G., Nielsen, T. O., Yorida, E., Peacock, M., Cheang, M. C. U., Dunn, S. E., Hayes, M., van de Rijn, M., Bajdik, C., & Gilks, C. B. (2004). Hierarchical clustering analysis of tissue microarray immunostaining data identifies prognostically significant groups of breast carcinoma. *Clinical Cancer Research, 18*(10), 6143 – 6151.

Maslov, S., Sneppen, K., & Zaliznyak, A. (2004). Detection of topological patterns in complex networks: Correlation profile of the Internet. *Physica A, 333*, 529 – 540.

Milligan, G. W. & Cooper M. C. (1985). An examination of procedures for determining the number of clusters in a dataset. *Psychometrika, 50*, 159-179.

Quakenbush, J. (2001). Computational analysis of microarray data. *Nature Review Genetics, 2*(6), 418 – 427.

Raser, J. M. & O' Shea E. K. (2005). Noise in gene expression data: Origins and control. *Science, 309*, 2010-2013.

Sander, J., Ester, M., Kriegel, K. P., & Xu, X. (1998). Density-based clustering in spatial databases: The algorithmic GDBSCAN and its applications. *Data Mining and Knowledge Discovery, 2*(2), 169 – 194.

Schulze, A. & Downward, J. Navigating gene expression using microarrays – A technology review. *Nature Cell Biology, 3*(8), E190 - 195.

Segal, E. Taskar, B., Gasch, A., Friedman, N., & Koller, D. (2003). Decomposing gene expression into cellular processes. *Proceedings of the Pacific Symposium on Biocomputing,* Lihue, Hawaii, USA, 89 – 100, World Scientific Press.

Scott A. J. & Symons, M. J. (1971). Clustering methods based on likelihood ratio criteria. *Biometrics, 27*(2), 387-397.

Sheng, Q., Moreau, Y., & De Moor, B. (2003). Biclustering microarray data by Gibbs sampling. *Bioinformaics, 19*(Supp. 2), ii196 – ii205.

Tamayo, D. Slonim, J. Mesirov, Q. Zhu, S. Kitareewan, E. Dmitrovsky, E. S. Lan-der, & Golub, T. R. (1999). Interpreting patterns of gene expression with self-organizing maps: Methods and application to hematopoietic differentiation. *Proceedings of the National Academy of Sciences of the United States of America, 96*(6), 2907-2912.

Tanay, A. Sharan, R., & Shamir, R. Discovering statistically significant biclusters in gene expression data. *Bioinformatics, 18*(1), S136-44.

Tavazoie, S., Hughes, J. D., Campbell, M. J. Cho, R. J., & Church, G. M. (1999). Systematic determination of genetic network architecture. *Nature genetics, 22*(3), 281-285.

Tibshirani, R., Walther, G., & Hastie, T. (2001). Estimating the number of clusters in a dataset via the gap statistic. *Journal of the Royal Statistical Society: Series B (Statistical Methodology), 63*(2), 411-423.

Toronen, P., Kolehmainen, M., Wong, G., & Castren, E. (1999). Analysis of gene expression data using self-organizing maps. *FEBS Letters, 451*(2), 142 – 146.

Troyanskaya, O., Cantor, M., Sherlock, G., Brown, P., Hastie, T., Tibshirani, R., Botstein, D., & Altman, R. B. (2001). Missing value estimation methods for DNA microarrays. *Bioinformatics, 17*(6), 520 – 525.

van der Laan, M. J. & Pollard, K. S. (2001). *Hybrid clustering of gene expression data with visualization and the bootstrap.* (Technical Report 93), *U.C. Berkeley Division of Biostatistics Working Paper Series, Berkeley, California, University of California, School of Public Health, Division of Biostatisitcs.*

Waters, K. M., Pounds, J. G. & Thrall B. D. (2006). Data merging for integrated microarray and proteomics analysis. *Briefings in Functional Genomics and Proteomics, 5(4)*, 261 – 272.

Wen, X., Fuhrman, S., Michaels, G. S., Carr, D. B., Smith, S., Barker, J. L., & Somogyi, R. (1998). Large Scale temporal gene expression mapping of central nervous system development. *PNAS, 95*(1), 334-339.

Yang, J., Wang, H., Wang, W., & Yu, P. (2003). Enhanced biclustering on expression data. *Proceedings of the 3rd IEEE Symposium on BioInformatics and BioEngineering (*BIBE '03). IEEE Computer Society, 321 - 327.

Zeeberg, B.R., Feng, W., Wang, Geoffrey, W., Wang, M. D., Fojo, A. T., Sunshine, M., Narasimhan, S., Kane, D. W., Reinhold, W. C., Lababidi, S., Bussey, K. J., Riss, J., Barrett, J. C., & Weinstein, J. N. (2003). GoMiner: A resource for biological interpretation of genomic and proteomics data. *Genome Biology, 4*, R28.

Zha, H., Ding, C., Gu, M., He, X., & Simon, H.D. (2002). Spectral relaxation for k-means clustering. *Proceedings Neural Information Processing Systems, 14*, 1057 – 1064.

ENDNOTES

[1] Microarray development timeline: 1989 – development of world's first microarray; 1991 – Photolithographic printing technique developed by Affymetrix; 1993 – Microarray containing over 1 million DNA sequences developed; 1994 – First cDNA collections developed by Stanford; 1995 – Quantitative monitoring of gene expression patterns with cDNA microarray; 1996 – Commercialisation of arrays (Affymetrix); 1997 – Genomewide expression monitoring in Yeast; 2000 – Portraits/Signatures of gene expression in cancer identified; 2002 - Genechip® Human Genome two array set developed for analysis of over 33,000 genes from public databases; 2003 – Microarray technology introduced to clinical practices; 2004 – Whole human genome on one microarray.

[2] The two most popular array platforms are complementary DNA (cDNA) and oligonucleotide microarrays. The former contains cDNA probes that are products synthesized from polymerase chain reactions generated from cDNA and clone libraries, the latter contain shorter synthesized oligonucleotide probes (prefect match and mismatch) generated directly from sequence data. A key difference between the two platforms is the manner in which the data is presented for analysis. Intensity measurements for cDNA arrays are the result of competitive hybridisation, (where two transcription samples of interest (labelled with two different dyes) are hybridised to the same array), resulting in a measurement of the ratio of transcript levels for each gene, (usually reported as a log ratio). Oligonucleotide arrays, on the other hand, results from non-competitive hybridisation (where one transcription sample is hybridised to a array and difference in expression levels between two samples are compared across arrays). Here, measurement level for a gene is presented as the average measurement of all probes representing the gene (depending on pre-processing technique this may have mismatch probes subtracted first). See Schulze and Downward (2001) for a review.

[3] Gene expression patterns with similar frequency and phase.

[4] These include likelihood ratios (Scott and Symons, 1971), cluster sums of squares (Milligan and Cooper, 1985), average silhouette (Kaufmann and Rousseeuw, 1990) or mean split silhouette (van der Laan and Pollard, 2001).

[5] Tools important for the management and understanding of large scale gene expres-

sion data: FatiGo (Al-Shahrour et al., 2003), GoMiner (Zeeberg et al., 2003), OntoExpress (Draghici et al., 2003), EASE (Hosack et al., 2003), DAVID Gene classification tool (Dennis et al., 2003).

6   Sequences of mRNA may vary considerably in stability. The balance between mRNA degradation and mRNA synthesis determines the level of mRNA in the cell.

7   The mechanisms, including regulatory proteins, which dictates which genes are expressed and at what level.

8   The method and rate at which protein is broken down in the body.

9   Before taking on a functional role in the cell an amino acid sequence must fold into its correct tertiary structure. Additional post-processing events may occur, such as proteolytic cleavage, chemical modifications, intein splicing. (Brown, 2002(b)).

Chapter IV
Using "Blackbox" Algorithms Such as TreeNet and Random Forests for Data–Mining and for Finding Meaningful Patterns, Relationships, and Outliers in Complex Ecological Data:
An Overview, an Example Using Golden Eagle Satellite Data and an Outlook for a Promising Future

Erica Craig
Western Ecological Studies, USA

Falk Huettmann
University of Alaska-Fairbanks, USA

ABSTRACT

The use of machine-learning algorithms capable of rapidly completing intensive computations may be an answer to processing the sheer volumes of highly complex data available to researchers in the field of ecology. In spite of this, the continued use of less effective, simple linear, and highly labor intensive techniques such as stepwise multiple regression continue to be widespread in the ecological community. Herein we describe the use of data-mining algorithms such as TreeNet and Random Forests (Salford Systems), which can rapidly and accurately identify meaningful patterns and relationships in subsets of data that carry various degrees of outliers and uncertainty. We use satellite data from a wintering

Golden Eagle as an example application; judged by the consistency of the results, the resultant models are robust, in spite of 30 % faulty presence data. The authors believe that the implications of these findings are potentially far-reaching and that linking computational software with wildlife ecology and conservation management in an interdisciplinary framework cannot only be a powerful tool, but is crucial toward obtaining sustainability.

INTRODUCTION

Individual species and even entire ecosystems are at risk because of climatic changes and destruction of native habitats that are occurring worldwide, simultaneous with increased pressures from the expansion of human populations (Bittner, Oakley, Hannan, Lincer, Muscolino, & Domenech, 2003; Braun, 2005; Knick, Dobkin, Rotenberry, Schroeder, Vander Haegen, & Van Riper, 2003; Millenium Ecosystem Assessment, 2005; Primack, 1998; Zakri, 2003). Knowing and understanding factors that affect species and even that drive entire systems is vital for assessing populations that are at risk, as well as for making land management decisions that promote species sustainability. Advances in geographic information system technology (GIS) and digital online data availability coupled with the ability to collect data on animal movements via satellite and GPS have given rise to large, highly complex datasets that have the potential to provide the global community with valuable information for pursuing these goals. However, the sheer volume and complexity of such animal location data can overwhelm biologists charged with making resource management decisions (Huettmann, 2005 for data overview). Further, it can affect the ability to obtain accurate results and to find the best possible solutions for making sustainable decisions. These major obstacles often result in under-utilization of data. Not only is it difficult to accurately filter out erroneous animal locations, it is challenging to identify meaningful patterns from data with multi-dimensional input variables (Braumoeller, 2004). Traditional

statistical regression methods are limited by the inability to truly meet the assumptions required for analysis, such as the distribution of variables, model fit, independence of variables and linearity of the data (James & McCulloch, 1990; Nielsen, Boyce, Stenhouse, & Munro, 2002). They also are incapable of explaining the relationships between response and predictor variables (De'ath 2007). However, researchers continue to use the very time consuming, general linear models which use stepwise multiple regression methods (e.g., Manly, McDonald, Thomas, McDonald, & Erickson, 2002; Nielsen et al., 2002) as the predominant analytical approach for such analyses (see Whittingham, Stephens, Bradbury, & Freckleton, 2006 for an assessment of use of these techniques in the ecological literature).

We propose that linking technology with biological applications is not only relevant, but crucial for obtaining sustainability (Chernetsov & Huettmann, 2005; Onyeahialam, Huettmann, & Bertazzon, 2005). Much of ecological data and factors that affect species and their distributions are highly complex and non-linear in nature. Elith et al. (2006) and Olden and Jackson (2002) found that alternative analytical techniques such as classification and regression trees for modeling species distribution widely outperformed traditional modeling methodologies on non-linear data and performed equally as well on linear data (see also Huettmann & Diamond 2006; Yen, Huettmann, & Cooke 2004). While many scientists still continue to propose the use of traditional methods (Kenward, 2001; Millspaugh & Marzluff, 2001; Braun, 2005), others are seeking alternative solutions because of the non-linearity of most ecological data (De'ath 2007; Olden & Jackson, 2002; Polikar, 2006; Prasad, Iverson, & Liaw, 2006). These non-traditional methods (sometimes referred to as "blackbox algorithms") involve computer-intensive data mining and analysis techniques and have a distinct advantage over classical statistical methods because they are fast and do not limit the number of predictor variables (e.g., model selection). They also require no *a priori* assumptions about the relationship between the response and predictor variables, and are effective in uncovering the underlying structure in data with non-additive or hierarchical variables (Prasad et al., 2006). However, there are criticisms of the use of traditional classification and regression trees because of the difficulty in estimating precision (Anderson, Burnham, & Thompson, 2000). Such models don't always produce the optimal tree, but can result in "over-fitting the data" (describing only a specific dataset with no capability for generalizing for broader application). Further, "messy datasets" with inaccuracies, missing data and outliers in the training data are believed to adversely affect the results (Prasad et al., 2006; Lawrence, Powell, &. Zambon, 2004).

To address some of these issues Friedman (2001, 2002) refined the traditional classification tree analyses (Breiman, Friedman, & Olshen, 1984) further, using stochastic gradient boosting (STG). STG (marketed as TreeNet: Salford Systems, 2002), theoretically, yields robust, highly accurate models that are resistant to the influence of missing data, outliers and other irregularities (i.e., "messy data"). TreeNet produces accurate predictive models, and an index of the relative importance of variables, graphic displays of dependence plots for single variables, and two way interactions among top variables and how they relate to the response variable (Friedman 2001,2002). These outputs greatly facilitate biologically relevant interpretation of complex and "messy" ecological datasets. A common example is animal locations data obtained via satellite.

SGB is ideal for analyzing the data obtained from satellite tracking, however, for a defendable analysis of satellite datasets using traditional statistical methods (Braun, 2005; Manly et al., 2002), potentially erroneous animal locations must be eliminated before any further analysis can occur. Various filtering methods have been developed for dealing with these errors (Austin, McMillan, & Bowen, 2003; Jonsen, Flemming, & Myers, 2005; Morales, Haydon, Friar, Holsinger, & Fryxell, 2004; Vincent, McConnell, Fedak, & Ridoux, 2002; David Douglas, http://alaska.usgs.gov/science/biology/ spatial/ index.html). Once data are filtered, there are a wide range of methods developed to aid in the interpretation of the data (see Guisan & Thuiller, 2005; James & McCulloch, 1990 for overviews).

In this chapter we propose that TreeNet may be used for modeling satellite-based wildlife location data and that it and a similar algorithm known as Random Forests may also be used to determine how best to filter data before analysis. TreeNet detects patterns associated with the most accurate locations, and Random Forests identifies outliers in a dataset. We also examine the feasibility of running computations on totally unfiltered satellite-based wildlife location data to determine if this algorithm is capable of identifying patterns and producing accurate predictions in spite of "messy" data. More specifically, we present the results of models constructed from satellite locations of a subadult female golden eagle, *Aquila chrysaetos*, wintering in east-central Idaho and Montana. We compare the results of totally unfiltered satellite data with datasets that are filtered based on parameters identified by TreeNet and verified with output from Random Forests, filtered using the Douglas Argos-Filter Algorithm, or simulated, based on patterns observed in the data and in the field (expert opinion). We propose the use of these algorithms as fast and accurate methods for analyzing extensive, complex datasets.

METHODS AND MATERIALS

Animal location data and study area. Satellite data used to develop the models were from a regional migrant golden eagle, identified as 5707 in the subsequent text. Bird 5707 was outfitted with a Platform Transmitting Terminal (PTT) and monitored for portions of two winters (January 8 through March 31, 1996 and November 3 through November 26, 1996) as it ranged over native shrub-steppe habitats in portions of Idaho and Montana (Craig & Craig, 1998).

Eagle presence data (base data for models). Eagle presence locations were based on PTT transmission receptions, categorized in location classes (LC) 3-Z according to their estimated accuracy. These are based on satellite positions and a number of other variables, including number of messages used to calculate PTT position and frequency (see Argos, 2007 for description of LC's). Our base dataset consist of all data n = 187 (Argos quality classes 0,1,2, A, B and Z), except extreme and obvious outliers from the east coast (>1600 km from previous location).

Table 1. List of GIS environmental layers and point data used to develop models for subadult golden eagle, 5707, wintering in Idaho and Montana

Data Subject	Name of dataset	Data source	Data type	Units
Golden Eagles	Golden eagle winter location data determined by satellite telemetry	WesternEcological Studies; P.O. Box 81291, Fairbanks, AK 99708	Discrete	Individual locations
Pseudo-absence data points	Random data points	Generated in ArcMap 9.0 using Hawth's Tools http://www.spatialecology.com/htools/tooldesc.php	Discrete	Individual locations
Regularly Spaced Data Points Distributed over Local Scale Study Areas	Evaluation points	Generated in ArcMap 9.0 using Hawth's Tools http://www.spatialecology.com/htools/tooldesc.php	Discrete	Individual locations
Climate	Average minimum monthly temperature over an 18 year period	Daymet http://www.daymet.org/	Continuous	Degrees
	Average monthly precipitation	Daymet	Continuous	Inches
	Average hillshade on the 15th of each month during the winter	Calculated in ArcMap 9.0	Continuous	Classified
Topography	Digital elevation models for Idaho and Montana (datasets were merged)	Idaho and Montana Gap Analysis Programs http://gapanalysis.nbii.gov	Continuous	Meters
	Slope derived from DEM layer	ArcMap 9.0 or ArcView 3.3 Spatial Analyst	Discrete	Classified
	Aspect derived from DEM layer	ArcMap 9.0 or ArcView 3.3 Spatial Analyst	Discrete	Classified
Landcover	Vegetation cover for Idaho and Montana	Idaho and Montana Gap Analysis Programs	Discrete	Classified
Human population density	Census Blocks 2000 with Associated Data on Human Population in the Western United States (1900 - 2000)	http://sagemap.wr.usgs.gov/ftp/regional/usgs/us_population_1900-2000_sgca.zip	Continuous	people/ square mile

Removing these extreme points does not affect our investigations further and we use this dataset as our test case. We constructed our models from satellite location data from a single eagle in spite of pseudo-replication of the data (multiple locations from the same animal treated as multiple observations; Aebischer, Robertson, & Kenward, 1993). For the purposes of this paper, we were interested in identifying selection preferences of the individual bird based on the overall data and specific subsets. Further, we treated all presence locations as point data, regardless of their inherent bias because such analysis is reported to overcome the limitations imposed by using buffers around each location (Frair, Nielsen, Merrill, Lele, Boyce, Munro, Stenhouse, & Beyer, 2004). This dataset presents the base data from which all models were developed; specific descriptions of data for model development are described by model in the following sections.

Environmental GIS data. Models were developed using eight compiled GIS environmental layers which were reformatted and merged to suit our modeling and research goals (see Table 1 for details and sources for individual layers). Aspect and slope were derived from the original data layers in either ArcView 3.3 or ArcMap 9.0; pixel size was set at 30 m for all layers obtained from GAP project data in Idaho and Montana (www.wildlife.uidaho.edu/idgap/; www.wru.umt.edu/reports/gap/). Layers for temperature, precipitation, and human population density had a pixel size of 1km. Aspect was reclassified from a continuous variable (0-360°) to the following five categories: F=flat, N=315-44°, E=45-34°, S=135-224°, W=225-314°. Vegetation classes were reclassified from those defined in the GAP project to nine general categories: 1=urban or developed land; 2=agricultural land; 3=grasslands and shrublands; 4=forest uplands; 5=water; 6=riparian and wetland areas; 7=barren land such as exposed rock, sand dunes, shorelines, and gravel bars; 8=alpine meadow; 9=snow, ice, cloud, or cloud shadow. Such data are typically used in distribu-

tion modeling studies (Elith, Ferrier, Huettmann & Leathwick, 2005; Elith et al., 2006; Manly et al., 2002 for examples). The resolution (pixel size) of the GIS layers determines the degree to which the models can be interpreted (see Huettmann & Diamond, 2006 for scale issues). Coarse layers can result in information loss through the simplification of heterogeneous landscapes thus providing correlations rather than actual detailed, causal, relationships among parameters and the target variable (Karl, Heglund, Garton, Scott, Wright, & Hutto, 2000).

Pseudo-absence and evaluation data points. The study design is based on a commonly used presence-available model as described by Manly et al. (2002). We generated pseudo-absence random (available) points at the winter home range scale (minimum convex polygon as determined by the Animal Movements Extension in ArcView 3.3) at a ratio of approximately 2:1 for all eagle satellite locations (or presence points); this ratio varied with the datasets that were filtered and the resultant presence point sample size of each particular filtering process. Evaluation points were generated evenly across the home range area and were used for prediction purposes. Data from the environmental layers were extracted and attached to the data points for model building and evaluation.

Description of algorithms used for model development. We constructed all models for eagle 5707 using non-parametric, stochastic gradient boosting (SGB) algorithms (TreeNet software by Salford Systems, 2002). SGB is a hybrid between the boosting and bagging approaches (Friedman 2001, 2002; Kotsiantis & Pintelas, 2004; Lawrence, 2004; Llew, Bartlett, & Frean, 2000) used in "voting" or "ensemble" trees. This software is an attempt to improve the accuracy of machine learning classification and regression trees. In general, TreeNet randomly selects subsets of the sample data (without replacement) to sequentially fit a series of simple trees at each iteration (tree complexity and total tree number being defined by the user, and can vary from a few hundred to several thousand) to current "pseudo"-residuals by least-squares. "Pseudo" residuals are evaluated at each step and are defined as the gradient of the loss function that is reduced relative to the model values at each training data step (Friedman, 2002). Each successive tree is built from the prediction residuals of the preceding tree(s) and the final model is a summation of the best partitioning of the input variables, which explains the target variation (Salford Systems, 2002).

TreeNet provides various options for constructing models. We used binary logistic regression and the "balanced" option under class weights, which automatically reweighted each class to take into account unequal sample sizes between presence and absence points. This option yielded more generalizable models for eagle occurrences. All other selections in TreeNet were default settings, except for the ones outlined below. The number of trees built was held constant at 5,000 trees. Ideally, the optimal number of trees should be no more than 75 % of the total number of trees constructed. To identify simple models similar to those that might be constructed for traditional linear models and general patterns from the data, we built all models using only two node trees (known as "stumps;" Kotsiantis, Kanellopoulos, & Pintelas, 2006). A minimum number of 20 observations was set for each terminal node for achieving the same purpose. Because each simple tree contained a single variable and a single split, the resultant models did not detect interactions among variables. These settings produced simple, main-effects, additive models that can still be powerful (Salford Systems, 2002) for finding patterns in the data and for analyzing and assessing different scenarios. Models constructed with six nodes and fewer observations in the terminal node (typically 10) show interactions among variables. However, for the purpose of simplicity, in this paper we present only models with the single split trees.

Model prediction and evaluation. Models were tested in TreeNet by randomly selecting and withholding 20 % of the learning data to later be used for testing. We evaluated the resultant models based on the confusion matrices generated for each model that reported the percent of presences and absences accurately depicted (sensitivity and specificity) for both training and test data (cutoff = 0.5). The prediction accuracy is a relative index of occurrence (ROI) for golden eagle presence location points rather than a true probability (see Keating & Cherry, 2004). We also used receiver operating characteristic Curve (ROC) integral values and graphs of the ROC curve for a measure of model quality. Resource selection of wintering eagle 5707 for Model 1 was identified based on graphic displays of the relative influence of the input variables on the targeted response. The environmental factor with the most influence is listed as 100 % with all other variables listed relative to it. Graphs of the partial dependence of wintering eagle location on each single variable are given for each of the predictor variables; these graphs show only additive effects. Three-dimensional graphs of the top predictors for eagle distribution are provided by this software if multi-node trees are constructed. However, they were not relevant for this application since single split trees do not allow interpretation of the interaction effect between top predictor variables identified by the model. TreeNet's output of single factor graphic displays, coupled with descriptive statistics for used vs. unused locations, were used to interpret the data and identify factors for filtering. We evaluated the ability of the algorithm to identify meaningful ecological relationships from "messy" data by comparing all of these results between the various filtered and unfiltered data subsets. Random Forests was used to validate outliers selected by TreeNet for filtering the dataset.

Model 1. We merged the unfiltered satellite data as described above with the pseudo-absence dataset generated within the home range area to produce a single dataset of presence/pseudo-absence points for model construction.

Filtering data for Models 2, 3, 4, 5 and 6. Data were filtered for model development using several different methods. Initially, we used the data mining algorithms themselves to filter the data for most accurate results (Figures 1 and 2) by determining the parameters that had the greatest influence on predicting LC's of the highest resolution and by using summary statistics for each location class. Parameters considered for these first models were those most commonly considered in the development of other filtering algorithms.

*   **Net displacement:** Total straight line distance traveled in meters between first and last animal locations.
*   **Step length:** Distance between a satellite eagle location and the previous location in meters.
*   **Turn angle:** Absolute value of the angle calculated using 3 consecutive satellite locations and the angle between the 2 resultant legs of an animal's path.
*   **Bearing angle:** The compass bearing of an animal's movement from it's previous location.
*   **Speed:** Time taken to travel between locations.

An exploratory model with no independent testing was constructed in TreeNet to aid in determining which factors were most useful in identifying "outliers" in the dataset. From this initial investigation, we selected steplength, described as the distance an eagle moved from the previous location and turnangle as two parameters to assist in the identification of erroneous data. Before deriving comparative datasets for Models 2, 3, 4, 5 and 6 to be compared with Model 1, and with each other, we plotted the steplength against the difference of Model 1 prediction for all satellite location data (Figure 1). The y-axis shows the dif-

Figure 1. Steplength (distance between satellite eagle locations and the previous location in meters) plotted on the x- axis against the relative index of occurrence of Model 1 predictions for all satellite location data. The y-axis shows the predicted relative index of occurrence (ROI) produced by TreeNet relative to actual presence points ("truth"), reported on a scale of 0.0 to 1.0 (1.0 = 100 percent accuracy in predicting presence and 0.0 = 0 percent accuracy in predicting presence. Values on the y axis indicate the liklihood that a predicted eagle location is false.

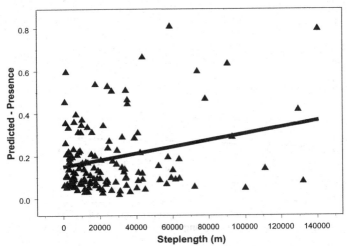

ference between the relative index of occurrence produced by TreeNet to presence points ("truth"), reported on a scale of 0.0 to 1.0, with 1.0 being 100 % accuracy in predicting presence and 0.0 being 0 % accuracy in predicting presence. This concept does not apply to pseudo-absence data because the truth is not known for these locations. Figure 2 shows the same concept but using turnangle as the x-axis to assess the ability of turnangle alone to accurately predict eagle presence locations. Figure 3 shows a frequency distribution of steplengths in our data set; such a figure is used to determine cut-offs for using a subset of the overall dataset, (e.g., what percentage should be included in the subset from the overall dataset). Based on the results of these two, we used the following thresholds to derive subsamples of the data: Model 2: 93 % of the original data (thresh-

old steplength 100,000m), Model 3: 70 % of the original data (threshold steplength 40,000m). We also used a fourth data selection criteria, the best points selected by "Expert Knowledge" to obtain "truth" (Model 4). This filtering process used a combination of visual assessment of the path of 5707 (calculated using Hawth's tools, http://www.spatialecology.com/htools/tooldesc.php, in Arc-Map 9.0, http://www.esri.com/) to identify erroneous data fixes, in addition to filtering based on steplength (greater than 40,000m and turnangles greater than an absolute value of 140°). The data for model 5 were filtered using The Douglas Argos-Filter Algorithm (http://alaska.usgs.gov/science/biology/spatial/index.html). The filtering criteria for these data might be considered "moderate," with all standard class locations (LC's 1,2, or 3) not filtered, a spatial redundancy

Figure 2. Turnangle (absolute value of the angle calculated using three consecutive satellite locations and the angle between the two resultant legs of eagle 5707's path) plotted on the x-axis plotted against the relative index of occurrence of Model 1 predictions for all satellite location data. The y-axis is the difference between the relative predicted index of occurrence (ROI) produced by TreeNet relative to actual presence points ("truth"), reported on a scale of 0.0 to 1.0 (1.0 = 100 percent accuracy in predicting presence and 0.0 = 0 percent accuracy in predicting presence. Values on the y axis indicate the likelihood that a predicted eagle location is false.

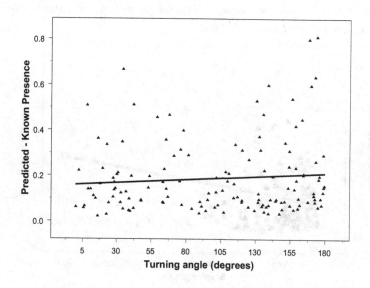

Figure 3. Frequency distribution of steplengths in our data set expressed as a percent. These data were used to determine cut-offs for filtering the overall dataset into subsets with fewer erroneous satellite locations.

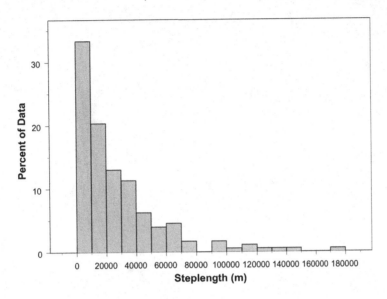

threshold equal to 5 km, and the bird was allowed to travel distances greater than 5 km at speeds up to 75 km/hr. We used the highest quality-filtered dataset in which, to reduce temporal autocorrelation (animal relocations obtained frequently over a short time period; Otis & White, 1999); one location per duty cycle that passed the filtering criteria was included in the final filtered dataset; n =39 (D. Douglas, pers. comm.). A sixth criteria was used for another comparison dataset that is based on simulation (Model 6). Here only high quality locations were used (Argos LC 2), and these were extrapolated to obtain 140 samples. In addition to these "good" presence points, 30 % of noise was added using 60 random points from within the study area. This allows for an additional assessment on how "good presence points" and a known set of noise will behave and compare to the other scenarios.

Description and construction of Models 2, 3, 4, 5 and 6. We used the filtered presence datasets described above, and merged them with pseudo-absences, as done with Model 1 to obtain binomial data (presence/pseudo-absence). We then ran TreeNet with the same settings as for Model 1, and quantitatively compared the findings based on performance metrics.

Locating outliers visually using random forests. We ran Random Forests on our "messy data" from Model 1 (the main data set for all the other scenarios). This was done to identify the outliers, and compare them to "truth" as judged by steplength alone (models 2, and 3). The Random Forests algorithm is similar to the TreeNet algorithm and is valuable for not only its predictive performance and for finding patterns and outliers in complex data (Prasad et al., 2006; see also Elith et al., 2006), but also because it records the unique ID of outlier data points in its output.

Figure 4. Functional relationships of predictor variables (using "messy" data, Model 1)

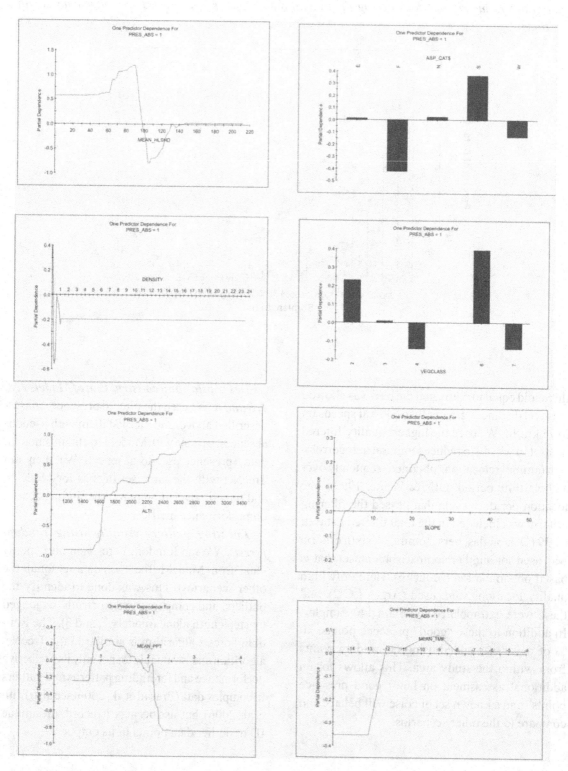

RESULTS

Effects of steplength and turnangle. Figures 1 and 2 show that there is a linear relationship between steplength and what TreeNet predicts as "truth" (presence). However, such an effect is not clear with absolute turnangle, in which the there is no slope to the regression line. Therefore, we concluded that when using a very simple filtering system and only one movement parameter for this dataset, steplength was a better measure than turnangle for determining the validity of telemetry locations. We only used that parameter to filter data for models 2 and 3. This is a parsimonious approach, and other filters often consider interaction among these variables.

Model 1. Results of this model using the entire "messy" dataset yielded an average of 80 % accuracy for test data for predicting both presence and absence eagle locations (Table 2; the optimal model was developed after the formation of approximately 1500 trees). Variable rankings by relative importance are shown in Table 3 with hillshade (positive correlation) the top predictor of eagle 5707 presence during winter, followed by altitude. The graphic displays of the functional relationships of predictor variables to presence/pseudo-absence are shown in Figure 4 with a presence location directly correlated with positive y values on the graph, relative to the correspond-

ing region of the predictor variable plotted on the x-axis. Negative values on the y axis indicate a negative relationship with eagle presence locations for the corresponding region of the predictor variable as it is plotted on the x axis (or a positive relationship with absence locations). The graphic displays indicate that this eagle tended to winter in areas of low human population density, on hillsides at higher elevations, and where hillshading ranged from 60 to 90 at temperatures of -8 to -10 degrees Fahrenheit. Animal 5707 generally selected south facing slopes in riparian areas (6) or ranch hayfields (2)

Model 2. With 3 % of the outliers removed, this model yielded approximately 79 % overall accuracy for predicting both presence and absence points (Table 2); the optimal model was developed after the formation of approximately 1500 trees. The variables were ranked in the same order as those for Model 1, with minor differences between the percent of influence by each variable on prediction outcome (Table 3). The optimal model was developed after the formation of approximately 1500 trees. Since the graphic displays of the functional relationships of presence/pseudo-absences and continuous variables are virtually identical to the ones shown in Figure 4, they are not discussed further. However, although the major categories are still the same, there are some differences for the lower ranked, categorical variables Aspect and Landcover (see Figure 5 a,b).

Table 2. Prediction accuracy of test data (rounded to the nearest percent) across models. Percent of test data points correctly identified as presences (row 1) and pseudo-absences (row 2) are listed above the average (row 3) of the two preceding values. The receiver operating characteristic curve score for the test data from each model is listed in the last row.

Category	Model 1	Mode 2	Model 3	Model 4	Model 5	Model 6
Presence	80	83	86	95	40	77
Pseudo-Absence	80	75	83	79	75	89
Average	80	79	85	87	53	84
ROC Integral	92	93	94	94	90	92

Table 3. Variable importance (rounded to the nearest percent) across models. The top predictor variable is listed as 100 percent for each model with the remaining factors ranked in order of importance below it and relative to the top predictor (ranking of each variable is listed in parentheses; variables listed within 5 percentage points of one another are given the same rank).

Name of Variable	Model 1	Model 2	Model 3	Model 4	Model 5	Model 6
Mean Hill-shade	100	100	100	100	100	100
Density	56(5.5)	55(5.5)	66(6.5)	62(6)	48(5.5)	43(4)
Altitude	58(5.5)	61(7)	65(6.5)	57(6)	46(5.5)	51(6)
Mean PPT	52(5.5)	52(5.5)	57(5)	54(6)	46(5.5)	43(4)
Aspect	35(4)	32(4)	43(4)	33(4)	20(2.5)	39(4)
Vegclass	23(2)	25(2)	29(3)	25(2.5)	0(1)	27(2)
Slope	23(2)	20(2)	20(2)	24(2.5)	41(5.5)	65(7)
Mean Temp	23(2)	16(2)	19(2)	17(1)	18(2.5)	16(1)

Model 3. Filtered data with 30 % of the outliers removed yielded an overall model accuracy of approximately 85 % (Table 2). The optimal model was developed after the formation of approximately 1500 trees. Like the two previous models, Model 3 ranked Hillshade as the top predictor variable (Table 3). Although, human population density initially was listed above elevation, a reversal of the order in the two previous models, the percent of influence by this variable on presence/absence of eagle location points differs only marginal from the previous two models. Further, graphic displays of the functional relationships of presence/pseudo-absences and continuous variables are virtually identical to the ones shown in Figure 4, and therefore are not discussed further. Although the major categories are still the same, there are only some minor differences between the lower ranked categorical variables (Aspect and Landcover); see Figure 5a,b.

Model 4. This model is based on data filtered by expert opinion. The cabability of this model remained fairly constant with that of the previous three models for predicting pseudo-absences but

increased by about 15 % in the ability to correctly predict presence locations. Overall prediction accuracy for the resultant model is approximately 87 % (Table 2). The optimal model was developed after the formation of approximately 1500 trees. The variable rankings are identical to Model 3 and similar to all the previous models (Table 3). The graphic displays of functional relationships of presence/pseudo-absences and continuous variables are virtually identical to the ones shown in Figure 4, and therefore not further discussed. A difference exists for the lower ranked categorical variables (Aspect and Landcover); see Figure 5a,b.

Model 5. This model is based on high quality filtered data using the Douglas_Argos Filter Algorithm. It has a very small sample size of presence records and yielded a model with approximately 53 % accuracy (Table 2); the optimal model was developed after the formation of approximately 1,500 trees. Similar to the previous models, hillshade is the top ranked variable; changes occur in the remaining variables, which all are lower in their ranking. Vegetation type showed no influence on the eagle winter distribution in this model, with the vegetation variable dropping out completely (Table 3). The functional relationships of presence/pseudo-absences and continuous variables are still virtually the same as the ones shown in the other models. A difference exists for the lower ranked categorical variable Aspect; see Figure 5 a,b). Overall, it has to be concluded for Model 5 that only using the "best" and highest quality presence points resulted in such a small sample size, that the accuracy assessment of the resultant model was affected.

Figure 5a. Functional relationships of categorical predictor variables (Aspect and Vegetation class) across six models (Model 1 to 3, downward)

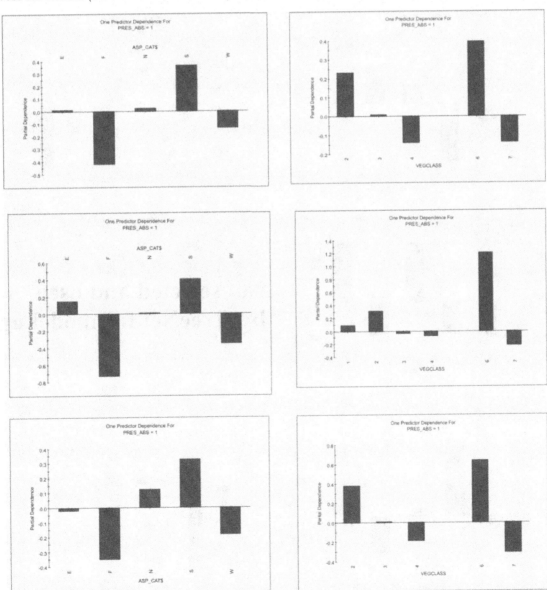

Model 6. This model is based on the simulated dataset. We obtained a model with approximately 84 % accuracy (Table 2); the optimal model was found after the formation of approximately 2,800 trees. Again, hillshade is the top ranked variable for this model (Table 3), and the functional relationships of presence/pseudo-absences and continuous variables are similar to the ones shown in the other models. A difference exists for the categorical variables (see Figure 5 a,b).

Identifying outliers according to Random Forests. We were able to identify accurately

Figure 5b. Functional relationships of categorical predictor variables (Aspect and Vegetation class) across six models (Models 4 to 6, downward)

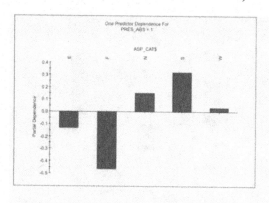
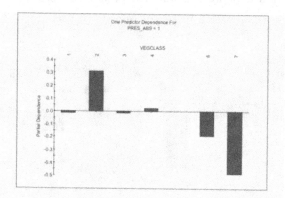

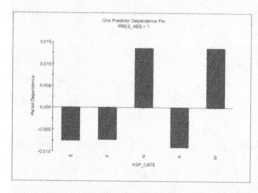

Not selected and used by TreeNet for modeling

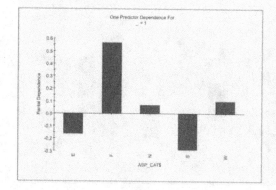
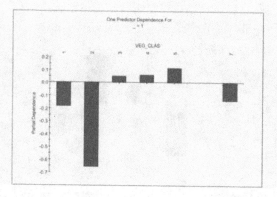

approximately 30 % of outliers using Random Forests. The outliers identified in Random Forests matched very well with the cases that had greater differences between predicted and eagle satellite locations. This analysis was done within a few seconds; a graph of the outliers (Figure 6) allowed visual highlighting of the relevant "outliers" in the data table.

DISCUSSION

We show that the overall biological findings are robust when using TreeNet and Random Forests, even when data are filtered out and subsampled. The model runs on our sample dataset were done within seconds allowing for fast results on "messy" data. In instances where it is necessary to filter data before further analysis, these algorithms proved to be effective in identifying factors to be used in filtering and/or individual outliers to be eliminated from the dataset. In our example dataset, we found that turnangle alone was not a good indicator of incorrect satellite eagle locations for this dataset; steplength was a more powerful single predictor. These two variables analyzed in relationship to one another and filtered by expert opinion (Model 4) did perform highest of the first five models. A very strict, high quality filter, the Douglas_Argos Filter Algorithm, gave different results than the other models. However, this method eliminated enough relevant presence data points that small sample size likely affected the accuracy assessment of the resultant model; final results may be different given larger initial datasets. The results of this example analysis emphasize that valid results are difficult to obtain from datasets with initial sample sizes that are relatively small. In such cases, filtering is not an option prior to developing models. That makes the results of our research all the more valuable because our simple models are effective in identifying generalized, additive patterns in continuous variable data. These results are fairly consistent among all models regardless of the filtering process used on the dataset. Excluding the top 3 % of

Figure 6. Outlier graph using Random Forests with messy data (Model 1) identifying cases (= data rows) in the data table to be used to create the model

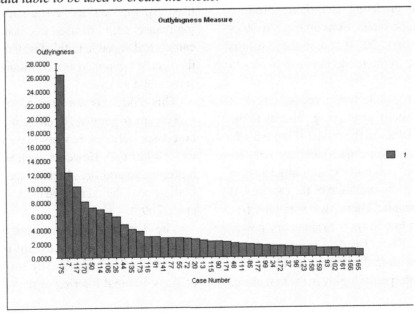

outliers had virtually no effect on the improvement of model performance. Even when using 30 % of "noisy" data, the findings remain rather robust in the TreeNet algorithm. However, when filters exclude more than 50 % of the presence points in a small dataset (as done in Model 5) effects occur that constrain reliable model interpretation. These findings manifest themselves the most in categorical variables, which rely on a sufficient point distribution by category.

It should be remembered that the models developed herein for demonstration of a process are representative for ecological studies, but are still relatively simplistic "additive-effects" models. While this purely additive approximation (2 node trees; >20 samples per terminal branch) is valuable for determining very general patterns in data, it is not capable of indicating interactive effects among the input variables and "finer scale" influences on eagle presence or absence. The results of our analysis appear to be robust at this scale. Further analysis allowing higher order complexities would be warranted in the future to determine if there is interaction among variables that could affect interpretation of the results; trees with larger nodes would have to be constructed for such analyses. However, many traditional, labor-intensive modeling techniques produce no information on interactions among variables (Keating & Cherry, 2004) and so these results are comparable to the predominant analyses in ecology.

TreeNet's two-node tree models were less effective in correctly identifying patterns in the categorical variables in the model (Figure 5 a,b; Aspect and Landcover classes) and, as such, we observed greater variability in the output among models, making interpretation of the categorical results questionable. These two variables frequently ranked low in their explanatory power (Table 3) and are not the key drivers for explaining where eagles occur in the landscape. Thus, they should not be interpreted highly in the first place.

Nevertheless, the resulting differences in these variables are likely due to variations in presence data sample sizes among the various categorical bins. This problem would have been exacerbated by the fact that the dataset is somewhat small, and minimum number of observations allowed in each terminal node was set fairly high (20). This was done in order to obtain more general models but the result was a trade-off that may have precluded identifying consistent patterns in these types of data. This is a general problem when using categorical variables, and well recognized by the modeling and statistical communities (Agresti, 2002). Valid analysis of categorical variables using this algorithm may not be possible and should potentially be avoided when using small sample sizes and "stumps." Alternatively, valid analysis might simply require consideration of terminal node size dependent upon overall sample size of presence points and/or, combining some categories with few observations in them. Another option, which we have not explored, is to define more than 30 individual categories that are ranked in the shape of a bell curve using literature or expert opinion to place the more likely categories at the center of an imagined bell-shaped histogram, grading out to the edges with categories less likely to be used. Simple descriptive statistics of the existing dataset could be used to construct the input categorical variable in this fashion. The variable then could be treated as a continuous variable in subsequent analyses.

This study has not used spatial predictions as a means to show differences in inference and outcomes between models (e.g., in a spatially explicit fashion). However, such an effort would represent an additional metric for assessing our findings and should receive more studying (Elith et al., 2005).

The TreeNet algorithm can very quickly achieve similar results to a usually labor-intensive process that has traditionally involved a series of steps: manual filtering of the telemetry data, applying software filtering, and then habitat analysis of GIS data. Once the GIS overlays are completed, these steps are achieved by TreeNet within seconds. We emphasize that despite these major achievements, alternative data are still crucial to assess the validity of these steps, but the potential for using machine learning algorithms to identify patterns in ecological data, or "modeling" data first (e.g., for data mining, locating outliers, creating predictions and for drawing inferences that are assessed by alternative data) are considerable. Because of the speed and accuracy with which machine learning algorithms for data mining allow researchers to identify patterns in data and construct models, they are an important, but not the only tool for exploring and interpretation of ecological concepts. This information can be used as a baseline for conducting additional research, or even, in some cases as an end product (see Graeber, 2006 for an application). Linking wildlife ecology and conservation management with computational tools in an interdisciplinary framework can be a very powerful tool for the wildlife biologist, in particular, and the field of conservation biology on the whole.

The ultimate and "true" model probably will be very difficult to detect in "messy" data (Chatfield, 1995). Here we find best approximations to the true biological model, which is still a trade-off between number of points and their accuracy. Based on this model, our fast and convenient approach can identify major patterns for habitat selection, and potentially find relevant outliers. Because we rarely have clean data in Ecology, we judge the application of machine learning algorithms as a relevant improvement.

The implications of our findings are potentially far-reaching. Running accurate models and results on datasets that have 30 % of faulty presence data is a major advancement in science, and ecology, for that matter. More study is needed to consolidate these findings, but if confirmed with ecological, wildlife and GIS applications elsewhere, our findings have the potential for major implications on database analysis, research design, GIS, and ecological studies for more sustainable decision-making world-wide.

ACKNOWLEDGMENT

We acknowledge T.H. Craig for sharing his data, for the publicly available environmental GIS data, H.Beyers for his freely available Hawth's tools online, D. Douglas for filtering the data using his algorithm, and M.R. Fuller of USGS, Raptor Research Center for support in earlier portions of this work. We are grateful to the EWHALE lab, UAF, Salford Systems, D. Steinberg, R. O'Connor, and A.W. Diamond, and the NCEAS working group on "Alternative Modeling" methods lead by C. Moritz and T. Peterson for support and discussions. EH acknowledges R., J. & H. Craig, for their considerable contributions in earlier phases of this research and L. Schueck for help in interpretation of the satellite data information. FH acknowledges S. & J. Linke, E. Bruenning and L. Strecker for contributions while developing some of the research leading to this publication. This is EWHALE lab publication # 36.

REFERENCES

Aebischer, N.J., Robertson, P.A., & Kenward, R.E. (1993). Compositional analysis of habitat use from animal radio-tracking data. *Ecology, 74*(3), 1313-1323.

Agresti, A. (2002). *Categorial data analysis. Wiley series in probability and statistics*. Second Edition. New Jersey: Wiley Publishers.

Anderson, D.R., Burnham, K.P., & Thompson W.L. (2000). Null hypothesis testing: Problems, prevalence, and an alternative. *Journal of Wildlife Management, 64*(4), 912-923.

Argos. (2007). *Argos user's manual online.* Retrieved March 15, 2007, from https://www.argos-system.org/manual/

Austin, D., McMillan, J.I., & Bowen, W.D. (2003). A three-stage algorithm for filtering erroneous Argos satellite locations. *Marine Mammal Science, 19*(2), 371-383.

Bittner, J.D., Oakley, J., Hannan, J., Lincer, J., Muscolino, N., & Domenech, R. (2003). *Reproduction of Golden Eagles in a Drought Period.* Paper presented at the Annual Raptor Research Foundation Meetings, September, Anchorage, Alaska.

Braun, C.E. (2005). *Techniques for wildlife investigations and management.* Bethesda, Maryland: The Wildlife Society (TWS).

Braumoeller, B.F. (2004). Hypothesis testing and multiplicative terms. *International Organization, 58*(Fall), 807-820.

Breiman, L., Friedman, J. H., Olshen, R. A., & Stone, C. J. (1984). *Classification and regression trees.* Boca Raton, Florida: CRC Press.

Chatfield, C. (1995). Model uncertainty, data mining and statistical inference. *Journal of Royal Statistical Society*, A 158, part 3, 419-466.

Chernetsov, N. & F. Huettmann. (2005). Linking global climate grid surfaces with local long-term migration monitoring data: Spatial computations for the Pied Flycatcher to assess climate-related population dynamics on a continental scale. Lecture Notes In *Computer Science (LNCS) 3482, International Conference on Computational Science and its Applications (ICCSA) Proceedings Part III,* (pp.133-142).

Craig, E.H., & Craig, T.H. (1998). *Lead and mercury levels in Golden and Bald Eagles and annual movements of Golden Eagles wintering in east central Idaho 1990 -1997.* (Technical Bulletin No. 98-12). Boise, ID: Idaho Bureau of Land Management.

De'ath, G. (2007). Boosted trees for ecological modeling and prediction. *Ecology, 88*(1), 243-251.

Elith, J., Ferrier, S., Huettmann, F., & Leathwick, J.R. (2005). The evaluation strip: A new and robust method for plotting predicted responses from species distribution models. *Ecological Modeling, 186,* 280-289.

Elith, J., & Graham, C., NCEAS working group (2006). Comparing methodologies for modeling species' distributions from presence-only data. *Ecography, 29*(2), 129-151.

Frair, J.L., Nielsen, S.E., Merrill, E.H., Lele, S.R., Boyce, M.S., Munro, R.H.M., Stenhouse, G.B., & Beyer, H.L. (2004). Removing GPS collar bias in habitat selection studies. *Journal of Applied Ecology, 41*(2), 201-212.

Friedman, J.H. (2001). Greedy function approximation: A gradient boosting machine. *Annals of Statistics, 2,* 1189-1232.

Friedman, J.H., & (2002). Stochastic Gradient Boosting: Nonlinear methods and data mining. *Computational Statistics and Data Analysis, 38,* 367-378.

Graeber, R. (2006). *Modeling the distribution and abundance of brown bears as a biodiversity component in the Northern Pacific Rim.* Unpublished M.S. Thesis, University of Hannover, Hannover, Germany.

Guisan, A., & Thuiller, W. (2005). Predicting species distribution: Offering more than simple habitat models. *Ecology Letters, 8,* 993-1009.

Huettmann, F. (2005). Databases and science-based management in the context of wildlife and habitat: Towards a certified ISO standard for objective decision-making for the global community by using the internet. *Journal of Wildlife Management, 69,* 466-472.

Huettmann, F., & Diamond, A.W. (2006). Large-scale effects on the spatial distribution of seabirds in the northwest atlantic. *Landscape Ecology, 21,* 1089-108.

James, F.C., & McCulloch, C.E. (1990). Multivariate analysis in ecology and systematics: Panacea or Pandora's box? *Annual Review of Ecology and. Systematics, 21,* 129-66.

Jonsen, I.D., Flemming, J.M., & Myers, R.A. (2005). Robust state-space modeling of animal movement data. *Ecology, 86*(11), 2874-2880.

Karl, J.W., Heglund, P.J., Garton, E.O., Scott, J.M., Wright, N.M., & Hutto, R.I. (2000). Sensitivity of species habitat-relationship model performance to factors of scale. *Ecological Applications, 10*(6), 1690-1705.

Keating, K. A., & Cherry, S. (2004). Use and interpretation of logistic regression in habitat-selection studies. *Journal of Wildlife Management, 68,* 774-789.

Kenward, R.E. (2001). *A manual for wildlife radio tagging.* San Diego: Academic Press

Knick, S.T., Dobkin, D.S., Rotenberry, J.T., Schroeder, M.A., Vander Haegen, W.M., & Van Riper III, C. (2003). Teetering on the edge or too late? Conservation and research issues for avifauna of sagebrush habitats. *The Condor, 105,* 611-634.

Kotsiantis, S., Kanellopoulos, D., & Pintelas, P. (2006). Local boosting of decision stumps for regression and classification problems. *Journal of Computers (JCP), 4*(1), 30-37.

Kotsiantis, S., & Pintelas, P. (2004). Combining bagging and boosting. *International Journal of Computational Intelligence, 1*(4), 324-333.

Lawrence, R. A., Powell, B.S., &. Zambon, M. (2004). Classification of remotely sensed imagery using stochastic gradient boosting as a refinement of classification tree analysis. *Remote Sensing of Environment, 90,* 331-336.

Llew Mason, J.B., Bartlett, P., & Frean, M. (2000). Boosting algorithms as gradient descent. In S.A. Solla, T.K. Leen, & K.-R. Muller (Ed.), *Advances in Neural Information Processing Systems 12,* pp. 512-518. MIT Press.

Manly, B.F.J., McDonald, L.L., Thomas, D.L., McDonald, T.L., & Erickson W.P. (2002). *Resource selection by animals, statistical design and analysis for field studies. 2nd Edition.* Dordrecht: Kluwer Academic Publishers.

Millenium Ecosystem Assessment. (2005). Ecosystems and Human Well-being: Biodiversity Synthesis. Retrieved August 6, 2007 from http://www.milenniumassessment.org

Millspaugh, J.J., & Marzluff, J.M. (Eds) (2001). *Radio tracking and animal populations.* Orlando, FL: Academic Press.

Morales, J.M., Haydon, D.T., Friar, J., Holsinger, K.E., & Fryxell, J.M. (2004). Extracting more out of relocation data: Building movement models as mixtures of random walks. *Ecology, 85,* 2436-2445.

Nielsen, S.E., Boyce, Stenhouse, G.B., & Munro, R.H.M. (2002). Modeling grizzly bear habitats in the Yellowhead Ecosystem of Alberta: Taking autocorrelation seriously. *Ursus, 13,* 45-56.

Olden, J.D., & Jackson, D.A. (2002). A comparison of statistical approaches for modeling fish species distributions. *Freshwater Biology, 47,* 1-20.

Onyeahialam, A., Huettmann, F., & Bertazzon, S. (2005). Modeling sage grouse: Progressive computational methods for linking a complex set of local biodiversity and habitat data towards global conservation statements and decision support systems. Lecture Notes In *Computer Science (LNCS) 3482, International Conference on Computational Science and its Applications (ICCSA) Proceedings Part III,* pp.152-161.

Polikar, R. (2006). Ensemble based systems in decision making. A tutorial article on ensemble systems including pseudocode, block diagrams and implementation issues for AdaBoost and other ensemble learning algorithms. *IEEE Circuits and Systems Magazine, 6*(3), 21-45.

Popp, J., Neubauer, D., Paciulli, L.M., & Huettmann, F. (in press). Using TreeNet for identifying management thresholds of mantled howling monkeys' habitat preferences on Ometepe Island, Nicaragua, on a tree and home range scale. *Journal Scientific International.*

Prasad, A.M., Iverson, L.R., & Liaw, A. (2006). Newer classification and regression tree techniques: Bagging and random forests for ecological prediction. *Ecosystems, 9*, 181-199.

Primack, R. B. (1998). *Essentials of conservation biology.* Second Edition. New York: Sinauer Associates Publishers

Ritter, J. (2007). *Wildlife habitat modeling in the Toklat basin study area of Denali National Park and Preserve, Alaska.* Unpublished M.Sc. Thesis. University of Alaska-Fairbanks.

Salford Systems. (2002). *TreeNet version 1.0 data mining software documentation.* Retrieved on February 25, 2007, from http://www.salford-systems.com/. San Diego, CA.

Vincent, C., McConnell, B.J., Fedak, M.A., & Ridoux, V. (2002). Assessment of Argos location accuracy from satellite tags deployed on captive grey seals. *Marine Mammal Science, 18,* 301-322.

Whittingham, M.J., Stephens, P.A., Bradbury, R.B., & Freckleton, R.P. (2006). Why do we still use stepwise modelling in ecology and behavior? *Journal of Animal Ecology, 75,* 1182-1189.

Yen, P., Huettmann, F. & Cooke, F. (2004). Modelling abundance and distribution of Marbled Murrelets (*Brachyramphus marmoratus*) using GIS, marine data and advanced multivariate statistics. *Ecological Modelling, 171,* 395-413.

Zakri, A.H. (2003). *Millennium ecosystem assessment: Integrated assessment through the millennium ecosystem assessment.* United Nations University Institute for Advanced Studies. Retrieved August 6, 2007 from http://www.milenniumassessment.org

Chapter V
A New Approach to Classification of Imbalanced Classes via Atanassov's Intuitionistic Fuzzy Sets[1]

Eulalia Szmidt
Polish Academy of Sciences, Poland

Marta Kukier
Polish Academy of Sciences, Poland

ABSTRACT

We present a new method of classification of imbalanced classes. The crucial point of the method lies in applying Atanassov's intuitionistic fuzzy sets (which are a generalization of fuzzy sets) while representing the classes during the first training phase. The Atanassov's intuitionistic fuzzy sets are generated according to an automatic and mathematically justified procedure from the relative frequency distributions representing the data. Next, we use the information about so-called hesitation margins (which besides membership and non-membership values characterize Atanassov's intuitionistic fuzzy sets) making it possible to improve the results of data classification. The results obtained in the testing phase were examined not only in the sense of general error/accuracy but also by using confusion matrices, that is, exploring a detailed behavior of the intuitionistic fuzzy classifiers. Detailed analysis of the errors for the examined examples has shown that applying Atanassov's intuitionistic fuzzy sets gives better results than the counterpart approach via fuzzy sets. Better performance of the intuitionistic fuzzy classifier concerns mainly the recognition power of a smaller class. The method was tested using a benchmark problem from UCI machine learning repository.

INTRODUCTION

Imbalanced and overlapping classes are a real challenge for the standard classifiers. The problem is not only theoretical but it concerns many different types of real tasks. Examples are given by Kubat, Holte, and Matwin (1998); Fawcett and Provost (1997); Japkowicz (2003); Lewis and Catlett (1994); and Mladenic and Grobelnik (1999). The problem of imbalanced classes occurs when the training set for a classifier contains far more examples from one class (majority *illegal* class) than the other (minority *legal* class).

To deal with the imbalance problems, up-sampling and down-sampling usually are used. Alas, both methods interfere in the structure of the data, and in a case of overlapping classes even the artificially obtained balance does not solve the problem (some data points may appear as valid examples in both classes). As the problem is still open, the new methods are investigated and trying to be improved (Chawla, Hall, & Kegelmeyer, 2002; Maloof, 2003; Visa & Ralescu, 2004; Zhang & Mani, 2003).

In this chapter we propose a new approach to the problem of classification of imbalanced and overlapping classes. The method proposed uses Atanassov's intuitionistic fuzzy sets (A-IFSs for short) (Atanassov, 1983, 1986, 1999). We consider a two-class classification problem (*legal* and *illegal* class).

Atanassov's theory of intuitionistic fuzzy sets (Atanassov, 1983, 1986, 1999) is one among many extensions of fuzzy sets (Zadeh, 1965) which has gained popularity in recent. Basically, it introduces, for each element of a universe of discourse, a degree of membership and a degree of non-membership, both from interval [0,1], but which do not sum up to 1 as in the conventional fuzzy sets. Such an extended definition can help more adequately represent situations when, for instance, decision makers abstain from expressing their testimonies, some assessments can not be classified but also can not be discarded, and so on.

Therefore, A-IFSs provide a richer apparatus to grasp the inherent imprecision of information than the conventional fuzzy sets by assigning to each element of the universe besides membership and non-membership functions also the corresponding lack of knowledge called hesitation margin, or intuitionistic fuzzy index (Atanassov, 1999).

The classification method which will be presented here (using A-IFSs) has its roots in the fuzzy set approach given in (Baldwin, Lawry, & Martin 1998). In that approach the classes are represented by fuzzy sets. The fuzzy sets are generated from the relative frequency distributions representing the data points used as examples of the classes (Baldwin et al., 1998). In the process of generating fuzzy sets a mass assignment based approach is adopted (Baldwin, Martin, & Pilsworth, 1995), (Baldwin et al., 1998). For the obtained model (fuzzy sets describing the classes), using a chosen classification rule, a testing phase is performed to assess the performance of the proposed method.

The approach proposed in this paper is similar to the above one in the sense of the same steps are performed. The main difference lies in using A-IFSs for the representation of classes, and next —in exploiting the structure of A-IFSs to obtain a classifier better recognizing the smaller classes.

The crucial point of the method is in representing the classes by A-IFSs (first, training phase). The A-IFSs are generated from the relative frequency distributions representing the data points used as examples of the classes. A-IFSs are obtained according to the automatic, and mathematically justified procedure given in (Szmidt, & Baldwin, 2005, 2006).

Having in mind recognition of the smaller class as good as possible we use the information about hesitation margins making it possible to improve the results of data classification in the (second) testing phase. The results obtained in the testing phase were examined not only in the sense of general error/accuracy but also with using confusion matrices making possible to explore a detailed behavior of the classifiers.

The material in this chapter is organized as follows: In the next section, a brief introduction to A-IFSs is given. We then present the mechanism converting relative frequency distributions into A-IFSs, and then the models of the classifier errors are described. In the following section, a simple classification problem is considered in detail using a fuzzy classifier and using an intuitionistic fuzzy classifier. We compare the performance of both classifiers analyzing the errors. Finally, the method proposed is verified while solving a benchmark classification problem from the UCI machine learning repository. We end with some conclusions.

A Brief Introduction to Atanassov's Intuitionistic Fuzzy Sets

One of the possible generalizations of a fuzzy set in X (Zadeh, 1965), given by

$$A' = \left\{ < x, \mu_{A'}(x) > \mid x \in X \right\} \qquad (1)$$

where $\mu_{A'}:X \rightarrow [0,1]$ is the membership function of the fuzzy set A', a so-called A-IFS (Atanassov, 1983, 1986, 1999) A is given by

$$A = \left\{ < x, \mu_A(x), v_A(x) > \mid x \in X \right\} \qquad (2)$$

where: $\mu_A:X \rightarrow [0,1]$ and $v_A:X \rightarrow [0,1]$ such that

$$0 \leq \mu_A(x) + v_A(x) \leq 1 \qquad (3)$$

and $\mu_A:X \rightarrow [0,1]$, $v_A:X \rightarrow [0,1]$ denote a degree of membership and a degree of non-membership of $x \in A$, respectively.

Obviously, each fuzzy set may be represented by the following A-IFS

$$A = \left\{ < x, \mu_{A'}(x), 1 - \mu_{A'}(x) > \mid x \in X \right\} \qquad (4)$$

For each A-IFS in X, we will call

$$\pi_A(x) = 1 - \mu_A(x) - v_A(x) \qquad (5)$$

an *intuitionistic fuzzy index* (or a *hesitation margin*) of $x \in A$ and, it expresses a lack of knowledge of whether x belongs to A or not (cf. Atanassov, 1999). It is obvious that $0 \leq \pi_A(x) \leq 1$ for each $x \in X$.

It turns out that the hesitation margins play an important role while considering distances (Szmidt & Kacprzyk, 2000, 2006), entropy (Szmidt & Kacprzyk, 2001, 2007), similarity (Szmidt & Kacprzyk, 2007a) for A-IFSs, and so on; that is, that play crucial role in all information processing tasks.

The application of A-IFSs instead of fuzzy sets means the introduction of another degree of freedom into a set description. Such a generalization of fuzzy sets gives us an additional possibility to represent imperfect knowledge what leads to describing many real problems in a more adequate way. We refer an interested reader to (Szmidt & Kacprzyk, 1998, 2002a, 2002b, 2004a, 2004b, 2005, 2006a, 2006b) where the applications of A-IFSs to group decision making, negotiations and other situations are presented.

Converting Relative Frequency Distributions Into A-IFSs

The mechanism of converting a relative frequency distribution into an A-IFS is mediated by the relation of an A-IFS to the mass assignment theory. Detailed description is given by Szmidt and Baldwin (2003, 2004, 2005).

A fuzzy set can be converted into a mass assignment (Baldwin, 1991; Dubois & Prade, 1982). This mass assignment represents a family of probability distributions. The theory of mass assignment has been developed by Baldwin (Baldwin, 1992; Baldwin et al., 1995, 1995a) to provide a formal framework for manipulating both probabilistic and fuzzy uncertainty.

Definition 1 (Mass Assignment)

Let A' be a fuzzy subset of a finite universe Ω, such that the range of the membership function of A', is $\{\mu_1, \mu_2, ..., \mu_n\}$ where $\mu_i > \mu_{i+1}$ Then the mass assignment of A' denoted $m_{A'}$ is a probability distribution on 2^Ω satisfying

$$m_{A'}(F_i) = \mu_i - \mu_{i+1} \qquad (6)$$

where $F_i = \{x \in \Omega \,|\, \mu(x) \geq \mu_i\}$ for $i = 1, ..., n$

The sets $F_1, ..., F_n$ are called the focal elements of $m_{A'}$.

The detailed introduction to mass assignment theory is given in (Baldwin et al., 1995).

Example 1 (Baldwin et al., 1995b)

Consider the discrete domain X={1, 2, 3, 4, 5, 6}, corresponding to the numbers of die. We may define the fuzzy set *low_numbers* as

low_numbers = 1/1 +2/1 + 3/0.5 + 4/0.2 + 5/0 + 6/0

such that 1 and 2 are definitely low numbers, 5 and 6 are definitely not low numbers and 3 and 4 have memberships of 0.5 and 0.2 to the fuzzy set respectively.

The mass assignment of the fuzzy set **low_numbers** is

$m_{low\_numbers}$ = {1, 2}:0.5, {1, 2, 3}:0.3, {1, 2, 3, 4}:0.2

Table 1. Counterparts of the parameters in Baldwin's voting model and A-IFS voting model

	Baldwin's voting model	A-IFS voting model
voting in favour	N	μ
voting against	1-p	ν
abstaining	p-n	π

In Table 1 equality of parameters from Baldwin's voting model and from A-IFS voting model is presented (Szmidt & Baldwin, 2003, 2004). The equivalence occurs under the condition that each value of membership/non-membership of A-IFS occurs with the same probability for each x_i (for a deeper discussion of the problem we refer an interested reader to (Szmidt & Baldwin, 2003, 2004). In other words both Support Pairs (mass assignment theory) and A-IFS models give the same intervals containing the probability of the fact being true, and the difference between the upper and lower values of intervals is a measure of the uncertainty associated with the fact (Szmidt & Baldwin, 2003, 2004).

The mass assignment structure is best used to represent knowledge that is statistically based such that the values can be measured, even if the measurements themselves are approximate or uncertain (Baldwin et al., 1995b).

Definition 2 (Least Prejudiced Distribution) (Baldwin et al., 1995)

For A' a fuzzy subset of a finite universe Ω such that A' is normalized, the least prejudiced distribution of A', denoted $lp_{A'}$, is a probability distribution on Ω given by

$$lp_{A'}(x) = \sum_{x \in F_i} \frac{m_{A'}(F_i)}{|F_i|} \qquad (7)$$

where $m_{A'}$ is the mass assignment of A' and $\{F_i\}$ is the corresponding set of focal elements.

Theorem 1 (Baldwin et al., 1998)

Let P be a probability distribution on a finite universe Ω taking as a range of values $\{p_1, p_2, ..., p_n\}$ where $0 \leq p_{i+1} \leq p_i \leq 1$ and $\sum_{i=1}^{n} p_i = 1$. Then P is the least prejudiced distribution of a fuzzy set A' if and only if A' has a mass assignment given by

$$\mu_{A'}(F_i) = \mu_i - \mu_{i+1} \text{ for } i = 1,\ldots,n-1 \qquad (8)$$
$$m_{A'}(F_n) = \mu_n$$

where

$$F_i = \{x \in \Omega \mid P(x) \geq p_i\}$$
$$\mu_i = |F_i|p_i + \sum_{j=i+1}^{n}\left(|F_j| - |F_{j-1}|\right)p_j$$

Proof in Baldwin et al. (1998).

It is worth mentioning that the above algorithm is identical to the bijection method proposed by Dubois and Prade (1983) although the motivation in (Baldwin et al., 1998) is quite different. Also Yager (1979) considered a similar approach to mapping between probability and possibility. A further justification for the transformation was given by Yamada (2001).

In other words, Theorem 1 gives a general procedure converting a relative frequency distribution into a fuzzy set, that is gives us means for generating fuzzy sets from data. As non-membership values for a fuzzy set are univocally assigned by membership values, Theorem 1 gives a full description of a fuzzy set.

Example 2 (Baldwin et al., 1998)

Let $\Omega = \{a, b, c, d\}$ and P be a probability distribution on Ω such that

$$P(a) = 0.15, \quad P(b) = 0.6, \quad P(c) = 0.2, \quad P(d) = 0.05$$

so that $p_1 = 0.6,\ p_2 = 0.2, p_3 = 0.15, p_4 = 0.05$.

Hence if A' is a normalized fuzzy subset of Ω such that $lp_{A'} = P$ then we can determine A' as follows:

Given the ordering constraint imposed by P we have that

$$m_{A'}(F_4) = \mu_4,\ m_{A'}(F_3) = \mu_3 - \mu_4,\ m_{A'}(F_2) = \mu_2 - \mu_3,$$
$$m_{A'}(F_1) = 1 - \mu_2$$

where

$$(F_4) = \{a, b, c, d\},\ (F_3) = \{a, b, c\},\ (F_2) = \{a, b\},$$
$$(F_1) = \{b\}$$

This implies that $A' = b/1 + c/\mu_2 + a/\mu_3 + d/\mu_4$ and using the formula from Theorem 1 we obtain

$$\mu_4 = 4p_4 = 4(0.05) = 0.2$$

$$\mu_3 = 3p_3 + p_4 = 3(0.15) + 0.05 = 0.5$$

$$\mu_2 = 2p_2 + p_3 + p_4 = 2(0.2) + 0.15$$

Therefore, $A' = b/1 + c/0.6 + a/0.5 + d/0.2$

This way it was shown that using Theorem 1 we can convert a relative frequency distribution into a fuzzy set.

But Theorem 1 gives also an idea how to convert the relative frequency distributions into A-IFSs.

When discussing A-IFSs we consider memberships and independent non-memberships so Theorem 1 gives only a part of the description we look for. To receive the full description of an A-IFS (with independently given membership and non-membership values), it is necessary to repeat the procedure as in Theorem 1 two times. In result we obtain two fuzzy sets. To interpret them properly in terms of A-IFSs we recall first a semantic for membership functions.

Dubois and Prade (1997) have explored three main semantics for membership functions—depending on the particular applications. Here we apply the interpretation proposed by Zadeh (1978) when he introduced the possibility theory that is, "membership $\mu(x)$ is there the degree of possibility that a parameter x has value μ."

In effect of repeating the procedure as in Theorem 1 two times (first: for data representing memberships, second: for data representing non-memberships), and taking into account interpretation that the obtained values are the degrees of possibility we receive the following results.

- First time we perform the steps from Theorem 1 for the relative frequencies connected to membership values. In effect we obtain (fuzzy) possibilities $Pos^+(x) = \mu(x) + \pi(x)$ that x has value Pos^+.

Pos^+ left side of the above equation) mean the values of a membership function for a fuzzy set (possibilities). In terms of A-IFSs (right side of the above equation) these possibilities are equal to possible (maximal) membership values of an A-IFS, that is $\mu(x) + \pi(x)$ where $\mu(x)$—the values of the membership function for an A-IFS, $\pi(x)$—the values of the hesitation margins.

- Second time we perform the steps from Theorem 1 for the (independently given) relative frequencies connected to non-membership values. In effect we obtain (fuzzy) possibilities $Pos^-(x) = v(x) + \pi(x)$ that x has not value Pos^-.

Pos^- (left side of the above equation) mean the values of a membership function for another (than in the previous step) fuzzy set (possibilities). In terms of A-IFSs (right side of the above equation) these possibilities are equal to possible (maximal) non-membership values, that is $v(x) + \pi(x)$, where $v(x)$—the values of the non-membership function for an A-IFS, $\pi(x)$—the values of the hesitation margins.

The Algorithm of Assigning The Parameters of A-IFSs

1. From Theorem 1 we calculate the values of the left sides of the equations:

$$Pos^+(x) = \mu(x) + \pi(x) \qquad (9)$$

$$Pos^-(x) = v(x) + \pi(x) \qquad (10)$$

2. From (9) - (10), and taking into account that $\mu(x) + v(x) + \pi(x) = 1$, we obtain the values $\pi(x)$

$$Pos^+ + Pos^- = \mu(x) + \pi(x) + v(x) + \pi(x) = 1 + \pi(x) \qquad (11)$$

$$\pi(x) = Pos^+ + Pos^- - 1 \qquad (12)$$

3. Having the values $\pi(x)$, from (9) and (10) we obtain for each x: $\mu(x)$, and $v(x)$.

This way, starting from relative frequency distributions, and using Theorem 1, we receive full description of an A-IFS. For more details we refer an interested reader to (Szmidt & Baldwin, 2005, 2006).

Example 3 (Szmidt & Baldwin, 2006)

The problem consists in classifying products (taking into account presence of 10 different levels of an element) as legal and illegal. The data describing relative frequencies for legal and illegal products are respectively

- relative frequencies $p^+(i)$ for *legal* products (for each i-th level of the presence of the considered element), $i=1, \ldots, 10$

$p^+(1)= 0$, $p^+(2)= 0$, $p^+(3)= 0.034$, $p^+(4)= 0.165$, $p^+(5)= 0.301$, $p^+(6)= 0.301$, $p^+(7)= 0.165$, $p^+(8)= 0.034$, $p^+(9)= 0$, $p^+(10)= 0$ $\qquad (13)$

- relative frequencies $p^-(i)$ for *illegal* products (for each i-th level of the presence of the considered element), $i=1, \ldots, 10$

$p^-(1)= 0.125$, $p^-(2)= 0.128$, $p^-(3)= 0.117$, $p^-(4)= 0.08$, $p^-(5)= 0.05$, $p^-(6)= 0.05$, $p^-(7)= 0.08$, $p^-(8)= 0.117$, $p^-(9)= 0.128$, $p^-(10)= 0.125$ $\qquad (14)$

From Theorem 1 and the data (13) we obtain possibilities $Pos^+(i)$ for legal products

$Pos^+(1)=0$, $Pos^+(2)=0$, $Pos^+(3)=0.205$, $Pos^+(4)=0.727$, $Pos^+(5)=1$, $Pos^+(6)=1$, $Pos^+(7)=0.727$, $Pos^+(8)=0.205$, $Pos^+(9)=0$, $Pos^+(10)=0$, (15)

From Theorem 1 and the data (14) we obtain possibilities $Pos^-(i)$ for illegal products

$Pos^-(1)=1$, $Pos^-(2)=1$, $Pos^-(3)=0.961$, $Pos^-(4)=0.737$, $Pos^-(5)=0.503$, $Pos^-(6)=0.503$, $Pos^-(7)=0.737$, $Pos^-(8)=0.961$, $Pos^-(9)=1$, $Pos^-(10)=1$,
(16)

This way, we have obtained two fuzzy sets describing legal products (15) and illegal products (16). Now we will find an intuitionistic fuzzy set representing legal and illegal products.

From (15), (16), and (12), we obtain the following values $\pi(i)$

$\pi(1)=0.$, $\pi(2)=0.$, $\pi(3)=0.166$, $\pi(4)=0.464$, $\pi(5)=0.503$, $\pi(6)=0.503$, $\pi(7)=0.464$, $\pi(8)=0.166$, $\pi(9)=0.$, $\pi(10)=0.$ (17)

Finally, from (15), (17), and (9) we obtain $\mu(i)$

$\mu(1)=0.$, $\mu(2)=0.$, $\mu(3)=0.039$, $\mu(4)=0.263$, $\mu(5)=0.497$, $\mu(6)=0.497$, $\mu(7)=0.263$, $\mu(8)=0.039$, $\mu(9)=0.$, $\mu(10)=0$ (18)

and from (16), (17), and (10) we obtain $v(1)$

$v(1)=1.$, $v(2)=1.$, $v(3)=0.795$, $v(4)=0.273$, $v(5)=0.$, $v(6)=0.$, $v(7)=0.273$, $v(8)=0.795$, $v(9)=1.$, $v(10)=1.$ (19)

This way starting from relative frequencies we have obtained the values μ (18), v (19), and π (17) characterizing the counterpart intuitionistic fuzzy set. The values of the membership function of the

legal elements are from intervals $[\mu(i), \mu(i)+\pi(i)]$, whereas the values of the membership function of the *illegal* elements are from the intervals $[v(i), v(i)+\pi(i)]$. As it will be shown later, the knowledge of the intuitionistic fuzzy indices $\pi(i)$ is rather important as it can be exploited to see better the relatively smaller classes.

The Models of a Classifier Error

Traditionally *accuracy* of a classifier is measured as the percentage of instances that are correctly classified, and *error* is measured as the percentage of incorrectly classified instances (unseen data). But when the considered classes are imbalanced or when misclassification costs are not equal both the accuracy and the error are not sufficient.

Example 4

For a data set consisting of 95 majority examples and only 5 minority examples, by assigning all the data to the majority class, 95 % accuracy is achieved. Assuming that the minority class represents a rare illness, and it is a class of interest, the classifier is rather useless although the accuracy seems not bad.

Confusion Matrix

The confusion matrix (Table 2) is often used to assess a two-class classifier.

The meaning of the symbols in Table 2 is:

a: **the number of correctly classified legal points,**

Table 2. The confusion matrix

		Tested:	
		Legal	Illegal
Actual:	Legal	a	b
	Illegal	c	d

Figure 1. Ellipse inequality in Cartesian space. Points in darker region satisfy the ellipse inequality and are classified as legal, points in light region are classified as illegal.

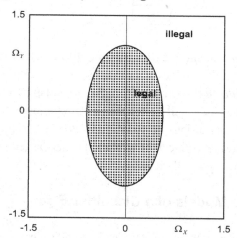

b: **the number of incorrectly classified legal points,**

c: **the number of incorrectly classified illegal points,**

d: **the number of correctly classified illegal points,**

$$TPR = \frac{legals \quad correctly \quad classified}{total \quad legals} = \frac{a}{a+b} \quad (20)$$

$$FPR = \frac{illegals \quad incorrecty \quad classified}{total \quad illegals} = \frac{c}{c+d} \quad (21)$$

A Simple Classification Problem

To illustrate the usefulness of A-IFSs in the classification problems we consider a toy prob-lem—elipse classification problem (Figure 1). The data set D consists of 288 data points from a regular grid with universes Ω_x and Ω_y being [-1.5, 1.5]. Legal points lie within the elipse $x^2 + y^2 \leq 1$, illegal points outside the elipse. We divide D into two equal parts: D_1—the training set, and D_2—the testing set. Each data sample consists of a triple <X,Y,CLASS> where class is *legal* when the point (X,Y) satisfies the elipse inequality and *illegal* otherwise.

Classification via Fuzzy Sets

In the ellipse problem we have two single attribute input features: X and Y. We formed Cartesian granule fuzzy sets corresponding to the legal and illegal classes over the Cartesian product space of the partitions P_X and P_Y. The number of fuzzy sets to form the fuzzy partition of each universe is a separate problem. We verified several pos-sibilities and decided for 10 fuzzy sets over each universe—for more fuzzy sets no significant gain in terms of model prediction was made. We divided the training database D_1 into two smaller databases according to the output classification. Then we took the points corresponding to the *legal* class and formed a Cartesian granule fuzzy set for the *legal* class. We repeated the procedure for the *illegal* class.

In order to generate the body fuzzy sets we partitioned X and Y universes with the following 10 fuzzy sets

Table 3. Model of the data—probability distributions on the fuzzy partition

	Interval									
	1	2	3	4	5	6	7	8	9	10
$P_X(p_i \mid legal)$	0	0	0.0341	0.1648	0.3011	0.3011	0.1648	0.0341	0	0
$P_X(p_i \mid illegal)$	0.1266	0.1266	0.1169	0.0796	0.0503	0.0503	0.0796	0.1169	0.1266	0.1266
$P_Y(p_i \mid legal)$	0	0.0227	0.1080	0.1477	0.2216	0.2216	0.1477	0.1080	0.0227	0
$P_Y(p_i \mid illegal)$	0.1266	0.1201	0.0958	0.0844	0.0731	0.0731	0.0844	0.0958	0.1201	0.1266

$$p_{X_1} = p_{Y_1} = [-1.5\!:\!1, -1.167\!:\!0\,]$$

$$p_{X_2} = p_{Y_2} = [-1.5\!:\!0, -1.167\!:\!1, -0.833\!:\!0\,]$$

$$p_{X_3} = p_{Y_3} = [-1.167\!:\!0, -0.833\!:\!1, -0.5\!:\!0\,]$$

$$p_{X_4} = p_{Y_4} = [-0.833\!:\!0, -0.5\!:\!1, -0.167\!:\!0\,]$$

$$p_{X_5} = p_{Y_5} = [-0.5\!:\!0, -0.167\!:\!1, 0.167\!:\!0]$$

$$p_{X_6} = p_{Y_6} = [-0.167\!:\!0, 0.167\!:\!1, 0.5\!:\!0\,]$$

$$p_{X_7} = p_{Y_7} = [0.167\!:\!0, 0.5\!:\!1, 0.833\!:\!0]$$

$$p_{X_8} = p_{Y_8} = [0.5\!:\!0, 0.833\!:\!1, 1.167\!:\!0]$$

$$p_{X_9} = p_{Y_9} = [0.833\!:\!0, 1.167\!:\!1, 1.5\!:\!0]$$

$$p_{X_{10}} = p_{Y_{10}} = [1.167\!:\!0, 1.5\!:\!1]$$

$$P_X\!\left(p_i \mid illegal\right) = \frac{\displaystyle\sum_{x \in D_1 : CLASS = illegal} \mu_{p_i}(X)}{\left|\{x \in D_1 \big| CLASS = illegal\}\right|} \tag{23}$$

$$P_Y\!\left(p_i \mid legal\right) = \frac{\displaystyle\sum_{y \in D_1 : CLASS = legal} \mu_{p_i}(Y)}{\left|\{y \in D_1 \big| CLASS = legal\}\right|} \tag{24}$$

$$P_Y\!\left(p_i \mid illegal\right) = \frac{\displaystyle\sum_{y \in D_1 : CLASS = illegal} \mu_{p_i}(Y)}{\left|\{y \in D_1 \big| CLASS = illegal\}\right|} \tag{25}$$

Next, from the training data set D_1 (144 triples) we evaluated the probability distributions on the above fuzzy partition, taking

$$P_X\!\left(p_i \mid legal\right) = \frac{\displaystyle\sum_{x \in D_1 : CLASS = legal} \mu_{p_i}(X)}{\left|\{x \in D_1 \big| CLASS = legal\}\right|} \tag{22}$$

The obtained results (the probability distributions on Ω_X and Ω_Y) are given in Table 3.

Then Theorem 1 was used to find the following approximation of the fuzzy sets (for data $D1$): (see Box 1).

As approximations (26) – (29) are discrete, they were extended to a continuous version by

Box 1.

---

legal data Ω_X

$CLASS(legal_X)$: $F_{X_1}/0 + F_{X_2}/0 + F_{X_3}/0.204545 + F_{X4}/0.72727 + F_{X_5}/1 + F_{X_6}/1 +$
$+ F_{X_7}/0.72727 + F_{X_8}/0.204545 + F_{X_9}/0 + F_{X_{10}}/0$ $\tag{26}$

illegal data Ω_X

$CLASS(illegal_X)$: $F_{X_1}/1 + F_{X_2}/1 + F_{X_3}/0.96104 + F_{X4}/0.73701 + F_{X_5}/0.503247 + F_{X_6}/503247 +$
$+ F_{X_7}/0.737013 + F_{X_8}/0.96104 + F_{X_9}/1 + F_{X_{10}}/1$ $\tag{27}$

legal data Ω_Y

$CLASS(legal_Y)$: $F_{Y_1}/0 + F_{Y_2}/0.181818 + F_{Y_3}/0.693182 + F_{Y4}/0.852273 + F_{Y_5}/1 + F_{Y_6}/1 +$
$+ F_{Y_7}/0.852273 + F_{Y_8}/0.693182 + F_{Y_9}/0.181818 + F_{Y_{10}}/0$ $\tag{28}$

illegal data Ω_Y

$CLASS(illegal_Y)$: $F_{Y_1}/1 + F_{Y_2}/0.98701 + F_{Y_3}/0.88961 + F_{Y4}/0.82143 + F_{Y_5}/0.73052 + F_{Y_6}/0.73052 +$
$+ F_{Y_7}/0.82143 + F_{Y_8}/0.88961 + F_{Y_9}/0.98701 + F_{Y_{10}}/1$ $\tag{29}$

Box 2.

$$Ag_{\max} : (X, Y) \in legal \Leftrightarrow legal = \arg\max[\mu_{CLASS_X}(X, Y); CLASS_X \in \{legal, illegal\}] \text{ and }$$
$$legal = \arg\max[\mu_{CLASS_Y}(X, Y); CLASS_Y \in \{legal, illegal\}] \tag{30}$$

Table 4. The confusion matrix for fuzzy classifier

		Tested:	
		Legal	Illegal
Actual:	Legal	16	16
	Illegal	0	112

the standard approach, that is, piecewise linear approximation. Having the fuzzy sets describing legal and illegal data in X and in Y we tested the model (on the test data D_2—another 144 triplets). We used a very simple classification rule—assigning a data point (X,Y) to the class to which it belongs most (highest membership values for both universes)

The accuracy on the test data D_2 using (30) (see Box 2.) was 88,9 %. We also assessed the results using the confusion matrix—Table 4.

It turned out that the classifier had difficulties with recognition of the *legal* (smaller) class. Only 16, that is the half of the tested points belonging to the *legal* class were correctly classified ($TPR=0.5$). On the other hand, all 112 points belonging to

the bigger *illegal* class were correctly classified ($FPR = 0$).

The results show that the fuzzy classifier should not be used for "seeing" the small classes although the accuracy seems to be acceptable.

Classification via Intuitionistic Fuzzy Sets

We solved the same problem but with additional possibilities giving by A-IFSs. In Section 3 it was shown how to convert relative frequencies to A-IFSs (and the meaning of all the parameters was discussed). So first we converted our training data set D_1 obtaining A-IFSs describing *legal* and *illegal* classes in X and in Y - Table 4. We exploited the information about hesitation margins (making use of the fact that *legal* and *illegal* classes overlap). Taking into account that hesitation margins assign (the width of the) intervals where the unknown values of memberships lies, we applied in the model the following values:

- Maximal possible values of the memberhips describing the *legal* class (see Table 5 - the

Table 5. Model of the data – A-IFS description in each of 10 intervals

	Interval									
	1	2	3	4	5	6	7	8	9	10
X=legal: Possibility	0	0	0.2045	0.7273	1	1	0.7273	0.2045	0	0
X=legal: hesitation margin	0	0	0.1656	0.4643	0.5033	0.5033	0.4643	0.1656	0	0
X=legal membership	0	0	0.2045	0.7273	1	1	0.7273	0.2045	0	0
X=illegal: Possibility	1	1	0.9610	0.7370	0.5033	0.5033	0.7370	0.9610	1	1
X=illegal: hesitation margin	0	0	0.1656	0.4643	0.5033	0.5033	0.4643	0.1656	0	0
X=illegal: membership ↓	1	1	0.7955	0.2727	2.2E-16	2.2E-16	0.2727	0.7955	1	1
Y=legal: Possibility	0	0.1818	0.6932	0.8523	1	1	0.8523	0.6932	0.1818	0
Y=legal: hesitation margin	0	0.1688	0.5828	0.6737	0.7305	0.7305	0.6737	0.5828	0.1688	0
Y=legal membership	0	0.1818	0.6932	0.8523	1	1	0.8523	0.6932	0.1818	0
Y=illegal: Possibility	1	0.9870	0.8896	0.8214	0.7305	0.7305	0.8214	0.8896	0.9870	1
Y=illegal: hesitation margin	0	0.1688	0.5828	0.6737	0.7305	0.7305	0.6737	0.5828	0.1688	0
Y=illegal: membership ↓	1	0.8182	0.3068	0.1477	1.1E-16	1.1E-16	0.1477	0.3068	0.8182	1

Table 6. The confusion matrix for intuitionistic fuzzy classifier

		Tested:	
		Legal	Illegal
Actual:	Legal	28	4
	Illegal	4	108

values of memberhips for the legal class both in Ω_X and Ω_Y are given in bolds).

- Minimal possible values of the memberhips describing the illegal class (see Table 5 - the minimal possible values of the memberships for illegal class were obtained, both in Ω_X and Ω_Y, by subtracting the hesitation margins from the maximal possible values of the memberships for the illegal class - this operation is signed by: $\downarrow$ - Table 4.

This way in the training phase we formed Cartesian granule A-IFSs corresponding to the *legal* and *illegal* classes in such a way that the *legal* class should be seen as good as possible.

The results for tested data D_2 (the same rule (23) was used) are the following: the accuracy is equal to 94, 4 % better result than 88.9 % obtained when applying fuzzy classifier (Table 4). But the most interesting is the difference in separate classification of *legal* and *illegal* classes by both classifiers. Detailed results are in Tables 4 and 6. The smaller *legal* class is better classified by intuitionistic fuzzy classifier—28 legal ele-

ments were correctly classified instead of 16 for fuzzy classifier (Tables 4). In effect *TPR* is bigger (0.875 instead of 0.5). Of course, in effect *FPR* is a little bigger (0.036 instead of 0) as the result of decreasing membership values for *illegal* class (four incorrectly classified elements instead of zero for fuzzy classifier). But intuitionistic fuzzy classifier better classifies the smaller *legal* class, and the general *accuracy* is also better.

It is also interesting to compare the results obtained by both classifiers while increasing the number of training and testing data. In Table 7 there are results obtained for equal numbers of points in D_1 and D_2, that is, 144, 255, 400, and 655. The *accuracy* of intuitionistic fuzzy classifier is generally better (from 6 % better for 144 points, to 4 % better for 655 points) than for fuzzy classifier. More, the highest *TPR* of fuzzy classifier is equal to 0.58 (for 655 points) whereas for intuitionistic fuzzy classifier the worst *TPR* is equal to 0.81 (for 144 points) and increases up to 0.99 (for 655 points). It is a big difference in favor of intuitionistic fuzzy classifier. Certainly, better *accuracy* and *TPR* are obtained at the expense of *FPR* but the cost is not big—only 1.7 % of *illegal* points are incorrectly classified (for 144 points) and 5.6 % (for 655 points).

So to sum up, we pay for the improved classification of the smaller *legal* class in the sense of increasing the values of *FPR*. But the changes of *FPR* are small and they do not decrease the *accuracy* of the classifier. Opposite—the general

Table 7. Classification results for different number of elements in data sets D_1 and D_2

a) fuzzy classifier

Number of training and testing data	A_{max}		
	Accuracy	TPR	FPR
144	0.88	0.5	0
255	0.89	0.51	0
400	0.90	0.56	0
655	0.91	0.58	0

b) intuitionistic fuzzy classifier

Number of training and testing data	A_{max}		
	accuracy	TPR	FPR
144	0.94	0.81	0.017
255	0.95	0.94	0.045
400	0.96	0.98	0.038
655	0.95	0.99	0.056

Table 8. Statistics of the glass data set. The fourth column shows the natural distribution of each class (treated as the minority class) percentage of the whole data set.

Glass	Name	Size	Minority class %
1	building window - float processed	70	33.7.
2	building window - nonfloat processed	76	36.5
3	vehicle windows - float processed	17	8.2
4	vehicle windows - nonfloat processed	0	0.0
5	Containers	13	6.3
6	Tableware	9	4.3
7	Headlamps	23	11.0

accuracy of the intuitionistic fuzzy classifier is bigger than the fuzzy classifier for the example considered.

Now we will verify if the above conclusions are true as well for a more complicated, benchmark problem.

Results Obtained for a Benchmark Classification Problem

We considered a benchmark problem from the web site (UCI Machine Learning Repository) regarding the classification of glass fragments divided into seven possible classes, although the database only contains examples of six (without examples of class 4). The classification was made on the basis of nine attributes relating to certain chemical properties of the glass.

To illustrate the performance of the considered classifiers designed for imbalance classes, we solved a two-class classification problem—class by class was treated as *legal* class (minority class) and the rest of the six classes as one (majority) *illegal* class. In Table 8 are listed the natural class distributions of the data sets expressed as the minority class percentage of the whole data set. For example, if *glass 1* (70 instances) is the

minority class, all other classes (138 instances) are treated as one majority class.

Six separate experiments were performed—each one for classifying one type of glass. In each experiment (for a chosen class to be classified as *legal*) the database consisting of 208 instances was split into a training set D_1 and test set D_2 in such a way that the instances of a *legal* (minor) class, and *illegal* (major class consisting of the sum of the rest classes) were divided equally between D_1 and D_2. Asymmetric triangular fuzzy partitioning was then defined for each attribute (Baldwin & Karale, 2003), that is, the training data set was divided so that each fuzzy partition had almost the same number of data points associated with it. Next, for each case, the fuzzy models of data

Table 9. Classification results obtained by a fuzzy classifier and intuitionistic fuzzy classifier (for Ag_2, and $\alpha = 0.9$).

		Fuzzy classifier		Intuitionistic fuzzy classifier	
		Training	Testing	Training	Testing
Glass 1 $\alpha = 0.9$	Accuracy	**90.385**	**84.615**	70.192	61.538
	TPR	0.829	0.686	**1.000**	**1.000**
	FPR	0.058	0.072	0.449	0.580
Glass 2 $\alpha = 0.9$	Accuracy	**83.654**	**76.923**	38.462	38.462
	TPR	0.684	0.579	**1.000**	1,000
	FPR	0.076	0.121	0.970	0.970
Glass 3 $\alpha = 0.9$	Accuracy	**91.346**	**92.308**	81.731	68.269
	TPR	0.00	0.00	**1.0**	**0.38**
	FPR	0.00	0.00	0.20	0.29
Glass 4	-	-	-	-	-
Glass 5 $\alpha = 0.9$	Accuracy	96.20	93.30	**98.1**	**96.2**
	TPR	0.33	0.14	**1.0**	**0.57**
	FPR	0.00	0.01	0.02	0.01
Glass 6 $\alpha = 0.9$	Accuracy	98.1	98.1	**100**	**100**
	TPR	0.6	0.5	**1**	**1**
	FPR	0	0	0	0
Glass 7 $\alpha = 0.9$	Accuracy	96.154	90.385	**99.038**	**94.231**
	TPR	0.636	0.167	**1.000**	0.583
	FPR	0.000	0.000	0.011	0,011

(for *legal* and *illegal* classes) were constructed (as described previously—separately for each attribute). In effect, for each experiment (each type of glass) nine classifiers (for each of nine attributes) were derived, and next aggregated. The following aggregation was used

$$Ag_1: \quad Ag_1^{CLASS}(e) = \sum_{k=1}^{n} w_k \mu_{CLASS}^k(e) \qquad (31)$$

where: e – an examined instance from a database;

$w_k = \dfrac{n_k}{\sum_{k=1}^{n} n_k}$ for $k=1,\ldots,n$ is a weight for each attribute: n_k is the number of correctly classified training data by k-th attribute;

Having the aggregation Ag_1, the classification of an examined instance was done by evaluating

$$D_1(e) = \arg\max[Ag_1^{CLASS}(e); CLASS \in \{legal, illegal\}] \qquad (32)$$

The described above procedure concerns a fuzzy classifier (*legal* and *illegal* data were given as fuzzy sets). The same procedure was repeated to construct an intuitionistic fuzzy classifier. The difference was that the data (given originally in the form of the frequency distributions) were converted (cf. Section 3) into A-IFSs. In effect each examined instance e was described (due to the definition of A-IFSs) by a triplet: membership value to a *legal* (smaller) class, non-membership value to a *legal* class (equal to membership value to *illegal* – bigger class) and hesitation margin, that is e: (μ_e, ν_e, π_e).

To enhance the possibility of a proper classification of the instances belonging to a smaller (*legal*) class, while training the intuitionistic fuzzy classifier, the values of the hesitation margins were divided so to "see" better the smaller class. e: $(\mu_e + \alpha\pi_e, \nu_e + (1-\alpha)\pi_e)$ where $\alpha \in (0.5, 1)$.

In Table 9, there are results given by a fuzzy and intuitionistic fuzzy classifiers for $\alpha = 0.9$.

Table 10. Classification results

		Fuzzy classifier		Intuitionistic fuzzy classifier	
		Training	Testing	Training	Testing
Glass 2 $\alpha = 0.6$	*Accuracy*	**83.654**	**76.923**	76,923	75,000
	TPR	0.684	0.579	**0,895**	**0,868**
	FPR	0.076	0.121	0,303	0,318

The results obtained by intuitionistic fuzzy classifier are better for glass 6, 5, 7 (better results are given in bolds in Table 9) as far as both *accuracy* and *TPR* are concerned. For glass 3, *accuracy* is lower but what is worth noticing—fuzzy classifier incorrectly classified all(!) *legal* instances (*TPR* = 0) whereas while training intuitionistic fuzzy classifier *TPR* = 1 (all *legal* instances were correctly classified). Unfortunately, while testing intuitionistic fuzzy classifier, *TPR* = 0.38 only. It seems to be the result of the fact that the structure of the learning sample (glass 3) is different than the testing sample (we took just first 8 of 17 instances). *Accuracy* for glass 1 and glass 2 (big classes – 70 and 76 instances, giving 33.7 % and 36.5 % of all data, respectively) are worse for intuitionistic fuzzy classifier but again - all *legal* instances were correctly classified (in comparison to 68 % and 58 % for fuzzy classifier for glass 1 and glass 2, respectively). Certainly, we might increase the *accuracy* but at the expense of *TPR*. It could be done by decreasing α - from value 0.9 for glass 2 until $\alpha = 0.5$; for $\alpha = 0.6$ the results are given in Table 10 – *accuracy* (test data) of intuitionistic fuzzy classifier is now (only) 1.9 % worse (75 % instead of 76.9 %) than of fuzzy classifier but *TPR* is still far better, that is, 0.868 instead of 0.579 for fuzzy classifier.

The obtained results compare favorably with other methods. For instance, mass assignment ID3 (Rodriguez, Lawry, & Baldwin, 2002) gave an *accuracy* of 68 % on the test set and a neural network with topology 9-6-6 gave 72 % on a smaller test set where the network was trained on 50 % of the data validated on 25 % and tested on 25 %. The accuracy obtained, using the prototypes for classifications (Baldwin, Lawry, & Martin, 1999) was 85 % on the training set and 71 % on the test set. In this context, the examined fuzzy classifier may be seen as a very good one in the sense of the accuracy, so the detailed analysis of how the fuzzy classifier sees the minor classes in comparison to the intuitionistic fuzzy classifier makes it possible to conclude about the abilities of the intuitionistic fuzzy classifier to recognize minor classes.

To sum up, the results of our experiment have shown that the intuitionistic fuzzy classifier may be successfully applied for seeing minor *legal* classes.

CONCLUSION

We proposed a new approach to classification of imbalanced and overlapping classes (for a two-class classification problem that is, with *legal* and *illegal* class). The idea lies in applying Atanassov's intuitionistic fuzzy sets with their additional possibilities (in comparison to fuzzy sets) to represent data in such a way so to see better the smaller *legal* class. Intuitionistic fuzzy index is the parameter making it possible to control the power of seeing *legal* and *illegal* classes.

Detailed analysis of the errors for the examined examples has shown that applying Atanassov's intuitionistic fuzzy sets gives better results than the counterpart approach via fuzzy sets. Better performance of the intuitionistic fuzzy classifier concerns mainly the recognition power of a smaller class (*TPR*). But for substantially imbalanced classes, the advantage of intuitionistic fuzzy classifier may be seen as well for *accuracy*. The approach proposed is being verified on other benchmark data.

REFERENCES

Atanassov, K. (1983). Intuitionistic Fuzzy Sets. *VII ITKR Session*. Sofia (Deposed in Central Scientific-Technical Library of Bulgarian Academy of Sciences, 1697/84) (in Bulgarian).

Atanassov, K. (1986). Intuitionistic fuzzy sets. *Fuzzy Sets and Systems, 20*, 87-96.

Atanassov, K. (1999). *Intuitionistic fuzzy sets: Theory and applications*. Heidelberg: Physica-Verlag.

Atanassov, K. (2005). Answer to D. Dubois, S. Gottwald, P. Hajek, J. Kacprzyk and H. Prade's paper, "Terminological difficulties in fuzzy set theory - The case of 'Intuitionistic Fuzzy Sets.'" *Fuzzy Sets and Systems, 156*, 496-499.

Baldwin, J.F. (1991). Combining evidences for evidential reasoning. *International Journal of Intelligent Systems, 6*, 569-616.

Baldwin, J.F. (1992). The management of fuzzy and probabilistic uncertainties for knowledge based systems. In S.A. Shapiro (Ed.), *Encyclopaedia of AI*, (2nd ed.), 528-537. John Wiley.

Baldwin, J.F. (1994). Mass assignments and fuzzy sets for fuzzy databases. In R. Yager et al. (Ed.) *Advances in the Dempster-Shafer theory of evidence*, pp.577-594. John Wiley.

Baldwin, J.F., Coyne, M.R., & Martin, T.P. (1995b). Intelligent reasoning using general knowledge to update specific information: A database approach. *Journal of Intelligent Information Systems, 4*, 281-304.

Baldwin, J.F., Lawry, J., & Martin, T.P. (1995a). A mass assignment theory of the probability of fuzzy events. *ITRC Report 229*. UK: University of Bristol.

Baldwin, J.F., Martin, T.P., & Pilsworth, B.W. (1995). *FRIL - Fuzzy and evidential reasoning in artificial intelligence*. John Wiley & Sons Inc.

Baldwin, J.F., Lawry, J., & Martin, T.P. (1998). The application of generalized fuzzy rules to machine learning and automated knowledge discovery. *International Journal of Uncertainty, Fuzziness and Knowledge-Based Systems, 6*(5), 459-487.

Baldwin, J.F., Lawry, J., & Martin, T.P. (1999). A mass assignment method for prototype induction. *International Journal of Intelligent Systems, 14,* 1041-1070.

Baldwin, J.F., & Karale, S.B. (2003). Asymmetric triangular fuzzy sets for classification models. In V. Palade, R.J. Howlett, & L.C. Jain (Eds.), *Lecture notes in artificial intelligence,* 2773, 364-370. Berlin, Heidelberg: Springer-Verlag.

Chawla, N., Bowyer, K., Hall, L., & Kegelmeyer, W. (2002). Smote: Synthetic minority over-sampling technique. *Artificial Intelligence Research, 16,* 321-357.

Dubois, D., Gottwald S., Hajek, P., Kacprzyk, J., & Prade, H. (2005). Terminological difficulties in fuzzy set theory: The case of "intuitionistic fuzzy sets." *Fuzzy Sets and Systems, 156*(3), 485-491.

Dubois, D., & Prade, H. (1982). On several representations of an uncertain body of evidence. In M.M. Gupta & E. Sanchez (Eds.), *Fuzzy information and decision processes*, pp. 167-181. North-Holland.

Dubois, D., & Prade, H. (1983). Unfair coins and necessity measures: towards a possibilistic interpretation of histograms. *Fuzzy Sets and Systems, 10,* 15-20.

Dubois, D., & Prade, H. (1997). The three semantics of fuzzy sets. *Fuzzy Sets and Systems, 90,* 141-150.

Fawcett, T., & Provost, F. (1997). Adaptive fraud detection. *Data Mining and Knowledge Discovery, 3*(1), 291-316.

Japkowicz, N. (2003). Class imbalances: Are we focusing on the right issue? *Workshop on Learning from Imbalanced Data II*, ICML, Washington 2003.

Kubat, M., Holte, R., & Matwin S. (1998). Machine learning for the detection of oil spills in satellite radar images. *Machine Learning, 30,* 195-215.

Lewis, D., & Catlett, J. (1994). Heterogeneous uncertainty sampling for supervised learning. Proceedings of 11th Conference on Machine Learning, 148-156.

Mladenic, D., & Grobelnik, M. (1999). Feature selection for unbalanced class distribution and naive Bayes. 16th International Conference on Machine Learning, 258-267.

Rodriguez, I., Lawry, J., & Baldwin, J. (2002). A hierarchical linguistic clustering algorithm for prototype induction. *Ninth International Conference Information Processing and Management of Uncertainty in Knowledge-based Systems IPMU 2002*, Annecy, 195-202.

Szmidt, E., & Baldwin, J. (2003). New similarity measure for intuitionistic fuzzy set theory and mass assignment theory. *Notes on Intuitionistic Fuzzy Sets, 9*(3), 60-76.

Szmidt, E., & Baldwin, J. (2004). Entropy for intuitionistic fuzzy set theory and mass assignment theory. *Notes on Intuitionistic Fuzzy Sets, 10*(3), 15-28.

Szmidt, E., & Baldwin, J. (2005). Assigning the parameters for intuitionistic fuzzy sets. *Notes on Intuitionistic Fuzzy Sets, 11*(6), 1-12.

Szmidt, E., & Baldwin, J. (2006). Intuitionistic fuzzy set functions, mass assignment theory, possibility theory and histograms. *Proceedings of 2006 IEEE World Congress on Computational Intelligence*, Vancouver, Canada, 234-243, Omnipress (IEEE Catalog Number: 06CH37726D; ISBN: 0-7803-9489-5).

Szmidt, E., & Kacprzyk, J. (1998). Group decision making under intuitionistic fuzzy preference relations. *Seventh International Conference Information Processing and Management of Uncertainty in Knowledge-based Systems,* 172-178. Paris, La Sorbonne.

Szmidt, E., & Kacprzyk, J. (2000). Distances between intuitionistic fuzzy sets. *Fuzzy Sets and Systems, 114*(3), 505-518.

Szmidt, E., & Kacprzyk, J. (2001). Entropy for intuitionistic fuzzy sets. *Fuzzy Sets and Systems, 118*(3), 467-477.

Szmidt, E., & Kacprzyk, J. (2002a). Analysis of agreement in a group of experts via distances between intuitionistic fuzzy preferences. *Ninth International Conference Information Processing and Management of Uncertainty in Knowledge-based Systems IPMU 2002,* Annecy, 1859-1865. ESIA: Universite de Savoie, France.

Szmidt, E., & Kacprzyk, J. (2002b). An intuitionistic fuzzy set based approach to intelligent data analysis (an application to medical diagnosis). In A. Abraham, L. Jain, & J. Kacprzyk (Eds.), *Recent advances in intelligent paradigms and applications,* pp. 57-70. Springer-Verlag.

Szmidt, E., & Kacprzyk, J. (2004a). A similarity measure for intuitionistic fuzzy sets and its application in supporting medical diagnostic reasoning. *Lecture Notes on Artificial Intelligence, 3070,* 388-393.

Szmidt, E., & Kacprzyk, J. (2004b). A concept of similarity for intuitionistic fuzzy sets and its use in group decision making. *Proceedings 2004 IEEE International Conference on Fuzzy Systems,* Budapest, 1129-1134. FUZZY IEEE 2004 CD-ROM Conference Proceedings. IEEE Catalog Number: 04CH37542C, ISBN: 0-7803-8354-0.

Szmidt, E., & Kacprzyk, J. (2005). A new concept of a similarity measure for intuitionistic fuzzy sets and its use in group decision making. In V. Torra, Y. Narukawa, & S. Miyamoto (Eds.), *Modelling decisions for artificial intelligence.*

Lecture notes on artificial intelligence, 3558, 272-282. Springer-Verlag.

Szmidt, E., & Kacprzyk, J. (2006). Distances between intuitionistic fuzzy sets: Straightforward approaches may not work. *3rd International IEEE Conference Intelligent Systems IS'06,* London, 716-721.

Szmidt, E., & Kacprzyk, J. (2006a). A model of case based reasoning using intuitionistic fuzzy sets. *2006 IEEE World Congress on Computational Intelligence,* 8428-8453.

Szmidt, E., & Kacprzyk, J. (2006b). An application of intuitionistic fuzzy set similarity measures to a multi-criteria decision making problem. *Lecture Notes on Artificial Intelligence, 4029,* 314-323. Springer-Verlag.

Szmidt, E., & Kacprzyk, J. (2007). Some problems with entropy measures for the Atamnassov intuitionistic fuzzy sets. *Applications of Fuzzy Sets Theory. Lecture Notes on Artificial Intelligence,* 4578, 291-297. Springer-Verlag.

Szmidt, E., & Kacprzyk, J. (2007a). A new similarity measure for intuitionistic fuzzy sets: Straightforward approaches may not work. *2007 IEEE Conference on Fuzzy Sytems,* 481-486. IEEE Catalog Number: 07CH37904C, ISBN: 1-4244-1210-2.

Szmidt, E., & Kukier, M. (2006). Classification of imbalanced and overlapping classes using intuitionistic fuzzy sets. Third International IEEE Conference "Intelligent Systems", 722-727, University of Westminster. IEEE Catalog Number: 06EX1304C, ISBN: 1-4244-0196-8.

UCI Machine Learning Repository, http://www. ics.uci.edu/~mlearn/MLRepository.html

Visa S., & Ralescu A. (2004). Experiments in guided class rebalance based on class structure. *Proceedings of the 15th Midwest Artificial Intelligence and Cognitive Science Conference.* Dayton, USA, 8-14.

Yager, R.R. (1979). Level sets for membership evaluation of fuzzy subsets. Technical Report RRY-79-14, Iona Colledge, New York. Also in: R.Yager (Ed.), *Fuzzy set and possibility theory - Recent developments,* 1982, 90-97. Oxford: Pergamon Press.

Yamada, K. (2001). Probability-possibility transformation based on evidence theory. Proceedings. IFSA-NAFIPS'2001, 70-75.

Zadeh, L.A. (1965). Fuzzy sets. *Information and Control, 8,* 338 - 353.

Zadeh, L.A. (1978). Fuzzy sets as the basis for a theory of possibility. *Fuzzy Sets and Systems, 1,* 3 - 28.

Zhang, J., & Mani, J. (2003). knn approach to unbalanced data distributions: A case study involving information extraction. *Proceedings of the ICML-2003 Workshop: Learning with Imbalanced Data Sets II,* 42-48.

Section II
Pattern Discovery from Huge Data Set:
Methodologies

Chapter VI
Fuzzy Neural Networks for Knowledge Discovery

Arun Kulkarni
The University of Texas at Tyler, USA

Sara McCaslin
The University of Texas at Tyler, USA

ABSTRACT

This chapter introduces fuzzy neural network models as means for knowledge discovery from databases. It describes architectures and learning algorithms for fuzzy neural networks. In addition, it introduces an algorithm for extracting and optimizing classification rules from a trained fuzzy neural network. As an illustration, multispectral satellite images have been analyzed using fuzzy neural network models. The authors hope that fuzzy neural network models and the methodology for generating classification rules from data samples provide a valuable tool for knowledge discovery. The algorithms are useful in a variety of data mining applications such as environment change detection, military reconnaissance, crop yield prediction, financial crimes and money laundering, and insurance fraud detection.

INTRODUCTION

Our ability to collect data has increased rapidly in the last decade with the growing use of computers and the Internet; contributing factors include computerization of businesses, advances in data collection tools and wide spread use of bar codes for commercial products, (Han & Kamber, 2006).

Government agencies, scientific institutes, and business all have dedicated enormous resources to collecting and gathering data. This explosive growth in data has generated an urgent need for new techniques to analyze large, complex, and information-rich data sets and to extract useful information. The ability to extract useful knowledge hidden in large data sets and to act on that knowledge is becoming important in today's competitive world (Kantardzic, 2001). The term *knowledge discovery from databases* (KDD) refers to the overall process of discovering and extracting useful knowledge from databases (Fayyad, Shapiro, & Smyth, 1996). The process of knowledge extraction consists of many steps. Data mining is a particular step in the process and it deals with clustering, classification, estimation and prediction. The evaluation step involves interpreting models or extracting rules for classification from sample data points. Classification and clustering tasks can be carried out using a number of techniques such as conventional statistical methods, neural networks, fuzzy inference systems, and fuzzy neural network models. Fuzzy neural networks provide a powerful and reasonable alternative to conventional statistical methods of classification. Fuzzy neural networks are capable of learning and decision making. In addition, after learning, it is possible to decode fuzzy neural networks and extract knowledge in terms of classification rules. Many fuzzy neural network models have been developed and used successfully for data mining applications. Until recently, fuzzy neural networks (FNNs) have been viewed as "black boxes," which successfully classify data samples, but without anything for the user to see that explains how the network reaches decisions. Recently there is a growing interest in the research community not only to understand how the network arrived at a decision but how to decode information stored in the form of connection strengths in the network. One of the directions taken in this endeavor involves the extraction of fuzzy *if-then* rules from FNNs. Many articles that deal with fuzzy neural networks and their applications have been published in the literature (Jang, 1993; Keller, Yager, & Tahani, 1992; Kulkarni & McCaslin, 2004; Lin & Lee, 1991; Mitra & Acharya, 2003; Zadeh, 1994). In this chapter, we introduce fuzzy inference systems and fuzzy neural network models with supervised and unsupervised learning. In addition, we discuss

Figure 1. Knowledge discovery from databases (KDD) process

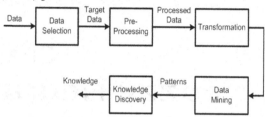

various methods of extracting fuzzy rules from neural networks and fuzzy neural networks, and present case studies that deal with real life data mining applications. The applications include analysis of multispectral satellite images and extracting rules for identification of various objects on the ground.

BACKGROUND

The process of knowledge discovery from databases (KDD) is outlined in Figure 1. This process is described in the following sections.

Data Selection, Pre-Processing, and Transformation

The first stage in the KDD process is data selection, where data relevant to the analysis task are retrieved from the database. In this stage, we focus on a subset of data records or attributes in the database on which knowledge discovery can be attempted. Several criteria can be used to select a subset of data. For example, data records may be selected based on geographic locations or time intervals.

Real-world data are often incomplete, inconsistent, and noisy. The preprocessing stage includes basic operations such as removing noise, filling up missing values, accounting for time sequence information and known changes, as well as database issues such as data types and schema. The problem of missing data is especially acute in business databases. Missing data can result from operator errors, actual system or measurement failure, or from a revision of the data collecting process. Commonly used approaches to fill missing values are to use a global constant, attribute mean, or the most probable value that is obtained by a regression model. The preprocessing stage also deals with mapping non numeric attributes in the database to numeric values that can be used for data mining.

The transformation stage involves data reduction and projection. It includes finding useful attributes to represent data depending on the goal of the task. Often, data attributes in a record are correlated and represent redundant information. The transformation stage uses data dimensionality reduction or transformation methods to reduce the effective number of attributes or to find invariant representation of the data (Fayyad, et al., 1996). To reduce the number of affective attributes while retaining most of the information attributes, values are mapped into a feature space using orthogonal transforms such as the principal component analysis (PCA), Fourier transform (FT), or the wavelet transform (WT) (Gonzalez & Woods, 2002). Attributes in the transformed domain can be ranked according to the degree of significance of their contribution to the information content. Other techniques such as histograms, moment invariants, and texture features also are employed for reduction of dimensionality (Kulkarni, 2001).

Data Mining

Data mining involves fitting models to or determining patterns from observed data. The fitted models play the role of inferred knowledge. A fitted model is used for classification, clustering, estimation, or prediction. Classification deals with labeling input samples to various categories. For example, records in the database can be classified on the basis of their properties or attribute values

in various categories. In supervised classification, the model learns from training samples. Statistical methods for supervised classification techniques include minimum distance classifier, Bayes classifier, K-nearest neighbor classifier, and induction trees (Duda, Hart, & Stork, 2000; Murthy, 1998; Quilan, 1986, 1993). Neural network models such as the perceptron, back-propagation networks, radial basis function networks, and fuzzy perceptron learn from training set data, can make decisions and are well suited for classification. Clustering is unsupervised classification of patterns or observations into groups or clusters. A wide variety of algorithms are described in the literature, including K-means clustering, hierarchical clustering, and Isodata. Self organizing networks with learning algorithms such as competitive learning, Kohonen learning, and fuzzy competitive learning are suitable for clustering (Jain, Murty, & Flynn, 1999). Estimation is similar to classification except that output values are continuous and not discrete. Prediction is similar to classification or estimation, except that the input vector represents past or present values and the output vector represents future values. Supervised classification techniques can be used for prediction. Training set data for the model consist of pairs of input-output vectors. In prediction, we use a sequence of data obtained over a period of time. We generate training set data in the form of input-output vectors by using past data for input vectors and present data for the output vector. The past and future data sets are determined on the basis of a reference point on the time axis.

Knowledge Discovery and Rule Extraction Techniques

The last stage in the KDD process is knowledge discovery. It deals with interpreting the discovered patterns or knowledge extraction. The observed patterns are translated into terms or rules understandable by users. In the data mining stage, we represent data by a model. Once the parameters that define the model are known, it is always possible to extract rules that characterize the model. Many times, rules that will be used elsewhere require expert validation and possible addition of expert heuristics. Duch, Adamczak, and Grabczewski (2001) comment that when an excessive number of rules are obtained, information gained is not much more comprehensible than the "black box" form of the network.

There are number of ways to extract rules from training data, including the use of fuzzy rule extraction from fuzzy neural systems. Many fuzzy neural network models have been proposed in the literature (Jang, 1993; Kulkarni, 1998; Lin & Lee, 1991; Pal & Mitra, 1992). Often, fuzzy neural networks are treated as "black boxes" which classify data samples but do not explain how the decisions were reached. Recent research has emphasized how the network reaches a decision, as well has how that information is stored in the network connection strengths. A major direction in this endeavor involves the extraction of *if-then* rules from fuzzy neural networks.

Andrews, Diederich, and Tickles (1995) provide an overview of most important features of the published techniques for extracting rules from trained artificial neural networks. They also describe techniques for extracting fuzzy rules from neuro-fuzzy systems. Survey articles by Mitra, Pal, and Mitra (2002) and Mitra and Hayashi (2000) describe various methodologies for generating fuzzy rules from fuzzy neural networks. Mitra, De, and Pal (1997) have proposed two methods for rule generation. In the first method, they have treated the network as a black box and have used the training set input and the network output to generate a set of *if-then* rules. The second method is based on the backtracking algorithm (Mitra & Pal, 1995). In this method, a path is traced from active nodes in the output layer back to the input layer based on the maximal paths through the network. The path is calculated as the sum of the input to a node in the network multiplied by the weight of its associated link. At least one

rule can be obtained for each data point using this methodology. Any input feature to which a path may be found is considered in producing the if portion of the rules. A confidence factor looking only at the inputs and the outputs is calculated for each rule. Setiono and Leow (2000) have suggested the methodology Fast Extraction of Rules from Neural Networks (FERNN), which builds a decision tree based on the relevant hidden units in the network, after the training phase. After irrelevant inputs to each activated hidden node are removed, the node splitting condition is replaced by an equivalent set of symbolic rules.

Ishibuchi, Nii, and Turksen (1998) demonstrated that fuzzy-rule based classification systems could be designed using rules that are extracted from neural networks, and that neural networks can be trained by both numerical data and linguistic type knowledge. They used fuzzy partitioning for classification problems in two steps. To achieve the partitioning, they first uniformly partition the fuzzy space and split the regions until the rule can be regarded as having a high certainty, then they use sequential partitioning of the region into fuzzy subspaces until some stopping criterion is reached.

One of the general methodologies for producing fuzzy rules from data involves partitioning the data. Abe and Lan (1995) presented a method of extracting rules directly from data. They group data samples in the feature space in two types of hyper-boxes, called activation hyper-boxes (to represent existence regions for classes) and inhibition hyper-boxes (to inhibit data existence within an activation hyper-box). Rules are extracted by resolving the overlap among these boxes, and each rule consists of an activation box and possibly an inhibition box. Wang and Mendel (1992) developed a five-step algorithm for directly extracting rules from a training data set. First, the input and output spaces are divided into fuzzy regions followed by determining the degrees of the inputs and outputs in different regions. Next, the inputs are assigned to a region with a maximum degree, and a rule is extracted from the input/output data pair. A degree is then assigned to each rule using the degree of membership of each part of the antecedent multiplied with the degree of membership of the consequent. After the rules are extracted, a combined fuzzy rule base, or a fuzzy associative memory (FAM) bank, is created to store the rules such that each box of possible input combinations has in it only the rule with the highest degree. After all samples from the data set have been processed, inputs can then be applied to determine a mapping based on the fuzzy associative memory using a centroid defuzzification method (Cox, 1994). In order to compare various rule extraction methods, many quantitative measures for rule evaluation have been suggested in the literature. They include overall accuracy, producer's accuracy, user's accuracy, kappa coefficient, and fidelity (Congalton, 1991; Mitra et al., 2002; Taha & Ghosh, 1999).

METHODOLOGY

In this section, we describe a fuzzy inference system and fuzzy-neural network models for supervised classification and clustering, as well as a method for rule generation and optimization (Kulkarni, 1995, 1998, 2000; Mitra et al, 1997; Pal & Mitra, 1992). The optimization step, which will

utilize a multidimensional associative memory bank, is required because a generated rule set often includes redundant or contradicting rules.

Fuzzy Inference System

The past few years have witnessed a rapid growth in a number of applications of fuzzy logic (Jang & Sun, 1995; Kulkarni & McCaslin, 2006; Mamdani, 1977; Zadeh, 1973, 1994; Zhang & Foody, 1998). Fuzzy logic provides a way to design a system using linguistic terms. A fuzzy set is an extension of a crisp set. Crisp sets allow only full membership or no membership at all, whereas fuzzy sets allow partial memberships. Fuzzy inference is the process of formulating the mapping from a given input to an output using fuzzy logic. The processing of fuzzy inference involves membership functions, fuzzy logic operators, and *if-then* rules. Fuzzy logic techniques in the form of approximate reasoning provide decision support and expert systems with powerful reasoning capabilities. A general model of a fuzzy inference system (FIS) with multiple inputs and a single output is shown in Figure 2. The FIS maps an input vector to an output value. The FIS contains four principal components: the fuzzifier, inference engine, rule base, and defuzzifier. The fuzzifier maps input variables to the corresponding fuzzy membership values. The fuzzifier takes input

Figure 2. Fuzzy inference system

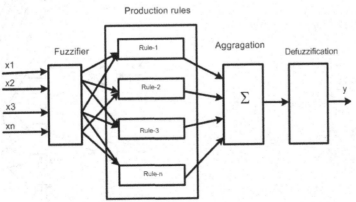

values and determines the degree to which they belong to each of the fuzzy sets via the membership functions. The rule base contains linguistic rules. The rules are provided by experts or they can be extracted from training set data. Once the rules have been established the FIS can be viewed as a system that maps input values to the corresponding output values.

The inference engine defines the mapping from input fuzzy sets to output fuzzy sets. It determines the degree to which the antecedent of each rule is satisfied. If the antecedent of a given rule has more than one part, the fuzzy operator is applied to obtain one number that represents the result of the antecedent for that rule. A consequent is a fuzzy set represented by a membership function. The consequent is reshaped using a single number associated with the antecedent. It is possible that for a given input more than one rule may fire at the same time, thus the outputs of each rule are aggregated. Aggregation is the process by which the fuzzy sets that represent the output of each rule are combined into a single fuzzy set. The output of the aggregation process is a fuzzy set. The defuzzifier maps the aggregated fuzzy set to a number.

Several methods of defuzzification are available in practice; the most commonly used method is the centroid method (Cox, 1994). As an illustrative example, we have considered a FIS with two inputs and a single output. The input represents two variables namely the education and experience,

and the output of the system represents salary. In this example, we used nine rules to define the mapping. The system was implemented using the MATLAB fuzzy logic tool box (MATLAB, 1998). The mapping surface for the FIS is shown Figure 3.

Fuzzy-Neural Network Models with Supervised Learning

Neural networks such as perceptron, multi-layered perceptron and back-propagation, have been successfully used in many classification tasks (Atkinson & Tatnall, 1997; Herrman & Khazenie, 1992; Yodhida & Omatu, 1994). One of the ways to combine neural networks and fuzzy logic is to use a neural network as an inference engine to develop a classification system (Kulkarni & Lulla, 1999). The main advantage of such a fuzzy-neural network is that the network can learn from training samples, and after learning it is then possible to decode the network to extract fuzzy classification rules. A three-layer fuzzy perceptron model is shown in Figure 4. The first layer is an input layer; the second layer is used for fuzzification wherein

Figure 4. Three-layer fuzzy neural network

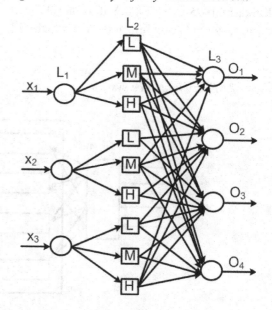

Figure 3. Input-output Mapping surface

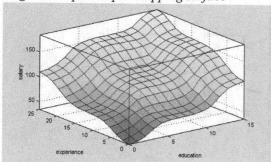

input feature values (numbers) are mapped to membership values (such as *low* or *very-high*), and the last layer implements a fuzzy inference engine. Membership functions of shapes such as the Gaussian, triangular or bell-shaped can be used. Initially, membership functions are determined using the mean and standard deviation of input variables. Subsequently, during learning, these functions are updated. Layers L_2 and L_3 represent a two-layer feed-forward network. The connection strengths connecting these layers encode fuzzy rules used in decision-making. In order to encode decision rules, a gradient descent technique is used. The algorithm minimizes the mean squared error between the desired output and the actual output. Layers in the model are described below (Kulkarni, 1998).

Layer L_1. The number of units in this layer is equal to the number of input features. Units in this layer correspond to input features, and they just transmit the input vector to the next layer. The output for ith unit is given by

$$o_i = x_i \qquad (1)$$

where x_i indicates the input for unit i.

Layer L_2. This layer implements membership functions. We have used five term sets {*very-low, low, medium, high, very-high*} for each input feature value. The number of units in layer L_2 is equal to the number of term sets times the number of units in L_1. The net-input and activation function for units are chosen so as to implement Gaussian membership functions, which are given by

$$f\left(x, \sigma, m\right) = \exp\left\{-\frac{\left(x-m\right)^2}{2\sigma^2}\right\} \qquad (2)$$

where m represents the mean value and σ represents, the standard deviation for a given membership functions. The net-input and output for units in L_2 are given by

$$net_i = x_i$$
$$out_k = f(net_i, \sigma_{ij}, m_{ij}) \qquad (3)$$

where $k = i \times j$, and out_k represents the output corresponds to the jth membership function that corresponds to the input x_i.

Layer L_3. This layer implements the inference engine. Layers L_2 and L_3 represent a simple two-layer feed-forward network. Layer L_2 serves as the input layer and L_3 represents the output layer. The number of units in the output layer is equal to the number of output classes. The net-input and output for units in L_3 are given by

$$net_i = \sum_{j=1}^{n} out_j w_{ij} \qquad (4)$$

$$out_i = \frac{1}{1 + \exp\left\{-\left(net_i + \phi\right)\right\}} \qquad (5)$$

where out_i is the output of unit i, and ϕ is a constant. Initially, weights between layers L_2 and L_3 are chosen randomly, and subsequently updated during learning. The membership functions are initially determined based on the minimum and maximum values for input features. The algorithm minimizes the mean squared error between the

Figure 5. Four-layer fuzzy backpropagation network

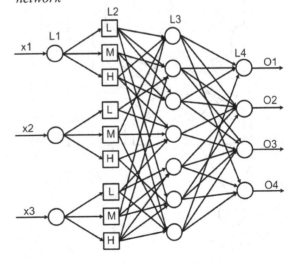

desired and the actual outputs. The model learns in two phases. During the first phase of learning the weights between layers L_2 and L_3 are updated and during the second phase membership function parameters are updated to minimize the mean squared error (Kulkarni & Cavanaugh, 2000). Once the learning is completed the model can be used to classify any unknown input sample. A four-layer fuzzy back-propagation network is shown in Figure 5. The first two layers of this network are the same as the fuzzy perceptron network. Layers L_2, L_3, and L_4 represent a three-layer back-propagation network that encodes the fuzzy rules and implements the inference engine. The model learns using the gradient descent procedure (Rumelhart & Zipser, 1985).

Fuzzy Neural Network Models for Clustering

Supervised neural networks require input that includes not only the feature values but the classification for each input pattern so that they can learn to recognize which patterns match which classes. Clustering networks, also called self-organizing networks or unsupervised networks, detect similarities among input patterns and adjust

Figure 6. Fuzzy Kohonen network

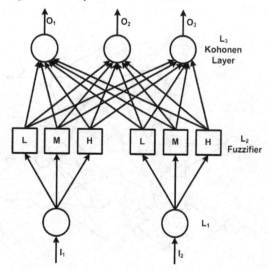

their weights. Two such learning algorithms are the Kohonen learning algorithm and the competitive learning algorithm. Kohonen (1982, 1988) introduced self organizing networks and the competitive learning algorithm was introduced by Rumelhart & Zipser (1985).

The fuzzy Kohonen network is shown in Figure 6. Layer L_1 is the input layer, which feeds directly into layer L_2, the fuzzifier block. Layer L_2 implements the fuzzifier. It maps input values to the corresponding fuzzy membership values. Layer L_3 is known as the Kohonen layer, which is fully interconnected with L_2. The input vector is presented to L_1 and fuzzified by L_2. The degree of mismatch is then calculated for each unit in L_2 as shown in Equation (6). Note that w_{ij} is the connection strength for a weight between unit j in L_2 and unit i in the Kohonen layer, x_j represents the fuzzified output of each membership function for each input, i is the number of units in the Kohonen layer and n is the total number of units in the fuzzifier block.

$$v_i = \sum_{j=1}^{n} \left(w_{ij} - x_j \right)^2 \qquad (6)$$

The degree of mismatch is the distance between the vectors represented by $\mathbf{w}_i$ and input vector $x = (x_1, x_2, ... x_n)^T$. The unit with the lowest degree of mismatch wins. The weights corresponding to the winning unit are updated by a change of Δw_{ij} given by Equation (7), where α represents a learning rate such that $0 \le \alpha \le 1$, and it is decremented according to a schedule.

$$\Delta w_{ij} = \alpha \left(x_j - w_{ij} \right) \qquad (7)$$

The weights are updated with each input sample. The process of comparing input samples to the weight vectors is repeated for each sample in the data set.

A fuzzy competitive network is shown in Figure 7. Layer L_1, is the input layer and Layer L_2 is the fuzzifier layer. Layer L_2 and L_3 implements the competitive learning algorithm (Rumelhart &

Zipser, 1985). To start with, the number of clusters is set to zero. Let $\mathbf{x}_1$ be the fuzzified form of the first input vector, and let it form the prototype for the first cluster. With each input vector, the unit in layer L_3 with the minimum distance (or the dot product) is declared as the winner. If the input vector satisfies the distance criteria it is assigned to that cluster and weights are updated using output fuzzy membership values. If no unit satisfies the distance criterion a new cluster with the input vector as the prototype is formed. The process is described in steps below.

***Step* 1**. To start with the number of cluster m is assumed to be zero. Let $\mathbf{x}_1$ be the first fuzzified vector. Assume the first fuzzified vector as the prototype for the first cluster, and assign the weights accordingly, that is, $\mathbf{w}_1 = \mathbf{x}_1$, where $\mathbf{w}_1$ represents weights connecting to the first unit in layer L_3. Note that input to the competitive layer is a normalized vector such that vector $\mathbf{x}_1$ satisfies Equation (8).

$$\sum_{j=1}^{n} x_{ij} = 1 \qquad (8)$$

***Step* 2**. Let $\mathbf{x}_j$ be the fuzzified vector for the next input vector. Find the winner unit in L_3 using the minimum distance as the criterion.

$$d_{\min} = \min \left\| \mathbf{x}_j - \mathbf{w}_i \right\|^2 \text{ for } i \in M \qquad (9)$$

$$\text{where } \left\| \mathbf{x}_j - \mathbf{w}_i \right\|^2 = \sum_{k=1}^{M} \left(x_{jk} - w_{ik} \right) \qquad (10)$$

and m represents the number of clusters.

***Step* 3**. If the winner unit does not satisfy the distance criterion $d_{\min} \leq \tau$, where τ is a threshold value, then add a unit to layer L_3. The new unit represents a new cluster. Set the weight vector of the new unit same as $\mathbf{x}_j$.

***Step* 4**. Otherwise, update weights corresponding to the winner unit by calculating new centroids and membership values using Equations (11) and (12).

$$\Delta w_{ij} = \alpha \left(\frac{x_j}{m} - w_{ij} \right) \qquad (11)$$

where α is a learning rate parameter ($0 < \alpha \ll 1$). Typical values of α range from 0.01 to 0.3, and m represents the number of active lines in layer L_2. Active lines are defined as connections for which x_j values are grater than the average x_j value.

$$w_{ij}^{new} = w_{ij}^{old} + \Delta w_{ij} \qquad (12)$$

***Step* 5**. If no more input samples then stop, else go to *Step* 2.

In competitive learning, weights that are connected to the winner unit only are updated. Weights corresponding to winner are increased, and weights corresponding to inactive lines are decreased. At each iteration, weights are normalized. The network learns by shifting a fraction of its weights from inactive lines to active lines (Rumelhart & Zipser, 1985)

Rule Generation and Optimization

The rule generation method combines the backtracking rule extraction technique with the fuzzy associative bank technique for rule reduction and optimization (Kulkarni & McCaslin, 2004, 2006). Figure 8 illustrates the process to extract and reduce the number of rules. The input to the rule extraction algorithm is a set of weight matrices of the trained neural network and training data samples. In these models, *if-then* rules are not explicitly represented in the knowledge base; they are generated by the inference system from the connection weight matrices. In the decision making phase, the network has already made the decision. A subset of the currently known information is taken to justify the decision. The next step in rule generation is backtracking (Pal & Mitra, 1992). The output of a backtracking algorithm is a collection of rules, many of which may be redundant and/or conflicting. These rules are then presented to a FAM bank, where redundant and conflicting rules are discarded using the measure of a degree of significance of the rule. The final output of a rule generation system is a set of non-redundant

Figure 8. Block diagram for rule generation and optimization

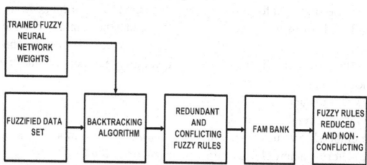

classification rules extracted from a sample data set. The three major components of this process are training the fuzzy neural network, extracting rules, and optimizing the rule set.

For a neural network model as shown in Figure 4, in order to extract classification rules, we start with layer L_3. For every node in layer L_3 that has output value greater than the active node value (i.e., $o_j \geq 0.5$), a path is traced to the input features. After selecting a neuron in the output layer, we select those neurons j in the layer L_2 that have positive impact on the conclusion at output neuron j. The activity level z_{ij} of any link is calculated as the product of the weight w_{ij} between node i and j and the output o_j of node j in layer L_2; and a path backward from that node was considered only if the activity level is greater than the user set active link threshold value.

$$z_{ij} = w_{ij}o_j \qquad (13)$$

If z_{ij} is greater than the active link threshold, the feature and the membership function involved are recorded. These form the antecedent of the fuzzy rules. After all paths back to layer L_1 have been investigated as described, rules encompassing all possible combinations of features and membership functions recorded are produced.

For a fuzzy-neural network model with four layers the rule extraction process is more complex because of the existence of a hidden layer. In this model the path with the maximum impact from the output neuron to the input features is traced using Equation (14).

$$z_{ij} = \max [\ \max_o (w_{ij}o_j) + \max_h (w_{ij}o_j) \qquad (14)$$

The value $\max_o$ refers to the maximum link value between the output layer active node and the hidden layer, and $\max_h$ refers to the value between the fuzzy layer and the node corresponding to the maximum link value in the hidden layer.

Since there are many input samples, and each sample generates one or more rules, it is highly probable that there will be some conflicting rules, that is, rules may have the same antecedent but different consequence. One way to resolve the conflict is to assign a degree of confidence to each rule generated from the sample, and to accept only the rule from a conflict group that has the maximum degree of confidence. We define the degree of confidence of a rule as

$$D = \mu_0 \mu_1 ... \mu_n o_i \qquad (15)$$

where D is the degree of confidence of the rule, and μ_i represents the degree of membership for feature i. For example, consider a rule "*if x_1 is low and x_2 is medium then* class is ω_3*.*" The degree of confidence is given by Equation (16). In Equation (16) o_3 represents output of the unit corresponding to class ω_3

$$D = \mu_{x1}^{low} \mu_{x2}^{medium} o_3 \qquad (16)$$

Figure 9. Fuzzy associative memory

	X1				
	VL	L	M	H	VH
VL					1
L		1			
X2 M				1	
H	1			1	
VH	1				

The extracted rules are then placed in the FAM bank. Figure 9 shows a FAM bank with two input feature system that uses five membership functions. The "1" in a cell indicates the existence of a rule. For example, a cell in the upper right hand corner is a rule that corresponds to the antecedent "*if x_1 very-high* and x_2 *very-low*".

In order to place a rule in a cell in the FAM bank, the rule needs each of the features specified. One issue in the backtracking algorithm is to account for rules with one or more features absent. For example, suppose after tracking through all active nodes and links in the network there is one feature that is never tracked back to the input layer. This would indicate that the feature in question has minimal effect on the final outcome. For the purpose of placing the rule in the FAM bank, one possibility would be to treat the missing feature as a "wild card," where that feature is allowed to have any value as far as that particular rule is concerned. If a rule with a missing feature (such as "*if x_2 medium then* class ω_1") was to be added to the FAM bank using this methodology, it would be added all the way down the x_2 *medium* column because there is no portion of the antecedent specifying a particular membership for feature x_2. For example, if feature x_1 was never tracked to and x_2 was *medium*, five rules would result:

if x_1 very-low and x_2 medium then class ω_1
if x_1 low and x_2 medium then class ω_1
if x_1 medium and x_2 medium then class ω_1
if x_1 high and x_2 medium then class ω_1
if x_1 very-high and x_2 medium then class ω_1

The missing features in cases such as this would not be used to calculate the degree of confidence of the rule. We have used two different techniques to handle rules with missing features. The first technique produces all rules using the "wild card" concept just discussed. When the rules go through a final reduction process, any rule with all possible values of a feature merely eliminates that feature from the rule producing a rule such as "*if x_2 medium then class is ω_1.*" The second method, called "highest membership value method," determines what feature is missing, then finds which fuzzy term has the highest membership value for that feature. The highest membership value is assigned to that feature/term combination in the rule, but the membership value is not used to calculate the degree of confidence of the rule. Note that neither technique uses the missing feature in calculation of the degree of confidence of the rule.

For both types of networks, the FAM bank rule reduction methodology is the same. First, the degree of confidence file is normalized such that the degree is replaced by its percentage of the maximum degree found. In order to map a rule to a cell of the FAM bank the first step is to determine whether each feature is represented in the rule. If so, then the corresponding cell to that combination of features is checked. The rule is added if either there is no rule present in the cell or the degree of significance of the rule under consideration is greater than the degree of confidence of the rule already present in the cell. This method eliminates redundant and/or conflicting rules by recording only rules with the highest degree of confidence.

Figure 10 shows a four-layer fuzzy neural network with two inputs, two output classes, and a single hidden layer with two hidden nodes (the number of hidden nodes was limited to only two to simplify the example and its illustration).

Figure 10. Four-layer fuzzy neural network illustrating the backtracking rule extraction methodology

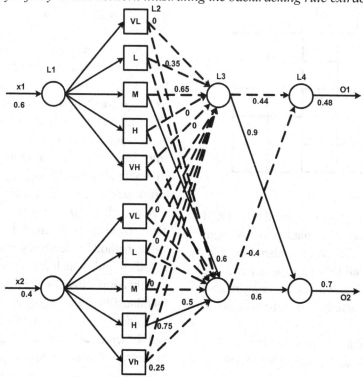

Note that the feature input values, resulting fuzzy term values, and output for each layer are shown in Figure 10. The active links are shown by solid lines and the inactive links are shown by dotted lines. A value of 0.6 was applied to the crisp input for feature 1, while a value of 0.4 was applied at feature 2 with two classes possible. An activity level threshold of 0.3 was assumed (a link was assumed active if its weight times the input to that link was at least 0.3), as was a degree threshold of 0.2 (a rule was considered acceptable if it had a degree greater than 0.2). We tried a number of the activity threshold and degree threshold values, and chose those which provided the optimum number of rules.

The output from the neural network indicated that the applied sample belonged to class 2 (output for class 2 was 0.7 as opposed to 0.48 for class 1). The activity level of the various links tracing back to the hidden layer were calculated using Equation (14). We found one active link leading to hidden node 2 with an activity level of 0.6 (which is greater than the 0.3 threshold), and no active links leading to hidden node 1 (all other links are below the threshold). Thus we give our full attention to backtracking from node 2. Using the same method, we find two active links from hidden node 2: one tracing back to fuzzy term member *medium* of feature 1 and another link to fuzzy term member *high* of feature 2. Figure 10 illustrates which of the links were determined to be active and visually illustrates the backtracking methodology just described. Two antecedents were thus produced for the final fuzzy rule. From these results, our resulting rule would be *if feature 1 medium and feature 2 high then class* ω_2.

To calculate the degree confidence of the rule, Equation (15) is used. For this example, the degree confidence would be 0.34. Note that this value does fall within the required degree threshold, and thus the rule would be accepted. The rule is placed into the corresponding cell in the FAM bank if the degree of confidence of the extracted rule is higher than the degree of confidence of the rule already recorded in the same cell of the FAM bank.

CASE STUDIES

Knowledge discovery by rule extraction has been successfully used in many applications such as

medical diagnosis (Duch et al., 2001; Taha & Ghosh, 1999) and remote sensing (Kulkarni & McCaslin, 2004, 2006). The authors developed software to simulate fuzzy neural network models, generate classification rules, and subsequently used the software to classify pixels in multispectral images and to generate fuzzy rules. Two satellite scenes, obtained with Landsat-4 Thematic Mapper sensor, were analyzed.

The first scene represents a nuclear plant in Chernobyl and was classified using the fuzzy perceptron, with each pixel represented by a vector of five reflectance values. We used reflectance values in bands 2, 3, 4, 5, and 7 as input features because these bands showed the maximum variance. Five linguistic term sets {*very-low, low, medium, high, very-high*} were used to represent reflectance values of a pixel. During the training phase, the network was trained using training set data; five training areas were selected, each of the size 10x10 pixels that represented five classes: matured crop, harvested field, vegetation, built-up area, and water. Each class was represented

Figure 11. Spectral Signatures for Chernobyl scene

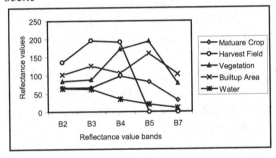

Figure 12. Classified Chernobyl scene output

by a small clear region. The training set areas were chosen interactively by a trained geologist from the raw image displayed on the computer screen. The target output vectors for five classes were defined as (1, 0, 0, 0, 0), (0, 1, 0, 0, 0), (0, 0, 1, 0, 0), (0, 0, 0, 1, 0), and (0, 0, 0, 0, 1). Only a small fraction (500 pixels) of the entire data set (256134 pixels) was used for training samples. We have considered a portion of the scene and it is of the size 512 columns and 512 rows. The spectral signatures used for the five classes are shown in Figure 11.

The optimum rule set was defined as a rule set with comparatively fewer rules and over all accuracy above 90 % (Kulkarni & McCaslin 2004). In order to evaluate a generated rule set, a FIS with the generated rule set as a rule base was built. It is obvious that the classification accuracy of the FIS depends on the quality of the rule set. Conversely, the quality of the rule set can be evaluated by measuring classification accuracy. For each rule set, the training set data were reclassified using the FIS that was built using the MATLAB fuzzy logic toolbox. In order to evaluate quality of a rule set, measures such as the overall accuracy, user's accuracy, and kappa coefficient were calculated (Congalton, 1991;

Mitra et al, 2002). The optimum rule set that was generated with the trained fuzzy perceptron models is shown below. Figure 12 shows the classified Chernobyl scene output.

R1: If band-2 is *low* and band-3 is *low* and band-4 is *low* and band-5 is *very-low* and band-7 is *very-low* then *class* is *water*.

R2: If band-2 is *low* and band-3 is *low* and band-4 is *medium* band-5 is *medium* and band-7 is *low* then *class* is *matured-crop*.

R3: If band-2 is *medium* and band-3 is *medium* and band-4 is *high* and band-5 is *very-high* and band-7 is medium then *class* is *vegetation*.

R4: If band-2 is *medium* and band-3 is *high* and band-4 is *medium* and band-5 is *high* and band-7 is *medium* then *class* is *built-up area*.

R5: If band-2 is *high* and band-3 is *very-high* and band-4 is *very-high* and band-5 is *very-low* and band-7 is *very-low* then *class* is *harvested-field*.

The second scene represents the Mississippi River bottomland area; the classified image is shown in Figure 13. It represents three different classes: water, land, and forest. In the case of a fuzzy perceptron network layer L_1 contained five units that represent input features, L_2 contained 25 units, and L_3 contained three units that represent three output classes. The optimized rule set is shown below.

Figure 13. Classified Mississippi scene output

R_1: If band 2 is *high* and band 3 is *high* and band 4 is *low* and band 5 is *very-low* and band 7 is *very-low*, then *class* is *water*

R_2: If band 2 is *high* and band 3 is *medium* and band 4 is *medium* and band 5 is *medium* and band 7 is *low*, then *class* is *land*

R_3: If band 2 is *high* and band 3 is *medium* and band 4 is *medium* and band 5 is *medium* and band 7 is *medium*, then *class* is *land*.

R_4: If band 2 is *high* and band 3 is *high* and band 4 is *high* and band 5 is *high* and band 7 is *high,* then *class* is *forest.*

SUMMARY

In this chapter, we described fuzzy neural network models for classification and clustering and introduced an algorithm for extracting and optimizing fuzzy classification rules from a trained network. The authors have developed software to implement these models and to generate classification rules, and demonstrated that these models are effective in analyzing multispectral data and extracting classification rules from data samples.

FNNs provide a valuable data mining tool that can be used in many practical applications such as crop yield prediction, environmental change detection, climate change impacts and assessments, and managing our planet's resources and health. Other uses include military reconnaissance, medical diagnosis and imaging, urban planning, biometric applications, multidimensional analysis of telecommunication data, identification of unusual patterns from homeland security databases, DNA analysis, and the discovery of structural patterns of genetic networks and protein pathways. Valuable business applications of knowledge discovery would be loan payment prediction, targeted marketing, financial crimes and money laundering, insurance fraud detection, product design, and customer profiling.

ACKNOWLEDGMENT

The authors are thankful to anonymous reviewers whose suggestions have helped us to improve the manuscript significantly.

REFERENCES

Abe, S. & Lan, M. (1995). A method for fuzzy rules extraction directly from numerical data and its application to pattern classification. *IEEE Transactions on Fuzzy Systems, 3*(1), 18-28.

Andrews, R., Diederich, J., & Tickles, A. B. (1995). Survey and critique of techniques for extracting rules from trained artificial neural networks. *Knowledge-Based Systems, 8*(6), 373-389.

Atkinson P. M. & Tatnall, A. R. L. (1997). Introduction: neural networks in remote sensing. *International Journal of Remote Sensing, 18*(4), 699-709.

Congalton, R. G. (1991). A review of assessing the accuracy of classifications of remotely sensed data. *Remote Sensing of Environment, 37,* 35-46.

Cox, E. (1994). *The fuzzy systems handbook.* Cambridge, MA: Academic Press.

Duda, R. O., Hart, P. E., & Stork, D. G. (2000). *Pattern classification.* New York, NY: John Wiley & Sons.

Duch, W, Adamczak, R., & Grabczewski, K. (2001). A new methodology of extraction, optimization and application of crisp and fuzzy logical rules. *IEEE Transactions on Neural Networks, 12*(2), 277-306.

Fayyad, U., Shapiro, G.P., & Smyth, P. (1996). The KDD process for extracting useful knowledge from volumes of data. *Communications of the ACM, 39,* 27-34.

Gonzalez, R. C. & Woods, R. E. (2002). *Digital image processing.* Upper Saddle River, NJ: Prentice Hall.

Han, J., & Kamber, M. (2006). *Data mining: Concepts and techniques.* Amsterdam, Netherlands: Morgan Kaufman.

Heermann P. D. & Khazenie, N. (1992). Classification of multispectral remote sensing data using a back-propagation neural network. *IEEE Transactions* on *Geosciences and Remote Sensing, 30*(1), 81-88.

Ishibuchi, H. Nii, M., & Turksen, I. B. (1998). Bidirectional bridge between neural networks and linguistic knowledge: Linguistic rule extraction and learning from linguistic rules. *Proceedings of the IEEE Conference on Fuzzy Systems FUZZ-IEEE '98*, Anchorage, 1112-1117.

Jang, J. S. R. (1993). ANFIS Adaptive network based fuzzy inference systems. *IEEE Trans. on Systems, Man, and Cybernetics, 23*(3), 665-685.

Jain A. K., Murty, M. N, & Flynn, P. J. (1999). Data clustering: A Review. *ACM Computing Surveys, 31*(3), 264-323.

Jang, J. S. R. & Sun, C. T. (1997). *Neuro-fuzzy and soft computing: A computational approach to learning and machine intelligence.* Upper Saddle River, NJ: Prentice Hall.

Kantardzic, M. (2001). *Data mining: Concepts, models, methods, and algorithms.* Hoboken, NJ: Wiley – IEEE Press.

Keller, J. K., Yager R. R., & Tahani, H. (1992). Neural network implementation of fuzzy logic. *Fuzzy Sets and Systems, 45*, 1-12.

Kohonen, T. (1982). Self-organized formation of topologically corrected feature maps. *Biological Cybernetics, 43*, 59-69.

Kohonen, T. (1988). *Self organization and associative memory.* Berlin: Springer-Verlag.

Kulkarni, A. D., Giridhar, G. B., & Coca, P. (1995). Neural network based fuzzy logic decision systems for multispectral image analysis. *Neural, Parallel, & Scientific Computations, 3*(2), 205-218.

Kulkarni, A.D. (1998). Neural fuzzy models for multispectral image analysis. *Applied Intelligence, 8*, 173-187.

Kulkarni, A. D. (2001). *Computer vision and fuzzy-neural systems.* Upper Saddle River, NJ: Prentice Hall PTR.

Kulkarni, A. D. & Cavanaugh, C. D. (2000). Fuzzy neural network models for classification. *Applied Intelligence, 12*, 207-215.

Kulkarni, A. D. & McCaslin S. (2004). Knowledge discovery from multispectral satellite images. *IEEE Geoscience and Remote Sensing Letters, 1*(4), 246-250.

Kulkarni, A. D. & McCaslin S. (2006). Knowledge discovery from satellite images. *WSEAS Transactions on Signal Processing, 11*(2), 1523-1530.

Kulkarni, A.D. & Lulla, K. (1999). Fuzzy neural network models for supervised classification: Multispectral image analysis. *Geocarto International, 14*(4), 41-49.

Lin, C. T. & Lee, George C. S. (1991). Neural network based fuzzy logic control and decision system. *IEEE Transactions on Computers, 40*, 1320-1336.

Mamdani, E. H. (1977). Applications of fuzzy logic to approximate reasoning using linguistic synthesis. *IEEE Transactions on Computers, 26*(12), 1182-1191.

MATLAB (1998). *Fuzzy logic tool box: User's Guide.* Natick, MA: The Math Works Inc.

Mitra S. & Acharya, T. (2003). *Data mining: Multimedia, soft computing, and bioinformatics.* Hoboken, NJ: Wiley-Interscience.

Mitra, S. & Hayashi, Y. (2000). Neuro-fuzzy rule generation: survey in soft computing framework. *IEEE Transactions on Neural Networks, 11*(3), 748-768.

Mitra, S. &. Pal, S. K. (1995). Fuzzy multi-layer perceptron inferencing and rule generation. *IEEE Transactions on Neural Networks, 6*(1), 51-63.

Mitra, S., De, R. K., & Pal, S. K. (1997). Knowledge-based fuzzy MLP for classification and rule generation. *IEEE Transactions on Neural Networks, 8*(6), 1338-1350.

Mitra, S., Pal, S. K. & Mitra, P. (2002). Data mining in a soft computing framework: A survey. *IEEE Transactions on Neural Networks, 13*(1), 3-14.

Murthy S. K. (1998). Automatic construction of decision trees from data: multi-disciplinary survey. *Data Mining and Knowledge Discovery, 2*, 345-389.

Pal, S. K. & Mitra, S. (1992). Multilayer perceptron, fuzzy sets, and classification. *IEEE Transactions on Neural Networks, 3*, 683-697.

Quilan J. R. (1986). Induction decision trees. *Machine Learning, 1*, 86-106.

Quilan J. R. (1993). C4.5: *Programs for machine learning.* San Mateo, CA: Morgan Kaufmann.

Rumelhart, D. E., McClelland, J. L., & PDP Group (1986). *Parallel distributed processing,* Vol I, Cambridge, MA: MIT Press.

Rumelhart, D. E. & Zipser, (1985). Feature discovery by competitive learning. *Cognitive Science, 9*, 75-112.

Setiono, R. & Leow, W. K. (2000). FERNN An algorithm for fast extraction of rules from neural networks. *Applied Intelligence, 12*, 15-25.

Taha, I. A. & Ghosh, J. (1999). Symbolic interpretation of artificial neural networks. *IEEE Transactions on Knowledge and Data Engineering, 11*(3), 448-463.

Wang L. & Mendel, J. M. (1992). Generating fuzzy rules by learning from examples. *IEEE Transactions on Systems, Man, and Cybernetics, 22*(6), 414-1427.

Yodhida, T. & Omatu, S. (1994). Neural network approach to land cover mapping. *IEEE Transactions on Geosciences and Remote Sensing, 32*(5), 1103-1109.

Zadeh, L. A. (1973). Outline of a new approach to analysis of complex systems and decision processes. *IEEE Transactions on Systems, Man, and Cybernetics, 3*, 28-44.

Zadeh, L. A. (1994). Fuzzy logic, neural networks, and soft computing. *Communications of the ACM, 37*, 77-84.

Zhang, J. & Foody, G. M. (1998). A fuzzy classification of land cover from remotely sensed imagery. *International Journal of Remote Sensing, 19*(14), 2621-2738.

Chapter VII
Genetic Learning:
Initialization and Representation Issues

Ivan Bruha
McMaster University, Canada

ABSTRACT

This chapter discusses the incorporation of genetic algorithms into machine learning. It does not present the principles of genetic algorithms (because it has been already done by many more or less large monographs) but rather focuses particularly on some important issues and enhancements of genetic algorithms design is faced by, namely: (a) the ways of initialization of a population for a genetic algorithm, (b) representation of chromosomes (individuals) in genetic algorithms (because it plays an influential role in the entire processing), and (c) discretization and fuzzification of numerical attributes for genetic algorithms (since they are not in its genuine form able to process these attributes). Furthermore, this chapter surveys new trends of dealing with the variable-length chromosomes and other issues related to the genetic learners. It concludes by discussing some directions of further improvement of the genetic learners, namely two topologies with the 'meta' level.

INTRODUCTION

A machine learning algorithm induces descriptions of concepts (classes) of a given problem. The induction of concepts from databases consists of searching usually a huge space of possible concept descriptions. There exist several paradigms how to control this search, e.g., various statistical methods, logical/symbolic algorithms, neural nets, and the like. This chapter presents the paradigm of genetic algorithms for such a search. There are several projects of incorporating genetic algorithms into machine learning (ML); we would like to present our contribution to this field, called *genetic learning*.

Genetic algorithms (GAs) represent a relatively new efficient optimization technique for inducing new concepts. They emulate biological evolution and are utilized in optimization processes, similarly to simulated annealing, rough sets, and neural nets. The optimization is performed by processing a *population* (a set) of individuals. Each *individual* (*chromosome*) is usually divided into several substructures, called *genes*. An individual as a unit is in most applications represented by a binary string. For representation purposes, we distinguish fixed- and variable-length strings.

A designer of a GA has to provide an evaluation function, called *fitness*; it evaluates any individual (chromosome). Also the formulas/procedures for so-called *genetic operators* must be provided by the user (see their definitions below).

GAs have become an attractive alternative to classical search algorithms for exploring large spaces of hypotheses (models, concept descriptions). They are two important characteristics of the search performed by a GA: the search is usually global and is parallel in nature since a GA processes not just a single individual (chromosome) but a large set (population) of individuals.

There exist both theoretical and experimental results showing that GAs can rapidly locate individuals with high fitness rating (even for very huge search spaces) by using a relatively small population of 50-100 individuals (chromosomes). This chapter, of course, does not present the principles of genetic algorithms; detailed and exhausted discussion can be found, e.g. in (Holland, 1975; De Jong, 1980; Grefenstette, 1986).

BACKGROUND

Research projects of incorporating (merging) genetic algorithms into the field of learning algorithms inducing concept descriptions can be divided into two categories.

In the first category, called *external* one, the actual concept description (model) is derived (induced) by a traditional machine learning algorithm and a GA serves as an *evaluation* or *parameter-optimizing* device. Behaviour of any performance system (not only a ML algorithm) exhibits several parameters that affect its behaviour; a suitable

strategy for changing these parameters' values improves performance of the system. How can a GA serve in this issue?

In one application, a GA plays a role of an evaluation device, and the performance system itself modifies its internal structure by GA's evaluation characteristics.

In a more sophisticated application, a GA itself searches for a combination of parameters that improve the performance of a machine learning (performance) system. Here, the parameters are viewed as genes, and the genetic material of individuals (chromosomes) as a fixed-length string of genes.

Another application of GAs (De Jong, 1988): in some tasks, a simple vector of parameters is not adequate, but rather a more complex data structure of parameters is involved in controlling the behaviour of the performance system. Such a data structure can be 'linearized' into a binary string representation; however, the traditional genetic operators (namely, crossover and mutation) could produce illegal data structures (not having the sense in a given task). Therefore, representation-sensitive operators are to be designed and applied.

To illustrate this fashion, we introduce a few existing systems. For instance, (Kelly & Davis, 1991) describes a hybrid learning system that utilizes the k-nearest-neighbour classification algorithm in a standard way and a genetic algorithm that learns weights associated with the attributes. Similar hybrid system may be found in (Turney, 1995): C4.5 generates decision trees and the genetic algorithm evolves a population of bias parameters that control C4.5's performance.

In the other fashion (called *genuine* one), a genetic algorithm itself generates concept descriptions (models), usually in a form of decision trees or sets of decision rules. Regal (Giordana & Saitta, 1993; Neri & Saitta, 1996) is a large system that utilizes genetic search for deriving first-order-logic concept descriptions. Samuel (Grefenstette et al., 1990), another genetic algorithm generating decision rules, works together with simulation models. (De Jong et al., 1993; Janikow, 1993) describe two applications of genetic algorithms in incremental learning.

This chapter concentrates on the following problem: GAs themselves exhibit various parameters that must be selected by a designer; there are, however, two important parameters whose selection and/or definition are the most important, namely the initialization of the population of individuals and their representation. Besides, the GAs in its original fashion can process individuals represented by discrete attributes only. Therefore, the other important issue is the way how to discretize these attributes (Bruha et al., 2000).

The next section (Main Thrust of the Chapter) briefly introduces the idea of genetic learners, then discusses discretization/fuzzification of numerical attributes, various ways of generating an initial population, representation of rules and decision sets, and the issue of variable-length chromosomes. The last section compares various approaches and suggests the future trends in research: dynamic and adaptive fitness, and an idea of a metalearner.

MAIN THRUST OF THE CHAPTER: RULE-INDUCING GENETIC LEARNER

Genetic-Based Learner

As we already stated, the optimization within a genetic algorithm is performed by processing a population of individuals (chromosomes). A designer of a GA must provide an evaluation function, called *fitness*, that evaluates all individuals. The fitter individual has the greater chance in forming a new population. Given an initial population of individuals, a genetic algorithm processes it by choosing individuals to become parents and then replacing members of the current population by the new individuals (*offsprings*) that

are modified copies of their parents. This process of reproduction and population replacement continues until, e.g. a performance goal achieved, or the maximum time limit exhausted.

Genetic algorithms exploit several *genetic operators*:

- *Selection* operator chooses chromosomes as parents depending on their fitness. The fittest individuals have on average more children (offsprings) than the less fit ones.
- *Crossover* operator creates offsprings by combining the information involved in the parents.
- *Mutation* causes that offsprings may differ from their parents by introducing a localized change.

There exist many research projects that merge genetic algorithms into machine learning systems, mostly the symbolic ones. These ML systems induce concept (class) descriptions in form of either decision trees or decision (production) set of decision (production) rules. We focus here on the latter structure.

Let us describe the induction process more formally. The input to such a symbolic ML system is a training set of K training examples (objects), each accompanied by its *desired class* C_r, r = 1,...,R. Examples are formally represented by N discrete (symbolic) *attributes*. A discrete attribute A_n, n=1,...,N, comprises $J(n)$ distinct values $V_1,...,V_{J(n)}$. The algorithm yields (induces) a list (decision set) of decision rules of the form

```
Rule: if Cond then class is C_r
```

The condition *Cond* is represented by a conjunction of selectors (a *selector* is defined as a pair of an attribute name and its value).

It should be noted that the author of this chapter designed and implemented a system that integrates a domain-independent genetic algorithm into the covering learning algorithm CN4 (Bruha, 1996), a large extension of the well-known algorithm CN2 (Clark & Boswell, 1991); the induction procedure of CN4 (beam search methodology) was removed and the GA has been implanted into this shell. We call it GA-CN4. Similarly to CN2 and CN4, GA-CN4 is a rule-inducing algorithm, i.e., it generates a set of decision rules. – The next discussion presents the internal structure of GA-CN4, however, it demonstrates the common characteristics of incorporating GAs into machine learning generally.

Since the beginning of 1980's, there has been an increasing interest in merging GAs in machine learning, particularly to learning (inducing) decision rules. Since, there have been existing two major approaches of representing of decision sets and decision rules in GAs by chromosomes (individuals). Using a rule-based concept representation brings the following problem: since the number of rules of a decision set (production system) is unknown a priori, the traditional fixed-length representation of chromosomes is unsuitable in some applications. Each of the two approaches solves this problem in a different way. From the historical viewpoint, they are called by the cities where the researches invented their approaches: Michigan and Pittsburgh ones.

(M) Michigan Approach

A chromosome (individual) represents a single decision rule. It has a fixed length given by the number N of attributes that describe a given problem. Therefore, the traditional genetic operators can be used. This methodology, known also as the classifier systems, along with a special 'bucket brigade' mechanism, was originally developed by (Holland, 1986). In this original version, the solution (set of decision rules) is represented by a set of all the chromosomes from a population. The newer versions possess a mechanism for selecting a useful subset of chromosomes (rules) from a population; this subset then forms an appropriate decision set of rules.

Our inductive rule-inducing system GA-CN4 exploits the latter version. When the algorithm stops, only one decision rule is selected. More precisely, at each learning sweep (loop), the algorithm finds the current best individual (decision rule) and appends it to the list of the decision rules. It stops as soon as no significant best rule has been found. The top-flow chart of the algorithm in this direction is identical to that of the original one. One learning loop is thus depicted by this domain-independent genetic algorithm GA() that, as already mentioned, processes the fixed-length chromosomes:

procedure GA()
1. Initialize a new population
2. **Until** stopping condition of GA is satisfied **do**
    > 2.1   Select individuals by the tournament selection operator
    > 2.2   Generate offsprings by the two-point crossover operator
    > 2.3   Perform the bit mutation
    > 2.4   Execute the hill-climbing local-optimization
    > 2.5   Check whether each new individual has the correct attribute and class values (within their ranges); if not the individual's fitness is set to 0 (i.e., to the worst value)
    enddo
3. Select the fittest individual (decision rule)
4. **If** this object is statistically significant **then**
    > return this object
    else return nil

Details of our genetic learner can be found in (Bruha et al., 2000); the default parameter values are: size of population is 50, probability of mutation $Pmut = 0.002$, probability of hill-climbing $Phc = 0.05$, width of hill-climbing (the number of iterations) $Whc = 2$. The fitness function is calculated by the Laplacian criterion for expected accuracy (for the class C_r)

$$Lapl(C_r, Cond) = \frac{K_r(Cond) + 1}{K(Cond) + R}$$

where $K_r(Cond)$ is the number of training examples of the class C_r covered by the condition *Cond*, called *class-sensitive* coverage, $K(Cond)$ is the total number of examples covered by the condition (*overall* coverage), and R is the number of classes involved in the given task. The GA stops the search when the above Laplacian criterion is not improved after 10000 generations.

(P) Pittsburgh Approach

This approach was originally proposed by Smith (1983) at University of Pittsburgh. Here, each individual (chromosome) of a population represents the entire decision set of rules.

Since the size of the decision set induced (the number of decision rules) is not known in advance, a decision set is represented by a variable-length individual (chromosome). The decision rules are thus depicted by substructures (genes) of the entire variable-length string. Similarly to the Michigan approach, the rules (genes) have fixed length given by the number N of attributes which represent the objects (examples) of a given task. If the corresponding genetic learner applied the traditional genetic operators, namely crossover and mutation, it would mostly produce offsprings having no physical sense. Therefore, it usually utilizes domain-specific operators that reflect the structure of chromosomes.

We could not use the original top flow chart; the genetic learner in this approach generates the best chromosome (the fittest one) as a result of the entire induction process. The fitness function may be formulated by various equations. (Bruha, 2006) introduces the *decision set quality* as the suitable fitness function; this statistics is derived from the idea of the *rule qualities* (Bruha, 1996; Tkadlec & Bruha, 2003).

Pittsburgh approach with variable-length individuals is faced by another problem. As we already know, the result of the inductive process is the best individual that represents the entire set of decision rules. It happens quite often that the decision set is redundant, i.e., it contains several redundant rules. However, dealing with this issue goes beyond the scope of this chapter.

Discretization/Fuzzification of Numerical Attributes

The traditional genetic algorithms are not able to process numerical (continuous) attributes, or their processing is not so straightforward as that of discrete attributes; some discretization/fuzzification procedure has to be performed. As an example of such a procedure, we can briefly present the procedure used in our genetic learner; we discretize numerical attributes by invoking the discretization off-line preprocessor of the learning algorithm KEX (Bruha et al., 2000) before a generic algorithm is called. It works off-line (what we need if we do not want to intervene the GA's code) and generates several intervals in an iterative manner.

The KEX discretization preprocessor discretizes (categorizes) each numerical attribute A_n separately. The rudimentary idea is to create intervals for which the *aposteriori* distribution of classes $P(C_r|interval)$ significantly differs from the *apriori* distribution of classes $P(C_r)$, r=1,...,R, in the entire training set. This can be achieved by simply merging such values, for which most objects (examples) belong to the same class. Thus, the performance of this procedure leads to a rule of the above form where one of the selectors of the condition *Cond* is $A_n \in interval$. The x^2 goodness-of-fit criterion is used. For more information see (Bruha et al., 2000).

Discretization of numerical attributes into crisp intervals (more precisely: sharp bounds between intervals) does not correspond to real situations in many application areas. Such crisp intervals may result in capturing training objects from various classes into one interval which consequently will not be consistent; this happens near to the interval borders. Therefore, KEX can also generate fuzzy intervals in order to eliminate such an impurity around the interval borders.

When fuzzifying values of a numerical attribute, we can observe that objects close to the borders may fall into two or more fuzzy intervals. Consequently, the original object with this numerical attribute can be split (according to the value of this attribute) into two or more (*fragmentary*) objects, each having the global membership (a product of membership functions of values of all attributes) lower than 1. The splitting procedure is repeated for each numerical attribute of every object. The genetic learner then processes each fragmentary object in the same way as 'complete' (not fragmentary) one.

Initial Population

A genetic algorithm starts with an initial population of individuals (chromosomes) and lets them evolve by combining them by means of genetic operators. Its behaviour generally depends on the selection of types of genetic operators, the shape of the fitness function, and the population's initialization procedure. It is known from both theoretical and experimental results that one important issue of defining or selecting parameters for a genetic algorithm is the forming of an initial population.

In both Michigan and Pittsburgh approaches, there are three types to fill the population initially:

1. Random Initialization

A pseudo-random number generator is utilized to initialize each individual as a random number of genes.

2. Initialization with Data

Each individual is a random positive training example (a positive example is one that belongs to a desired class).

3. Initialization with Prior Hypotheses

Each individual is formulated by a hypothesis from a set of hypotheses given a priori, usually in a form of a domain-specific ('external') knowledge base. This knowledge base (set of decision rules) is usually provided by an 'external' agent, expert system, or domain expert (a knowledge engineer). Consequently, a GA utilizing this type of initialization can be viewed as a knowledge refinement tool.

More specifically, Michigan approach utilizing this initialization works in our genetic learner according to the following procedure; details in (Bruha & Kralik, 2002):

procedure Initialize()
1. Convert all the external rules to chromosomes of the initial population
2. **Until** the required number of initial chromosomes (size of population) is generated **do**
    2.1 **If** there is no external (generalized) rule left **then**
    generate randomly the rest of initial chromosomes and **exit**
    2.3 Generalize the external rules by removing the last selector from their conditions
    2.4 Convert all these new rules into initial chromosomes
    enddo

Next, we have to realize that a population is initialized before a new rule is generated (step 1 of the procedure GA() above). There exist two possibilities: either

a. to initialize a new population for each new rule, or

b. to initialize a new population for the first rule only, thus using the final population from the last call (loop) as the new one for the current call of the procedure GA().

The flow chart for Pittsburgh approach utilizing the initialization with prior hypotheses looks as follows. Chromosomes in the initial population are formed by various combinations of the external rules (hypotheses) until the required size of population is reached.

Representation of Decision Rules/ Sets

(M) Michigan Approach

As we have already stated, each decision rule generated by the genetic learner is portrayed by a chromosome (individual) of fixed length. It comprises two portions:

- A condition portion (representing *Cond*) has always the length of N fields (genes) because the number N of attributes for a task (problem) is given;
- A class portion depicts the class attached to the rule.

The class portion is usually represented by one byte that can thus exhibit 256 different classes. Therefore, we will focus on the condition portion of a decision rule only. As we already stated, it consists of N fields; consequently, it is represented by a fixed-length chromosome of N genes.

There exist various ways of actual representation of these fields that form the entire string (chromosome). We now survey the most interesting ones. As one can see some of them allow even the internal disjunction and negation of selectors, i.e. attributed pairs (attribute name and its value).

a. Byte Representation

It exhibits the simplest but very inefficient representation of chromosomes (decision rules); each attribute field is placed in one byte (8 bits); i.e., maximum range of values of any attribute is from 0 to 255.

Let us illustrate this representation on the well-known 'weather' problem (Quinlan, 1987) with these attributes:

windy:	false, true
humidity:	normal, high
temperature:	cool, mild, hot
outlook:	rain, overcast, sunny

Each rule's condition is represented by a string of 4 bytes, each attribute value by an integer from the range 0 to $J(n)$ -1 . If a byte is within this range, then it is interpreted as the corresponding attribute value; otherwise, the given selector (attribute-value pair) is excluded from the rule. For instance, the string

```
00000001   10111101   01011111   11001011
```

corresponds to the decimal values 1, 189, 95, 203; since only the value of the first field falls into the permissible interval, the above string is converted to the rule

```
if windy=true then class is C
```

where C is the majority class of the training examples covered by this rule.

Evidently, this representation requires *Lchrom* $= 8 * N$ bits. The probability of inserting a selector of attribute A_n into a rule's condition is thus

$$Pins(A_n) = \frac{J(n)}{256}$$

i.e. usually very small. In our example, the probability $Pins(\texttt{windy}) = 0.0078$ (0.78%).

However, this representation allows to introduce a negation of a selector. The left-most bit in any byte can serve as a flag for negation (equal 1 if the selector is to be negated). The maximum range of attribute values is consequently half, i.e. from 0 to 127.

b. Reduced Mask Representation

Each attribute A_n in a chromosome representation is depicted by $Lmask(n)$ bits which is the minimum integer so that $2^{Lmask(n)} \geq J(n)$. The probability of inserting a selector of A_n into a rule looks thus better:

$$Pins(A_n) = \frac{J(n)}{2^{Lmask(n)} + 1}$$

In our example, $Pins(\texttt{windy}) = 0.75$.

Also, by adding an extra bit for each rule allows to introduce a negation of the corresponding selector.

c. Bit Representation

Although there exist several other rule representations in genetic algorithms, this one seems to be one of the most efficient. Each attribute A_n here is represented by $J(n)+1$ bits. Each attribute field (gene) begins with one bit (toggle) for negation. Each of the remaining bits exhibits one value of this attribute; it is set up to 1 if the corresponding value is present in the selector of the rule's condition. For instance, the string

```
0 01   1 00   1 101   1 001
```

in our task represents the condition of this rule:

```
if windy=true && temperature\=[cool or hot]
    && outlook\=sunny
then class is C
```

Hence, this representation allows negation, internal disjunction, and negation of the internal disjunction. The length of a chromosome is:

$$Lchrom = N + \sum_{n=1}^{N} J(n)$$

and the probability of inserting a selector of A_n into a rule is always 0.5 .

d. Representation of a Numerical Attribute

The above representations are valid for the discrete attributes. A selector for a numerical attribute A_n is represented by a field of two real numbers; the first corresponds to the lower bound $Lbound_n$ of an interval, the latter to its upper bound $Ubound_n$, i.e. this field depicts the selector (interval)

$$Lbound_n < A_n \leq Ubound_n$$

If a bound does not fit to the entire range of the numerical attribute, then it is eliminated from the above interval; if both bounds do not fit, or if the lower bound is greater than the upper one, then the entire selector is eliminated from the corresponding rule.

(P) Pittsburgh Approach

In Pittsburgh approach, a chromosome (individual) represents the entire set of decision rules. Each rule is usually symbolized by a gene of the fixed length of N sub-genes. Consequently, the representation discussed above can be used for expressing the decision rules. Since we do not know the size of the decision set (the number of decision rules) a priori, the variable-length chromosome must be utilized for representing the entire decision set. The length of such an individual (in bits) is thus equal to

$$Lchrom = Lgene * Nrules$$

where $Lgene$ is the length (in bits) of a gene for a single rule, and $Nrules$ is the current number of the decision rules involved in the given individual (chromosome).

It is to be noted that there exist in fact two fashions to variable-length chromosome's representation.

- In the first fashion, *pseudo* variable-length chromosomes, maximum number of rules in a decision set *Nmax* is a priori given, see, e.g. (Bandyopadhyay et al, 2000).

A decision set is then represented by a chromosome of the length *Lchrom = Lgene * Nmax* . In this type of representation, a variable-length chromosome is padded by special symbols # . Consequently, only *Nrules* genes portray existing decision rules, and the remaining genes are padded with #s. This new representation scheme thus involves ternary alphabet set {0, 1, #} . This allows to use the traditional genetic operators as much as possible, see, e.g. (Yang, 2004). However, some extra processing steps have to be defined in order to tackle the presence of #s in the string. The genetic operators are modified in such a way that the inclusion of # in the string does not affect the binary characteristics of coding. Replacing 0s and 1s by #s or vice versa can thus change the actual length of a chromosome (the actual number of rules in the decision set).

- The other fashion, the *genuine* variable-length chromosomes, works with individuals of different lengths; there is no padding issue involved. Consequently, the genetic operators have to be defined in a different, non-traditional way. Details are, e.g. in (Kotani et al, 2001).

The fitness function is equal to the decision set quality which is derived from the rule qualities. The crossover operator is to be defined in such a way that it carefully handles the situation when it 'cuts' the internal representations (genes) of two rules; however, a change within each rule

(gene) can be performed in the way equivalent to Michigan approach. Similarly the mutation operator.

CONCLUSION AND FUTURE TRENDS

We have presented some issues of genetic algorithms, namely (a) discretization and fuzzification of numerical attributes, (b) introducing two approaches to represent a decision set: Michigan and Pittsburgh approaches, (c) representation of decision rules/set for the above approaches, (d) the ways of initialization of a GA population. Various papers and experiments have revealed that all these directions in enhancing the genetic learners' behaviour can improve the entire mechanism of learning and pattern recognition.

The experiments with various chromosome representation have not brought anything substantial as for the classification accuracy; the t-test exhibited no significant difference in their behaviour. The tests performed for various initialization procedures revealed that (as we have intuitively expected) that the initialization by an external knowledge base has become significantly better than the other ones.

Generally speaking, the genetic learners have better classification performance than the traditional learning algorithms. We explain this better behaviour by the fact that the traditional ML algorithms explore a small number of hypotheses at a time, whereas the genetic algorithm carries out a search within a robust population, in parallel in nature. The only disadvantage of a genetic learner is time consumption. If one requests faster processing, some special hardware is required, compare, e.g. the system Regal (Giordana & Saitta, 1993) that runs on CM5 connection machine with 64 processors.

We are convinced that the idea of genetic learners is promising and some additional enhancements could be performed for improving their performance:

- The fitness function is another important parameter of genetic algorithms. Here we have used the Laplacian formula as the fitness; it is commonly applied in the inductive learning algorithms. However, it is constant during the entire process and does not change from population to population. It would be better to have a fitness formula where one of its parameters is the number (order) of the population; e.g., fitness values could decrease for newer and newer populations.

  Another possibility is *dynamically* changing fitness; its value can change according to user-specified parameters of the genetic process. One such an attempt can be found in (Dilimulati & Bruha, 2007). Ever more sophisticated is an *adaptive* fitness that not only changes its value according to defined genetic parameters but also it remembers these changes.

- One possible direction in genetic learners is to define a second-level genetic algorithm (or *metaGA*). This metaalgorithm could modify genetic operators (either by adding or deleting some of them), modify their parameters, population size, and the fitness function (either by weighting sum of existing formulas, or by generating new formulas).

- We can also combine the best topologies/ procedures together to get a more precise decision-making system. This concept is commonly called multiple knowledge, multi-strategy learning, and metalearning, particularly by the concept of *metacombiner* (*metalearner*) (Bruha, 2004). Several genetic learners work independently at the first (base) level, and their decision is then processed at the second (meta) level. (Note: do not mix it with the metaGA discussed above.)

REFERENCES

Bandyopadhyay, S., Murthy, C.A., & Pal, S.K. (2000). VGA-classifier: Design and applications. *IEEE Transactions Systems, Man, and Cybernetics*, 30, 6, 890-895.

Bruha, I. (1996). Quality of decision rules: Definitions and classification schemes for multiple rules. In: Nakhaeizadeh, G., & Taylor, C.C. (Eds.), *Machine Learning and Statistics: The Interface*, John Wiley, 107-131.

Bruha, I. (2004). Metalearner for unknown attribute values processing: Dealing with inconsistency of metadatabases. *J. Intelligent Information Systems*, 22, 1, 71-84.

Bruha, I. (2006). From quality of decision rules to quality of sets of decision rule. Submitted to journal.

Bruha, I., Kralik, P., & Berka, P. (2000). Genetic learner: Discretization and fuzzification of numerical attributes. *Intelligent Data Analysis J.*, 4, 445-460.

Bruha, I., & Kralik, P. (2002). Genetic learner GA-CN4: The ways of initializations of new populations, (Tech. Rep.), Dept Computing & Software, McMaster University.

Clark, P., & Boswell, R. (1991). Rule induction with CN2: Some recent improvements. *EWSL-91*, Porto, Springer-Verlag, 151-163.

De Jong, K. (1980). Adaptive system design: A genetic approach. *IEEE Transactions on Systems, Man, and Cybernetics*, 10, 556-574.

De Jong, K. (1988). Learning with genetic algorithms: An overview. *Machine learning*, 3, 121-138.

De Jong, K.A., Spears, W.M., & Gordon, D.F. (1993). Using genetic algorithms for concept learning. *Machine Learning*, 13, Kluwer Academic Publ., 161-188.

Dilimulati, B., & Bruha, I. (2007). Genetic Algorithms in Dynamically Changing Environment. In:Zanasi, A., Brebbia, C.A., & Ebecken, N.F.F. (Eds.), *Data Mining VIII: Data , Text and Web Mining and Their Business Applications*, WIT Press, 65-73.

Giordana, A., & Saitta, L. (1993). REGAL: An integrated system for learning relations using genetic algorithms. *Proc. 2nd International Workshop Multistrategy Learning*, 234-249.

Grefenstette, J. (1986). Optimization of control parameters for genetic algorithms. *IEEE Transactions on Systems, Man, and Cybernetics*, 16, 122-128.

Grefenstette, J., Ramsey, C.L., & Schultz, A.C. (1990). Learning sequential decision rules using simulation models and competition. *Machine Learning J.*, 5, Kluwer Academic Publ., 355-381.

Holland, J.H. (1975). *Adaptation in natural and artificial systems*. Ann Arbor: University of Michigan Press.

Holland, J.H. (1986). Escaping brittleness: The possibilities of general-purpose learning algorithms applied to parallel rule-based systems. In: Michalski, R.S., Carbonell, J.G., & Mitchell, T.M. (Eds.), *Machine learning: An artificial intelligence approach*, Vol. 2, Morgan Kaufmann.

Janikow, C.Z. (1993). A knowledge-intensive genetic algorithm for supervised learning. *Machine Learning J.*, 5, Kluwer Academic Publ., 189-228.

Kelly, J.D., & Davis, L. (1991). A hybrid genetic algorithm for classification. *Proc. IJCAI-91*, 645-650.

Kotani, M., Ochi, M., Ozawa, S., & Akazawa, K. (2001). Evolutionary discriminant functions using genetic algorithms with variable-length chromosome. *IEEE Transactions Systems, Man, and Cybernetics*, 31, 761-766.

Neri, F., & Saitta, L. (1996). Exploring the power of genetic search in learning symbolic classifiers. *IEEE Transaction Pattern Analysis and Machine Intelligence*, 18, 11, 1135-1141.

Quinlan, J.R. (1987). Simplifying decision trees. *International J. Man-Machine Studies*, 27, 221-234.

Smith, S.F. (1983). Flexible learning of problem solving heuristics through adaptive search. *Proceedings Eight International Conference on Artificial Intelligence*. Karlsruhe, Germany: Morgan Kaufmann, 422-425.

Tkadlec, J., & Bruha, I. (2003). Formal aspects of a multiple-rule classifier. *International Journal of Pattern Recognition and Artificial Intelligence*, 17, 4, 581-600.

Turney, P.D. (1995). Cost-sensitive classification: Empirical evaluation of a hybrid genetic decision tree induction algorithm. *J. Artificial Intelligence Research*.

Yang, W.X. (2004). An improved genetic algorithm adopting immigration operator. *Intelligent Data Analysis*, 8, 385-401.

Chapter VIII
Evolutionary Computing

Robert M. Patton
Oak Ridge National Laboratory, USA

Xiaohui Cui
Oak Ridge National Laboratory, USA

Yu Jiao
Oak Ridge National Laboratory, USA

Thomas E. Potok
Oak Ridge National Laboratory, USA

ABSTRACT

The rate at which information overwhelms humans is significantly more than the rate at which humans have learned to process, analyze, and leverage this information. To overcome this challenge, new methods of computing must be formulated, and scientist and engineers have looked to nature for inspiration in developing these new methods. Consequently, evolutionary computing has emerged as new paradigm for computing, and has rapidly demonstrated its ability to solve real-world problems where traditional techniques have failed. This field of work has now become quite broad and encompasses areas ranging from artificial life to neural networks. This chapter specifically focuses on two sub-areas of nature-inspired computing: Evolutionary Algorithms and Swarm Intelligence.

INTRODUCTION

Information and data continue to overwhelm humans. Yet, this same information and data often holds the key of success to many human endeavors through the patterns they contain. Unfortunately, the rate at which information overwhelms humans is significantly more than the rate at which humans have learned to process, analyze, and leverage this information. To overcome this challenge, new methods of computing must be formulated, and scientist and engineers have looked to nature for inspiration in developing these new methods.

For centuries, nature has amazed and inspired humanity. From paintings to sculptures to weapons of war, evidence of this inspiration from nature abounds. Now, as computing technology continues to advance, this inspiration continues. Evolutionary computing has emerged as new paradigm for computing and has rapidly demonstrated its ability to solve real-world problems where traditional techniques have failed. This field of work has now become quite broad and encompasses areas ranging from artificial life to neural networks. This chapter focuses specifically on two sub-areas of nature-inspired computing: Evolutionary Algorithms and Swarm Intelligence.

The following sections will discuss the theoretical background of these sub-areas as well demonstrate some real-world applications based on each. Finally, the chapter will conclude with future trends and directions in these areas.

EVOLUTIONARY ALGORITHMS

Charles Darwin radically changed the way evolutionary biology is viewed in his work entitled "Origin of Species" published in 1859 (Darwin, 1859). In this work, Darwin describes his theory of natural selection based on his experience and observations of nature around the world. Darwin states that there is an implicit struggle for survival because of species producing more offspring than can grow to adulthood and that food sources are limited. Because of this implicit struggle, sexually reproducing species create offspring that are genetic variants of the parents. Darwin theorizes that it is this genetic variation that enables some offspring to survive in a particular environment much better than other offspring with different genetic variations. As a direct result of this "enhanced"

genetic variation, these offspring not only survive in the environment, but go on to reproduce new offspring that carry some form of this enhanced genetic variation. In addition, those offspring that are not as suited for the environment do not pass on their genetic variation to offspring, but rather die off. Darwin then theorizes that over many generations of reproduction, new species that are highly adapted to their specific environments will emerge. It is this theory of natural selection that forms the theoretical foundation for the field of Evolutionary Algorithms (EA).

Following in the footsteps of Darwin, John Holland dramatically altered the computer science and artificial intelligence fields in 1975 with his publication entitled "Adaptation in Natural and Artificial Systems" (Holland 1975). In this work, Holland describes a mathematical model for the evolutionary process of natural selection, and demonstrates its use in a variety of problem domains. This seminal work by Holland created the fertile soil by which the field of Evolutionary Algorithms grew and thrived. In the same year and under the direction of Holland, Ken De Jong's dissertation entitled "An Analysis of the Behavior of a Class of Genetic Adaptive Systems" helps fully demonstrate the possibilities of using evolutionary algorithms for problem solving (De Jong, 1975). In 1989, the field of evolutionary algorithms received a fresh injection of enthusiasm with the publication of David Goldberg's work entitled "Genetic Algorithms in Search, Optimization, and Machine Learning" (Goldberg, 1989). The momentum of development continued with Melanie Mitchell's 1996 work entitled "An Introduction to Genetic Algorithms," which helped to further solidify the theoretical foundations of EAs (Mitchell, 1996). Ever since then, the field has continued to grow and the practical applications of EA's are abounding with success stories (Chambers, 2000; Coley, 2001; Haupt, 1998).

With the explosive growth of the EA field, there has also been an expansion in the variety of EA types. Some of these variations include genetic algorithms (GAs), evolutionary strategy (ES), genetic programming (GP), and learning classifier systems (LCS). In addition to these, a new variety is beginning to emerge known as quantum-inspired EA (QEA) (Han, 2003). The primary distinction between each of these is the representation used for the population of individuals. For example, GAs are traditionally associated with using a binary number representation, while GPs use a tree structure to represent individuals. In some cases, such as LCS, a distinction is also made in the form of the fitness function used to evaluate the individual. These different forms of EAs are necessary to solve different types of problems depending on the domain. Despite these differences, the fundamental philosophy behind each is the same: natural selection and survival of the fittest.

In brief, an EA is a search algorithm, but with key features that distinguish it from other search methods including:

- A population of individuals where each individual represents a potential solution to the problem to be solved
- A fitness function that evaluates the utility of each individual as a solution
- A selection function that selects individuals for reproduction based on their fitness.
- Idealized genetic operators that alter selected individuals to create new individuals for further testing. These operators, e.g. crossover

and mutation, attempt to explore the search space without completely losing information (partial solutions) that is already found.

Figure 1 illustrates the basic steps of an EA. The population may be initialized either randomly or with user-defined individuals. The EA then iterates through an evaluate-select-reproduce cycle until either a user-defined stopping condition is satisfied or the maximum number of allowed generations is exceeded.

The use of a population allows the EA to perform parallel searches into multiple regions of the solution space. Operators such as crossover allow the EA to combine discovered partial solutions into more complete solutions. As a result, the EA searches for small building blocks in parallel, then iteratively recombine small building blocks to form larger and larger building blocks. In the process, the EA attempts to maintain a balance between explorations for new information and exploitation of existing information. Over time, the EA is able to evolve populations containing more fit individuals or better solutions. For more information about EAs, the reader is referred to (Coley, 2001; Mitchell, 1996).

SWARM INTELLIGENCE

More than 50 years ago, biologists have reported that a different kind of intelligence form could

Figure 1. Basic steps of a typical evolutionary algorithm

```
procedure EA
{
        initialize population;
        while termination condition not satisfied do
        {
                evaluate current population;
                select parents;
                apply genetic operators to parents to create
offspring;
                set current population equal to be the new
offspring population;
        }
```

emerge from some social insects, fish, birds, and mammals (Bonabeau, Dorigo et al., 1999; Bonabeau, Henaux et al., 1998). Inside an anthill, a termite swarm, a bee colony, a bird flock, or a fish school, each individual does not have the requisite neuronal capacity. However, the mere interaction among a great number of individually simple creatures can lead to the emergence of intelligence, which is reactive and adaptable to the environment (Bonabeau et al., 1999). In insect societies, the whole system is organized in a decentralized model. A large amount of autonomous units with a relatively simple and probabilistic behavior is distributed in the environment. Each unit is provided only with local information. Units do not have any representation or explicit knowledge of the global structure they are supposed to produce or in which they evolve. They have no plan at all. In other words, the global "task" is not programmed explicitly within individuals, but emerges after the succession of a high number of elementary interactions between individuals, or between individual and environment. This type of collective intelligence model built from multiple simple individual entities inspired a new discipline in computer science: Swarm Intelligence (SI).

Swarm Intelligence is an artificial intelligence technique involving studies of collective behaviors in decentralized systems. It is the modeling and application of group interactions found in social insects (Dorigo, Bonabeau et al. 2000). Beni and Wang (Wang & Beni, 1988, 1989, 1990) first introduced the term of Swarm Intelligence in the context of cellular robotic systems. In their experiments, many agents occupy one or two-dimensional environments to generate patterns and to self-organize through interaction with the nearest neighbor. Bonabeau (Bonabeau et al., 1999; Bonabeau et al., 1998) extended the concept of swarm intelligence to any work involved with algorithm design or distributed problem-solving devices. He gave a definition of Swarm Intelligence as "any attempt to design algorithms or distributed problem-solving devices inspired by

the collective behavior of social insect colonies and other animal societies." This last definition is wider and more up-to-date than the original one that only referred to the cellular robotics framework.

Currently, popular research directions in Swarm Intelligence are grounded on following four research areas: Flocking (Reynolds, 1987), Swarm Robotics (Wang & Beni, 1988, 1990), Ant Colony Optimization (ACO) (Bonabeau et al., 1999) and Particle Swarm Optimization (PSO) (Eberhart & Kennedy, 1995).

Flocking

Flocking model was first proposed by Craig Reynolds(Reynolds, 1987). It is a bio-inspired computational model for simulating the animation of a flock of entities called "boid." It represents group movement as seen in bird flocks and schools of fish in nature. In this model, each boid makes its own decisions on its movement according to a small number of simple rules that react to the neighboring mates in the flock and the environment it can sense. The simple local rules of each boid generate complex global behaviors of the entire flock.

The Flocking model consists of three simple steering rules that need to be executed at each instance over time. Three basic rules include: (1) Separation: Steering to avoid collision with other boids nearby. (2) Alignment: Steering toward the average heading and match the velocity of the neighbor flock mates. (3) Cohesion: Steering to the average position of the neighbor flock mates. The three basic rules are sufficient to reproduce the moving behaviors of a single species bird flock on the computer. However, experiments indicate these three rules will eventually result in all boids in the simulation forming a single flock. It cannot reproduce the real phenomena in the nature: the birds or other herd animals not only keep themselves within a flock that is composed of the same species or the same colony creatures,

Ant Colony Optimization

The Ant Colony Optimization is a heuristic algorithm that is inspired from the food foraging behavior of ants. Ant colonies would be able to accomplish tasks that would be impossible to be accomplished by a single individual ant. One type of task is seeking the shortest path from their nest to the food source. As ants forage they deposit a trail of slowly evaporating pheromone. Ants then use the pheromone as a guide for them to find the between the nest and the food source if they find one. All foraging ants use the pheromone as a guide regardless of whether the pheromone is deposited by itself or other ants. Pheromones accumulate when multiple ants travel through same path. The pheromones on the tail evaporate as well. Those ants that reach the food first return before the others. Their return trail's pheromone is now stronger than the other ant trails that have not found food or have longer distances from the food source to nest because the return trail has been traveled twice. This high pheromone volume trail attracts other ants following the trail. The pheromone content on this trail become stronger as the trail is increasing traveled and other trail's pheromone content will become weaker because fewer ants travel those trails and pheromone evaporates. Eventually, the trail with highest content of pheromone and traveled by most of foraging ants will be shortest tail between food sources to nest.

Marco Dorigo introduced the first ACO system in his Ph.D. thesis (Dorigo, 1992). The idea of the ACO algorithm is to mimic the ant's foraging behavior with "simulated ants" walking around the graph searching for the optimal solution. In the ACO algorithm, each path followed by a "simulated ant" represents a candidate solution for a given problem. The simulated ant "deposits" pheromone on the path and the volume of the pheromone is proportional to the quality of the corresponding candidate solution for the target problem. The searching ants choose the path(s) with the higher volume of pheromone with greater probability than the path(s) with low pheromone volume. Eventually, the searching ants will converge on the path that represent the optimum or near optimum solution for the target problem.

Particle Swarm Optimization

Particle Swarm Optimization is a population based stochastic optimization technique that can be used to find an optimal, or near optimal, solution to a numerical and qualitative problem. PSO was originally developed by Eberhart and Kennedy in 1995 (Eberhart & Kennedy, 1995), inspired by the social behavior of flocking birds or a school of fish.

In the PSO algorithm, birds in a flock are symbolically represented as particles. These particles can be considered as simple agents "flying" through a problem space. A problem space in PSO may have as many dimensions as needed to model the problem space. A particle's location in the multi-dimensional problem space represents one solution for the problem. When a particle moves to a new location, a different solution is generated. This solution is evaluated by a fitness function that provides a quantitative value of the solution's utility.

The velocity and direction of each particle moving along each dimension of the problem space are altered at each generation of movement. It is the particle's personal experience combined with its neighbors' experience that influences the movement of each particle through a problem space. For every generation, the particle's new location is computed by adding the particle's current velocity V-vector to its location X-vector.

Mathematically, given a multi-dimensional problem space, the $i th$ particle changes its velocity and location according to the following equations (Clerc, 1999; Clerc & Kennedy, 2002):

$$v_{id} = w * (v_{id} + c_1 * rand_1 * (p_{id} - x_{id}) + c_2 * rand (p_{gd} - x_{id}))$$

Equation 1

$$x_{id} = x_{id} + v_{id}$$

Equation 2

where, p_{id} is the location of the particle where it experiences the best fitness value; p_{gd} is the location of the particle experienced the highest best fitness value in the whole population; x_{id} is the particle current location; c_1 and c_2 are two positive acceleration constants; d is the number of dimensions of the problem space; $rand_1$, $rand_2$ are random values in the range of (0,1); v_{id} is the particle current velocity. w is called the constriction coefficient (Clerc & Kennedy, 2002) and it is computed according to Equation 3:

$$w = \frac{2}{2 - \varphi - \sqrt{\varphi^2 - 4\varphi}}$$

Equation 3

$$\varphi = c1 + c2, \varphi > 4$$

Equation 4

PSO versus Evolutionary Computing

PSO shares many similarities with evolutionary computational techniques. Both systems are initialized with a collection of random solutions for searching the optima in a problem space by updating generations. However, unlike most other population-based evolutionary algorithms, PSO is motivated by cooperative social behavior instead of survival of the fittest. In evolutionary computation, the solution change is driven by the genetic recombination and mutations. In the case of PSO, it is by learning from peers. Each particle in PSO has memory to track the best solution it has experienced, as well as that of its

neighbors. This history of the best solutions plays an important role in generating a new position, that is, a potential problem solution.

APPLICATIONS OF EA AND SI

To illustrate the value of EA and SI techniques for revealing data patterns, this section discusses two different methods for analyzing data. For each of these methods, the focus area is that of text analysis. However, their applicability is not limited to this domain.

In text analysis, there is a variety of challenges. For illustration purposes, the primary challenge is that a massive data set in the form of unstructured text within individual documents must be analyzed. For example, a data set may consist of 1,000 documents (of various lengths), and a human must analyze and understand the data that is contained within these 1,000 documents. To make matters more complicated, this document set may even be streaming, so that 1,000 documents may arrive every hour from various sources. To address this daunting challenge, this section will illustrate the application of EA and SI for pattern analysis.

Adaptive Sampling using an Evolutionary Algorithm

To characterize effectively a large and streaming set of news articles, the following goals are proposed in order to create an algorithm that provides a useful result to a human analyst, it must:

1. Be capable of sufficiently reducing the data to manageable levels
2. Be able to provide a fast and accurate processing of massive amounts of data
3. Efficiently and effectively deal with duplicate data

4. Be able to work with streaming data
5. Not require prior knowledge concerning the data set

To address the five goals identified, an evolutionary algorithm will be discussed that performs an adaptive, maximum variation sampling (MVS) technique. This technique is a sampling technique and therefore does not require prior knowledge of the data set, and will naturally reduce the data set to the appropriate size as determined by the analysts.

Two of the most critical components of implementing a GA are the encoding of the problem domain into the GA population and the fitness function to be used for evaluating individuals in the population. To encode the data for this particular problem domain, each individual in the population represents one sample of size N. Each individual consists of N genes where each gene represents one document (each document is given a unique numeric identifier) in the sample. For example, if the sample size were 15, each individual would represent one possible sample and consist of 15 genes that represent 15 different documents. This representation is shown in Figure 2.

The fitness function evaluates each individual according to some predefined set of constraints or goals. In this particular application, the goal was to achieve an ideal sample that represents the maximum variation of the data set without applying clustering techniques or without prior knowledge of what the categories of the population are. To measure the variation (or diversity) of our samples, the summation of the similarity

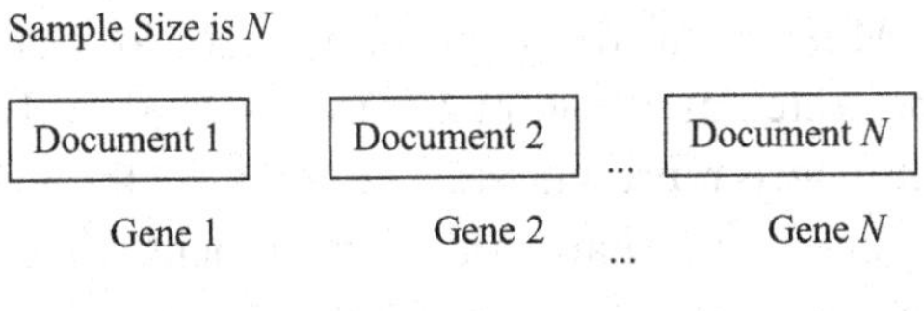

Equation 5. Fitness function

$$Fitness(i) = \sum_{j=0}^{N} \sum_{k=j+1}^{N} Similarity(Gene(i,j), Gene(i,k))$$

between the vector space models of each document (or gene) in the sample is calculated as shown in Equation 5.

In Equation 5, the Similarity function calculates the distance between the vector space models of gene j and k of the individual i. The vector space models are represented in Equation 5 as Gene(i, j) and Gene(i, k), respectively. This distance value ranges between 0 and 1 with 1 meaning that the two documents are identical and 0 meaning they are completely different in terms of the words used in that document. This similarity is based on the words used in the content of the documents. Therefore, in order to find a sample with the maximum variation, Equation 5 must be minimized. In this fitness function, there will be $(N^2 - N) / 2$ comparisons for each sample to be evaluated.

The defined fitness function can be computationally intensive for large sample sizes or for data sets with lengthy news articles. To compensate for this, the GA developed for this work was designed as a global population parallel GA. For this particular work, the selection process used an "above average" measure for the selection. For each generation, an average fitness value is calculated for the population. Individuals with fitness values that are above this average are selected as parents, while the other individuals are discarded. The crossover and mutation operators are 1-point operators. The crossover rate was set to 0.6. The mutation rate was set to 0.01.

The data set used for the tests described previously was the Reuters-21578 Distribution 1.0 document collection (Lewis, 1997). This corpus consists of 21,578 Reuters news articles from 1987 and was specifically developed for categorization research purposes. As a result, this corpus includes additional information concerning the documents

Figure 2. Genetic representation of each individual

Sample Size is N

Document 1	Document 2	...	Document N
Gene 1	Gene 2	...	Gene N

Table 1. List of tests performed

Test Num.	Corpus Size	Sample Size	Known Duplicates
1-3	1,000	15	No
4-6	9,494	135	No
7-9	21,578	200	No
10-12	1,000	15	Yes
13-15	9,494	135	Yes

in the set. This corpus was chosen due to its availability, its size and for the additional information (e.g., category information) for each document, which will be used for future comparisons and research. To evaluate the performance of this implementation, several tests were conducted, and are briefly summarized in the following table.

For each test, ten runs were performed with a population size of 100 and 100 generations. However, on test 7 – 9, only three runs of 400 generations each with a population size of 100 were performed due to time constraints. After conducting the defined test and analyzing the results, several interesting observations are evident. The hypothesis that the MVS-GA would be "immune" to duplicate data or take advantage of it did appear to hold true. There is a very slight decrease in fitness values as duplicates are added. While this is not as big of a decrease as was expected, it still supports the hypothesis that the MVS-GA is not dramatically affected by duplicate data. In addition, this approach successfully reduces massive data amounts to manageable levels. Finally, while the results demonstrated several significant relationships and behaviors, future work will be needed to further understand these relationships and to develop improved parameter control functions.

Distributed Flocking Algorithm for Information Stream Clustering Analysis

Document clustering analysis plays an important role in improving the accuracy of information retrieval. In this section, a novel Flocking-based algorithm for document clustering analysis is presented. This approach uses principles discovered from observing bird flocks or fish schools. Inspired by the self-organized behavior of bird flocks, each document object is represented as a flock boid (i.e., bird). The simple local rules followed by each flock boid results in the entire document flock generating complex global behaviors, which eventually result in a clustering of the documents. The efficiency of the algorithm is evaluated with both a synthetic dataset and a real document collection that includes 100 news articles collected from the Internet. Results show that the Flocking-clustering algorithm achieves better performance compared to the K-means and the Ant clustering algorithm for real document clustering.

In (Cui, Gao et al. 2006), a new Multiple Species Flocking (MSF) model is proposed to model the multiple species bird flock behaviors. In the MSF model, in addition to the three basic action rules in the Flocking model, a fourth rule, "feature similarity rule," is added into the basic action rules of each boid to influence the motion of the boids. Based on this rule, the flock boid tries to stay close to other boids that have similar features and stay away from other boids that have dissimilar features. The strength of the attracting force for similar boids and repulsion force for dissimilar boids is inversely proportional to the distance between the boids and the similarity value between the boids' features.

One application of the MSF model is document clustering (Cui & Potok 2006). Inspired by the bird's ability of maintaining a flock as well as separating different species or colony flocks, the MSF clustering algorithm uses a simple and heuristic way to cluster document datasets. In the MSF clustering algorithm, each document is projected as a boid in a 2D virtual space. The document is represented as the feature of the boid. The boids that share similar document features (same as the bird's species and colony in nature) will automatically group together and became a boid flock. Other boids that have different document features will stay away from this flock. After several iterations, the simple local rules followed by each boid results in generating complex global behaviors of the entire document flock, and eventually a document clustering result is emerged.

One synthetic dataset and one real document collection dataset were used for evaluating the performance of the clustering algorithms. The synthetic dataset consists of four data types, each including 200 two dimensional (x, y) data objects. x and y are distributed according to Normal distribution. This is the same dataset that has been used by Lumer and Faieta (1994)for their Ant clustering algorithm. There are many references in the document clustering literature (Handl & Meyer, 2002; Ramos & Merelo, 2002) to the use of this synthetic dataset as a performance evaluation benchmark. In the real document collection dataset, a document collection that contains 100 news articles was used. These articles are collected from the Internet at different time stages and have been categorized by human experts and manually clustered into 12 categories. A description of the test dataset is given in Table 2.

Table 2. The document collection dataset

	Category/Topic	Number of articles
1	Airline Safety	10
2	Amphetamine	10
3	China and Spy Plane and Captives	4
4	Hoof and Mouth Disease	9
5	Hurricane Katrina	5
6	Iran Nuclear	8
7	Korea and Nuclear Capability	10
8	Mortgage Rates	10
9	Ocean and Pollution	6
10	Saddam Hussein and WMD	8
11	Storm Irene	10
12	Volcano	10

In order to reduce the impact of the length variations of different documents, each document vector is normalized so that it is of unit length. Each term represents one dimension in the document vector space. The total number of terms in the 100 stripped test documents is 4,790, which means the document collection has 4,790 dimensions.

The different clustering methods were evaluated over data sets representing distinct clustering difficulties in the same experimental conditions in order to appreciate better the performance of each clustering algorithm. The number of iterations in each algorithm was fixed at 300 iterations. First, the K-Means, Ant clustering, and Flocking clustering were evaluated over the synthetic dataset. Second, the algorithms were tested over the real document datasets. For each dataset, each algorithm was run 20 times and the mean number of clusters found (since the K-Means algorithm uses the prior knowledge of the cluster number of the data collection, the clustering number it produces is exactly equal to the real class number) and the F-measure of the clustering results. Table 3 shows the results obtained from both the synthetic and the real datasets. The three clustering algorithms all work well in the synthetic dataset. When these three algorithms are applied to the 100 news article dataset, according to the results shown in Table 3, it was determined that 300 iterations was not enough for the Ant clustering algorithm to generate an acceptable clustering result. However, 300 iterations are sufficient for the Flocking-clustering algorithm to generate good clustering results from the document dataset.

Results show that the K-means algorithm implementation needs much less computing time and iterations to reach a stable clustering result than the other two algorithms. However, the drawback of the K-means clustering algorithm is that the average F-measure value of the clustering results are lower than Flocking algorithm. The K-means algorithm also requires the probable number of clusters of a dataset before clustering it. For the Flocking clustering implementation and the Ant clustering implementation, the major computing time cost is the document similarity and dissimilarity calculations. Our experiment results show that it takes both implementations nearly same computing time to finish the initial 20-30 iterations. However, after that, the flocking implementation's computing time of each iteration quickly increases. The reason for this is that, in the Flocking implementation, the clustering result is generated very quickly and the boids with similar features quickly converge together, therefore, boids need to calculate the similarity values with multiple neighboring flock mates during the cluster refining stage. For the Ant clustering algorithm implementation, our experiments show that even after thousands of iterations, the implementation still cannot generate an acceptable visual clustering result. The fact that, after several thousands of iterations, the computing time of each iteration is still low may indicate most document objects are still randomly distributed in the grid space.

The advantage of the Flocking-clustering algorithm is the heuristic principle of the flock's searching mechanism. This heuristic searching mechanism helps boids quickly form a flock. Results from experiments evaluating these three different clustering algorithms illustrate that the Flocking-clustering algorithm can generate a better clustering result with fewer iterations than that of the Ant clustering algorithm. The clustering results generated by the Flocking algorithm can be easily visualized and recognized by an untrained human user. Since the boid in the algorithm continues flying in the virtual space and joining the flock it belongs to, new results can be quickly re-generated when adding or deleting document boids at run time. This feature allows the Flocking algorithm to be applied in clustering and analyzing dynamically changing information stream and real time visualizing of results for a human.

FUTURE TRENDS & CONCLUSION

As discussed in the previous sections, the area of Evolutionary Computing is rich in application, and has very rapidly become a new paradigm for computing. However, the potential for such computing has not been completely harnessed. Several areas are now emerging that will extend the power of Evolutionary Computing even further. For example, Quantum-Inspired Evolutionary Algorithms are currently being explored and show tremendous promise based on its novel representation schema. Much of the driving force behind these areas stems from the challenge of dynamic and multi-objective optimization problems. Consequently, the future trends of EC will involve hybrid approaches that leverage the strengths of each technique to create a new technique that will be more robust to changing problem spaces. For example, SI techniques that can learn and adapt via the use of EA techniques, or EA techniques that utilize SI techniques for evaluating potential solutions. In addition, creative evolutionary techniques will be explored that will help expand the capability of current EC technique to create new hypothetical solutions that even the EC designers would not have imagined. These future capabilities will only strengthen the value of EC for data pattern analysis.

Table 3. The results of K-means, ant clustering and flocking clustering algorithm on synthetic and real datasets after 300 iterations

	Algorithms	Average cluster number	Average F-measure value
Synthetic Dataset	Flocking	4	0.9997
	K-means	(4)	0.9879
	Ant	4	0.9823
Real	Flocking	10.083	0.8058
	K-means	(12)	0.6684
	Ant	1	0.1623

REFERENCES

Bonabeau, E., Henaux, F., Guerin S., Snyers, D., Kuntz, P., & Theraulaz, G. (1998). *Routing in telecommunications networks with ant-like agents*. 1437: 60.

Bonabeau, E., Dorigo, M., et al. (1999). *Swarm intelligence from natural to artificial systems*. New York, Oxford University Press.

Chambers, L.(Ed.) (2000). *The practical handbook of genetic algorithms: Applications, Second Edition*. Chapman & Hall / CRC.

Clerc, M. (1999). The swarm and the queen: Towards a deterministic and adaptive particle swarm optimization. *Proceedings of the 1999 Congress on Evolutionary Computation*, Washington, DC, IEEE.

Clerc, M. & Kennedy, J. (2002). The particle swarm-explosion, stability, and convergence in a multidimensional complex space. *IEEE Transactions on Evolutionary Computation*, 6(1), 58-73.

Coley, D.A. (2001). *An introduction to genetic algorithms for scientists and engineers*. River Edge, NJ: World Scientific.

Cui, X., Gao, J., Potok, T. E. (2006). A flocking based algorithm for document clustering analysis. *Journal of System Architecture* (Special issue on Nature Inspired Applied Systems).

Cui, X. & Potok, T. E. (2006). A distributed flocking approach for information stream clustering analysis. *Proceedings of the Seventh ACIS International Conference on Software Engineering, Artificial Intelligence, Networking, and Parallel/Distributed Computing (SNPD'06)*. Las Vegas, NV, United States, IEEE Computer Society.

Darwin, C. (1859). *On the origin of species by means of natural selection, or the preservation of favoured races in the struggle for life*. London: John Murray.

De Jong, K. (1975). *An analysis of the behavior of a class of genetic adaptive systems*. Doctoral Dissertation, University of Michigan.

Dorigo, M. (1992). *Optimization, learning and natural algorithms* (in Italian). Doctoral Dissertation, Dipartimento di Elettronica, Politecnico di Milano, Milan, Italy.

Dorigo, M., Bonabeau, E., & Theraulaz, G. (2000). Ant algorithms and stigmergy. *Future Generation Computer Systems, 16*(8), 851-871.

Eberhart, R. & Kennedy, J. (1995). A new optimizer using particle swarm theory. *Proceedings of the Sixth International Symposium on Micro Machine and Human Science*, Nagoya, Japan, IEEE.

Goldberg, D.E. (1989). *Genetic algorithms in search, optimization, and machine learning*. Addison-Wesley.

Han, K.H. (2003). *Quantum-inspired evolutionary algorithm*. Doctoral Dissertation, Korea Advanced Institute of Science and Technology.

Handl, J. & Meyer, B. (2002). *Improved ant-based clustering and sorting in a document retrieval interface*. Granada, Spain: Springer-Verlag.

Haupt, R.L. & Haupt, S.E. (1998). *Practical genetic algorithms*. New York: John Wiley & Sons, Inc.

Holland, J.H. (1975). *Adaptation in natural and artificial systems*. University of Michigan Press.

Lewis, D.D. (1997). *Reuters-21578 Distribution 1.0*. Retrieved March 2007 from http://kdd.ics.uci.edu/databases/reuters21578/

Lumer, E. D. & Faieta, B. (1994). Diversity and adaptation in populations of clustering ants. *Proceedings of 3rd International Conference on Simulation of Adaptive Behaviour*, August 8-12, Brighton, UK, MIT Press.

Mitchell, M. (1996). *An introduction to genetic algorithms*. MIT Press.

Ramos, V. & Merelo, J. (2002). Self-organized stigmergic document maps: Environment as a mechanism for context learning. *1st Spanish Conference on Evolutionary and Bio-Inspired Algorithms*, Merida, Spain.

Reynolds, C. W. (1987). Flocks, herds, and schools: A distributed behavioral model. *Computer Graphics (ACM), 21*(4), 25-34.

Wang, J. & Beni, G. (1988). *Pattern generation in cellular robotic systems.* Arlington, VA/Piscataway, NJ: IEEE.

Wang, J. & Beni, G. (1989). *Cellular robotic system with stationary robots and its application to manufacturing lattices.* Albany, NY/Piscataway, NJ: IEEE.

Wang, J. & Beni, G. (1990). *Distributed computing problems in cellular robotic systems.* Ibaraki, Japan: IEEE.

Chapter IX
Particle Identification Using Light Scattering:
A Global Optimization Problem

M.C. Bartholomew-Biggs
University of Hertfordshire, Hatfield, UK

Z. Ulanowski
University of Hertfordshire, Hatfield, UK

S. Zakovic
Imperial College, UK

ABSTRACT

We discuss some experience of solving an inverse light scattering problem for single, spherical, homogeneous particles using least squares global optimization. If there is significant noise in the data, the particle corresponding to the "best" solution may not correspond well to the "actual" particle. One way of overcoming this difficulty involves the use of peak positions in the experimental data as a means of distinguishing genuine from spurious solutions. We introduce two composite approaches which combine conventional data fitting with peak-matching and show that they lead to a more robust identification procedure.

INTRODUCTION

Developments in the theory of light scattering from particulate matter mean that, in many situations, we can accurately compute the properties of scat-tered electromagnetic fields. There are rigorous solutions to this *direct scattering problem* for numerous particle types, such as homogeneous and inhomogeneous spheres, ellipsoids, and others. However it is the *inverse scattering problem* that is of greater practical importance. This involves the determination of properties of scatterers from the knowledge of scattered fields. Here, we will concentrate on the case where the angular dependence of the scattered field is known. This type of problem arises in numerous applications, ranging from astronomy and remote sensing, through aerosol and emulsion characterization, to non-destructive analysis of single particles and living cells (Barth & Flippen, 1995; De Pieri, Ludlow, & Waites, 1993; Gousbet & Grehan, 1988; Hull & Quinby-Hunt, 1997; Kolesnikova, Potapov, Yurkin, Hoekstra, Maltsev, & Semyanov, 2006; Nascimento, Guardani, & Giulietti, 1997; Semyanov, Tarasov, Soini, Petrov, & Maltsev, 2000; Ulanowski, Ludlow, & Waites, 1987; Ulanowski & Ludlow, 1989; Wyatt, 1980).

The inverse problem has proved to be much harder to solve, even for the simplest particle shapes. Some approaches are based on generating solutions to the direct problem (after making assumptions concerning the shape, internal structure of the particle, etc.) and matching these solutions to experimental data (Ulanowski 1988; Ulanowski & Ludlow, 1989; Wyatt, 1980). More recently, various neural network methods have been used (Berdnik, Gilev, Shvalov, Maltsev, & Loiko, 2006; Hull & Quinby-Hunt, 1997; Nascimento et al., 1997; Ulanowski, Wang, Kaye, & Ludlow, 1998). The inverse scattering problem has also been approached using global minimization of a sum of squares error function (Zakovic, 1997; Zakovic, Ulanowski, & Bartholomew-Biggs, 1998). In this chapter we consider ways of counteracting the influence of data noise when using this approach. We use ideas discussed by Bartholomew-Biggs, Ulanowski, and Zakovic (2005) and apply them in the context of unconstrained optimization of a composite performance function which seeks to match the experimental data in more than one way.

Experimental data are inevitably distorted by the presence of noise and numerous sources of error. These include optical aberrations, nonlin-earity of the detection system, multiple scattering, and particle nonsphericity. All existing inversion algorithms are sensitive to such distortion to a greater or lesser extent, which results in error (Gousbet & Grehan 1988; Shimizu & Ishimaru, 1990). This problem is especially acute in, but not limited to, measurements on single particles, and we will confine ourselves to this case.

A good starting point for the development of methods for solving the inverse scattering problem for small particles is the case of a homogeneous, isotropic, non-absorbing sphere. If there is a known medium surrounding the particle and if we assume a plane incident wave of known wave-length and state of polarization then the particle can be completely described using its radius r and refractive index n.. The direct problem then can be solved using the series expansions of Lorenz-Mie theory (e.g., Bohren & Huffman, 1983). In the scattering geometry considered in the present study, the intensity of the light scattered by the particle is measured in one plane only and can be regarded as a function of the scattering angle $I_1(\theta) = j(\theta, r, n)$ (θ being the angle between the direction of propagation of the incident wave and the direction of observation). This arrangement leads to a one-dimensional scattering pattern which is representative of the properties of the particle and has been used as a basis for characterization of both single particles and particle distributions (Barth & Flippen, 1995, Dubovik, Sinyuk, Lapyonok, Holben, Mishchenko, Yang, 2006; Gousbet & Grehan, 1988; Hull & Quinby-Hunt, 1997; Maltsev & Lopatin, 1997, Nascimento et al., 1997; Semyanov et al., 2000; Ulanowski & Ludlow, 1989; Vargas-Ubera, Aguilar, & Gale, 2007; Wyatt, 1980). Typical scattering patterns are shown in Figures 4.1 – 4.4. We should note that although the present work concentrates on multi-angle scattering data, the results should also be applicable to some extent to multi-wavelength measurements.

We now give a brief outline of the Lorenz-Mie model of intensity to indicate the work involved in a typical function evaluation in the global optimization calculations discussed below. Suppose the incident light has intensity I_0 and wavelength *in vacuo* λ. Suppose also that the refractive index of the scattering medium is n_0. If we let R be the radial coordinate and write $k = 2\pi n_0 / \lambda$ then the intensity of scattered light is given by

$$I_1 = I_0 / \{ k^2 R^2 |S_1|^2 \}$$

where $S_1 = \sum_j \dfrac{2j+1}{j(j+1)} (a_j \pi_j + b_j \tau_j)$.

The values of π_j and τ_j depend on the scattering angle θ and are obtained from recurrence relations involving Legendre polynomials π_j. Specifically

$$\pi_j = (2_j - 1) P_j + \pi_{j-2} \text{ and } \tau_j = j(j+1) P_j - \pi_j \cos\theta$$

with initial conditions $\pi_0 = 0$, $\pi_1 = 1$, $\tau_0 = 0$, $\tau_1 = \cos\theta$. The values of a_j, b_j depend on Bessel-Riccati functions

$$\psi_j = \sqrt{x} J_{j+\frac{1}{2}}(x) \text{ and } \chi_j(x) = \sqrt{x} Y_{j+\frac{1}{2}}(x)$$

where J and Y respectively denote half-order Bessel functions of the first and second kinds. If we now define the relative refractive index $n_r = n/n_0$, set the function argument to be the sphere size parameter $x = kr$, and let $\xi_j = \psi_j(x) + i\chi_j(x)$ then

$$a_j = \frac{(n_r \psi_j(n_r x) \psi'_j(x) - \psi_j(x) \psi_j(n_r x))}{(n_r \psi_j(n_r x) \chi'_j(x) - \chi_j(x) \psi_j(n_r x))}$$

and

$$b_j = \frac{(\psi_j(n_r x) \psi'_j(x) - n_r \psi_j(x) \psi_j(n_r x))}{(\psi_j(n_r x) \chi'_j(x) - n_r \chi_j(x) \psi_j(n_r x))}$$

The summation for S_1 continues until the magnitudes of a_j, b_j are sufficiently small. We note that the computation of objective function gradients can be speeded up through the use of analytic derivatives of the coefficients a_j, b_j with respect to the independent variables describing particle properties (Grainger, Lucas, Thomas & Ewen, 2004).

PARTICLE IDENTIFICATION USING LEAST-SQUARES

Given a set of experimental measures of scattered light intensity $I_1(\theta_1), ..., I_1(\theta_m)$ we wish to determine corresponding values for r and n. A standard approach involves finding r and n to minimize the function

$$E_1 = \sum_{i=1}^{m} (I_1(\theta_i) - k\varphi(\theta, r, n))^2 \qquad (2.1)$$

where $I_1(\theta) = \varphi(\theta, r, n)$ denotes the Lorenz-Mie model of light-scattering (Bohren & Huffman, 1983). The additional variable k appears in (2.1) because experimental measurements usually give only relative intensities at the angles θ_i and so a scaling is necessary to match the theoretical model. This model is valid for the situations we wish to consider which involve refractive indices, n, and radii, r, such that $1.34 \leq n \leq 1.675$ and $0.52\ \mu m \leq r \leq 2\mu m$. These ranges are appropriate for living cells suspended in water. The lower limit on r is the wavelength of the incident light.

Since, in practice, the intensities may vary widely in magnitude over the typical range $0^0 \leq \theta_i \leq 180^o$, experimental results are often presented in the form $\log I_l$ against θ. Hence we may need to consider an objective function of the form

$$E_2 = \sum_{i=1}^{m} (i(\theta_i) - \psi(\theta_i, r, n) - c)^2 \qquad (2.2)$$

which is related to (2.1) via $i = \log I_1$, $\psi = \log\varphi$, $c = \log k$. The minimization of either E_1 or E_2 can be reduced to a two-variable problem. In the case of E_1 we can write

$$\frac{\partial E_1}{\partial k} = -2 \sum_{i=1}^{m} \varphi(\theta_i, r, n)(I_1(\theta_i) - k\varphi(\theta_i, r, n))$$

and since this must be zero at the minimum of (2.1) we can obtain the optimal value of k in terms of the other two variables:

$$k = \frac{\sum_{i=1}^{m} \varphi(\theta, r, n)(I_1(\theta))}{\sum_{i=1}^{m} \varphi(\theta, r, n)^2}.$$

In a similar way we obtain the optimal value for c in (2.2) as

$$c = \frac{1}{m} \sum_{i=1}^{m} (i(\theta_i) - \psi(\theta_i, r, n)) \qquad (2.3)$$

There are a number of optimization techniques which can be used to minimize (2.2). However, since this is a sum of squared terms, an obvious choice would be the Gauss-Newton method. Briefly, this minimizes functions of the form

$$F(x) = \sum_{i=1}^{m} f_i(x)^2$$

using the fact that

$$\nabla F(x) = 2J^T f(x)$$

and $\nabla^2 F(x) = 2J^T J + \sum_{i=1}^{m} f_i(x) \nabla^2 f_i(x)$

where $f(x)$ denotes $(f_1(x),...,f_m(x))^T$ and $J(x)$ is the Jacobian matrix whose (i,j)-th element is $\partial f_i(x)/\partial x_j$. If the minimum value of F is near-zero and/or the subfunctions f_i are near-linear then the second term in $\nabla^2 F(x)$ may be neglected; and hence we can use an approximate form of the Newton iteration which avoids the computation of second derivatives. The Gauss-Newton iteration is

$$x^{(k+1)} = x^{(k)} + \alpha d^{(k)} \qquad (2.4)$$

where

$$d^{(k)} = -(J^{(k)T} J^{(k)})^{-1} J^{(k)T} f \qquad (2.5)$$

and α is a scalar step length, chosen to ensure that $F(x^{(k+1)}) < F(x^{(k)})$.

The minimization of the error function (2.2) is not as straightforward as might be expected because it may have many *local* minima. This is true even in the idealised case when the data is perfect—that is, when the values of I_1 are generated from the Lorenz-Mie model and so (2.2) has a global minimum of zero. Thus, although the Gauss-Newton method is capable of fast convergence when close to the global optimum, it can be difficult to determine the correct values of r and n because, as shown by Zakovic (1997), the region of attraction to the global solution is relatively small. Hence, unless we have very good initial estimates of the correct particle parameters, we must use the Gauss-Newton method within the framework of a multi-start global optimization technique.

The application of the clustering approach of Rinnooy-Kan and Timmer (1987) to particle identification problems is described by Zakovic (1997). Essentially, each *major* iteration of this technique performs a number of minimizations of the objective function using multiple, randomly selected, starting points. *Cluster analysis* is used to identify, and hence reject, starting points which are too close to one another or too close to any minima that have already been found. In this way, wide exploration of the search region is encouraged and the amount of unnecessary work, due to minimizations duplicating one another, is reduced. After each set of minimizations is completed, a Bayesian estimate can be made of the probable total number of minima. If this significantly exceeds the number of minima found so far then another major iteration must be performed with a new set of starting points for the local minimizations.

As an alternative to the multi-start approach we can minimize (2.2) via the global optimization algorithm DIRECT devised by Jones, Perttunen, and Stuckman (1993). This is a direct-search method which minimizes $F(x)$ by systematically subdividing an initial region of search $l_i \le x_i \le \mu_i$ into *hyperboxes*. These are characterized by size (mid-point to corner) and function value at their centres. Each iteration determines which hyper-boxes are *potentially optimal*, using Lipschitz constant arguments to identify those which could contain the lowest function value. The boxes which pass the relevant tests are further subdivided. The algorithm has proved to be quite successful in practice (see Bartholomew-Biggs, Parkhurst, & Wilson, 2003, and the references therein); the process of exploration by subdivision of promising hyperboxes often locates the neighbourhood of a global optimum quite efficiently.

GLOBAL OPTIMIZATION APPLIED TO PARTICLE IDENTIFICATION

As a first illustration we consider two datasets **pd1log** and **pd2log** which contain log-intensity values generated directly from the Lorenz-Mie model using, respectively, $n=1.525$, $r=1.475$ and $n=1.4$, $r=1$. We begin by considering the global minimization of (2.2) for the data set **pd1log**, in the search region $1.475 \leq n \leq 1.575$, $1.375 \leq r \leq 1.575$. The RKT clustering approach (Rinnooy-Kan & Timmer, 1987) finds six local minima in this box, including of course the global optimum with $E_2 = 0$, which identifies the particle. The best three local minima are:

$n = 1.525$, $r = 1.475$ giving $E_2 = 0$
$n = 1.519$, $r = 1.387$ giving $E_2 = 26.5$
$n = 1.526$, $r = 1.563$ giving $E_2 = 28.9$

For the dataset **pd2log** the search region is $1.3 \leq n \leq 1.5$, $0.85 \leq r \leq 1.15$. Here the RKT clustering approach finds seven local minima of which the best three are

$n = 1.40$, $r = 1.0$ giving $E_2 = 0$
$n = 1.418$, $r = 1.090$ giving $E_2 = 37.8$
$n = 1.482$, $r = 0.928$ giving $E_2 = 52.5$

If DIRECT is applied to (2.2) it also finds the correct global minimum for each of these two

Table 1. Global optimization of (2.2) with perfect data

Dataset	RKT & GN Iterations	DIRECT Iterations & function calls
pd1log	1100	50/1300
pd2log	1500	60/1400

datasets. The work done by the two methods is summarised in Table 1.

The cost of each Gauss-Newton iteration includes the calculation of a search direction from (2.5) and as well as one or more function evaluations. Hence, the results in Table 1 suggest that DIRECT is quite competitive with the RKT method. In a later section, we shall compare DIRECT with the RKT clustering approach on problems involving experimental data. First, however, we discuss some difficulties which arise due to the presence of noise in such data.

Particle Identification with Noisy Data

When we solve the particle identification problem using real-life experimental data, the difficulties caused by the presence of multiple minima of E_2 may be more severe than when the data is perfect. In the idealized case, we can be sure that a minimum with the value zero is the global solution and the corresponding values of r and n do identify the true particle. The presence of experimental noise in real-life data means that we can no longer assume the true solution is associated with a value $E_2 = 0$. Indeed, as we shall see in the examples quoted below, several of the best local optima may have rather similar values and it may be hard to say which of them most closely identifies the actual particle.

Consider a particle whose radius and refractive index are r^* and n^* but suppose that there are errors ε_i (with zero mean and standard deviation σ_m) in the log-intensity measurements, $i_i = \psi_i +$

ε_i. If we calculate ψ_i using the correct value of x^* ($= (n^*, r^*, c)$), the expected value of E_2 is

$$E_2(x^*) = \sum_i \varepsilon_i^2 = m\sigma_m^2$$

where m is the number of measurements. Hence experimental noise can cause the minimum of the least-squares error function to be very different from zero. Indeed, if we could estimate σ_m, it might be better to adjust the particle parameters so as to make E_2 approximately equal to σ_m, rather than trying to drive the errors to zero. If we make E_2 "too small" we may be modeling the noise just as much as the underlying intensity pattern and thus producing a spurious "identification" of the particle. Let us assume $x^* = (n^*, r^*, c)$ and that $x^\sim$ is the solution found by minimizing E_2. Then we can show

$$x^\sim \approx x^* + (J^T J)^{-1} J^T \varepsilon$$

where J is the Jacobian matrix of normals appearing in the Gauss-Newton algorithm. Thus, if the eigenvalues of $(J^T J)^{-1}$ are large, even small perturbations in data can cause a large perturbation in the computed solution. In the rest of this chapter we shall consider some practical consequences of these remarks.

PARTICLE IDENTIFICATION FROM EXPERIMENTAL DATA

We now consider four sets of experimental data, representing varying levels of pattern distortion. The first two sets (denoted by **py12log**, **lp29log**) are scattering patterns for fungal spores and the second two (**n1log**, **p1log**) are measurements from polystyrene microspheres. All patterns were obtained from single particles suspended in water (Ulanowski, 1988; Ulanowski & Ludlow, 1989), leading to the presence of distortion and/or noise at quite high levels in some cases. The last two patterns came from particles which were known to

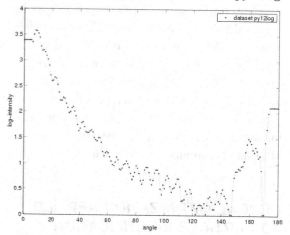

Figure 1. Scattering pattern for dataset py12log

have good sphericity and homogeneity of refractive index; the refractive index was larger than for the first two particles, leading to a relatively stronger scattering pattern with respect to noise. In addition, **n1log** came from a larger particle than **p1log**, giving a further improvement in the signal-to-noise ratio.

In realistic situations we have, at best, only a rough estimate of the "true" solution. Before using global optimization of (2.2) to attempt to identify the particles, we consider the appearance of the experimental data, since this shows some of the practical difficulties that an identification process has to contend with. Figure 1 shows the data pattern **py12log**.

Knowledge of the original experiment suggests that the particle has refractive index approximately 1.5 and radius about 1.8 μm. We see that parts of the pattern are truncated, meaning that intensity measurements are cut off at some maximum or minimum value. These cut-offs appear in both the forward and back-scattering regions; hence, we shall attempt an identification based only on the range angular range between 20° and 160°.

Figure 2 shows the data pattern for **lp29log**. Prior knowledge suggests the refractive index is again 1.5 and the radius approximately 1.5 μm. Because of cut offs in the forward region and the

Figure 2. Scattering pattern for dataset lp29log

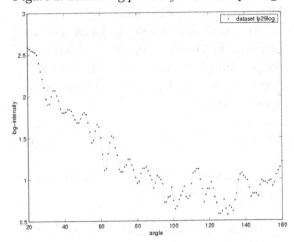

Figure 3. Scattering pattern for dataset n1log

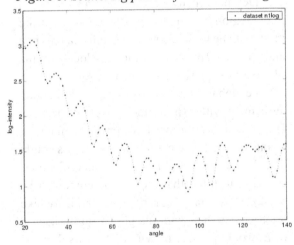

Figure 4. Scattering pattern for dataset p1log

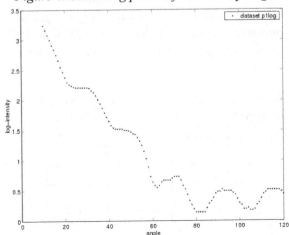

presence of a large peak at high angles, we shall again only use data for the range 20° to 160°.

For the data set **n1log** (Figure 3), we expect n and r to be about 1.6 and 1 µm, respectively. In this case, the data is regarded as reliable only between 20° and 140°.

The last data set, **p1log,** is shown in Figure 4. The expected values of the refractive index and radius are 1.6 and 0.6 µm. This dataset appears nearly complete in the forward region but there is some truncation in the back-scattering region, so the identification is based on the range 10° to120°.

Global Optimization Applied to the Experimental Data Sets

Taking advantage of prior expectations about the particles which generated our experimental datasets we can choose reasonable search regions for the global optimization algorithms to explore. These are

For **py12log:** $\quad 1.4 \leq n \leq 1.6 \quad$ and $\quad 1.7 \leq r \leq 1.9$
$$(4.1)$$

For **lp29log:** $\quad 1.4 \leq n \leq 1.6 \quad$ and $\quad 1.4 \leq r \leq 1.6$
$$(4.2)$$

For **n1log:** $\quad 1.5 \leq n \leq 1.7 \quad$ and $\quad 0.8 \leq r \leq 1.5$
$$(4.3)$$

For **p1log:** $\quad 1.45 \leq n \leq 1.75$ and $0.35 \leq r \leq 0.75$
$$(4.4)$$

Table 2 summarises the results produced by the RKT clustering method and by DIRECT within

Table 2. Global optimization of (2.2) with noisy data

Dataset	E_2^*	N_{min}	RKT iterations	DIRECT iterations & function calls
py12log	19.1	19	8000	40/1300
lp29log	17.9	12	3500	40/1300
n1log	1.6	29	1700	50/1000
p1log	3.2	4	700	60/1000

these search regions. We show the optimum value of (2.2), E_2^*, and the number of local optima found by the RKT algorithm. We also show how many Gauss-Newton iterations were performed by the RKT process for comparison with the numbers of iterations and function evaluations needed by DIRECT.

The figures in Table 2 suggest that DIRECT is usually more efficient than the clustering approach on these problems. Hence we shall use DIRECT as our preferred global optimization method throughout the rest of this chapter. However, in order not to go beyond any conclusion that should be drawn from a specific set of results, we must point out that the performance of global optimization methods can be quite sensitive to a number of factors. For instance, the computational cost of the RKT approach will obviously depend on how many random points are generated as possible starting points for local minimizations (even though this number is automatically reduced by the clustering analysis). Again, the number of iterations performed by both DIRECT and the clustering approach will depend on the (semi-) heuristic rule used to decide that the global optimum has been found. As mentioned already, the clustering approach uses a formula which gives a Bayesian estimate, W_t, of the total number of local minima. In the results reported in this chapter, the algorithm has continued until $W_t < W + 0.5$, where W is the actual number of minima found so far. In many cases, the algorithm might have produced the same results with less computing effort if we had used a weaker threshold—for instance $W_t < W + 0.9$. DIRECT does not have a natural stopping rule and Jones et al. (1993) recommend simply that it should be run for a fixed number of iterations. In these tests we have chosen to terminate when the best function value has not changed significantly for a specified number of hyperbox subdivisions. For these two-variable problems we have usually set this number as 25.

It is worth noting that, even if the clustering algorithm is more expensive than DIRECT, it has

the advantage of producing information about all local minima of the function.

We now consider the results for each data set in more detail. In doing so, we will also consider the possibility that no *a priori* estimates of the particle were available and that a bigger global optimization "box"

$$1.34 \leq n \leq 1.675, \; 0.52 \leq r \leq 2 \qquad (4.5)$$

would have to be used instead of the more restricted problem-specific regions (4.1) – (4.4).

More Detailed Results for Dataset py12log

The fact that nineteen local minima were found in the region (4.1) shows that the light-scattering model can be very sensitive to small changes in n and r. Table 4.2 presents the four best local minima of the least-squares error function E_2.

The global solution in row one seems in good agreement with expectations about the particle. However, if we did not have prior estimates of n and r then the second and third rows might also be regarded as acceptable identifications (bearing in mind that the data is corrupted by noise). More worrying is the fact that, if we take a larger search region, the global minimization of E_2 would provide us with different solutions. Specifically, suppose we search within the range (4.5), which covers the whole region of interest for our applications. Within this box, the global minimum is at $n = 1.6604$, $r = 0.5328$ with the error function $E_2 = 16.1$. While this might appear

Table 3. py12log - best 4 local minima of (2.2) in region (4.1)

Refractive index	Radius (μm)	Error (2.2)
1.50316	1.80139	19.1
1.47371	1.82105	19.6
1.49090	1.82189	19,9
1.49969	1.78799	20.9

Table 4. lp29log - best 3 local minima of (2.2) in region (4.2)

refractive index	Radius (μm)	Error (2.2)
1.53730	1.44106	17.9
1.52455	1.56270	19.5
1.55896	1.49713	22.4

Table 6. n1log - best 3 local minima of (2.2) in region (4.3)

Refractive index	Radius (μm)	Error (2.2)
1.58695	1.10817	1.7
1.59481	0.82549	7.5
1.60132	0.87394	7.6

to be a better solution, our prior knowledge of the experiment excludes the possibility of such a small particle radius and so this "identification" is entirely spurious.

A more extreme indication that a small value of E_2 is no guarantee that we have found the true particle, occurs when we use the box $0 \leq n \leq 2$, $0 \leq r \leq 2$. Now the global minimum occurs at $n = 0.8951$, $r = 0.4352$ with $E_2 = 12.2$ – a mathematically correct solution which is physically impossible!

More Detailed Results for Dataset lp29log

Table 4 shows the best three solutions obtained by the clustering approach within the search region (4.2).

In this case the global minimum stands out a little more clearly from its competitors than was the case for **py12log.** However we observe that the corresponding values of n and r are not particularly close to the expected refractive index and radius.

If we enlarge the search region to that given in (4.5) then the global optimum of E_2 is found at $n = 1.65$, $r = 0.5825$ where the error function (2.2) is approximately 10.3. Once again this seemingly "better" result, in terms of the value of E_2, is completely at variance with our prior knowledge about the size of the particle in the experiment.

Table 5. lp29log - global minimum of (2.2) in region (4.5)

Refractive index	Radius (μm)	Error (2.2)
1.54280	1.62180	17.8

However, during the search within the region (4.5), we also find another *local* optimum which is slightly better than the solution in the first row of Table 4. This solution is shown in Table 5.

As with the dataset **py12log**, we now have two candidate solutions which are very close in terms of error function value but quite different in terms of particle identification.

More Detailed Results for Dataset n1log

The best three of the 29 local minima in the region (4.3) are shown in Table 6.

The value of the error function at the global minimum is very much smaller than for the previous two datasets (and also much smaller than at the other optima). This suggests that there is not too much noise in the dataset **n1log**. It is interesting to note therefore that when the search region is enlarged to (4.5) the global optimum is still given by row one. This shows that, when the noise levels are relatively low we are not so dependent upon having a good initial estimate of n and r in order to avoid spurious solutions to the identification problem.

More Detailed Results for Dataset p1log

When we apply the RKT algorithm in the box (4.4) we obtain just four local minima which are listed in Table 7. While the global minimum of E_2 is not as small as for dataset **n1log**, it still stands out as being significantly better than its nearest competitor and it does correspond to a

Table 7. p1log - best 4 local minima of (2.2) in region (4.4)

Refractive index	Radius (μm)	Error (2.2)
1.65370	0.58107	3.2
1.71955	0.45543	7.9
1.61993	0.70499	8.1
1.62134	0.65349	12.4

refractive index and radius that agree well with what was already known about the particle which produced the data.

Increasing the search range to (4.5) does not change the global optimum. Hence, as for **n1log**, it seems as if the noise level for this example is small enough to mean that there is much less uncertainty involved in basing an identification procedure on the global minimization of (2.2).

Identification Based on other Error Norms

It is worth mentioning that the difficulties and ambiguities of particle identification are not peculiar to the least-squares approach. We have tried replacing (2.2) with a minimax error function and also one which involves the L_1 norm of the errors. In both cases the results are similar to what we obtained with the least-squares approach. Hence, we need to consider a different approach to the matching of scattering data.

IDENTIFICATION USING A COMPOSITE ERROR FUNCTION

On two of the four examples discussed above we have seen that, unless we restrict the search range on the basis of reasonably good expected values for n and r, the solutions given by global optimization of (2.2) may not give a good approximation to the particle which produced the scattering data. There are some instances when

good estimates might be available—examples include microbial cells (these can be quite uniform in size when originating from a cell culture and/or single species of organism) or microparticles produced in an industrial process. Nevertheless, we recognize that it is inadvisable to rely too much on prior information and so we present an alternative approach.

If we do not have reliable estimates of n and r then we can seek to mimic a heuristic approach to particle identification based on visual comparison of experimental and theoretical data. It has been noted that the *positions* of intensity peaks can be useful in particle identification (Maltsev & Lopatin, 1997; Ulanowski 1988; Ulanowski & Ludlow, 1989). Hence, we now consider a way of automating a process of *peak-matching* first suggested by Bartholomew-Biggs et al. (2005). For brevity we let i_k denote the data value $i(\theta_k) = \log I_l(\theta_k)$. We also let K be the set of indices of reference angles θ_k at which the given log-intensities satisfy

$$i_{k-2} < i_{k-1} < i_k \text{ and } i_{k+2} < i_{k+1} < i_k.$$

These conditions hold when the data has a peak in the region of θ_k. (In practice, the weaker condition $i_{k-1} < i_k$ and $i_{k+1} < i_k$ has been found unreliable as a way of detecting peaks.) If $\delta\theta$ is the spacing between the θ-values in the data then we can estimate first and second derivatives using finite difference formulae such as:

$$i'(\theta_k) = \frac{i_{k+1} - i_{k-1}}{2\delta\theta} \text{ and } i''(\theta_k) = \frac{i_{k+1} - 2i_k + i_{k-1}}{\delta\theta^2}.$$

By Newton's method we can then deduce that a peak in the data occurs at

$$\hat{\theta}_k \approx \theta_k - \frac{i'(\theta_k)}{i''(\theta_k)}.$$

Similarly, for all k in the set K, corresponding peaks in the model data can be estimated to be at

$$\bar{\theta}_k(n,r) \approx \theta_k - \frac{\psi'(n,r,\theta_k)}{\psi''(n,r,\theta_k)}$$

where the expressions for ψ' and ψ'' are similar to those for i' and i''. We can define

$$E_3 = \sum_{k \in K} (\bar{\theta}_k - \hat{\theta}_k)^2 \qquad (5.1)$$

and then minimizing (5.1) with respect to n and r gives a "best" match between the peak positions of the data and the Lorenz-Mie model. Using E_3 on its own would ignore much of the data included in E_2; but we can use *both* criteria in the *composite error function*

$$E_4 = E_2 + E_3. \qquad (5.2)$$

Using the Composite Error Function with Dataset py12log

If we minimize (5.2) by DIRECT using an initial box (4.5) we get the global minimum as $n = 1.4993$, $r = 1.7993$ where E_4 is about 22.4. This solution is obtained in 64 DIRECT iterations (about 1200 function calls). We note first that this result is almost exactly equal to the *a priori* estimate of the particle. This is pleasing in itself; but what is more encouraging is the following comparison of accuracy measures at the global minimum of E_2 (from Table 3) and the result we have just obtained using (5.2).

global minimum of E_2: $n = 1.5032$, $r = 1.8014$ with $E_2 = 19.1$ and $E_3 = 70.5$

global minimum of E_4: $n = 1.4993$, $r = 1.7993$ with $E_2 = 19.9$ and $E_3 = 2.5$

Hence the new approach gives a solution where E_2 is only about 4 percent worse than the least-squares minimum while the peak-matching function is reduced by about 95 percent. It also is important to notice that we have now avoided the spurious solution which occurs when we minimize the standard error function E_2 in the larger box (4.5). In other words, the use of E_4 has enabled us to make a good identification of the actual particle *without* using an initial solution estimate to restrict the region of search.

Figure 1. Scattering patterns for dataset py12log and model based on (2.2)

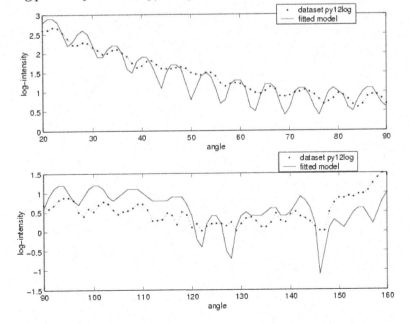

Figure 2. Scattering patterns for dataset py12log and model based on (5.2)

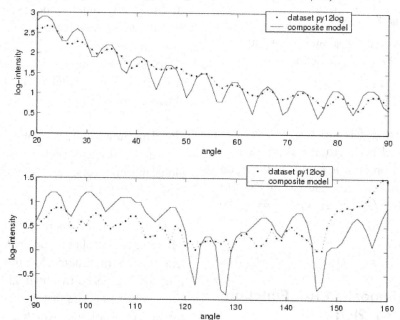

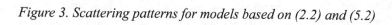

Figure 3. Scattering patterns for models based on (2.2) and (5.2)

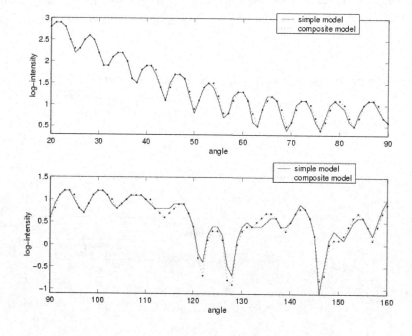

In Figures 1 and 2, we compare the scattering patterns corresponding to the solutions given by minimizing (2.2) and (5.2). For greater clarity, these plots are split between the forward and backward parts of the pattern. Somewhat surprisingly, there are few obvious differences between the scattering patterns produced by the original least-squares data fit and the peak-matching composite model. With care, one can pick out certain points where the composite model gives a closer match to the data—for instance, at the trough between 110° and 115°, at the peak near 130° and at the trough just before 140°. However, these quite local features would not necessarily have been expected to produce such an overall improvement in the peak-matching function E_3.

Figure 3 compares the scattering patterns produced by the two models. They are very similar in the forward section up to 90° and the main differences occur in the part between about 115° and 150°. A modest improvement in peak-matching in this fairly limited range appears to have rather significant consequences for correct particle identification.

Using the Composite Error Function with Dataset lp29log

For the scattering pattern **lp29log** the global minimum of the function (5.2) within the region (4.5) is at $n = 1.5453$, $r = 1.6244$ with $E_2 = 18.3$ and $E_3 = 2.4$. We observe that this is closer to the result in Table 4, for which the corresponding figures are

$n = 1.5428$, $r = 1.6218$ with $E_2 = 17.8$ and $E_3 = 132$.

Thus, when compared with the best result from (2.2), the identification using (5.2) has reduced peak-matching errors by 98 percent while causing an increase in the overall least-squares error-function of less than 3 percent. Moreover, as with the previous example, minimization of the composite

function E_4 within the search region (4.5) has not led to a false identification of the particle of the kind which occurs when we use (2.2).

For this example, the minimization of (5.2) proved more difficult for DIRECT than in the previous case. The global solution given above was only obtained after some 250 iterations (costing around 9500 function calls), which suggests that the region of attraction around the optimum is quite small relative to the size of (4.5).

Graphical comparison of solutions given by (2.2) and (5.2) produces results like those obtained for dataset **py12log**—namely that the scattering patterns are broadly quite similar and the improvement in E_3 corresponds to small—but presumably significant—differences over quite a small range of θ.

Using the Composite Error Function with Dataset n1log

For dataset **n1log**, DIRECT takes 50 iterations (1000 function calls) to find the global minimum of (5.2) in the search region (4.5) as $n = 1.584$, $r = 1.108$. This agrees quite well both with the expected solution and also with the identification obtained using the standard error function E_2. Hence the use of the composite error function has no adverse effect on performance in a case where straightforward least-squares fitting was already adequate. A closer comparison of the solutions given by (2.2) and (5.2) is as follows.

global minimum of E_2: $n = 1.5870$, $r = 1.1082$ with $E_2 = 1.64$ and $E_3 = 0.643$
global minimum of E_4: $n = 1.5840$, $r = 1.1080$ with $E_2 = 1.65$ and $E_3 = 0.618$.

Using the Composite Error Function with Dataset p1log

The global minimum of (5.2) in the region (4.5) is at $n = 1.6557$, $r = 0.5747$. Again, this is in fairly good agreement with the expected solution and with the result obtained by minimizing the error function E_2. The global optimization problem seems rather more difficult in this case than for **n1log** and DIRECT uses about 140 iterations and 3500 function calls. The errors associated with the global minima of (2.2) and (5.2) are:

global minimum of E_2: $n = 1.6537$, $r = 0.5811$ with
$\quad E_2 = 3.2$ and $E_3 = 2.7$
global minimum of E_4: $n = 1.6557$, $r = 0.5747$ with
$\quad E_2 = 3.7$ and $E_3 = 0.735$.

Hence, as with the previous three examples, the identification based on E_4 improves the peak-match error appreciably (by about 73%). The corresponding 16 percent increase in the error function E_2 is rather more significant than in the other examples, however. This suggests that we could give more attention to the balance between the peak-matching and overall data-fitting aspects of the composite approach.

The Balance Between E_2 and E_3

The examples presented so far show that we can avoid spurious solutions to the inverse light-scattering problem if we minimize (5.2) rather than the standard error function (2.2). Moreover, the presence of the peak-matching term E_3 in (5.2) causes some "refinement" of the particle identifications provided by simple least-squares fitting to experimental data. In the case of datasets **py12log** and **lp29log**, for instance, the minimum of (5.2) seems better than the minimum of (2.2) in the sense that the peaks in the Lorenz-Mie scattering pattern agree better with the experimental data. It has to be recognized, however, that in the definition of (5.2) we have quite arbitrarily made E_2 and E_3 of equal importance. More generally we could define E_4 as

$$E_4(\rho) = E_2 + \rho E_3 \qquad (5.3)$$

where ρ is some constant weighting parameter.

To illustrate the effects of varying ρ in (5.3) we consider some scattering patterns which have been obtained by introducing errors into perfect data. The datasets **n123log**, **n133log**, **n12xlog**, and **n13xlog** are all based on **pd1log** from an earlier section. In each case, noise has been added which is normally distributed with zero mean and standard deviation 0.45. In the data sets **n12xlog** and **n13xlog** the data has also been truncated so that negative values of log-intensity are replaced by zero. Ideally, we want to be able to identify the "true" particle which underlies the noise—that is, to obtain $n = 1.525$, $r = 1.475$. The results below show how well the approaches based on (2.2) and (5.3) succeed in doing this when $\rho = 1$ and $\rho = 0.1$

For **n123log**
$\quad$ global minimum of E_2: $n = 1.5233$, $r = 1.4750$
$\quad$ with $E_2 = 36.5$ and $E_3 = 33.6$
$\quad$ global minimum of $E_4(0.1)$: $n = 1.5253$, $r = 1.4759$ with $E_2 = 36.8$ and $E_3 = 10.2$
$\quad$ global minimum of $E_4(1.0)$: $n = 1.529$, $r = 1.4758$ with $E_2 = 38.2$ and $E_3 = 6.2$.

For **n133log**
$\quad$ global minimum of E_2: $n = 1.5193$, $r = 1.4754$
$\quad$ with $E_2 = 35.7$ and $E_3 = 5.5$
$\quad$ global minimum of $E_4(0.1)$: $n = 1.5198$, $r = 1.4756$ with $E_2 = 35.7$ and $E_3 = 4.9$
$\quad$ global minimum of $E_4(1.0)$: $n = 1.5214$, $r = 1.4762$ with $E_2 = 36.0$ and $E_3 = 4.2$.

For **n12xlog**
$\quad$ global minimum of E_2: $n = 1.5217$, $r = 1.4797$
$\quad$ with $E_2 = 36.6$ and $E_3 = 10.6$
$\quad$ global minimum of $E_4(0.1)$: $n = 1.5233$, $r = 1.4799$ with $E_2 = 36.7$ and $E_3 = 8.2$
$\quad$ global minimum of $E_4(1.0)$: $n = 1.5287$, $r = 1.4783$ with $E_2 = 37.7$ and $E_3 = 5.5$.

For n13xlog

global minimum of E_2: $n = 1.5192$, $r = 1.4715$
with $E_2 = 31.6$ and $E_3 = 24.0$
global minimum of $E_4(0.1)$: $n = 1.5197$, $r = 1.4734$ with $E_2 = 31.8$ and $E_3 = 7.2$
global minimum of $E_4(1.0)$: $n = 1.5176$, $r = 1.4787$ with $E_2 = 32.7$ and $E_3 = 3.9$.

In each case the identification based on (5.3) has produced a result which is different from the standard approach using (2.2). The values of n and r from the composite function E_4 give scattering patterns whose peak-positions match the data better than those given by minimizing E_2 alone. As we would expect, the peak match error E_3 is smaller when we minimize E_4 with $\rho = 1$.

For all the datasets, the minimum of $E_4(0.1)$ is "better" than the minimum of E_2 in the sense that n is closer to 1.525, the actual value of refractive index. The value of r is relatively unaffected except in the case **n13xlog** when it becomes much closer to the target value 1.475. However, in only one instance (**n133log**) does the minimum of $E_4(1.0)$ give an improvement on the identification obtained using $\rho = 0.1$. In the other cases, the extra weight given to the peak-matching term seems to have caused *over*-correction so that n and/or r are further away from the desired values and the overall data errors in E_2 have become too large.

The examples in this section show that the choice of ρ can be a problem-dependent matter. One way of tackling this issue might be to use (5.3) in an iterative framework where several trial values of ρ are used until some acceptable balance is obtained between reductions in E_3 and increases in $\hat{E}_2$.

If $\hat{E}_2$ and $\hat{E}_3$ denote values of the point- and peak-match error functions at the minimum of (2.2) then a simple example of an iterative procedure could be as follows. Starting with the trial value $\rho = 1$ (say), ρ can be successively halved until the solution satisfies a condition such as

$$1 - \frac{E_3}{\hat{E}_3} \geq M\left(\frac{E_2}{\hat{E}_2} - 1\right) \qquad (5.4)$$

where $M \gg 1$ defines a threshold for the decrease in E_3 relative to the increase in E_2.

A way of avoiding the question of relative weighting of E_2 and E_3 in (5.3) might be to consider a constrained formulation of the particle identification problem. This idea has already been explored by Bartholomew-Biggs et al. (2005) who obtain particle identification solutions by using peak-matching in the context of a constrained optimization problem where E_3 is minimized subject to a constraint of the form (5.4). In the next section we give brief consideration to an alternative way of using constrained optimization.

IDENTIFICATION USING CONSTRAINTS ON PEAK-MATCHING

We can easily calculate the root-mean-square peak-match error as

$$E_3^{rms} = \sqrt{(E_3/m_p)} \qquad (6.1)$$

where m_p is the number of peaks in the data. If τ denotes the maximum acceptable value of E_3^{rms} then we could seek to identify the particle by solving the constrained problem

$$\text{Minimize } E_2 \text{ subject to } E_3^{rms} \leq \tau. \qquad (6.2)$$

A reasonable tolerance on peak-match errors is given by setting $\tau = 0.5$ in problem (6.2). This implies that there is typically an interval of about one degree around each peak in the data in which it is acceptable for the corresponding peak in the model to lie.

Problem (6.2) can in turn be solved by finding the (global) unconstrained minimum of

$$E_5 = E_2 + \xi \max (0, E_3^{rms} - \tau) \qquad (6.3)$$

where ξ is a *penalty parameter* that must be chosen sufficiently large. In the numerical results which follow, we have adopted the simple strategy of choosing an initial ξ and then increasing it, if necessary, after each minimization until the minimum of (6.3) satisfies the constraint in (6.2). Since (6.3) is a non-smooth function, DIRECT is a suitable algorithm for minimizing it.

If we choose $\tau = 0.5$ and then use (6.3) to identify particles from light-scattering patterns in datasets **py12log**–**p1log** we obtain results that are similar to those obtained by minimizing (5.2). If we consider the artificial data sets **n123log**–**n13xlog**, however, then it turns out to be advisable to use a slightly larger tolerance $\tau = 0.7$ on acceptable peak positions because the data is subject to higher noise levels than those in the experimental data. The identifications obtained from (6.3) are then similar to those are those given by (5.3) with $\rho = 1$. Using τ as a problem-dependent parameter in the calculation is somewhat preferable to using the weighting factor ρ because it can be related more directly to an accuracy requirement on the peak-matching aspect of the identification.

DISCUSSION AND CONCLUSION

In this chapter, we have addressed the problems caused by noise in the solution of the problem of identifying the radius and refractive index of a particle on the basis of a Lorenz-Mie light-scattering model. Light-scattering data for small particles is typically of the "jagged" form illustrated in Figures 1 – 4; and, even in the absence of experimental errors, a straightforward least-squares error function like (2.2) has many local minima. In the case of perfect (noise-free) data we can apply a global minimization method and be confident that a solution which gives a zero value of (2.2) corresponds to the true particle. When there is substantial noise in the data, however, we cannot

be sure that the global minimum of (2.2) is necessarily associated with the correct values of radius and refractive index. This is demonstrated by two examples (**py12log** and **lp29log**) where the global minimum of (2.2) yields a false "identification" of the particle.

To overcome the fact that global minima of (2.2) can give spurious solutions to identification problems, we have considered other features of the scattering data. In particular, we have sought to exploit the heuristic observation that the position of peaks in the data can be a good visual diagnostic tool. Hence we have constructed an additional error function which measures differences between (estimated) peak positions in the data and the Lorenz-Mie model. This error function has been included in a composite function (5.3) which combines the standard least-squares error function with the new peak-matching one. Numerical tests involving the global minimization of (5.3) show that it leads to more robust particle identification than the original least-squares approach based on (2.2). For the datasets **py12log, lp29log, n1log** and **p1log**, the global minima of (5.3) correspond quite well with prior knowledge about the particles which generated the data. Moreover, we do not need to have such prior knowledge in order to restrict the region of search and exclude spurious "solutions."

One feature of the proposed approach that may still need further attention is the balance between peak-match and overall errors in the composite function (5.3). In most of our examples we have taken the balancing parameter $\rho = 1$ and obtained quite good results. However, on some examples it may be preferable to use a smaller value of ρ to place less emphasis on peak-matching. Thus the choice of ρ can be a problem-dependent matter: at the minimum of (5.3), it is the value of ρ which governs how much E_3 has decreased and E_2 increased in comparison with the standard least-squares solution. Further consideration could still be given to the matter of making an *a priori* choice of ρ so that improvements in peak-matching are not accompanied by a "too big" increase in the overall errors. However we may be able to circumvent this question by using a constrained minimization approach based on (6.2) or (6.3). For these problems we need to set τ as an upper limit for the peak-matching errors but our experiments suggest that solutions are not over-sensitive to this choice. In any case, the choice of τ relates fairly directly to peak displacement, whereas the choice of ρ only influences peak errors in an indirect way.

The introduction of extra peak-matching errors into a standard least-squares data-fitting approach is a simple example of *data fusion*. This term denotes a class of techniques for identification problems which seek to incorporate as much prior knowledge as possible, rather than just performing some optimum fit to the raw experimental data. Clearly, for the problems under consideration, the inclusion of peak-match errors has been beneficial.

One final point emerges from the numerical results involving global optimization of (2.2). For this problem, the algorithm DIRECT (Jones et al., 1993) seems appreciably more efficient than the multi-start approach of Rinnooy-Kan & Timmer (1987) on problems where there are large numbers of local minima. The multi-start method only becomes competitive for the dataset **p1log**, for which (2.2) has just four local minima in the region of interest. We do not wish to draw sweeping conclusions from this, because we have been solving problems in only two variables and the systematic subdivision approach used by DIRECT may become less efficient as problem dimensions increase. However, it is also worth noting that DIRECT seems to be a robust algorithm and, because it does not require gradient information, it can easily be used for global minimization of non-smooth functions like (6.3).

REFERENCES

Barth, H. G. & Flippen, R. B. (1995). Particle-size analysis. *Analytical Chemistry, 67*, 257R-272R.

Bartholomew-Biggs, M. C., Parkhurst S. C., & Wilson S. P. (2003). Using DIRECT to solve an aircraft routing problem. *Computational Optimization and Applications, 21*, 311-323.

Bartholomew-Biggs, M. C., Ulanowski, Z., & Zakovic, S. (2005). Using global optimization for a microparticle identification problem with noisy data. *Journal of Global Optimization, 32*, 325-347.

Berdnik, V. V., Gilev, K., Shvalov, A., Maltsev, V., & Loiko, V. A. (2006). Characterization of spherical particles using high-order neural networks and scanning flow cytometry. *Journal of Quantitative Spectroscopy & Radiative Transfer, 102*, 62-72.

Bohren, C. F. & Huffman, D. F. (1983). *Absorption and scattering of light by small particles.* New York: Wiley.

De Pieri, L. A., Ludlow, I. K., & Waites, W. M. (1993). The application of laser diffractometry to study the water content of spores of Bacillus sphaericus with different heat resistances. *Journal of Applied Bacteriology, 74*, 578-582.

Dubovik, O., Sinyuk, A., Lapyonok, T., Holben, B. N., Mishchenko, M., Yang, P. (2006). Application of spheroid models to account for aerosol particle nonsphericity in remote sensing of desert dust. *Journal of Geophysical Research, 111*, D11208.

Gousbet, G. & Grehan, G. (1988). *Optical particle sizing.* New York: Plenum.

Grainger, R. G., Lucas, J., Thomas, G. E. & Ewen, G. B. L. (2004). Calculation of Mie derivatives. *Applied Optics, 43*, 5386-5393.

Hull, P. G. & Quinby-Hunt, M. (1997). A neural-network to extract size parameter from light-scattering data. *SPIE Proceedings, 2963*, 448-454.

Jones, D. R., Perttunen, C. P. & Stuckman, B. E. (1993). Lipschitzian optimization without the Lipschitz constant. *Journal of Optimization Theory and Applications, 79*, 157-181.

Kolesnikova, I. V., Potapov, S. V., Yurkin, M. A., Hoekstra, A. G., Maltsev, V. P. & Semyanov, K. A. (2006). Determination of volume, shape and refractive index of individual blood platelets. *Journal of Quantitative Spectroscopy & Radiative Transfer, 102*, 37-45.

Maltsev,V. P. & Lopatin, V. N. (1997). Parametric solution of the inverse light-scattering problem for individual spherical particles. *Applied Optics, 36*, 6102-6108.

Nascimento, C.A.O., Guardani, R. & Giulietti, M. (1997). Use of neural networks in the analysis of particle size distributions by laser diffraction. *Powder Technology, 90*, 89-94.

Rinnooy-Kan, A. & Timmer, G. T. (1987a). Stochastic global optimization methods. Part I: Clustering methods. *Mathematical Programming, 39*, 27-56.

Rinnooy-Kan, A. & Timmer, G. T. (1987b). Stochastic global optimization methods. Part II: Multilevel methods. *Mathematical Programming, 39*, 57-78.

Semyanov, K. A., Tarasov, P. A., Soini, J. T., Petrov, A. K. & Maltsev, V. P. (2000). Calibration-free method to determine the size and hemoglobin concentration of individual red blood cells from light scattering. *Applied Optics, 39*, 5884-5889.

Shimizu, K. & Ishimaru, A. (1990). Differential Fourier-transform technique for the inverse scattering problem. *Applied Optics, 29*, 3428-3433.

Ulanowski, Z. (1988). PhD thesis: *Investigations of microbial physiology and cell structure using laser diffractometry*. Hatfield: Hatfield Polytechnic.

Ulanowski, Z., Ludlow, I. K. & Waites, W. M. (1987). Water-content and size of spore components determined by laser diffractometry. *FEMS Microbiology Letters, 40*, 229-232.

Ulanowski, Z. & Ludlow, I. K. (1989). Water distribution, size, and wall thickness in Lycoperdon pyriforme spores. *Mycological Research, 93*, 28-32.

Ulanowsk,i Z., Wang, Z., Kaye, P. H., & Ludlow, I. K. (1998). Application of neural networks to the inverse light scattering problem for spheres. *Applied Optics, 37*, 4027-4033.

Vargas-Ubera, J., Aguilar, J. F., & Gale, D. M. (2007). Reconstruction of particle-size distributions from light-scattering patterns using three inversion methods. *Applied Optics, 46*, 124-132.

Wyatt, P.J. (1980). Some chemical, physical and optical properties of fly ash particles, *Applied Optics, 7*, 975-983.

Zakovic, S. (1997). PhD thesis: *Global optimization applied to an inverse light scattering problem*. Hatfield: University of Hertfordshire.

Zakovic, S., Ulanowski, Z. & Bartholomew-Biggs, M. C. (1998). Application of global optimization to particle identification using light scattering. *Inverse Problems, 14*, 1053-1067.

Chapter X
Exact Markov Chain Monte Carlo Algorithms and their Applications in Probabilistic Data Analysis and Inference

Dominic Savio Lee
University of Canterbury, New Zealand

ABSTRACT

*This chapter describes algorithms that use Markov chains for generating **exact** sample values from complex distributions, and discusses their use in probabilistic data analysis and inference. Its purpose is to disseminate these ideas more widely so that their use will become more widespread, thereby improving Monte Carlo simulation results and stimulating greater research interest in the algorithms themselves. The chapter begins by introducing **Markov chain Monte Carlo** (MCMC), which stems from the idea that sample values from a desired distribution f can be obtained from the stationary states of an ergodic Markov chain whose stationary distribution is f. To get sample values that have distribution f exactly, it is necessary to detect when the Markov chain has reached its stationary distribution. Under certain conditions, this can be achieved by means of **coupled** Markov chains—these conditions and the resulting **exact MCMC** or **perfect sampling** algorithms and their applications are described.*

INTRODUCTION

The use of probability models to represent uncertainty is a proven and effective way to derive useful information from uncertain data. Prob-ability models shift the focus from individual data values to their pattern of occurrence or *probability distribution*. Probability distributions in real-world applications are often too complex for analysis and inference to proceed analytically.

A practical way forward is Monte Carlo simulation, whereby a collection of sample values is generated from a distribution and then used for analysis and inference. Clearly, the quality of the Monte Carlo results depends on the ability to produce sample values that have the desired distribution. Generic methods for generating from common parametric distributions, such as the inverse distribution function method and the rejection method, often cannot be used for complex distributions. A generic approach that is applicable is based on the simple idea that if a Markov chain is designed with a desired distribution as its stationary distribution, then the states of the stationary chain will provide the required sample values. This approach is known as *Markov chain Monte Carlo (MCMC)*.

MCMC algorithms make it easy to implement a Markov chain that has a given distribution as its stationary distribution. When used on their own, however, MCMC algorithms can only provide sample values that approximate a desired distribution because of the practical difficulty in detecting whether the Markov chain has converged to its stationary distribution. Under certain conditions, this can be resolved by means of *coupled* Markov chains, resulting in *exact MCMC* or *perfect sampling* algorithms that give sample values whose distribution is exactly the required distribution. Thus, when applicable, exact MCMC is better than MCMC at recovering the underlying distribution, and is therefore a more intelligent choice to get sample values for use in a Monte Carlo analysis of data.

The objective of this chapter is to describe exact MCMC algorithms and discuss some of their applications in Monte Carlo data analysis and inference, so as to promote their usage and stimulate greater interest in their research.

MARKOV CHAIN MONTE CARLO

MCMC is based on the observation that the state of an *ergodic* Markov chain (see Appendix to this chapter for a glossary of Markov chain properties) will eventually converge to a stationary distribution, no matter which state the chain starts in. Thus, to obtain a sample from a desired distribution f, an ergodic Markov chain with f as its stationary distribution can be constructed and then run till it is stationary. The required sample values are given by the states of the stationary chain. Let $X^{(0)}, X^{(1)}, ...$ represent a sequence of states for an ergodic Markov chain and suppose that it reaches its stationary distribution f after transition T, then a *dependent* sample with distribution f is given by $\{X^{(t)} : t > T\}$. This sample can be used in the same way as an independent sample for the estimation of expectations; by the *strong law of large numbers*, the sample average for a measurable function h will converge, almost surely, to the expectation under f:

$$\lim_{n \to \infty} \frac{1}{n} \sum_{i=1}^{n} h(X^{(T+i)}) \overset{\text{a.s.}}{=} \mathrm{E}_f[h(X)] \qquad (1)$$

Note, however, that the sample variance cannot simply be used as an estimate of Monte Carlo standard error because of the dependency within the sample (Kass, Carlin, Gelman, & Neal, 1998). Instead, the autocorrelation in the sample must be estimated and used to estimate the standard error. If an independent sample is required, multiple chains with independent starting states must be used.

Generic algorithms are available that allow an ergodic Markov chain with a specified stationary distribution to be constructed easily. Many of these algorithms can be regarded as variants of the *Metropolis-Hastings algorithm*, commonly attributed to Metropolis, Rosenbluth, Rosenbluth, Teller, and Teller (1953) and Hastings (1970). Let $U(0, 1)$ represent the uniform distribution on the interval (0, 1).

Metropolis-Hastings Algorithm

Choose initial state $X^{(0)}$ and *proposal distribution g*.

At iteration t,

Generate $\widetilde{X} \sim g(x \mid X^{(t-1)})$ and $U \sim U$

$(0,1)$,

Compute *acceptance probability*

$$\alpha = \min\left\{1, \frac{f(\widetilde{X})g(X^{(t-1)} \mid \widetilde{X})}{f(X^{(t-1)})g(\widetilde{X} \mid X^{(t-1)})}\right\}$$

(2)

If $U \le \alpha$:

Set $X^{(t)} = \widetilde{X}$, (accept $\widetilde{X}$ with probability α)

Else:

Set $X(t) = X^{(t-1)}$.

Since f is used only to compute the acceptance probability, and appears both in the numerator and denominator, the algorithm is applicable even if f is not known completely but only up to a multiplicative constant. This frequently is the case in practice, where f is available as an un-normalized distribution. Some common variants of the Metropolis-Hastings algorithm include the *Metropolis sampler, independent Metropolis-Hastings sampler, single-component Metropolis-Hastings sampler* and *Gibbs sampler*.

The *Metropolis sampler* is obtained when a symmetric proposal distribution is used, that is, $g(\widetilde{X} \mid X^{(t-1)}) = g(X^{(t-1)} \mid \widetilde{X})$. In this case, the acceptance probability simplifies to:

$$\alpha = \min\left\{1, \frac{f(\widetilde{X})}{f(X^{(t-1)})}\right\}$$

(3)

A special case, where $g(\widetilde{X} \mid X^{(t-1)}) = g(\mid \widetilde{X} - X^{(t-1)} \mid)$, is known as the *random walk Metropolis-Hastings sampler*.

When the proposal distribution is independent of $X^{(t-1)}$, the *independent Metropolis-Hastings (IMH) sampler* is obtained, with acceptance probability given by:

$$\alpha = \min\left\{1, \frac{f(\widetilde{X})g(X^{(t-1)})}{f(X^{(t-1)})g(\widetilde{X})}\right\}$$

(4)

This algorithm usually works well if g is close to f and has heavier tails than f.

In general, X may be multivariate, and the idea behind the *single-component Metropolis-Hastings sampler* is to update X using a series of steps at each iteration, rather than a single step. To do this, X is partitioned into d parts: $X = (X_{[1]}, X_{[2]},...,X_{[d]})$. Let $X_{[-j]}$ denote X with the j-th part omitted, and suppose that the conditional distributions, $f(x_{[j]} \mid x_{[-j]})$, are known.

Box 1.

$$\alpha_j = \min\left\{1, \frac{f(\widetilde{X}_{[j]} \mid X_{[1]}^{(t)},...,X_{[j-1]}^{(t)}, X_{[j+1]}^{(t-1)},...,X_{[d]}^{(t-1)})}{f(X_{[j]}^{(t-1)} \mid X_{[1]}^{(t)},...,X_{[j-1]}^{(t)}, X_{[j+1]}^{(t-1)},...,X_{[d]}^{(t-1)})} \cdot \frac{g(X_{[j]}^{(t-1)} \mid X_{[1]}^{(t)},...,X_{[j-1]}^{(t)}, \widetilde{X}_{[j]}, X_{[j+1]}^{(t-1)},...,X_{[d]}^{(t-1)})}{g(\widetilde{X}_{[j]} \mid X_{[1]}^{(t)},...,X_{[j-1]}^{(t)}, X_{[j]}^{(t-1)}, X_{[j+1]}^{(t-1)},...,X_{[d]}^{(t-1)})}\right\},$$

(5)

Single-Component Metropolis-Hastings Sampler

Choose initial state $X^{(0)}$ and *proposal distribution g*.

At iteration t,

For $j = 1, 2, \ldots, d$,

Generate

$$\widetilde{X}_{[j]} \sim g(x_{[j]} \mid X_{[1]}^{(t)}, \ldots, X_{[j-1]}^{(t)}, X_{[j]}^{(t-1)}, \ldots, X_{[d]}^{(t-1)})$$

and $U_j \sim U(0,1)$

Compute (see Box 1).

If $U_j \le \alpha$:

Set $X_{[j]}^{(t)} = \widetilde{X}_{[j]}$, (accept $\widetilde{X}_{[j]}$ with probability α_j)

Else:

Set $X_{[j]}^{(t)} = X_{[j]}^{(t-1)}$.

If it is possible to generate from the conditional distributions, $f(x_{[j]} \mid x_{[-j]})$, then by choosing them as the proposal distribution in the single-component Metropolis-Hastings sampler, the acceptance probabilities will always be one and the proposals will always be accepted. The resulting algorithm is known as the *Gibbs sampler*, which effectively generates from the conditional distributions.

Gibbs Sampler

Choose initial state $X^{(0)}$.

At iteration t,

For $j = 1, 2, \ldots, d$,

Generate:

$$X_{[j]}^{(t)} \sim f(x_{[j]} \mid X_{[1]}^{(t)}, \ldots, X_{[j-1]}^{(t)}, X_{[j+1]}^{(t-1)}, \ldots, X_{[d]}^{(t-1)})$$

Hybrid combinations of single-component Metropolis-Hastings and Gibbs sampling are possible, with some parts of X updated using Gibbs updates and others (which cannot be generated from their conditional distributions) using Metropolis-Hastings updates.

An indirect, but insightful, way of generating X from f is to introduce an *auxiliary variable*, V, generate the joint quantity, (X, V), from the uniform distribution over the set, $\{(x, v) : 0 < v < f(x)\}$, and then take the X component. This works because f is the marginal density of X from the joint uniform distribution:

$$f(x) = \int_0^{f(x)} dv \qquad (6)$$

Generating from the joint uniform distribution may not be easy, but the conditional distributions are uniform as well:

$$f(V \mid X = x) = U(\{v : v \le f(x)\}) \qquad (7)$$

and

$$f(X \mid V = v) = U(\{x : v \le f(x)\}) \qquad (8)$$

Therefore, (X, V) can be generated using the Gibbs sampler. The resulting algorithm is called the *slice sampler* because it alternates between uniform generation from a vertical slice, $\{v : v \le f(x)\}$, and uniform generation from a horizontal slice, $\{x : v \le f(x)\}$. The second uniform generation may be difficult to perform.

Slice Sampler

Choose initial state $X^{(0)}$.

At iteration t,

Generate $V^{(t)} \sim U(0, f(X^{(t-1)}))$, (vertical slice)

Generate $X^{(t)} \sim U\{(x : V^{(t)} \le f(x))\}$. (horizontal slice)

There are still other MCMC algorithms (see Cappe & Robert, 2000; Gamerman, 1997; Gilks, Richardson, & Spiegelhalter, 1996) but those given here will suffice for the description of exact MCMC in the next section.

In practice, a MCMC sampler is used to generate a long sequence of Markov chain states. After an initial *burn-in period*, the states are assumed to have the required stationary distribution, at least approximately. The Achilles' heel in MCMC is the difficulty in determining how long the burn-in period should be. Various convergence diagnostics have been suggested (Brooks & Roberts, 1998; Cowles & Carlin, 1996; Mengersen, Robert, & Guihenneuc-Jouyaux, 1999) but none can indicate convergence with complete certainty. For this reason, MCMC has been described as "what you get is what you see," suggesting that the resulting sample values may not represent *f* fully because the Markov chain has not yet become stationary. The breakthrough came when Propp & Wilson (1996) showed how to generate exact sample values from the stationary distribution of a Markov chain with finite state space.

EXACT MCMC (PERFECT SAMPLING)

MCMC convergence diagnostics based on *multiple* independent (Gelman & Rubin, 1992) or *coupled* (Johnson, 1996) Markov chains running *forward* in time have been suggested, but are not completely reliable. The chains are coupled if the same sequence of random numbers is used to propagate all of them. By adopting a different perspective—running multiple coupled chains from the past or *backward coupling*—Propp & Wilson (1996) developed the *coupling from the past (CFTP)* algorithm, which allowed exact sample values to be obtained from the stationary distribution of an ergodic Markov chain with *finite* state space.

Coupling from the Past

The CFTP algorithm starts multiple Markov chains, one for each possible state, at some time $t_0 < 0$ in the past, and uses coupled transitions to propagate them to time 0. If all the chains *coalesce*, that is, end up having the same state, at or before time 0, then they will have "forgotten" their starting values and will evolve as a single chain from that point onwards, and the common state at time zero ($X^{(0)}$) is an exact sample value from the stationary distribution. Intuitively, if coalescence occurs at some finite time, $t^* < 0$, then if the chains had been started in the infinite past, coupling with the same sequence of random numbers will ensure that they coalesce at t^*, and the common chain at time 0 must be stationary because it had been running for an infinitely long time. Thus, the existence of a finite coalescence time can give a stationary sample value in finite time. The use of coupling is essential to induce coalescence in a finite length of time.

Consider a Markov chain with finite state space, $S = \{1, 2, ..., K\}$. The CFTP algorithm starts K Markov chains, one from each state in S, at some time $t_0 < 0$ in the past. A sequence of t_0 random vectors, $R^{(t_0+1)}, R^{(t_0+2)}, ..., R^{(0)}$, is generated and used to propagate all K Markov chains to time 0. Let $X^{(t,k(t_0))}$ represent the state of the Markov chain at time t, starting from state $k \in S$ at time $t_0 < t$, and let ϕ be the update function of the Markov chain, such that

$$X^{(t+1,k(t_0))} = \phi(X^{(t,k(t_0))}, R^{(t+1)}) \qquad (9)$$

Coupling from the Past

Set $t_0 = 0$.
Repeat:
  Set $t_0 = t_0 - 1$, (take 1 time-step back)
  Generate $R^{(t_0+1)}$,
  For $k = 1, 2, ..., K$, (for each state)
    Set $X^{(t_0,k(t_0))} = k$, (start chain in that state)
    For $t = t_0, t_0 + 1, ..., -1$, (propagate chain to time 0)
      Set $X^{(t+1,k(t_0))} = \phi(X^{(t,k(t_0))}, R^{(t+1)})$.
Until $X^{(0,1(t_0))} = X^{(0,2(t_0))} = \cdots = X^{(0,K(t_0))}$.
  (check for coalescence at time 0)
Return $X^{(0)}$.

The following example, adapted from Casella, Lavine, and Robert (2001), illustrates the CFTP algorithm. Suppose that the Markov chain has state space, $S = \{0, 1, 2\}$, and transition matrix,

$$Q = \begin{pmatrix} 0.6 & 0.3 & 0.1 \\ 0.4 & 0.4 & 0.2 \\ 0.3 & 0.4 & 0.3 \end{pmatrix},$$

where the (i,j)-element is the conditional probability, $P(X^{(t+1)} = j \mid X^{(t)} = i)$. The matrix of conditional cumulative probabilities is

$$C = \begin{pmatrix} 0.6 & 0.9 & 1 \\ 0.4 & 0.8 & 1 \\ 0.3 & 0.7 & 1 \end{pmatrix},$$

where the (i, j)-element is the probability, $P(X^{(t+1)} \leq j \mid X^{(t)} = i)$. Beginning at $t_0 = -1$, three chains are started at 0, 1 and 2. A uniform (0, 1) random number, $U^{(0)}$, is generated (in this example, $R^{(0)} = U^{(0)}$) and used to propagate all three chains to time 0. Suppose that $U^{(0)} \in (0.8, 0.9)$, then the three chains are updated as shown:

$$U^{(0)}$$

$$\begin{array}{ccc} 2 & \longrightarrow & 2 \\ 1 & \nearrow & 1 \\ 0 & \nearrow & 0 \end{array}$$

$$t = \quad -1 \qquad\qquad 0$$

The chains have not coalesced at $t = 0$, so move one time-step back to $t_0 = -2$, start three chains

at 0, 1 and 2, generate a second uniform (0, 1) random number, $U^{(-1)}$, and use it together with the previous $U^{(0)}$, to propagate the chains to time 0. Suppose that $U^{(-1)} \in (0.3, 0.4)$, then the three chains evolve as shown:

		$U^{(-1)}$		$U^{(0)}$	
	2		2		2
	1		1		1
	0		0		0
t =	−2		−1		0

The chains have still not coalesced at $t = 0$, so move another time-step back to $t_0 = -3$ and start again, generating a third uniform (0, 1) random number, $U^{(-2)}$. Suppose that $U^{(-2)} \in (0.3, 0.4)$. This is used with $U^{(-1)}$ and $U^{(0)}$ from before, giving the following transitions:

		$U^{(-2)}$		$U^{(-1)}$		$U^{(0)}$	
	2		2		2		2
	1		1		1		1
	0		0		0		0
t =	−3		−2		−1		0

All three chains have now coalesced at $t = 0$ and so $X^{(0)} = 1$ is accepted as a sample value from the stationary distribution. The whole process is repeated to get another independent sample value. It is important to note that even though the chains have coalesced at $t = -1$, with common value, $X^{(-1)} = 0$, this value at the time of coalescence is not accepted as being from the stationary distribution. This is because the time of coalescence is a *random* time that depends only on the sequence of random numbers, $U^{(0)}, U^{(-1)}, ...,$ whilst the time at which a coalesced state has the

Box 2.

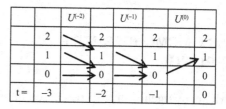

$$\Phi(\mathbf{X}^{(t)}, R^{(t+1)}) = \{\phi(X^{(t,1)}, R^{(t+1)}), \phi(X^{(t,2)}, R^{(t+1)}), ..., \phi(X^{(t,K)}, R^{(t+1)})\} \qquad (10)$$

required stationary distribution must be a *fixed* time. In the CFTP algorithm, this fixed time has been arbitrarily specified to be $t = 0$.

To see that the state at the time of coalescence does not have the stationary distribution, consider the following example, also taken from Casella, et al. (2001). Suppose that the state space is $S = \{1, 2\}$ and the transition matrix is

$$Q = \begin{pmatrix} 0.5 & 0.5 \\ 1 & 0 \end{pmatrix}$$

Since $Q(2, 1) = 1$, the two coupled chains must be in state 1 at the time of coalescence. However, the stationary distribution of this Markov chain is $f(1) = 2/3$ and $f(2) = 1/3$, and so the state at the time of coalescence cannot be from the stationary distribution.

Instead of taking a single step back when the chains fail to coalesce, any decreasing sequence of time-steps may be used. Propp & Wilson (1996) showed that the "double-until-overshoot" choice of $t_0 = -2^0, -2^1, -2^2,...$ is optimal in the sense that it minimizes the worst-case number of steps and almost minimizes the expected number of steps for coalescence.

An alternative description of CFTP, in terms of set updates, will be useful later on for extensions to general state spaces. Let $\mathbf{X}^{(t)} = \{X^{(t,1)}, X^{(t,2)},..., X^{(t,K)}\}$ be the set of states of Markov chains at time t, starting from all possible states in S. Define the set-valued update function, Φ, as (see Box 2).

Starting with $\mathbf{X}^{(t_0)} = S$ at some time t_0 in the past, the set of states is updated by Φ at each time-step. When coalescence occurs, the set degenerates into a singleton, and so a singleton at time 0 is an exact sample value from the stationary distribution.

Coupling from the Past (Set Version)

Set $k = -1$.
Repeat
    Set $k = k + 1$ and $t_0 = -2^k$, (take 2^k time-steps back)
    Generate $R^{(t_0+1)}, R^{(t_0+2)},..., R^{(\lceil t_0/2 \rceil)}$,
    Set $\mathbf{X}^{(t_0)} = S$, (initialize starting set to S)
    For $t = t_0, t_0 + 1,..., -1$, (propagate set to time 0)
        Set $\mathbf{X}^{(t+1)} = \Phi(\mathbf{X}^{(t)}, R^{(t+1)})$,
Until $|\mathbf{X}^{(0)}| = 1$. (check whether $\mathbf{X}^{(0)}$ is a singleton)
Return $\mathbf{X}^{(0)}$.

In line 4 of the algorithm, $\lceil c \rceil$ denotes the smallest integer that is greater than or equal to c. Thus, when $t_0 = -1$, a random vector, $R^{(0)}$, is generated; when $t_0 = -2$, $R^{(-1)}$ is generated; when $t_0 = -4$, $R^{(-3)}$ and $R^{(-2)}$ are generated; and so on.

Monotone Coupling from the Past

If the state space is large, the CFTP algorithm becomes computationally expensive. In this case, Propp and Wilson (1996) suggested a more efficient algorithm for a Markov chain that satisfies the following additional conditions: a partial ordering can be defined on the state space together with a minimal state and a maximal state, and the Markov chain is *monotone* with respect to this partial ordering. If two states, $x, y \in S$, satisfy the partial order, $x \le y$, then the Markov chain is monotone when $\phi(x, R) \le \phi(y, R)$, that is, when the partial order is preserved after a coupled transition. For a monotone Markov chain with minimal state s_{min} and maximal state s_{max}, instead of starting chains from every state in the state space, it is necessary to use only two bounding chains, starting from s_{min} and s_{max}. When these two bounding chains coalesce, the monotone property guarantees that all other chains starting from any intermediate states would coalesce as well.

The monotone CFTP algorithm, with optimal sequence of steps back, proceeds as follows:

Monotone CFTP

Set $k = -1$.
Repeat
  Set $k = k + 1$ and $t_0 = -2^k$, (take 2^k time-steps back)
  Generate $R^{(t_0+1)}, R^{(t_0+2)}, ..., R^{(\lceil t_0/2 \rceil)}$,
  Set $X^{(t_0, s_{min}(t_0))} = s_{min}$ and $X^{(t_0, s_{max}(t_0))} = s_{max}$ (start chains in extremal states)
  For $t = t_0, t_0 +1, ..., -1$, (propagate coupled chains to time 0)
    Set $X^{(t+1, s_{min}(t_0))} = \phi(X^{(t, s_{min}(t_0))}, R^{(t+1)})$,
    $X^{(t+1, s_{max}(t_0))} = \phi(X^{(t, s_{max}(t_0))}, R^{(t+1)})$,
  Until $X^{(0, s_{min}(t_0))} = X^{(0, s_{max}(t_0))}$.
  (check for coalescence at time 0)
Return $X^{(0)}$.

Monotonicity not only provides computational efficiency, but also suggests a way to extend CFTP to general state spaces.

Extensions of CFTP to General State Space

Foss and Tweedie (1998) showed that a necessary and sufficient condition for using the CFTP algorithm is that the Markov chain be *uniformly ergodic*, that is, the rate at which the Markov chain converges to its stationary distribution is *geometric* and *uniform* over all starting values. When convergence to the stationary distribution is at a geometric rate but not uniform over starting values, the Markov chain is described as *geometrically ergodic*. For a finite state space, the situation is straightforward because an ergodic Markov chain is uniformly ergodic (Robert & Casella, 2004: Theorem 6.59).

For a general (countable or continuous) state space, one way to get a uniformly ergodic Markov chain with stationary distribution, f, is to use the

IMH sampler with a proposal distribution, g, that makes $f(x)/g(x)$ bounded for all $x \in S$ (Mengersen & Tweedie, 1996). In particular, this holds when g is over-dispersed relative to the target distribution f. The boundedness of $f(x)/g(x)$ is essential because when $f(x)/g(x)$ is not bounded, the sampler is not even geometrically ergodic. Even with a uniformly ergodic IMH chain, however, implementation of CFTP is more delicate because of the infiniteness of the state space. Generally, chains with different starting values may come arbitrarily close but not coalesce in finite time. Fortunately, when $f(x)/g(x)$ is bounded, not only is the IMH chain uniformly ergodic, it is monotone with respect to the ordering: $x \leq y$ if, and only if, $f(x)/g(x) \geq f(y)/g(y)$ (Corcoran & Tweedie, 2002). Furthermore, a state that maximizes f/g is a minimal state under the ordering; denote it by s_{min}, if it exists. s_{min} may be regarded as a state with highest inertia because it is hardest for the IMH chain to change state when it is in s_{min}. Thus, when a chain in state s_{min} at time t changes to state s at time $t+1$, all other coupled chains in any other state at time t will also change to state s at time $t+1$. This means that all coupled chains will coalesce at the time-step when the chain starting in s_{min} changes to a new state. Therefore, a version of monotone CFTP requiring a single IMH chain is available.

IMH CFTP

Choose proposal distribution g.
Find $s_{min} = \arg \max f(x)/g(x)$.
Set $k = -1$ and *coalesce* = 0.
Repeat
  Set $k = k + 1$ and $t_0 = -2^k$. (take 2^k time-steps back)
  Generate $\tilde{X}^{(t_0+1)}, \tilde{X}^{(t_0+2)}, ..., \tilde{X}^{(\lceil t_0/2 \rceil)} \sim g$,
    $U^{(t_0+1)}, U^{(t_0+2)}, ..., U^{(\lceil t_0/2 \rceil)} \sim U(0,1)$,
  Set $X^{(t_0, s_{min}(t_0))} = s_{min}$, (start IMH chain in minimal state)
  For $t = t_0, t_0 + 1, ..., -1$, (propagate IMH chain to time 0)

Compute $\alpha = \min\left\{1, \dfrac{f(\widetilde{X})g(X^{(t-1)})}{f(X^{(t-1)})g(\widetilde{X})}\right\}$,

If $U^{(t+1)} \leq \alpha$

    Set $X^{(t+1,s_{\min}(t_0))} = X^{(t,s_{\min}(t_0))}$, (accept $\widetilde{X}^{(t+1)}$
with probability α)

    Set *coalesce* = 1,

Else:

    Set $X^{(t+1,s_{\min}(t_0))} = X^{(t,s_{\min}(t_0))}$,

Until *coalesce* = 1. (check for coalescence at time 0)

Return $X^{(0)}$.

IMH CFTP requires $f(x)/g(x)$ to be bounded, which is not always achievable in practice. Even if $f(x)/g(x)$ is bounded, it may be difficult to find the maximizing point (minimal state) in a complex high-dimensional situation. When the state space is compact, a convenient choice of g is the uniform distribution.

Roberts and Rosenthal (1999) showed that a Markov chain given by the slice sampler is monotone with respect to the partial ordering: $x \leq y$ if, and only if, $f(x) \leq f(y)$. Mira, Moller, and Roberts (2001) used this to propose a perfect slice sampling algorithm. The *perfect slice sampler* has the same practical impediment as the slice sampler: it can be difficult to simulate from the uniform distribution on the horizontal slice. Philippe and Robert (2003) used the perfect slice sampler to simulate from a truncated multivariate normal distribution.

Monotonicity provides a way for defining and detecting coalescence in an infinite state space. When monotonicity is unavailable, some other way for determining coalescence must be found. One approach, proposed by Murdoch and Green (1998), is to use a *bounding* or *dominating process*,

together with some means of coupling it to the Markov chain. Consider the one-dimensional case where the state space is the real line, and suppose that the Markov chain is uniformly ergodic, with transition kernel density, q, satisfying

$$q(y \mid x) \geq v(y) \tag{11}$$

for all $x, y \in S = \mathbf{R}$, and some non-negative function v, for which

$$\rho = \int v(y)dy > 0 \tag{12}$$

Thus, v serves as a bounding process for the Markov chain. Using *gamma coupling* (Lindvall, 2002, pp. 18-20) to couple v to the Markov chain, Murdoch and Green (1998) pointed out that (see Box 3.) where

$$V(y) = \frac{1}{\rho}\int_{-\infty}^{y} v(z)dz \tag{14}$$

and

$$W(y \mid x) = \frac{1}{1-\rho}\int_{-\infty}^{y}[q(z \mid x) - v(z)]dz \tag{15}$$

Equation (13) provides the following update function:

$$\Phi(\mathbf{X},U) = \begin{cases} V^{-1}(U_2), & \text{if } U_1 \leq \rho, \\ W^{-1}(U_2 \mid \mathbf{X}), & \text{if } U_1 > \rho \text{ and } |\mathbf{X}| = 1, \\ S, & \text{otherwise,} \end{cases} \tag{16}$$

where $U = (U_1, U_2)$ is a pair of uniform $(0, 1)$ random numbers. Starting with $\mathbf{X}^{(t_0)} = S$ at some time t_0 in the past, the resulting algorithm is called the *multi-gamma coupler*.

Box 3.

$$\boxed{P(X^{(t+1)} \leq y \mid X^{(t)} = x) = \int_{-\infty}^{y} q(z \mid x)dz = \rho V(y) + (1-\rho)W(y \mid x)} \tag{13}$$

Multi-Gamma Coupler

Set $k = -1$.
Repeat
    Set $k = k + 1$ and $t_0 = -2^k$, (take 2^k time-steps back)
    Generate ,

$$(U_1^{(t_0+1)}, U_2^{(t_0+1)}), (U_1^{(t_0+2)}, U_2^{(t_0+2)}), ..., (U_1^{(\lceil t_0/2 \rceil)}, U_2^{(\lceil t_0/2 \rceil)})$$

    Set $\mathbf{X}^{(t_0)} = S$, (initialize starting set to S)
    For $t = t_0, t_0 + 1, ..., -1$, (propagate set to time 0)
        If $|\mathbf{X}^{(t+1)}| = \infty$
          If $U_1^{(t+1)} \leq \rho$
            Set $\mathbf{X}^{(t+1)} = V^{-1}(U_2^{(t+1)})$,
          Else
            Set $\mathbf{X}^{(t+1)} = S$,
        Else
          If $U_1^{(t+1)} \leq \rho$
            Set $\mathbf{X}^{(t+1)} V^{-1}(U_2^{(t+1)})$,
          Else
            Set $\mathbf{X}^{(t+1)} = W^{-1}(U_2^{(t+1)} | \mathbf{X}^{(t)})$,
Until $|\mathbf{X}^{(0)}| = 1$. (check whether $\mathbf{X}^{(0)}$ is a singleton)
Return $\mathbf{X}^{(0)}$.

In practical applications, the bounding process v may be too small to be useful, and may even be equal to 0. Moreover, the algorithm requires the distributions in the update function to be known completely; usually, only the unnormalized distributions are known. Some ways to get around these limitations are described in Murdoch and Green (1998).

Murdoch and Green (1998) also provide an alternative simpler algorithm that does not require backward simulations, showing that exact MCMC can be achieved by forward simulations.

Multi-Gamma Sampler

Generate $\tau \sim$ geometric (ρ) and $U \sim U(0,1)$.
Set $t = 0$ and $X^{(0)} = V^{-1}(U)$.
While $t < \tau$
    Set $t = t + 1$,
    Generate $U^{(t)} \sim U(0,1)$,
    Set $X^{(t)} = W^{-1}(U^{(t)} | X^{(t-1)})$.
Return $X^{(\tau)}$.

An explanation of this algorithm in terms of an infinite mixture representation of the stationary distribution is given in Hobert and Robert (2004). For a uniformly ergodic Markov chain on the real line, the stationary distribution can be expressed as

$$F(y) = \int_{-\infty}^{y} f(x)dx = \sum_{k=0}^{\infty} \rho(1-\rho)^k W^k(V, y) \quad (17)$$

where

$$W^k(V, y) = \int_S W^k(y | x) dV(x) \quad (18)$$

and

$$W^k(y | x) = P(Y^{(t+k)} \leq y | Y^{(t)} = x) \quad (19)$$

for process, $(Y^{(t)})$, propagating according to W. Therefore, a sample value from the stationary distribution can be generated from the mixture component, $W^k(V, y)$, with probability $\rho(1-\rho)^k$, which is a geometric probability for k= 0, 1,.... Hobert and Robert (2004) also show how the *read-once coupler* by Wilson (2000) can be derived from the representation in (17). The read-once coupler is another algorithm that employs forward coupling, not backward. Breyer and Roberts (2001) extend these methods to geometrically ergodic Markov chains by proposing a general methodology (*catalytic coupling*) that allows sample values from the stationary distribution to be read off the sample path in a forward simulation of the chain.

The idea of a bounding process can be used to adapt monotone CFTP for an *anti-monotone* Markov chain, that is, when $s_1 \leq s_2$ implies $\phi(s_1, R) \geq \phi(s_1, R)$. This is achieved by replacing the lower and upper bounding chains in the monotone CFTP algorithm by the bounding sequences,

$$\underline{X}^{(t+1, s_{\min}(t_0))} = \phi(\overline{X}^{(t, s_{\max}(t_0))}, R^{(t+1)}) \qquad (20)$$

$$\overline{X}^{(t+1, s_{\max}(t_0))} = \phi(\underline{X}^{(t, s_{\min}(t_0))}, R^{(t+1)}) \qquad (21)$$

Note that the two bounding sequences, $(\underline{X}^{(t, s_{\min}(t_0))})$ and $(\overline{X}^{(t, s_{\max}(t_0))})$, are individually *not* Markov chains, but the augmented sequence, $(\underline{X}^{(t, s_{\min}(t_0))}, \overline{X}^{(t, s_{\max}(t_0))})$, is a Markov chain and, upon coalescence, the common chain is Markov and has the required stationary distribution. Details can be found in Haggstrom and Nelander (1998).

Extensions of the bounding idea to geometrically ergodic Markov chains are reported in Kendall (1998), Moller (1999), and Kendall and Moller (2000). Suppose a partial order can be defined on the state space and two coupled *bounding sequences*, $(\underline{X}^{(t)})$ and $(\overline{X}^{(t)})$, can be constructed such that

$$\underline{X}^{(t)} \leq X^{(t)} \leq \overline{X}^{(t)} \qquad (22)$$

for any starting state $X^{(0)}$, then coalescence of the bounding sequences implies that all coupled chains starting from all possible states would have coalesced as well. There is great flexibility in this approach because the bounding sequences can be defined on a larger state space and there can be different ways of coupling them to $(X^{(t)})$.

The bounding sequences, $(\underline{X}^{(t)})$ and $(\overline{X}^{(t)})$ can be regarded as the lower and upper limits of a sequence of bounding sets, $\mathbf{X}^{(t)} = [\underline{X}^{(t)}, \overline{X}^{(t)}]$, for the states of the Markov chain, that is, $X^{(t)} \in \mathbf{X}^{(t)}$. When coalescence occurs, the bounding set degenerates into a singleton, and so a singleton at time 0 is an exact sample value from the stationary distribution. In general, depending on the

application, the bounding set is initialized using some starting set, say S_0, and propagated by a set-valued update function, Φ, such that

$$\mathbf{X}^{(t+1)} = \Phi(\mathbf{X}^{(t)}, R^{(t+1)}) \qquad (23)$$

The key to implementing this lies in finding suitable bounding processes and coupling schemes so that coalescence will happen in a finite time. Some specific implementations are described in Kendall (1998), Huber (1998), Moller (1999), Green and Murdoch (1999), Kendall and Moller (2000), Huber (2004) and Cai (2005).

An example of such an algorithm is *dominated CFTP*, suggested by Kendall (1998). Consider a Markov chain, $(X^{(t)})$, on the state space, $S = [0, \infty)$, and suppose that for $r \leq t$ and $s \leq t$, the Markov chain can be coupled such that

$$X^{(t, x(r))} \leq X^{(t, y(s))} \quad \Rightarrow \quad X^{(t+1, x(r))} \leq X^{(t+1, y(s))} \qquad (24)$$

for $x, y \in S$. Suppose a stationary dominating process, Y, can be constructed on S, with stationary distribution, f_Y, and which can be coupled to X such that

$$X^{(t, x(r))} \leq Y^{(t)} \quad \Rightarrow \quad X^{(t+1, x(r))} \leq Y^{(t+1)} \qquad (25)$$

for $r \leq t$. The algorithm proceeds by generating $Y^{(0)}$ from f_Y and propagating it backwards to time t_0 in the past. Two chains for X are then started at t_0, one in state 0 and the other in state $Y^{(t_0)}$. These two chains, coupled to each other and to Y, are propagated forward in time to time 0. If they coalesce by the time they reach 0, then the common value has distribution f.

Dominated CFTP

Set $k = -1$.
Generate $Y^{(0)} \sim f_Y$
Repeat

Set $k = k + 1$ and $t_0 = -2^k$, (take 2^k time-steps back)

Generate $R^{(t_0+1)}, R^{(t_0+2)}, \ldots, R^{(\lceil t_0/2 \rceil)}$,

For $t = \lceil t_0/2 \rceil - 1, \lceil t_0/2 \rceil - 2, \ldots, t_0$, (propagate Y chain backwards to time t_0)

Set $Y^{(t)} = \phi_Y(Y^{(t+1)}, R^{(t+1)})$,

Set $X^{(t_0, 0(t_0))} = 0$ and $X^{(t_0, Y^{(t_0)}(t_0))} = Y^{(t_0)}$, (initialize X chains)

For $t = t_0, t_0 + 1, \ldots, -1$, (propagate X chains forward to time 0)

Set $X^{(t+1, 0(t_0))} = \phi(X^{(t, 0(t_0))}, R^{(t+1)})$,

$X^{(t+1, Y^{(t_0)}(t_0))} = \phi(X^{(t, Y^{(t_0)}(t_0))}, R^{(t+1)})$,

Until $X^{(0, 0(t_0))} = X^{(0, Y^{(t_0)}(t_0))}$. (check for coalescence at time 0)

Return $X^{(0)}$.

Another related development, reported in Moller and Nicholls (1999), combines backward coupling via a dominating process with *simulated tempering* (Marinari & Parisi, 1992). The resulting algorithm is known as *perfect tempering.*

Other Exact MCMC Algorithms

Fill (1998) proposed an exact MCMC algorithm that uses forward coupling and is *interruptible.* This means that if a run is aborted, the sample values from other completed runs still constitute an *unbiased* sample from the stationary distribution. In contrast, algorithms based on backward coupling are generally not interruptible because a returned sample value is dependent on the run time. For example, if the CFTP algorithm is used and long runs are aborted, the resulting sample values may become biased and cease to be distributed according to the stationary distribution. Fill's algorithm is a form of generalized rejection sampling and requires an ergodic, monotone Markov chain on a finite state space, with minimal state, s_{min}, and maximal state, s_{max}. The algorithm works by reverse coupling two chains starting from s_{min} and s_{max}. Let $\underline{\phi}$ be the forward-chain update function and let $\overline{\phi}$ be the reverse-chain update function.

Fill's Algorithm

Set $k = -1$.

Repeat

Set $k = k + 1$, $\tau = 2^k$, $\underline{X}^{(0)} = s_{min}$ and $\overline{X}^{(0)} = s_{max}$.

For $t = 1, 2, \ldots, \tau$

Generate $\underline{R}^{(t)}$,

Set $\underline{X}^{(t)} = \underline{\phi}(\underline{X}^{(t-1)}, \underline{R}^{(t)})$,

For $t = 1, 2, \ldots, \tau$

Generate $\overline{R}^{(t)} \sim h(R \mid \underline{X}^{(\tau-t+1)}, \underline{X}^{(\tau-t)})$,

Set $\overline{X}^{(t)} = \overline{\phi}(\overline{X}^{(t-1)}, \overline{R}^{(t)})$,

Until $\overline{X}^{(\tau)} = s_{min}$.

Return $\underline{X}^{(\tau)}$.

In the algorithm, $\overline{R}^{(t)} \sim h(R \mid \underline{X}^{(\tau-t+1)}, \underline{X}^{(\tau-t)})$ is the conditional distribution of R given $\underline{X}^{(\tau-t+1)}$ and $\underline{X}^{(\tau-t)}$. Fill's algorithm is not as easy to implement as CFTP, and can be computationally more expensive in time and storage requirements. Fill, Machida, Murdoch, and Rosenthal (2000) contains an extension to general state spaces, and also discusses connections with CFTP.

Some other insights into exact MCMC can be found in the review papers by Casella, et al. (2001); Dimakos (2001); Djuric, Huang, and Ghirmai (2002); Kendall (2005); and Thonnes (2000). A valuable resource on exact MCMC is David Wilson's Web site: http://dbwilson.com/exact/.

The key idea in exact MCMC is the use of coupling. Two useful references for the coupling method are Lindvall (2002) and Thorisson (2000).

APPLICATIONS OF EXACT MCMC

Exact MCMC methods have been developed for a wide variety of models.

Markov Random Fields

Markov random fields are widely used in statistical physics and in image processing. A distribution for a Markov random field is given by

$$f(x) \propto e^{-H(x)} \qquad (26)$$

where $H(x)$ is an *energy function*. The normalizing constant for the distribution is usually not available in practice, thus hindering direct sampling from the distribution. Before exact MCMC was available, Geman and Geman (1984) suggested using the Gibbs sampler.

An example of a Markov random field in statistical physics is the *Ising model* for magnetic spins in ferromagnetic substances. This model was used by Propp and Wilson (1996) to demonstrate their CFTP algorithm, and also by Fill (1998) for his interruptible algorithm. For a two-dimensional lattice with N sites, let X_i represent the magnetic spin at site i, with $X_i = -1$ for spin down and $X_i = 1$ for spin up. The spin state of the entire lattice can then be represented by an N-dimensional vector in a state space of size 2^N. If the lattice is exposed to an external magnetic field, the energy function can be expressed as

$$H(x) = -\frac{1}{kT}\left(\sum_{i<j}\alpha_{i,j}x_i x_j + \sum_i \beta_i x_i\right) \quad (27)$$

where k is Boltzmann's constant, T is absolute temperature, $\alpha_{i,j}$ is the interaction strength between sites i and j, and β_i is the strength of the external field at site i.

When $\alpha_{i,j} \geq 0$, the Gibbs sampler is monotone with respect to the *component-wise partial ordering*: $x \leq y$ if, and only if, $x_i \leq y_i$ for all sites. To see this, let X_{-i} denote all lattice sites except the i-th one. It can be shown that (see Box 4.), which is larger when more sites have spin up. Therefore, if $x \leq y$, then $P(X_l = 1 \mid X_{-l} = x_{-l}) \leq P(Y_l = 1 \mid Y_{-l} = y_{-l})$ for any site l, and so $\phi(x,R) \leq \phi(y,R)$ for a coupled Gibbs sampler transition. Hence, monotone CFTP can be used in this case, with a minimal state made up of all spin down sites and a maximal state comprising all spin up sites.

Propp and Wilson (1996) describe applications of CFTP to other models in statistical physics, including the Potts model, which generalizes the Ising model to allow more than two "spins" per site; the random cluster model, which generalizes both the Ising and Potts models; ice models and dimer models.

In Haggstrom and Nelander (1999), an algorithm using the Gibbs sampler with bounding processes is developed for Markov random fields. Moller and Schladitz (1999) describe the extension and application of Fill's algorithm to antimonotone Markov random fields. Djuric, et al. (2002) contains an example in which CFTP with bounding processes is used for the restoration of binary images. Haran and Tierney (2005) applied the perfect tempering method to a Markov random field model used for disease mapping.

Linear Models

Consider the problem of fitting a response, y, to d predictors, $x_{\cdot,1},...,x_{\cdot,d}$, using n data points, $(y_1, x_{1,1},...,x_{1,d}),...,(y_n, x_{n,1},...,x_{n,d})$, with a *linear regression model* expressed as

Box 4.

$$P(X_l = 1 \mid X_{-l} = x_{-l}) = \left\{1 + \exp\left[-\frac{2}{kT}\left(\sum_{i<l}\alpha_{i,l}x_i + \sum_{l<j}\alpha_{l,j}x_j + \beta_l\right)\right]\right\}^{-1} \qquad (28)$$

$$y_i = \sum_{j=1}^{d} \gamma_j \beta_j x_{i,j} + \varepsilon_i \qquad (29)$$

where $\beta_1,...,\beta_d$ are regression coefficients, and $\varepsilon_1,...,\varepsilon_n$ are independent normal random variables with mean 0 and variance σ^2. $\gamma_1,...,\gamma_d \in \{0,1\}$ are called latent variables and they indicate which predictors contribute to the response. In the most general situation, the unknown parameters in the model are $\gamma = (\gamma_1,...,\gamma_d)$, $\beta = (\beta_1,...,\beta_d)$ and σ^2. Let X be the $n \times d$ matrix whose (i, j)-component is $x_{i,j}$, assumed to be known without error, and let $Y = (y_1,...,y_n)$. In a Bayesian analysis, the posterior distribution, $f(\gamma, \beta, \sigma^2 \mid Y, X)$, must be found. Using Bayes' theorem (see Box 5), where $\phi(\cdot \mid \mu, \nu)$ denotes the normal density with mean μ and variance ν, and $f(\gamma, \beta, \sigma^2)$ is a prior distribution. For predictor selection, the marginal distribution, $f(\gamma \mid Y, X)$, is of interest. Note that the support of this marginal distribution is discrete and finite.

Huang and Djuric (2002) looked at a simpler case, by assuming that β and σ^2 are known, and using algorithms based on CFTP to sample from $f(\gamma \mid Y, X)$. Schneider and Corcoran (2004) treated the general case by developing exact MCMC algorithms to sample from $f(\gamma, \beta, \sigma^2 \mid Y, X)$.

A similar problem is curve fitting for a set of n data points, $(x_1, y_1),...,(x_n, y_n)$, using a *basis functions model*,

$$y_i = \sum_{j=1}^{n} \gamma_j \beta_j \psi_j(x_i) + \varepsilon_i \qquad (31)$$

where $\psi_1,...,\psi_n$ are the basis functions, $\beta_1,...,\beta_n$ are the model coefficients, $\gamma_1,...,\gamma_n \in \{0, 1\}$ are binary

latent variables, and $\varepsilon_1,...,\varepsilon_n$ are independent normal random variables with mean 0 and variance σ^2. Let $y = (y_1,...,y_n)^T$, $\varepsilon = (\varepsilon_1,...,\varepsilon_n)^T$, $\gamma = (\gamma_1,...,\gamma_n)^T$ and $\beta = (\beta_1,...,\beta_n)^T$ be column vectors, and let Ψ be the $n \times n$ matrix whose (i, j)-component is $\psi_j(x_i)$, that is each column of Ψ is a basis function vector. Then equation (31) can be written as

$$y = \Psi(\gamma * \beta) + \varepsilon \qquad (32)$$

where $\gamma * \beta$ denotes the point-wise product of γ and β. Assuming that $x_1,...,x_n$ are known without error, the Bayesian approach to the selection or thresholding of model coefficients is based on the marginal posterior distribution, $f(\gamma \mid y)$.

Suppose that the basis functions are orthonormal, and let

$$\hat{\beta} = \Psi^T y \qquad (33)$$

By Bayes' theorem, the joint posterior distribution of the unknown quantities, γ, β and σ^2, is given by

$$f(\gamma, \beta, \sigma^2 \mid y) \propto f(y \mid \gamma, \beta, \sigma^2) f(\gamma, \beta, \sigma^2) \qquad (34)$$

where

$$f(y \mid \gamma, \beta, \sigma^2) \propto (\sigma^2)^{-n/2} \exp\left(-\frac{(\hat{\beta} - \gamma * \beta)^T (\hat{\beta} - \gamma * \beta)}{2\sigma^2}\right) \qquad (35)$$

is the likelihood function and $f(\gamma, \beta, \sigma^2)$ is a prior distribution. Following Holmes and Denison (2002), choose

Box 5.

$$f(\gamma, \beta, \sigma^2 \mid Y, X) \propto f(Y \mid \gamma, \beta, \sigma^2, X) f(\gamma, \beta, \sigma^2)$$

$$= \left[\prod_{i=1}^{n} \phi\left(y_i \mid \sum_{j=1}^{d} \gamma_j \beta_j x_{i,j}, \sigma^2\right)\right] f(\gamma, \beta, \sigma^2) \qquad (30)$$

$$f(\gamma, \beta, \sigma^2) = f(\gamma)f(\beta \mid \sigma^2)f(\sigma^2) \qquad (36)$$

where

$$f(\gamma) = q^m(1-q)^{n-m}, \quad q = P(\gamma_i = 1), \quad m = \gamma_1 + \ldots + \gamma_n \qquad (37)$$

$$f(\beta \mid \sigma^2) = N_n(0, v\sigma^2 I) \propto (\sigma^2)^{-n/2} \exp\left(-\frac{\beta^T \beta}{2v\sigma^2}\right) \qquad (38)$$

that is n-variate normal with mean 0 and covariance matrix $v\sigma^2 I$, and

$$f(\sigma^2) = IG(a, b) \propto (\sigma^2)^{-(a+1)} \exp(-b/\sigma^2) \qquad (39)$$

that is inverse gamma with shape parameter a and scale parameter b. Thus, the hyperparameters are q, v, a and b.

The marginal posterior distribution of γ is (Lee, Iyengar, Czanner, & Roscoe, 2005) (see Box 6) from which the following conditional probability can be derived: (see Box 7) where γ_{-j} represents γ with γ_j omitted, γ_{j1} denotes γ with $\gamma_j = 1$ and γ_{j0} is γ with $\gamma_j = 0$. Hence, the Gibbs sampler can be used to produce a Markov chain with stationary

distribution $f(\gamma \mid y)$. CFTP can be used to simulate from $f(\gamma \mid y)$, but the size of the state space is 2^n, which can be computationally intractable when n is large. Fortunately, the resulting Markov chain can be shown to be monotone with respect to the component-wise partial ordering, with minimal state, $(0,0,\ldots,0)$, and maximal state, $(1,1,\ldots,1)$, and so monotone CFTP can be used to sample from $f(\gamma \mid y)$.

In Lee, et al. (2005), this was applied to the wavelet representation of neuron spiking signals. Ambler and Silverman (2004) adopted a different approach to deal with correlated wavelet coefficients.

Mixture Models

A *finite mixture density* has the form,

$$h(x) = \sum_{j=1}^{k} p_j h_j(x \mid \theta_j) \qquad (42)$$

where $h_1, h_2, \ldots, h_k$ are known component densities, θ_j is the parameter of h_j, and the mixing proportions, $p_1, p_2, \ldots, p_k$, satisfy $0 < p_j \leq 1$ and

$$\sum_{j=1}^{k} p_j = 1 \qquad (43)$$

Box 6.

$$f(\gamma \mid y) = \iint f(\gamma, \beta, \sigma^2 \mid y) d\beta d\sigma^2$$

$$\propto \frac{q^m(1-q)^{n-m}}{(v+1)^{m/2}[2b(v+1) + (v+1)\hat{\beta}^T\hat{\beta} - v(\gamma * \hat{\beta})^T(\gamma * \hat{\beta})]^{(a+n/2)}} \qquad (40)$$

Box 7.

$$P(\gamma_j = 1 \mid y, \gamma_{-j})$$

$$= \left\{ 1 + (v+1)^{1/2} \frac{(1-q)}{q} \left[\frac{2b(v+1) + (v+1)\hat{\beta}^T\hat{\beta} - v(\gamma_{j1} * \hat{\beta})^T(\gamma_{j1} * \hat{\beta})}{2b(v+1) + (v+1)\hat{\beta}^T\hat{\beta} - v(\gamma_{j0} * \hat{\beta})^T(\gamma_{j0} * \hat{\beta})} \right]^{(a+n/2)} \right\}^{-1} \qquad (41)$$

In the most general situation, k, $p = (p_1, p_2, ..., p_k)$ and $\theta = (\theta_1, \theta_2, ..., \theta_k)$ may all be unknown and need to be inferred from data, say $x_1, ..., x_n$. The Bayesian approach seeks to find the posterior distribution of the unknown quantities, that is, $f(k, p, \theta \mid x_1, ..., x_n)$. By Bayes' theorem,

$$f(k, p, \theta \mid x_1, ..., x_n) \propto f(x_1, ..., x_n \mid k, p, \theta) f(k, p, \theta)$$
$$= \left[\prod_{i=1}^{n} \sum_{j=1}^{k} p_j h_j(x_i \mid \theta_j) \right] f(k, p, \theta), \tag{44}$$

where it is assumed that the data are independent, and $f(k, p, \theta)$ is a prior distribution. Clearly, the posterior distribution is analytically intractable, and so inference must proceed through sample values generated from it. The Bayesian analysis of finite mixture models is widely recognized as a challenging problem.

One of the first attempts in using CFTP for finite mixtures was Hobert, Robert, and Titterington (1999), where it was assumed that only the mixing proportions were unknown. Even for this simpler situation, Hobert et al. (1999) were only able to implement algorithms for $k \leq 3$. Consider the case with two component densities: $p h_0(x) + (1 - p) h_1(x)$. The likelihood function for $x = x_1, ..., x_n$ is

$$f(x \mid p) = \prod_{i=1}^{n} [p h_0(x_i) + (1 - p) h_1(x_i)] \tag{45}$$

By introducing a latent variable, $z_i \in \{0, 1\}$, for each x_i, to indicate which density component x_i originates from, the simpler completed likelihood function is given by

$$f(x, z \mid p) = \prod_{i=1}^{n} p_{z_i} h_{z_i}(x_i) \tag{46}$$

where $z = (z_1, ..., z_n)$, $p_0 = p$ and $p_1 = 1 - p$. By Bayes' theorem, the joint posterior distribution of p and z is

$$f(p, z \mid x) \propto f(x \mid p, z) f(p, z) = f(x, z \mid p) f(p). \tag{47}$$

Choosing a uniform prior for p,

$$f(p, z \mid x) \propto \prod_{i=1}^{n} p_{z_i} h_{z_i}(x_i) \tag{48}$$

and so

$$P(z_i = 0 \mid x, p) = \frac{p h_0(x_i)}{p h_0(x_i) + (1 - p) h_1(x_i)} \tag{49}$$

and, letting $m = z_1 + \cdots + z_n$,

$$f(p \mid x, z) \propto p^{n-m} (1 - p)^m \tag{50}$$

which is a beta distribution with parameters $n - m + 1$ and $m + 1$. Thus, the Gibbs sampler can be used to produce a Markov chain with stationary distribution $f(p, z \mid x)$. Since m can only take $n + 1$ possible values, $0, 1, ..., n$, CFTP can be used to simulate from $f(p \mid x)$. In fact, a more efficient monotone CFTP can be used by noting that a beta$(n - m + 1, m + 1)$ variate, p, can be obtained from

$$p = \frac{\sum_{i=1}^{m+1} y_i}{\sum_{i=1}^{n+2} y_i} \tag{51}$$

where $y_1, ..., y_{n+2}$ are independent exponential random variables with mean 1. Therefore, p is increasing with m, which provides the monotone structure needed to use monotone CFTP with two chains, one starting with $m = 0$ and the other with $m = n$. The case with three component densities is more delicate and requires the construction of a bounding process—see Hobert, et al. (1999) for details.

Machida (2004) pursued the implementation of extensions of Fill's algorithm for the same 2 and 3-component mixtures, under the same assumption that only the mixing proportions were unknown. Casella, et al. (2002) investigated the use of the perfect slice sampler and the catalytic coupling method of Breyer and Roberts (2001) for mixture models, under the weaker assumption that only k was known. They concluded that the perfect slice sampler was practical only for small sample sizes and that an algorithm using catalytic coupling can be used for larger sample sizes.

Other Applications

Exact MCMC has been most successful for point processes, with seminal work done by Kendall (1998); Haggstrom, van Liesholt, and Moller (1999); and Kendall and Moller (2000). At least two books—Moller (2003) and Moller and Waagepetersen (2003)—have already been written about this application. The interested reader can refer to these excellent resources and the references contained therein. See also the paper by Berthelsen and Moller (2002).

Propp and Wilson (1998) describes how the problem of simulating from the stationary distribution of a Markov chain is related to the problem of generating a random spanning tree of a directed graph and, therefore, how CFTP can be applied to the latter problem. Harvey and Neal (2000) used CFTP to perform inference for belief networks.

Huang and Djuric (2001) describe the use of exact MCMC for solving a problem in communications engineering—that of multiuser detection of synchronous code division multiple access signals.

Guglielmi, Holmes, and Walker (2002) used CFTP methods to simulate from bounded functionals of a Dirichlet process, which is of interest in the context of Bayesian nonparametric inference.

CONCLUSION

Tremendous advances have been made in exact MCMC since the publication of CFTP (Propp & Wilson, 1996). Exact MCMC has found great success in some niche applications, such as point processes, stochastic geometry and random fields. However, in other applications involving more general state spaces and more complex distributions, such as in computational Bayesian statistics, there is some way to go yet.

At the moment, the closest to a generic exact MCMC algorithm is possibly CFTP for finite state spaces. For large state spaces, CFTP can be computationally too expensive to implement and some monotone structure must be found for it to be practicable. This may or may not be available depending on the application, and so large finite state spaces with no monotone structure remain a problem.

For more general problems involving continuous state spaces, a key limitation of exact MCMC is the difficulty in devising effective bounding or dominating processes. This is a challenging task that requires advanced mathematical knowledge and skills to attempt, with no guarantee of a working algorithm. Successful implementations of exact MCMC for continuous state spaces will most likely comprise a collection of techniques or hybrid combinations of techniques. Further theoretical and methodological breakthroughs are needed to make exact MCMC easier to use, more computationally efficient and more widely applicable. Recent works, such as Hobert and Robert (2004), Breyer and Roberts (2001), and Wilson (2000), represent some efforts toward this goal.

REFERENCES

Ambler, G.K., & Silverman, B.W. (2004). Perfect simulation for Bayesian wavelet thresholding with correlated coefficients. Preprint from http://dbwilson.com/exact/

Berthelsen, K.K., & Moller, J. (2002). A primer on perfect simulation for spatial point processes. *Bulletin of the Brazilian Mathematical Society, 33*, 351 - 367.

Breyer, L.A., & Roberts, G.O. (2001). Catalytic perfect simulation. *Methodology and Computing in Applied Probability*, 3(2), 161-177.

Brooks, S.P., & Roberts, G.O. (1998). Diagnosing convergence of Markov chain Monte Carlo algorithms. *Statistics and Computing*, 8, 319-335.

Cai, Y. (2005). A non-monotone CFTP perfect simulation method. *Statistica Sinica*, 15, 927-943.

Cappe, O., & Robert, C.P. (2000). Markov chain Monte Carlo: 10 years and still running! *Journal of the American Statistical Association*, 95, 1282-1286.

Casella, G., Lavine, M., & Robert, C.P. (2001). Explaining the perfect sampler. *American Statistician*, 55(4), 299-305.

Casella, G., Mengersen, K., Robert, C., & Titterington, D. (2002). Perfect slice samplers for mixtures of distributions. *Journal of the Royal Statistical Society Series B*, 64(4), 777-790.

Corcoran, J., & Tweedie, R. (2002). Perfect sampling from independent Metropolis-Hastings chains. *Journal of Statistical Planning and Inference*, 104, 297-314.

Cowles, M.K., & Carlin, B.P. (1996). Markov chain Monte Carlo convergence diagnostics: A comparative review. *Journal of the American Statistical Association*, 91, 883-904.

Dimakos, X.K. (2001). A guide to exact simulation. *International Statistical Review*, 69(1), 27-48.

Djuric, P.M., Huang, Y., & Ghirmai, T. (2002). Perfect sampling: A review and applications to signal processing. *IEEE Transactions on Signal Processing*, 50(2), 345-356.

Fill, J.A. (1998). An interruptible algorithm for perfect sampling via Markov chains. *Annals of Applied Probability*, 8, 131-162.

Fill, J.A., Machida, M., Murdoch, D.J., & Rosenthal, J.S. (2000). Extension of Fill's perfect rejection sampling algorithm to general chains. *Random Structures and Algorithms*, 17, 290-316.

Foss, S., & Tweedie, R. (1998). Perfect simulation and backward coupling. *Stochastic Models*, 14, 187-203.

Gamerman, D. (1997). *Markov chain Monte Carlo*. Chapman & Hall.

Gelman, A., & Rubin, D.B. (1992). Inference from iterative simulation using multiple sequences. *Statistical Science*, 7, 457-511.

Geman, S., & Geman, D. (1984). Stochastic relaxation, Gibbs distributions and the Bayesian restoration of images. *IEEE Transactions on Pattern Analysis and Machine Intelligence*, 6, 721-741.

Gilks, W.R., Richardson, S., & Spiegelhalter, D.J. (Eds.) (1996). *Markov chain Monte Carlo in practice*. Chapman & Hall.

Green, P., & Murdoch, D. (1999). Exact sampling for Bayesian inference: Towards general purpose algorithms. In J. Berger, J. Bernardo, A. Dawid, D. Lindley, & A. Smith (Eds.), *Bayesian Statistics 6*, pp. 302-321. Oxford University Press.

Guglielmi, A., Holmes, C.C., & Walker, S.G. (2002). Perfect simulation involving functionals of a Dirichlet process. *Journal of Computational and Graphical Statistics*, 11(2), 306-310.

Haggstrom, O. (2002). *Finite Markov chains and algorithmic applications*. Cambridge University Press.

Haggstrom, O., & Nelander, K. (1998). Exact sampling from anti-monotone systems. *Statistica Neerlandica*, 52(3), 360-380.

Haggstrom, O., & Nelander, K. (1999). On exact simulation of Markov random fields using coupling from the past. *Scandinavian Journal of Statistics*, 26(3), 395-411.

Haggstrom, O., van Liesholt, M., & Moller, J. (1999). Characterisation results and Markov chain Monte Carlo algorithms including exact simulation for some spatial point processes. *Bernoulli, 5,* 641-659.

Haran, M., & Tierney, L. (2005). Perfect sampling for a Markov random field model. Preprint from http://www.stat.psu.edu/~mharan/

Harvey, M., & Neal, R.M. (2000). Inference for belief networks using coupling from the past. In C. Boutilier, & M. Goldszmidt (Eds.), *Proceedings of the 16th Conference on Uncertainty in Artificial Intelligence,* pp. 256-263.

Hastings, W.K. (1970). Monte Carlo sampling methods using Markov chains and their applications. *Biometrika, 57,* 97-109.

Hobert, J.P., & Robert, C.P. (2004). A mixture representation of π with applications in Markov chain Monte Carlo and perfect sampling. *The Annals of Applied Probability, 14*(3), 1295-1305.

Hobert, J.P., Robert, C.P., & Titterington, D.M. (1999). On perfect simulation for some mixtures of distributions. *Statistics and Computing, 9,* 287-298.

Holmes, C., & Denison, D.G.T. (2002). Perfect sampling for the wavelet reconstruction of signals. *IEEE Transactions on Signal Processing, 50*(2), 337-344.

Huang, Y., & Djuric, P.M. (2001). Multiuser detection of synchronous Code-Division-Multiple-Access signals by the Gibbs coupler. *Proceedings of the IEEE International Conference on Acoustics, Speech and Signal Processing,* Salt Lake City, Utah.

Huang, Y., & Djuric, P.M. (2002). Variable selection by perfect sampling. *EURASIP Journal on Applied Signal Processing, 2002*(1), 38-45.

Huber, M. (1998). Exact sampling and approximate counting techniques. *Proceedings of the 30th Annual ACM Symposium on the Theory of Computing,* 31-40.

Huber, M. (2004). Perfect sampling using bounding chains. *The Annals of Applied Probability, 14*(2), 734-753.

Johnson, V.E. (1996). Studying convergence of Markov chain Monte Carlo algorithms using coupled sample paths. *Journal of the American Statistical Association, 91*(433), 154-166.

Kass, R.E., Carlin, B.P., Gelman, A., & Neal, R.M. (1998). Markov chain Monte Carlo in practice: A roundtable discussion. *American Statistician, 52,* 93-100.

Kendall, W.S. (1998). Perfect simulation for the area-interaction point process. In L. Accardi & C.C. Heyde (Eds.), *Probability Towards 2000,* pp. 218-234. Springer.

Kendall, W.S. (2005). Notes on perfect simulation. Preprint from http://dbwilson.com/exact/

Kendall, W.S., & Moller, J. (2000). Perfect simulation using dominated processes on ordered spaces, with applications to locally stable point processes. *Advances in Applied Probability, 32,* 844-865.

Lee, D.S., Iyengar, S., Czanner, G., & Roscoe, J. (2005). *Bayesian wavelet representation of neuron signals via perfect sampling.* Paper presented at the 2nd IMS-ISBA Joint Meeting, Bormio, Italy.

Lindvall, T. (2002). *Lectures on the coupling method.* Dover Publications.

Machida, M. (2004). Perfect rejection sampling algorithm for simple mixture models. Preprint from http://www.math.tntech.edu/machida/

Marinari, E., & Parisi, G. (1992). Simulated tempering: A new Monte Carlo scheme. *Europhysics Letters, 19,* 451-458.

Mengersen, K., & Tweedie, R. (1996). Rates of convergence of the Hastings and Metropolis algorithms. Annals of Statistics, *24,* 101-121.

Mengersen, K.L., Robert, C.P., & Guihenneuc-Jouyaux, C. (1999). MCMC convergence diagnostics: A review. In J. Berger, J. Bernardo, A. Dawid, D. Lindley, & A. Smith (Eds.), *Bayesian Statistics 6,* pp. 415-440. Oxford University Press.

Metropolis, N., Rosenbluth, A., Rosenbluth, M., Teller, A., & Teller, E. (1953). Equations of state calculations by fast computing machines. *Journal of Chemical Physics, 21,* 1087-1092.

Meyn, S.P., & Tweedie, R.L. (1993). *Markov chains and stochastic stability.* Springer.

Mira, A., Moller, J., & Roberts, G. (2001). Perfect Slice Samplers. *Journal of the Royal Statistical Society Series B, 63*(3), 593-606.

Moller, J. (1999). Perfect simulation of conditionally specified models. *Journal of the Royal Statistical Society Series B, 61*(1), 251-264.

Moller, J. (2003). *Spatial statistics and computational methods.* Springer.

Moller, J., & Nicholls, G. (1999). Perfect simulation for sample-based inference. Preprint from http://www.math.auckland.ac.nz/~nicholls/linkfiles/papers.html

Moller, J., & Schladitz, K. (1999). Extension of Fill's algorithm for perfect simulation. *Journal of the Royal Statistical Society Series B, 61,* 955-969.

Moller, J., & Waagepetersen, R. (2003). *Statistical inference and simulation for spatial point processes.* Chapman & Hall/CRC.

Murdoch, D.J., & Green, P.J. (1998). Exact sampling from a continuous state space. *Scandinavian Journal of Statistics, 25,* 483-502.

Norris, J.R. (1997). *Markov chains.* Cambridge University Press.

Philippe, A., & Robert, C. (2003). Perfect simulation of positive Gaussian distributions. *Statistics and Computing, 13*(2), 179-186.

Propp, J.G., & Wilson, D.B. (1996). Exact sampling with coupled Markov chains and applications to statistical mechanics. *Random Structures and Algorithms, 9*(1/2), 223-252.

Propp, J.G., & Wilson, D.B. (1998). How to get a perfectly random sample from a generic Markov chain and generate a random spanning tree of a directed graph. *Journal of Algorithms, 27,* 170-217.

Robert, C.P., & Casella, G. (2004). *Monte Carlo statistical methods (2nd ed.).* Springer.

Roberts, G.O. (1996). Markov chain concepts related to sampling algorithms. In W.R. Gilks, S. Richardson & D.J. Spiegelhalter (Eds.), *Markov chain Monte Carlo in practice,* pp. 45-57. Chapman & Hall.

Roberts, G., & Rosenthal, J. (1999). Convergence of slice sampler Markov chains. *Journal of the Royal Statistical Society Series B, 61,* 643-660.

Schneider, U., & Corcoran, J.N. (2004). Perfect sampling for Bayesian variable selection in a linear regression model. *Journal of Statistical Planning and Inference, 126,* 153-171.

Thonnes, E. (2000). A primer in perfect simulation. In K.R. Mecke & D. Stoyan (Eds.), *Statistical Physics and Spatial Statistics,* pp. 349-378. Springer.

Thorisson, H. (2000). *Coupling, stationarity and regeneration.* Springer.

Tierney, L. (1996). Introduction to general state-space Markov chain theory. In W.R. Gilks, S. Richardson & D.J. Spiegelhalter (Eds.), *Markov chain Monte Carlo in practice,* pp. 59-74. Chapman & Hall.

Wilson, D.B. (2000). How to couple from the past using a read-once source of randomness. *Random Structures and Algorithms, 16*(1), 85-113.

APPENDIX: GLOSSARY ON MARKOV CHAINS FOR MCMC

This brief glossary provides a quick reference for the properties of Markov chains used in this chapter. For more details, excellent reviews of Markov chains for MCMC can be found in Robert and Casella (2004, pp. 205-265), Roberts (1996), and Tierney (1996). For more general expositions of Markov chains, see Meyn and Tweedie (1993), Norris (1997), and Haggstrom (2002).

Let $(X^{(t)} : t \geq 0)$ be a Markov chain with state space S and transition kernel Q. If the Markov chain has a stationary distribution, let it be denoted by f.

Continuous State Space

When S is continuous, Q represents a conditional density, such that

$$Q(x, A) = P(X^{(t+1)} \in A \mid X^{(t)} = x) = \int_A Q(x, y) dy \tag{52}$$

for $A \in \Sigma$, where Σ is the sigma-algebra induced by S. Thus, the notation, $q(y \mid x)$, may be used in place of $Q(x, y)$. Let τ_A be the first time that the Markov chain visits set A, and let n_A be the number of visits to A. For $n \in \{1, 2, \ldots\}$,

$$Q^n(x, A) = P(X^{(t+n)} \in A \mid X^{(t)} = x) \tag{53}$$

Definition. A Markov chain is *irreducible* with respect to probability measure ψ if, for every $A \in \Sigma$ with $\psi(A) > 0$, there exists $n > 0$ such that $Q^n(x, A) > 0$ or, equivalently, $P(\tau_A < \infty \mid X^{(0)} = x) > 0$, for all $x \in S$.

For MCMC, the Markov chain must be irreducible with respect to f. This ensures that the chain is free to move over the entire state space, since any set A with non-zero probability under f can be reached from any starting state x in a finite number of steps. Furthermore, the Markov chain must not be restricted by any deterministic pattern of movement. This is described by the *periodicity* of the chain.

Definition. A set $C \subseteq S$ is a *small set* of order $m > 0$ if there exist $\varepsilon > 0$ and a non-zero probability measure μ_n such that $Q^m(x, A) \geq \varepsilon \mu_m(A)$, for every $x \in C$ and every $A \in \Sigma$.

Definition. (a) An irreducible Markov chain has a *cycle of length d* if there exists a small set C of order M with respect to the probability measure μ_M, such that

$$d = \gcd\{m \geq 1 : C \text{ is a small set of order } m \text{ w.r.t. } \mu_m \geq \varepsilon_m \mu_M \text{ for some } \varepsilon_m > 0\} \tag{54}$$

where gcd denotes "greatest common divisor."

(b) A Markov chain is *aperiodic* if the length of its longest cycle is 1.

Irreducibility alone is not enough; the chain must not get stuck in any subset of the state space, but every path of the Markov chain must visit any subset infinitely often. This is provided by the property of Harris recurrence.

Definition. A Markov chain is *recurrent* if there exists a probability measure ψ for which the chain is irreducible and, for every $A \in \Sigma$ with $\psi(A) > 0$, $E(n_A \mid X^{(0)} = x) = \infty$, for all $x \in A$.

Definition. A Markov chain is *Harris recurrent* if there exists a probability measure ψ for which the chain is irreducible and, for every $A \in \Sigma$ with $\psi(A) > 0$, $P(n_A = \infty \mid X^{(0)} = x) = 1$, for all $x \in A$.

A recurrent Markov chain makes an infinite average number of visits to the set A, while a Harris recurrent chain makes an infinite number of visits for every path of the Markov chain. Hence, Harris recurrence is, in general, a stronger property than recurrence.

Definition. A recurrent or Harris recurrent Markov chain is *positive* if it has an invariant or stationary distribution f, that is, $X^{(t+1)} \sim f$ if $X^{(t)} \sim f$.

Positive Harris recurrence ensures that a Markov chain converges to the same stationary distribution for every starting state, whilst positive recurrence only ensures that the stationary distribution is the same for almost every starting state.

Definition. An *ergodic* Markov chain is positive Harris recurrent and aperiodic.

Therefore, for MCMC, the Markov chain must be ergodic so that a stationary distribution exists, and the chain converges, in total variation norm, to its stationary distribution regardless of its starting value.

Discrete State Space

When S is discrete, Q defines a matrix of conditional probabilities, called the *transition matrix*, with elements

$$Q(x, y) = P(X^{(t+1)} = y \mid X^{(t)} = x) \tag{55}$$

for $x, y \in S$. For $n \in \{1, 2, \ldots\}$,

$$Q^n(x, y) = P(X^{(t+n)} = y \mid X^{(t)} = x) \tag{56}$$

For a discrete-state Markov chain, irreducibility means that all states communicate.
Definition. A discrete-state Markov chain is *irreducible* if there exists n such that $Q^n(x, y) > 0$ or, equivalently, $P(\tau_y < \infty \mid X^{(0)} = x) > 0$, for all $x, y \in S$.

Definition. (a) For a discrete-state Markov chain, the period of a state, $x \in S$, is

$$d(x) = \gcd\{n \geq 1 : Q^n(x, x) > 0\} \tag{57}$$

(b) A discrete-state Markov chain is *aperiodic* if all of its states have period 1.

Definition. A discrete-state Markov chain is *recurrent* if $E(n_x \mid X^{(0)} = x) = \infty$, for all $x \in S$.

Definition. A recurrent discrete-state Markov chain is *positive* if $E(\tau_x \mid X^{(0)} = x) < \infty$, for all $x \in S$.

When the state space is discrete, recurrence is equivalent to Harris recurrence. Therefore, *an ergodic discrete-state Markov chain is positive recurrent and aperiodic.*

In a finite state space, a Markov chain is irreducible if, and only if, it is positive recurrent. Therefore, *an ergodic finite-state Markov chain is irreducible and aperiodic.*

Rates of Convergence to the Stationary Distribution

Definition. A Markov chain is *geometrically ergodic* if there are constants, $c_x > 0$ and $r \in (0, 1)$, such that

$$\sup_{A \in \Sigma} \mid Q^n(x, A) - f(A) \mid \leq c_x r^n \tag{58}$$

for all n and all $x \in S$.

A geometrically ergodic Markov chain converges to its stationary distribution at a geometric rate, with a geometric bound that depends on the starting value of the chain.

Definition. A Markov chain is *uniformly ergodic* if there are constants, $c > 0$ and $r \in (0, 1)$, such that

$$\sup_{A \in \Sigma} \mid Q^n(x, A) - f(A) \mid \leq c r^n \tag{59}$$

for all n and all $x \in S$.

Uniform ergodicity is a stronger property than geometric ergodicity because the geometric rate of convergence is uniform for all starting states.

Section III
Pattern Discovery from Huge Data Set:
Applications

Chapter XI
Design of Knowledge Bases for Forward and Reverse Mappings of TIG Welding Process

J. P. Ganjigatti
Siddaganga Institute of Technology, Tumkur, India

Dilip Kumar Pratihar
Indian Institute of Technology, Kharagpur, India

ABSTRACT

In this chapter, an attempt has been made to design suitable knowledge bases (KBs) for carrying out forward and reverse mappings of a Tungsten inert gas (TIG) welding process. In forward mapping, the outputs (also known as the responses) are expressed as the functions of the input variables (also called the factors), whereas in reverse mapping, the factors are represented as the functions of the responses. Both the forward as well as reverse mappings are required to conduct, for an effective online control of a process. Conventional statistical regression analysis is able to carry out the forward mapping efficiently but it may not be always able to solve the problem of reverse mapping. It is a novel attempt to conduct the forward and reverse mappings of a TIG welding process using fuzzy logic (FL)-based approaches and these are found to solve the said problem efficiently.

INTRODUCTION

We have a natural quest to know the input-output relationships of a process. To control the process efficiently, it might be required to know the said relationships beforehand. Forward mapping aims to determine the outputs as the functions of the inputs, whereas the inputs are expressed as the functions of the outputs in reverse mapping. Both the forward as well as reverse mappings of a process are to be carried out, to automate the same. It may be difficult to determine the input-output relationships for most of the processes mathematically, due to inherent complexity of their physics. Realizing this, several attempts were made by various investigators to express the said relationships through conventional statistical regression analysis. It is carried out based on the data collected experimentally, which may not be precise in nature. Forward mapping can be done easily but reverse mapping may sometimes offer difficulty. It happens, when the transformation matrix relating the outputs with the inputs becomes singular. In such cases, particularly when the transformation matrix becomes non-square, some investigators tried to determine the pseudo-inverse of the matrix. However, it may be far from being the true inverse of the transformation matrix and as a result of which, the deviation in predictions of the inputs for a set of desired outputs could be more. To ensure a square transformation matrix between the outputs and inputs of a process, the number of outputs should be equal to that of inputs. In order to make the reverse mapping possible, the interaction terms of linear regression model are to be neglected. It is important to mention that reverse mapping cannot be implemented accurately for the nonlinear regression model. Forward mapping can be carried out through the linear and non-linear regression models, if the experimental data are collected as per some standard

two-level and three-level designs of experiments, respectively. On the other hand, reverse mapping can be implemented using the conventional linear regression analysis involving main factors only, for a process having equal number of inputs and outputs (see Table 1).

In conventional statistical regression analysis, only one output parameter is tackled at a time and consequently, it may not be able to capture the dynamics of the process completely. Soft computing is a family consists of the techniques—**fuzzy logic** (FL), neural networks (NN), genetic algorithms (GAs), and their different combinations, in which the precision is traded for tractability, robustness, and a low cost solution. It may provide with some feasible solutions to the said problem.

The present chapter deals with the issues related to determination of the input-output relationships of a TIG welding process. Suitable **knowledge bases** (KBs) of the **fuzzy logic** Controller (FLC) have been designed and developed for carrying out the forward and reverse mappings of the process. The performance of an FLC depends on its KB, which consists of the **data base** (DB) (carrying information of the membership function distributions of the variables) and Rule Base (RB), that is, KB=DB+RB. A rule of an FLC is expressed with the help of the DB and represents the input-output relationship of a process. A RB consisting of a number of rules indicates the transformation matrix of the input-output relationships. A manually designed FLC may not work in an optimal sense and it may be required to train its KB with the help of a number of known scenarios. A large number of training cases are generally required for the said purpose. It may be difficult to gather such a huge training data through experiments. Thus, a less amount of data compared to that required for the training is collected according to the statistical designs of experiments (namely full-factorial design, fractional-factorial design, central composite design and others) and the regression equations are determined. If the developed regression models are found to be statistically

Table 1. Requirements for forward and reverse mappings

Mappings	Requirements
Forward	• Linear regression analysis based on two-level designs of experiments like full-factorial, fractional factorial. • Non-linear regression analysis based on three-level designs of experiments, namely central composite design, Box-Behnken design, and so on.
Reverse	• Linear regression analysis involving main factors only for a process having the same number of inputs and outputs.

adequate, they can be utilized to generate a large number of training scenarios artificially. A batch mode of training has been adopted to inject some amount of adaptability to the KB with the help of an optimizer, say genetic algorithm (GA).

BACKGROUND

Several methods had been tried by various researchers to predict bead-geometry in welding. Those methods include theoretical studies, conventional statistical regression analysis, soft computing-based approaches. Some of those studies are stated below.

Theoretical Studies

Rosenthal studied the temperature distributions on an infinite sheet subjected to a moving point heat source by considering the conduction mode of heat dissipation (Rosenthal, 1941). His analysis was later utilized by a number of investigators to study the weld bead geometry. Roberts and Wells (1954) estimated the weld bead width theoretically considering conduction heat transfer only in the plane of the plate, after assuming a complete penetration through it. Later on, Christensen, Davies, and Gjermundsen (1965) derived non-dimensional factors to relate bead dimensions with the operating parameters. Chandel, Seow, and Cheong (1997) determined the effect of current, electrode polarity, electrode diameter and electrode extension on the melting rate, bead height, bead width, and weld penetration theoretically, in a submerged arc welding. Jou (2003) could develop a numerical model for a single pass Gas Tungsten Arc (GTA) welding. The developed 3-D FEM model was able to predict the transient thermal histories and weld pool geometries.

Theoretical studies can be made after simplifying the model through a number of assumptions. Due to these assumptions, the theoretical studies may not be able to determine the input-output relationships of a process accurately.

Conventional Statistical Regression Analysis

Realizing the difficulties associated with theoretical estimation of input-output relationships of a welding process, various investigators tried to establish those through conventional statistical regression analysis based on some experimental data. Some of those works are mentioned below.

Kim, Jeong, Sona, Kima, Kimb, Kimb, and Yarlagadda, (2003a) and Kim, Son, Yang, and Yarlagadda (2003b) carried out nonlinear multiple regression analysis for modeling the process and determined the respective effects of process parameters on the weld bead geometric parameters. In another work, Kim, Son, Kim, Kim, and Kim (2003c) obtained both linear as well as non-linear multiple regression equations to relate the welding process parameters with the bead geometric parameters in robotic CO_2 arc welding. The weld bead geometry could be predicted accurately from the process parameters using the developed relations. Lee and Rhee (2000) reported an investigation of the gas metal arc welding (GMAW) process, where both forward as well as backward relations were established through multiple regression analysis and the mean deviations in prediction were found to lie within 9.5 and 6.5 percent, respectively. Kim, Park, Jeong, and Son (2001) also tried to determine the GMAW process parameters for the optimized weld bead geometry through the inversion of empirical equations obtained using the multiple regression analysis. Rowlands and Antony (2003) applied the concept of design of experiments (DOE), which indicates the way the experimental data are to be collected to make the regression analysis possible, to a spot welding process, in order to identify significant process parameters influencing mean tensile strength and its variability in welded joints.

Response surface methodology (RSM) was used to develop quadratic relations between welding process parameters and bead geometry for depositing 316L stainless steel onto structural steel using automated submerged arc welding (SAW) (Murugan, Parmer, & Sud, 1993) and MIG welding (Murugan & Parmer, 1994) separately. Gunaraj and Murugan (2000a) modeled the SAW process using five-level factorial technique using the RSM. In a continuation of this work, mathematical models were developed (together with sensitivity analysis) for minimization of total bead volume (keeping other bead parameters as the constraints) and determination of optimum process parameters for better weld quality, increased productivity, and minimum welding cost (Gunaraj & Murugan, 2000b). Tarng and Yang (1998) reported on the optimization of weld bead geometry in GTAW using the Taguchi method. Kim, Park, and Yarlagadda (2003d) tried to predict the process parameter values for optimum bead geometry settings in GMAW of mild steel using the Taguchi method. The above statistical analyses are able to provide with some satisfactory results, while predicting the responses from the process parameters. However, sometimes it offers difficulty in the reverse mapping due to the reason mentioned earlier.

It is also to be mentioned that the methods are global in nature, that is, the usual practice is to establish a single working relationship between the inputs and an output for the entire domain of interest, as a result of which, it will be possible to predict the results accurately at the anchor points (that is, the points which are used to carry out the regression analysis) only. However, there might be some significant deviation in prediction at the intermediate points.

Soft Computing-Based Approaches

Soft computing was also used by various investigators to determine input-output relationships in welding. Some of those attempts are mentioned below.

Andersen, Cook, Karsai, and Ramaswamy (1990) developed an artificial neural network

(ANN) model with actual welding data and concluded that the accuracy of ANN model could be comparable with that of other conventional control systems. Cook, Barnett, Andersen, and Strauss (1995) used an ANN to investigate three areas of welding analysis, namely weld process modeling, control, and bead profile analysis for quality control. Li, Simpson, and Rados (2000) developed a control system for GMAW, where an ANN received online arc voltage data and predicted the mode of transfer of molten metal and assessed whether the operating regime was appropriate for producing good quality welds. Nagesh and Datta (2002) used a back-propagation neural network (BPNN) to relate the shielded metal arc welding process parameters with weld bead geometry and penetration. The results showed good matching with the experimental values. Juang, Tarng, and Lii (1998) reported that both back-propagation (BP) as well as counter-propagation (CP) networks could successfully relate the welding process parameters to weld pool geometry in TIG welding. Tarng, Tsai, and Yeh (1999) utilized an NN to establish the relationships between welding process parameters and weld pool geometry in TIG welding. simulated annealing (SA) was then used to search for the process parameters that will ensure optimal weld geometry. The quality of welds was then classified and verified by a fuzzy clustering technique.

Wu, Polte, and Rehfeldt (2001) developed a **fuzzy logic** system for process monitoring and quality evaluation in GMAW. Kovacevic and Zhang (1997) reported an online welding control system comprising of a topside sensor (for bead width estimation), an image-processing algorithm coupled with a dynamic neuro-fuzzy predictive controller to achieve the desirable fusion states in the weld pool. Moon and Na (1996) adopted a neuro-fuzzy approach (with experimental verification) in horizontal fillet welding, where the NN predicted the appropriate welding parameters for a desired weld bead geometry and the fuzzy rule-based method chose appropriate welding conditions for avoidance of defects.

Soft computing could be an effective tool to determine the input-output relationships in welding. The main aim is to develop either an NN or FL-based expert system, which will be able to predict the outputs knowing the inputs and vice versa, accurately. The quality of prediction depends on the developed expert system. A considerable amount of work had been done to develop a suitable NN, for the said purpose. However, a back-propagation algorithm works based on the steepest descent method and thus, the developed NN may have a local minimum problem. Moreover, an NN works like a black box. A **fuzzy logic**-based expert system might be easier for the user to understand and use, because the input-output relationships are expressed using the IF...THEN rules.

The present chapter deals with design of some suitable **knowledge bases** (KBs) of the FLC for conducting both the forward as well as reverse mappings of a TIG welding process.

MAIN THRUST

Statement of the Problem

Tungsten inert gas (TIG) welding is a popular arc welding process performed using the heat of the arc established between a non-consumable tungsten electrode and the work-piece. An inert gas is used to protect the molten metal pool from the atmosphere. The intense heat generated by the arc melts the work metal and allows the joining with the solidification of molten metal. It can be used for welding of almost all metals. The quality of TIG weld is characterized by the bead geometric parameters, such as front height (FH), front width (FW), back height (BH) and back width (BW), which are dependent on a number of process parameters like welding speed (A), wire feed rate (B), percent cleaning (C), arc gap (D) and welding current (E). Figure 1 shows the inputs and outputs of the process.

Multiple Least-Square Regression Analysis Using Full-Factorial Design of Experiments (Montgomery, 1997)

Regression analysis is carried out to establish input-output relationships of a process. A least-square method is utilized to determine the coefficients of the regression model.

Let us consider a process having one response and three input variables as given below.

$$\hat{Y} = f(X_1, X_2, X_3)$$

Let us consider a response equation of the following form:

$$Y_i = \alpha_0 + \sum_{j=1}^{k} \alpha_j X_{ij} + e_i$$

where i = 1,........, n (sets of input-output relationships); $\alpha_0, \alpha_1, \alpha_2, \alpha_3$ are the coefficients; e indicates the error; k represents the number of input variables. The method of least-square chooses the values of α, such that the sum of the square of errors (e) becomes the minimum. The sum of the square of the errors can be written as follows.

$$e = \sum_{i=1}^{n} e_i^2 = \sum_{i=1}^{n} \left(Y_i - \alpha_0 - \sum_{j=1}^{k} \alpha_j X_{ij} \right)^2$$

Figure 1. A schematic diagram showing the inputs and outputs of a TIG welding process. Before planning the experiments, the maximum and minimum values of process parameters – A, B, C, D and E have been kept fixed to (46, 24 cm/min), (2.5, 1.5 m/min), (70%, 30%), (3.2, 2.4 mm) and (110, 80 amp), respectively.

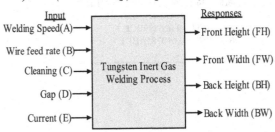

Box 1.

$$\begin{bmatrix} n & \sum_{i=1}^{n} X_{i1} & \sum_{i=1}^{n} X_{i2} & \cdots & \sum_{i=1}^{n} X_{ik} \\ \sum_{i=1}^{n} X_{i1} & \sum_{1}^{n} X_{i1}^{2} & \sum_{i=1}^{n} X_{i1}X_{i2} & \cdots & \sum_{i=1}^{n} X_{i1}X_{ik} \\ \vdots & \vdots & \vdots & & \vdots \\ \sum_{i=1}^{n} X_{ik} & \sum_{i=1}^{n} X_{ik}X_{i1} & \sum_{i=1}^{n} X_{ik}X_{i2} & \cdots & \sum_{i=1}^{n} X_{ik}^{2} \end{bmatrix} \begin{bmatrix} \hat{\alpha}_0 \\ \hat{\alpha}_1 \\ \vdots \\ \hat{\alpha}_k \end{bmatrix} = \begin{bmatrix} \sum_{i=1}^{n} Y_i \\ \sum_{i=1}^{n} X_{i1}Y_i \\ \vdots \\ \sum_{i=1}^{n} X_{ik}Y_i \end{bmatrix}$$

Equation 1.

FH = -17.250398 + 0.620178A + 4.676159B + 0.086647C + 7.447921D + 0.043108E - 0.186955AB - 0.005792AC - 0.220992AD - 0.002912AE + 0.001813BC - 1.839593BD + 0.019139BE - 0.058577CD + 0.001789CE -0.035219DE + 0.001406ABC + 0.062296ABD + 0.000206ABE + 0.002231ACD - 0.000007ACE + 0.001141ADE + 0.006098BCD - 0.001363BCE - 0.003033BDE - 0.000275CDE - 0.000424ABCD + 0.000019ABCE - 0.000046ABDE - 0.000001ACDE + 0.000376BCDE -0.000007ABCDE

Equation 2.

FW = - 329.675788 + 8.253936A + 167.104121B + 5.818671C + 101.462353D + 3.995271E - 4.070727AB - 0.141415AC - 2.548911AD - 0.099144AE + -2.915045BC - 54.137794BD - 1.988320BE - 1.851000CD - 0.068644CE - 1.214995DE + 0.069989ABC + 1.317491ABD + 0.048568ABE + 0.044112ACD + 0.001698ACE + 0.030810ADE + 0.939865BCD + 0.034547BCE + 0.652385BDE + 0.022294CDE - 0.022260ABCD - 0.000839ABCE - 0.015943ABDE - 0.000543ACDE - 0.011294BCDE + 0.000272ABCDE

Equation 3.

BH = 20.799936 - 0.383051A - 3.574492B + 0.107945C -9.328395D - 0.092436E + 0.005830AB - 0.005431 + 0.166515AD + 0.000491AE - 0.111449BC + 2.293608BD - 0.016822BE - 0.009152CD - 0.003683CE + 0.057568DE + 0.004416ABC - 0.023731ABD + 0.001457ABE - 0.001558ACD + 0.000124ACE - 0.000552ADE + 0.026228BCD + 0.002370BCE - 0.004131BDE + 0.000950CDE - 0.001348ABCD - 0.000077ABCE - 0.000315ABDE - 0.000039ACDE - 0.000684BCDE + 0.000025A BCDE

Equation 4.

BW = - 179.435443 + 4.120909A + 104.770811B + 4.111289C + 52.875341D + 2.436847E - 2.547364AB - 0.094617AC - 1.269519AD - 0.057292AE - 2.227246BC - 34.167652BD - 1.297342BE - 1.385604CD - 0.050824CE - 0.719793DE + 0.052044ABC + 0.818774ABD + 0.032125ABE + 0.031846ACD + 0.001216ACE + 0.018180ADE + 0.768436BCD + 0.026839BCE + 0.435309BDE + 0.017557CDE - 0.017848ABCD - 0.000643ABCE - 0.010785ABDE - 0.000421ACDE - 0.009350BCDE + 0.000225ABCDE

To minimize 'e', the following equations are to be satisfied:

$$\left.\frac{\partial e}{\partial \alpha_0}\right|_{\hat{\alpha}_0,\hat{\alpha}_1......,\hat{\alpha}_k} = -2\sum_{i=1}^{n}\left(Y_i - \alpha_0 - \sum_{j=1}^{k}\alpha_j X_{ij}\right) = 0$$

and

$$\left.\frac{\partial e}{\partial \alpha_j}\right|_{\hat{\alpha}_1,\hat{\alpha}_2,....,\hat{\alpha}_k} = -2\sum_{i=1}^{n}\left(Y_i - \hat{\alpha}_0 - \sum_{j=1}^{k}\hat{\alpha}_j X_{ij}\right)X_{ij} = 0$$

$j = 1, 2, ..., k$

Simplifying the previous equations, we get the following relationship among the responses and process parameters: (see Box 1).

Linear regression analysis has been carried out based on the data collected (see Equations 1 through 4) as per full-factorial DOE and the following response equations are obtained (Ganjigatti, 2006):

The following observations have been made from the study:

1. Weld bead geometry largely depends on the input parameters like welding current and welding speed.
2. Welding current has the maximum influence on front height, front width and back width, whereas welding speed is found to have the maximum contribution on back height.
3. Welding current has a positive effect on the front width, back height and back width where as front height is seen to decrease with the increase in current.
4. Back height of the weld bead is found to decrease with the welding speed.
5. Welding current and speed combination has a significant contribution on both front width as well as back width of the bead.

The above response equations have been utilized to generate a set of 1,000 training data required for tuning of the FL-based approaches.

Forward and Reverse Mappings Using FL-Based Approaches

The problems related to both the forward as well as reverse mappings of a TIG welding process have been solved using different approaches of FLC, the results of which are discussed below.

Design of FLC for Forward Mapping

Fuzzy logic controller (FLC) has been developed to model the input-output relationships of the above TIG welding process. An attempt has been made to manually design the **knowledge base** KB (consisting of the **data base** DB and Rule Base RB) of the FLC. It is important to mention that the KB of the FLC represents the transformation matrix of the input-output relationships of the process, indirectly. Three linguistic terms (L-Low, M-Medium, and H-High) have been used to represent each variable. For simplicity, the shape of the membership function distributions has been assumed to be triangular in nature.

Figure 2 shows the membership function distributions of the input-output variables of the FLC. As there are five input variables and each variable is expressed using three linguistic terms, there is a maximum of $3^5 = 243$ possible input combinations or rules. The RB has been designed based on the designer's knowledge of the process gathered after consulting the above regression equations. A typical rule will look as follows:

IF A is M AND B is H AND C is M AND D is M AND E is M, THEN FH is H, FW is H, BH is H, BW is L.

The manually designed KB of the FLC may not be optimal in any sense. Thus, attempts are made to optimize its KB off-line using a GA. Four approaches have been developed, which are explained below.

Figure 2. Manually constructed membership function distributions of the variables

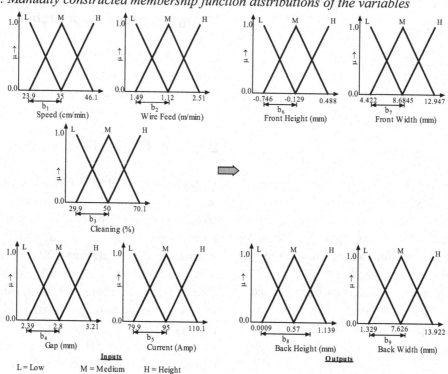

Approach 1: GA-Based Tuning of the DB (Symmetric) and RB of the Manually Constructed FLC

Figure 3 shows the schematic diagram of the genetic-fuzzy system, whose aim is to improve the performance of the FLC by providing a GA-based training off-line. As a GA is computationally expensive, it has been used off-line. In this approach, the membership function distributions of the variables have been assumed to be symmetrical in nature. As the performance of an FLC depends on both the DB as well as RB, both of them have been optimized simultaneously.

A binary-coded GA has been used, whose string will look as such in Box 2.

There are nine real variables, such as b_1, b_2,......, b_9 (refer to Figure 2) and each b represents the half base-width of the triangle used to represent the membership function distribution. As 10 bits are assigned to represent each b value, there is a total of 90 bits to indicate nine b values. Moreover, 243 bits are used to represent the presence or absence of the rules (1 is for presence and 0 is for absence). Thus, the GA-string is 90+243 = 333 - bits long. During optimization, b_1, b_2, b_3, b_4, b_5, b_6, b_7, b_8 and b_9 have been varied in the range of (11.1-14.1), (0.51- 0.81), (20.1-25.1), (0.41-0.61), (15.1-18.1), (0.617- 0.917), (4.2625 -5.2625), (0.5691 - 0.8691) and (6.2965 - 7.2965), respectively. Moreover, the fitness of a GA-string is made equal to average RMS deviation in prediction, which has been determined as follows:

Box 2.

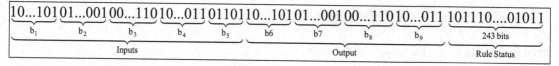

Figure 3. Genetic-Fuzzy system to model TIG welding process

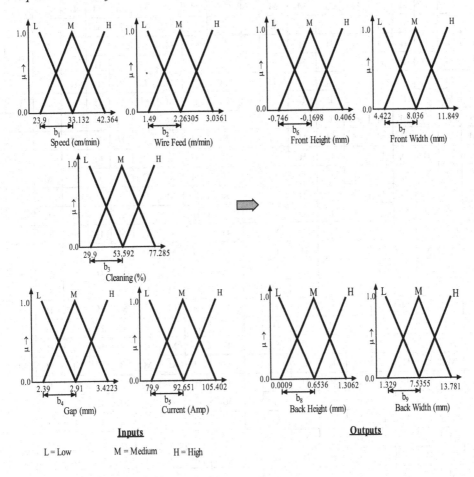

Figure 4. Optimized DB of the FLC obtained using Approach 1

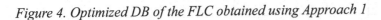

$$\text{Fitness} = \frac{1}{N}\sum_{i=1}^{N}\sqrt{\frac{1}{n}\sum_{j=1}^{n}(y_{ijt}-y_{ijp})^2}\,,$$

where y_t is the target output, y_p represents the predicted output, n indicates the number of responses and N is the number of training scenarios.

The performance of a GA depends on its parameters, namely crossover probability p_c, mutation probability p_m and population size P. Moreover, it is dependent on the number of generations, for which it is run. As a uniform crossover of fixed probability ($p_c = 0.5$) is used in the present study, a parametric study has been carried out to determine other optimal parameters, which are found to be as follows: $p_m = 0.001$, $P = 860$. The GA is run for a maximum of 200 generations. The optimized membership function distributions of variables as obtained above are shown in Figure 4.

The GA through search has identified 54 good rules from a total of 243, which are shown in Table 2.

Table 2. Optimized rule base of the FLC obtained using Approach 1

Rule. No	A	B	C	D	E	FH	FW	BH	BW	Rule. No	A	B	C	D	E	FH	FW	BH	BW
1	M	M	L	M	L	H	L	L	L	28	M	L	M	L	L	H	L	L	L
2	L	M	L	M	M	M	M	M	M	29	H	M	M	M	M	H	L	L	L
3	H	L	L	M	M	H	L	L	L	30	L	M	H	L	M	L	H	H	H
4	L	M	L	H	H	L	H	H	H	31	M	M	H	L	L	H	L	L	L
5	L	M	M	L	H	L	H	H	H	32	L	L	M	M	H	L	H	H	H
6	H	M	L	L	L	H	L	L	L	33	L	M	L	M	L	H	L	L	L
7	M	M	M	L	L	H	L	L	L	34	L	M	M	H	H	L	H	H	H
8	H	L	M	M	L	H	L	L	L	35	H	M	L	M	M	H	L	L	L
9	M	M	L	H	M	M	M	M	M	36	M	M	L	H	L	H	L	L	L
10	M	H	H	H	H	L	H	H	H	37	M	L	M	L	M	M	L	L	M
11	H	M	M	L	M	H	L	L	L	38	M	M	H	M	L	M	M	M	M
12	H	M	M	M	H	M	M	M	M	39	H	M	H	L	H	M	M	M	M
13	H	M	M	M	L	H	L	L	L	40	H	L	M	L	L	H	L	L	L
14	M	M	H	L	M	M	M	M	M	41	H	L	L	M	H	M	L	L	M
15	L	M	M	M	M	L	H	H	H	42	M	M	L	H	H	L	H	H	H
16	L	M	M	L	M	M	M	M	M	43	M	M	L	M	H	M	M	M	M
17	L	H	L	H	M	M	H	H	M	44	H	H	L	H	L	H	L	L	L
18	M	L	L	M	L	H	L	L	L	45	M	M	M	M	H	L	H	H	H
19	L	L	L	H	H	L	H	H	H	46	H	H	L	L	H	H	L	L	L
20	H	M	H	L	M	H	L	L	L	47	L	M	L	M	H	L	H	H	H
21	H	M	L	H	L	H	L	L	L	48	M	M	M	M	M	M	M	M	M
22	L	M	H	L	H	L	H	H	H	49	H	L	H	L	M	M	L	L	M
23	H	M	L	M	L	H	L	L	L	50	H	M	H	M	L	H	L	L	L
24	H	L	H	L	L	H	L	L	L	51	M	M	M	M	L	H	L	L	L
25	H	H	L	M	L	H	L	L	L	52	L	M	M	M	H	L	H	H	H
26	M	L	H	M	H	L	H	H	H	53	M	M	H	L	H	L	H	H	H
27	H	M	M	L	L	H	L	L	L	54	H	M	L	H	M	H	L	L	L

Box 3.

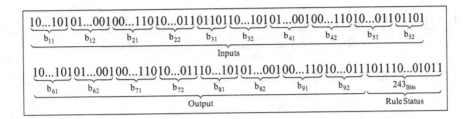

Approach 2: GA-Based Tuning of RB and DB (asymmetric) of the Manually Constructed FLC

Here, the membership function distributions of the variables are assumed to be asymmetric in nature and consequently, 2 x 9 = 18 real b values (such as b_{11}, b_{12}, b_{21}, b_{22}, b_{31}, b_{32}, b_{41}, b_{42}, b_{51}, b_{52}, b_{61}, b_{62}, b_{71}, b_{72}, b_{81}, b_{82}, b_{91}, b_{92}) are to be considered during optimization using a GA. Moreover, 243 bits have been used to represent the RB. Thus, the GA-string is 423–bits long, which is Box 3.

During optimization, the ranges of different b values have been kept the same as those considered in Approach 1, that is, the ranges of b_{11} and b_{12} are the same with that of b_1 (used in Approach 1) and so on. It is important to note that the GA has selected 53 good rules from a total of 243.

Approach 3: Automatic Design of FLC (Having Symmetrical DB) Using a GA

To develop the above two FL-based approaches, the KB has been designed initially based on the designer's knowledge of the process and later on it has been optimized using a GA. Thus, in Approaches 1 and 2, a considerable amount of time is spent on manual design of the KB. Moreover,

sometimes it might be difficult to design the KB beforehand. To overcome these difficulties, a method for automatic design of FLC is adopted in the present work. In this approach, the task of designing a good KB of an FLC is given to the GA and it tries to find an optimal KB through search. In this approach, the GA-string will look like that shown in Box 4.

It is to be noted that 10 bits are assigned to each b value. Thus, the first 90 bits will carry information of nine real variables (b1, b2, b3, b4, b5, b6, b7, b8, b9). The next 243 bits indicate the presence or absence of the rules. To indicate the first output of 243 rules, 243 x 2 = 486 bits have been assigned. Thus, 4 × 486 = 1944 bits are required to represent all the four outputs for 243 input conditions. The GA-string is 90+243+486×4 = 2277-bits long. The GA has selected 119 good rules from a total of 243 rules.

Approach 4: Automatic design of FLC (Having Asymmetric DB) Using GA

In this approach, the FL-based expert system is designed automatically using a GA, in which the membership function distributions of the variables are assumed to be asymmetric in nature. There are 18 real variables and 10 bits are used

Box 4.

Box 5.

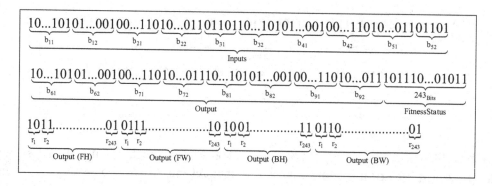

to represent each variable. The next 243 bits are utilized to represent the rules. There are 243 input combinations and for each of them, only two bits are used (00 for L, 01 and 11 for M and 11 for H) to represent the first output, that is, FH. Thus, for 243 input combinations, $243 \times 2 = 486$ bits are required to indicate the first output. Similarly, for four different outputs of 243 input combinations, 4×486 bits are necessary. Thus, each GA-string is composed of $180 + 243 + 4 \times 486 = 2367$ bits. A typical GA-string is shown in Box 5.

The fitness of a GA-string has been calculated in the same way, as done earlier. During optimization, the ranges of b-values have been set as those done in Approach 2.

The values of average RMS deviation (as discussed earlier) have been calculated by consider-

ing all the responses for both the manually–constructed FLC as well as GA-tuned/designed FLCs. Figure 5 shows the comparison of these above approaches and cluster-wise regression analysis (Ganjigatti, 2006) in terms of their average RMS deviation in predictions.

It is important to note that Approach 1 has slightly outperformed other approaches. In Approaches 1 and 2, initially the KB is designed manually and then it is further tuned using a GA, whereas in Approaches 3 and 4, the whole task of developing the KB of the FLC is given to the GA. Thus, the GA faces a more difficult problem in Approaches 3 and 4, compared to it does in Approaches 1 and 2, and it might be difficult for the GA to search for the globally optimal KB. However, there is a chance for further improve-

Figure 5. Comparison of different approaches of developing FLCs and cluster-wise regression analysis

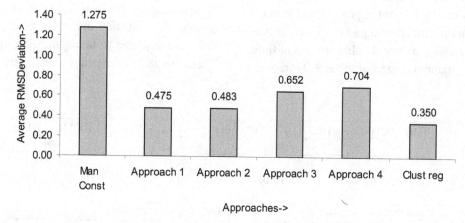

ment of the performance of the FLC. Moreover, the triangular membership function distributions may be replaced by some non-linear distributions for further improvement of the performance of the FLC. In Approaches 3 and 4, the GA through search is able to find the optimal KB of the FLC automatically. As no effort is made for manual design of the rule base, these approaches might be more interesting.

Design of FLC for Reverse Mapping

Figure 6 shows the schematic diagram of the reverse model of TIG welding process.

In reverse modeling, the prior information of the response-factor relationships are not available and as a result of which, the FLCs cannot be designed manually. Under these circumstances, automatic design of the FLC is the only option to go for. Two different approaches have been developed, which are explained below.

Approach 1: Automatic Design of FLC (Symmetric Membership Function Distribution)

For simplicity, the shape of the membership function distribution has been assumed to be triangular in nature and each variable is expressed using three linguistic terms – L, M, and H. As there are four variables on input side, there is a maximum of 3^4, that is, 81 feasible rules. A binary-coded GA is used to represent and optimize the KB of the FLC. A GA-string will look like that in Box 6.

There are nine real variables (b_1, b_2, b_3, b_4, b_5, b_6, b_7, b_8, b_9) and 10 bits are used to represent each. Thus, $10 \times 9 = 90$ bits will be used to represent nine real variables. The next 81 bits are utilized to represent the rule base. Two bits are used to represent each output of a rule. Thus, we used 81 $\times 2 = 162$ bits to indicate first output of 81 rules. A total of $5 \times 162 = 810$ bits are required to represent five outputs of all 81 rules. Thus, the string is 90 + 81 + 810 = 981-bits long. The GA has selected 51 good rules from a total of 81.

Figure 6. A schematic diagram showing the reverse mapping

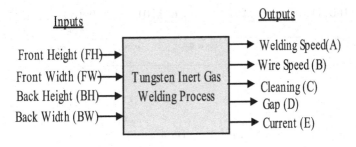

Box 6.

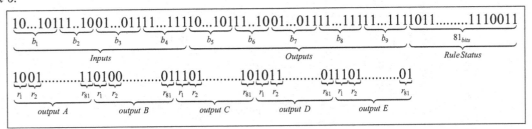

Approach 2: Automatic Design of FLC (Asymmetric Membership Function Distribution)

The membership function distributions are assumed to be asymmetric in nature and $9 \times 2 = 18$ real variables have been considered during optimization. Ten bits are assigned to represent each of these variables. Thus, the first 180 bits will carry information of the real variables. The next 81 bits will represent 81 rules. To represent one output of a particular rule, 2-bits are assigned. Thus, $81 \times 2 = 162$ bits are required to indicate the first output of 81 rules. The GA-string is found to be 1071-bits long. A typical GA-string is shown in Box 7.

The optimized RB of the FLC obtained using this approach is found to contain only 43 rules.

Figure 7 compares the performances of Approaches 1 and 2, in terms of average RMS deviation in prediction (as explained earlier) of the parameters. It is interesting to note that Approach 2 has slightly outperformed Approach1 in this regard. It is obvious because in Approach 2, the GA carries out its search in a wider space compared to that in Approach 1 to find the optimal FL-based expert system. In the above two approaches, the membership function distributions of the variables have been assumed to be triangular in nature. Non-linear membership function distributions of the variables may further improve the performance of the FL-based expert system.

Box 7.

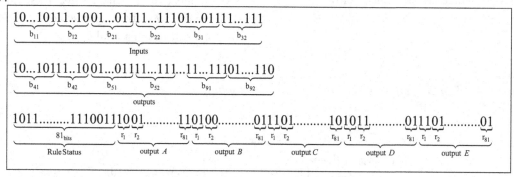

Figure 7. Comparison of Approaches 1 and 2 – reverse mapping.

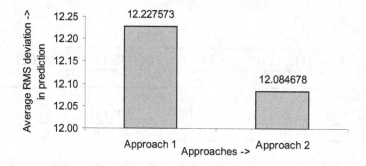

FUTURE TRENDS

To automate a process, the predictions in both the forward as well as reverse directions are necessary to have. Thus, the present study may be considered as a notable foundation work for successful development of an automatic **manufacturing** process. The developed FLCs are able to make the predictions within a reasonable accuracy limit. However, their performances may be further improved by selecting the proper distributions (say some form of non-linear) of the membership functions. An FL-based expert system using Takagi and Sugeno's approach may also be developed for the said purpose.

CONCLUSION

Both the forward as well as reverse mappings of a TIG welding process have been carried out using the FL-based approaches. An FLC is found to predict the responses for a set of input process parameters and vice versa, efficiently. Various approaches have been developed to design the FLC. The method of automatic design of the FLC with asymmetric membership function distributions is found to be more promising for both the forward as well as reverse mappings. It is obvious because in the above method, the GA carries out its search in a wider space to determine the optimized KB of the FLC.

REFERENCES

Andersen, K., Cook, G. E., Karsai, G., & Ramaswamy, K. (1990). Artificial neural network applied to arc welding process modeling and control. *IEEE Transactions on Industry Applications, 26*(5), 824-830.

Chandel, R. S., Seow, H. P., & Cheong, F. L. (1997). Effect of increasing deposition rate on the bead geometry of submerged arc welds. *Journal of Materials Processing Technology, 72,*124–128.

Christensen, N., Davies, V., & Gjermundsen, K. (1965). Distribution of temperature in arc welding. *British Welding Journal, 12*(2), 54-75.

Cook, G. E., Barnett, R. J., Andersen, K., & Strauss, A. M. (1995). Weld modeling and control using artificial neural networks. *IEEE Transactions on Industry Applications, 31*(6), 1484-1491.

Ganjigatti, J. P. (2006). *Application of statistical methods and fuzzy logic techniques to predict bead geometry in welding.* Unpublished doctoral dissertation, IIT Kharagpur, India.

Gunaraj, V., & Murugan, N. (2000a). Prediction and optimization of weld bead volume for the submerged arc process – Part 1. *Welding Research Supplement,* 287-294

Gunaraj, V., & Murugan, N. (2000b). Prediction and optimization of weld bead volume for the submerged arc process – Part 2. *Welding Research Supplement,* 331s-338s.

Jou, M. (2003). Experimental study and modeling of GTA welding process. *Journal of Manufacturing Science and Engineering, 125*(4), 801–808

Juang, S. C., Tarng Y. S., & Lii, H. R. (1998). A comparison between the back-propagation and counter-propagation networks in the modeling of the TIG welding process. *Journal of Material Processing Technology, 75,* 54–62.

Kim, I. S., Park, C. E., Jeong Y. J., & Son, J. S. (2001). Development of an intelligent system for selection of the process variables in gas metal arc welding processes. *International Journal of Advanced Manufacturing Technology, 18,* 98-102.

Kim, I. S., Jeong, Y. J., Sona, I. J., Kima, I. J., Kimb, J. Y., Kimb, I. K., & Yarlagadda, P. K. D. V. (2003a). Sensitivity analysis for process parameters influencing weld quality in robotic GMA welding process. *Journal of Material Processing Technology, 140,* 676-681.

Kim, I. S., Son, K. J., Yang, Y. S., & Yarlagadda, P. K. D. V. (2003b). Sensitivity analysis for process parameters in GMA welding processes using a factorial design method. *International Journal of Machine tools and Manufacture, 143,* 763-769.

Kim, I. S., Son, J. S., Kim, I. G., Kim, J. Y., & Kim, O. S. (2003c). A study on relationship between process variables and bead penetration for robotic Co_2 Arc Welding. *Journal of Material Processing Technology, (136),* 139-145.

Kim, I. S., Park, C. E., & Yarlagadda, P. K. D. V. (2003d). A study on the prediction of process parameters in the Gas-Metal Arc Welding (GMAW) of mild steel using Taguchi Methods. *Materials Science Forum,* 235 – 238.

Kovacevic, R., & Zhang, Y. M. (1997). Neurofuzzy model-based weld fusion state estimation. *IEEE Control Systems Magazine, 17*(2), 30-42.

Lee, J. I., & Rhee, S. (2000). Prediction of process parameters for gas metal arc welding by multiple regression analysis. *Proceedings of Institute of Mechanical Engineers Part. B, 214,* 443-449.

Li, X., Simpson, S. W., & Rados, M. (2000). Neural networks for online prediction of quality in gas metal arc welding. *Science and Technology of Welding and Joining, 5*(2), 71-79.

Montgomery, D. C. (1997). *Design and analysis of experiments.* New York: Wiley.

Moon, H., & Na, S. J. (1996). A neuro-fuzzy approach to select welding conditions for welding quality improvement in horizontal fillet welding. *ASME Journal of Manufacturing Systems, 15*(6), 392-402.

Murugan, N., Parmer, R. S., & Sud, S. K. (1993). Effect of submerged arc process variables on dilution and bead geometry in single wire surfacing. *Journal of Materials Processing Technology, 37,* 767-780.

Murugan, N., & Parmer, R. S. (1994). Effect of MIG process parameters on the geometry of the bead in the automatic surfacing of stainless steel. *Journal of Material Processing Technology, 41,* 381-398.

Nagesh, D. S., & Datta G. L., (2002). Prediction of weld bead geometry and penetration in shielded metal-arc welding using artificial neural networks. *Journal of Materials Processing Technology, 79,* 1–10.

Roberts, D. K., & Wells, A. A. (1954). Fusion welding of aluminium alloys. *British Welding Journal, 12,* 553-559.

Rosenthal, D. (1941). Mathematical theory of heat distribution during welding and cutting. *Welding Journal, 20*(5), 220-234.

Rowlands, H., & Antony, F. (2003). Application of design of experiments to a spot welding process. *Journal of Assembly Automation, 23*(3), 273-279.

Tarng, Y. S., & Yang, W. H. (1998). Optimization of the weld bead geometry in gas tungsten arc welding by the Taguchi method. *International Journal of Advanced Manufacturing Technology, 14,* 549–554.

Tarng, Y. S., Tsai, H. L., & Yeh, S. S. (1999). Modeling, optimization and classification of weld quality in tungsten inert gas welding. *International Journal of Machine Tools & Manufacturing, 39*(9), 1427-1438.

Wu, C. S., Polte, T., & Rehfeldt, D. (2001). A fuzzy logic system for process monitoring and quality evaluation in GMAW. *Welding Research Supplement, 2,* 33-38.

Chapter XII
A Fuzzy Decision Tree Analysis of Traffic Fatalities in the U.S.

Malcolm J. Beynon
Cardiff University, UK

ABSTRACT

This chapter considers the role of fuzzy decision trees as a tool for intelligent data analysis in domestic travel research. It demonstrates the readability and interpretability the findings from fuzzy decision tree analysis can pertain, first presented in a small problem allowing the fullest opportunity for the analysis to be followed. The investigation of the traffic fatalities in the states of the U.S. offers an example of a more comprehensive fuzzy decision tree analysis. The graphical representations of the fuzzy based membership functions show how the necessary linguistic terms are defined. The final fuzzy decision trees, both tutorial and U.S. traffic fatalities based, show the structured form the analysis offers, as well as more readable decision rules contained therein.

INTRODUCTION

In a wide discussion on the issue of data analysis, Breiman (2001) advocates the need for the development of new techniques, suggesting that the interpretation of results has an equal if not more important role to play than the simple predictive accuracy often only identified. Beyond the statistical inference from traditional regression type analyses of data, for many researchers, the set-up costs necessary to understand novel techniques can dissuade them from their employment. Domestic travel research is one such area that can benefit from the interpretable results accrued, since policy making is often the central desire of the study undertaken (see for example, Ewing, 2003; Noland, 2003; Shemer, 2004).

This self-induced doubt may be true with the possible employment of nascent techniques based on uncertain reasoning (Chen, 2001), which in one way or another, attempt to take into account the possible imperfection and/or relevance of the data to be studied. These imperfections include the imprecision of individual data values and in the more extreme case when a number of them are missing (incompleteness). One associated general methodology, fuzzy set theory (FST), introduced in Zadeh (1965), is closely associated with uncertain reasoning (Zadeh, 2005), including the opportunities to develop traditional techniques so that they incorporate vagueness and ambiguity in their operations. Within this fuzzy environment, data analysis is also extended to allow a linguistic facet to the possible interpretation of results.

In this chapter the technical emphasis is in the general area of decision trees within a fuzzy environment, a technique for the classification of objects described by a number of attributes. Armand, Watelain, Roux, Mercier, and Lepoutre (2007, p. 476) present a recent, succinct, description of what fuzzy decision trees offer;

"Fuzzy decision trees (FDT) incorporate a notion of fuzziness that permits inaccuracy and uncertainty to be introduced and allow the phenomena under consideration to be expressed using natural language."

Their application in gait analysis they believe benefits from the allowance for imprecision and interpretability. Pertinent for this edited book, Wang, Nauck, Spott, and Kruse (2007) consider fuzzy decision trees in relation to intelligent data analysis, motivation for their study was the belief that typical business users prefer softwares, which hide complexity from users and automate the data analysis process. There is a further implication when using fuzzy decision trees, namely that it inherently includes feature selection (Mikut, Jäkel, & Gröll, 2005), whereby small subsets of features are found with high-discriminating power.

The fuzzy approach employed here was presented in Yuan and Shaw (1995) and Wang, Chen,

Qian, and Ye (2000), and attempts to include the cognitive uncertainties evident in the imprecision inherent with the data values. This is, notably, through the construction of fuzzy membership functions (MFs), which enable levels of association to the linguistic variable representation of the numerical attributes considered (Kecman, 2001).

The problem considered in this study concerns road travel in the U.S., namely the discernment of the levels of traffic fatalities across the individual states. This issue has attracted much attention (see Noland, 2003), one reason being that these accidents account for a significant proportion of premature fatalities in the U.S. (and most other developed countries for that matter, see Shemer, 2004). As such they have been the focus of much attention in many fields of scientific study, from accident prevention to economic, social and behavioural analysis (Zobeck, Grant, Stinson, & Bettolucci 1994; Washington, Metarko, Fomumung, Ross, Julian, & Moran, 1999; Farmer & Williams, 2005).

State-to-state analysis can give valuable insights to policy makers interested in reducing the rate of accidents and fatalities. With the 50 states of the U.S. and the District of Columbia making up the considered objects, the relatively small data set offers every opportunity for the reader to follow the stages in the fuzzy decision tree construction process and the interpretation of the findings (beneficial when policy making is warranted). Indeed the inference from the tree structure employed takes advantage of the ability of humans to distinguish between patterns and observable characteristics (Chen, 2001).

BACKGROUND

Since the first paper introducing fuzzy set theory-FST (Zadeh, 1965), the interest in its utilisation and development continues to grow and grow (Zadeh, 1999).

Basic Concepts of Fuzzy Set Theory

The membership of an element x to a traditional (crisp) set A can be defined by the expression:

$$\mu_A(x) = \begin{cases} 1 & \text{if } x \in A, \\ 0 & \text{if } x \notin A, \end{cases}$$

where $\mu_A(x)$ is a dichotomous membership function (MF) that can indicate either the membership of x in A ($\mu_A(x) = 1$) or not the membership of x in A ($\mu_A(x) = 0$). It follows, a fuzzy set extends this to allow $\mu_A(x)$ to be a grade of membership, which means it takes a value over the domain $[0, 1]$. When x is a numerical value, the accompanying attribute domain can be described by a finite series of MFs that each offers a grade of membership to describe x, which collectively form its concomitant fuzzy number (see Kecman, 2001). It is the role played by, and structure of, the MFs that is fundamental to the utilisation of FST related methodologies (Medaglia *et al.*, 2002).

The finite set of MFs defining a numerical attribute's domain can be denoted a linguistic variable (Herrera *et al.*, 2000), which serves the purpose of providing a means of approximate characterization to attributes, which are too complex, or too ill-defined to be amenable to their description in conventional quantitative terms. The number of words (MFs) in a linguistic term set, which define a linguistic variable, determines the granularity of the characterization of an attribute's domain. The semantics of these words is given by the fuzzy numbers defined over the $[0, 1]$ interval, which are described by the associated MFs, see Janikow (1998) for further discussion.

Different types of MFs have been proposed to describe fuzzy numbers, including triangular and trapezoidal functions (Lin and Chen, 2002; Medaglia, Fang, Nuttle, & Wilson, 2002). Yu and Li (2001) highlight that MFs may be (advantageously) constructed from mixed shapes, supporting the use of piecewise linear MFs (see also Kecman, 2001). A functional form of a piecewise linear MF, the type utilised here (in the context of a linguistic term T_j^k), is given by:

$$\mu_{T_j^k}(x) \begin{cases} 0 & \text{if } x \leq \alpha_{j,1} \\ 0.5\dfrac{x-\alpha_{j,1}}{\alpha_{j,2}-\alpha_{j,1}} & \text{if } \alpha_{j,1} < x \leq \alpha_{j,2} \\ 0.5+0.5\dfrac{x-\alpha_{j,2}}{\alpha_{j,3}-\alpha_{j,2}} & \text{if } \alpha_{j,2} < x \leq \alpha_{j,3} \\ 1 & \text{if } x = \alpha_{j,3} \\ 1-0.5\dfrac{x-\alpha_{j,3}}{\alpha_{j,4}-\alpha_{j,3}} & \text{if } \alpha_{j,3} < x \leq \alpha_{j,4} \\ 0.5-0.5\dfrac{x-\alpha_{j,4}}{\alpha_{j,5}-\alpha_{j,4}} & \text{if } \alpha_{j,4} < x \leq \alpha_{j,5} \\ 0 & \text{if } \alpha_{j,5} < x \end{cases} \quad,$$

where $[\alpha_{j,1}, \alpha_{j,2}, \alpha_{j,3}, \alpha_{j,4}, \alpha_{j,5}]$ are the *defining values* for the above MF, in this case the these values are associated with the jth linguistic term of a linguistic variable A_k. A visual representation of this general MF form is presented in Figure 1, which elucidates its general structure along with the role played by the defining values.

The general form presented in Figure 1 shows how the value of an MF is constrained within 0 and 1. Furthermore, the implication of the defining values is also illustrated, including the idea of associated support (see Kovalerchuk & Vityaev,

Figure 1. General definition of a MF (including defining values)

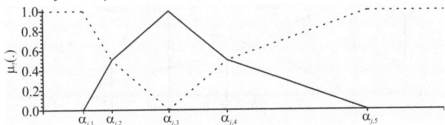

2000). That is, the support is the domain of the attribute value in question for which the MF has a positive value – the domain $[\alpha_{j,1}, \alpha_{j,5}]$. It follows, an attribute value is described by a series of fuzzy values found directly from the constructed MFs. Taking this further, the notion of dominant support can also be considered where that MF is most closely associated with the attribute value (largest fuzzy value) - the domain $[\alpha_{j,2}, \alpha_{j,4}]$.

To circumvent the influence of expert opinion in analysis the construction of the MFs should be automated. On this matter DeOliveria (1999) considers the implication of Zadeh's principle of incompatibility--that is, as the number of MFs increase, so the precision of the system increases, but at the expense of relevance decreasing (Zadeh, 1973). A small example MF is next considered which demonstrates the fuzzy modelling of a numerical attribute (and individual value), see Figure 2.

In Figure 2, two MFs $\mu_L(x)$ (labelled L) and $\mu_H(x)$ (H) are shown to cover the domain of a numerical attribute, the concomitant defining values are; for L: $[-\infty, -\infty, 2, 6, 14]$ and H: $[2, 6, 14, \infty, \infty]$ (the $-\infty$ and ∞ values denote finite domains for this numerical value may or may not exist). A linguistic interpretation could then simply be the association of a numerical value to being low (L) and/or high (H), with the two MFs showing the respective linguistic partition. Also shown in Figure 2 is the numerical value $x = 10$, which is decomposed into its grades of membership to L and H, here found to be $\mu_L(10) = 0.25$ and $\mu_H(10)$

$= 0.75$, respectively. With $\mu_H(10) > \mu_L(10)$, there is more association for the number 10 to high (H) than low (L), but with both membership values greater than 0.0 a level of vagueness exists.

The MFs constructed and shown in Figure 2 are within exact complete context spaces (ECCS), as described by Kovalerchuk and Vityaev (2000). That is, for a value x, the sum $(S(x))$ of the associated MF values equal 1.0. For example, when $x = 10$, $S(10) = \mu_L(10) + \mu_H(10) = 0.25 + 0.75 = 1.0$. Operating in ECCS it is suggested offers the potential to be able to use the near optimum number of MFs required (not considered here, see Chiang, Shieh, Hsu, and Wong 2005). Beyond ECCS, there exists incomplete context spaces $(S_{FTLS}(x) < 1.0$ possible) and over-complete context spaces $(S_{FTLS}(x) > 1.0$ possible).

Description Fuzzy Decision Trees

The catalyst for the development of fuzzy decision trees has been to resolve certain shortcomings of the crisp versions, including; their propensity to overfit the training data, so it is sensitive to noise in the data, and can be computationally inefficient when the domains of attributes are real numbers (see for example Jeng, Jeng, & Liang, 1997). As well as overcoming these shortcomings, fuzzy decision trees can offer the increased opportunity for linguistically interpreting the results (Chakraborty, 2001; Herrera, Herrera-Viedma, & Martinez, 2000). Janikow (1998) offers a general discussion on the issues and methods associated with fuzzy decision trees.

Figure 2. Example of two MFs (labeled L and H)

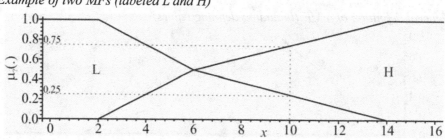

A detailed description on the current work of fuzzy decision trees is presented in Olaru and Wehenkel (2003). This latter work highlights how such methodologies include the fuzzification of a crisp decision tree post its construction (Jang, 1994), or approaches that directly integrate fuzzy techniques during the tree-growing phase (Yuan & Shaw, 1995). Recent examples of their successful application include in the areas of; optimising economic dispatch (Roa-Sepulveda, Herrera, Pavez-Lazo, Knight, & Coonick, 2003), the antecedents of company audit fees (Beynon, Peel, & Tang, 2004) and medical decision support (Chiang et al., 2005).

Appropriate for a wide range of problems, fuzzy decision trees allow a representation of information in a more direct and adequate form (with linguistic variables). The fuzzy formulizations of decision trees include derivatives of the well known ID3 approach utilizing fuzzy entropy (Peng, 2004), those that specifically take into account more cognitive uncertainties (Yuan & Shaw, 1995). This latter method is utilized here and focuses on the minimization of classification ambiguity in the presence of fuzzy evidence. With an inductive fuzzy decision tree, the underlying knowledge related to a decision outcome can be represented as a set of fuzzy "*if .. then …*" decision rules, each of the form:

If $(A_1$ is $T_{i_1}^1)$ and $(A_2$ is $T_{i_2}^2)$ … and $(A_k$ is $T_{i_k}^k)$ then C is C_j, where $A = \{A_1, A_2, .., A_k\}$ and C are linguistic variables in the multiple antecedents $(A_i\text{'s})$ and consequent (C) statements, respectively, and $T(A_k) = \{T_1^k, T_2^k, .. T_{S_i}^k\}$ and $\{C_1, C_2, …, C_L\}$ are their linguistic terms. Each linguistic term T_j^k is defined by the MF $\mu_{T_j^k}(x)$, which transforms a value in its associated domain to a grade of membership value between 0 and 1. The MFs, $\mu_{T_j^k}(x)$ and $\mu_{C_j}(y)$, represent the grade of membership of an object's antecedent A_j being T_j^k and consequent C being C_j, respectively (Wang et al., 2000; Yuan & Shaw, 1995).

A fuzzy set A in a universe of discourse U is characterized by a membership function $\mu_A(\cdot)$

which takes values in the interval [0, 1]. For all $u \in U$, the intersection $A \cap B$ of two fuzzy sets is given by $\mu_{A \cap B} = \min[\mu_A(u), \mu_B(u)]$. A membership function $\mu(x)$ from the set describing a fuzzy linguistic term Y defined on X, can be viewed as a possibility distribution of Y on X, that is $\pi(x) = \mu(x)$, for all $x \in X$ (also normalized so $\max_{x \in X} \pi(x) = 1$).

The possibility measure $E_\alpha(Y)$ of ambiguity is defined by:

$$E_\alpha(Y) = g(\pi) = \sum_{i=1}^n (\pi_i^* - \pi_{i+1}^*) \ln[i]$$

where $\pi^* = \{\pi_1^*, \pi_2^*, …, \pi_n^*\}$ is the permutation of the normalized possibility distribution $\pi = \{\pi(x_1), \pi(x_2), …, \pi(x_n)\}$, sorted so that $\pi_i^* \geq \pi_{n+1}^*$ for $i = 1, .., n$, and $\pi_{n+1}^* = 0$ (see Higashi & Klir, 1983). In the limit, if $\pi_2^* = 0$ then $E_\alpha(Y) = 0$ indicates no ambiguity, whereas if $\pi_n^* = 1$ then $E_\alpha(Y) = \ln[n]$, then all values are fully possible for Y, representing the greatest ambiguity.

The ambiguity of attribute A (over the objects $u_1, .., u_m$) is given as:

$$E_\alpha(A) = \frac{1}{m} \sum_{i=1}^m E_\alpha(A(u_i)),$$

where $E_\alpha(A(u_i)) = g(\mu_{Ts}(u_i) / \max_{1 \leq j \leq s}(\mu_{Tj}(u_i)))$,

with $T_1, …, T_s$ the linguistic terms of an attribute (antecedent) with m objects. When there is overlapping between linguistic terms (MFs) of an attribute or between consequents, then ambiguity exists. The fuzzy subsethood $S(A, B)$ measures the degree to which A is a subset of B (Kosko, 1986), and is given by:

$$S(A, B) = \sum_{u \in U} \min(\mu_A(u), \mu_B(u)) / \sum_{u \in U} \mu_A(u).$$

Given fuzzy evidence E, the possibility of classifying an object to consequent C_i can be defined as: $\pi(C_i|E) = S(E, C_i) / \max S(E, C_j)$, where $S(E, C_i)$ represents the degree of truth for the classification rule ("if E then C_i"). With a single piece of evidence (a fuzzy number for an attribute), then the classification ambiguity based on this fuzzy evidence is defined as: $G(E) = g(\pi(C | E))$, which is measured based on the possibility distribution $\pi(C | E) = (\pi(C_1 | E), ..., \pi(C_L | E))$.

The classification ambiguity with fuzzy partitioning $P = \{E_1, ..., E_k\}$ on the fuzzy evidence F, denoted as $G(P | F)$, is the weighted average of classification ambiguity with each subset of partition:

$$G(P | F) = \sum_{i=1}^{k} w(E_i | F) G(E_i \cap F),$$

where $G(E_i \cap F)$ is the classification ambiguity with fuzzy evidence $E_i \cap F$, and where $w(E_i | F)$ is the weight which represents the relative size of subset $E_i \cap F$ in F: $w(E_i | F) =$

$$\sum_{u \in U} \min(\mu_{E_i}(u), \mu_F(u)) \Big/ \sum_{j=1}^{k} \Big(\sum_{u \in U} \min(\mu_{E_j}(u), \mu_F(u)) \Big)$$

In summary, attributes are assigned to nodes based on the lowest level of classification ambiguity. A node becomes a leaf node if the level of subsethood is higher than some truth value β assigned to the whole of the fuzzy decision tree. The classification from the leaf node is to the decision group with the largest subsethood value. The truth level threshold β controls the growth of the tree; lower β may lead to a smaller tree (with lower classification accuracy), higher β may lead to a larger tree (with higher classification accuracy). Importantly, the selection of β depends on the individual situation.

To enable a process of matching an object to a fuzzy decision rule, the procedure described in Wang et al. (2000) can be followed:

i. Matching starts from the root node and ends at a leaf node along the branch of the

maximum membership of an object to each node (condition) met,

ii. If the maximum membership at the node is not unique, matching proceeds along several branches,

iii. The decision class with the maximum degree of truth from the leaf nodes is then assigned the classification for the associated rule (for example L or H).

Example Fuzzy Decision Tree Analysis

This subsection describes an example fuzzy decision tree analysis, using a very small data set, so that the intermediate calculations can be clearly exposed. The small data set consists of only two objects u_1 and u_2, described by two condition attributes, T1 and T2, and one decision attribute C, see Table 1.

In Table 1, all three attributes are each described by two linguistic terms (each denoting low (L) and high (H)), that make up their respective linguistic variable. These linguistic terms are individually defined by their concomitant MFs, like those described in Figures 1 and 2. It follows, the individual fuzzy values take a value between 0 and 1. For example, using the two MFs described in Figure 2, for the u_1 object and the T1 condition attribute, its linguistic term values of $\mu_{T1_L}(u_1) = 0.65$ and $\mu_{T1_H}(u_2) = 0.35$, would have come from a value of $x = 4.8$ along their domain.

For the construction of a fuzzy decision tree, the classification ambiguity of each condition attribute with respect to the decision attribute is first considered, namely the evaluation of the respective $G(E)$ values. Further, a threshold value of $\beta = 0.65$ for the minimum required truth level was used throughout this construction process. The evaluation of a $G(E)$ value is shown for the first attribute T1 (i.e., $g(\pi(C | T1))$), where it is broken down to the fuzzy labels L and H, for L; $\pi(C | T1_L) = S(T1_L, C_j)/\max S(T1_L, C_j)$, considering C_L and C_H with the information in Table 1: (see

Table 1. Small example fuzzy data set

Object	T1 = [T1$_L$, T1$_H$]	T2 = [T2$_L$, T2$_H$]	C = [C$_L$, C$_H$]
u_1	[**0.65**, 0.35]	[0.40, **0.60**]	[**0.90**, 0.10]
u_2	[**0.55**, 0.45]	[0.30, **0.70**]	[0.15, **0.85**]

Box 1.

$$S(T1_L, C_L) = \sum_{u \in U} \min(\mu_{T1_L}(u), \mu_{C_L}(u)) \Big/ \sum_{u \in U} \mu_{T_L}(u)$$

$$= \frac{\min(0.65, 0.90) + \min(0.55, 0.15)}{(0.65 + 0.55)} = \frac{0.65 + 0.15}{1.2} = \frac{0.8}{1.2} = 0.667$$

whereas

$$S(T1_L, C_H) = \frac{\min(0.65, 0.10) + \min(0.55, 0.85)}{(0.65 + 0.55)} = \frac{0.10 + 0.55}{1.2} = \frac{0.65}{1.2} = 0.542$$

Hence $\pi = \{0.667, 0.542\}$, giving the ordered normalized form of $\pi^* = \{1.000, 0.813\}$,

with π_3^*, then $G(T1_L) = g(\pi(C|\ T1_L)) = \sum_{i=1}^{2} (\pi_i^* - \pi_{i+1}^*) \ln[i]$

$$= (1.000 - 0.813)\ [1] + (0.813 - 0.000\ \ln[2] = 0.563,$$

Box 2.

$$S(T2_L, C_L) = \sum_{u \in U} \min(\mu_{T2_L}(u), \mu_{C_L}(u)) \Big/ \sum_{u \in U} \mu_{T2_L}(u)$$

$$= \frac{\min(0.4, 0.9) + \min(0.3, 0.15)}{0.4 + 0.3} = \frac{0.4 + 0.15}{0.7} = \frac{0.55}{0.7} = \mathbf{0.786}$$

Box 3.

$$G(T2_H \text{ and } T1|\ C) = \sum_{i=1}^{2} w(T1_i\ |\ T2_H) G(T2_H \cap T1_i).$$

Starting with the weight values, in the case of $T2_H$ and $T1_L$, it follows:

$$w(T1_L|\ T2_H) = \frac{\sum_{u \in U} \min(\mu_{T1_L}(u), \mu_{T2_H}(u))}{\sum_{j=1}^{k} \left(\sum_{u \in U} \min(\mu_{T1_j}(u), \mu_{T2_H}(u)) \right)},$$

$$= \frac{\min(0.65, 0.60) + \min(0.55, 0.70)}{(\min(0.65, 0.60) + \min(0.55, 0.70)) + (\min(0.35, 0.60) + \min(0.45, 0.70))}$$

$$= \frac{(0.60 + 0.55)}{0.60 + 0.55 + (0.35 + 0.45)} = \frac{1.15}{1.15 + 0.80} = \frac{1.15}{1.95} = 0.590$$

similarly $w(T1_H|\ T2_H) = 0.410$, hence:

$$G(T2_H \text{ and } T1|\ C) = 0.590 \times G(T2_H \cap T1_L) + 0.410 \times G(T2_H \cap T1_H),$$
$$= 0.590 \times 0.601 + 0.410 \times 0.630,$$
$$= 0.354 + 0.259 = 0.613,$$

Box 1.) along with $G(T1_H) = 0.630$, then $G(T1) = (0.563 + 0.630)/2 = 0.597$. Compared with $G(T2) = 0.577$, the T2 attribute, with less classification ambiguity (slightly), forms the root node for the desired fuzzy decision tree. The subsethood values in this case are, for T2:(see Box 2.) and $S(T2_L, C_H) = 0.571$, and $S(T2_H, C_L) = 0.577$ and $S(T2_H, C_H) = \mathbf{0.615}$. For $T2_L$ and $T2_H$, the larger subsethood value (in bold), defines the possible classification for that path. For $T2_L$ this is to C_L, with largest subsethood value (0.786), above the desired truth value of 0.65, previously defined. In the case of $T2_H$ its largest subsethood value is 0.615 ($S(T2_H, C_H)$), hence is not able to be a leaf node and further possible augmentation needs to be considered.

With only two condition attributes included in the example data set, the possible augmentation to $T2_H$ is with T1, where with $G(T2_H) = 0.650$, the ambiguity with partition evaluated for T1 ($G(T2_H$ and $T1| C)$) has to be less than this value, where: (see Box 3.) which is lower than the concomitant $G(T2_H) = 0.650$ value so less ambiguity would be found if the T1 attribute was augmented to the path T2 = H. The subsequent subsethood values in this case for each new path are; $T1_L$; $S(T2_H \cap T1_L, C_L) = \mathbf{0.652}$ and $S(T2_H \cap T1_L, C_H) = 0.565$; $T1_H$: $S(T2_H \cap T1_H, C_L) = 0.625$ and $S(T2_H \cap T1_H, C_H) = \mathbf{0.686}$. With each suggested classification path, the largest subsethood value is above the truth level threshold, therefore they are both leaf nodes leading from the T2 = H path.

Inspection of these results shows there are three fuzzy decision rules constructed, of the form:

If T2 = L, then C = L with truth level 0.786,
If T2 = H and T1 = L, then C = L with truth level 0.652,
If T2 = H and T1 = H, then C = H with truth level 0.686.

It is interesting to note from this example fuzzy decision tree analysis that there are three fuzzy decision rules to describe only two objects.

Wang et al. (2007) offers a reason for this, suggesting that associated fuzzy decision trees are normally larger than traditional crisp ones due to the membership degrees of the examples. Further elucidation of such fuzzy decision rules, and their representation in a tree structure, are presented in the more detailed analysis next given.

FUZZY DECISION TREE ANALYSIS OF U.S. TRAFFIC FATALITIES

The main thrust of this chapter is a fuzzy decision tree analysis of a U.S. traffic data set. The section is partitioned into two parts: firstly a description of the fuzzification of the included condition and decision attributes in the data, and secondly descriptions of the intermediate stages of the fuzzy decision tree analysis and the final results.

TRAFFIC FATALITIES IN THE U.S. AND FUZZIFICATION OF DATA

Traffic accidents have grown to account for a significant proportion of premature fatalities in the U.S. and most other developed countries (Shemer, 2004). State-to-state analysis can give valuable insights to policy makers interested in improving road safety and reducing the rate of road travel accidents and fatalities. However, state-to-state differences in road travel regulations and behaviour makes comparisons within the U.S. problematic.

Washington et al. (1999) provide an inter-regional comparison of the South Eastern States and suggest links between crash occurrence and differences in driver age, restraint use, vehicle miles travelled and type of road. However, it is apparent from the Fatality Analysis Reporting System of data and other studies that geographic variations exist in the incidence of vehicle accidents and fatalities. Studies have identified geographic variations alongside other, important, possible

Table 2. Descriptions of the independent condition attributes considered

Attribute	Function	Mean	St. Dev.
1: Youth cohort (YTC)	Proportion of state's population aged 15 to 24	0.145	0.010
2: Urban Proportion (UBP)	Urban road length/total road length	0.331	0.212
3: Income (INC)	Median household income ($)	53699.2	8306.2
4: Alcohol (ALC)	Proportion of fatalities alcohol related (BAC)	0.230	0.042
5: Driver's intensity (DVI)	Vehicle Miles Travelled/Licensed Drivers	0.152	0.026
6: Seat belt use (SBU)	None (0) / Secondary (1) / Primary (2)	1.431	0.533

contributory factors such as drinking patterns and seat belt usage (Houston & Richardson Jr., 2005; Zobeck et al., 1994). Indeed Noland (2003), argues that demographic and policy details, such as age cohorts and seat belt use legislation may account for fatality levels, more than infrastructure based details (such as number of lanes and lane widths).

To identify spatial variations of traffic fatalities across states in this study, the number of fatalities per 100,000 population is considered (FTLS), for each of the 50 states and DC for 2004. With mean value of 16.422 FTLS across this small data set, and the extremes of 7.42 for MS (Mississippi) and 32.38 for WY (Wyoming), there is noticeable variation in this measure of traffic fatalities. The attributes research question is then whether descriptive characteristics of each state can offer adequate discernment of their levels of FTLS, with the opportunity for the fullest interpretation to be given also.

The attributes chosen to describe each state are those based on previous research studies in the area (Noland, 2003; Zlatoper, 1991), see Table 2. The mean and standard deviation (St. Dev.) values given offer an indication to the levels of the considered attributes employed.

Inspection of the condition attributes reported in Table 2 shows a variety of general demographics are also present, such as the youth cohort and income. In the case of alcohol (ALC), *alcohol related* means at least one driver or non-occupant involved in the crash is determined to have had a blood alcohol concentration (BAC) level of .01 gram per deciliter (g/dL) or higher. The term "alcohol-related" does not indicate that a crash or fatality was caused by the presence of alcohol (Traffic Safety Facts, 2004).

The seat belt use (SBU) attribute is of interest, firstly because it is the only categorical attribute amongst the six considered, and secondly it is itself a policy based attribute. Moreover, most states have enacted safety belt laws, which can be classified as primary or secondary (or none if no law). The primary laws permit law enforcement officers to stop a vehicle and issue a citation for a safety belt violation, even if this is the only violation the officers' notice. The secondary laws allow the officers to issue safety belt citations to motorists only after they stop the drivers for other violations (Farmer & Williams, 2005).

To undertake a fuzzy analysis of the described traffic fatalities data set, the decision and condition attributes need to be fuzzified, with the creation

Table 3. Relevant information on the three groups of FTLS states

	Low (L)	Medium (M)	High (H)
Interval	L ≤ 12.393 (16)	12.393 < M ≤ 18.417 (16)	18.417 < H (17)
Mean	9.974	15.161	23.737

of sets of membership functions (MFs). With consideration to the size of the traffic fatality problem, here, three MFs are used to describe each attribute (one of only two constraints decided by an expert). It follows, there are three intervals used to identify an initial partitioning of the states based on their number of fatalities per 100,000 population (FTLS), defined Low (H), medium (M) and high (H) levels. Beyond the choice of the number of MFs describing each decision attribute, the prescribed approach to their specific construction given here, is only a demonstration of on such way. Using a simple equal-frequency partitioning of the states (49 used as in-sample with two retained, FL and NH, to illustrate the matching process), the midpoint between neighbouring, ordered, FTLS values in different groups are identified and initially used as the interval boundary points, see Table 3.

Also presented in Table 3, in parentheses, are the actual number of states included in each defined interval (supporting the equal-frequency approach adopted). To illustrate the presented information, for a medium level of traffic FTLS, the interval domain is between 12.393 and 18.417, for which there are 16 states associated with this interval (FTLS = M). These interval boundary values and within group means are used as the defining values for the construction of the associated MFs.

From Figure 1, the defining value, $\alpha_{j,3}$, is the modal value of the MF associated with the jth interval (single value where the MF equals one), for

Table 4. Attribute values and fuzzification with final labels presented for state of Vermont (VT)

Vermont (VT)	Crisp value	Fuzzy values	Label
YTC	0.144	[0.000, **0.878**, 0.122]	M
UBP	0.139	[**0.898**, 0.102, 0.000]	L
INC	55819.0	[0.000, 0.497, **0.503**]	H
ALC	0.184	[**1.000**, 0.000, 0.000]	L
DVI	0.143	[**0.530**, 0.470, 0.000]	L
SBU	S	[0.000, **1.000**, 0.000]	S
FTLS	15.77	[0.000, **0.907**, 0.093]	M

example $\alpha_{M,3} = 15.161$. The neighbouring defining values, $\alpha_{j,2}$ and $\alpha_{j,4}$, of $\alpha_{j,3}$, are simply the left and right boundary values of that interval (when $j = 1$ or k then the respective $\alpha_{j,2}$ and $\alpha_{j,4}$ are special cases). The final outer defining values, $\alpha_{j,1}$ and $\alpha_{j,5}$, are the modal defining values of its neighbouring intervals, for example $\alpha_{L,3} = \alpha_{M,1} = 9.974$ and $\alpha_{M,5} = \alpha_{H,3} = 23.737$. From these definitions of the defining values, the associated linear piecewise MFs can be constructed, see Figure 3.

The graphs in Figure 3, similar to those in Figure 1, show the MFs associated with the three decision classes describing the FTLS (L, M and H). These MFs are within ECCS, so for a value of FTLS the associated MF values equal 1.0. For example, when FTLS = 15.77 (fatalities per 100,000 population), $S_{FTLS}(15.77) = \mu_{FTLS,L}(15.77) + \mu_{FTLS,M}(15.77) + \mu_{FTLS,H}(15.77) = 0.000 + 0.907 + 0.093 = 1.0$. From Table 3, five of the six condition attributes are continuous in nature, and so

Figure 3. Set of MFs for FTLS decision attribute (including defining values)

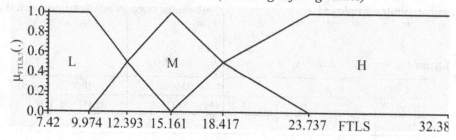

Figure 4. Sets of MFs for the five continuous condition attributes; YTC, UBP, INC, ALC, DVI

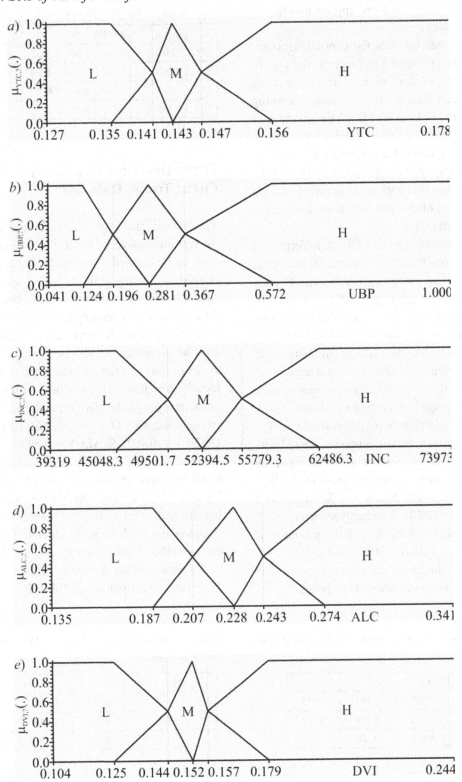

they require sets of three MFs to be constructed, see Figure 4 (using the same approach as for the FTLS attribute).

The fuzzification of the five continuous condition attributes presented in Figure 4, show three MFs describe each of them. The values along the base axis include the necessary defining values for the individual MFs. The structure of the linear piecewise MFs is similar for each MF produced. It follows, the information in Figures 3 and 4, allows the fuzzification of the attribute values that describe each state, see Table 4 for a demonstration of this process in the case of the state Vermont (VT).

The fuzzification details of the state Vermont's attributes show triplets of values, in each case representing the grades of membership to each linguistic term $(\mu_{\cdot,L}(x), \mu_{\cdot,M}(x)$ and $\mu_{\cdot,H}(x))$. The MF value that is the largest in each triplet is shown in bold and governs the linguistic variable the respective attribute value is most associated with (L, M or H). Since the SBU condition attribute is nominal, there is a 1.000 value associated with the seat belt usage legislation for that state, None, Secondary and Primary (in that order).

The variation in the vagueness associated with the fuzzification of the continuous attributes is demonstrated here by consideration of the INC and ALC attributes. Moreover, for ALC with $\mu_{ALC,L}(0.184) = 1.000$ it is certainly associated with being low, whereas for INC with the near equivalence of $\mu_{INC,M}(0.184) = 0.497$ and $\mu_{INC,H}(0.184) = 0.503$, they highlight noticeable vagueness is apparent about its linguistic description.

Table 5. Subsethood values of INC groups to FTLS groups

INC	FTLS = L	FTLS = M	FTLS = H
L	0.037	0.295	**0.835**
M	0.326	**0.650**	0.259
H	**0.671**	0.388	0.053

Table 6. Classification ambiguity values of attribute, after the partition INC = ·

INC	G(INC = ·)	G(·| INC = ·)				
		YTC	UBP	ALC	DVI	SBU
L	0.262	0.351	0.367	0.346	0.365	0.277
M	0.510	0.542	**0.462**	0.563	0.571	0.518
H	0.433	0.451	**0.350**	0.505	0.458	0.449

Fuzzy Decision Tree Analysis of Fuzzy Traffic Data Set

The second constraint offered by the analyst is the minimum level of truth (β) acceptable for a node to be defined a leaf node. Here, $\beta = 0.85$ is used, indicating at the technical level, only a subsethood value evaluated above 0.85 will define a leaf node (with accompanying decision rule). Using the MFs constructed in the previous section and the details of the 49 states considered (the states FL and NH not included), the root node is identified by finding the attribute with the lowest class ambiguity value ($G(E)$). For the six attributes in this case; $G(YTC) = 0.757$, $G(UBP) = 0.618$, $G(INC) = 0.402$, $G(ALC) = 0.849$, $G(DVI) = 0.492$ and $G(SBU) = 0.941$. With $G(INC) = 0.402$ the lowest amongst those identified, it infers the Income (INC) attribute has the lowest class ambiguity and so forms the root node for the fuzzy decision tree. With the root node (INC) identified, the subsethood $S(A, B)$ values of the INC classes to the classes of the decision attribute FTLS (L, M, H) are investigated, see Table 5.

Table 7. Subsethood values of INC groups to FTLS groups

INC = H then UBP	FTLS = L	FTLS = M	FTLS = H
L	0.121	**0.808**	0.290
M	0.654	**0.738**	0.093
H	**0.880**	0.277	0.015

Table 8. Attribute values and fuzzification with final labels presented for FL and NH states

	FL			NH		
	Crisp	Fuzzy	Label	Crisp	Fuzzy	Label
YTC	0.129	[**1.000**, 0.000, 0.000]	L	0.139	[**0.704**, 0.296, 0.000]	L
UBP	0.427	[0.000, 0.354, **0.646**]	H	0.239	[0.248, **0.752**, 0.000]	M
INC	49461.0	[**0.505**, 0.495, 0.000]	L	67848.0	[0.000, 0.000, **1.000**]	H
ALC	0.198	[**0.730**, 0.270, 0.000]	L	0.234	[0.000, **0.799**, 0.201]	M
DVI	0.150	[0.155, **0.845**, 0.000]	H	0.134	[**0.746**, 0.254, 0.000]	L
SBU	S	[0.000, **1.000**, 0.000]	S	N	[**1.000**, 0.000, 0.000]	N
FTLS	18.65	[0.000, 0.478, **0.522**]	H	13.16	[0.362, **0.638**, 0.000]	M

In each row in Table 5, the largest value identifies the decision class each of the paths from the root node should take. In the case of the INC = L path, the largest value is 0.835 (highlighted in bold with FTLS = H), since this value is just below the minimum truth level of 0.85 earlier defined, there is no leaf node defined. This is the case for all the paths from the root node INC, which means further checks for the lessening of ambiguity are made in each case, see Table 6.

In Table 6, the G(INC = ·) column of values identifies the level of classification ambiguity with each subset partition, these values are important since they benchmark the value below which a weighted average of classification ambiguity with each subset of partition G(P| F) must be to augment a node to a particular path. In the case of INC = L, the G(INC = L) = 0.262 is already quite low (supported by the large subsethood value in Table 5), so low in fact that there is no G(·| INC

Figure 5. Fuzzy decision tree of traffic fatalities (with minimum truth level b = 0.85)

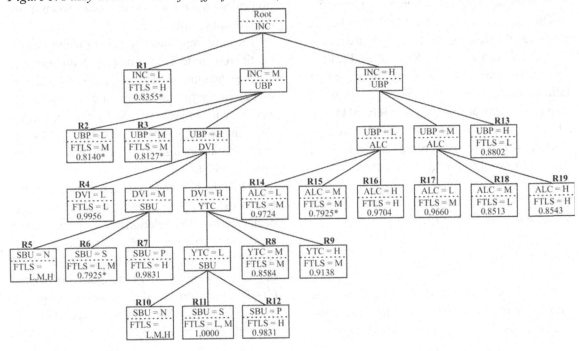

= L) value below this. This means that the node does become a leaf node with the classification to FTLS = H (with subsethood strength = 0.835). In the cases of INC = M and INC = H, there are lower $G(\cdot|\text{ INC} = \cdot)$ values, namely $G(\text{UBP}|\text{ INC} = M) = 0.462$ and $G(\text{UBP}|\text{ INC} = H) = 0.350$, respectively. Hence the two paths INC = M and INC = H are both augmented by the attribute UBP. The subsethood values associated with these two paths to the possible classification to FTLS = L, M or H, are reported in Table 7.

The results in Table 7 concern the progression from the INC = H then UBP path, the only largest subsethood value greater than the 0.85 boundary of minimum truth is associated with UBP = H (value 0.880). It follows, the path INC = H and UBP = H classifies to FTLS = L with 0.880 level of truth. For the other two paths there would be further checks on the possibility of minimising ambiguity by further augmenting other attribute, the same as for the INC = M then UBP path. This described process is repeated until all paths end with a leaf node, found from achieving the required level of subsethood, or no further augmentation is possible. The resultant fuzzy decision tree formed through this approach is presented in Figure 5.

The fuzzy decision tree in Figure 5 indicates that a total of 19 leaf nodes were established (fuzzy *"if .. then .."* decision rules, **R1** to **R19**). Further, the depth of the constructed fuzzy decision tree indicates each state is classified using a maximum of five condition attributes (rules **R10**, **R11** and **R12**), with all condition attributes used in the tree. To illustrate the practicality of the derived decision rules, the rule labeled **R18** interprets to:

If INC = H, UBP = M and ALC = M then FTLS = L with truth level 0.8513,

or (equivalently):

For a state with high median income, medium level of urban proportion of roads and a medium level of alcohol related fatalities, then a low level

of fatalities per 100,000 population is expected with truth level 0.8513.

or (equivalently):

For a state with median income greater than $55,779.3, proportional level of urban roads is between 0.196 and 0.367, and a proportional level of alcohol related fatalities is between 0.207 BAC and 0.243BAC, then a level of fatalities per 100,000 population less than 12.393 is expected with truth level 0.8513.

Either of the above three versions of the decision rule **R18** can be used, indeed it can be found that three states are classified by this rule, namely Minnesota (MN), New Hampshire (NH) and Washington (WA) (using details in Table A1). For the state Vermont (VT), for whose fuzzification is expressed in Table 4, the classification path through the fuzzy decision tree shows it is classified by the path ending at the leaf node labeled **R14**, in this case the correct classification (FTLS = M). As with the small example fuzzy decision tree exposed previously, a number of these decision rules do not classify any states when using the matching procedure.

The most important condition attribute, forming the root node, is income (INC), the immediate classification of states with INC = L (low) is supported by the understanding that normally wealthier areas seek to avoid riskier activities (here the wealthier states with INC = M or H need other attributes to further discern them with respect to FTLS).

While the influence of seat belt use is limited due to its utilisation towards the bottom of the decision tree, the relationship appears mixed in terms of whether the legislation is primary, secondary or none towards discerning the level of FTLS. This ambiguity is supported in Noland (2003), which concluded from their findings that primary laws have the expected effect of reducing both fatalities and injuries, while secondary laws unexpectedly seem to result in an increase in fatalities. It perhaps would be more pertinent to use actual levels of seat belt use rather than the concomitant legislation that may dictate the usage level (Noland, 2003).

The fuzzy decision tree reported in Figure 5, as well as elucidating the relationship between traffic fatality levels (FTLS) and state characteristics, can also be utilised to make predictions (matching) on the level of FTLS on other states not previously considered (following the matching procedure given previously). To illustrate the further matching properties of the fuzzy decision tree, the two states Florida (FL) and New Hampshire (NH), not utilised in its construction are next considered, starting with the fuzzification of the original attribute values, see Table 8.

In Table 8, the two states are described through their original crisp values, their fuzzification into triplets of membership values (to L, M and H) and their linguistic label based on the largest of the membership values (similar to that in Table 4). Using the fuzzy decision tree and matching procedure again, the two out-of-sample states are found to be classified by **R1** for the state FL (to FTLS = H) and **R18** for the state NH (to FTLS = L). For the case of the state NH, its classification follows from the different representations of the decision rule **R18**, given previously.

FUTURE TRENDS

As with any novel technique, there is the need for it to "bed in," that is, to be used a number of times before the full understanding to how it operates on a particular problem can be realised. Fuzzy decision trees are no exception, for example, the fuzzification of the data needs careful consideration, since the decisions here are present in the subsequent fuzzy decision rules presented.

Further future issues that surround fuzzy decision trees, include those that are specific to it and other that are more general. The specific

issues include checking for the comprehensibility and consistency of the results, acknowledging that fuzzy decision tree may produce larger trees than their crisp counterparts. One example general issue, is how to handle missing values in data, here decision trees have their approach, while operations in a fuzzy environment brings their own solutions.

CONCLUSION

The concurrent evolution of quantitative techniques, through the availability of desk top computing and the Internet, is able to be witnessed by researchers whether they are technical or non-technical minded. The modern communication mediums available also allow the opportunity to employ these techniques, due to their often availability over the Internet, and so on. However, to optimise the benefit of their employment, researchers need to understand the rudiments of them.

The emphasis in this chapter has been on the utilisation of fuzzy decision trees in domestic travel research. The analysis within a fuzzy environment brings with it the allowance for imprecision in the data considered, and a linguistic interpretation to the results found. The area of fuzzy decision trees clearly offer these advantages, the technique here taking into account inherent cognitive uncertainties. The U.S. traffic fatalities data set considered exemplifies the type of data investigated, from which policy decisions may be desired.

The resultant fuzzy decision tree constructed includes a number paths, from which fuzzy "*if* .. *then* .." decision rules are interpreted. The visual tree structure immediately offers the elucidation of the important attributes (feature selection), as well as possible relationships between condition attributes and some decision. In this case, the median income in U.S. states appearing to be the most important. The association of objects (U.S. states) to individual decision rules, can identify outliers, these may require specific policy understanding.

It is hoped this book chapter offers the necessary rudiments and references that will allow readers to further utilise this fuzzy decision tree technique (as well as others).

REFERENCES

Armand, S., Watelain, E., Roux, E., Mercier, M., & Lepoutre, F.-X. (2007). Linking clinical measurements and kinematic gait patterns of toe-walking using fuzzy decision trees. *Gait & Posture, 25*(3), 475-484.

Beynon, M. J., Peel, M. J., & Tang, Y-C. (2004). The application of fuzzy decision tree analysis in an exposition of the antecedents of audit fees. *OMEGA, 32*, 231-244.

Breiman, L. (2001). Statistical modelling: The two cultures. *Statistical Science, 16*(3), 199-231.

Chakraborty, D. (2001). Structural quantization of vagueness in linguistic expert opinion in an evaluation programme. *Fuzzy Sets and Systems, 119*, 171-186.

Chen, Z. (2001). *Data mining and uncertain reasoning: An integrated approach.* New York: John Wiley.

Chiang, I-J., Shieh, M-J., Hsu, J. Y-J., & Wong, J-M. (2005). Building a medical decision support system for colon polyp screening by using fuzzy classification trees. *Applied Intelligence, 22*, 61-75.

DeOliveria, J. V. (1999). Semantic constraints for membership function optimization. *IEEE Transactions on Systems, Man and Cybernetics – Part A: Systems and Humans, 29*(1), 128-138.

Ewing, R. (2003). Legal, status of traffic calming. *Transportation Quarterly, 57*(2), 11-23.

Farmer, C. M., & Williams, A. F. (2005). Effect on fatality risk of changing from secondary to primary seat belt enforcement. *Journal of Safety Research, 36*, 189-194

Herrera, F., Herrera-Viedma, E., & Martinez, L. (2000). A fusion approach for managing multi-granularity linguistic term sets in decision making. *Fuzzy Sets and Systems, 114*, 43-58.

Higashi, M., & Klir, G. J. (1983). Measures of uncertainty and information based on possibility distributions. *International Journal of General Systems, 9*, 43-58.

Houston, D. J., & Richardson, Jr., L. E. (2005). Getting Americans to buckle up: The efficacy of state seat belt laws. *Accident Analysis & Prevention, 37*, 1114-1120.

Jang, J.-S. R. (1994). Structure determination in fuzzy modeling: A fuzzy CART approach. *Proceedings of IEEE International Conference on Fuzzy Systems*, Orlando, Florida, *1*, 480-485.

Janikow, C. Z. (1998). Fuzzy decision trees: Issues and methods. *IEEE Transactions of Systems, Man and Cybernetics Part B, 28*(1), 1-14.

Jeng, B., Jeng, Y-M., & Liang, T-P. (1997). FILM: A fuzzy inductive learning method for automated knowledge acquisition. *Decision Support Systems, 21*, 61-73.

Kecman, V. (2001). *Learning and Soft Computing: Support Vector Machines, Neural Networks, and Fuzzy Logic.* London: MIT Press.

Kosko, B. (1986). Fuzzy entropy and conditioning. *Information Science, 30*, 165-74.

Kovalerchuk, B., & Vityaev, E. (2000). *Data mining in finance: Advances in relational and hybrid methods.* Dordrecht: Kluwer, Academic Publishers.

Lin, C-C., & Chen, A-P. (2002). Generalisation of Yang et al.'s method of fuzzy programming with piecewise linear membership functions. *Fuzzy sets and Systems*, *132*, 346-352.

Lo, K. L. (2004). The fuzzy decision tree application to a power system problem. *COMPEL*, *23*(2), 436-451.

Medaglia, A. L., Fang, S-C., Nuttle, H. L. W., & Wilson, J. R. (2002). An efficient and flexible mechanism for constructing membership functions. *European Journal of Operational Research*, *139*, 84-95.

Mikut, R., Jäkel, J., & Gröll, L. (2005). Interpretability issues in data-based learning of fuzzy systems, *Fuzzy Sets and Systems*, *150*, 179-197.

Noland, R. (2003). Traffic fatalities and injuries: the effect of changes in infrastructure and other trends. *Accident Analysis & Prevention*, *35*, 599-611

Olaru, C., & Wehenkel, L. (2003). A complete fuzzy decision tree technique. *Fuzzy Sets and Systems*, *138*, 221-254.

Peng, Y. (2004). Intelligent condition monitoring using fuzzy inductive learning. *Journal of Intelligent Manufacturing*, *15*, 373-380.

Roa-Sepulveda, C. A., Herrera, M., Pavez-Lazo, B., Knight, U. G., & Coonick, A. H. (2003). Economic dispatch using fuzzy decision trees. *Electric Power Systems Research*, *66*, 115-122.

Shemer, J. (2004). Traffic Accidents - The National Killer. *Harefuah*, *143*(2), 90-91.

Traffic Safety Facts (2004). State Alcohol Estimates, www.nhtsa.dot.gov.

Wang, X., Chen, B., Qian, G., & Ye, F. (2000). On the optimization of fuzzy decision trees. *Fuzzy Sets and Systems*, *112*, 117-125.

Wang, X., Nauck, D. D., Spott, M., & Kruse, R. (2007). Intelligent data analysis with fuzzy decision trees. *Soft Computing*, *11*, 439-457.

Washington, S., Metarko, J., Fomumung, I., Ross, R., Julian, F., & Moran, E. (1999). An inter-regional comparison: fatal crashes in the Southeastern and non-Southeastern United States: preliminary findings. *Accident Analysis & Prevention*, *31*, 135-146.

Yu, C-S., & Li, H-L. (2001). Method for solving quasi-concave and non-cave fuzzy multi-objective programming problems. *Fuzzy Sets and Systems*, *122*, 205-227.

Yuan, Y., & Shaw, M. J. (1995). Induction of fuzzy decision trees. *Fuzzy Sets and Systems*, *69*, 125-139.

Zadeh, L. A. (1965). Fuzzy sets. *Information and Control*, *8*(3), 338-353.

Zadeh L. A. (1973). Outline of a new approach to the analysis of complex systems and decision processes. *IEEE Transactions on Systems, Man and Cybernetics-Part A: Systems and Humans*, *SMC-3*, 28-44.

Zadeh, L. A. (1999). Some reflections o the anniversary of Fuzzy Sets and Systems. *Fuzzy Sets and Systems*, *100*, 1-3.

Zadeh, L. A. (2005). Toward a generalized theory of uncertainty (GTU) – An outline. *Information Sciences*, *172*, 1-40.

Zlatoper, T. J. (1991). Determinants of motor vehicles deaths in the Unites States: A cross sectional analysis. *Accident Analysis and Prevention*, *23*(5), 431-436.

Zobeck, T. S., Grant, B. F., Stinson, F. S., & Bettolucci, D. (1994). Alcohol involvement in fatal traffic crashes in the United States 1979–90. *Addiction*, *89*, 227-231.

Chapter XIII
New Churn Prediction Strategies in Telecom Industry

Dymitr Ruta
BT Group, Research and Venturing, UK

Christoph Adl
BT Group, Research and Venturing, UK

Detlef Nauck
BT Group, Research and Venturing, UK

ABSTRACT

In the telecom industry, high installation and marketing costs make it six to 10 times more expensive to acquire a new customer than it is to retain an existing one. Prediction and prevention of customer churn is therefore a key priority for industrial research. While all the motives of customer decision to churn are highly uncertain there is a lot of related temporal data generated as a result of customer interaction with the service provider. The major problem with this data is its time discontinuity resulting from the transactional character of events they describe. Moreover, such irregular temporal data sequences are typically a chaotic mixture of different data types, which further hinders its exploitation for any predictive task. Existing churn prediction methods like decision trees typically classify customers into churners and non-churners based on the static data collected in a snapshot of time while completely ignoring the timing of churn and hence the circumstances of this event. In this work, we propose new churn prediction strategies that are suitable for application at different levels of the information content available in customers' data. Gradually enriching the data information content from the prior churn rate and lifetime expectancy then typical static events data up to decay-weighted data sequences, we propose a set of new churn prediction tools based on: customer lifetime modelling, hidden markov model (HMM) of customer events, and the most powerful k nearest sequence (kNS) algorithm that deliver robust churn predictions at different levels of data availability. Focussing further on kNS we demonstrate how the sequential processing of appropriately pre-processed data streams lead to better performance of customer churn prediction. Given histories of other customers and the current customer data, the presented kNS uses an original combination of sequential nearest neighbour algorithm and original sequence aggregation technique to predict the whole remaining customer data sequence path up to the churn event. On the course of experimental trials, it is demonstrated that the new kNS model better exploits time-ordered customer data sequences and surpasses existing churn prediction methods in terms of performance and capabilities offered.

INTRODUCTION

Today's global telecommunication market environment can be characterised by the strong competition among different telcos and a decline in growth rate due to maturity of the market. Furthermore, there is a huge pressure on those companies to make healthy profits and increase their market shares. Most telecom companies are in fact customer-centric service providers and offer to their customers a variety of subscription services. One of the major issues in such environment is customer churn known as a process by which a company loses a customer to a competitor. Recent estimates suggest that churn rates in the telecom industry could be anywhere from 25 percent to 50 percent (Furnas, 2003). Moreover on average it costs around $400 to acquire a new customer, which takes years to recoup (Furnas, 2003). These huge acquisition costs are estimated to be five to eight times higher than it is to retain the existing customer by offering him some incentives (Yan, Miller, Mozer, & Wolniewicz, 2001). In this competitive and volatile environment, it makes every economic sense to have a strategy to retain customers, which is only possible if the customer intention to churn is detected early enough.

There are many different reasons for customers to churn, some of them, like moving home, unstoppable, others like sudden death, undetectable. The churn prediction systems

therefore should focus on detecting those churners that are deliberately moving to a competitor as these customers are most likely to leave data traces of their intent prior to churn and can

be potentially persuaded to stay. This work is not concerned with the effectiveness of actual actions preventing customer churn or rescuing customers who cancelled their contract. The only concern here is the prediction of customer churn in order to provide the information about which customers are most likely to leave the service in the near future.

Churn prediction attracts recently a lot of both scientific and business attention. In the presence of large data warehouses as well as terabytes of data from Web resources, data mining techniques are increasingly being appreciated and adopted to business applications (Lemmen, 2000; Morgan, 2003), in an attempt to explain drivers of customer actions, in particular sudden falls in customer satisfaction and value ultimately leading to churn. There is a number of churn prediction models used commercially at present, however churn is only being modelled statically by analysing event-driven customer data and running regression or predictive classification models at a particular time (Duda, Hart, & Stork, 2001) over aggregated customer data. Some improvement is obtained after segmenting customers into specific groups and dealing with different groups separately yet this segmentation only supports company's customer relationship management (CRM) and on its own does not improve weak performance in churn prediction. In practise the most common churn management systems are even simpler as they try to device a churn risk based on regression against available data variables. On the research arena the focus is shifted towards more complex classification and non-linear regression techniques like neural networks (Mozer, Wolniewicz, Grimes, Johnson, & Kaushansky, 2000), decision trees (Blundon, 2003) or support vector machines (Morik & Kopcke, 2004) yet applied in the same static context to customer data and hence not generating any promising results.

In this work, the weaknesses of static churn prediction systems are fully addressed and as a result a dynamic temporal churn prediction system called k nearest sequences has been developed. It uses a novel sequential nearest neighbour algorithm that learns from the whole available customer data path and takes into account the order of customer event history. As a result, the system is able to generate future data sequences along with precisely timed predicted churn events. While a more robust churn prediction system is a primary goal, the attempt is also to illustrate how the performance of churn prediction depends on the information content of the data. In the course of incremental enrichment of data informativeness, we illustrated using our originally developed models how the performance of churn prediction improves up to the state where it surpasses traditional churn prediction models. This has been achieved by applying sequential processing of temporal data transformed by the original weight-decay mechanism, allowing the incorporation of infrequent events' data and dealing with many missing patterns. The experiments carried out on real customer's data from a major telecom company illustrate the effectiveness of the method and highlight the need to maximally exploit absolutely all information describing customer relationship with the service provider.

The remainder of the chapter is organised as follows. First, we describe a customer life cycle and provide the context for the churn analysis. The following section explains the churn management problem on different layers of data quality and availability. The following subsections consider different churn prediction scenarios depending on the availability of the data and consider different prior churn rate strategies, lifetime-based churn predictions, HMM-based customer events predictions, and churn prediction systems based on temporal classification. We then provide the results from experiments carried out upon real customer data in these three scenarios. Finally, the concluding section summarises our result and makes some recommendations for further research.

CUSTOMER LIFECYCLE

The beginning of the 21st century brought an explosion of customer-centric service providers. The business cycle of such vendors very quickly converged to the customer life cycle. While customer relationship management (CRM) accounts for all customer interactions during company service, the management methodology depends on the stage and type of customer relationships with the company. Typically, the service provider would advertise its services to prospective customers, offer discounts for new customers to build up customer loyalty, set a quality care to retain the customers, and keep them satisfied. These distinct stages of customer relationship with the company are referred to as customer life cycle. There are many different ways the customer life cycle can be split into distinct stages. In one of the representations, a customer is shown to come through a cyclic process of stages as shown in Figure 1. After each cycle the customer may either leave the cycle or be reborn in terms of new services offered to him and that way stay in the cycle. The other model assumes customer acquisition and churn as separate beginning and end stages of the individual customer lifecycle while the cycle itself relates to the ongoing efforts of increasing customer value and retaining customers as shown in Figure 2.

A routine of many companies today is to group customers into many different customer segments based on their credit rating, value contribution, service usage, and so on. The stages shown in Figure 1 and Figure 2 reflect customer behaviour evolution along time, yet there could be many other ways the customers can be segmented. Despite this variety, all the evidence for customer segmentation comes in a form of sequential data portions customers generate on their way throughout their life with the service provider. If the goal is a prediction of customer churn, prediction mechanism should be based on original customer data if possible, because any intermediate pre-processing like customer segmentation is restricted by the informative power of the data evidence and could only result in the loss of information. In the experimental section, we compare the effectiveness of segmentation based churn prediction using a Hidden markov model (HMM) against classification models directly learning from source data.

1. **Identifying customer needs:** Customer segmentation and identification of target products or services
2. **Acquiring customers:** Advertising the product to the customer segment, offering discounts, promotions, tailored services
3. **Keeping in touch with the customer:** Collecting data, monitoring and increasing customers' loyalty and value.
4. **Customer retention:** The collected data is used to predict customer behaviour and

Figure 1. Five stages of recurrent customer life cycle

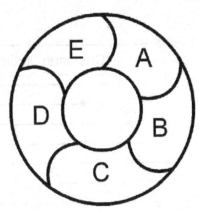

act proactively especially under high churn risk

5. **Loosing the customer:** Customer leaves the company, but may be reborn or re-acquired by new products/services or by special offers for former customers.

CHURN MANAGEMENT ON DIFFERENT DATA LAYERS

The telecom industry of today represents strongly customer-centric, service-oriented businesses operating mostly on minimum-period contracts.

Figure 2. Individual customer life cycle flow with typical data mining application domains

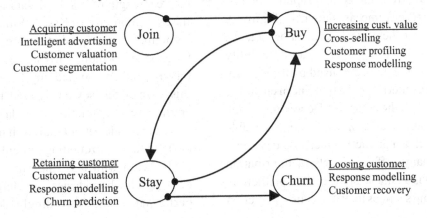

Figure 3. Illustration of the customer lifetime and the nature of the available data. Each horizontal line represents individual customer life with the service.

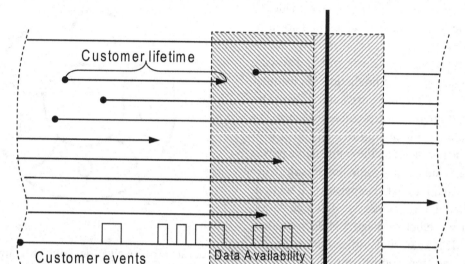

Throughout the duration of the contract there is a great deal of interaction between the customer and the service provider that generates a lot of time-stamped data. These data typically have transactional character and are reported in the database in a form of events characterised by many descriptive attributes. In a realistic scenario due to various privacy and security issues customer data is available only within a narrow timeframe compared to the customer lifetime. All churn analysis therefore is forced to be applied on this availability timeframe as shown in Figure 3. Customer data therefore is constrained on the one hand by the limits of the data availability timeframe and on the other hand by the sparsity of data-rich events along the timeline of customer interaction with the company. Depending on the availability and quality of the data, it is sensible to consider churn prediction methodology separately on many different levels of information content that is available at the time of prediction. The following sections look into churn prediction

methodologies on different layers of information content of the available data ranging from complete lack of data up to complete continuous sequences of customer data.

Prior Churn Rate

There are many approaches to predict customer churn. The ability to predict customer churn is strictly related to the availability and the discriminative strength of customer data with respect to the churn/non-churn classes. With this respect, it is common that the prediction rate reflects mostly the goodness of the data irrespective of the predictor type used. Acknowledging these observations, this chapter focuses on optimal representation and maximal exploitation of available evidence in order to provide better assured churn predictions along with its surrounding circumstances.

To begin with it is important to start from drawing the boundaries on churn prediction performance and accordingly determine the

Table 1. Confusion matrix representation $C_{0|0}$ – true negatives, $C_{1|0}$ – false negatives, $C_{0|1}$ – false positives, $C_{1|1}$ – true positives

Actual\Predicted	NonChurn	Churn
NonChurn	$C_{0|0}$	$C_{1|0}$
Churn	$C_{0|1}$	$C_{1|1}$

Table 2. Comparison of costs for retaining and acquiring new customers if all customers are treated as churners, assuming that the cost x of acquiring a new customer is f = 5 times higher than the cost of retaining an existing customer (Yan et al., 2001). In general the effective cost of retaining 1 customer would be expressed by: $cost_{ret} = x/(fp_{churn})$ where p stands for the prior churn rate. According to (Yan et al., 2001) in the wireless telecom industry x varies on average between 300\$ and 400\$.

Churn probability	50%	5%	3%	1%
Cost of acquiring 1 customer	x	x	x	x
Cost of retaining 1 customer	0.4x	4x	6.66x	20x
Difference	0.6x	-3x	-5.66x	-19x

relevant performance measures. Assuming a constant stream of N customers from whom n_{churn} customers churn while n_{new} customers join the company in a considered time window let $n_{churn} = n_{new}$ and let $p_{prior} = n_{churn} / N$ stand for a prior churn probability. Given this information at the very worst, for example by predicting k churners at random, on average there will be always kp_{churn} correctly recognised churners at the cost of $(1 - kp_{churn})$ wrong churn predictions. The prior churn probability p_{prior} sets therefore the lower bound on churn prediction rate which can be achieved with no prediction model at all. In the optimal scenario all the churn predictions are correct. The focus is put here just on churn predictions rather churn and non-churn predictions as only churn predictions are actionable and typically incur some costs. There is no action and no costs involved in a prediction of a non-churner but the rate of false positives predictions, that is non-churners that were incorrectly classified as churners, limits the maximum number of churners that can be picked. The prediction results are typically summarised in a form of confusion matrix as illustrated in Table 1.

$C_{a|b}$ means the number of customers coming from class a that were classified as class b (in our case churn is 1, non-churn is 0). Given the confusion matrix, by analogy to p_{prior}, the churn recognition rate understood as efficiency of churn predictions can be expressed by:

$$p_{churn} = c_{1|1}/(c_{1|1} + c_{1|0}) \qquad (1)$$

In order to truly reflect the performance of the prediction model compared to the random predictions, it is sensible to use a gain measure which expresses how many times the predictor's churn rate is better than the prior churn rate p_{prior}:

$$G = \frac{p_{churn}}{p_{prior}} = \frac{c_{1|1}/(c_{1|1} + c_{1|0} + c_{0|1} + c_{0|0})}{(c_{1|1} + c_{1|0})(c_{0|1} + c_{1|1})} \qquad (2)$$

In order to scale the gain within the achievable limits of $(1, 1/p_{prior})$ one could use the relative gain measure defined as follows:

$$G_r = \frac{p_{churn} - p_{prior}}{1 - p_{prior}} = \frac{c_{1|1}c_{0|0} - c_{1|0}c_{0|1}}{(c_{1|1} + c_{1|0})(c_{0|0} + c_{1|0})} \qquad (3)$$

Finally, let us now consider the effect that different prior churn rates have on customer retention costs. Assuming that, as mentioned above, the costs of acquiring a new customer is about five times higher than retaining an existing customer (Yan et al., 2001) the retention costs can be expressed in terms of acquisition costs. Table 2 shows the economic problems of proactive churn management for different churn rates, when the prediction strategy advises all the customers as potential churners. Table 2 clearly illustrates that in the realistic scenario of around 3 percent churn rate customer retention is unprofitable in the naive "all-churner" based prediction strategy.

Customer Lifetime

Customer lifetime provides additional vital information for churn prediction purposes. Historical lifetime data from different customers gives extra information about the lifetime distribution which then allows to link the churn event to a random process with a certain probability distribution and hence describe churn in probabilistic terms. Consider a random series of customer lifetimes x_i extracted from the available data. The first goal is to fit some standard distribution to it. Customer lifetime and the termination point of churn can be modelled as a random process where the waiting time (i.e., lifetime) before the event (i.e., churn) is relatively long. Moreover, the distribution of lifetimes is certainly asymmetric due to the enforced starting point of $x_i = 0$ for each lifetime. The three distributions that match these assumptions have been identified: exponential, Gamma and Weibull distributions. All of these distributions have reported applications to lifetime modelling

(Finkelstein, 2002). Yet further analysis in which distributions were fitted to the certain ranges of lifetimes, for example for lifetimes greater than five years, showed that only the Gamma distribution consistently fits the data well despite its changing characteristics. Settling on the Gamma distribution, the probability density function (PDF) of the lifetime x is defined by:

$$y = f(x \mid a,b) = \frac{x^{a-1}e^{-x/b}}{b^a \Gamma(a)} \quad where \quad \Gamma(a) = \int_0^\infty e^{-t}t^{a-1}dt \tag{4}$$

where a,b are distribution parameters and $\Gamma(a)$ is a well known gamma function. Given the density (4) the cumulative distribution function (CDF) can be obtained by:

$$p = F(x \mid a,b) = \int_0^x f(x)dx = \frac{1}{b^a \Gamma(a)} \int_0^x t^{a-1}e^{-t/b}dt \tag{5}$$

The CDF function $F(x)$ returns the probability that the event drawn from the gamma distribution will occur no later than at time period x. In the case of customer lifetime modelling, the only event expected is customer churn, hence the CDF

Figure 4. Gamma probability density (PDF) distribution fitted to customer lifetime data 3(a) Comparison of the real lifetime distribution with the fitted gamma distribution 3(b) Cumulative probability distribution of the fitted gamma distribution

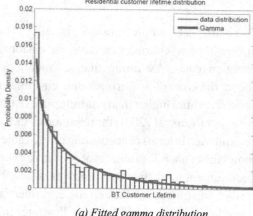

(a) Fitted gamma distribution

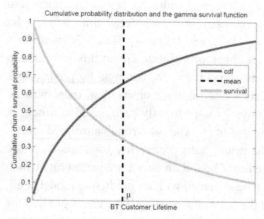

(b) Cumulative PDF and survival function

becomes immediately the unconditional churn risk expressed as a function of the customer life with the service provider. Assigning churn to a certain event, for example $S(x)=1-F(x)$ gives the customer survival function showing the probability $S(x)$ of a customer surviving up to the period x with the service provider. Figure 4 shows an example of a fitted gamma distribution along with the corresponding cumulative probability distribution and the survival function. Exploiting further the properties of the gamma distribution one can immediately obtain the average customer lifetime expectancy and its variability which correspond to the gamma mean $\mu=ab$ and variance $v=ab^2$.

The lifetime analysis carried out so far applies to a customer who just joined the service. In reality at any time period one might need to ask about the remaining lifetime of a customer who already stayed with the service provider for some time. The problem of remaining lifetime from the mathematical point of view is quite simple. The remaining lifetime of a customer at age t can be found by an integration of the survival function from t to ∞ and renormalisation which can be expressed by:

$$L(t) = \frac{1}{S(t)} \int_{T}^{\infty} S(x)dx \qquad (6)$$

Note that if the customer has just joined the company, that is when $t=0$, the remaining lifetime simplifies to the Gamma mean parameter:

$$L(0) = \int_{0}^{\infty} S(x)dx = \mu \qquad (7)$$

Figure 5(a) shows the plot of the remaining lifetime for incremental periods that the customer already stayed with the company obtained by numerical integration according to (6). Finally the most interesting characteristic from the churn prediction point of view is the churn risk evolution over time. Assuming that the churn probability relates to fixed time ahead τ, its evolution over time $H(t)$ can be calculated by the integration of gamma PDF function from t to $t + \tau$ and renormalisation, that is:

$$H_\tau(t) = \frac{\int_{t}^{t+\tau} f(x)dx}{\int_{t}^{\infty} f(x)dx} = \frac{F(t+\tau)-F(t)}{1-F(t)} = \frac{S(t)-S(t+\tau)}{S(t)} \qquad (8)$$

Using formula (8) examples of churn risk evolution curves were obtained for one, three, six, and 12 months as shown in Figure 5(b). The presented analysis indicates that entrants have much higher churn rate than the customers who stayed long with the service provider. For churn prediction purposes, this information means that the random churn prediction strategy from previous section would give much higher performance if applied only to entrants or in general to customers with the service age at which the churn risk is the highest.

HMM-Based Binary Events Prediction

In the following, we assume that the binary information of customer events is available along the sequence of temporal slots that is "1" if the event took place in a time slot say a week or "0" otherwise. Given a number of different events that could happen to a customer, the data take a form

Table 3. Description of the visible state encoding scheme used for churn prediction with hidden markov models. For confidentiality purposes event type names other than churn are not revealed.

Digit position	Event type	Negative/positive value decision
1 (2^0)	type 1	0 – none reported / 1 – at least 1 reported this month
2 (2^1)	type 2	0 – none reported / 1 – at least 1 reported this month
3 (2^2)	type 3	0 – none reported / 1 – at least 1 reported this month
4 (2^3)	churn	0 – none reported / 1 – exactly 1 reported this month

of binary strings of the length consistent with the number of different events that are monitored. Each combination of such a string represents a certain state that a customer is in and since long historical sequences of such states are available it is possible to use Hidden markov model to model and predict such sequences.

Markov models represent a family of stochastic methods focused on the analysis of temporal sequences of discrete states. In traditional first-order models, the current state depends only on the prior state which means no prior history of sequence evolution has any effect on the current state. In hidden markov models, the states are hidden from observation, but each of them emits a number of observable variables which could take either discrete or continuous values. A hidden markov model is fully described by its parameters, which are the transition probabilities between the hidden states and the probabilities or probability densities of the emission of observables. Given a coarse model structure there are three central issues in hidden markov models (Duda et al., 2001):

- **The evaluation problem:** Determination of the probability of a particular given sequence of visible states (emissions) in a fully defined hidden markov model.
- **The decoding problem:** Similar to the evaluation problem, a hidden markov model and a visible state sequence are given. The aim is now to find the most likely sequence of hidden states that led to those observations.
- **The learning problem:** A coarse structure of the model (number of hidden and visible states) is given, but neither the transition probabilities between the hidden states nor the probabilities of the emission of observables are known. The aim is to determine these with a set of training observations of visible symbols.

Data preparation. In our model, the state space consists of 16 (2^4) states corresponding to the combination of different events within consecutive monthly periods. Each state represents a four digit binary string with each digit indicating presence of particular event types (see Table 3). For every month, one state is created, providing basic information about the customer provisions, repairs, complaints, and churns.

This model allows not only to predict churn events but also to model customer behaviour in a form of a prediction of most likely sequences of events that the customer may experience in the near future. Prediction of individual events like churn can be considered in the two contexts. The churn event can be predicted whenever the most likely sequence of states terminates with a state containing churn. Moreover, the model can be used to predict the churn likelihood at each time period just by calculating the sum of all probabilities of sequences that lead to churn at a particular time.

Implementation. The presented HMM model has been implemented in JAVA with the support of JaHMM (Java Hidden markov model) (Francois, 2006) developed by Jean-Marc Francois, see Figure 10 for visualisation of generated HMM. JaHMM supports discrete state HMMs and provides algorithms to address the three central issues for hidden markov models. Some of the exact algorithms (e.g. the one for solving the decoding problem) have been replaced with stochastic algorithms due to a low prior churn probability that prevented finding churn among the most likely states.

Temporal Classification on Events Data

Churn prediction can also be seen as a classification problem with 2 classes. Because we only need to act on predicted churn it can be even considered as 1-class classification problem of identifying churners. Customers' data is tem-

Figure 5. Typical remaining lifetime (5(a)) and churn risk (5(b)) evolution curves in service-oriented business. Due to data confidentiality issues we can not reveal the real numbers behind the graphs.

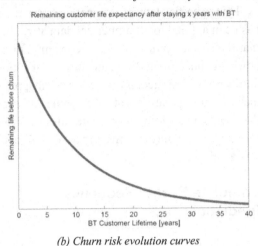

(b) Churn risk evolution curves

(a) Remaining lifetime expectancy curve

poral in nature and as a consequence valid only in selected narrow time frames from where they originate. For the classification model the most significant consequence is that the predictions are always related to and depend on a particular time window in the future. The width of the prediction time window should be consistent with the time distance between data and class label used for training. That means, the temporal classification model needs to work adaptively on a moving window of customer data and use data with advance time distance labels for training in order to make consistent predictions in the same time distance forward in time. The concept of such a temporal classification is schematically illustrated in Figure 6.

Formally, temporal classification means simply embedding the traditional static classifier into a temporal framework described above. Given the historical sequence of customer data vectors x_t and the corresponding labels ω_t the objective of a temporal classifier is to learn the relationship $\omega_{t+dt} = f(x_t)$ and apply learned function to the current time customer data x_{t+k} in order to predict their future class label ω_{t+k+dt}. In the experimental section a number of different temporal classifiers are evaluated in terms of their gain above the random predictor performance.

Continuous data generation using decay function. The classification model presented above is driven by events distributed in a discrete time domain and ignores time periods when no

Figure 6. Schematic illustration of the temporal classification process.

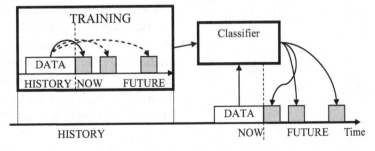

data is generated. This model is supported by the optimal database storage of customer data by recording observations in the time they happen. The question is what happens with the customer in-between these events. Although no data is available it is certainly possible to deduct from the characteristics of previous events what impact they may cause upon the customer. For example, repetitive faults followed by multiple complaints will be well remembered by the customer for quite a while although their significance will inevitably fade away with time. In an attempt to incorporate this observation a weight decay mechanism is introduced to fill data gaps between the events and that way eliminate the problem of missing data. Data decay methodology is commonly used in psychology to model emotion evolution over time [13]. Here the missing data have been filled in using an exponential continuous decay function of the form $y(t)=e^{-\ln(2)t/T}$, where T stands for the half-decay period. In this model a half-decay period of T=2 would mean that a customer emotional level two months after the fault occurred is only half of what it was at the time of the fault. Whenever the events reoccur the new data "intensity" unit is added to the remainder from the decaying se-

quence of events after which the decaying process reinitialises as shown in Figure 7.

This specific data pre-processing treatment has been applied to all numerical data attributes that match the emotional decay concept. For all other attributes including categorical data standard missing data techniques have been applied including interpolation of attribute values between the events and adding a separate missing value for categorical data or whenever no data reference was available.

Complete Events Sequence Prediction

Temporal classification struggles from its underlying static form in which a single model can only give the answer whether the churn will occur or not in the next time slot. They instantly forget about the preceding history and make no use of the dynamics of data evolution in time, unless an explosion of features results in an attempt to cover all feature values in all preceding time slots. The most needed predictions about when the churn might happen and in what future circumstances is beyond the capabilities of temporal classification models.

In an answer to these challenges an original yet simple and efficient non-parametric model called k nearest sequence (kNS) is presented. This model uses all available sequences of customer data as input and generates a complete future data sequence up to the churn event as an output. An interesting part is that this model does not require learning prior to the prediction process. Instead it uses customer sequences as templates and automatically finds the k best matching data subsequences of customers who already churned and based on their remaining subsequences kNS predicts the most likely future data sequence up to the time-stamped churn event as shown schematically in the imaginary example in Figure 8. The model is further supported by the remaining

Figure 7. Visualisation of the exponential decay of customer events intensity with half-decay period of T = 4 weeks.

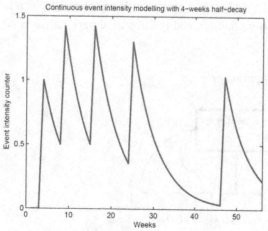

Figure 8. Visual demonstration of the k nearest sequence algorithm. First for all the customers it finds the sub-sequences that best match to the trajectory of a customer in question (right diagram). Then it compares them and selects k closest subsequences. The remainders of these sebsequences that is parts of sequences that start after the matched subsequences until the end of sequences are then aggregated to obtain the expected sequence prediction for the customer in question.

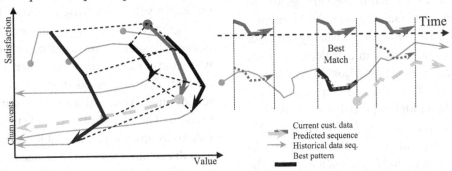

lifetime estimate which is recommended in case of a narrow data availability timeframe.

k nearest sequence Algorithm. Let $S(c, t, \tau)$ stand for a data sequence for a customer identified by c, starting at time period t and having the length τ that is:

$$S(c,t,\tau) = \{x_{c,t},...,x_{c,t+\tau}\} \quad \tau = 1,2,... \quad (9)$$

Where $x_{x,t}$ is a data vector of a customer c at time period t. Formally the objective of kNS is to predict the future sequences of customer data $S(c,t_{cur}+1, R)$, where R is the remaining customer lifetime and t_{cur} is the current time, given the existing customer data sequence to date $S(c,t_{cur}-\tau, \tau)$, where τ is the data availability timeframe, and the historical and live data of former and current customers $S(c_i,0,L_i)$, where L_i is a lifetime of the customer identified by c_i. In the first step kNS finds the k nearest neighbours in the sequential sense, that is the customers whose data sequences match the considered sequence the most. This task is split

into 2 subtasks. First all customer sequences are exhaustively scanned to find the best matching subsequences that is the subsequences $S(c_i,t_i-\tau, \tau)$ that have the closest corresponding points to the considered sequence pattern $S(c,t_{cur}-\tau, \tau)$ in the Euclidean distance sense, that is: (see Box 1).

Then all best subsequences $S(c_i,t_i-\tau, \tau)$ are sorted according to their distance from the sequence in question in order to determine first k best matching patterns. The remaining subsequences of these best matches that is $S(c_i,t_i,L_i-t)$, $i=1,...,k$, are referred to as k nearest remainders, and are used directly for predicting the future sequence in question $S(c,t_{cur},L)$. The prediction is done by a specific aggregation of the k nearest remainders which in general could be of different lengths. The aggregation method first re-scales all the nearest remainders subsequences along the time so that their lengths are equal and thereby terminate at the same time determined by the average length of these subsequences. This average length defines the predicted remaining lifetime of the customer in question that can be simply calculated by:

Box 1.

$$t_i = \arg\min_{t=\tau}^{L_i} \|S(c,t_{cur}-\tau,\tau) - S(c_i,t-\tau,\tau)\| = \arg\min_{t=\tau}^{L_i} \sqrt{\sum_{j=0}^{\tau} \|x_{c,t_{cur}-j} - x_{c_i,t-j}\|} \quad (10)$$

$$R = \frac{1}{k}\sum_{i=1}^{k} L_i - t_i \qquad (11)$$

Let $s_i=(L_i-t_i)/R$, where $i=1,...,k$ stand for the transition step for each of k nearest remainder subsequence, which define the timings of the predicted remaining subsequence of the customer in question. Each jth point $x_{c,t_{cur}+j}$ where $j=1,...,R$ of the predicted sequence can be calculated using the following formula: (see Box 2.) which uses interpolation of in-between sequence points spaces to obtain higher precision when dealing with sequence reminders of different length. This way the kNS algorithm would predict churn taking place in time period $L = t_{cur}+R$ along with the data path $S(c,t_{cur},R)$ leading to this event.

In a realistic scenario the data availability time frame is very narrow compared to the customer lifetime, which means that instead of having complete data sequences of customers from their acquisition up to churn there is only a tiny time slice of data available. In this time slice the turnover of customers and hence the number of churners that can be observed is on average $\tau N/L$. It is therefore expected that the vast majority of the data relate to the existing customers who did not churn yet. In this case it is very likely that among the k nearest neighbouring sequences most or even all would relate to existing customers for which the point of churn is unknown. In this case the kNS algorithm is aided by the unconditional remaining lifetime estimate covered in previous sections. The data sequence predictions are provided only up to the data availability limit and then overall customer average sequence is filled in up to the time determined by the remaining lifetime expectancy given by equation (6). The complete kNS algorithm is visualised in Figure 9.

Sequential data model. To support the presented kNS model the available data has to be organised in an appropriate structure to provide an easy and fast access to customer event sequences.

Box 2.

$$x_{c,t_{cur}+j} = \frac{1}{k}\sum_{i=1}^{k}\left[\left(\lceil js_i \rceil - js_i\right)x_{c_i,t_i+\lfloor js_i \rfloor} + \left(js_i - \lfloor js_i \rfloor\right)x_{c_i,t_i+\lceil js_i \rceil} \right] \qquad (12)$$

Figure 9. Flowchart of the sequential k nearest neighbour algorithm

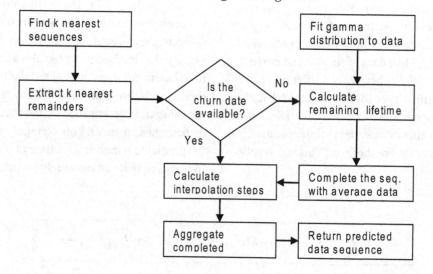

Mathematically customer event sequences can be interpreted as time-directed trajectories in a multidimensional data space. The kNS model assumes periodical sequences of customer data collected or calculated at regularly spread time intervals. The duration of each time interval will form the time resolution for customer behaviour analysis and should be selected in line with company routines, data availability and the required time-resolution of generated predictions. Once this is decided, the elementary data unit x_{cti} represents a value of the ith column (feature), collected at time interval t for the customer identified by c. For each customer c the complete life cycle would be defined by the time ordered sequence of customer data:

$$X_c = \begin{bmatrix} x_{c,1,1} & x_{c,1,2} & \cdots & x_{c,1,M} \\ x_{c,2,1} & \cdots & \cdots & \cdots \\ \cdots & \cdots & \cdots & \cdots \\ x_{c,T,1} & \cdots & \cdots & x_{c,T,M} \end{bmatrix} \quad (13)$$

where T is the total number of time intervals of a sequence and M stands for the number of features. For storage purposes it is more convenient to keep a single table of data rather than many tables corresponding to different customers. Hence both customer identifier and the time interval index have been moved into the customer data as the two first identifying columns, thereby reducing the storage data model from 3-dimensional to 2-dimensional:

$$X^{[C,T,M]} \Rightarrow X^{[C \times T, M]} \quad (14)$$

where C denotes the number of customers. This model representation is more suitable for all sorts of manipulations on the data from accessing, and retrieving up to complex transformations and can be easily handled by means of SQL. An additional benefit of such a storage model is that the data does not have to be sorted and hence the update is instant and effortless. The sorting would be done on the fly using the time interval column only when needed to obtain an ordered customer data sequence. For prediction, however, the first two identification columns will not be used.

Due to data availability issues, in our models the time resolution has been set to 1 month such that the annual customer data form an ordered sequence of 12 points and any prediction of churn or any other customer behaviour/event can be positioned in at least a one month time window. The imaginary example of the data table is shown in (15):

$$X_c = \begin{bmatrix} 5553234567 & Mar/2005 & x_{1,3} & \cdots & x_{1,M} \\ 5555987654 & Jan/2005 & x_{2,3} & \cdots & x_{2,M} \\ \cdots & \cdots & \cdots & \cdots \\ 5554321234 & Nov/2004 & x_{C \times T,3} & \cdots & x_{C \times T,M} \end{bmatrix}$$

EXPERIMENTS

The experiments have been organised in four slots demonstrating increasing informational content extracted from data. The reference point is a prior churn rate which cannot be disclosed due to confidentiality reasons. All the performance measures presented in these experiments will be shown in a form of gain measure defined in (2). In the first experiment the lifetime analysis on its own was applied. The random churn prediction

Table 4. Gain measures obtained for the 6 linear classifiers applied to the last month data

Classifier	Dec. Tree	LDA	Fisher	Quadratic	Nueral Net	SVM
Aggregated	9.34	9.23	8.79	9.12	9.89	10.56
Decayed	11.28	10.24	10.58	10.86	9.97	11.06

Figure 10. Screenshot of the best HMM generated (18 hidden states). The HMM was created using the iCan Churn Predictor (Intelligent Customer Analytics) software, which uses JaHMM library (http://www. run.montefiore.ulg.ac.be/~francois/software/jahmm/).

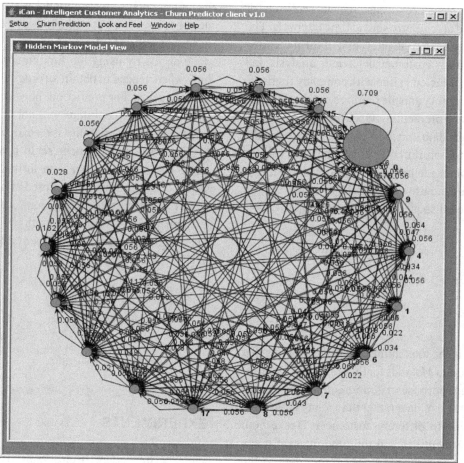

was applied to the lifetime period where churn probability density is the highest. Using analysis summarised in equations (4) to (8), the optimal period was identified to be the first year of the contract duration and accordingly random churn prediction was applied to customers who stayed less than a year at the time of measurement. The resulting performance resulted in a gain of $G_{lifetime}$ = 1.46 achieving 46% improvement in correct churn predictions compared to random selection of churners. In the next experiment the information content of the data has been further improved by the including evidence of customer events like faults, provisions, complaints and churn. This data represented in a binary string form, as described the section dedicated to HMM above have been collected and stored as 10-months sequences for which, for simplicity, churn was only allowed to occur in the last month. The data set with 20000 of such sequences have been split into halves with one part used to train the HMM model and the other part used for testing. Then the roles of the two sets of sequences were swapped and testing was repeated effectively realising a 2-fold cross-validation performance evaluation. Out of the summed confusion matrices the gain measure showed further improvement reaching the value of *GHMM* = 6.43 obtained for an HMM with 18 hidden states as shown in Figure 10.

In the next experiments all available attributes of the 20000 customers were used within temporal classification churn prediction framework for two case scenarios. In the first scenario, all the data were aggregated within the 10 monthly bins of the time domain. In the second scenario instead of aggregation the data were subjected to the decay function which on the one hand filled in the missing values and on the other hand transformed some of the features such that they better reflect the historical circumstances of current events. Following a quick manual optimisation a 2-weeks half-decay period has been selected as it produced the best classification results. All the data were then used to train 6 different classifiers and subsequently test them via 10-fold cross-validation method. In case of decay-filtered data only last month's data weights were used for classification. The results are shown in Table 4.

Clearly a visible improvement has been obtained for decay-filtered data particularly for a pruned decision tree. The high performance gains have been obtained under relatively low sensitivity scores, such that the most of churners still remain undetected due to their data overlapping with the non-churners data.

Finally the presented sequential nearest neighbour algorithm was tested using all 20000 10-months customer sequences with missing data approximated when necessary. Due to the fact that SNN returns precise churn timing it has been assumed that correct churn recognition occurs when the predicted timing deviates no more than 2 months from the actual churn date. The experiment was run for 5 different nearest neighbours parameters $k=1,\ldots,5$ and for 5 different lengths of the matching template that is for $\tau=1,\ldots,5$ months. For each setup the performances have been converted to the gain measures which are shown in Figure 11 along with the diagram depicting differences between these measures. The results show very clearly that above $k \geq 3$ the performance gain obtained for SNN becomes higher than for any other tested classifier, shown in Table 4. When $\tau=1$ the algorithm converges to a standard k nearest neighbour algorithm for which the performance is comparable to other classifiers from Table 4. The sequential strength starts to take effects from $\tau>1$ and the results shown in Figure 11 confirm that the highest performance gains are observed for τ ranging between 2 and 4 months with the highest gain of 13.29 obtained for 3-months sequences matched to 4 nearest sequences. These results outperform static non-sequential classification by around 20% and thereby confirm the contribution of the sequential modelling to the churn prediction performance. Due to lack of space the broad problem of complete sequence predictions, that kNS can produce solutions for, was ignored and left for further investigations within a wider framework of customer behaviour modelling.

Figure 11. Gain performance measures obtained for SNN predictors for 5 different nearest neighbour parameters k and template sequence lengths τ, shown in a tabular form and graphical diagram. The darker the colour the higher gain measure as consistent with numerical results.

$k \setminus \tau$	1	2	3	4	5
1	6.53	6.53	8.05	7.37	7.58
2	8.80	11.20	10.71	7.61	9.06
3	9.00	11.25	10.75	12.87	9.09
4	10.62	12.82	**13.29**	13.18	12.87
5	11.05	13.02	12.35	12.33	12.42

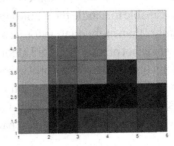

CONCLUSION

Summarising, this work uncovered a new perspective on customer churn prediction and highlighted the importance of the maximal extraction of all the available data along with their temporal evolution. It has also been demonstrated that the information of how the predictions are going to be exploited is very important and could significantly influence the design of the prediction model.

In case of churn prediction it has been shown that the improved performance can be obtained when event-driven data are appropriately transformed to a continuous representation using an exponential decay function. Deployment of such a system produced significant improvement of churn prediction in case of static classification, yet more importantly allowed for the application of sequential models to predict churn.

In the first sequential scenario a standard hidden markov model was applied to churn prediction yet effectively was used to model all the events in a sequential framework. It has been shown that although very limited information is provided to a discrete HMM like kNS it is capable of predicting not only churn but the complete sequences of customer events leading to churn. Although the performance of such predictions is not yet satisfactory it offers significant improvement over random predictions. Further research will be directed towards continuous data HMMs and their interesting properties related to hidden states which could form the basis for an automated segmentation of customer behavioural patterns.

The newly proposed, more flexible predictor called k nearest sequence was designed specifically to learn from customer data sequences and is capable to handle the whole customer life cycle rather than individual customer states captured in a snapshot of time. The kNS algorithm is prepared for a limited data availability time frame and can effectively handle missing data. Moreover kNS is capable of exploiting both former customers with completed lifetime data paths and existing

customer sequences by using a Gamma distribution to model expected customer lifetime. kNS significantly outperformed state-of-the-art temporal classifiers and like HMM offered the capacity to predict complete customer sequences of events up to a given point in time and with the precision subject to the quality of evidence.

Due to lack of space the broad problem of complete sequence predictions, that kNS can produce solutions for, was ignored and left for further investigations within a wider framework of customer behaviour modelling.

REFERENCES

Becker, C., Kopp, S., & Wachsmuth I. (2004). Simulating the emotion dynamics of a multimodal conversational agent. In E. Andr et al. (Eds.), *Affective Dialogue Systems Workshop 2004, (LNAI 3068)*, pp. 154-165. Berlin/Heidelberg: Springer-Verlag.

Blundon, W. (2003). Predicting success: Using analytics to drive more profitable customer interactions. *Data Mining Direct Newsletter*, December 05 Issue.

Duda, R.O., Hart, P.E., & Stork, D.G. (2001). *Pattern classification*. John Wiley & Sons.

Finkelstein, M.S. (2002). On the shape of the mean residual lifetime function. *Applied Stochastic Models in Business and Industry, 18*(2), 135 - 146.

Francois, J.-M. (2006). JaHMM – Hidden markov models – Java implementation, http://www.run.montefiore.ulg.ac.be/ francois/software/jahmm

Furnas, G. (2003). Framing the wireless market. *The Future of Wireless, WSA News:Bytes, 17*(11), 4-6.

Lemmen, S. (2000). Building loyalty and minimising churn in telecoms. Presentation of Telfort's loyalty programme: http://www.pimonline.nl/

activities/tshistory/ 2000/pim20001031Telfort-copyright.ppt

Lu, J. (2002). Predicting customer churn in the telecommunications industry - An application of survival analysis modeling using SAS°R. *SUGI 27 Proceedings.*

Morgan, M. (2003). Unearthing the customer: data mining is no longer the preserve of mathematical statisticians. Marketeers can also make a real, practical use of it (Revenue-Generating Networks). *Telecommunications International.*

Morik, K., & Kopcke, H. (2004). Analysing customer churn in insurance data - A case study. *Proceedings of the European Conf. on Principles and Practice of Knowledge Discovery in Databases*, Pisa, Italy, pp 325-336.

Mozer, M., Wolniewicz, R.H., Grimes, D.B., Johnson, E., & Kaushansky, H. (2000). Churn reduction in the wireless industry. *Advances in Neural Information Processing Systems, 12,* 935-941.

Sun, B., Wilcox, R.T., & Li, S. (2005). Cross-selling sequentially ordered products: an application to consumer banking services. Forthcoming, in *Journal of Marketing Research.*

Yan, L., Miller, D.J., Mozer, M.C., & Wolniewicz, R. (2001). Improving prediction of customer behaviour in non-stationary environments. *Proceedings of International Joint Conference on Neural Networks*, pp. 2258-2263.

Chapter XIV
Intelligent Classification and Ranking Analyses Using CaRBS:
Bank Rating Application

Malcolm J. Beynon
Cardiff University, UK

ABSTRACT

This chapter demonstrates intelligent data analysis, within the environment of uncertain reasoning, using the recently introduced CaRBS technique that has its mathematical rudiments in Dempster-Shafer theory. A series of classification and ranking analyses are undertaken on a bank rating application, looking at Moody's bank financial strength rating (BFSR). The results presented involve the association of each bank to being low or high BFSR, with emphasis is on the graphical exposition of the results including the use of a series of simplex plots. Throughout the analysis there is discussion on how the present of ignorance in the results should be handled, whether it should be excluded (belief) or included (plausibility) in the evidence supporting the classification or ranking of the banks.

INTRODUCTION

One direction of intelligent data analysis is within the environment that facilitates uncertain reasoning, which by its definition acknowledges the often imperfection of the considered data (Chen, 2001). Amongst the general methodologies associated with uncertain reasoning, is, Dempster-Shafer theory (DST), introduced in Dempster (1967) and Shafer (1976). Indeed, an alternative term for DST, regularly employed, is evidential reasoning, which

further epitomises the computational intelligence domain worked in (see for example, Smets, 1991; Srivastava & Liu, 2003).

The reasoning associated with DST has been contentiously argued as a generalisation of Bayesian probability calculus (Shafer & Srivastava, 1990), in contrast, Cobb and Shenoy (2003) suggest they have "roughly" the same expressive power. Specific techniques that are based around DST include, in multi-criteria decision making DS/AHP (Beynon, 2002) and belief decision trees (Vannoorenberghe, 2004). Pertinent to this chapter's analysis, inherent with DST based analyses is their close association with the ability to undertake such analysis in the presence of ignorance (Safranek, Gottschlich, & Kak, 1990).

A nascent DST based technique for object classification and ranking is CaRBS, which has the full title classification and ranking belief simplex, introduced in Beynon (2005a). It facilitates this analysis by constructing bodies of evidence (DST terminology), from characteristics describing the objects, which are then combined to offer the evidence used to classify or rank them. The CaRBS technique offers a visual representation of the contribution of characteristics to the classification and ranking of objects using simplex plots, including the concomitant levels of ambiguity and ignorance (Beynon, 2005b). While only recently introduced, it has been applied in the areas of; education (Jones & Beynon, 2007), finance (Beynon, 2005b) and medicine (Jones Beynon, Holt, & Roy, 2006).

In this chapter, the two directions of analysis offered by the CaRBS technique, namely classification and ranking, are exposited. In the case of object classification, the objects are known to be classed to a given hypothesis or its complement. It follows, a quantifying objective function is described which places emphasis on the minimising of ambiguity in the objects' classifications, but not the inherent ignorance associated with their individual classifications (Beynon, 2005b). In the case of the ranking of objects across the domain of the potential classifications, based on the objects' characteristic values describing them, this is between the extremes of a given hypothesis and its complement. How the inherent ignorance is included depends on whether more formulaic belief or plausibility measures are employed (Beynon & Kitchener, 2005).

A sample bank rating problem is analysed using the CaRBS technique, with classification and ranking analyses performed on the associated data set. The relative simplicity of the CaRBS technique and visual presentation of the findings allows the reader the opportunity to succinctly view a form of DST based data analysis. This analysis includes an elucidation of the notions of ambiguity and ignorance in object classification, and belief or plausibility based ranking of objects. Moreover, the analysis, using CaRBS, is encompassing of the presence of ignorance in its facilitation of intelligent data analysis.

It is intended for this chapter to offer the reader a benchmark outline in the ability to intelligently analyse data, through classification and/or ranking, in an environment based on uncertain reasoning.

BACKGROUND

The background to this chapter describes the general rudiments of the CaRBS technique, which is itself illustrative of the technical details surrounding Dempster-Shafer theory (DST). This is followed by separate descriptions of its utilisation within the data analysis problems of object classification and ranking, with further general measures also presented. Throughout the description of CaRBS it is considered to be working on a data set made up of a number of objects each described by a series of characteristic values.

The General CaRBS Technique

Drawing from DST (see Dempster, 1967; Shafer, 1976), the rudimentary aim of the CaRBS technique (Beynon, 2005a) is to construct a body of evidence (BOE), defined $m(\cdot)$, for each characteristic value describing an object, which includes levels of exact belief (mass values) in the support for the association of an object to a given hypothesis ($\{x\}$ - $m(\{x\})$), its complement ($\{\neg x\}$ - $m(\{\neg x\})$) and concomitant ignorance ($\{x, \neg x\}$ - $m(\{x, \neg x\})$). In the DST literature, the sets $\{x\}$, $\{\neg x\}$ and $\{x, \neg x\}$ are termed focal elements, in the case of $\{x, \neg x\}$, its association with the term ignorance is since its mass value is unable to be assigned specifically to either $\{x\}$ or $\{\neg x\}$ (see Srivastava & Liu, 2003).

Within the CaRBS technique, the notions of $\{x\}$ and $\{\neg x\}$ take on different connotations when considered with respect to classification and ranking oriented analyses. Moreover; with classification, they are a pair of exhaustive states, where the objects are known to be classed to either of them; with ranking, they are the limits of the domain that the association of the objects can exist on. To briefly describe the general stages of the CaRBS technique, Figure 1 reports its approach to the transformation of an object's characteristic value into a *characteristic* BOE.

In Figure 1, stage *a)* shows the transformation of a characteristic value $v_{j,i}$ (j^{th} object, i^{th} characteristic) into a confidence value $cf_i(v_{j,i})$, using a sigmoid function, defined with the control variables k_i and θ_i. Stage *b)* transforms a characteristic value's confidence value $cf_i(v_{j,i})$ into a characteristic BOE, defined $m_{j,i}(\cdot)$, made up of the three mass values, $m_{j,i}(\{x\})$, $m_{j,i}(\{\neg x\})$ and $m_{j,i}(\{x, \neg x\})$, from Safranek et al. (1990), these are defined by:

$$m_{j,i}(\{x\}) = \frac{B_i}{1 - A_i} cf_i(v_{j,i}) - \frac{A_i B_i}{1 - A_i}, \; m_{j,i}(\{\neg x\}) =$$

$$\frac{-B_i}{1 - A_i} cf_i(v_{j,i}) + B_i, \text{ and}$$

$$m_{j,i}(\{x, \neg x\}) = 1 - m_{j,i}(\{x\}) - m_{j,i}(\{\neg x\}),$$

where A_i and B_i are two further control variables utilized within the CaRBS technique. When either $m_{j,i}(\{x\})$ or $m_{j,i}(\{\neg x\})$ are negative they are set to zero (before the calculation of $m_{j,i}(\{x, \neg x\})$). Stage *c)* shows the mass values in a BOE $m_{j,i}(\cdot)$; $m_{j,i}(\{x\})$, $m_{j,i}(\{\neg x\})$ and $m_{j,i}(\{x, \neg x\})$, can be represented as a simplex coordinate (single point -$p_{j,i,v}$) in a simplex plot (equilateral triangle). That is, a point $p_{j,i,v}$ exists within an equilateral triangle such that the least distance from $p_{j,i,v}$ to each of the sides of the equilateral triangle are in the same proportion (ratio) to the values, $v_{j,i,1}$, $v_{j,i,2}$ and $v_{j,i,3}$. Each corner (vertex) of the equilateral triangle is labelled with one of the three focal elements in the BOE (in the case of a binary frame of discernment—as here).

Figure 1. Stages within the CaRBS technique with respect to a single characteristic value

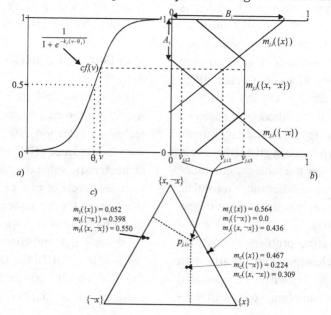

When a series of characteristics describe each object, a similar number of characteristic BOEs are constructed. Within DST, Dempster's rule of combination is used to combine the characteristic BOEs (assuring they are independent), the combination of two BOEs $m_{j,i}(\cdot)$ and $m_{j,k}(\cdot)$, defined $(m_{j,i} \oplus m_{j,k})(\cdot)$, results in a combined BOE whose mass values are given by: (see Box 1).

To illustrate the method of combination employed here, two example BOEs, $m_1(\cdot)$ and $m_2(\cdot)$ are considered, with mass values in each BOE given in the vector form $[m_j(\{x\}), m_j(\{\neg x\}), m_j(\{x, \neg x\})]$ as, $[0.564, 0.000, 0.436]$ and $[0.052, 0.398, 0.550]$, respectively. The combination of $m_1(\cdot)$ and $m_2(\cdot)$, to a further BOE $m_c(\cdot)$, is evaluated to be $[0.467, 0.224, 0.309]$, further illustrated in Figure 1c, where the simplex coordinates of the BOEs, $m_1(\cdot)$ and $m_2(\cdot)$, are shown along with that of the combined BOE $m_c(\cdot)$. Inspection of the simplex coordinate representation of the BOEs shows the effect of the combination of the BOEs, $m_1(\cdot)$ and $m_2(\cdot)$, which includes a decrease in the ignorance associated with the resultant BOE $m_c(\cdot)$. It is important to note that the combination process can be visually presented.

The Use of CaRBS for Object Classification

The utilisation of the CaRBS technique as a classification tool is dependent on the objects considered having known classifications to either a given hypothesis ($\{x\}$) or its complement ($\{\neg x\}$). The effectiveness of the CaRBS technique to op-timally classify objects is governed by the values assigned to the incumbent control variables (for each characteristic considered), k_i, θ_i, A_i and B_i, $i = 1, ..., n$. It follows, this assignment problem is able to be defined as a constrained optimisation issue. Since the control variables are continuous in nature, the recently introduced trigonometric differential evolution (TDE) method is utilised (Fan & Lampinen, 003; Storn & Price, 1997).

In summary, TDE is an evolutionary algorithm that iteratively generates improved solutions to a problem through the marginal changes in previous solutions with the differences in pairs of other previous solutions. When the classification of a number of objects to some hypothesis and its complement is known, the effectiveness of a configured CaRBS system can be measured by a defined objective function (OB), next described.

For objects in the equivalence classes E(x) and E($\neg x$), the optimum solution considered here is to maximise the difference values $(m_j(\{x\}) - m_j(\{\neg x\}))$ and $(m_j(\{\neg x\}) - m_j(\{x\}))$, respectively. That is, for those objects known to be classified to $\{x\}$ (E(x)) it would be desirable to have $m_j(\{x\})$ as larger than $m_j(\{\neg x\})$ as possible, similarly for those objects in E($\neg x$) it is desirable to have $m_j(\{\neg x\})$ as larger than $m_j(\{x\})$. The subsequent objective function, defined OB, where optimisation is minimisation with a general lower limit of zero, is given by (from Beynon, 2005b): (see Box 2).

In the limit, each of the difference values $(m_j(\{x\}) - m_j(\{\neg x\}))$ and $(m_j(\{\neg x\}) - m_j(\{x\}))$ can attain -1 and 1, then $0 \leq \text{OB} \leq 1$. It is noted,

Box 1.

$$(m_{j,i} \oplus m_{j,k})(\{x\}) = \frac{m_{j,i}(\{x\})m_{j,k}(\{x\}) + m_{j,k}(\{x\})m_{j,i}(\{x, \neg x\}) + m_{j,i}(\{x\})m_{j,k}(\{x, \neg x\})}{1 - (m_{j,i}(\{\neg x\})m_{j,k}(\{x\}) + m_{j,i}(\{x\})m_{j,k}(\{\neg x\}))},$$

$$(m_{j,i} \oplus m_{j,k})(\{\neg x\}) = \frac{m_{j,i}(\{\neg x\})m_{j,k}(\{\neg x\}) + m_{j,k}(\{x, \neg x\})m_{j,i}(\{\neg x\}) + m_{j,k}(\{\neg x\})m_{j,i}(\{x, \neg x\})}{1 - (m_{j,i}(\{\neg x\})m_{j,k}(\{x\}) + m_{j,i}(\{x\})m_{j,k}(\{\neg x\}))},$$

$$(m_{j,i} \oplus m_{j,k})(\{x, \neg x\}) = 1 - (m_{j,i} \oplus m_{j,k})(\{x\}) - (m_{j,i} \oplus m_{j,k})(\{\neg x\}).$$

Box 2.

$$\text{OB} = \frac{1}{4}\left(\frac{1}{|\,E(x)\,|}\sum_{o_j \in E(x)}(1 - m_j(\{x\}) + m_j(\{\neg x\})) + \frac{1}{|\,E(\neg x)\,|}\sum_{o_j \in E(\neg x)}(1 + m_j(\{x\}) - m_j(\{\neg x\}))\right).$$

maximising a difference value such as $(m_j(\{x\}) - m_j(\{\neg x\}))$ only indirectly affects the associated ignorance $(m_j(\{x, \neg x\}))$, rather than making it a direct issue.

The Use of CaRBS for Object Ranking

The utilisation of the CaRBS technique as a ranking tool, unlike the classification role that required a time consuming optimisation step, is to utilise the considered data in a one step approach. Importantly, it does not necessarily require explicit knowledge on their classification to $\{x\}$ or $\{\neg x\}$ (as in the classification role the CaRBS technique can adopt).

The basis for the described ranking approach was included in the original introduction of the CaRBS technique in Beynon (2005a). In this chapter, two sets of ranking results are later presented that utilise the original approach with different assumption levels. Here the rudiments of the ranking approach as outlined in Beynon (2005a) are presented, again it centres on the assignment of values to the control variables, k_i, θ_i, A_i, and B_i, for each characteristic, which configure a particular CaRBS system.

In summary, for a characteristic c_i, the control variable $k_i = \pm 1/\sigma_i$, where σ_i is the respective standard deviation of the characteristic values. The ± 1 term identifies the requirement to identify the known association, positive or negative sign, of the characteristic to the preference of an object (either through expert choice or an alternative method), and the use of σ_i takes into account the level of spread of the values over a single characteristic. The θ_i control variable (see Figure 1a) is the point in the ith characteristic's

domain where the evidence supporting either $\{x\}$ or $\{\neg x\}$ is equal $(m_{j,i}(\{x\}) = m_{j,i}(\{\neg x\}))$ in a characteristic BOE), subsequently $\theta_i = v_i$ (the mean value for that characteristic) is chosen which may at least minimise the possibility for over bias to either $\{x\}$ or $\{\neg x\}$ in the constructed evidence (in characteristic BOEs).

The process for the assignment of values to the control variables, A_i and B_i, requires a set of characteristic importance weights, $w_1, \ldots, w_K$, and *a priori* general knowledge on the inherent ignorance in the ranking problem considered, see Beynon (2005a). The prior knowledge on ignorance required relates specifically to the general limits on the domain of possible ignorance associated with the evidence from the considered characteristics, defined $[\Theta_L, \Theta_U]$. Based on these limits and the importance weights, values for the control variables, A_i and B_i, are found for each characteristic.

For a characteristic c_i, its associated specific domain of ignorance is defined by $[\Theta_{L,i}, \Theta_{U,i}]$. Each pair of boundary values, $\Theta_{L,i}$ and $\Theta_{U,i}$, are found using the associated weight w_i, and are based on a movement up from the Θ_L and down from the Θ_U general ignorance domain boundary values. Defining $I_i = (w_i - \underline{w})/(\overline{w} - \underline{w})$, as the index value of the weight w_i, where $\underline{w}$ and $\overline{w}$ are the lowest and highest weights in the set of weights, then $\Theta_{L,i} = \Theta_L + 0.5\,(1 - I_i)(\Theta_U - \Theta_L)$ and $\Theta_{U,i} = \Theta_U - 0.5 I_i(\Theta_U - \Theta_L)$, $i = 1, \ldots, K$ (see Beynon, 2005a). It follows, the respective A_i and B_i can be found from knowing that characteristic's ignorance interval $[\Theta_{L,i}, \Theta_{U,i}]$, and are given by:

$$A_i = \frac{\Theta_{L,i} - \Theta_{U,i}}{2\Theta_{L,i} - \Theta_{U,i} - 1} \text{ and } B_i = 1 - \Theta_{L,i}.$$

As mentioned earlier, this approach was outlined when the CaRBS technique was first introduced, in this chapter two variants of this are later utilised.

Further Associated Measures Included with CaRBS

Beyond the processes for the configuration of a CaRBS system (assigning values to the respective control variables), further measures are available to describe the objects (using the object BOEs), as well as the evidence associated with the objects (using the characteristic BOEs).

An indication of the evidential support offered by a characteristic is made with the evaluation of the respective *average characteristic* BOE. More formally, considering an equivalence class of objects, defined E(*o*), then an average characteristic BOE, for the characteristic c_i, defined $am_{i,o}(\cdot)$, is given by; (see Box 3) where o_j is an object. As a BOE, it can also be represented as a simplex coordinate in a simplex plot (see Figure 1c), describing the evidential support for that characteristic and the equivalence class of objects it is associated with.

Using CaRBS, the ability to rank alternatives may be with respect to {*x*} or {¬*x*} (the extremes of the domain of classification), but the inherent ignorance ({*x*, ¬*x*}) needs to be possibly taken into account also. From DST, the belief and plausibility confidence measures allow the opportunity for the required ranking subject to whether they take into account the inherent ignorance (belief)

or not (plausibility). In general, a *belief* measure is a function *Bel*: $2^{\Theta} \rightarrow [0, 1]$, defined by:

$$Bel(s_1) = \sum_{s_2 \subseteq s_1} m(s_2),$$

for $s_1 \subseteq \Theta$ (Θ is the frame of discernment - {*x*, ¬*x*} in this case). It represents the confidence that a proposition *x* lies in s_1 or any subset of s_1. A *plausibility* measure is a function *Pls*: $2^{\Theta} \rightarrow [0, 1]$, defined by:

$$Pls(s_1) = \sum_{s_1 \cap s_2 \neq \varnothing} m(s_2), \text{ for } s_1 \subseteq \Theta.$$

Clearly, $Pls(s_1)$ represents the extent to which we fail to disbelieve s_1.

CaRBS CLASSIFICATION AND RANKING ANALYSIS OF BANK DATA SET

The main thrust of this chapter briefly describes the bank ratings data set considered and then undertakes respective classification and ranking orientated CaRBS analyses of it. Throughout the section the emphasis is on the visual representation of the results.

Bank Data Set

Since the work of John Moody and his involvement with the Manual of Industrial and Miscellaneous Securities in 1900 and the Analyses of Railroad Investments in 1909, the issue of credit ratings has

Box 3.

$$am_{i,o}(\{x\}) = \sum_{o_j \in E(o)} \frac{m_{j,i}(\{x\})}{|E(o)|}, \, am_{i,o}(\{\neg x\}) = \sum_{o_j \in E(o)} \frac{m_{j,i}(\{\neg x\})}{|E(o)|} \text{ and}$$

$$am_{i,o}(\{x, \neg x\}) = \sum_{o_j \in E(o)} \frac{m_{j,i}(\{x, \neg x\})}{|E(o)|},$$

become increasingly influential (see for example, Levich, Majnoni, & Reinhart, 2002). This has meant the creation of a number of rating agencies, which include the two most well known, Moody's Investors Services (Moody's) and Standard & Poor's Corporation (S&P), as well as others such as Fitch Investors Service (Fitch).

One overriding facet associated with the rating agencies, such as Moody's, S&P's and Fitch, is that they have stated that statistical models cannot be used to replicate their ratings (Singleton & Surkan, 1991). Hence here, it will be of interest to see how well this novel technique, CaRBS, performs in classifying and ranking banks to certain known ratings. The specific rating considered here is the bank financial strength rating (BFSR). Introduced in 1995 by Moody's Investors Services, it represents Moody's opinion of a bank's intrinsic safety and soundness - a measure of the likelihood that a bank will require assistance from third parties (Moody's, 2006)

The actual BFSR classification of the individual banks, can be rated from A to E - 13 ordinal values (+ and – modifiers below and above A to E,

Moody's (2006)). A small, demonstrative sample of the full data is considered here, pertinently it is as much as possible made up of a balance of the 13 classifiers. Moreover, 58 banks are considered, the breakdown of these banks with respect to the 13 classifiers is given in Table 1.

The suggested balance of the banks considered, with respect to their known BFSR classification, is clearly shown in Table 1, with the majority of BFSR classifiers having five banks representing them (the more extreme classifiers have less than five due to the availability of banks with these classifications). These 58 banks are here described by six characteristics (financial ratios), known to be potentially influential in deciding bank ratings (see Poon, Firth, & Fung, 1999), which are themselves described in Table 2.

In Table 2, the descriptions of the six characteristics are explicitly described, alongside their mean and standard deviation values (utilised later).

With respect to the CaRBS analyses later presented, an *a priori* binary partitioning of the 58 considered banks in next briefly undertaken.

Table 1. Breakdown of numbers of considered banks in each classifier

Classifier	A	A–	B+	B	B–	C+	C	C–	D+	D	D–	E+	E
Number	1	5	5	5	5	5	5	5	5	5	5	5	2

Table 2. Description of six characteristics of banks

Index	Description	Mean	Standard Deviation σ_i	Association r_i
c_1	Equity / Total Assets (%)	8.142	4.222	−0.053
c_2	Return on Average Assets (ROAA) (%)	1.349	1.103	−0.031
c_3	Return on Average Equity (ROAE) (%)	16.524	7.769	0.013
c_4	Liquid Assets / Cust & ST Funding (%)	15.360	14.739	−0.231
c_5	Impaired Loans / Gross Loans (%)	2.837	3.575	−0.533
c_6	Total Capital Ratio (%)	13.894	5.086	−0.262

This partitioning of the banks was based on them being categorized as having, low BFSR (L) - below or equal to the C classifier or high BFSR (H) - equal to or above the C+ classifier, from Table 1, this confers a partitioning of 32 and 26 banks, respectively. The Pearson's correlation coefficient in Table 2 offers an indication of the strengths of association of each bank characteristic to their known BFSR binary group classification (adopting a numerical scale of 0 and 1 for those banks in the low BFSR and high BFSR categories, respectively).

Binary Classification of Bank Data Set using CaRBS

The first analysis presented here utilises the CaRBS technique in its role as a classification technique. Moreover, here the binary classification of the 58 considered banks is outlined. With respect to the CaRBS technique, the high BFSR is considered the given hypothesis ($x \equiv H \equiv 1$, within the configuration process) and the low BFSR is not the hypothesis ($\neg x \equiv L \equiv 0$). It is acknowledged that the original BFSR classifiers are more ordinal (A to E), rather than this binary simplification, so the neighbour classifiers, such as C and C+, while close to each other, are differently classified here, suggesting total classification certainty to low or high BFSR may not be attained.

Concentrating on the characteristics describing the banks, these are standardised, so they have zero mean and unit standard deviation (each characteristic value has that characteristic's mean

deducted from it and then divided by its standard deviation value, using the information contained in Table 2). This standardisation of the characteristic values allows a standard set of domains to be fixed for the control variables associated with each characteristic, as; $-3 \leq k_i \leq 3$, $-2 \leq \theta_i \leq 2$ and $0 \leq A_i < 1$. For the B_i control variable, from previous studies it is set at a constant, here equal to 0.600, consigning a minimum level of ignorance of 0.400 ($m_{j,i}(\{x, \neg x\})$) present in each characteristic BOE $m_{j,i}(\cdot)$ constructed (see Beynon, 2005b, for associated discussion).

The trigonometric differential evolution (TDE) approach for constrained optimisation was then employed to minimise the associated objective function OB defined in the previous section. Following Storn and Price (1997) and Fan and Lampinen (2003), the TDE based parameters to enable its running were assigned as; amplification control $F = 0.99$, crossover constant $CR = 0.85$, trigonometric mutation probability $M_t = 0.05$ and number of parameter vectors $NP = 10 \times$ number of control variables $= 180$. It follows, the TDE was allowed to run, and the objective function found to converge to the value OB $= 0.2940$, the resultant control variables from the TDE run are reported in Table 3.

In Table 3, the sets of k_i, θ_i, A_i and B_i values are shown for each characteristic considered, noticeably the k_i values are all at a limit of its domain, indeed are all -3.000. Of the other values, θ_i and A_i show little consistency, but A_i has a number of values near the upper bound of 1.000, which from Figure 1c, may indicate limited

Table 3. Control variable values associated with bank characteristics, after a binary classification of banks' based configuration of a CaRBS system

Characteristic	c_1	c_2	c_3	c_4	c_5	c_6
k_i	−3.000	−3.000	−3.000	−3.000	−3.000	−3.000
θ_i	−0.263	−0.171	−0.335	0.330	−0.223	−1.208
A_i	0.925	0.944	0.981	0.747	0.231	0.948
B_i	0.600	0.600	0.600	0.600	0.600	0.600

evidential contribution by these characteristics, B_i has the consistent value 0.600, as previously discussed (shown for completeness and future comparison).

The utilisation of these control variables is in the direct construction of characteristic BOEs ($m_{j,i}(\cdot)$), describing the evidence from the characteristics to the classification of the individual banks (see Figure 1). Due to the novelty of the associated calculation process, the evaluation of one characteristic BOE is next briefly shown. Considering a single bank o_1 and c_4 characteristic, its original value was 5.65, when standardised it is $v = -0.534$, then:

$$cf_4(-0.534) = \frac{1}{1 + e^{3.000(-0.534-0.330)}} = \frac{1}{1 + 0.075} = 0.930,$$

using the control variables in Table 3. This confidence value is used in the expressions making up the mass values in the characteristic BOE $m_{1,4}(\cdot)$, namely; $m_{1,4}(\{H\})$, $m_{1,4}(\{L\})$ and $m_{1,4}(\{L, H\})$, found to be: (See Box 4).

For the bank o_1, this characteristic BOE is representative of the characteristic BOEs $m_{1,i}(\cdot)$, that describe the evidence associating the bank with its classification to low BFSR (L) or high BFSR (H).

The characteristic BOEs for any book are then combined, using Dempster's combination rule, to produce the respective *bank* BOEs ($m_j(\cdot)$) that offer the final classification of the individual bank (examples of their construction are given in Beynon, 2005a, 2005b). The final bank BOEs for the 58

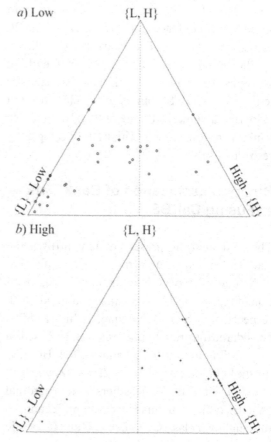

Figure 2. Simplex plot based classification of objects, after a binary classification of banks' based configuration of a CaRBS system

considered banks, found through the configured CaRBS system using the control variables in Table 3, are presented visually in Figure 2.

The results reported in Figure 2 centre around the domain of the simplex plot, with its utilisation

Box 4.

$$m_{1,4}(\{H\}) = \frac{0.6}{1 - 0.747}0.930 - \frac{0.747 \times 0.6}{1 - 0.747} = 2.203 - 1.768 = 0.435,$$

$$m_{1,4}(\{L\}) = \frac{-0.6}{1 - 0.747}0.930 + 0.6 = -2.203 + 0.6 = -1.604 < 0 \text{ so} = 0.000,$$

$$m_{1,4}(\{L, H\}) = 1 - 0.435 - 0.000 = 0.565.$$

a direct consequence of a BOE, here a bank BOE $m_j(\cdot)$, being made up of a triplet of mass values, $m_j(\{L\})$, $m_j(\{H\})$ and $m_j(\{L, H\})$, which sum to one. This is the standard domain that the CaRBS technique works with, where each vertex is labelled with one of the focal elements in the previously described mass values, to $\{L\}$, $\{H\}$ or $\{L, H\}$. In Figures 2a and 2b, the simplex coordinates representing the bank BOEs are shown for the banks known to be classified as having low BFSR (circles) and high BFSR (crosses), respectively.

The positions of the bank BOEs appear over much of the simplex plot domains, noticeably at different heights, which is an indication of the remit within the objective function, used in the CaRBS configuration, not to attempt to minimise the concomitant ignorance in each bank BOE (the overall evidence for a bank's classification). Instead, only the associated ambiguity has been attempted to be minimised in the classification of the banks, in relation to the simplex plot domain this is an attempt to minimise the presence of simplex coordinates at its centre In other words, away from the vertical dashed lines that partition either side of where there is majority evidence towards one class over the other (dictated by the base vertex in that half of the domain).

In a simplex plot, the positions of the bank BOEs on both sides of the vertical dashed line indicate correct and incorrect classification of certain banks. In terms of classification accuracy, there were, 24 out of 32 (75.0%) low and 24 out of 26 (92.3%) high BFSR known banks correctly classified (on the respective correct side of the vertical dashed lines in Figures 2a and 2b). This gives, in total, 48 out of 58 (82.8%) banks were correctly classified.

The simplex plot representation of results can be used to investigate the individual classification of a bank, through the presentation of the evidence from individual characteristics (characteristic BOEs) and final evidence (bank BOE) in the same simplex plot. Here this is not considered, but

Figure 3. Simplex coordinates of $am_{i,L}(\cdot)$ '?L' and $am_{i,H}(\cdot)$ '?H' average characteristic BOEs, after a binary classification of banks' based configuration of a CaRBS system

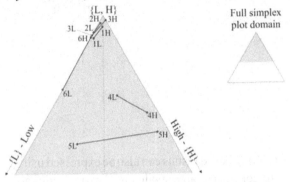

the overall influence of the characteristics in the classification of the banks is next shown, using the *average characteristic* BOEs, defined in the background section, see Figure 3.

In Figure 3, a shaded sub-domain of the simplex plot is shown (compare with inset full simplex plot domain), where each characteristic is described by two points, representing the average characteristic BOEs, $am_{i,L}(\cdot)$ and $am_{i,H}(\cdot)$, labelled with '?L' and '?H', respectively. The average characteristic BOEs are discerning the influence of characteristics over the low and high BFSR banks.

For a characteristic, increased influence associated with it is shown by its position towards the base of the presented sub-domain, and its discernibility power, between L and H, is also shown by the horizontal distance between the two points (further elucidated by the joining line). For the characteristics included in Figure 3, the c_5 especially, and also c_4, are shown to have the most influence, followed by c_6, with the other three characteristics, c_1, c_2 and c_3, having all their associated average characteristic BOEs towards the vertex $\{L, H\}$, indicating little influence on their behalf.

Beyond the binary classification of the banks to the general groups of low BFSR and high BFSR,

Figure 4. Ranking of 58 banks based on their Bel$_j$({H}) values, after a binary classification of banks' based configuration of a CaRBS system

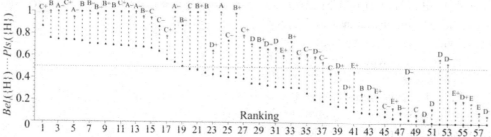

ranking based results can also be expressed using the control variables evaluated. Two measures are available to rank the banks, namely the $Bel_j(\cdot)$ and $Pls_j(\cdot)$ values described in the previous section, on top of this is whether the ranking is to either low or high BFSR that is considered. Here, only the ranking of the banks to the high (H) class is considered, starting with the rank order of the banks based on their $Bel_j(\{H\})$ values, see Figure 4.

In Figure 4, the representation of each bank includes two points, the bottom one is the respective $Bel_j(\{H\})$ value, used here to rank the banks, and the top one that is the respective $Pls_j(\{H\})$ value (since $Bel_j(\{H\}) \leq Pls_j(\{H\})$). As can be seen in the previous section, the difference between the respective $Bel_j(\{H\})$ and $Pls_j(\{H\})$ values is the level of concomitant ignorance associated with that bank's classification (the $m_j(\{L, H\})$ mass

value of a bank BOE), its size further signified by the dashed line joining the two points.

For each bank, their original BFSR class is given, ranging from A down to E BFSR. Since the banks are ranked, left to right, from highest $Bel_j(\{H\})$ down to lowest, the appropriate ranking of the banks would be from the A BFSR banks down to those which are E BFSR. Inspection of the rank order of the BFSR classes shows an ordered trend of A to C+ BFSR group then C to E group, with out-of-place banks BFSR present across the two groups. However, there is little discernment of the BFSR classes within these two groups. It is clear the level of concomitant ignorance varies between the classification of banks, through looking at the differences in the $Bel_j(\{H\})$ and $Pls_j(\{H\})$ values.

A further ranking is given for the banks based on their respective $Pls_j(\{H\})$ values, which is

Figure 5. Ranking of 58 banks based on Pls$_j$({H}), after a binary classification of banks' based configuration of a CaRBS system

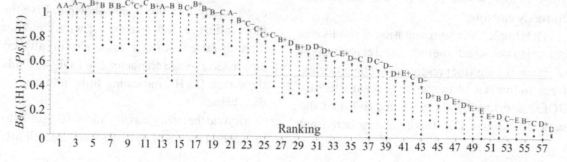

inclusive of the concomitant ignorance in each banks' final classification evidence displayed in their respective bank BOEs $m_j(\cdot)$, see Figure 5.

The results in Figure 5 show the ranking of the banks based on their $Pls_j(\{H\})$ values, dictated by the top points in this case (compared to the bottom points used in Figure 4), with the bottom points again representing the respective $Bel_j(\{H\})$ values. The rank order of the banks, with respect to their original BFSR classes, shows a trend of discernment of the two BFSR groups, A to C+ and C to E. However, there is noticeable discernment within the groups, for example the top eight ranked banks have BFSR classes in a correct order A to B.

The differences in the ranking results exhibited in Figures 4 and 5, the first ranking results presented, asks the question of which results should be used in future decision making. The choice here is considered through the type of decision making desired, whether the concomitant ignorance is ignored (belief - Figure 4) or it is taken into account (plausibility - Figure 5). Indeed, the dashed lines presented in Figures 4 and 5, between belief and plausibility values, could be used to evaluate a proportional distance (e.g., midpoint) between the two values to acquire a single value for ranking purposes.

First Ranking Analysis of Bank Data Set

This section considers a ranking based analysis of the banks, that takes a relatively naïve use of

the characteristics used to describe the banks. It follows, in part, the ranking-based approach using CaRBS outlined in the previous section.

Using the standardised data (where standard deviation $\sigma_i = 1$ for all characteristics c_i), the k_i values are all set to $3.000 \times \text{sgn}(r_i)$, where $\text{sgn}(r_i)$ is the sign of the correlation coefficient value associated with that characteristic (referring to Table 2). For the θ_i values, they are all set to 0.000 (the means of the standardised characteristic values). Next considered are the evaluation of the A_i and B_i control variables, to achieve this, the characteristics are all considered of equal importance, with the required interval of ignorance as $[\Theta_{L,i}, \Theta_{U,i}] = [0.4, 0.9]$ associated with each characteristic (in line with the general range shown in the classification analysis, see Figure 3). Using this interval for a characteristic, it follows, each $B_i = 1 - \Theta_{L,i} = 1 - 0.4 = 0.6$ (the same value used in the classification analysis), and

$$A_i = \frac{\Theta_{L,i} - \Theta_{U,i}}{2\Theta_{L,i} - \Theta_{U,i} - 1} = \frac{0.4 - 0.9}{2 \times 0.4 - 0.9 - 1} = 0.455.$$

These control variables are briefly presented in Table 4.

The values in Table 4 clearly illustrate the naivety of the approach taken here, with almost the same set of control variables used for each characteristic, the exception being for c_3, where $k_3 = -3.000$ unlike the others (all 3.000). Based on these control variables, the necessary characteristic BOEs and subsequent bank BOEs can be found for all banks. Following the previous analysis, results pertaining to the ability to clas-

Table 4. Control variable values associated with bank characteristics, after a naïve ranking based configuration of a CaRBS system

Characteristic	c_1	c_2	c_3	c_4	c_5	c_6
k_i	−3.000	−3.000	3.000	−3.000	−3.000	−3.000
θ_i	0.000	0.000	0.000	0.000	0.000	0.000
A_i	0.455	0.455	0.455	0.455	0.455	0.455
B_i	0.600	0.600	0.600	0.600	0.600	0.600

Figure 6. Simplex plot based classification of objects, after a naïve ranking based configuration of a CaRBS system

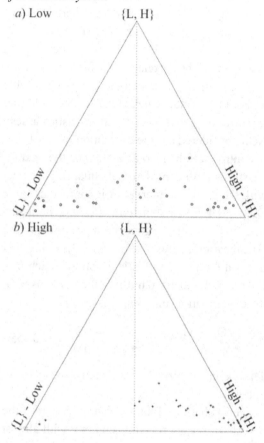

a) Low

b) High

sify the banks to the low and high BFSR groups are considered, see Figure 6.

In Figure 6, the final bank BOEs of the 58 banks are represented as simplex coordinates in the simplex plots, with their positions across much of the presented domain. This includes at different heights, but not to the extent as in the previous analysis (compare with Figure 2). To offer some quantification to the comparison of this classification with that given previously, using this sequence of control variables, the associated objective function value is OB = 0.365, higher than the 0.2940 value found previously. This indicates, in classification terms, the results here are understandably worse than when an optimally

configured CaRBS system based classification was specifically attempted.

In terms of classification accuracy, there were 15 out of 32 (46.9%) low and 24 out of 26 (92.3%) high BFSR banks correctly classified (on the correct side of the vertical dashed lines). This gives in total, 39 out of 58 (67.2%) banks were correctly classified, and less than that found in the classification based analysis. The next consideration is on the influence of the characteristics, see Figure 7.

In Figure 7, the positions of the average characteristic BOEs are all grouped together (compare with their further dispersion shown in Figure 3), a feature of the equal importance weight given to the characteristics (in particular the same values assigned to the A_i and B_i control variables across the different characteristics). Beyond this tight grouping, there is some difference in the horizontal positions of the respective "?L" and "?H" points of certain characteristics, most noticeably with c_5 and c_6 (in line with the findings in Figure 3). In conclusion, there is little variation in the influences offered by the individual characteristics, pertinent to the notion of "naïve" overshadowing this analysis.

Figure 7. Simplex coordinates of $am_{i,L}(\cdot)$ "?L" and $am_{i,H}(\cdot)$ "?H" average characteristic BOEs, after a naïve ranking based configuration of a CaRBS system

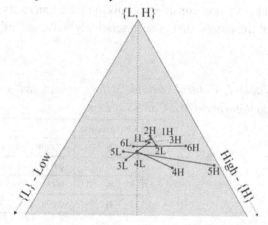

Figure 8. Ranking of 58 banks based on $Bel_j(\{H\})$, after a naïve ranking based configuration of a CaRBS system

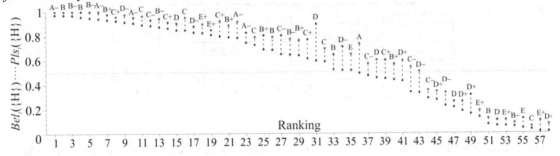

Figure 9. Ranking of 58 banks based on $Pls_j(\{H\})$, after a naïve ranking based configuration of a CaRBS system

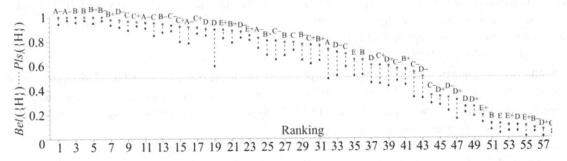

Attention now turns to ranking of the banks, including referral to their original BFSR, see Figures 8 and 9.

A noticeable result in Figures 8 and 9, when compared with the similar findings shown in Figures 4 and 5, is the generally less level of ignorance associated with each bank's ranking shown here (referring to the lengths of the dashed lines), representing the difference between the $Bel_j(\{H\})$ and $Pls_j(\{H\})$ values. In particular, in Figure 8, at the limits of the ranking there is less associated ignorance with a bank's BFSR, than towards the middle of the ranking. Inspection of the original BFSR given shows a general trend in decreasing from A to E BFSR.

Second Ranking Analysis of Bank Data Set

This section considers another ranking based analysis of the banks, this time taking into account more information accrued from the classification analysis first undertaken than what was used in the previous ranking based analysis.

As before, the k_i control variables were again fixed at $3.000 \times sgn(r_i)$ (the same as in Table 4). The θ_i variable in this case, take into account the differences in the low and high BFSR grouped banks considered in the first CaRBS analysis, Moreover, the θ_i variable is the difference between the mean values of the equivalence classes of banks associated with the low and high BFSR groups.

Table 5. Control variable values associated with bank characteristics, after an informative ranking based configuration of a CaRBS system

Characteristic	c_1	c_2	c_3	c_4	c_5	c_6
k_i	−3.000	−3.000	3.000	−3.000	−3.000	−3.000
θ_i	−0.0055	−0.0033	0.0013	−0.0240	−0.0555	−0.0273
A_i	0.385	0.417	0.402	0.338	0.294	0.365
B_i	0.399	0.372	0.372	0.491	0.600	0.436

The calculation of the A_i and B_i control variables starts with consideration on the importance of the characteristics. Here, an incorporation of a specific expression for the evaluation of weights (w_is) describing characteristic importance is utilised, based on a rank order of their importance. Moreover, the rank order centroid (ROC) weights are employed, given by $ROC_i = (1/K) \sum_{k=i}^{K} (1/k)$, K-number of characteristics (see Solymosi & Dombi (1986) and Barron and Barrett (1996)). One reason for the employment of the ROC weights is that they are considered to resemble more, weights associated with an *a priori* known ranking, rather than weights directly elucidated from a decision maker.

For the case of six characteristics, a rank order of importance was based on their perceived influence shown in Figure 3, a consequence of the classification based analysis. The resultant set of ROC weights are; 0.408 (c_5), 0.242 (c_4), 0.158 (c_6), 0.103 (c_1), 0.061 (c_3) and 0.028 (c_2), with the characteristics' the weights are assigned to shown in brackets. As just mentioned, the assignment of the weights was made with inspection of the influences found in the first classification based analysis using CaRBS, see Figure 3, hence largest weight was assigned to the c_5 characteristic, etc. These weights can be used to find the respective A_i and B_i control variables, along with the general ignorance interval of $[\Theta_L, \Theta_U] = [0.4, 0.9]$ again adopted, see Table 5.

The values presented in Table 5 are more varied than the respective variable values reported in Tables 3 and 4. For convenience, the θ_i values are given to four decimal places to discern the differences of these values amongst the characteristics. As in the previous analyses presented, the first results shown are the subsequent classifications of the individual banks (their bank BOEs), using these control variables, see Figure 10.

Figure 10. Simplex plot based classification of objects, after an informative ranking based configuration of a CaRBS system

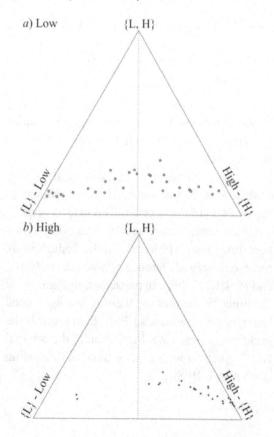

The simplex coordinates representing the bank BOEs in the simplex plots in Figure 10, are shown to extend across the lower part of the simplex plot, but not as near to the base as in the previous analyses. The associated objective function value is OB = 0.356, showing, in classification terms it to be an improvement on the naïve ranking results, but still worse than the classification based results. These findings are in line with what was expected.

In terms of classification accuracy, there were 17 out of 32 (53.1%) low and 24 out of 26 (92.3%) high BFSR banks correctly classified (on the correct side of the vertical dashed lines). This gives in total, 41 out of 58 (70.7%) banks were correctly classified. This accuracy value is in between those found from the previous two analyses. Moreover, it is better than the value associated with the naïve ranking analysis, but worse than the classification specific analysis previously described. To again gauge the influence of the characteristics, this time from an informative ranking based analysis, the average characteristic BOEs are considered, see Figure 11.

In Figure 11, a level of dispersion of the levels of influence exists between the characteristics, in line with the importance weights assigned to each of them (which themselves came from the identified influences of the characteristics in the classification based analysis). As such, the whole influence domain graph shown is a compromise

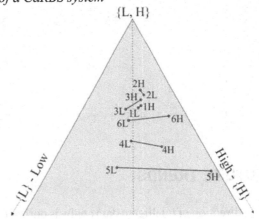

Figure 11. Simplex coordinates of am$_{i,L}$(·) "?L" and am$_{i,H}$(·) "?H" average characteristic BOEs, after an informative ranking based configuration of a CaRBS system

between the two previous graphs of this type (see Figures 3 and 7). The final results presented consider the ranking of the banks, with respect to their association with being H BFSR, based on $Bel_j(\{H\})$ and $Pls_j(\{H\})$, see Figures 12 and 13.

In the rankings presented in Figures 12 and 13, there is a relatively consistent level of ignorance associated with each bank's rank position. In particular, this consistency is prevalent in Figure 12, using $Bel_j(\{H\})$, that doesn't take into account the concomitant ignorance in a bank BOE for a bank.

Figure 12. Ranking of 58 banks based on Bel$_j$({H}), after an informative ranking based configuration of a CaRBS system

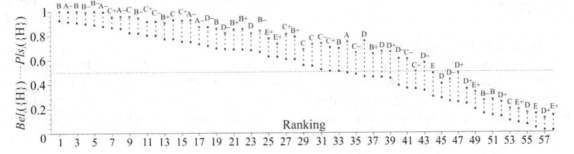

Figure 13. Ranking of 58 banks based on $Pls_j(\{H\})$, after an informative ranking based configuration of a CaRBS system

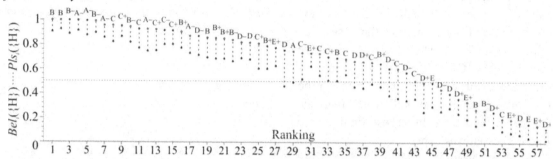

FUTURE TRENDS

The direction of intelligent data analysis outlined in this chapter has, in particular, been through the prevalence of ignorance in such analysis. One issue is that through the term ignorance used here, it could be argued that it is only a label to a mathematical expression. The relative newness of the notion of uncertain reasoning, including in such methodologies as Dempster-Shafer theory, suggests this continued representation is necessary to allow it to become an accustomed part of the analysis literature.

The ranking results presented highlight the issue of how the concomitant ignorance is used in the ranking of objects. That is, here, the two measures of belief and plausibility employed do and do not take into account the level of ignorance present, respectively. A future technical issue is how the interval created between the belief and plausibility values should be fully used.

CONCLUSION

The presented chapter considers two streams of data analysis, namely the classification and ranking of objects. Further, the elucidation of the concomitant analyses through the novel CaRBS technique brings the issue of uncertain reasoning to the forefront of this discussion, in the form of the prevalence of ignorance in the evidence from the characteristics describing the objects.

From the results presented, one identified conclusion, ironically, is that with intelligent data analysis it may be appropriate to encompass the prevalence of ignorance throughout its operation. That is, allowing for ignorance in such analysis can facilitate more pertinent analysis than if there is an incumbency to ascertain as certain as results as possible, as in more traditional techniques. In conclusion, the strengthening of this potential allowance for ignorance will come from the continued application of the technique CaRBS and techniques like it.

REFERENCES

Barron, F. H., & Barrett, B. E. (1996). Decision quality using ranked attribute weights. *Management Science*, *42*(11), 1515-1523.

Beynon, M. (2002). DS/AHP method: A mathematical analysis, including an understanding of uncertainty. *European Journal of Operational Research*, *140*(1), 149-165.

Beynon, M. J. (2005a). A novel technique of object ranking and classification under ignorance: An application to the corporate failure risk problem. *European Journal of Operational Research*, *167*(2), 493-517.

Beynon, M. J. (2005b). A novel approach to the credit rating problem: Object classification under ignorance. *International Journal of Intelligent Systems in Accounting, Finance and Management, 13*, 113-130.

Beynon, M. J., & Kitchener, M. (2005). Ranking the "balance" of state long-term care systems: A comparative exposition of the SMARTER and CaRBS techniques. *Health Care Management Science, 8*, 157-166.

Chen, Z. (2001). *Data mining and uncertain reasoning: An integrated approach.* New York: John Wiley.

Cobb, B. R., & Shenoy, P. P. (2003). A comparison of Bayesian and belief function reasoning. *Information Systems Frontiers, 5*(4), 345-358.

Dempster, A. P. (1967). Upper and lower probabilities induced by a multiple valued mapping. *Ann. Math. Statistics, 38*, 325-339.

Fan, H.-Y., & Lampinen, J. (2003). A trigonometric mutation operation to differential evolution. *Journal of Global Optimization, 27*, 105-129.

Jones, A. L., Beynon, M. J., Holt C. A., & Roy, S. (2006). A novel approach to the exposition of the temporal development of post-op osteoarthritic knee subjects. *Journal of Biomechanics, 39*(13), 2512-2520.

Jones, P., & Beynon, M. J. (2007). Temporal support in the identification of e-learning efficacy: An example of object classification in the presence of ignorance. *Expert Systems, 24*(1), 1-16.

Levich R. M., Majnoni, G., & Reinhart C. (2002). *Ratings, rating agencies and the global financial system.* Boston: Kluwer Academic Publishers.

Moody's (2006). Rating Definitions - Bank Financial Strength Ratings. Retrieved on June 26, 2006, from http://www.moodys.com.

Poon W. P. H., Firth, M., & Fung, M. (1999). A multivariate analysis of the determinants of Moody's bank financial strength ratings. *Journal of International Financial Markets Institutions and Money, 9*, 267-283.

Safranek, R. J., Gottschlich, S., & Kak, A. C. (1990). Evidence accumulation using binary frames of discernment for verification vision. *IEEE Transactions on Robotics and Automation, 6*, 405-417.

Shafer, G. A. (1976). *Mathematical theory of evidence.* Princeton: Princeton University Press.

Shafer G., & Srivastava, R. (1990). The Bayesian and belief-function formalisms: A general perspective for auditing. In *Auditing: A Journal of Practice and Theory.* Reprinted in J. Pearl & G. Shafer (Eds.) *Readings in uncertain reasoning,* pp. 482-521. San Mateo, CA: Morgan Kaufmann.

Singleton, J. C., & Surkan, J. S. (1991). Modelling the judgement of bond rating agencies: Artificial intelligence applied to finance. *Journal of the Midwest Finance Association, 20*, 72-80.

Smets, P. (1991). Varieties of ignorance and the need for well-founded theories. *Information Sciences, 57-58*, 135-144.

Solymosi, T., & Dombi, J. (1986). A method for determining weights of criteria: The centralized weights. *European Journal of Operational Research, 26*, 35-41.

Srivastava, R. P., & Liu, L. (2003). Applications of belief functions in business decisions: A review. *Information Systems Frontiers, 5*(4), 359-378.

Storn, R., & Price, K. (1997). Differential evolution - A simple and efficient heuristic for global optimization over continuous spaces. *Journal of Global Optimisation, 11*(4), 41-359.

Vannoorenberghe, P. (2004). On aggregating belief decision trees. *Information Fusion, 5*, 179-188.

Chapter XV
Analysis of Individual Risk Attitude for Risk Management Based on Cumulative Prospect Theory

Fei-Chen Hsu
National Tsing Hua University, Taiwan, ROC

Hsiao-Fan Wang
National Tsing Hua University, Taiwan, ROC

ABSTRACT

In this chapter, we used Cumulative Prospect Theory to propose an individual risk management process (IRM) including a risk analysis stage and a risk response stage. According to an individual's preferential structure, an individual's risk level for the confronted risk can be identified from risk analysis. And based on a response evaluation model, the appropriate response strategy is assessed at the risk response stage. The applicability of the proposed model is evaluated by an A-C court case. The results have shown that the proposed method is able to provide more useful and pertinent information than the traditional method of decision tree by using the expected monetary value (EMV).

INTRODUCTION

Risk management has been widely applied in various fields, such as economics, insurance, industry, and so on. While the word "risk" means that uncertainty may be expressed through probability, risk management is a process comprising two main segments: risk analysis and risk response.

Most studies on risk management have focused on the causes and effects of a risk event. While this is important, follow-up considerations for assessing risks and response can provide valuable information in the face of risks. In addition, different individuals take the same risk event with different degrees of impacts. In consequence, the adopted actions will be different from different types of individuals. The studies from individual's viewpoint were rarely found in the literature, yet it is significant, in particular, if an effective strategy is going to be proposed. Thus, in this chapter we intend to base on individual's preference to propose an Individual Risk Management process call IRM in brief, which includes two parts of risk analysis and risk response. The risk analysis procedure is to identify the degree of risk with respect to the individual's tolerance level; and the risk response process is to assess the considered response strategy, in order to provide an appropriate action.

Piney (2003) has introduced an idea of linking risk management and cognitive psychology to identify four personal risk zones with respect to the gains and losses of the outcomes. In light of the magnitude of influence, these four zones are the dead zone, the rational zone, the sensitivity zone, and the saturation zone. Since Piney's paper did not provide a measure to classify these zones, in this chapter, we shall first investigate such issue to define an appropriate measure and then propose a systematic approach to analyze the risk magnitude, based on an individual's tolerance level.

BASIC CONCEPTS

Much research has been done on risk management (e.g., Tummala & Leung, 1996; Tummala & Burchett, 1999). The risk management process (RMP) provides a systematic structure to assess the consequences and the likelihood of occurrence associated with a given risk event. Risk analysis and risk response are two major parts of RMP. At the risk analysis stage, we begin by identifying the risk management mission, aims, and objectives, followed by the identification of potential risk factors, enumeration of the associated consequences and their severity, and the assessment of the likelihood of these consequences occurrence. At the risk response stage, the managers should

be able to evaluate several risk response strategies, based on risk profiles generated by the risk analysis phases, choosing the most appropriate course of action to avoid or control the identified risks. This may be accomplished in four useful categories of response strategy of: risk acceptance, risk mitigation, risk transfer, and risk avoidance (Piney, 2003). Finally, by applying the risk control and monitoring steps, the risk management process is reviewed and the suitable response actions are implemented. The entire process is outlined in Figure 1.

Although risk management procedures have been developed extensively, the considered factors are not comprehensive. Most of the existing studies have focused on objective evaluation and ignored subjective factors which, however, can help us to discriminate the different impacts of risk events for different individuals and thus allow the adopted actions to be more effective. Based on this idea, we introduce the individual's subjective values into the process of risk management.

Personal judgments about uncertainty and values are important inputs for making any decisions.

Figure 1. Risk management process (Tummala & Burchett, 1999)

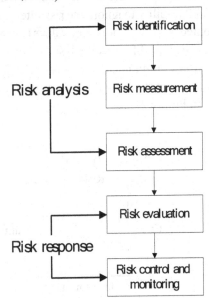

Therefore, how to define individual value function is a preliminary step towards risk analysis.

The concept of utility was proposed by Bernoulli and Cramer (1982). They suggested that risky monetary options be evaluated not by their expected return but rather by the expectations of the utilities of their return. The utility of a gain or loss is measured by the degree of pleasure (rejoicing) or pain (regret) that the amount gained or lost generates (Piney, 2003). Expected utility theory under risk was proposed by Von Neumann and Morgenstern (Von Neumann & Morgenstern, 2004), and was based on the strict logic of a human being's behavioral assumptions. This is the guiding principle of decision making under risk conditions.

According to the risk attitudes of being risk averse, risk neutral, and risk seeking, one may obtain a parameter of a function by a lottery (Clemen & Reilly, 1982; Goicoechea, Hansen, & Duckstein, 1982). Individuals who are afraid of risk or sensitive to risk are called risk aversion. Their typical utility curve is upward and concave. A convex utility curve indicates a risk seeker; these kinds of people are eager to enter the game. Finally, the utility function of a risk neutral person is a straight line. The characteristics of being risk neutral are a lack of concern about risk and the ability to ignore the risk alternatives confronted. expected monetary values (EMV) as conventional used for risk analysis are based on risk neutral assumptions (Clemen & Reilly, 2001). The figures representing these risk attitudes are shown in Figure 2.

Prospect Theory (PT) was proposed by Kahneman and Tversky (1979). They discovered that decision preferences of human beings violated the axioms of expected utility theory. The overall value of a risk event, denoted by V, is expressed in terms of two functions: one is a value function v and the other is a weighting function π. Therefore the function of PT is presented by
$$V(x_i, p_i) = \sum_i \pi(p_i) v(x_i).$$

There remain some theoretical issues for PT. The main problem is that the functional form of PT violates "stochastic dominance" (Fennema & Wakker, 1997). This problem has been solved by Quiggin's Rank-Dependent Utility (Chateauneuf & Wakker, 1999). Therefore, Tversky and Kahneman (1992) adopted Quiggin's idea to propose a Cumulative Prospect Theory (CPT) that incorporated the descriptive advantages of original PT and the theoretical advantages of rank-dependent utility.

CPT treats gains and losses separately (Neilson & Stowe, 2002). Instead of using a probability distribution, CPT uses cumulative probability to measure the effect on likelihood of occurrence. Therefore, suppose a gamble is composed of n monetary outcomes, $x_1 \le \cdots \le x_k \le 0 \le x_{k+1} \le \cdots \le x_n$ which occur with probabilities $p_1, \cdots, p_n$ respectively. Then the CPT value of the prospect $(x_1, p_1; \cdots; x_n, p_n)$ may be given by the following formula: (see Box 1).

The expression V^+ measures the contribution of gains, while V^- measures the contribution of losses.

Figure 2. Three types of risk attitude

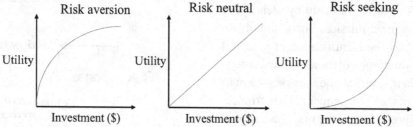

Box 1.

$$V(x, p) = V^-(x, p) + V^+(x, p)$$

$$= \sum_{i=1}^{k} \pi^- v(x_i) + \sum_{i=k+1}^{n} \pi^+ v(x_i)$$

$$\text{where } \pi_1^- = w^-(p_1), \ \pi_i^- = w^-\left(\sum_{j=1}^{i} p_j\right) - w^-\left(\sum_{j=1}^{i-1} p_j\right) \ 2 \leq i \leq k$$

$$\pi_n^+ = w^+(p_n) \ \pi_i^+ = w^+\left(\sum_{j=i}^{n} p_j\right) - w^+\left(\sum_{j=i+1}^{n} p_j\right) \ k+1 \ i \leq \leq n-1$$

$$(1)$$

RMP is a useful tool to deal with risk events. Most applications concentrated on searching risk factors and ignored the individual differences of risk influence which, however, are critical and what we concern. .

As regards the risk response stage, studies were emphasized on the method of developing the strategies, giving no consideration to the impact of the response action. Hence, we shall propose a method of combining RMP with individual's risk tolerance to classify the personal tolerance zones; then, to develop an analytical model to assess the risk response strategies in order to develop an effective response plan to reduce the overall cost.

However, individual feelings towards magnitude of risk may differ in the risk management process, so attempting to describe individual values is difficult. By making use of CPT to represent an individual's preference, a general utility function is defined as a value function as below:

$$v(x) = \begin{cases} 1 - e^{-x/R} & \text{for Risk aversion} \\ e^{-x/R} - 1 & \text{for Risk seeking} \end{cases} \quad (2)$$

The parameter R represents the risk tolerance of an individual and controls the curve of the utility function. The value of R can be derived from a reference game (Clemen & Reilly, 2001; Goicoechea et al., 1982).

As regards the probability weighting function, the form proposed by Prelec (1998) is adopted as below because it is based on behavioral axioms rather than the convenience of computation:

$$w(p) = e^{-(-\ln p)^\gamma} \quad (3)$$

Furthermore, in order to complete the risk management procedure, we proposed an optimization model to determine whether the risk response strategy is cost effective. Figure 3 summarizes the framework of this chapter, in which the focused issues are addressed by the questions in the diamond blocks, while those in the hexagon blocks are the models for proposing the optimal solutions.

The Proposed Individual Risk Management Process (IRM)

Based on the framework proposed in Figure 3, in this section we shall describe the analysis procedure in details. First we illustrate the risk analysis and then develop the risk strategies of which an evaluation model is proposed. Finally, we summarize the proposed IRM.

Risk Analysis

In this section, a method for assessing risk levels based on individual preferences is introduced of

Figure 3. *Framework of the proposed risk management*

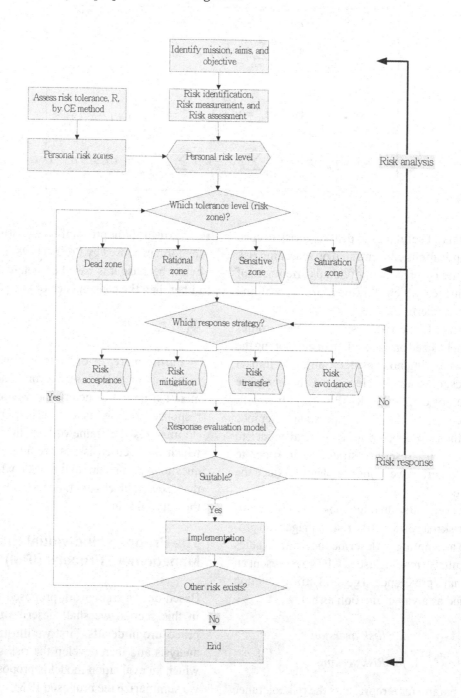

which a measure of risk level is defined and the risk zones are classified accordingly.

Individual's Risk Levels and Risk Zones

Based on the cumulative prospect theory (Neilson & Stowe, (2002)), an individual's preference towards a risk event can be described by a value function, weighted by probability as follows (see Box 5.):

$$\text{where } v(x) = \begin{cases} 1 - e^{-x/R} & \text{for Risk aversion} \\ e^{-x/R} - 1 & \text{for Risk seeking} \end{cases}$$

(x_i, p_i): outcome x_i of risk event and its corresponding probabilities, p_i

n: a risk event composed of n monetary outcomes

k: the number of negative outcomes

V: the CPT value of the prospect $(x_1, p_1; \cdots; x_n, p_n)$

v: value function

π: probability weighting function

γ: control parameter of the curvature of probability weighting function

R: risk tolerance: when $R > 0$, it is risk aversion; when $R < 0$, it is risk seeking

According to the idea of Piney (2003), the slope is the main criterion dividing utility functions into four risk zones. Therefore, by differentiating the function V, we define **Risk Level** by the slope of V as shown in Box 6.

$$\text{where } v'(x_i) = \begin{cases} \dfrac{e^{-x_i/R}}{R} & \text{for risk aversion} \\ -\dfrac{e^{-x_i/R}}{R} & \text{for risk seeking} \end{cases}$$

Box 5.

$$V(x,p) = V^-(x,p) + V^+(x,p)$$

$$= \sum_{i=1}^{k} \pi^- v(x_i) + \sum_{i=k+1}^{n} \pi^+ v(x_i)$$

$$= \sum_{i=1}^{k} \left[e^{-\left(-\ln \sum_{j=1}^{i} p_j\right)^\gamma} - e^{-\left(-\ln \sum_{j=1}^{i-1} p_j\right)^\gamma} \right] v(x_i) + \sum_{i=k+1}^{n} \left[e^{-\left(-\ln \sum_{j=i}^{n} p_j\right)^\gamma} - e^{-\left(-\ln \sum_{j=i+1}^{n} p_j\right)^\gamma} \right] v(x_i) \quad (4)$$

Box 6.

$$V'(x,p) = \sum_{i=1}^{k} \left[\left(\frac{\gamma}{\sum_{j=1}^{i} p_j} \right) \left(-\ln \sum_{j=1}^{i} p_j \right)^{\gamma-1} \left(e^{-\left(-\ln \sum_{j=1}^{i} p_j\right)^\gamma} \right) - \left(\frac{\gamma}{\sum_{j=1}^{i-1} p_j} \right) \left(-\ln \sum_{j=1}^{i-1} p_j \right)^{\gamma-1} \left(e^{-\left(-\ln \sum_{j=1}^{i-1} p_j\right)^\gamma} \right) \right] v'(x_i) +$$

$$\sum_{i=k+1}^{n} \left[\left(\frac{\gamma}{\sum_{j=i}^{n} p_j} \right) \left(-\ln \sum_{j=i}^{n} p_j \right)^{\gamma-1} \left(e^{-\left(-\ln \sum_{j=i}^{n} p_j\right)^\gamma} \right) - \left(\frac{\gamma}{\sum_{j=i+1}^{n} p_j} \right) \left(-\ln \sum_{j=i+1}^{n} p_j \right)^{\gamma-1} \left(e^{-\left(-\ln \sum_{j=i+1}^{n} p_j\right)^\gamma} \right) \right] v'(x_i)$$

(5)

Given the number of clusters (four clusters) and the attribute (slope), we used the c-means clustering method (Kaufman & Rousseeuw, 1990) to classify the weighted value function into four risk zones, based on the slope of V.

In order to illustrate this procedure, we used the MATLAB to execute the clustering procedure. Let's consider the initial data as follows

1. Each risk event is composed of three possible outcomes, that is, $n = 3$.
2. Each clustering process includes 1000 risk events.
3. Number of iteration = 30
4. Number of clusters = 4

Then, by giving the risk tolerance, R with the incremental value of 100 each time from 50 ~ 10000 for $R \leq 1000$ and 1000 for $R > 1000$, and $\gamma = 0.74$ as suggested by Wu and Gonzalez (1996) for model (5), the results are shown in Table 1 and Table 2 for negative $\sum_i p_i x_i$ and positive $\sum_i p_i x_i$ respectively.

After the person's risk zones have been determined, risk analysis of a risk event can be done by first obtaining the slope interval of each risk zone, according to his/her risk tolerance. Then, the risk level for the risk event can be calculated and which risk zone the risk event falls into can be determined. Thus, the severity of the confronted risk event can be revealed. Based on this result, a suitable response action can then be recommended.

In order to apply the results from the risk analysis, we used regression analysis to determine the relations between risk tolerance and the possibility of each risk zone as well as the slope interval of each risk zone.

Regression Model for the Possibility of Each Risk Zone

According to the clustering result, a polynomial regression model was applied to fit the number of risk events falling into each risk zone of which the regression variable R represents the risk tolerance, and the response y represents the number of each risk zone. So, we can obtain four regression models for each risk zone, as shown below.

$$y^{Zone\,i} = \left(\beta_0 + \beta_1 R + \beta_2 R^2 + \cdots + \beta_n R^n + \varepsilon \right)_i, \quad i = 1 \sim 4 \tag{6}$$

Then, the possibility of each risk zone can be obtained by its percentage as seen in Bo

According to these functions, we can understand the possibility for the risk zone each person falls into. This helps us comprehend the distribution of risk events for a specific individual, and the tolerance for risk, in general.

For example, with the same data above, we obtained the regression models for the numbers in each risk zone as listed in Box 7.

Therefore, the possibility of each risk zone is obtained as shown in Table 4. Then, once the risk tolerance is known, the possibility of the risk zone this individual might fall in can be identified with respect to the outcomes of the risk event one faced.

Analysis of the Slope Interval of Each Risk Zone

To facilitate the prediction and applications, the possible slope interval of each risk zone with respect to R is investigated in this section. Since the interval regression analysis can be served for this

Box 7.

$$\text{Possibility of Zone } i = \frac{y^{Zone\,i}}{y^{Zone\,1} + y^{Zone\,2} + y^{Zone\,3} + y^{Zone\,4}}, \quad i = 1 \sim 4 \tag{7}$$

Table 1. Slope interval of each risk zone for negative $\sum_i p_i x_i$

Negative $\sum_i p_i x_i$ Risk Tolerance	Zone 1		Zone 1		Zone 3		Zone 4	
	Lower bound	Upper bound	Lower bound	Upper bound	Lower bound	Upper bound	Lower bound	Upper bound
10000	1.1797E-04	2.0656E-04	2.0656E-04	2.5649E-04	2.5649E-04	3.2141E-04	3.2141E-04	5.0666E-04
9000	1.1768E-04	2.3938E-04	2.3938E-04	3.0302E-04	3.0302E-04	3.8154E-04	3.8154E-04	6.1740E-04
8000	1.4545E-04	2.8735E-04	2.8735E-04	3.7055E-04	3.7055E-04	4.7522E-04	4.7522E-04	7.8622E-04
7000	1.5797E-04	3.4672E-04	3.4672E-04	4.6047E-04	4.6047E-04	6.0896E-04	6.0896E-04	1.0796E-03
6000	1.9489E-04	4.6661E-04	4.6661E-04	6.4077E-04	6.4077E-04	8.5671E-04	8.5671E-04	1.5057E-03
5000	2.3074E-04	6.4626E-04	6.4626E-04	9.4183E-04	9.4183E-04	1.2968E-03	1.2968E-03	2.5717E-03
4000	2.9714E-04	1.0887E-03	1.0887E-03	1.7279E-03	1.7279E-03	2.4576E-03	2.4576E-03	5.1738E-03
3000	4.2698E-04	2.4795E-03	2.4795E-03	4.4295E-03	4.4295E-03	6.5526E-03	6.5526E-03	1.4759E-02
2000	7.0315E-04	1.2828E-02	1.2828E-02	2.7267E-02	2.7267E-02	4.3846E-02	4.3846E-02	1.0605E-01
1000	1.7418E-03	2.3761E+00	2.3761E+00	6.4820E+00	6.4820E+00	1.1565E+01	1.1565E+01	2.6799E+01
900	1.4667E-03	7.3436E+00	7.3436E+00	2.0871E+01	2.0871E+01	3.8122E+01	3.8122E+01	8.4790E+01
800	2.4846E-03	3.3044E+01	3.3044E+01	9.4394E+01	9.4394E+01	1.7042E+02	1.7042E+02	3.4926E+02
700	2.7630E-03	2.1778E+02	2.1778E+02	6.3563E+02	6.3563E+02	1.1772E+03	1.1772E+03	2.6626E+03
600	3.5148E-03	2.6080E+03	2.6080E+03	7.8762E+03	7.8762E+03	1.4537E+04	1.4537E+04	3.1900E+04
500	5.4926E-03	8.1553E+04	8.1553E+04	2.5353E+05	2.5353E+05	4.7929E+05	4.7929E+05	1.0192E+06

Table 2. Slope interval of each risk zone for positive $\sum_i p_i x_i$

Positive $\sum_i p_i x_i$ Risk Tolerance	Zone 1		Zone 2		Zone 3		Zone 4	
	Upper bound	Lower bound	Upper bound	Lower bound	Upper bound	Lower bound	Upper bound	Lower bound
10000	3.5300E-04	2.2337E-04	2.2337E-04	1.6941E-04	1.6941E-04	1.2331E-04	1.2331E-04	5.9293E-05
9000	4.1491E-04	2.5593E-04	2.5593E-04	1.9069E-04	1.9069E-04	1.3500E-04	1.3500E-04	5.6600E-05
8000	5.2176E-04	3.1013E-04	3.1013E-04	2.2398E-04	2.2398E-04	1.5198E-04	1.5198E-04	5.9172E-05
7000	6.5062E-04	3.9951E-04	3.9951E-04	2.7512E-04	2.7512E-04	1.7462E-04	1.7462E-04	5.1763E-05
6000	9.4892E-04	5.3723E-04	5.3723E-04	3.5280E-04	3.5280E-04	2.0874E-04	2.0874E-04	5.3678E-05
5000	1.4737E-03	8.3337E-04	8.3337E-04	5.1617E-04	5.1617E-04	2.7734E-04	2.7734E-04	4.5127E-05
4000	2.8939E-03	1.6415E-03	1.6415E-03	9.5943E-04	9.5943E-04	4.5301E-04	4.5301E-04	3.5789E-05
3000	8.5551E-03	4.7929E-03	4.7929E-03	2.6413E-03	2.6413E-03	1.0623E-03	1.0623E-03	2.1672E-05
2000	6.7023E-02	3.6778E-02	3.6778E-02	1.9108E-02	1.9108E-02	6.4563E-03	6.4563E-03	6.8033E-06
1000	1.9776E+01	1.0800E+01	1.0800E+01	5.3947E+00	5.3947E+00	1.5957E+00	1.5957E+00	1.2834E-07
900	6.6938E+01	3.5507E+01	3.5507E+01	1.7810E+01	1.7810E+01	5.1735E+00	5.1735E+00	5.5793E-08
800	3.0398E+02	1.6605E+02	1.6605E+02	8.2407E+01	8.2407E+01	2.3848E+01	2.3848E+01	1.5209E-08
700	2.0103E+03	1.2550E+03	1.2550E+03	6.7126E+02	6.7126E+02	-1.9852E+02	1.9852E+02	1.8627E-09
600	2.5149E+04	1.3909E+04	1.3909E+04	7.1882E+03	7.1882E+03	2.1692E+03	2.1692E+03	5.5264E-10
500	8.6187E+05	4.7395E+05	4.7395E+05	2.3650E+05	2.3650E+05	6.8192E+04	6.8192E+04	2.5839E-11

Table 3 Regression Models for the Number of Each Risk Zone

Zone	Regression Model of number for each zone (Negative $\sum_i p_i x_i$)	R-square value	Regression Model of number for each zone (Positive $\sum_i p_i x_i$)	R-square value
1	$4608.73 - 1.7038R + 0.0002218R^2$	95.9%	$1.89277 + 0.130237R - 0.0000048R^2$	100%
2	$224.885 + 0.727092R - 0.0000925R^2$	94.4%	$-4.15135 + 0.212562R + 0.0000073R^2$	100%
3	$74.8246 + 0.598495R - 0.0000638R^2$	99.3%	$-13.6073 + 0.411139R + 0.0000195R^2$	100%
4	$-34.7599 + 0.737643R - 0.0002523R^2$	95.6%	$5019.9 - 0.752437R + 0.0000313R^2$	100%

Table 4. Regression models of possibility for each zone

Zone	Regression Model of possibility for each zone (Negative $\sum_i p_i x_i$)	Regression Model of possibility for each zone (Positive $\sum_i p_i x_i$)
1	$\dfrac{4608.73 - 1.70383R + 0.0002218R^2}{4873.6797 + 0.3594R - 0.0001876R^2}$	$\dfrac{1.89277 + 0.130237R - 0.0000048R^2}{5004.12412 + 0.001501R - 0.0000758R^2}$
2	$\dfrac{224.885 + 0.727092R - 0.0000925R^2}{4873.6797 + 0.3594R - 0.0001876R^2}$	$\dfrac{-4.15135 + 0.212562R + 0.0000073R^2}{5004.12412 + 0.001501R - 0.0000758R^2}$
3	$\dfrac{74.8246 + 0.598495R - 0.0000638R^2}{4873.6797 + 0.3594R - 0.0001876R^2}$	$\dfrac{-13.6073 + 0.411139R + 0.0000195R^2}{5004.12412 + 0.001501R - 0.0000758R^2}$
4	$\dfrac{-34.7599 + 0.737643R - 0.0002523R^2}{4873.6797 + 0.3594R - 0.0001876R^2}$	$\dfrac{5019.99 - 0.752437R + 0.0000313R^2}{5004.12412 + 0.001501R - 0.0000758R^2}$

purpose, (Lee & Tanaka, 1999; Tanaka, Uejima, & Asai, 1982), the model formulated in (5) is used to estimate the boundaries of each zone.

Assuming the interval regression function for each zone is $y = A_0 + A_1 R + \varepsilon$, then, four interval regression models for each risk zone are shown below.

$$y^{Zone\,i} = (A_0 + A_1 R + \varepsilon)_i = ((a_0, c_0) + (a_1, c_1)R + \varepsilon)_i, \ i = 1 \sim 4 \tag{8}$$

Then, using this result we can predict and analyze the risk level of a risk event.

Taking the same data for illustration., the regression models for the slope interval of each risk zone are shown in Table 5 when the risk tolerance was larger than 1000_and Table 6 when the risk tolerance was smaller than or equal to 1000.

Risk Response

Based on the results of a previous section, we consider the second phase of IRM—assessment of risk response.

Response Strategy

After the risk analysis, we know by giving each individual's value function with its specified risk level, which risk zone the risk event belongs to; and what are the boundaries of each risk zone. Then, based on the risk zone levels, the appropri-

Table 5. Regression models of slope interval for each zone (R >1000)

Zone	Regression model of slope interval for each zone (Negative $\sum_i p_i x_i$)	Regression model of slope interval for each zone (Positive $\sum_i p_i x_i$)
1	$y = (3.3075E - 04, 0) + (0, 2.264333E - 08)R$	$y = (7.4308E - 04, 0) + (0, 3.43075E - 08)R$
2	$y = (5.53688E - 04, 0) + (0, 1.45145E - 08)R$	$y = (4.4502E - 04, 0) + (0, 1.536917E - 08)R$
3	$y = (7.4874E - 04, 0) + (0, 1.79955E - 08)R$	$y = (2.8077E - 04, 0) + (0, 1.2005E - 08)R$
4	$y = (1.18121E - 03, 0) + (0, 5.40825E - 08)R$	$y = (1.31209E - 04, 2.609225E - 05) + (0, 8.573126E - 09)R$

Table 6. Regression models of slope interval for each zone (R ≤ 1000)

Zone	Regression model of slope interval for each zone (Negative $\sum_i p_i x_i$)	Regression model of slope interval for each zone (Positive $\sum_i p_i x_i$)
1	$y = (1.652324E + 01, 0) + (0, 2.065095E - 02)R$	$y = (2.35015E + 02, 0) + (0, 8.620625E - 02)R$
2	$y = (6.371875E + 01, 0) + (0, 3.834375E - 02)R$	$y = (1.242285E + 02, 0) + (0, 5.227688E - 02)R$
3	$y = (1.324042E + 02, 0) + (0, 4.751344E - 02)R$	$y = (5.312725E + 01, 0) + (0, 3.659969E - 02)R$
4	$y = (2.598375E + 02, 0) + (0, 1.117781E - 01)R$	$y = (1.192375E + 01, 0) + (0, 1.490469E - 02)R$

ate strategies of avoidance, transfer, mitigation and acceptance considered by Piney (2003) can be proposed with their interpretation shown in Table 7.

Response Evaluation Model

In order to check the adequacy of the suggested strategy, a response evaluation model is needed and developed in this subsection. This is done by considering the embedded costs as listed below (Hsu, 2005):

1. **Investment cost:** The resources used to gain the ownership of the risk event

2. **Impact of primary risk:** The influence produced from the risk event

3. **Response cost:** The resources used to implement the response strategy

4. **Impact of second risk:** the influence of other risk arising from the implementation of a response

5. **Impact of responded primary risk:** influence of risk arising as a direct result of implementing a response (remaining risk)

Table 7. Meaning and applications of four response strategies w.r.t. 4 risk zones

Strategy	Avoidance	Transfer	Mitigation	Acceptance
Meaning	Taking action, so the risk event no longer impacts. Seeking to eliminate the uncertainty.	To transfer ownership and/or liability to a third party.	To reduce the "size" of the risk event to below a threshold of "risk acceptance". The size means reducing probability or/and outcomes of risk event.	Passively accept it. To deal with the risk event if it occurs, rather than attempting to influence its probability or outcomes.
Application zone	Sensitive zone Saturation zone	Rational zone	Adjunct to the other strategies	Dead zone

Table 8. Costs vs. response strategies

		Acceptance	Mitigation	Transfer	Avoidance
Investment cost		No	No	No	No
		None	None	None	None
Impact of primary risk		Yes	Yes	Yes	Yes
		Low	Medium	High	Higher
Response cost		No	Yes	Yes	Yes
		None	Low	Medium	High
Impact of second risk		No	Yes/No	Yes/No	Yes/No
		None	Depend	Depend	Depend
Impact of responded primary risk		Yes	Yes	Yes	No
		High	Medium	Low	None

The relations between the response strategies and these costs are analyzed in Table 8.

Therefore, from the analysis in Table 8, it can be realized that completely avoiding the risk, the implementation cost would be very high; yet if one is able to shoulder the risk by oneself, the cost of implementation would be zero. Besides, if the response action of avoidance is taken, there is no remaining risk. In the other hand, acceptance doesn't completely remove the risk because the responded risk is the same as for the original risk. Therefore, there is a trade off between the response cost and the impact of the responded primary cost.

Therefore, to minimize total costs, the following model was proposed to evaluate the suitability of the response strategy. In this model, function

(b) checks the impact of the risk response which includes primary risk; and the impact of other risks should be smaller than that of the original one. The response action is worth implementing when the condition conforms to the model. Function (c) measures the value of response cost relative to the reduced risk. This gives the ratio of the improvement in risk exposure to the cost of obtaining that improvement. The larger the ratio, the more is the cost-effective of the response. As a guideline, effective response ratios should have values above 20 (Hillson, 1999). If the corresponding strategy conforms to the model constraints, the strategy is recommended (see Box 8).

This is a typical binary integer programming model and only two alternatives exist in the feasible solution set $\{(x_1, x_2)|(x_1, x_2) = (0,1), (1,0)\}$.

Box 8.

$$Min \quad (investment \ \cos t) + (impact \ of \ primary \ risk)x_1 +$$
$$\left[(response \ \cos t) + (impact \ of \ other \ risk) + (impact \ of \ responded \ primary \ risk)\right]x_2$$

$s.t.$ (a) $x_1 + x_2 = 1$

(b) $(impact \ of \ responded \ primary \ risk) + (impact \ of \ other \ risk) < (impact \ of \ primary \ risk)$

(c) $\dfrac{(impact \ of \ primary \ risk) - (impact \ of \ responded \ primary \ risk)}{(response \ \cos t)} \geq 20$

$x_i = \begin{cases} 0 \\ 1 \end{cases} \quad i = ,2$

Because this is a minimization problem, it is easy to find the optimal solution from these two alternatives. Therefore, if x_1 is 1, the response strategy is not suitable and requires another strategy. If x_2 is 1, this response strategy is implemented.

Summary

So far, we have proposed a complete risk management process. In the risk analysis, we are able to derive the risk level of a risk event and the risk zone it belongs to, before deciding the corresponding response strategy. In the risk response, we have assessed the impact of the response strategies via the response evaluation model to determine the most suitable response action.

An example is presented below to explain how this risk management process works.

Illustrative Example

We adopted the court case of A-C to illustrate the proposed procedure and compare the result with EMV as formally suggested (Clemen & Reilly, 2001).

Problem Description and Analysis

This case involved two persons, A and B, who agreed to the terms of a merger. However, person C offered B a substantially better price, and B reneged on the deal with A and sold to C. Naturally, A felt if it had been dealt with unfairly and immediately filed a lawsuit against C, alleging that C had legally interfered in the A-B negotiations. A won the case and it was awarded $10300. C had said that it would file for bankruptcy if A obtained court permission to secure the judgment by filing liens against C's assets. Furthermore, C was determined to fight the case all the way to the U.S. Supreme Court, if necessary, arguing in part that A had not followed the Security and Exchange Commission regulations in its negotiations with B. In April 1987, just before A began to file the liens, C offered to pay $2000 to A, to settle the entire case. A indicated that he had been advised that a settlement between $3000 and $5000 would be fair.

What do you think A should do? Should he accept the offer of $2000, or should he refuse and make a counteroffer? If he refuses the certainty

Figure 4. Decision tree for A-C court (Clemen & Reilly, 2001)

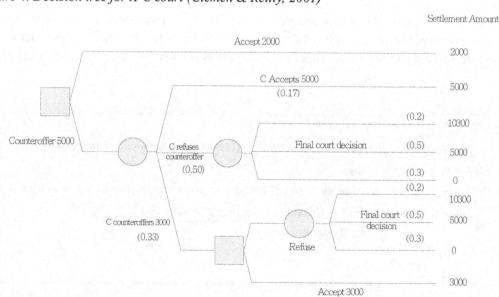

of $2000, he faced with a risky situation. C may, indeed, agree to pay $5000, a reasonable amount in A's mind. On the other hand, if he places a counter-offer of $5000 as a settlement amount, C may perhaps counter with $3000 or simply pursue a further appeal. In Figure 4, a decision tree shows a simplified version of A's problem.

This risk problem can be separated into two stages for risk analysis. The first is that if C counters with $3000, what A should do? The other is, should A refuse the offer and make a counter-offer? A's risk tolerance is 1000 and is regarded as a risk averter. We can evaluate this risk problem using our proposed RMP, as follows.

Using the interval regression results of Table 6, we can predict the interval of slope for risk tolerance = 1000 as follows:

Risk Analysis

Decision 1

The stage 1 arrangement can be viewed in Figure 5.

Based on Equation (5), the value of risk level V' = 1.42E-02 falls in the Saturation zone (Zone 4); thus, the corresponding strategy is Avoidance.

Decision 2

The stage 2 arrangement can be viewed in Figure 6.

Based on Equation (5), the value of risk level V' = 6.06E-03 again falls within the Saturation zone (Zone 4) and again, the corresponding strat-

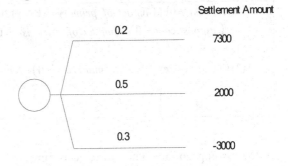

Figure 5 Decision Tree for Decision 1

Settlement Amount

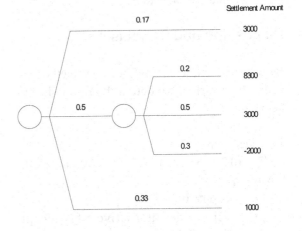

Figure 6. Decision tree for Decision 2

Settlement Amount

egy is avoidance. This means that A should not make a counter-offer to C and should accept the alternative of $2000.

Risk Response

The response evaluation model solution is x_1 = 0 x_2 = 1, which suggests that the "Avoidance"

Table 9. The interval of slope for risk tolerance=1000

Positive $\sum_i p_i x_i$							
Zone 1		Zone 2		Zone 3		Zone 4	
Upper bound	Lower bound	Upper bound	Lower bound	Upper bound	Lower bound	Upper bound	Lower bound
3.2122E+02	1.4881E+02	1.7651E+02	7.1952E+01	8.9727E+01	1.6528E+01	2.6828E+01	-2.9809E+00

Box 9. Risk response

$$Min \quad (invest\ \cos t = 0) + (impact\ of\ primary\ risk = 2120)x_1 +$$
$$[(response\ \cos t = 0) + (impact\ of\ other\ risk = 0) + (impact\ of\ responded\ primary\ risk = 0)]x_2$$
$$s.t. \quad (1)\ x_1 + x_2 = 1$$
$$(2)\ (impact\ of\ responded\ primary\ risk = 0) + (impact\ of\ other\ risk = 0) < (impact\ of\ primary\ risk = 2120)$$
$$x_i = \begin{cases} 0 \\ 1 \end{cases} \quad i = 1,2$$

strategy is appropriate. Therefore, according to our risk management process (IRM), we suggest that A accept C's offer of $2000, and forgets about making a counter-offer to C.

Discussion and Conclusion

For comparison, let us use the EMV method to make the decision, we obtain the result shown below:

1. Decision 1
$EMV = (0.2 \times 10300) + (0.5 \times 5000) + (0.3 \times 0)$
$= 4560$

- 4560>3000
- reject the alternative of "Accept $3000"

2. Decision 2
$EMV = (0.17\ 5000) + (0.5\ 4560) + (0.33\ 4560)$
$= 4630$

- 4630>2000
- reject the alternative of "Accept $2000"

Therefore, A should turn down C's offer but place a counter-offer for a settlement of 5000.

If C turns down the $5000 and makes another counteroffer of $3000, A should refuse the $3000 and take his chance in court.

To compare these two risky decision methods, we offer the following conclusions:

1. IRM is analyzed according to individual's risk attitude, whereas EMV is applied for types of individuals and thus the recom-

mended action will be the same for each one.

2. In this case, since A is a risk averter. According to our analysis, this risk event was at a high level of risk (Saturation zone) for A. Therefore, we recommended A to implement the response strategy of "Avoidance" and accept the offer from C because the response cost is the minimum. This result matches our common knowledge, yet different from that suggested by EMV.

Now, using the regression model, we further analyzed the tolerance ranges for this case and showed in Table 10.

CONCLUSION

The risk management process is an essential tool in decision-making, helping to evaluate the influence of a risk, step by step. The more precise the analysis process, the more appropriate the response action recommended.

Since different people may evaluate the same event as having different levels of risk, in this chap-

Table 10. Tolerance analysis

	Zone 1	Zone 2	Zone 3	Zone 4
Range of risk tolerance	~2376	2376~1451	1451~799	799~0
Belonging zone	Dead zone	Rational zone	Sensitive zone	Saturation zone
Corresponding strategy	Acceptance	Transfer	Avoidance	Avoidance

ter, we explored risk tolerance based on individual preferences. In order to develop a complete analysis of risk management, we studied and proposed a risk management process called Individual Risk Management by adopting cumulative prospect theory to describe individual preferences, and used the slope as a measure to separate individual risk levels when c-means clustering method was used. In order to construct tolerance analysis, we examined clustering results to discover the relation between risk tolerance and risk level. After these analyses, risk response strategies, based on the properties of four risk zones were considered. Acceptance of the recommended strategy was based on the proposed evaluation model, which assessed response strategies based on the overall costs of both operation and impact, embedded in the implemented results.

IRM has shown to provide more precise assessment at the risk analysis stage, and consider more thorough evaluation factors at the risk response stage. This is a systematic process, which includes follow-up consideration in assessing risks and response and provides more useful information for coping with the risks one faces. In addition, we solved the division problem of Piney's four risk zones by the clustering method. Therefore, the guidelines outlined in this paper offer a framework for developing effective risk analysis and response, and for minimizing the influence resulting from that risk.

Acknowledgement: The authors acknowledge the financial support from the National Science Council with project number NSC 93-2213-E007-016.

REFERENCES

Bleichrodt, H., & Pinto, J. L. (2000). A parameter-free elicitation of the probability weighting function in medical decision analysis. *Management Science, 46*(11), 1485-1496.

Chateauneuf, A., & Wakker, P. (1999). An axiomatization of cumulative prospect theory for decision under risk. *Journal of Risk and Uncertainty, 18*(2), 137-145.

Clemen, R. T., & Reilly, T. (2001). *Making hard decisions with decision tools*. Belmont, CA: Duxbury.

Fennema, H., & Wakker, P. (1997). Original and cumulative prospect theory: A discussion of empirical differences. *Journal of Behavioral Decision Making, 10*, 53-64.

Fishburn, P. C. (1982). *The foundations of expected utility*. Dordrecht, Holland: Reidel.

Goicoechea, A., Hansen, D. R., & Duckstein, L. (1982). Multiobjective decision analysis with engineering and business applications. New York: John Wiley.

Hillson, D. (1999). Developing effective risk responses. *Proceedings of 30th Annual Project Management Institute 1999 Seminar & Symposium*, Philadelphia, Pennsylvania, USA, Papers Presented October 10 to 16.

Hojati, M., Bector, C. R., & Smimou, K. (2005). A simple method for computation of fuzzy linear regression. *European Journal of Operational Research, 166*, 172-184.

Hsu, F. C. (2005). *Risk management of crisp and fuzzy events based on individual's preference*. Masters Thesis, Department of IEEM, National Tsing Hua University, Hsichu, Taiwan, ROC.

Kahneman, D., & Tversky, A. (1979). Prospect theory: An analysis of decision under risk. *Econometrica, 47*(2), 263-292.

Kaufman, L., & Rousseeuw, P. J. (1990). Finding groups in data: An introduction to cluster analysis. New York: John Wiley & Sons.

Lee, H., & Tanaka, H. (1999). Upper and lower approximation models in interval regression using regression quantile techniques. *European Journal of Operational Research, 116*, 653-666.

Neilson, W., & Stowe, J. (2002). A further examination of cumulative prospect theory parameterizations. *The Journal of Risk and Uncertainty, 24*(1), 31-46.

Piney, C. (2003). Applying utility theory to risk management. *Project Management Journal, 34*,(3), 26-31.

Prelec, D. (1998). The probability weighting function. *Econometrica, 66*(3), 497-527.

Tanaka, H., Uejima, S., & Asai, K. (1982). Linear regression analysis with fuzzy model. *IEEE Transactions on Systems, Man, and Cybernetics, 12*, 903-907.

Tummala, V. M. & Rao Leung, Y. H. (1996). A risk management model to assess safety and reliability risks. *International Journal of Quality & Reliability Management, 13*(8), 53-62.

Tummala, V M R., & Burchett, J. F. (1999). Applying a risk management process (RMP) to manage cost risk for an EHV transmission line project. *International Journal of Project Management, 17*(4), 223-235.

Tversky, A., & Kahneman, D. (1992). Advanced in prospect theory: Cumulative representation of uncertainty. *Journal of Risk and Uncertainty, 5*(4), 297-323.

Von Neumann J., & Morgenstern, O. (2004). *Theory of games and economic behavior.* Princeton: Princeton University Press, New Work.

Wu, G., & Gonzalez, R. (1996). Curvature of the probability weighting function. *Management Science, 42*, 1676-1690.

Section III
Pattern Recovery from Small Data Set:
Methodologies and Applications

Chapter XVI
Neural Networks and Bootstrap Methods for Regression Models with Dependent Errors

Francesco Giordano
University of Salerno, Italy

Michele La Rocca
University of Salerno, Italy

Cira Perna
University of Salerno, Italy

ABSTRACT

This chapter introduces the use of the bootstrap in a nonlinear, nonparametric regression framework with dependent errors. The aim is to construct approximate confidence intervals for the regression function which is estimated by using a single hidden layer feedforward neural network. In this framework, the use of a standard residual bootstrap scheme is not appropriate and it may lead to results that are not consistent. As an alternative solution, we investigate the AR-Sieve bootstrap and the Moving Block bootstrap, which are used to generate bootstrap replicates with a proper dependence structure. Both approaches are nonparametric bootstrap schemes, a consistent choice when dealing with neural network models which are often used as an accurate nonparametric estimation and prediction tool. In this context, both procedures may lead to satisfactory results but the AR sieve bootstrap seems to outperform the moving block bootstrap delivering confidence intervals with coverages closer to the nominal levels.

INTRODUCTION

One of the main difficulties in building a model for time series data is related to the detection of the nonlinear nature of the relationship among variables and to the specification of a nonlinear pattern. To overcome the problem of prior knowledge about the functional form of the model, a number of nonparametric methods have been proposed and widely used in statistical applications. Research focused on techniques such as kernel and local polynomial regression (for a review see Hardle, Lutkepohl, & Chen, 1997) but, feedforward neural networks have received increasing attention in many different fields due to their flexibility, forecasting accuracy, and absence of the curse of dimensionality. Feedforward neural networks can be seen as parallel distributed models made up of simple data processing units. This parallel structure gives reason to their well known approximation capability: given a sufficiently large number of nonlinear terms and a suitable choice of the parameters, feedfoward neural networks are able to approximate arbitrary functions of variables arbitrarily well. Because of their flexibility and because of demonstrated success in a variety of empirical applications, artificial neural networks have become the focus of considerable research activity.

In neural network modelling, a key issue is the construction of confidence intervals for the network output at any input value. Unfortunately, the sampling distribution of the estimators has a difficult and complex analytic derivation and, even if some asymptotic results are available, their complexity makes them not feasible for applications and practical usage. A feasible alternative solution, available due to the increase in computer power, is the usage of resampling techniques, powerful nonparametric approaches for estimating the distribution of a given statistic.

In this chapter we investigate some of the main issues in the use of two different bootstrap schemes, the AR-Sieve bootstrap and the Moving Block bootstrap, in the context of neural network regression models with dependent errors. These approaches have a wide range of applications and give consistent results under general conditions. They are genuine non parametric bootstrap methods which seem the best choice when dealing with non parametric estimates for dependent data. In our context, no specific and explicit structures for the noise must be assumed. This can be particularly useful in neural networks where there is no need to assume a specific parametric structure for the innovation process.

The chapter is organised as follows. In the next section we briefly review the use of single hidden feedforward neural networks for nonparametric estimation of regression functions and the use of the bootstrap in *iid* settings. In the third section, we propose and discuss the use of some bootstrap techniques to take into account the dependent structure of the innovation process. Particularly, we consider the AR-Sieve and the moving block bootstrap, two non parametric resampling techniques useful to construct confidence intervals for the output of neural networks. In the fourth section, in order to evaluate the performance of the proposed bootstrap techniques, we report the results of a Monte Carlo simulation experiment, while in the fifth section an application to real data is also discussed. Some remarks close the chapter.

NEURAL NETWORKS IN REGRESSION MODELS

Let $\{Y_t\}$, $t \in \{0, \pm 1, \pm 2, \ldots\}$, be a (possibly non stationary) process modelled as:

$$Y_t = f(\mathbf{x}_t) + Z_t, \qquad (1)$$

where f is a non linear continuous function, $\mathbf{x}_t = (x_{1t}, \ldots, x_{dt})$ is a vector of d non stochastic explanatory variables, and $\{Z_t\}$ is a stationary noise process with zero mean. The unknown function f in the model (1) can be approximated with a *single hidden layer feedforward neural network* of the form:

$$g(\mathbf{x}_t;\theta) = \sum_{k=1}^{m} c_k \phi\left(\sum_{j=1}^{d} a_{kj} x_{jt} + a_{0j}\right) + c_0 \quad (2)$$

where $\theta = (c_1,...,c_m, \mathbf{a}_1',...,\mathbf{a}_m')$ with $\mathbf{a}_k' = (a_{k1},...,a_{kd})$; c_k, $k = 1,...,m$ is the weight of the link between the k-th neuron in the hidden layer and the output; a_{ki} is the weight of the connection between the j-th input neuron and the k-th neuron in the hidden level. We suppose that the activation function of the hidden layer is the logistic function $\phi(x) = 1/(1+e^{-x})$ and that of the output layer is the identity function. Hornik, Stinchcombe, & White (1989) showed that this class of nonlinear functions can approximate any continuous function uniformly on compact sets, by increasing the size of the hidden layer. Barron (1993) showed that for sufficiently smooth functions the L_2 approximation with these activation functions is of order $O(1/m)$.

Clearly, looking at equation (2), a single hidden feedforward neural network with independent inputs and noisy output is a particular nonlinear regression model with parameters coinciding with the weights of the network connections. Therefore, the usual iterative estimation procedures available for nonlinear statistical regression models can be used as a more efficient alternative to traditional neural network estimation techniques, such as the backpropagation (Kuan & White, 1994; White, 1989).

Given a training observation set, $(Y_t, \mathbf{x}_t)$, $t = 1, 2,...,T$, the vector θ can be estimated by minimising the least squares criterion:

$$\varphi(Y_t, \mathbf{x}_t;\theta) = \frac{1}{2T}\sum_{t=1}^{T}(Y_t - g(\mathbf{x}_t;\theta))^2 \quad (3)$$

that is:

$$\hat{\theta}_T = \arg\min_{\theta} \varphi(Y_t, \mathbf{x}_t;\theta). \quad (4)$$

Consistency and asymptotic normality of the weight vector estimator has been established by

White (1989) for *iid* data and by Kuan and White (1994) for dependent data by considering neural networks as particular (possibly) misspecified nonlinear regression models. These results make possible to test hypotheses about the connection strengths, which can be of great help in defining pruning strategies with a strong inferential base. Of great interest in many applications is the construction of confidence intervals for the output of the network.

$$\hat{f}(Y_t, \mathbf{x}_t) = g(\mathbf{x}_t;\hat{\theta}_T) = \sum_{k=1}^{m} \hat{c}_k \phi\left(\sum_{j=1}^{d} \hat{a}_{kj} x_{jt} + \hat{a}_{k0}\right) + \hat{c}_0.$$

$$(5)$$

For a discussion about alternative analytical approaches see Hwang and Ding (1997), De Veaux, Schemi, Schweinsberg, Shellington, and Ungar (1998), Rasmussen and Hines (2004) *inter alia*. An interesting comparison among alternative confidence intervals construction methods for neural networks can be found in Papadopoulos, Edwards, and Murray (2000).

Unfortunately, the variance covariance matrix of the estimators and the forecast distribution have quite complex structures which is not feasible for the applications and for an easy practical usage. This is quite common in the setting of nonparametric estimation where asymptotic techniques, even if available in principle and very useful to study the theoretical properties of the statistics involved, are only rarely used. It is much more common to carry out stochastic simulations such as bootstrapping to provide feasible estimators for sampling variability or, more generally, for sampling distributions. The bootstrap is a good alternative to analytical results and it often provides higher accuracy in finite samples. It can be used for calculating approximate critical values for statistical tests, for confidence intervals for predictions as well as for model selection.

Several authors use the bootstrap in a neural network framework for estimating sampling variability (Baxt & White, 1995; Refenes & Zapranis, 1999 *inter alia*) and for calculating critical values for statistical tests (White & Racine, 2001). LeBaron (1997) proposes a technique which combines evolutionary optimization algorithms, for searching the large number of potential network architecture, along with bootstrap based statistical tests, for estimating objectives out of sample. Weigend and LeBaron (1994) and Tibshirani (1996) discuss the use of the bootstrap to determine the quality and reliability of a neural network predictor. LeBaron and Weigend (1998) discuss, by using the bootstrap, the effect of data splitting, a common practice for model selection in neural networks, on financial time series.

If the model is correctly specified, that is the mapping *f* can be represented exactly by a network of the form considered, the neural network can be considered the particular case of parametric nonlinear regression models. In this case the validity and second-order efficiency of the bootstrap has been described and investigated in practice (Huet Jolivet, & Messean, 1990 *inter alia*) and those results extent immediately to neural network models. In the more general case of misspecified models, formal proof of the consistency of the bootstrap can be found in Franke and Neumann (2000).

All the mentioned procedures assume independent random samples that are free of outlying observations. However, it is well known that the existence of outliers in a sample has serious effects on the bootstrap scheme leading to resamples with possible higher contamination levels than the initial sample. As a consequence, estimated models can be seriously affected by those deviations resulting on a poor performance and confidence intervals and tests that can be seriously biased. To solve the problem, a robust bootstrap procedure is proposed and discussed in Allende, Nanculef, and Salas (2004).

Nevertheless, all previous approaches are designed in the *iid* setting, where the bootstrap works by creating many independent pseudo-rep-

licates of the training set and then re-estimating the statistics of interest on each bootstrap sample. These schemes are not consistent for different specifications of the error structures and specifically when neural networks are used in a time series framework. It is well known (Kunsh, 1989) that for dependent data the classical bootstrap approach fails and so modifications of the original procedure are needed in order to preserve the dependence structure of the original data in the bootstrap samples.

When dealing with time series data, two different classes of bootstrap methods have been proposed. The first is a model based approach where the dependence structure of the series is modelled explicitly and the bootstrap sample is drawn from the fitted model. Of course, if the model is not correctly specified the generated series will not have the same statistical properties of the original data and, as a consequence, the bootstrap estimators will not be consistent (Davidson & Hinkley, 1997). This issue is a serious drawback when dealing with neural network models that are intrinsically misspecified.

In the next section we focus on two resampling techniques, namely the AR-Sieve and the Moving block bootstrap (MBB) which are nonparametric, purely model free bootstrap schemes. They are suitable to be employed in neural network frameworks for the construction of confidence intervals for the output of the network in a time series setting. A moving block bootstrap scheme has also been proposed in Giordano, La Rocca, and Perna (2004) for variable selection. Alternatively, the dependence structure which is present in the training set could be captured by using the subsampling (Politis, Romano, & Wolf, 1999) which gives consistent results when constructing test procedure and confidence intervals in a neural network framework (see La Rocca & Perna, 2005a, 2005b). This latter approach will not be further discussed here.

RESAMPLING SCHEMES FOR NEURAL NETWORK REGRESSION MODELS

The classical approach for dealing with time series data is the moving block bootstrap. In this scheme, the time series is divided into blocks of consecutive observations and replicates are generated by resampling the overlapping blocks with replacement. These schemes enjoy the property of being valid under weak conditions and robust against misspecifications, since they do not require a selection of a proper model and the only parameter to be estimated is the block length. This approach, known as blockwise bootstrap or moving block bootstrap (MBB), generally works satisfactory and enjoys the properties of being robust against misspecified models.

The MBB bootstrap procedure can be adapted to possibly non-stationary time series, in a neural network context, as follows.

- STEP 1. Compute the neural network estimates $\hat{f}(Y_t, \mathbf{x}_t)$ for $t = 1,...,T$.
- STEP 2. Compute the residuals $\hat{Z}_t = Y_t - \hat{f}(Y_t, \mathbf{x}_t)$ with $t = 1,...,T$ and the centred residuals $\widetilde{Z}_t = \hat{Z}_t - \sum_{t=1}^{T} \hat{Z}_t / T$.
- STEP 3. Fix $l < T$ and form blocks of length l of consecutive observations from the original data, i.e. the bootstrap sample is

$$Z^*_{(j-1)l+t} = \widetilde{Z}_{S_j+t}, \ 1 \leq j \leq b, \ 1 \leq j \leq l.$$

where $b = [T/l]$ denoting with $[x]$ the smallest integer greater or equal to x. Let $S_1, S_2,...,S_b$ are *iid* uniform on $\{0,1,..., T-l\}$. If T is not a multiple of l, only $T + l - b$ observations from the last block are used. Given bootstrap replicate $\{Z^*_1,...,Z^*_T\}$, generate the bootstrap observations by setting. $Y^*_t = \hat{f}(Y_t, \mathbf{x}_t) + Z^*_t$ with $t = 1,...,T$.

MBB schemes are very popular and conceptually very simple. The idea that underlies the block resampling scheme is that if blocks are long enough, the original dependence will be reasonably preserved in the resampled series. Clearly, this approximation is better if the dependence is weak and the blocks are as long as possible, thus preserving the dependence more faithfully. On the other hand, the distinct values of the statistics must be as numerous as possible to provide a good estimate of the distribution of the statistics and this points toward short blocks. Thus, unless the length of the series is considerable to accommodate longer and more number of blocks the preservation of the dependence structure may be difficult, especially for complex, long range dependence structure. In such cases, the block resampling scheme tend to generate resampled series that are less dependent than the original ones. Moreover, the resampled series often exhibits artifacts which are caused by joining randomly selected blocks. As a consequence, the asymptotic variance-covariance matrices of the estimators based on the original series and those based on the bootstrap series are different and a modification of the original scheme is needed. A further difficulty, is that the bootstrap sample is not (conditionally) stationary. This can be overcome by taking blocks of random length, as proposed by Politis and Romano (1994), but a tuning parameter, which seems difficult to control, has to be fixed. Anyway, a recent study of Lahiri (1999) shows that this approach is much less efficient than the original one and so no clear choice is possible.

A more effective solution seems to be the AR-Sieve bootstrap, first proposed by Kreiss (1992) and extensively studied by Buhlmann (1998; 1999). It uses a sequence of AR(p) models with the order p that increases as a function of the sample size to approximate the unknown data generating process. This scheme even if based on a sequence of parametric models it is nonparametric in its spirit being model free within the class of linear processes. This technique is effective for linear and "weak" nonlinear processes.

It can be implemented in the neural network framework considered in this chapter as follows.

- STEP 1. Compute the neural network estimates $\hat{f}(Y_t, \mathbf{x}_t)$ for $t = 1, \ldots, T$.
- STEP 2. Compute the residuals $\hat{Z}_t = Y_t - \hat{f}(Y_t, \mathbf{x}_t)$ with $t = 1, \ldots, T$ and the centred residuals $\widetilde{Z}_t = \hat{Z}_t - \sum_{t=1}^{T} \hat{Z}_t / T$.
- STEP 3. Fit an autoregressive model of order p to the residuals $\widetilde{Z}_t$ and compute another set of residuals

$$\hat{\varepsilon}_t = \sum_{j=0}^{p} \hat{\phi}_j \, \widetilde{Z}_{t-j}, \; \hat{\phi}_0 = 1, \, t = p + 1, \ldots, T.$$

A guideline for approximating p is given by the Akaike information criterion in the increasing range $[0, 10 \log_{10}(T)]$, the default option of the S-plus package.

Compute $\widetilde{\varepsilon}_t = \hat{\varepsilon}_t - \sum_{t=p+1}^{T} \hat{\varepsilon}_t / (T - p)$, $t = 1, \ldots, T.$

- STEP 4. Denote by $\hat{F}_{\widetilde{\varepsilon}}$ the empirical cumulative distribution function of $\widetilde{\varepsilon}_t$, $t = p + 1, \ldots, T$. Resample $\{\varepsilon_t^*\}$ *iid* from $\hat{F}_{\widetilde{\varepsilon}}$ with $t = 1, \ldots, T$.
- STEP 5. Generate the bootstrap error series $\{Z_t^*\}$, $t = 1, \ldots, T$, defined by

$$\varepsilon_t^* = \sum_{j=0}^{p} \hat{\phi}_j \, Z_{t-j}^*, \; \hat{\phi}_0 = 1, \, t = 1, \ldots, T.$$

Here we start the recursion with some starting value (the initial conditional if available or some resampled innovations) and wait until stationarity is reached.

- STEP 6. Then generate a bootstrap series by $Y_t^* = \hat{f}(Y_t, \mathbf{x}_t) + Z_t^*$ with $t = 1, \ldots, T$.

Observe that even if the sieve bootstrap is based on a parametric model it is basically non parametric in its spirit. The AR(p) model here is just used to filter the residuals series.

The bootstrap series generated by using one of the previous methods can be used to approximate the sampling distribution of the statistic of interest. Given the bootstrap series Y_t^*, $t = 1, \ldots, T$, compute the bootstrap analogue of the neural network parameters

$$\hat{\theta}_T^* = \arg\min_{\theta} \frac{1}{2T} \sum_{t=1}^{T} \left(Y_t^* - g(\mathbf{x}_t; \theta) \right)^2$$

and the bootstrap analogue of the neural network estimates

$$\hat{f}^* \left(Y_t^*, \mathbf{x}_t \right) = g\left(\mathbf{x}_t; \hat{\theta}_T^* \right) = \sum_{k=1}^{m} \hat{c}_k^* \phi \left(\sum_{j=1}^{d} \hat{a}_{kj}^* x_{jt} + \hat{a}_{k0}^* \right) + \hat{c}_0^*.$$

Then, estimate the sample distribution of $\hat{f}(Y_t, \mathbf{x}_t)$ with the distribution of $\hat{f}^*(Y_t^*, \mathbf{x}_t)$, conditional on the observed data $(Y_t, \mathbf{x}_t)$ $t = 1, \ldots, T$.

Such a distribution can be used to estimate the quantiles $q_{\alpha/2}^*(x)$ and $q_{1-\alpha/2}^*(x)$ to obtain a pointwise confidence interval of nominal level $1 - \alpha$ for the network output.

As usual the bootstrap distribution can be approximated through a Monte Carlo approach. That is:

- STEP 1. Generate B different bootstrap series, $Y_{t,b}^*$, $t = 1, \ldots, T$, $b = 1, \ldots, B$.
- STEP 2. Compute $\hat{\theta}_{T,b}^* = \arg\min_{\theta} \frac{1}{2T} \sum_{t=1}^{T} \left(Y_{t,b}^* - g(\mathbf{x}_t; \theta) \right)^2$, $b = 1, \ldots, B$.
- STEP 3. Evaluate $\hat{f}_b^* \left(Y_{t,b}^*, \mathbf{x}_t \right) = g \left(\mathbf{x}_t; \hat{\theta}_{b,T}^* \right)$, $b = 1, \ldots, B$.
- STEP 4. Define the estimated bootstrap distribution as the empirical distribution function of $\hat{f}_b^* \left(Y_{t,b}^*, \mathbf{x}_t \right)$, $b = 1, \ldots, B$, that is

$$\hat{G}_{T,B}^*(x) = B^{-1} \sum_{b=1}^{B} I \left(\hat{f}_b^* \leq x \right),$$

where $I(\cdot)$ is the indicator function and, moreover, define the quantile of order $1 - \alpha$ as

$$\hat{q}^*(1 - \alpha) = \inf \left\{ x : \hat{G}_{T,B}^*(x) \geq 1 - \alpha \right\}.$$

- STEP 5. Compute the approximated bootstrap confidence interval of nominal level $1 - \alpha$ as:

$$\left[\hat{q}^*(\alpha/2), \hat{q}^*(1-\alpha/2)\right]$$

SOME MONTE CARLO RESULTS

To evaluate the performance of the proposed bootstrap procedures to construct pointwise confidence intervals in the context of neural network estimators, a Monte Carlo experiment was performed. For illustration purposes we have considered the important problem of interval estimation for a trend in a time series framework. More precisely, we have considered as data generating process the model $Y_t = f(t) + Z_t$ where $\{f(t)\}$, $t \in \{0, \pm 1, \pm 2, \dots\}$, is a deterministic trend (or signal) and $\{Z(t)\}$, $t \in \{0, \pm 1, \pm 2, \dots\}$ is a stationary noise process with zero mean.

The simulated data set has been generated according to the following trend structures:

(M1) $f(t) = 1 + 3t$, $t \in [0,1]$
(M2) $f(t) = \sin(2\pi t)$, $t \in [0,1]$
(M3) $f(t) = 4.26(e^{-t} - 4e^{-2t} + 3e^{-3t})$, $t \in [0, 2.5]$

in order to cover both linear and nonlinear models as well as periodic structures.

The noise process has been generated according to the AR(1) model

$$Z_t = 0.8Z_{t-1} + \varepsilon_t$$

while for the innovations two different specifications have been considered:

(N1) $\sqrt{1.8}\varepsilon$, $i.i.d. \sim t_6$
(N2) $\varepsilon_t = (\eta_t - E[\eta_t])/\sqrt{1.2}$ with $\eta_t \sim Exp(1)$

in order to consider both symmetric and nonsymmetric error distributions. The noise level (inverse of signal to noise ratio) is fixed to 0.10.

To approximate the function $f(\cdot)$, we have used a single input-single output feedforward neural network with one hidden layer. The hidden layer size has been fixed by using the bayesian information criterion (BIC) as reported in Faraway and Chatfield (1998). The complexity of the network has been estimated on the original training data set and kept fixed in all bootstrap replicates.

The simulations are based on 100 Monte Carlo runs and 999 bootstrap series. We fixed $T = 300, 500, 1000$ in order to simulate the time series length usually available in real applications. The block length l in the MBB scheme is computed using the Buhlmann procedure and it has based on the influence function of the quantiles (Buhlmann & Kunsch, 1999). The nominal level of the confidence intervals is $1 - \alpha = 0.90$.

All bootstrap runs have been computed by using a "Local" Bootstrap scheme. That is, at each bootstrap replicate the initial values for the Neural Network training algorithm are fixed to the values that minimise the objective function (3) in the original sample.

In our simulation study we investigated the actual pointwise coverages against the nominal one fixed equal to 0.90.

By looking at figure 1, where we report a typical realization of the processes considered along with and the "true" trend function, it is evident the non standard structure of the noise with heavy tails and non symmetric behaviour, especially for (N2). Moreover, to motivate the use of bootstrap schemes which take into account the dependence structure of the residuals, we reported the autocorrelation function computed on the residuals from neural network models estimated on the original data (see Figure 2). Clearly, the estimated network, when properly identified, does not add any spurious structure to the residuals when the innovation process is white noise. Moreover, the original dependence structure is still present in the residuals after filtering the original data set with a proper estimated network, when the innovation process has a linear dependent structure. In

Figure 1. A typical realization of the processes (M1), (M2) and (M3) with noise (N1) and (N2) along with the trend function.

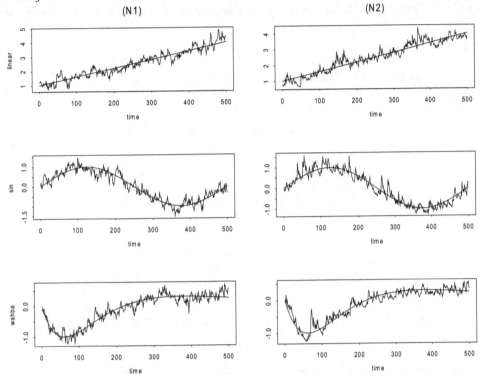

Figure 2. A typical realization of the model (M3) with noise (N1) and (N2) (top panels) along with the trend function (solid line), neural network estimate (dashed line) and residual autocorrelation functions (bottom panels) from trend neural network estimates.

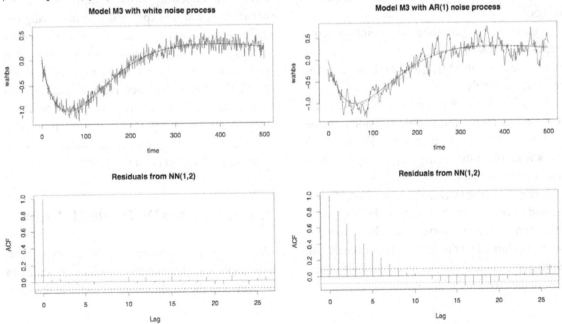

Figure 3. Pointwise coverages using model (M1) with noise (N1) and (N2). Solid line refers to AR-Sieve bootstrap coverages, dashed line refers to MBB coverages. The reference line is the nominal level 0.90. The two horizontal point lines denote an acceptance region for the observed coverages at a 0.95 confidence level.

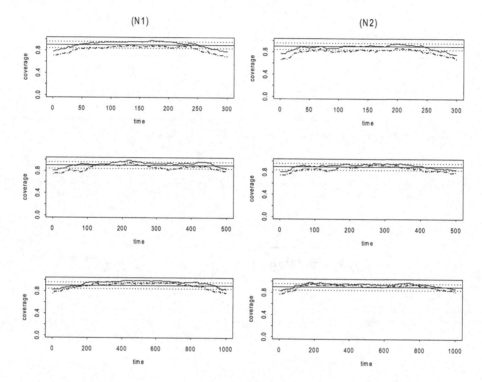

this latter case, the residual bootstrap is clearly not appropriate and it may lead to inconsistent results.

Figures 3 – 5 report the actual pointwise coverages on 100 Monte Carlo iterations according to the three models (M1), (M2) and (M3) for the trend, respectively.

Each figure shows at the left column the case of the noise model (N1) while the noise model (N2) is shown at the right column. Finally, each row shows three different sample lengths {300, 500, 1000}.

It is evident the so called "edge effect" that is the bad coverages to the points at the beginning and the end of the time series data. This behaviour can be explained by the nature of neural network estimators, which are basically global estimators, and by the structure of the noise.

In general, in all the cases considered, the AR-Sieve bootstrap always outperforms the MBB. This can be explained by considering the different rate of convergence for the two bootstrap techniques. In fact the MBB estimators have a polynomial rate of convergence (Kunsch, 1989) while the AR-Sieve ones have an exponential rate of convergence (Buhlmann, 1999). So, for a time series length equal to 300, we can observe a wide gap which becomes narrower when the time series length is equal to 1000.

AN APPLICATION TO REAL DATA

We have applied the neural network estimator with AR-Sieve bootstrap on the residuals presented in section 3 to the world's longest series of monthly

Figure 4. Pointwise coverages using model (M2) with noise (N1) and (N2). Solid line refers to AR-Sieve bootstrap coverages, dashed line refers to MBB coverages. The reference line is the nominal level 0.90. The two horizontal point lines denote an acceptance region for the observed coverages at a 0.95 confidence level.

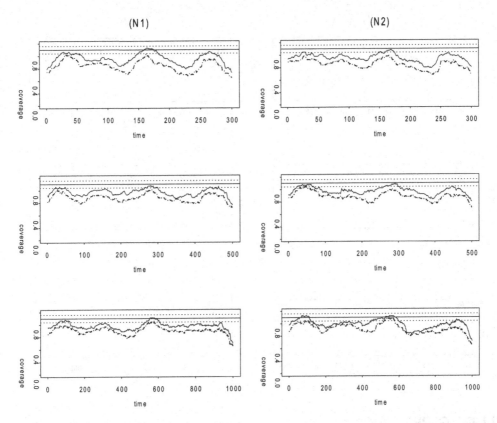

total ozone measurements from Arosa, Switzerland. The range of the observations is from July, 1926 to May, 2005. The measures are performed by the Swiss Meteorological Institute All data are direct sun measurements the total ozone amount is given in DU (Dobson units). The data, which are reported in Figure 6, has been filtered to remove the seasonal component.

The data set has been deeply studied. A trend analysis has been given by Staehelin, Kegel, and Harris (1997); based on a linear trend model, including other exogenous variables and an AR(2) noise process, a significantly decreasing trend has been found, up to 1996. The same decreasing trend has been found by Buhlmann (1998) by using a nonparametric kernel smoother (without including any exogenous variables). It is now of interest, to see whether our neural network trend model exhibits a decreasing trend, without using any other exogenous explanatory variables (as in Buhlmann), when considering the data set up to 1996 and a different behaviour when considering the updated data set up to 2005.

By looking at Figure 6 it is evident that the procedure is able to capture not only the decreasing trend in the observation up to 1996 but also an increasing trend for the sample from 1996 up to 2005. Moreover the confidence band, constructed by using the AR-Sieve bootstrap on the neural network filtered data, supports the evidence of a different behaviour of the trend for the updated data set.

Figure 5. Pointwise coverages using model (M3) with noise (N1) and (N2). Solid line refers to AR-Sieve bootstrap coverages, dashed line refers to MBB coverages. The reference line is the nominal level 0.90. The two horizontal point lines denote an acceptance region for the observed coverages at a 0.95 confidence level.

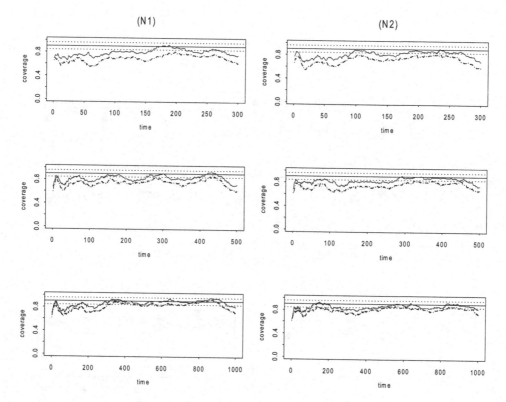

CONCLUDING REMARKS

In this chapter we have investigated the use of the AR-Sieve bootstrap and the Moving Block bootstrap in the framework of nonparametric, nonlinear regression models with dependent errors. The resampling schemes are used to construct confidence intervals for the regression function estimated by a feedforward neural network.

Unfortunately, the sampling distribution of the estimators has a difficult and complex analytic derivation and, even if some asymptotic results are available, their complexity makes them not feasible for applications and practical usage. A possible alternative solution, available due to the increase in computer power, is the usage of resampling techniques, powerful nonparametric approaches for estimating the distribution of a given statistics.

The use of simulation approaches seems to be appropriate in this context since the estimators involved have a complex probabilistic structure, which is difficult to deal with from an analytical point of view. Even if some asymptotic results are available, their complexity makes them not feasible for applications and practical usage. A feasible alternative solution, available due to the increase in computer power, is the use of resampling techniques which can be effective employed to get an approximate sampling distribution.

However, in this framework the use of a standard residual bootstrap is not appropriate and it may lead to results that are not consistent. To overcome the problem, we have investigated

Figure 6. Total ozone measurements and trend estimation by neural network model (solid line); confidence band with AR-Sieve bootstrap (dashed lines).

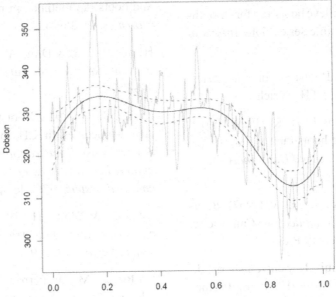

bootstrap schemes which are able to generate bootstrap replicates with a proper dependence structure. The proposed schemes, based on the AR-Sieve and the Moving block bootstrap, are nonparametric and do not relay on the specification of a proper parametric bootstrap model. This aspect seems to be particularly relevant for neural network models, which are used as an accurate nonparametric estimation tool. In a Monte Carlo experiment designed to evaluate the performances of the proposed schemes, both procedures give satisfactory results, but the AR sieve bootstrap seem to outperform the moving block bootstrap delivering confidence intervals with coverages closer to nominal levels. Moreover, the AR-Sieve bootstrap avoids the need of the specification of the block length, a critical parameter for all blockwise bootstrap schemes.

Finally, observe that one of the main disadvantages of the bootstrap method is that the computational cost could be high when datasets or networks are large. However, Tibshirani (1996) found that the bootstrap approach provided more accurate confidence intervals than the delta method or other analytical approximations. A reason for this success is that bootstrap sampling takes into account the variability of feedforward neural networks due to different initial network weights.

REFERENCES

Allende, H., Nanculef, R., & Salas R. (2004). Robust bootstrapping neural networks. In R. Monroy, G. Arroyo-Figueroa, L. E. Sucar, H. Sossa (Eds.), *MICAI 2004*, LNAI 2972, pp. 813–822. Berlin/Heidelberg: Springer-Verlag.

Barron, A.R. (1993). Universal approximation bounds for superpositions of a sigmoidal function. *IEEE Transactions on Information Theory*, *39*, 930-945.

Baxt, W. G., & White, H. (1995). Bootstrapping confidence intervals for clinical input variable effects in a network trained to identify the presence of acute myocardial infarction. *Neural Computation, 7,* 624–638.

Buhlmann, P. (1998). Sieve bootstrap for smoothing in nonstationary time series. *The Annals of Statistics, 26,* 48-83.

Bühlmann, P. (1999). Bootstrap for time series. *Research report n. 87,* ETH, Zürich.

Buhlmann, P., & Kunsch, H. R. (1999). Block length selection in the bootstrap for time series. *Computational Statistics and Data Analysis, 31,* 295-310.

Davidson, A.C., & Hinkley, D. V. (1997). *Bootstrap methods and their application.* Cambridge, UK: Cambridge University Press.

De Veaux, R., Schemi, J., Schweinsberg, J., Shellington, D., & Ungar, L. H. (1998). Prediction intervals for neural networks via nonlinear regression. *Technometrics, 40,* 277-282.

Efron, B. (1979). Bootstrap methods: Another look at the jackknife. *The Annals of Statistics, 7,* 1-26.

Faraway J., & Chatfield C. (1998). Time series forecasting with neural networks: a comparative study using the airline data. *Applied Statistics, 47,* 231-250.

Franke J., & Neumann M.H. (2000). Bootstrapping neural networks. *Neural Computation, 12,* 1929-1949.

Giordano, F., La Rocca, M., & Perna, C. (2004). Bootstrap variable selection in neural network regression models. In H. H. Bock, M. Chiodi, & A. Mineo (Eds.), Advances in multivariate data analysis. Heidelberg-Berlin: Springer-Verlag.

Hardle, W., Lutkepohl, H., & Chen, R. (1997). A review of non parametric time series analyisis. *International Statistical Review, 65,* 49-72.

Hornik, K., Stinchcombe, M., & White, H. (1989). Multi-layer feedforward networks are universal approximators. *Neural Networks, 2,* 359-366.

Huet, S., Jolivet, E., & Messean, A. (1990). Some simulation results about confidence intervals and bootstrap methods in nonlinear regression. *Statistics, 21,* 369-432.

Hwang, J. T. G., & Ding, A. A. (1997). Prediction intervals for artificial neural networks. *JASA, 92,* 748-757.

Kreiss, J.-P. (1992). Bootstrap procedures for AR(1)-processes. In K.H. Jöckel, G. Rothe, & W. Sender (Eds), *Bootstrapping and Related Techniques. Lecture Notes in Economics and Mathematical Systems 376.* Heidelberg: Springer.

Kuan C., & White, H. (1994). Artificial neural networks: An econometric perspective. *Econometric Review, 13,* 1–91.

La Rocca, M., & Perna C. (2005a). Variable selection in neural network regression models with dependent data: A subsampling approach. *Computational Statistics and Data Analysis, 48,* 415-429.

La Rocca, M., & Perna C. (2005b). Neural network modeling by subsampling. In J. Cabestany, A. Prieto, & F. Sandoval (Eds), *Computational intelligence and Bioinspired Systems, Lecture Notes in Computer Science 3512,* pp. 200-207. Springer.

Kunsch, H.R. (1989). The jackknife and the bootstrap for general stationary observations. *The Annals of Statistics, 17,* 1217-1241.

Lahiri, S. N. (1999). Theoretical comparisons of block bootstrap methods. *The Annals of Statistics, 27,* 386-404.

LeBaron, B. (1997). *An evolutionary bootstrap approach to neural network pruning and generalization.* Working paper, Dept. of Economics, University of Winsconsin, Madison.

LeBaron, B., & Weigend, A. S. (1998). A bootstrap evaluation of the effect of data splitting on financial time series. *IEEE Transactions on Neural Networks, 9,* 213–220.

Papadopoulos, G., Edwards, P. J., & Murray, A. F. (2000). Confidence estimation methods for neural networks: A practical comparison. *Proceedings of ESANN 2000,* Bruges (Belgium), April 26 – 28, 2000, D-facto public., 75-80.

Politis, D. N., & Romano, J. P. (1992). A circular block-resampling procedure for stationary data. In C. Page & R. LePage (Eds.), *Exploring the limits of the bootstrap.* New York: Springer-Verlag.

Politis, D. N., & Romano, J. P. (1994). The stationary bootstrap. *JASA, 89,* 1303-1313.

Politis, D. N., J. P. Romano, & Wolf, M. (1999). *Subsampling.* Springer.

Rasmussen, B., & Hines, J. W. (2004). Prediction interval estimation techniques for empirical modelling strategies and their applications to signal validation tasks. *Applied Computational Intelligence,* Proceedings of the 6th International FLINS Conference, Blankenberge, Belgium, September 1-3, 2004.

Refenes, A.P.N., & Zapranis, A.D. (1999). Neural model identification, variable selection and model adequacy. *Journal of Forecasting, 18,* 299-332

Staehelin, J., Kegel, R. & Harris, N. R. P. (1997). Trend analysis of the homogenised total ozone series of AROSA (Switzerland), 1926 – 1996. *Journal of Geophysical Research.*

Tibshirani, R. (1996). A comparison of some error estimates for neural network models. *Neural Computation, 8,* 152-163.

Weigend, A. S., & LeBaron, B. (1994). Evaluating neural network predictors by bootstrapping. In *Proceedings of the International Conference on Neural Information Processing,* ICONIP'94, Seoul, Korea, 1207-1212.

White, H. (1989). Learning in artificial neural networks: A statistical perspective. *Neural Computation, 1,* 425-464.

White H., & Racine J.(2001). Statistical inference, the bootstrap and neural network modelling with application to foreign exchange rates. *IEEE Transaction on neural Networks, 12,* 657-673.

Chapter XVII
Financial Crisis Modeling and Prediction with a Hilbert–EMD–Based SVM Approach

Lean Yu
Chinese Academy of Sciences, China & City University of Hong Kong, Hong Kong

Shouyang Wang
Chinese Academy of Sciences, China

Kin Keung Lai
City University of Hong Kong, Hong Kong

ABSTRACT

Financial crisis is a kind of typical rare event, but it is harmful to economic sustainable development if occurs. In this chapter, a Hilbert-EMD-based intelligent learning approach is proposed to predict financial crisis events for early-warning purpose. In this approach a typical financial indicator currency exchange rate reflecting economic fluctuation condition is first chosen. Then the Hilbert-EMD algorithm is applied to the economic indicator series. With the aid of the Hilbert-EMD procedure, some intrinsic mode components (IMCs) of the data series with different scales can be obtained. Using these IMCs, a support vector machine (SVM) classification paradigm is used to predict the future financial crisis events based upon some historical data. For illustration purposes, two typical Asian countries including South Korea and Thailand suffered from the 1997-1998 disastrous financial crisis experience are selected to verify the effectiveness of the proposed Hilbert-EMD-based SVM methodology.

INTRODUCTION

In the past decades, some important economic and financial events like the Black October 1987, the December 1994 devaluation of the Mexican peso, and the October 1997 Asia financial turmoil after the devaluation of the Thai baht justify the considerable concerns with financial and currency crisis in the financial literature. These unprecedented and peculiar crisis events brought large change not only to their economy but also to their society, and since then much attention has been focused on study of the financial crisis from the theoretical and empirical standpoints (Flood & Marion, 1999; Goldstein, 1996; Kaminsky, Lizondo, & Reinhart, 1998; Sachs, Tornell, & Velasco, 1996). The main reason for much research attention is that financial market practitioners have different reasons for undertaking financial crises analysis. For example, macro policymakers are interested in leading indicators of pressure on economic growth; market participants are increasingly concerned to measure and limit their risk to large currency fluctuation; and financial regulators are keen to understand the currency risk exposure of the institutions they supervise (Yu, Lai, & Wang, 2006).

In order to predict whether one country will reach financial crisis level, it is important to be clear exactly how a crisis is defined. Much relevant literature looks at crisis indices (termed currency pressure indicators) defined as weighted sums of percentage change in exchange rates, interest rates and foreign currency reserves (Kumar, Moorthy, & Perraudin, 2003). Use of such indices is appropriate if one views crises from the view of a macro policymaker and is equally interested in "successful" and "unsuccessful" speculative attacks. From the standpoint of an investor, manager of foreign reserve positions, or a macro policymaker who cares primarily about a "successful attack" on the currency, it is more appropriate to consider a simpler definition of financial crisis based on large depreciations of currency exchange rates.

To distinguish our research from those of studies which employ currency pressure indicators, a large devaluation of currency which far exceeds previous devaluations is defined as a financial crisis event.

In the existing studies, much effort has been made to build an appropriate model that could detect a possible crisis in advance. Accordingly various financial crisis forecasting models and early warning systems (e.g., Edison, 2000; Frankel & Rose, 1996; Goldstein, Kaminsky, & Reinhart, 2000; Kim, Hwang, & Lee, 2004; Kim, Oh, Sohn, & Hwang, 2004; Yu et al., 2006) have been constructed. In general, there are four types of financial crisis modeling and analysis model. The first type is to use structural models to analyze the financial crisis. There are case studies into specific financial episodes, often employing explicit structural models of balance of payments crises. Notable examples include Blanco and Garber (1986), Cumby and van Wijnbergen (1989), Jeanne and Masson (2000), Cole and Kehoe (1996), and Sachs et al. (1996). These studies are informative about the episodes in question and revealing with regard to structural model proposed by some theorists (Kumar et al., 2003).

The second type of financial crisis modeling is signal approach. Typical examples include Kaminsky et al. (1998), Berg and Pattillo (1999), Kaminsky and Reinhart (1999), and Goldstein et al., (2000). In their models, individual variables such as real effective exchange rate or debt to GDP levels are considered as a "signal" that a country is potentially in a crisis state when they exceed a specified threshold. While intuitively appealing, signal models are essentially univariate in nature. Kaminsky (1999) suggested a way of combining individual signals to form a composite index for prediction purposes, but this does not solve all problems. For illustration, assume that some of the signal variables are very closely correlated. They may each have a very high noise-to-signals ratio, even though all but one of them adds almost nothing to the collective analysis. The problem here is that the noise-to-signal weights are themselves based on univariate analysis.

The third type of financial crisis analysis looks at pooled panel data, employing discrete choice techniques in which macroeconomic and financial data are used to explain discrete crisis events in a range of countries. For instance, Eichengreen, Rose and Wyplosz (1996) adopted a probit model to analyze and predict the crisis for industrial countries using quarterly data between 1959 and 1993. Likewise, Berg and Pattillo (1999) also used a probit model to predict the currency crisis. Similarly, Kumar et al. (2003) utilized a logit model to predict emerging market currency crashes. However, these models are parametrically statistical models, which include several statistical assumptions and have weak robustness. Since a currency crisis is a rare event with nonlinear characteristics, it is difficult for these statistical models to capture the all possible crises for all the time. Furthermore, a great deal of data about different variables must be collected to construct these models.

The fourth or final type of financial crisis modeling is to employ some emerging artificial intelligent (AI) technique to predict the financial crisis state. Typical examples include Kim et al., (2004), Kim et al., (2004), and Yu et al. (2006). The first two studies applied a back-propagation neural network (BPNN) to predict the economic crisis level of South Korea using the Korean stock market index. While the last work presented by Yu et al. (2006) employed a general regression neural network (GRNN) to predict the currency crisis of Southeast Asia economies using some currency volatility indicators. However, some important shortcomings such as local minima, overfitting and slow convergence rate are often occurred in the neural network learning. These shortcomings lead to some unreliable prediction for financial crisis events when applying neural networks. In such backgrounds, it is therefore necessary to devise a new approach to assessing financial vulnerability and predicting financial crises level.

In this chapter, we attempt to develop a Hilbert-EMD-based support vector machine (SVM) approach to judging the financial crisis level using currency exchange rates. The EMD is the abbreviation of empirical mode decomposition, which is an effective time-frequent algorithm, based on the Hilbert-Huang-Transform (HHT), for the analysis of nonlinear and nonstationary data (Huang, Shen, Long, Wu, Shih, Zheng, Yen, Tung, & Liu, 1998). The support vector machine (SVM) used in this chapter is the support vector classification algorithm firstly proposed by Vapnik (1995), a quite popular tool for pattern recognition, and hence the process of building a financial crisis early-warning system or crisis forecasting model is transformed into a pattern recognition problem. Before applying SVM classification algorithm, the original exchange rate data are decomposed into multiple independent intrinsic mode components (IMCs) by Hilbert-EMD technique. These IMCs can represent different factors affecting currency exchange rate movement. Therefore the IMCs are considered as the independent variables for constructing a pattern recognition model. Using these IMCs, a SVM classification algorithm is used to predict the future financial crisis events based upon some historical data. For the applications of EMD and SVM, see Huang (2001) and Cristianini and Shawe-Taylor (2000) for more details.

A distinct characteristic of the proposed approach is that only currency exchange rate data are used. While in most previous studies, statistical methodologies for crisis forecasting require a large amount of data related to crisis which are usually difficult to obtain in reality because such a disastrous economic crisis occurs rarely or over a very short period of time. In addition, the exchange rate data is used to judge whether the economic condition reaches the crisis level. The main reasons of selecting exchange rate as a crisis judgment indicator rather than other economic indicators (e.g., stock index and interest rate) reflect two-fold. On the one hand, currency exchange rate is an important "indicator," which can reflect the economic condition fairly well. On the other hand, exchange rate usually shows the highest variability to economic volatility, which implies that they are more sensitive to economic changes.

The main motivation of this chapter is to employ a Hilbert-EMD-based SVM approach to constructing an early-warning system of financial crisis or financial crisis forecasting. The rest of the chapter is organized as follows. The first section describes the Hilbert-EMD-based SVM approach to financial crisis forecasting in detail. For illustration purposes, two typical Asian countries including South Korea and Thailand suffered from the 1997 disastrous financial crisis experience are selected to verify the effectiveness of the proposed Hilbert-EMD-based SVM methodology in the next section. The final section concludes the chapter.

HILBERT-EMD-BASED SVM APPROACH TO FINANCIAL CRISIS FORECASTING

In this section, an overall process of the Hilbert-EMD-based SVM approach is proposed for financial crisis forecasting. First of all, the Hilbert-EMD technique and SVM approach are briefly reviewed. Then the Hilbert-EMD-based SVM learning paradigm is presented.

Overview of Hilbert-EMD Technique

The empirical mode decomposition (EMD) method first proposed by Huang et al. (1998) is a form of adaptive time series decomposition technique using spectral analysis via Hilbert-Huang-Transform (HHT) for nonlinear and nonstationary time series data. Traditional forms of spectral analysis, like Fourier, assume that a time series (either linear or nonlinear) can be decomposed into a set of linear components. As the degree of nonlinearity and nonstationarity in a time series increases, the

Fourier decomposition often produces large sets of physically meaningless harmonics when applied to nonlinear time series (Huang, Shen, & Long, 1999). For wavelet analysis, it needs to select a filter function beforehand (Li, 2006), which is difficult for some unknown time series. Naturally, a new spectrum analysis method, EMD based on Hilbert-Huang-transform, is emerged.

The basic principle of EMD is to decompose a time series into a sum of intrinsic mode components (IMCs) with the following sifting procedure:

1. Identify all the local extrema including local maxima and minima of $x(t)$,
2. Connect all local extrema by a cubic spline line to generate its upper and lower envelopes $x_{up}(t)$ and $x_{low}(t)$.
3. Compute the point-by-point envelope mean $m(t)$ from upper and lower envelopes, that is, $m(t) = \left(x_{up}(t) + x_{low}(t)\right)/2$.
4. Extract the details, $d(t) = x(t) - m(t)$.
5. Check the properties of $d(t)$: (i) if $d(t)$ meets the above two requirements, an IMC is derived and replace $x(t)$ with the residual $r(t) = x(t) - d(t)$; (ii) if $d(t)$ is not an IMC, replace $x(t)$ with $d(t)$.
6. Repeat Steps (1) – (5) until the residual satisfies the following stopping condition:

$$\sum\nolimits_{t=1}^{T} \frac{\left[d_j(t) - d_{j+1}(t)\right]^2}{d_j^2(t)} < SC,$$

where $d_j(t)$ is the sifting result in the jth iteration, and SC is the stopping condition. Typically, it is usually set between 0.2 and 0.3.

Figure 1 shows the above steps with a real example, as illustrated below. Note that the arrow direction represents the sifting process of the EMD.

The EMD extracts the next IMC by applying the above procedure to the residual term $r_1(t) = x(t) - c_1(t)$, where $c_1(t)$ denotes the first IMC. The

Figure 1. The illustrative example for EMD sifting process

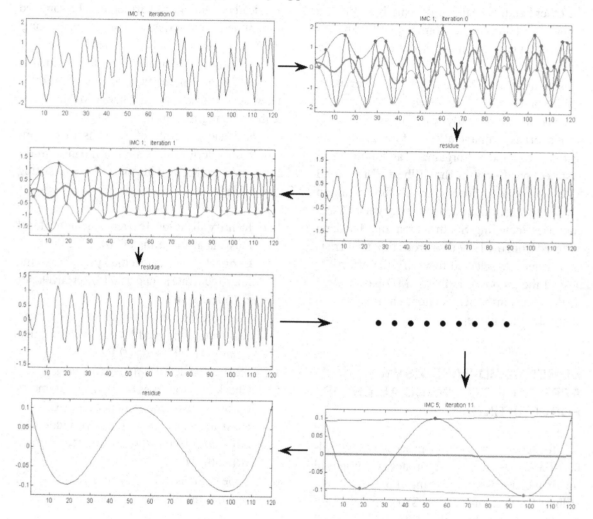

decomposition process can be repeated until the last residue $r(t)$ only has at most one local extremum or becomes a monotonic function from which no more IMCs can be extracted. A typical sifting process can be represented by a tree graph, as illustrated in Figure 2.

At the end of this sifting procedure, the time series $x(t)$ can be expressed by

$$x(t) = \sum_{j=1}^{p} c_j(t) + r_p(t) \qquad (1)$$

where p is the number of IMCs, $r_p(t)$ is the final residue, which is the main trend of $x(t)$, and $c_j(t)$

$(j = 1, 2, ..., p)$ are the IMCs, which are nearly orthogonal to each other, and all have nearly zero means. Thus, one can achieve a decomposition of the data series into m-empirical modes and a residue. The frequency components contained in each frequency band are different and they change with the variation of time series $x(t)$, while $r_p(t)$ represents the central tendency of time series $x(t)$. For later analysis, the residue can be seen as the $(p+1)$th IMC (i.e., c_{p+1}). Then the equation (1) can be rewritten as

Figure 2. The tree graph representation of the EMD sifting process

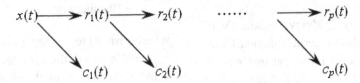

$$x(t) = \sum_{j=1}^{p+1} c_j(t) \qquad (2)$$

Overview of SVM

Support vector machine (SVM) was originally introduced by Vapnik (1995) in the 1990s. Before the SVM is introduced, many traditional statistical theories and neural network models had implemented the empirical risk minimization (ERM) principle. Different from the previous statistical and neural network models, the SVM implements the structure risk minimization (SRM) principle. The statistical and neural network models seek to minimize the mis-classification error or deviation from correct solution of the training data but the SVM searches to minimize an upper bound of generalization error. SVM mainly has two classes of applications: classification and regression. In this study, application of classification is discussed.

The basic idea of SVM is to use linear model to implement nonlinear class boundaries through some nonlinear mapping the input vector into the high-dimensional feature space. A linear model constructed in the new space can represent a nonlinear decision boundary in the original space. In the new space, an optimal separating hyperplane is constructed. Thus SVM is known as the algorithm that finds a special kind of linear model, the maximum margin hyperplane. The maximum margin hyperplane gives the maximum separation between the decision classes. The training examples that are closest to the maximum margin hyperplane are called support vectors. All other training examples are irrelevant for defining the binary class boundaries. Usually, the separating hyperplane is constructed in this high dimension feature space. The SVM classifier takes the form as

$$y = f(x) = \mathrm{sgn}(w \cdot \psi(x) + b) \qquad (3)$$

where $\psi(x) = \varphi_1(x), \varphi_2(x), \ldots, \varphi_N(x)$ is a nonlinear function employed to map the original input space R^n to N-dimensional feature space, w is the weight vector and b is a bias, which are obtained by solving the following optimization problem:

$$\begin{cases} \mathrm{Min} & \phi(w, \xi) = (1/2)\|w\|^2 + C\sum_{i=1}^{m}\xi_i \\ \mathrm{s.t.} & y_i[\varphi(x_i) \cdot w + b] \geq 1 - \xi_i \\ & \xi_i \geq 0, i = 1,2,\ldots,m \end{cases} \qquad (4)$$

where $\|w\|$ is a distance parameter, C is a margin parameter and ξ_i is positive slack variable, which is necessary to allow misclassification. Through computation of Equation (4), the optimal separating hyperplane is obtained in the following form:

$$y = \mathrm{sgn}\left(\sum_{SV}\alpha_i y_i \varphi(x_i)\varphi(x_j) + b\right) \qquad (5)$$

where SV are the support vectors. If there exist a kernel function such that $K(x_i, x_j) = (\varphi(x_i), \varphi(x_j))$, it is usually unnecessary to explicitly know what $\varphi(x)$ is, and we only need to work with a kernel function in the training algorithm, i.e., the optimal classifier can be represented by

$$y = \text{sgn}\left(\sum\nolimits_{SV} \alpha_i y_i K(x_i, x_j) + b\right) \qquad (6)$$

Any function satisfying Mercy condition (Vapnik, 1995) can be used as the kernel function. Common examples of the kernel function are the polynomial kernel $K(x_i, x_j) = (x_i x_j^T + 1)^d$ and the Gaussian radial basis function $K(x_i, x_j) = \exp\left(-(x_i - x_j)^2 / 2\sigma^2\right)$. The construction and selection of kernel function is important to SVM, but in practice the kernel function is often given directly. It is interesting that the structure of SVM model is similar to that of neural networks, as illustrated in Figure 3. In the same way, the SVM consists of an input layer, middle layer or transformation layer and output layer. The difference is that every node output of the middle layer is a support vector transformed by the kernel function $k(x, \hat{x})$. Note that the SVM could overcome the important drawbacks of the neural networks, such as local minima and overfitting (Vapnik, 1995).

Hilbert-EMD-Based SVM Approach to Financial Crisis Forecasting

As earlier noted, a financial crisis event is defined as a large devaluation of currency which far exceeds previous devaluations. From this definition and some previous studies such as Kumar et al. (2003) and Edison (2000), a crisis can be defined as an event where the rate of change (ROC) of exchange rate ($ROC_t = (e_t - e_{t-1})/ e_{t-1}$) exceeds an extreme value:

$$\text{Crisis} = \begin{cases} 1, & \text{if } ROC > \mu_{ROC} + 2.5\sigma_{ROC}, \\ 0, & \text{otherwise.} \end{cases} \qquad (7)$$

where crisis = 1 represents the occurrence of crisis, μ_{ROC} and σ_{ROC} are the sample mean and sample standard deviation of the ROC respectively. A crisis is said to occur when the ROC is more than 2.5 standard deviations above the mean. Although the choice of 2.5 as a threshold value is somewhat arbitrary, the cataloging of crises obtained by this method tends to follow closely the chronology of currency market disruptions described in the literature (Kaminsky et al., 1998; Kaminsky & Reinhart, 1999). From Equation (7), the main task of crisis forecasting model is to judge whether the crisis occurs or not. Therefore two patterns, that is, crisis occurrence and un-occurrence, will be recognized using the exchange rates. Note that currency exchange rates against the US dollar are specified in advance. Different from previous studies, our proposed crisis forecasting approach attempts to apply exchange rates only to judge the occurrence of crisis. To construct a SVM classification model, the Hilbert-EMD technique is used to formulate the independent variables of SVM. Generally speaking, the Hilbert-EMD-based SVM classification model for crisis forecasting consists of three stages: data decomposition stage, SVM training stage, and crisis forecasting stage.

Stage I: Data decomposition. In order to construct a SVM classification model, the original exchange rate series are decomposed into various independent intrinsic mode components (IMCs) with a range of frequency scales. As earlier noted, these IMCs can be seen as different factors affecting financial crisis. Therefore, the produced different IMCs can formulate the inputs of SVM classification model. Figure 4 presents an illustrative decomposition example of a time series with p IMCs and one residue. From Figure 4, it is easy to find that the SVM has $p+1$ input variables.

Figure 3. The generic structure of SVM model

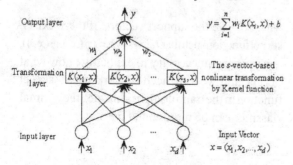

Figure 4. The EMD decomposition to form the inputs of the SVM model

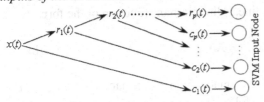

EXPERTMENT STUDY

For verification purposes, some experiments with two typical Asian countries are conducted in this chapter. First of all, the data description and experimental design are presented and then the experimental results are reported.

Data Description and Experiment Design

In our experimental analysis, we set out to examine the financial crisis condition using two typical Asian economies such as South Korea and Thailand. As previously mentioned, financial crisis research is an important and meaningful topic for macro policymakers, financial regulators, institutional managers and a variety of investors. Main reasons are that the financial crisis prediction can provide some effective decision suggestions in establishing and carrying out some macro economic policies for macro policymakers and financial regulators, and meantime, the financial crisis forecasting can create new profit making opportunity for market speculators and arbitrageurs and hedge against potential market risks for financial managers and many investors. Therefore, it has profound implications for researchers and practitioners alike to accurately predict the financial crisis conditions (Yu et al., 2006).

The data used in this study are daily exchange rate data for two currency exchange rates against the US dollar (Korean won, Thai baht) and are obtained from the PACIFIC Exchange Rate Service (http://fx.sauder.ubc.ca/) provided by Professor Werner Antweiler, University of British Columbia, Vancouver, Canada. The main reason for choosing the two countries in this study is that these two countries are typical representatives of Asian economies suffered from the 1997 disastrous financial crisis experience. Particularly, our sample data span the period from January 2, 1996 to December 31, 1998 with a total of 755 observa-

Stage II: SVM training. Once the input variables or independent variables are determined, the SVM training stage can be started. In SVM, the Gaussian radial function is used as the kernel function in this study. Thus two parameter kernel parameters σ and margin parameters C are needed to be tuned by cross-validation (CV) technique. In addition, the 1997 exchange rate series data are adopted to train the SVM. The main reason for using this data is that the 1997 experience can set a good benchmark for all Asian economic sectors.

Stage III: Crisis forecasting. After training the SVM, we can use the trained SVM to predict the future financial crisis conditions for out-of-sample data in the final stage. In terms of above work, we classify the financial crisis conditions for the period from 1999-2004 for Asian economies. When an unknown vector with $p+1$ dimensions is input, the one with the highest output value is to be picked as the final SVM output, that is, the pattern to which the given financial condition belongs. Particularly, output "0" is classified as non-crisis pattern, while output "1" is classified as crisis pattern, implying the financial condition might be trapped in a crisis period.

In order to verify the effectiveness of the proposed Hilbert-EMD-based SVM approach to crisis forecasting, two typical Asian countries including South Korea and Thailand suffered from the 1997 disastrous financial crisis experience are used as testing objects.

tions. For purposes of training and testing, we take daily data from January 2, 1996 to December 31, 1997 as in-sample (training periods) data sets (506 observations). We also take data from January 2, 1998 to December 31, 1998 as out-of-sample (test periods) data sets (249 observations), and these are used to evaluate the good or bad performance of our currency crisis prediction. There are two main reasons for such a data partition. The one is that the 1997-1998 Asian financial turmoil provides a good experimental example. That is, both crisis samples and non-crisis samples are provided for the training and testing periods, which are useful for the intelligent learning algorithms. The other is that we are difficult to test the effectiveness of the proposed approach if we use other samples without crisis occurrence. In order to save space, the original data are not listed here, detailed data can be obtained from the above Web site.

To evaluate the forecasting ability of the proposed Hilbert-EMD-based SVM approach to financial crisis forecasting, we select some other forecasting methods from the existing literature—such as logit model (Kumar et al., 2003), probit model (Berg & Pattillo, 1999; Eichengreen et al., 1996), signal approach (Kaminsky et al., 1998; Berg & Pattillo, 1999; Goldstein et al., 2000; Eichengreen et al., 1996) and GRNN model (Yu et al., 2006)—for comparative purposes.

In addition, we also compare the forecasting performance with two typical discriminant analysis models, that is, linear discriminant analysis (LDA) and quadratic discriminant analysis (QDA). LDA can handle the case in which the within-class frequencies are unequal and its performance has been examined on randomly generated test data. This method maximizes the ratio of between-class variance to the within-class variance in any particular data set, thereby guaranteeing maximal separability. QDA is similar to LDA, only dropping the assumption of equal to be a quadratic surface (e.g., ellipsoid, hyperboloid, etc.) in the maximum likelihood argument with normal distributions. Interested readers can refer

to Hair, Anderson, Tatham, and Black (1995) for a more detailed description. In this study, we derive a linear discriminant function of the form:

$$L(X) = \mathbf{A}X^T \tag{8}$$

and a quadratic discriminant function that has the following form:

$$Q(X) = \mathbf{A} + \mathbf{B}X^T + X\mathbf{K}X^T \tag{9}$$

where a_i ($i = 0, 1, 2, …, 6$), $\mathbf{A}$, $\mathbf{B}$, $\mathbf{K}$ are coefficients to be estimated. Note that the independent variable X is composed of IMCs obtained from Hilbert-EMD in these two discriminant analysis approaches. Finally, the classification accuracy is used to measure the prediction performance of the proposed approach.

Finally, in the proposed approach, the stop criterion of the Hilbert-EMD procedure is set to $SC = 0.3$. For the SVM model, the Gaussian kernel with $\sigma^2 = 45$ and margin parameter $C = 10$ are used. Note that the above parameters are obtained by trial and error testing based on the experimental data.

Experimental Results

In this section, a detailed process of the proposed approach is first presented via the testing examples. Then we report classification results for the training data and testing data. For further comparison, the results for different models are also provided.

A. Methodology Implementation Process

Following the proposed approach, the first step is that exchange rates data of the two typical economies can be decomposed into some intrinsic mode components via Hilbert-Huang transformation technique. Figure 5 presents the decomposed results for Korean Won (KRW) and Figure 6 gives

Figure 5. The EMD decomposition results of Korean Won (KRW)

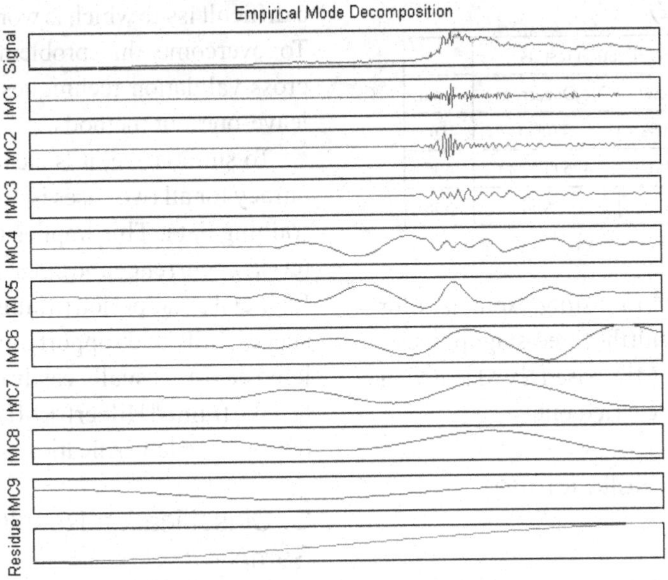

the graphical decomposition representation for Thai Baht (THB). From Figures 5 and 6, it is easy to find that the KRW data consists of nine IMCs and one residue, while THB data are composed of seven IMCs and one residual term. These IMCs can formulate a basis of the Hilbert-EMD-based SVM learning paradigm.

The second step is to utilize the IMCs to training the SVM classification models, that is, SVM training. In this stage, the first work is to determine the training targets. Using Equation (7), the training targets can be obtained. Using the IMCs and training targets, the SVM training process are easy to be implemented. The third step is to

Figure 6. The EMD decomposition results of Thai Baht (THB)

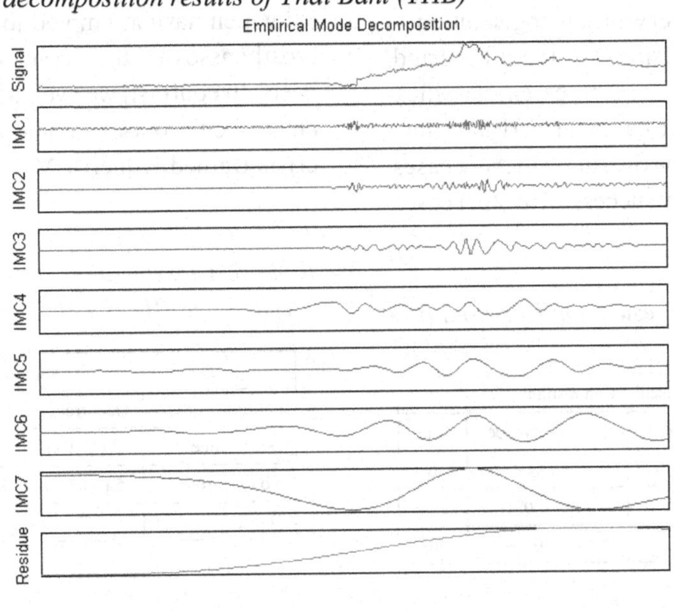

Table 1. Classification results for Korean Won (Periods: 96:01-97:12)

Patterns	Classification results		Total
	Occurrence	No Occurrence	
Occurrence	10 (100%)	0 (0%)	10
No Occurrence	0 (0%)	496 (100%)	496
Total	10	496	506

apply the trained SVM to testing exemplars for verification purpose. With the three-stage process, the proposed Hilbert-EMD-based SVM learning approach is easy to be carried out.

B. Classification Results for the Training Samples

As earlier indicated, the 1996-1997 exchange rates series data are used as the training sample for training purpose. Accordingly, the classification results are shown in Tables 1 and 2.

From Tables 1 and 2, we can find two distinct features. On the one hand, the two patterns of the financial crisis can be classified correctly in all cases. In particular, the accuracy in classifying two patterns is very high in the two cases. The classification accuracy arrives at 100 percent. This implies that the proposed Hilbert-EMD-based SVM approach is a very promising solution to financial crisis forecasting. On the other hand, there may be a problem for 100 percent classification accuracy of the two cases. The crisis-trained SVM model seems to be overfitted in these cases, though it is usually very successful in other cases.

Table 2. Classification results for Thai Baht (Periods: 96:01-97:12)

Patterns	Classification results		Total
	Occurrence	No Occurrence	
Occurrence	6 (100%)	0 (0%)	6
No Occurrence	0 (0%)	500 (100%)	500
Total	6	500	506

The question of how to avoid SVM overfitting is a difficult issue which is worth exploring further. To overcome this problem, we suggest using cross-validation techniques, such as *k*-fold and leave-one-out methods.

To summarize, it is clear that the overall accuracy for all two cases is quite promising for the training data. This implies that the two patterns (crisis occurrence and not occurrence) in the 1997 financial crisis period (training data) are captured successfully and support our claim that crisis-related data are usually easily classified. In order to test the trained Hilbert-EMD-based SVM model, out-of-sample verification is necessary.

C. Classification Results for Testing Sample

To verify the effectiveness of the proposed currency crisis forecasting approach, we take the data from January 2, 1998 to December 31, 1998 as our out-of-sample data (249 observations). This is a distinct feature of our study, which differs from many previous studies in that we focus on the degree to which currency crises can be predicted. Earlier studies take a more descriptive approach, relating the occurrence of crises to contemporaneous rather than lagged variables. Studies which have attempted to predict crises have mostly assessed their results on an "in-sample" basis. In contrast, we evaluate the predictions on an explicitly out-of-sample basis. Applying the crisis-trained Hilbert-EMD-based SVM model,

Table 3. Classification results for Korean Won (Periods: 98:01-98:12)

Patterns	Classification results		Total
	Occurrence	No Occurrence	
Occurrence	2 (100%)	0 (0%)	2
No Occurrence	5 (2.02%)	242 (97.98%)	247
Total	7	242	249

Table 4. Classification results for Thai Baht (Periods: 98:01-98:12)

Patterns	Classification results		Total
	Occurrence	No Occurrence	
Occurrence	5 (83.33%)	1 (16.67%)	6
No Occurrence	3 (1.23%)	240 (98.77%)	243
Total	8	241	249

empirical testing is performed. The detailed test results are shown in Tables 3 and.4.

From the results shown in Tables 3 and 4, we can draw the following three conclusions. First of all, the classification accuracy for the test period is not as good as that for the training period. In general, however, the results obtained are quite satisfactory. Secondly, among the two cases, the classification accuracy for the Korean Won is 97.99 percent (244/249) and the accuracy for Thai Baht arrives at 98.39 percent (245/249). These classification results for testing data also demonstrate the effectiveness of the proposed Hilbert-EMD-based SVM learning paradigm. Thirdly, as a rare event, financial crisis is difficult to be captured in the economic life. In our study, the proposed approach is rather promising. Finally, one of the main contributions of our results is that the crisis trained Hilbert-EMD-based SVM model is able to provide an efficient decision sign and an early warning signal about whether the financial condition has entered a crisis state.

To summarize, application of the crisis-trained Hilbert-EMD-based SVM approach to the test data shows very accurate classification results in all cases in the sense that the proposed model is worth generalizing for more countries.

D. Results of Comparison with Other Methods

Each of the forecasting models described in the last section is estimated and validated by in-sample data. The model estimation and selection process is then followed by an empirical evaluation, which is based on the out-of-sample data. At this stage, the models' performance is measured using the total classification accuracy for simplicity. Table 5 shows the results of comparison.

From Table 5, we can conclude three aspects: (i) QDA outperforms LDA in terms of the total classification ratio for all tested cases. The main reason for this is that LDA assumes that all classes have equal covariance. In fact, different classes often have different covariances. hus, heteroscedastic models are more appropriate than homoscedastic ones. (ii) Although the signal, logit and probit models yield confused results, their performance is better than that of the LDA and QDA models. One possible reason is that it is easier for the former to capture possible crisis signals. The reasons for the confused results of the three approaches are worth exploring further. (iii) Another distinct characteristic of the proposed Hilbert-EMD-based SVM approach is that this approach only depends on one variable. This is distinctly different from previous approaches, such as sign approach, logit and probit models presented in the last studies. Most previous studies depend on many independent variables, which increase the difficulty of collecting related data. (iv) The Hilbert-EMD-based SVM approach performs the best, implying that our proposed approach is a competitive alternative model for financial crisis forecasting among the methods tested.

Table 5. Comparisons of forecasting performance for different methods (%)

	LDA	QDA	Signal	Logit	Probit	GRNN	SVM
KRW	68.67	75.10	79.52	78.31	84.74	92.77	97.99
THB	57.77	63.61	78.95	84.73	87.64	93.82	98.39

CONCLUSION

In this chapter, a Hilbert-EMD-based SVM learning approach to financial crisis forecasting model is proposed using data from the 1996-1998 Asian financial crisis. Applications of the proposed Hilbert-EMD-based SVM learning paradigm to test data display surprisingly high accuracy in judging the financial crisis level of each country, revealing that the proposed Hilbert-EMD-based SVM approach might also be useful for other countries trying to build a financial crisis forecasting model or a financial crisis early-warning system. Furthermore, comparing our model with the other forecasting methods, experimental results show that the proposed Hilbert-EMD-based SVM approach is superior to the other classification methods in financial crisis prediction, implying that our proposed approach can be used as a promising tool for financial crisis forecasting. More important, our proposed approach can provide an intelligent financial risk management solution for complex financial systems.

However, there are still some problems for the proposed approach in the financial crisis forecasting. For example, a financial crisis is actually a continuous rare event because it would hold on an inestimable period once a financial crisis really started. But in the study, the financial crisis is treated as a discrete rare event for simplicity. In addition, if one country are adopting basket-money policy or pegging their money significantly for US dollar (i.e., adopting a "dirty-floating" policy), it may be intractable with the proposed approach. That is, the proposed intelligent methodology is only suitable for the countries which are adopting the free-floating exchange rate policy. For these potential problems, we will look into these issues in the future.

ACKNOWLEDGMENT

This work is supported by the grants from the National Natural Science Foundation of China (NSFC No. 70221001, 70601029), the Chinese Academy of Sciences (CAS No. 3547600), the Academy of Mathematics and Systems Sciences (AMSS No. 3543500) of CAS, and the Strategic Research Grant of City University of Hong Kong (SRG No. 7001677, 7001806).

REFERENCES

Berg, A., & Pattillo, C. (1999). Predicting currency crises: The indicators approach and an alternative. *Journal of Money and Finance, 18*, 561–586.

Blanco, H., & Garber, P.M. (1986). Recurrent devaluations and speculative attacks on the Mexican peso. *Journal of Political Economy, 94*, 148-166.

Cole, H.L., & Kehoe, T.J. (1996). A self-fulfilling model of Mexico's 1994-95 debt crisis. *Journal of International Economics, 41*, 309-330.

Cristianini, N., & Shawe-Taylor, J. (2000). *An introduction to support vector machines and other Kernel-based learning methods*. London: Cambridge University Press.

Cumby, R., & van Wijnbergen, S. (1989). Financial policy and speculative runs with a crawling peg—Argentina 1979–1981. *Journal of International Economics, 17*, 111-127.

Edison, H. (2000). *Do indicators of financial crises work? An evaluation of an early warning system*. International Finance Discussion Papers No. 675, Board of Governors of the Federal Reserve Systems.

Eichengreen, B., Rose, A.K., & Wyplosz, C. (1996). Exchange market mayhem: The antecedents and aftermath of speculative attacks. *Economic Policy, 21*, 249-312.

Flood, R.P., & Marion, N.P. (1999). Perspectives on the recent currency crisis literature. *International Journal of Finance and Economics*, *4*(1), 1-26.

Frankel, J.A., & Rose, A.K. (1996). Currency crashes in emerging markets: An empirical treatment. *Journal of International Economics*, *41*, 351-366.

Goldstein, M. (1996). *The seven deadly sins: Presumptive indicators of vulnerability to financial crises in emerging economies: Origin and policy options*. Economic papers 46, Bank for International Settlements (BIS).

Goldstein, M., Kaminsky, G.L., & Reinhart, C.M. (2000). *Assessing financial vulnerability: An early warning system for emerging markets*. Washington, DC: Institute for International Economics.

Hair, J.F., Anderson, R.E., Tatham, R.L., & Black, W.C. (1995). *Multivariate data analysis*. New York: Prentice-Hall.

Huang, N.E. (2001). Review of empirical mode decomposition. *Proceedings of SPIE*, 3, pp. 71-80, Orlando, USA.

Huang, N.E., Shen, Z., & Long, S.R. (1999). A new view of nonlinear water waves: The Hilbert spectrum. *Annual Review of Fluid Mechanics*, *31*, 417-457.

Huang, N.E., Shen, Z., Long, S.R., Wu, M.C., Shih, H.H., Zheng, Q., Yen, N.C., Tung, C.C., & Liu, H.H. (1998). The empirical mode decomposition and the Hilbert spectrum for nonlinear and nonstationary time series analysis. *Proceedings of the Royal Society A: Mathematical, Physical & Engineering Sciences*, *454*, 903-995.

Jeanne, O., & Masson, P. (2000). Currency crises, sunspots, and Markov-switching regimes. *Journal of International Economics*, *50*(2), 327-350.

Kaminsky, G.L. (1999). *Currency and banking crises: the early warnings of distress*. IMF Working Paper 99-178, International Monetary Fund, Washington, DC.

Kaminsky, G.L., Lizondo, S., & Reinhart, C. (1998). *Leading indicators of currency crises*. International Monetary Fund (IMF) Staff Papers, 45, 1-48.

Kaminsky, G.L., & Reinhart, C.M. (1999). The twin crises: Te causes of banking and balance-of-payments problems. *American Economic Review*, *89*(3), 473-500.

Kim, T.Y., Hwang, C., & Lee, J. (2004). Korean economic condition indicator using a neural network trained on the 1997 crisis. *Journal of Data Science*, *2*, 371-381.

Kim, T.Y., Oh, K.J., Sohn, I., & Hwang, C. (2004). Usefulness of artificial neural networks for early warning systems of economic crisis. *Expert Systems with Applications*, *26*, 583-590.

Kumar, M., Moorthy, U., & Perraudin, W. (2003). Predicting emerging market currency crashes. *Journal of Empirical Finance*, *10*, 427-454.

Li, X. (2006). Temporal Structure of Neuronal Population Oscillations with Empirical Mode Decomposition. *Physics Letters A*, *356*, 237-241.

Sachs, J.D., Tornell, A., & Velasco, A. (1996). *Financial crises in emerging markets: the lessons from 1996*. Brookings Papers on Economic Activity, 147-215.

Vapnik, V.N. (1995). *The nature of statistical learning theory*. New York: Springer.

Yu, L., Lai, K.K., & Wang, S.Y. (2006). Currency crisis forecasting with general regression neural networks. *International Journal of Information Technology and Decision Making*, *5*(3), 437-454.

Chapter XVIII
Virtual Sampling with Data Construction Method

Chun-Jung Huang
National Tsing Hua University, Taiwan, ROC

Hsiao-Fan Wang
National Tsing Hua University, Taiwan, ROC

ABSTRACT

*One of the key problems in supervised learning is due to the insufficient size of the training data set. The natural way for an intelligent learning process to counter this problem and successfully generalize is to exploit prior information that may be available about the domain or that can be learned from prototypical examples. According to the concept of creating **virtual samples**, the intervalized kernel method of density estimation (IKDE) was proposed to improve the learning ability from a small data set. To demonstrate its theoretical validity, we provided a theorem based on Decomposition Theory. In addition, we proposed an alternative approach to achieving the better learning performance of IKDE.*

INTRODUCTION

Lack of referenced data is very often responsible for poor performances of learning. In many cases, difficulty, if not impossible, in collecting additional data often cause unsatisfactory solutions. For example, due to the shorter life cycle of a product, prior management is very important, because it acquires management knowledge in the early stages, yet the accumulated information is often not sufficient for supporting the decisions. It indeed has been a challenge for managers. Because of insufficient data in the initial period of a manufacturing system, the derived management model may not be reliable and stable.

One major contribution to the above issue has been given by Abu-Mostafa (1993) who developed a methodology for integrating different kinds of "hints" (prior knowledge) into usual learning-from-example procedure. By this way, the "hints" can be represented by new examples, generated from the existing data set by applying transformations that are known to leave the function to be learned invariant. Then, Niyogi, Girosi, and Tomaso (1998) modified "hints" into "*virtual samples*" and applied it to improve the learning performances of artificial neural networks such as Back- Propagation and Radial Basis Function Networks. In fact, it is evident that generating more resembling samples from the small training set can make the learning tools perform well.

Recently, Li and Lin (2006) combined the concept of *virtual sample* generation and the method of intervalized kernel density estimation (IKDE) to overcome the difficulty of learning with insufficient data at the early manufacturing stages. From the Li and Lin's results, it can be noted that, when the size of virtual data increases, the average learning accuracy would decrease. This is because that when using IKDE for *virtual sample* generation, an actual probability density function should firstly be estimated from the original data set. Then, due to the unbounded universal discourse of the density estimation function, the more are

the *virtual samples* generated, the larger is the Type Two error in Statistics as shown in Figure 1 (Wackerly, Mendenhall, & Scheaffer, 1996). Therefore, even though creating *virtual samples* by an estimated function is a way to overcome the difficulty in learning with insufficient data, the prediction capability remains a critical issue.

In this chapter, after introducing the main concept and procedure of IKDE, we used Decomposition Theory to provide a theoretical support for using IKDE to improve the learning ability from a small data set. In addition, to overcome the possible Type Two error in prediction, an alternative method named *Data Construction Method (DCM)* was proposed. To compare their performance, we demonstrated a numerical case adopted from Li and Lin's and finally, discussion and conclusions were drawn.

The Procedure of Virtual Sample Generation

Because insufficient data is very often responsible for poor performances of learning, how to extract the significant information for inferences is a critical issue. It is well known that one of the basic theories in Statistics is the *Central Limit Theorem* (Ross, 1987). This theorem asserts that when a sample size is *large* (≥ 25 or 30), the x-bar distribution is approximately normal without considering the population distribution. Therefore, when a given sample is less than 25 (or 30), it is regarded as a *small sample*. Although "*small*" is not well defined, it is in general related to the concept of accuracy. Huang (2002) has clarified this concept which will be adopted in our study and thus presented by the following definition:

Definition 2.1 Small Samples (Huang, 2002)

Let $X = \{x_i | i = 1, 2, \ldots, n\}$ be a given sample drawn from a population. We assume that X will

Figure 1. The relationship among the population, obtained data and virtual data (Li & Lin, 2006)

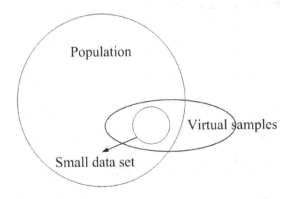

be employed to estimate a relationship R defined on Ω. The set of all models by which we can estimate R with a given sample is called the operator space, denoted by Γ. We use $r(x)$ to denote the value of R at a point $x \in \Omega$, $r_X^\gamma(x)$ to denote the estimate with X by γ, and $|r_X^\gamma(x) - r(x)|$ to denote the estimate bias $\forall \gamma \in \Gamma, \exists x \in \Omega$.

X is called a ***small sample*** or an insufficient data set if and only if its size n is too small to provide the necessary accuracy which means the similarity between $r_X^\gamma(x)$ and $r(x)$ for recognizing a relationship of the population from which X was drawn.

Due to the key problem in prediction from insufficient size of the training data set, IKED was developed and used for estimating the actual probability density function. Then, using the estimation function, more data can be generated to contribute a new training data set. The detailed concept is explained below:

The Intervalized Kernel Density Estimation (IKDE)

In Figure 2, when a set of observations with size n, $\{x_1, ..., x_n\}$ is given with a bandwidth (one half of bin width) h, the probability of observations can be estimated by

$$f(x) = \lim_{h \to \infty} \frac{1}{2h} P(x - h < X < x + h) \qquad (1)$$

or (see Box 1).

To express the naive density estimator, formula (3) below is employed

$$\widehat{f}(x) = \frac{1}{n} * \sum_{i=1}^{n} \frac{1}{h} w\left(\frac{x - X_i}{h}\right), \text{ where}$$

$$w\left(\frac{x - X_i}{h}\right) = \begin{cases} 0.5, & |(x - X_i)/h| < 1 \\ 0, & \text{otherwise} \end{cases} \qquad (3)$$

Giving m different smoothing parameters, $h_j, j = 1, ..., m$, n data can be intervalized, where each h_j is tied to a number of samples, n_j. Then, using a kernel function, $K_j(\cdot)$ with its central location, c_j, the method of IKDE can be formulated as

$$\widehat{f}(x) = \sum_{j=1}^{m} \frac{1}{n_j} \frac{1}{h_j} K_j\left(\frac{x - c_j}{h_j}\right),$$

$$\text{where } n = \sum_{j=1}^{m} n_j \qquad (4)$$

Since the value of h will affect the distribu-

Box 1.

$$\widehat{f}(x) = \frac{1}{2h} * \frac{\text{number of } X_1 \ ..., X_n \text{ falling in } (x - h, x + h)}{n} \qquad (2)$$

Figure 2. A histogram has identical bandwidth for each bin (Li & Lin, 2006)

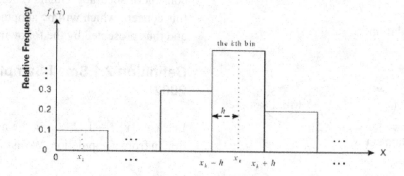

tion of the function, many researches have been devoted to finding an appropriate h by minimizing the empirical error such as mean square error, and mean integrated square error; or by maximizing the likelihood of estimators. Different from these approaches, Li and Lin (2006) has proposed the following intuitive rules for the selection of h, which have shown to be able to provide a reliable density estimate function for a small data set:

- **Rule 1:** if a data set with size n concentrated on one location, then $h = \sigma_X/n$, where σ_X is the standard deviation of variable X in the selected data set.
- **Rule 2:** if n data separately concentrated on two locations or more, then $h_j = \sigma_X^{0.5}/n_j$, $1 \leq j \leq m$, and $n = n_1 + n_2 + \ldots + n_m$.
- **Rule 3:** if n data grouped around one location, then $h = \sigma_{X|Y}$, where $\sigma_{X|Y}$ is the corresponding conditional standard deviation.
- **Rule 4:** if n data separately grouped around two locations or more, then $h_j = \sigma_X^{0.5}/n_j$, $1 \leq j \leq m$, and $n = n_1 + n_2 + \ldots + n_m$.

After refining the form of kernel estimator into a Gaussian function, $(\sqrt{2\pi})^{-1} e^{-\frac{t^2}{2}}$, $t \in (-\infty, \infty)$, Equation (4) can be rewritten into (see Box 2).

For fitting **small samples** in the learning process, IKDE can assist in generating **virtual samples** as additional instances added to the learning system. Although IKDE is intuitively valid and numerically superior to the other methods, lack of theoretical evidence still can not guarantee its performance. We hereby demonstrate its theoretical background as follows.

The Validation of IKDE

Giving a set of observations A with size n, let $A = \{a_i(k_i) | 1 \leq i \leq n, a_i \in \mathbb{R}, k_i \in \mathbb{N}, a_i \leq a_{i+1}\}$ where k_i are the frequency of a_i. Because A is bounded and closed (Huang & Wang, 2006) in $\mathbb{R}$, based on *Heine-Borel Theory*, A is *compact* (Marsden, 1993).

With a compact A, there exists a finite number of *classes* (*covers*) to contain A. According to equation (5), different h values will produce different numbers of classes as shown in Figure 3.

To verify the validity of the h value derived from four rules above, let us first define some concepts:

Definition 2.2 Possibility Function (Spott, 1999; Steuer, 1986)

Let X be a universe of discourse and $A \subseteq X$. Define the relative frequency of appearance of each datum a_i by the degree of compatibility of $a_i(k_i)$. Then a possibility function $\pi_A(a_i)$ defined by A: $X \rightarrow [0, 1]$ is postulated by $\pi_A(a_i) = k_i / |A|$, $1 \leq i \leq n$ where $|A|$ is the cardinality of A.

Then, referred to equation (5), let us define the possibility distribution and the maximal respective possibility of each class be K_j and c_j, $1 \leq j \leq m$, respectively where m is the class number, then all kernel functions can be aggregated as a density estimation function defined below.

Definition 2.3 The Density Estimation Function

Giving K_j and c_j, $1 \leq j \leq m$, when K_j are discrete, a density estimation function, $L(K_1, K_2, \ldots, K_m)$, is defined by aggregating $\{(c_j, K_j) | 1 \leq j \leq m\}$ as equation (5).

Box 2.

$$\widehat{f}(x) = \sum_{j=1}^{m} \frac{1}{n_j} \frac{1}{h_j} ((\sqrt{2\pi})^{-1} \exp(-(x - c_j)^2 / 2 * h_j^2)), (x \in -\infty, \infty) \text{ and } n = \sum_{j=1}^{m} n_j \quad (5)$$

Figure 3. (a) The original data with a four-modal shape; (b), (c) the internalization of 1 bin and 2 bins; (d) the internalization with various h (Li & Lin, 2006)

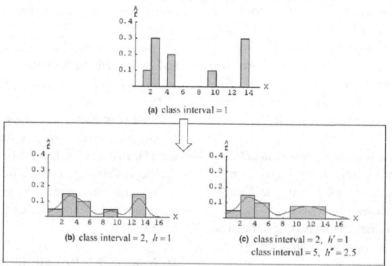

Then, an *Extended Decomposition Theorem* proved in Theorem 2.1 shows that $L(K_1, K_2,..., K_m)$ is a sufficient representative to the original set A.

Theorem 2.1 The Extended Decomposition Theorem

$$\{(a_i, \pi_A(a_i)) \mid 1 \le i \le n\} \cong L(K_1, K_2,..., K_m).$$

Proof

Since the distribution of $\{(a_i, \pi_A(a_i)) \mid 1 \le i \le n\}$ can be decomposed into finite modals K_j with respect to central locations c_j, $1 \le j \le m$, based on *Decomposition Theorem* [3], we have

$$\pi_A(a_i) = \max_{0 \le \alpha \le 1}\left[\alpha \cdot \chi_{A,\alpha}(a_i)\right], \forall a_i \in A, 1 \le i \le n \quad (6)$$

where $\chi_{A,\alpha}$ is the Characteristic function of A_α with .

Then, equation (6) can be rewritten as seen in Box 3.

Therefore, based on Theorem 2.1, we have proved the equivalence between $\{(a_i, \pi_A(a_i)) \mid 1 \le i \le n\}$ and $L(K_1, K_2,..., K_m)$. Therefore, $L(K_1, K_2,..., K_m)$ can be approximated a small-data-set A. This, in turn, provides a theoretical support for IKDE.

Box 3.

$$\pi_A(a_i) = \{\frac{\pi_A(a_1)}{a_1} + \frac{\pi_A(a_2)}{a_2} + \cdots + \frac{\pi_A(a_n)}{a_n}\} = \{K_1 \cup K_2 \cup \cdots \cup K_m\}$$
$$\{= \max_{0 \le \alpha \le 1}[\alpha \cdot \chi_{K_j,\alpha}(a_i)] \mid 1 \le j \le m, 1 \le i \le n\}$$
$$\supseteq \{\max[\max_{\alpha \ge \pi_A(c_j)}(\alpha \cdot \chi_{K_j,\alpha}(c_j)), \max_{\alpha < \pi_A(c_j)}(\alpha \cdot \chi_{K_j,\alpha}(c_j)) \mid 1 \le j \le m]\}$$

Box 3.

Step 0: Given a $k>1$ and set $t=1$;

Step 1: Set an arbitrary set $B=\{1, b\}$ with $b>1$, and input a sample set $\Omega=\{A_j \mid 1\le j\le n\}$ are categorical data with m attributes, and each datum $A_j=\{a_i^j \mid 1\le i\le m\}$. Then let $U_i=\{a_i^1, a_i^2, \cdots, a_i^n\}$ be the total count of each attribute;

Step 2: Let $\text{mod}_{1\le i\le m}$ equal to the mode of $\{a_i^1, a_i^2, \cdots, a_i^n\}$. Translate A_j into $A_j' = \{a_i^1-\text{mod}_{i=1}, a_i^2-\text{mod}_{i=2}, \cdots, a_i^n-\text{mod}_{i=m}\}$, and then U_i into $U_i'=\{a_i^1-\text{mod}_i, a_i^2-\text{mod}_i, \cdots, a_i^n-\text{mod}_i\}$;

Step 3: Let $Z_{i,t} \equiv U_i'(:)B^{(t)} = \{z_i^{q_t} \mid 1\le q\le Q, 1\le i\le m\}$ be the **multiset division** procedure where the division time is defined as $t=0, 1, 2, \ldots$;

Step 4: Rescaling the generated data: Suppose $t=T$, compute $\{(z_1^{1_T}+\text{mod}_{i=1}, z_2^{1_T}+\text{mod}_{i=2}, \cdots, z_m^{1_T}+\text{mod}_{i=m}), \ldots, (z_1^{Q_T}+\text{mod}_{i=1}, z_2^{Q_T}+\text{mod}_{i=2}, \cdots, z_m^{Q_T}+\text{mod}_{i=m})\}$ the final data set $\Omega_T = \{A_1, A_2, \ldots, A_Q\}$ of size Q with m attributes.

The Proposed Method, Data Construction Method (DCM)

Recalling that IKDE has the unbounded property of the universal discourse of the density estimation function, this property leads to a large Type Two error when more *virtual samples* are generated. Although $L(K_1, K_2, \ldots, K_m)$ has shown to be useful for generating *virtual samples*, the related prediction risk should not to be ignored. So, depending on the procedure of *multiset division* (Huang & Wang, 2006), we have developed a method named *Data Construction Method (DCM)* for prediction from a small data set.

In order to compare with IKDE, we first list the procedure of the *DCM* as shown in Box 4.

When giving a data set Ω with size n and doing T times of *multiset division*, the amount of generated data set, $|\Omega_T|$, will be equal to $2^T*|\Omega|$ which means $Q= 2^T*n$ (Huang & Wang, 2006). Because Ω_T will always include Ω the size of the generated data is equal to $|\Omega|*(2^T -1)$. For convenience, the resultant data, Ω_T, is named a *DCM* sample set.

While both the DCM and IKDE were designed similarly for creating more *virtual samples* from the original small-data-set, IKDE will result in a density estimation function and DCM will obtain a specific amount of data. To compare the prediction performance, we applied the IKDE and DCM to the case of 20 data provided by Li and Lin (2006) in the following section.

Comparative Study

As the case of Li and Lin (2006), 20 data were obtained in the early stages in a manufacturing system for building up management knowledge. The task of this supervised learning process employed a common artificial neural network, back propagation network (BPN), to find scheduling knowledge, the relationship between three controlling factors (X_1, X_2, X_3) on the production line and the scheduling rule (Y) which includes

Table 1. The training data set with size 20 (Y=1: FCFS, Y=2: SPT, Y=3: EDD) (Li and Lin, 2006)

No.	X_1	X_2	X_3	Y	No.	X_1	X_2	X_3	Y
1	8	20	50	1	11	10	20	70	2
2	10	30	110	1	12	7	30	90	2
3	7	20	110	1	13	10	30	70	2
4	8	30	80	1	14	7	20	60	2
5	8	30	70	1	15	10	20	70	2
6	10	20	60	2	16	10	30	70	2
7	11	30	90	2	17	7	20	60	2
8	7	30	60	2	18	13	20	90	3
9	8	30	50	2	19	9	20	100	3
10	9	40	60	2	20	7	30	50	3

the first come first serve (FCFS), shortest processing time (SPT), and earliest due data (EDD) dispatching rules. The corresponding network had three input units, four computational units located at one hidden layer and one output unit; that was, a 3-4-1 structure. The output unit had linear activation while the computational units in the hidden layer had sigmoid function defined by $f(x) = (1+\exp(-x))^{-1}$. Then the training and testing data sets, each with size 20, were listed below:

By setting the parameter of **DCM**, $B=\{1, 2\}$, we applied the **DCM** to the source data in Table

Table 2 The testing data set with size 20 (Y=1: FCFS, Y=2: SPT, Y=3: EDD) (Li & Lin, 2006)

No.	X_1	X_2	X_3	Y	No.	X_1	X_2	X_3	Y
1	10	40	70	1	11	10	20	60	2
2	7	20	110	1	12	10	20	80	2
3	7	20	60	2	13	11	30	90	2
4	8	30	50	2	14	7	30	70	3
5	8	40	90	2	15	7	30	60	3
6	9	30	50	2	16	7	20	70	3
7	9	30	60	2	17	7	20	70	3
8	9	20	60	2	18	9	20	100	3
9	10	30	50	2	19	9	20	100	3
10	10	30	60	2	20	10	30	120	3

Table 3. The learning accuracies resulted from doing DCM

Division times	The size of **DCM** samples	The learning accuracy
0	0	0.33
1	40	0.66
2	80	0.47
3	160	0.21
4	320	0.21

1; and for comparative sake, we set the times of doing **multiset division** as $t = 1, 2, 3$, and 4 for data generation before running the BPN. After testing, the respective accuracies were showed in Table 3 of which $t = 0$ means no data being generated and thus the training data set is the original set. For example, when doing **multiset division** procedure twice, the accuracy is 0.47, and the size of **DCM** samples is equal to $20*(2^2) = 80$. Therefore, without using **DCM** or IKDE, the accuracy is only 0.33.

From the above results, when $t=1$ the performance of which the learning accuracy is 0.66 is the best among these five test runs. Using **DCM** samples at $t=1$, the learning accuracy of BPN is significantly improved from 0.33 to 0.66.

As regard to IKDE, Li and Lin (2006) used the same source data in Table 1 to derive three density estimation functions as see in Box 4.

From equations (7), (8), and (9), the required amounts of **virtual samples** can be generated right away. Then, after making 10 trials to compute

Table 4. The learning accuracies resulted from IKDE

The size of **virtual samples**	The learning accuracy
40	0.59
80	0.27
160	0.15
320	0.12

Box 4.

$$f(x_1, x_2, x_3 \mid Y = 1) = 0.0728e^{-0.4167(x_1-8.2)^2} * (0.1631(e^{-0.3343(x_2-20)^2} + e^{-0.7522(x_2-30)^2})) * \quad (7)$$
$$(0.0915(e^{-0.0021(x_3-66.67)^2} + e^{-0.1053(x_3-110)^2}))$$

$$f(x_1, x_2, x_3 \mid Y = 2) = 0.0915(e^{-2.5(x_1-7.5)^2} + e^{-1.5(x_1-10)^2}) * (0.0915e^{-0.0118(x_2-26.67)^2}) * \quad (8)$$
$$(0.0915(e^{-0.0110(x_3-63)^2} + e^{-0.1053(x_3-90)^2}))$$

$$f(x_1, x_2, x_3 \mid Y = 3) = (0.0915e^{-0.25(x_1-8)^2} + 0.3084e^{-0.2988(x_1-13)^2}) * \quad (9)$$
$$(0.1631(e^{-0.3343(x_2-20)^2} + e^{-0.0836(x_2-30)^2})) * (0.0915 * (e^{-0.0263(x_3-50)^2} + e^{-0.01(x_3-95)^2}))$$

the average accuracies with respective to the specific amounts of *virtual sample* sizes of 40, 80, 160, and 320, the corresponding results were listed in Table 4.

The results from *DCM* and IKDE in this case were summarized in Figure 4. The rule of which more *virtual samples* being generated will cause more cumulative errors was verified from experiments. Although when the size of *virtual samples* increases the learning accuracy decreases drastically, a better performance can be obtained by using *DCM*. The reason for this is not hard to see: due to the bounded property of the universal discourse of *DCM* samples, *DCM* can help to avoid Type Two error in Statistics effectively.

Conclusions and Discussion

Depending on the *intervalized kernel methods of density estimation* (IKDE), Li and Lin (2006) proposed the way of creating *virtual samples* to improve the inference ability from a small data set. Although using IKDE, the *virtual sample* generation can overcome the difficulty of learning with insufficient data, it is lack of theoretical validity. To compensate this shortage, this study provides a theorem for this purpose. Additionally, we also proposed an alternative method named *Data Construction Method (DCM)* from the concept of set division for comparison.

To compare their performance, we have demonstrated a numerical case adopted from Li and

*Figure 4. The comparative plot of **DCM** and IKDE (Note that the examining target is the corresponding 20 testing data)*

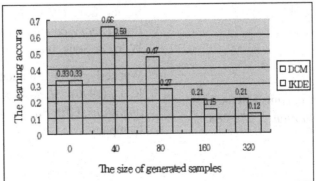

Lin's paper. From the obtained results, it is noted that, when the size of generated data increases, the learning accuracy decreases. Referred to Figure 1, this situation means that the more amounts of generated samples will make the Type Two error bigger in the viewpoint of Statistics, and that is the reason why we emphasized the universal discourse of the generated data shall be bounded. Therefore, owing to the bounded property of the **DCM**, whenever adopting it to be the way of data generation, its accuracy can be better than the one of the IKDE though more of the generated samples have an exactly opposite effect upon the learning accuracy.

Although these two methods have shown to be able to help inference from a ***small sample*** set, they both cannot be applied to the system with nominal variables. Especially for the IKDE, different forms of the kernel function and other ways of the central location, medium, mode, and so on, should further be discussed. While almost all aspects of technologies, environment, social-economics etc. have been changed drastically in a short time, collection of sufficient amount of data for just-in-time inferences is almost impossible. How to develop a theoretically and practically valid tool for analyzing ***small sample*** data remains a critical and challenging issue for researchers.

ACKNOWLEDGMENT

The authors acknowledge the financial support from the National Science Council, ROC with project number NSC94-2213-E007-018.

REFERENCES

Abu-Mostafa, Y. S. (1993). Hints and the VC-dimension. *Neural Computation, 5*, 278-288.

Huang, C. (2002). Information diffusion techniques and small-sample problem. *International Journal of Information Technology & Decision Making, 1*(2), 229-249.

Huang C. -J., & Wang, H. -F. (2006). Resolution of rare event by set division. *Proceedings from the 36th International Conference on Computers and Industrial Engineering*, Taipei, Taiwan, R.O.C., June, 20-23.

Li, D.-C., Chen, L.-S., & Lin, Y.-S. (2003). Using Functional Virtual Population as assistance to learn scheduling knowledge in dynamic manufacturing environments. *International Journal of Production Research, 17*, 4011–4024.

Li, D.-C., & Lin, Y.-S. (2006). Using virtual sample generation to build up management knowledge in the early manufacturing stages. *European Journal of Operational Research, 175*, 413-434.

Marsden Jerrold E., & Hoffman, M.J. (1993). *Elementary classical analysis*, Second Edition. W. H. Freeman and Company.

Niyogi, P., Girosi, F., & Tomaso, P. (1998). Incorporating prior information in machine learning by creating virtual examples. *Proceeding of the IEEE, 86*(11), 275-298.

Ross, M. S. (1987). *Introduction to probability and statistics for engineers and scientists*. John Wiley & Sons, Inc.

Spott, M. (1999). A theory of possibility distributions. *Fuzzy Sets and Systems, 102*, 135-155.

Steuer, E. R. (1986). *Multiple criteria optimization: Theory, computation and application*. John Wiley & Sons, Inc.

Wackerly, D. D., Mendenhall, W., & Scheaffer, R. L. (1996). *Mathematical statistics with applications*, Fifth Edition. Wadsworth Publishing Company.

Compilation of References

Abe, S. & Lan, M. (1995). A method for fuzzy rules extraction directly from numerical data and its application to pattern classification. *IEEE Transactions on Fuzzy Systems, 3*(1), 18-28.

Abu-Mostafa, Y. S. (1993). Hints and the VC-dimension. *Neural Computation, 5*, 278-288.

Aebischer, N.J., Robertson, P.A., & Kenward, R.E. (1993). Compositional analysis of habitat use from animal radio-tracking data. *Ecology, 74*(3), 1313-1323.

Agresti, A. (2002). *Categorial data analysis. Wiley series in probability and statistics*. Second Edition. New Jersey: Wiley Publishers.

Aiello, W, Chun, F., & Lu, L. (2000). A random graph model for massive graphs. *Proceedings of the 32nd Annual ACM symposium on Theory of computing*, Portland, Oregon, USA, 171 – 180, ACM Press.

Aittokallio, T. & Schwikowski, B. (2006). Graph-based methods for analyzing networks in cell biology. *Briefings in Bioinformatics, 7*(3), 243 – 255.

Alizadeh, A. A., Eisen, M. B., Davis, R. E., Ma, C., Lossos, I. S., Rosenwald, A., C. Boldrick, J. C., Sabet, J., Tran, T., Yu, X. Powell, J. I. Yang, L., Marti, G. E., Moore, T., Hudson Jr., J. Lu, L., Lewis, D. B., Tibshirani, R., Sherlock, G., Chan, W. C., Greiner, T. C., Weisenburger, D. D., Armitage, J. O., Warnke, R., Levy, R., Wilson, W., Grever, M. R., Byrd, J. C., Botstein, D., Brown, P. O., & Staudt, L. M. (2000). Distinct types of diffuse large b-cell lymphoma identified by gene expression profiling. *Nature, 403*(6769), 503-511.

Allende, H., Nanculef, R., & Salas R. (2004). Robust bootstrapping neural networks. In R. Monroy, et al. (Eds.), *MICAI 2004*, LNAI 2972, pp. 813–822. Berlin/Heidelberg: Springer-Verlag.

Al-Shahrour, F., Díaz-Uriarte, R., & Dopazo, J. (2003). FatiGO: A Web tool for finding significant associations of Gene Ontology terms with groups of genes. *Bioinformatics, 20*(4), 578 – 580.

Ambler, G.K., & Silverman, B.W. (2004). Perfect simulation for Bayesian wavelet thresholding with correlated coefficients. Preprint from http://dbwilson.com/exact/

Andersen, K., Cook, G. E., Karsai, G., & Ramaswamy, K. (1990). Artificial neural network applied to arc welding process modeling and control. *IEEE Transactions on Industry Applications, 26*(5), 824-830.

Anderson, D.R., Burnham, K.P., & Thompson W.L. (2000). Null hypothesis testing: Problems, prevalence, and an alternative. *Journal of Wildlife Management, 64*(4), 912-923.

Andrews, R., Diederich, J., & Tickles, A. B. (1995). Survey and critique of techniques for extracting rules from trained artificial neural networks. *Knowledge-Based Systems, 8*(6), 373-389.

Argos. (2007). *Argos user's manual online*. Retrieved March 15, 2007, from https://www.argos-system.org/manual/

Armand, S., Watelain, E., Roux, E., Mercier, M., & Lepoutre, F.-X. (2007). Linking clinical measurements and kinematic gait patterns of toe-walking using fuzzy decision trees. *Gait & Posture, 25*(3), 475-484.

Ashburner, M., Ball, C.A., Blake, J.A., Botstein, D., Butler, H., Cherry, J. M., Davies, A. P., Dolinski, K., Dwight, S. S., Epping, J. T., Harris, M. A., Hill, D. P. Issel-Tarver, L., Kasarskis, A., Lewis, S., Matese, J.C., Richardson, J. E., Ringwald, M., Rubin, G. M., & Sherlock, G. (2000). Gene ontology: Tool for the unification of biology. The Gene Ontology Consortium. *Nature Genetics, 25*(1), 25-29.

Atanassov, K. (1983). Intuitionistic Fuzzy Sets. *VII ITKR Session.* Sofia (Deposited in Central Scientific-Technical Library of Bulgarian Academy of Sciences, 1697/84) (in Bulgarian).

Atanassov, K. (1986). Intuitionistic fuzzy sets. *Fuzzy Sets and Systems, 20,* 87-96.

Atanassov, K. (1999). *Intuitionistic fuzzy sets: Theory and applications.* Heidelberg: Physica-Verlag.

Atanassov, K. (2005). Answer to D. Dubois, S. Gottwald, P. Hajek, J. Kacprzyk and H. Prade's paper, "Terminological difficulties in fuzzy set theory - The case of 'Intuitionistic Fuzzy Sets.'" *Fuzzy Sets and Systems, 156,* 496-499.

Atkinson P. M. & Tatnall, A. R. L. (1997). Introduction: neural networks in remote sensing. *International Journal of Remote Sensing, 18*(4), 699-709.

Austin, D., McMillan, J.I., & Bowen, W.D. (2003). A three-stage algorithm for filtering erroneous Argos satellite locations. *Marine Mammal Science, 19*(2), 371-383.

Azvine, B., Ho, C., Kay, S., Nauck, D., & Spott, M. (2003). Estimating travel times of field engineers. *BT Technology Journal, 21*(4), 33-38.

Azvine, B., Nauck, D.D., Ho, C., Broszat, K., & Lim, J. (2006). Intelligent process analytics for CRM. *BT Technology Journal, 24*(1), 60-69.

Baldwin, J.F. (1991). Combining evidences for evidential reasoning. *International Journal of Intelligent Systems, 6,* 569-616.

Baldwin, J.F. (1992). The management of fuzzy and probabilistic uncertainties for knowledge based systems. In S.A. Shapiro (Ed.), *Encyclopaedia of AI,* (2nd ed.), 528-537. John Wiley.

Baldwin, J.F. (1994). Mass assignments and fuzzy sets for fuzzy databases. In R. Yager et al. (Ed.) *Advances in the Dempster-Shafer theory of evidence,* pp.577-594. John Wiley.

Baldwin, J.F., & Karale, S.B. (2003). Asymmetric triangular fuzzy sets for classification models. In V. Palade, R.J. Howlett, & L.C. Jain (Eds.), *Lecture notes in artificial intelligence,* 2773, 364-370. Berlin, Heidelberg: Springer-Verlag.

Baldwin, J.F., Coyne, M.R., & Martin, T.P. (1995). Intelligent reasoning using general knowledge to update specific information: A database approach. *Journal of Intelligent Information Systems, 4,* 281-304.

Baldwin, J.F., Lawry, J., & Martin, T.P. (1995). A mass assignment theory of the probability of fuzzy events. *ITRC Report 229.* UK: University of Bristol.

Baldwin, J.F., Lawry, J., & Martin, T.P. (1998). The application of generalized fuzzy rules to machine learning and automated knowledge discovery. *International Journal of Uncertainty, Fuzziness and Knowledge-Based Systems, 6*(5), 459-487.

Baldwin, J.F., Lawry, J., & Martin, T.P. (1999). A mass assignment method for prototype induction. *International Journal of Intelligent Systems, 14,* 1041-1070.

Baldwin, J.F., Martin, T.P., & Pilsworth, B.W. (1995). *FRIL - Fuzzy and evidential reasoning in artificial intelligence.* John Wiley & Sons Inc.

Bandyopadhyay, S., Murthy, C.A., & Pal, S.K. (2000). VGA-classifier: Design and applications. *IEEE Transactions Systems, Man, and Cybernetics, 30,* 6, 890-895.

Barron, A.R. (1993). Universal approximation bounds for superpositions of a sigmoidal function. *IEEE Transactions on Information Theory, 39,* 930-945.

Barron, F. H., & Barrett, B. E. (1996). Decision quality using ranked attribute weights. *Management Science, 42*(11), 1515-1523.

Barth, H. G. & Flippen, R. B. (1995). Particle-size analysis. *Analytical Chemistry, 67,* 257R-272R.

Bartholomew-Biggs, M. C., Parkhurst S. C., & Wilson S. P. (2003). Using DIRECT to solve an aircraft routing problem. *Computational Optimization and Applications, 21,* 311-323.

Bartholomew-Biggs, M. C., Ulanowski, Z., & Zakovic, S. (2005). Using global optimization for a microparticle identification problem with noisy data. *Journal of Global Optimization, 32,* 325-347.

Baxt, W. G., & White, H. (1995). Bootstrapping confidence intervals for clinical input variable effects in a network trained to identify the presence of acute myocardial infarction. *Neural Computation, 7,* 624–638.

Becker, C., Kopp, S., & Wachsmuth I. (2004). Simulating the emotion dynamics of a multimodal conversational agent. In E. Andr et al. (Eds.), *Affective Dialogue Systems Workshop 2004, (LNAI 3068),* pp. 154-165. Berlin/Heidelberg: Springer-Verlag.

Ben-Dor, A., Chor, B., Karp, R., & Yakhini, Z. (2002). Discovering local structure in gene expression data: The order-preserving submatrix problem. *Proceedings of the 6th International Conference on Computational Biology (RECOMB '02),* Washington DC, USA, 49 – 57, ACM Press.

Berdnik, V. V., Gilev, K., Shvalov, A., Maltsev, V., & Loiko, V. A. (2006). Characterization of spherical particles using high-order neural networks and scanning flow cytometry. *Journal of Quantitative Spectroscopy & Radiative Transfer, 102,* 62-72.

Berg, A., & Pattillo, C. (1999). Predicting currency crises: The indicators approach and an alternative. *Journal of Money and Finance, 18,* 561– 586.

Bernstein, A. & Provost, F. (2001). *An intelligent assistant for the knowledge discovery process* (CeDER Working Paper IS-01-01). New York: Center for Digital Economy Research, Leonard Stern School of Business, New York University.

Bernstein, A., Hill, S., & Provost, F. (2002). *Intelligent assistance for the data mining process: An ontology-based approach* (CeDER Working Paper IS-02-02). New York: Center for Digital Economy Research, Leonard Stern School of Business, New York University.

Berthelsen, K.K., & Moller, J. (2002). A primer on perfect simulation for spatial point processes. *Bulletin of the Brazilian Mathematical Society, 33,* 351 - 367.

Beynon, M. (2002). DS/AHP method: A mathematical analysis, including an understanding of uncertainty. *European Journal of Operational Research, 140*(1), 149-165.

Beynon, M. J. (2005). A novel technique of object ranking and classification under ignorance: An application to the corporate failure risk problem. *European Journal of Operational Research, 167*(2), 493-517.

Beynon, M. J. (2005). A novel approach to the credit rating problem: Object classification under ignorance. *International Journal of Intelligent Systems in Accounting, Finance and Management, 13,* 113-130.

Beynon, M. J., & Kitchener, M. (2005). Ranking the "balance" of state long-term care systems: A comparative exposition of the SMARTER and CaRBS techniques. *Health Care Management Science, 8,* 157-166.

Beynon, M. J., Peel, M. J., & Tang, Y-C. (2004). The application of fuzzy decision tree analysis in an exposition of the antecedents of audit fees. *OMEGA, 32,* 231-244.

Bittner, J.D., Oakley, J., Hannan, J., Lincer, J., Muscolino, N., & Domenech, R. (2003). *Reproduction of Golden Eagles in a Drought Period.* Paper presented at the Annual Raptor Research Foundation Meetings, September, Anchorage, Alaska.

Bittner, M., Meltzer, P., Chen, Y., Jiang, Y., Seftor, E., Hendrix, M., Radmacher, M., Simon, R., Yakhini, Z., Ben-Dor, A., Sampas, N., Dougherty, E., Wang, E., Marincola, F., Gooden, C., Lueders, J., Glatfelter, A., Pollock, P., Carpten, J., Gillanders, E., Leja, D., Dietrich, K., Beaudry, C., Berens, M., Alberts, D., & Sondak, V. (2000). Molecular classification of cutaneous malignant melanoma by gene expression profiling. *Nature, 406*(6795), 536-540.

Blanco, H., & Garber, P.M. (1986). Recurrent devaluations and speculative attacks on the Mexican peso. *Journal of Political Economy, 94,* 148-166.

Bleichrodt, H., & Pinto, J. L. (2000). A parameter-free elicitation of the probability weighting function in medical decision analysis. *Management Science, 46*(11), 1485-1496.

Blundon, W. (2003). Predicting success: Using analytics to drive more profitable customer interactions. *Data Mining Direct Newsletter,* December 05 Issue.

Bohren, C. F. & Huffman, D. F. (1983). *Absorption and scattering of light by small particles.* New York: Wiley.

Bolstad, B. M., Irizarry, R. A., Astrand, M., & Speed, T. P. (2003). A comparison of normalization methods for high density oligonucleotide array data based on variance and bias. *Bioinformatics, 19*(2), 185-93.

Bonabeau, E., Dorigo, M., et al. (1999). *Swarm intelligence from natural to artificial systems*. New York, Oxford University Press.

Bonabeau, E., Henaux, F., et al. (1998). *Routing in telecommunications networks with ant-like agents*. 1437: 60.

Botia, J.A., Skarmeta, A.F., Velasco, J.R., & Garijo, M. (2000). A proposal for Meta-Learning through a MAS. In T. Wagner & O. Rana (Eds.), *Infrastructure for agents, multi-agent systems, and scalable multi-agent systems* (pp. 226-233). Lecture notes in artificial intelligence 1887. Berlin: Springer-Verlag.

Botia, J.A., Velasco, J.R., Garijo, M., & Skarmeta, A.F.G. (1998). A generic datamining system. Basic design and implementation guidelines. In H. Kargupta & P.K. Chan (Eds.), *Workshop in distributed datamining at KDD-98*. New York: AAAI Press.

Bouchon-Meunier, B., Rifqi, M., & Bothorel, S. (1996). Towards general measures of comparison of objects. *Fuzzy Sets & Systems, 84*(2), 143–153.

Braumoeller, B.F. (2004). Hypothesis testing and multiplicative terms. *International Organization, 58*(Fall), 807-820.

Braun, C.E. (2005). *Techniques for wildlife investigations and management*. Bethesda, Maryland: The Wildlife Society (TWS).

Brazma, A., Hingamp, P., Quackenbush, J., Sherlock, G., Spellman, P., Stoeckert, C., Aach, J., Ansorge, W., Ball, C.A., Causton, H.C., Gaasterland, T., Glenisson, P., Holstege, F.C., Kim, I.F., Markowitz, V., Matese, J.C., Parkinson, H., Robinson, A., Sarkans, U., Schulze-Kremer, S., Stewart, J., Taylor, R., Vilo, J., & Vingron, M. (2001). Minimum information about a microarray experiment (MIAME)-toward standards for microarray data. *Nature Genetics, 29*(4), 365-371.

Breiman, L. (2001). Statistical modelling: The two cultures. *Statistical Science, 16*(3), 199-231.

Breiman, L., Friedman, J. H., Olshen, R. A., & Stone, C. J. (1984). *Classification and regression trees*. Boca Raton, Florida: CRC Press.

Breyer, L.A., & Roberts, G.O. (2001). Catalytic perfect simulation. *Methodology and Computing in Applied Probability, 3*(2), 161-177.

Brooks, S.P., & Roberts, G.O. (1998). Diagnosing convergence of Markov chain Monte Carlo algorithms. *Statistics and Computing, 8*, 319-335.

Brown, T. A. (2002). Transcriptomes and proteomes. In *Genomes, 2 edition*, pp. 70 – 91. Manchester, UK: Wiley-Liss.

Brown, T. A. (2002). Synthesis and processing of the proteome. In *Genomes, 2 edition*, pp. 314 – 344. Manchester, UK: Wiley-Liss.

Bruha, I. (1996). Quality of decision rules: Definitions and classification schemes for multiple rules. In: Nakhaeizadeh, G., & Taylor, C.C. (Eds.), *Machine Learning and Statistics: The Interface*, John Wiley, 107-131.

Bruha, I. (2004). Metalearner for unknown attribute values processing: Dealing with inconsistency of metadatabases. *J. Intelligent Information Systems*, 22, 1, 71-84.

Bruha, I. (2006). From quality of decision rules to quality of sets of decision rule. Submitted to journal.

Bruha, I., & Kralik, P. (2002). Genetic learner GA-CN4: The ways of initializations of new populations, (Tech. Rep.), Dept Computing & Software, McMaster University.

Bruha, I., Kralik, P., & Berka, P. (2000). Genetic learner: Discretization and fuzzification of numerical attributes. *Intelligent Data Analysis J.*, 4, 445-460.

Buhlmann, P. (1998). Sieve bootstrap for smoothing in nonstationary time series. *The Annals of Statistics, 26*, 48-83.

Bühlmann, P. (1999). Bootstrap for time series. *Research report n. 87*, ETH, Zürich.

Buhlmann, P., & Kunsch, H. R. (1999). Block length selection in the bootstrap for time series. *Computational Statistics and Data Analysis, 31*, 295-310.

Busygin, S., Jacobsen, G., & Kramer, E. (2002). Double conjugated clustering applied to leukaemia microarray data. *Proceedings of the 2nd SIAM International Conference on Data Mining, Workshop on Clustering High Dimensional data,* Arlington, Virgina, USA, 420 – 436, Soc for Industrial & Applied Math.

Cai, Y. (2005). A non-monotone CFTP perfect simulation method. *Statistica Sinica, 15,* 927-943.

Califano, A., Stolovitzky, G., & Tu, Y. (2000). Analysis of gene expression microarrays for phenotype classification. *Proceedings of the International Conference on Computational Molecular Biology,* Tokyo, Japan, 75 – 85, ACM Press.

Cappe, O., & Robert, C.P. (2000). Markov chain Monte Carlo: 10 years and still running! *Journal of the American Statistical Association, 95,* 1282-1286.

Casella, G., Lavine, M., & Robert, C.P. (2001). Explaining the perfect sampler. *American Statistician, 55*(4), 299-305.

Casella, G., Mengersen, K., Robert, C., & Titterington, D. (2002). Perfect slice samplers for mixtures of distributions. *Journal of the Royal Statistical Society Series B, 64*(4), 777-790.

Chakraborty, D. (2001). Structural quantization of vagueness in linguistic expert opinion in an evaluation programme. *Fuzzy Sets and Systems, 119,* 171-186.

Chambers, L.(Ed.) (2000). *The practical handbook of genetic algorithms: Applications, Second Edition.* Chapman & Hall / CRC.

Chandel, R. S., Seow, H. P., & Cheong, F. L. (1997). Effect of increasing deposition rate on the bead geometry of submerged arc welds. *Journal of Materials Processing Technology, 72,*124–128.

Chateauneuf, A., & Wakker, P. (1999). An axiomatization of cumulative prospect theory for decision under risk. *Journal of Risk and Uncertainty, 18*(2), 137-145.

Chatfield, C. (1995). Model uncertainty, data mining and statistical inference. *Journal of Royal Statistical Society,* A 158, part 3, 419-466.

Chawla, N., Bowyer, K., Hall, L., & Kegelmeyer, W. (2002). Smote: Synthetic minority over-sampling technique. *Artificial Intelligence Research, 16,* 321-357.

Chen, Z. (2001). *Data mining and uncertain reasoning: An integrated approach.* New York: John Wiley.

Cheng, Y. & Church, G. M. (2000). Biclustering of expression data. *Proceedings of the International Conference on Intelligent Systems for Molecular Biology*; ISMB. International Conference on Intelligent Systems for Molecular Biology 8, 93-103.

Chernetsov, N. & F. Huettmann. (2005). Linking global climate grid surfaces with local long-term migration monitoring data: Spatial computations for the Pied Flycatcher to assess climate-related population dynamics on a continental scale. Lecture Notes In *Computer Science (LNCS) 3482, International Conference on Computational Science and its Applications (ICCSA) Proceedings Part III,* (pp.133-142).

Chiang, I-J., Shieh, M-J., Hsu, J. Y-J., & Wong, J-M. (2005). Building a medical decision support system for colon polyp screening by using fuzzy classification trees. *Applied Intelligence, 22,* 61-75.

Cho, R.J., Campbell, M.J., Winzeler, E. A., Steinmetz, L., Conway, A., Wodicka, L., Wolfsberg, T. G., Gabrielian, A. E., Landsman, D., Lockhart, D. J., & Davis, R. W. (1998). A genome-wide transcriptional analysis of mitotic cell cycle. *Molecular Cell 2, 1,* 65-73.

Christensen, N., Davies, V., & Gjermundsen, K. (1965). Distribution of temperature in arc welding. *British Welding Journal, 12*(2), 54-75.

Clark, P., & Boswell, R. (1991). Rule induction with CN2: Some recent improvements. *EWSL-91,* Porto, Springer-Verlag, 151-163.

Clemen, R. T., & Reilly, T. (2001). *Making hard decisions with decision tools.* Belmont, CA: Duxbury.

Clerc, M. & Kennedy, J. (2002). The particle swarm-explosion, stability, and convergence in a multidimensional complex space. *IEEE Transactions on Evolutionary Computation, 6*(1), 58-73.

Clerc, M. (1999). The swarm and the queen: Towards a deterministic and adaptive particle swarm optimization. *Proceedings of the 1999 Congress on Evolutionary Computation,* Washington, DC, IEEE.

Cobb, B. R., & Shenoy, P. P. (2003). A comparison of Bayesian and belief function reasoning. *Information Systems Frontiers, 5*(4), 345-358.

Cole, H.L., & Kehoe, T.J. (1996). A self-fulfilling model of Mexico's 1994-95 debt crisis. *Journal of International Economics, 41*, 309-330.

Coley, D.A. (2001). *An introduction to genetic algorithms for scientists and engineers.* River Edge, NJ: World Scientific.

Congalton, R. G. (1991). A review of assessing the accuracy of classifications of remotely sensed data. *Remote Sensing of Environment, 37*, 35-46.

Cook, G. E., Barnett, R. J., Andersen, K., & Strauss, A. M. (1995). Weld modeling and control using artificial neural networks. *IEEE Transactions on Industry Applications, 31*(6), 1484-1491.

Corcoran, J., & Tweedie, R. (2002). Perfect sampling from independent Metropolis-Hastings chains. *Journal of Statistical Planning and Inference, 104*, 297-314.

Cornelis, C., Van der Donck, C., & Kerre, E. (2003). Sinha-Dougherty approach to the fuzzification of set inclusion revisited. *Fuzzy Sets & Systems, 134*, 283–295.

Cowles, M.K., & Carlin, B.P. (1996). Markov chain Monte Carlo convergence diagnostics: A comparative review. *Journal of the American Statistical Association, 91*, 883-904.

Cox, E. (1994). *The fuzzy systems handbook.* Cambridge, MA: Academic Press.

Craig, E.H., & Craig, T.H. (1998). *Lead and mercury levels in Golden and Bald Eagles and annual movements of Golden Eagles wintering in east central Idaho 1990 -1997.*(Technical Bulletin No. 98-12). Boise, ID: Idaho Bureau of Land Management.

Cristianini, N., & Shawe-Taylor, J. (2000). *An introduction to support vector machines and other Kernel-based learning methods.* London: Cambridge University Press.

Cui, X. & Potok, T. E. (2006). A distributed flocking approach for information stream clustering analysis. *Proceedings of the Seventh ACIS International Conference on Software Engineering, Artificial Intelligence, Networking, and Parallel/Distributed Computing (SNPD'06).* Las Vegas, NV, United States, IEEE Computer Society.

Cui, X., Gao, J., et al. (2006). A flocking based algorithm for document clustering analysis. *Journal of System*

Architecture (Special issue on Nature Inspired Applied Systems).

Cumby, R., & van Wijnbergen, S. (1989). Financial policy and speculative runs with a crawling peg—Argentina 1979–1981. *Journal of International Economics, 17*, 111-127.

Dantsin, E., Kreinovich, V., Wolpert, A., & Xiang, G. (2006). Population variance under interval uncertainty: A new algorithm. *Reliable Computing, 12*(4), 273-280.

Darwin, C. (1859). *On the origin of species by means of natural selection, or the preservation of favoured races in the struggle for life.* London: John Murray.

Davidson, A.C., & Hinkley, D. V. (1997). *Bootstrap methods and their application.* Cambridge, UK: Cambridge University Press.

De Jong, K. (1975). *An analysis of the behavior of a class of genetic adaptive systems.* Doctoral Dissertation, University of Michigan.

De Jong, K. (1980). Adaptive system design: A genetic approach. *IEEE Transactions on Systems, Man, and Cybernetics, 10*, 556-574.

De Jong, K. (1988). Learning with genetic algorithms: An overview. *Machine learning, 3*, 121-138.

De Jong, K.A., Spears, W.M., & Gordon, D.F. (1993). Using genetic algorithms for concept learning. *Machine Learning, 13*, Kluwer Academic Publ., 161-188.

De Pieri, L. A., Ludlow, I. K., & Waites, W. M. (1993). The application of laser diffractometry to study the water content of spores of Bacillus sphaericus with different heat resistances. *Journal of Applied Bacteriology, 74*, 578-582.

De Veaux, R., Schemi, J., Schweinsberg, J., Shellington, D., & Ungar, L. H. (1998). Prediction intervals for neural networks via nonlinear regression. *Technometrics, 40*, 277-282.

De'ath, G. (2007). Boosted trees for ecological modeling and prediction. *Ecology, 88*(1), 243-251.

Dempster, A. P. (1967). Upper and lower probabilities induced by a multiple valued mapping. *Ann. Math. Statistics, 38*, 325-339.

Dennis, G., Sherman, B. T., Hosack, D. A., Yang, J., Gao, W., Lane, H. C., & Lempicki, R. A. (2003). DAVID: Database for Annotation, Visualization and Integrated Discovery. *Genome Biology, 4*, R60.

DeOliveria, J. V. (1999). Semantic constraints for membership function optimization. *IEEE Transactions on Systems, Man and Cybernetics – Part A: Systems and Humans, 29*(1), 128-138.

Dilimulati, B., & Bruha, I. (2007). Genetic Algorithms in Dynamically Changing Environment. In:Zanasi, A., Brebbia, C.A., & Ebecken, N.F.F. (Eds.), *Data Mining VIII: Data , Text and Web Mining and Their Business Applications*, WIT Press, 65-73.

Dimakos, X.K. (2001). A guide to exact simulation. *International Statistical Review, 69*(1), 27-48.

Djuric, P.M., Huang, Y., & Ghirmai, T. (2002). Perfect sampling: A review and applications to signal processing. *IEEE Transactions on Signal Processing, 50*(2), 345-356.

Dorigo, M. (1992). *Optimization, learning and natural algorithms* (in Italian). Doctoral Dissertation, Dipartimento di Elettronica, Politecnico di Milano, Milan, Italy.

Dorigo, M., Bonabeau, E., et al. (2000). Ant algorithms and stigmergy. *Future Generation Computer Systems, 16*(8), 851-871.

Draghici, S., Khatri, P., Martins, R. P., Ostermeier, G. C., & Krawetz, S. A. (2003). Global functional profiling of gene expression. *Genomics, 81*(2), 98 – 104.

Dubois, D., & Prade, H. (1982). On several representations of an uncertain body of evidence. In M.M. Gupta & E. Sanchez (Eds.), *Fuzzy information and decision processes*, pp. 167-181. North-Holland.

Dubois, D., & Prade, H. (1983). Unfair coins and necessity measures: towards a possibilistic interpretation of histograms. *Fuzzy Sets and Systems, 10*, 15-20.

Dubois, D., & Prade, H. (1997). The three semantics of fuzzy sets. *Fuzzy Sets and Systems, 90*, 141-150.

Dubois, D., Fargier, H., & Fortin, J. (2005). The empirical variance of a set of fuzzy intervals. *Proceedings of the 2005 IEEE International Conference on Fuzzy Systems FUZZ-IEEE'2005*, Reno, Nevada, May 22–25, pp. 885-890.

Dubois, D., Gottwald S., Hajek, P., Kacprzyk, J., & Prade, H. (2005). Terminological difficulties in fuzzy set theory: The case of "intuitionistic fuzzy sets." *Fuzzy Sets and Systems, 156*(3), 485-491.

Dubovik, O., Sinyuk, A., Lapyonok, T., Holben, B. N., Mishchenko, M., Yang, P. et al. (2006). Application of spheroid models to account for aerosol particle nonsphericity in remote sensing of desert dust. *Journal of Geophysical Research, 111*, D11208.

Duch, W, Adamczak, R., & Grabczewski, K. (2001). A new methodology of extraction, optimization and application of crisp and fuzzy logical rules. *IEEE Transactions on Neural Networks, 12*(2), 277-306.

Duda, R. O., Hart, P. E., & Stork, D. G. (2000). *Pattern classification*. New York, NY: John Wiley & Sons.

Duda, R.O., Hart, P.E., & Stork, D.G. (2001). *Pattern classification*. John Wiley & Sons.

Eberhart, R. & Kennedy, J. (1995). A new optimizer using particle swarm theory. *Proceedings of the Sixth International Symposium on Micro Machine and Human Science*, Nagoya, Japan, IEEE.

Edison, H. (2000). *Do indicators of financial crises work? An evaluation of an early warning system*. International Finance Discussion Papers No. 675, Board of Governors of the Federal Reserve Systems.

Efron, B. (1979). Bootstrap methods: Another look at the jackknife. *The Annals of Statistics, 7*, 1-26.

Eichengreen, B., Rose, A.K., & Wyplosz, C. (1996). Exchange market mayhem: The antecedents and aftermath of speculative attacks. *Economic Policy, 21*, 249-312.

Eisen, M B., Spellman, P. T., Brown, P. O., & Botstein, D. (1998). Cluster analysis and display of genome wide expression patterns. *PNAS, 95*(25), 14863-14868.

Elith, J., & Graham, C., NCEAS working group (2006). Comparing methodologies for modeling species' distributions from presence-only data. *Ecography, 29*(2), 129-151.

Elith, J., Ferrier, S., Huettmann, F., & Leathwick, J.R. (2005). The evaluation strip: A new and robust method for plotting predicted responses from species distribution models. *Ecological Modeling, 186*, 280-289.

Ewing, R. (2003). Legal, status of traffic calming. *Transportation Quarterly, 57*(2), 11-23.

Fan, H.-Y., & Lampinen, J. (2003). A trigonometric mutation operation to differential evolution. *Journal of Global Optimization, 27*, 105-129.

Faraway J., & Chatfield C. (1998). Time series forecasting with neural networks: a comparative study using the airline data. *Applied Statistics, 47*, 231-250.

Farmer, C. M., & Williams, A. F. (2005). Effect on fatality risk of changing from secondary to primary seat belt enforcement. *Journal of Safety Research, 36*, 189-194

Fawcett, T., & Provost, F. (1997). Adaptive fraud detection. *Data Mining and Knowledge Discovery, 3*(1), 291-316.

Fayyad, U., Shapiro, G.P., & Smyth, P. (1996). The KDD process for extracting useful knowledge from volumes of data. *Communications of the ACM, 39*, 27-34.

Fell, J. M. G. (1961). The structure of algebras of operator fields. *Acta Mathematics, 101,* 19-38.

Fell, J. M. G. (1962). A Hausdorff topology for the closed sets of a locally compact non-Hausdorff space. *Proceedings of the American Mathematical Society, 13*, 472–476.

Fennema, H., & Wakker, P. (1997). Original and cumulative prospect theory: A discussion of empirical differences. *Journal of Behavioral Decision Making, 10*, 53-64.

Ferson, S., & Hajagos, J. (2007). Interval versions of statistical techniques, with applications to environmental analysis, bioinformatics, and privacy in statistical databases. *Journal of Computational and Applied Mathematics, 199*(2), 418-423.

Ferson, S., Ginzburg, L., Kreinovich, V., Longpre, L., & Aviles, M. (2005). Exact bounds on finite populations of interval data. *Reliable Computing, 11*(3), 207-233.

Fill, J.A. (1998). An interruptible algorithm for perfect sampling via Markov chains. *Annals of Applied Probability, 8*, 131-162.

Fill, J.A., Machida, M., Murdoch, D.J., & Rosenthal, J.S. (2000). Extension of Fill's perfect rejection sampling algorithm to general chains. *Random Structures and Algorithms, 17*, 290-316.

Finkelstein, M.S. (2002). On the shape of the mean residual lifetime function. *Applied Stochastic Models in Business and Industry, 18*(2), 135 - 146.

Fishburn, P. C. (1982). *The foundations of expected utility.* Dordrecht, Holland: Reidel.

Flood, R.P., & Marion, N.P. (1999). Perspectives on the recent currency crisis literature. *International Journal of Finance and Economics, 4*(1), 1-26.

Foss, S., & Tweedie, R. (1998). Perfect simulation and backward coupling. *Stochastic Models, 14*, 187-203.

Frair, J.L., Nielsen, S.E., Merrill, E.H., Lele, S.R., Boyce, M.S., Munro, R.H.M., Stenhouse, G.B., & Beyer, H.L. (2004). Removing GPS collar bias in habitat selection studies. *Journal of Applied Ecology, 41*(2), 201-212.

Francois, J.-M. (2006). JaHMM – Hidden markov models – Java implementation, http://www.run.montefiore.ulg.ac.be/ francois/software/jahmm

Franke J., & Neumann M.H. (2000). Bootstrapping neural networks. *Neural Computation, 12*, 1929-1949.

Frankel, J.A., & Rose, A.K. (1996). Currency crashes in emerging markets: An empirical treatment. *Journal of International Economics, 41*, 351-366.

Fridlyand, J. & Dudoit, S. (2001). *Applications of resampling methods to estimate the number of clusters and to improve the accuracy of a clustering method.* (Technical Report 600), Berkeley, California: University of California, Department of Statistics.

Friedman, J.H. (2001). Greedy function approximation: A gradient boosting machine. *Annals of Statistics, 2*, 1189-1232.

Friedman, J.H., & (2002). Stochastic Gradient Boosting: Nonlinear methods and data mining. *Computational Statistics and Data Analysis, 38*, 367-378.

Friemert, C., Erfle, V., & Strauss, G. (1989). Preparation of radiolabeled cDNA probes with high specific activity for rapid screening of gene expression. *Methods Molecular Cell Biology, 1*, 143 -153.

Furnas, G. (2003). Framing the wireless market. *The Future of Wireless, WSA News:Bytes, 17*(11), 4-6.

Gamerman, D. (1997). *Markov chain Monte Carlo.* Chapman & Hall.

Ganjigatti, J. P. (2006). *Application of statistical methods and fuzzy logic techniques to predict bead geometry in welding.* Unpublished doctoral dissertation, IIT Kharagpur, India.

Gasch, A. P. & Eisen, M.B. (2002). Exploring the conditional coregulation of yeast in gene expression through fuzzy K-Means clustering. *Genome Biology, 3*(11), RESEARCH0059.1 – RESEARCH0059.22.

Gebhardt, J. & Kruse R. (1993). The context model – An integrating view of vagueness and uncertainty. *International Journal of Approximate Reasoning, 9*, 283–314.

Gelman, A., & Rubin, D.B. (1992). Inference from iterative simulation using multiple sequences. *Statistical Science, 7*, 457-511.

Geman, S., & Geman, D. (1984). Stochastic relaxation, Gibbs distributions and the Bayesian restoration of images. *IEEE Transactions on Pattern Analysis and Machine Intelligence, 6*, 721-741.

Getz, G., Levine, E., & Domany, E. (2000). Coupled two-way clustering analysis of gene microarray data. *PNAS, 97*(22), 12079 – 12084.

Gierz, G., Hofmann, K. H., Keimel, K., Lawson, J. D., Mislove, M., & Scott, D. S. (1980). *A compendium of continuous lattices.* Berlin, Heidelberg, New York: Springer-Verlag.

Gilks, W.R., Richardson, S., & Spiegelhalter, D.J. (Eds.) (1996). *Markov chain Monte Carlo in practice.* Chapman & Hall.

Giordana, A., & Saitta, L. (1993). REGAL: An integrated system for learning relations using genetic algorithms. *Proc. 2nd International Workshop Multistrategy Learning, 234-249.*

Giordano, F., La Rocca, M., & Perna, C. (2004). Bootstrap variable selection in neural network regression models. In H. H. Bock, M. Chiodi, & A. Mineo (Eds.), Advances in multivariate data analysis. Heidelberg-Berlin: Springer-Verlag.

Goicoechea, A., Hansen, D. R., & Duckstein, L. (1982). Multiobjective decision analysis with engineering and business applications. New York: John Wiley.

Goldberg, D.E. (1989). *Genetic algorithms in search, optimization, and machine learning.* Addison-Wesley.

Goldstein, M. (1996). *The seven deadly sins: Presumptive indicators of vulnerability to financial crises in emerging economies: Origin and policy options.* Economic papers 46, Bank for International Settlements (BIS).

Goldstein, M., Kaminsky, G.L., & Reinhart, C.M. (2000). *Assessing financial vulnerability: An early warning system for emerging markets.* Washington, DC: Institute for International Economics.

Golub, T. R., Slonim, D. K., Tamayo, P., Huard, C., Gaasenbeek, M., Mesirov, J. P., Coller, H., Loh, M. L., Downing, J. R., Caligiuri, M. A., Bloomfield, C. D., & Lander, E. S. (1999). Molecular classification of cancer: Class discovery and class prediction by gene expression monitoring. *Science 286*(5439), 531-537.

Gonzalez, R. C. & Woods, R. E. (2002). *Digital image processing.* Upper Saddle River, NJ: Prentice Hall.

Gousbet, G. & Grehan, G. (1988). *Optical particle sizing.* New York: Plenum.

Goutsias, J., Mahler, R. P. S., & Nguyen, H. T. (Eds.) (1997). *Random sets: Theory and applications.* New York: Springer-Verlag.

Graeber, R. (2006). *Modeling the distribution and abundance of brown bears as a biodiversity component in the Northern Pacific Rim.* Unpublished M.S. Thesis, University of Hannover, Hannover, Germany.

Grainger, R. G., Lucas, J., Thomas, G. E. & Ewen, G. B. L. (2004). Calculation of Mie derivatives. *Applied Optics, 43*, 5386-5393.

Green, P., & Murdoch, D. (1999). Exact sampling for Bayesian inference: Towards general purpose algorithms. In J. Berger, J. Bernardo, A. Dawid, D. Lindley, & A. Smith (Eds.), *Bayesian Statistics 6*, pp. 302-321. Oxford University Press.

Grefenstette, J. (1986). Optimization of control parameters for genetic algorithms. *IEEE Transactions on Systems, Man, and Cybernetics, 16*, 122-128.

Grefenstette, J., Ramsey, C.L., & Schultz, A.C. (1990). Learning sequential decision rules using simulation models and competition. *Machine Learning J., 5*, Kluwer Academic Publ., 355-381.

Gress, T.M., Hoheisel, J.D., Sehetner, G., & Leahrach, H. (1992). Hybridization fingerprinting of high-density cDNA-library arrays with cDNA pools derived from whole tissues. *Mammalian Genome, 3,* 609⁻-619.

Guglielmi, A., Holmes, C.C., & Walker, S.G. (2002). Perfect simulation involving functionals of a Dirichlet process. *Journal of Computational and Graphical Statistics, 11*(2), 306-310.

Guillaume, J. L. & Latapy, M. (2006). Bipartite graphs as models of complex networks. *Physica A, 317,* 795 – 813.

Guisan, A., & Thuiller, W. (2005). Predicting species distribution: Offering more than simple habitat models. *Ecology Letters, 8,* 993-1009.

Gunaraj, V., & Murugan, N. (2000a). Prediction and optimization of weld bead volume for the submerged arc process –Part 1. *Welding Research Supplement,* 287-294

Gunaraj, V., & Murugan, N. (2000b). Prediction and optimization of weld bead volume for the submerged arc process –Part 2. *Welding Research Supplement,* 331s-338s.

Haggstrom, O. (2002). *Finite Markov chains and algorithmic applications.* Cambridge University Press.

Haggstrom, O., & Nelander, K. (1998). Exact sampling from anti-monotone systems. *Statistica Neerlandica, 52*(3), 360-380.

Haggstrom, O., & Nelander, K. (1999). On exact simulation of Markov random fields using coupling from the past. *Scandinavian Journal of Statistics, 26*(3), 395-411.

Haggstrom, O., van Liesholt, M., & Moller, J. (1999). Characterisation results and Markov chain Monte Carlo algorithms including exact simulation for some spatial point processes. *Bernoulli, 5,* 641-659.

Hair, J.F., Anderson, R.E., Tatham, R.L., & Black, W.C. (1995). *Multivariate data analysis.* New York: Prentice-Hall.

Han, J., & Kamber, M. (2006). *Data mining: Concepts and techniques.* Amsterdam, Netherlands: Morgan Kaufman.

Han, K.H. (2003). *Quantum-inspired evolutionary algorithm.* Doctoral Dissertation, Korea Advanced Institute of Science and Technology.

Handl, J. & Meyer, B. (2002). *Improved ant-based clustering and sorting in a document retrieval interface.* Granada, Spain: Springer-Verlag.

Haran, M., & Tierney, L. (2005). Perfect sampling for a Markov random field model. Preprint from http://www.stat.psu.edu/~mharan/

Hardle, W., Lutkepohl, H., & Chen, R. (1997). A review of non parametric time series analyisis. *International Statistical Review, 65,* 49-72.

Hartigan, J.A. (1972). Direct clustering of a data matrix. *Journal of the American Statistical Association, 67*(337), 123-129.

Harvey, M., & Neal, R.M. (2000). Inference for belief networks using coupling from the past. In C. Boutilier, & M. Goldszmidt (Eds.), *Proceedings of the 16th Conference on Uncertainty in Artificial Intelligence,* pp. 256-263.

Hastings, W.K. (1970). Monte Carlo sampling methods using Markov chains and their applications. *Biometrika, 57,* 97-109.

Haupt, R.L. & Haupt, S.E. (1998). *Practical genetic algorithms.* New York: John Wiley & Sons, Inc.

Heermann P. D. & Khazenie, N. (1992). Classification of multispectral remote sensing data using a back-propagation neural network. *IEEE Transactions on Geosciences and Remote Sensing, 30*(1), 81-88.

Heitjan D. F., & Rubin, D. B. (1991). Ignorability and coarse data. *Ann. Stat., 19*(4), 2244-2253.

Herrera, F., Herrera-Viedma, E., & Martinez, L. (2000). A fusion approach for managing multi-granularity linguistic term sets in decision making. *Fuzzy Sets and Systems, 114,* 43-58.

Higashi, M., & Klir, G. J. (1983). Measures of uncertainty and information based on possibility distributions. *International Journal of General Systems, 9,* 43-58.

Higgins, J. P., Shinghal, R., Gill, H., Reese, J. H., Terris, M., Cohen, R. J., Fero, M., Pollack, J. R. van de Rijn, M., & Brooks, J. D. (2003). Gene expression patterns in renal cell carcinoma assessed by complementary DNA microarray. *The American Journal of Pathology, 162(3)*, 925 – 932.

Hillson, D. (1999). Developing effective risk responses. *Proceedings of 30ᵗʰ Annual Project Management Institute 1999 Seminar & Symposium*, Philadelphia, Pennsylvania, USA, Papers Presented October 10 to 16.

Hobert, J.P., & Robert, C.P. (2004). A mixture representation of π with applications in Markov chain Monte Carlo and perfect sampling. *The Annals of Applied Probability, 14*(3), 1295-1305.

Hobert, J.P., Robert, C.P., & Titterington, D.M. (1999). On perfect simulation for some mixtures of distributions. *Statistics and Computing, 9*, 287-298.

Hojati, M., Bector, C. R., & Smimou, K. (2005). A simple method for computation of fuzzy linear regression. *European Journal of Operational Research, 166*, 172-184.

Holland, J.H. (1975). *Adaptation in natural and artificial systems*. Ann Arbor: University of Michigan Press.

Holland, J.H. (1986). Escaping brittleness: The possibilities of general-purpose learning algorithms applied to parallel rule-based systems. In: Michalski, R.S., Carbonell, J.G., & Mitchell, T.M. (Eds.), *Machine learning: An artificial intelligence approach*, Vol. 2, Morgan Kaufmann.

Holmes, C., & Denison, D.G.T. (2002). Perfect sampling for the wavelet reconstruction of signals. *IEEE Transactions on Signal Processing, 50*(2), 337-344.

Hornik, K., Stinchcombe, M., & White, H. (1989). Multilayer feedforward networks are universal approximators. *Neural Networks, 2*, 359-366.

Hosack, D. A., Dennis, G. Jr., Sherman, B. T., Lane, H. C., & Lempicki, R. A. (2003). Identifying biological themes within lists of genes with EASE. *Genome Biology, 4*, R70.

Houston, D. J., & Richardson, Jr., L. E. (2005). Getting Americans to buckle up: The efficacy of state seat belt laws. *Accident Analysis & Prevention, 37*, 1114-1120.

Hsu, F. C. (2005). *Risk management of crisp and fuzzy events based on individual's preference*. Masters Thesis, Department of IEEM, National Tsing Hua University, Hsichu, Taiwan, ROC.

Huang C. -J., & Wang, H. -F. (2006). Resolution of rare event by set division. *Proceedings from the 36ᵗʰ International Conference on Computers and Industrial Engineering*, Taipei, Taiwan, R.O.C., June, 20-23.

Huang, C. (2002). Information diffusion techniques and small-sample problem. *International Journal of Information Technology & Decision Making, 1*(2), 229-249.

Huang, N.E. (2001). Review of empirical mode decomposition. *Proceedings of SPIE*, 3, pp. 71-80, Orlando, USA.

Huang, N.E., Shen, Z., & Long, S.R. (1999). A new view of nonlinear water waves: The Hilbert spectrum. *Annual Review of Fluid Mechanics, 31*, 417-457.

Huang, N.E., Shen, Z., Long, S.R., Wu, M.C., Shih, H.H., Zheng, Q., Yen, N.C., Tung, C.C., & Liu, H.H. (1998). The empirical mode decomposition and the Hilbert spectrum for nonlinear and nonstationary time series analysis. *Proceedings of the Royal Society A: Mathematical, Physical & Engineering Sciences, 454*, 903-995.

Huang, Y., & Djuric, P.M. (2001). Multiuser detection of synchronous Code-Division-Multiple-Access signals by the Gibbs coupler. *Proceedings of the IEEE International Conference on Acoustics, Speech and Signal Processing*, Salt Lake City, Utah.

Huang, Y., & Djuric, P.M. (2002). Variable selection by perfect sampling. *EURASIP Journal on Applied Signal Processing, 2002*(1), 38-45.

Huber, M. (1998). Exact sampling and approximate counting techniques. *Proceedings of the 30ᵗʰ Annual ACM Symposium on the Theory of Computing*, 31-40.

Huber, M. (2004). Perfect sampling using bounding chains. *The Annals of Applied Probability, 14*(2), 734-753.

Huet, S., Jolivet, E., & Messean, A. (1990). Some simulation results about confidence intervals and bootstrap methods in nonlinear regression. *Statistics, 21*, 369-432.

Huettmann, F. (2005). Databases and science-based management in the context of wildlife and habitat: Towards a certified ISO standard for objective decision-making for the global community by using the internet. *Journal of Wildlife Management, 69*, 466-472.

Huettmann, F., & Diamond, A.W. (2006). Large-scale effects on the spatial distribution of seabirds in the northwest atlantic. *Landscape Ecology, 21*, 1089-108.

Hull, P. G. & Quinby-Hunt, M. (1997). A neural-network to extract size parameter from light-scattering data. *SPIE Proceedings, 2963*, 448-454.

Hwang, J. T. G., & Ding, A. A. (1997). Prediction intervals for artificial neural networks. *JASA, 92*, 748-757.

Ishibuchi, H. Nii, M., & Turksen, I. B. (1998). Bidirectional bridge between neural networks and linguistic knowledge: Linguistic rule extraction and learning from linguistic rules. *Proceedings of the IEEE Conference on Fuzzy Systems FUZZ-IEEE '98*, Anchorage, 1112-1117.

Jains, A.K., Murty M.N., & Flynn P.J. (1999). Data clustering: A review. *ACM Computing Surveys, 31*(3), 264-323.

James, F.C., & McCulloch, C.E. (1990). Multivariate analysis in ecology and systematics: Panacea or Pandora's box? *Annual Review of Ecology and. Systematics, 21*, 129-66.

Jang, J. S. R. & Sun, C. T. (1997). *Neuro-fuzzy and soft computing: A computational approach to learning and machine intelligence.* Upper Saddle River, NJ: Prentice Hall.

Jang, J. S. R. (1993). ANFIS Adaptive network based fuzzy inference systems. *IEEE Trans. on Systems, Man, and Cybernetics, 23*(3), 665-685.

Jang, J.-S. R. (1994). Structure determination in fuzzy modeling: A fuzzy CART approach. *Proceedings of IEEE International Conference on Fuzzy Systems*, Orlando, Florida, *1*, 480-485.

Janikow, C. Z. (1998). Fuzzy decision trees: Issues and methods. *IEEE Transactions of Systems, Man and Cybernetics Part B, 28*(1), 1-14.

Janikow, C.Z. (1993). A knowledge-intensive genetic algorithm for supervised learning. *Machine Learning J.*, 5, Kluwer Academic Publ., 189-228.

Japkowicz, N. (2003). Class imbalances: Are we focusing on the right issue? *Workshop on Learning from Imbalanced Data II*, ICML, Washington 2003.

Jaulin L., Kieffer, M., Didrit, O., & Walter, E. (2001). *Applied interval analysis.* London: Springer-Verlag.

Jeanne, O., & Masson, P. (2000). Currency crises, sunspots, and Markov-switching regimes. *Journal of International Economics, 50*(2), 327-350.

Jeng, B., Jeng, Y-M., & Liang, T-P. (1997). FILM: A fuzzy inductive learning method for automated knowledge acquisition. *Decision Support Systems, 21*, 61-73.

Johnson, V.E. (1996). Studying convergence of Markov chain Monte Carlo algorithms using coupled sample paths. *Journal of the American Statistical Association, 91*(433), 154-166.

Jones, A. L., Beynon, M. J., Holt C. A., & Roy, S. (2006). A novel approach to the exposition of the temporal development of post-op osteoarthritic knee subjects. *Journal of Biomechanics, 39*(13), 2512-2520.

Jones, D. R., Perttunen, C. P. & Stuckman, B. E. (1993). Lipschitzian optimization without the Lipschitz constant. *Journal of Optimization Theory and Applications, 79*, 157-181.

Jones, P., & Beynon, M. J. (2007). Temporal support in the identification of e-learning efficacy: An example of object classification in the presence of ignorance. *Expert Systems, 24*(1), 1-16.

Jonsen, I.D., Flemming, J.M., & Myers, R.A. (2005). Robust state-space modeling of animal movement data. *Ecology, 86*(11), 2874-2880.

Jou, M. (2003). Experimental study and modeling of GTA welding process. *Journal of Manufacturing Science and Engineering, 125*(4), 801–808

Juang, S. C., Tarng Y. S., & Lii, H. R. (1998). A comparison between the back-propagation and counter-propagation networks in the modeling of the TIG welding process. *Journal of Material Processing Technology, 75*, 54–62.

Kahneman, D., & Tversky, A. (1979). Prospect theory: An analysis of decision under risk. *Econometrica, 47*(2), 263-292.

Kaminsky, G.L. (1999). *Currency and banking crises: the early warnings of distress.* IMF Working Paper 99-178, International Monetary Fund, Washington, DC.

Kaminsky, G.L., & Reinhart, C.M. (1999). The twin crises: Te causes of banking and balance-of-payments problems. *American Economic Review, 89*(3), 473-500.

Kaminsky, G.L., Lizondo, S., & Reinhart, C. (1998). *Leading indicators of currency crises.* International Monetary Fund (IMF) Staff Papers, 45, 1-48.

Kantardzic, M. (2001). *Data mining: Concepts, models, methods, and algorithms.* Hoboken, NJ: Wiley – IEEE Press.

Karl, J.W., Heglund, P.J., Garton, E.O., Scott, J.M., Wright, N.M., & Hutto, R.I. (2000). Sensitivity of species habitat-relationship model performance to factors of scale. *Ecological Applications, 10*(6), 1690-1705.

Kass, R.E., Carlin, B.P., Gelman, A., & Neal, R.M. (1998). Markov chain Monte Carlo in practice: A roundtable discussion. *American Statistician, 52*, 93-100.

Kaufman, L., & Rousseeuw, P. J. (1990). Finding groups in data: An introduction to cluster analysis. New York: John Wiley & Sons.

Kaufmann, L. & Rousseeuw, P. J. (1990). *Finding groups in data: An introduction to cluster analysis.* New York: John Wiley and Sons Inc., Chinchester, Weinheim.

Keating, K. A., & Cherry, S. (2004). Use and interpretation of logistic regression in habitat-selection studies. *Journal of Wildlife Management, 68,* 774-789.

Kecman, V. (2001). *Learning and Soft Computing: Support Vector Machines, Neural Networks, and Fuzzy Logic.* London: MIT Press.

Keller, J. K., Yager R. R., & Tahani, H. (1992). Neural network implementation of fuzzy logic. *Fuzzy Sets and Systems, 45*, 1-12.

Kelly, J.D., & Davis, L. (1991). A hybrid genetic algorithm for classification. *Proc. IJCAI-91,* 645-650.

Kendall, W.S. (1998). Perfect simulation for the area-interaction point process. In L. Accardi & C.C. Heyde (Eds.), *Probability Towards 2000,* pp. 218-234. Springer.

Kendall, W.S. (2005). Notes on perfect simulation. Preprint from http://dbwilson.com/exact/

Kendall, W.S., & Moller, J. (2000). Perfect simulation using dominated processes on ordered spaces, with applications to locally stable point processes. *Advances in Applied Probability, 32,* 844-865.

Kenward, R.E. (2001). *A manual for wildlife radio tagging.* San Diego: Academic Press

Kerr, M.K. & Churchill, G.A. (2001). Experimental design for gene expression microarrays, *Biostatistics, 2*(2), 183 – 201.

Khodursky, A. B., Peter, B. J., Cozzarelli, N. R., Botstein, D., Brown, P. O., Yanofsky, C. (2000). DNA microarray analysis of gene expression in response to physiological and genetic changes that affect tryptophan metabolism in Escherichia coli. *PNAS, 97*(22), 12170 - 12175

Kim, I. S., Jeong, Y. J., Sona, I. J., Kima, I. J., Kimb, J. Y., Kimb, I. K., & Yarlagadda, P. K. D. V. (2003a). Sensitivity analysis for process parameters influencing weld quality in robotic GMA welding process. *Journal of Material Processing Technology, 140,* 676-681.

Kim, I. S., Park, C. E., & Yarlagadda, P. K. D. V. (2003d). A study on the prediction of process parameters in the Gas-Metal Arc Welding (GMAW) of mild steel using Taguchi Methods. *Materials Science Forum,* 235 – 238.

Kim, I. S., Park, C. E., Jeong Y. J., & Son, J. S. (2001). Development of an intelligent system for selection of the process variables in gas metal arc welding processes. *International Journal of Advanced Manufacturing Technology, 18,* 98-102.

Kim, I. S., Son, J. S., Kim, I. G., Kim, J. Y., & Kim, O. S. (2003). A study on relationship between process variables and bead penetration for robotic Co_2 Arc Welding. *Journal of Material Processing Technology, (136),* 139-145.

Kim, I. S., Son, K. J., Yang, Y. S., & Yarlagadda, P. K. D. V. (2003b). Sensitivity analysis for process parameters in GMA welding processes using a factorial design method. *International Journal of Machine tools and Manufacture, 143,* 763-769.

Kim, T.Y., Hwang, C., & Lee, J. (2004). Korean economic condition indicator using a neural network trained on the 1997 crisis. *Journal of Data Science, 2,* 371-381.

Kim, T.Y., Oh, K.J., Sohn, I., & Hwang, C. (2004). Usefulness of artificial neural networks for early warning systems of economic crisis. *Expert Systems with Applications, 26,* 583-590.

Kishnapuram R. and Keller J.M. (1993) A possibilistic approach to clustering. *Fuzzy Systems, IEEE Transactions on, 1*(2), 98-110.

Klir, G., & Yuan, B. (1995). *Fuzzy sets and fuzzy logic: Theory and applications*. Upper Saddle River, NJ: Prentice Hall.

Kluger, Y., Basri, R., Chang, J. T., & Gerstein, M. (2003). Spectral biclustering of microarray data: Coclustering genes and conditions. *Genome research, 13*(4), 703-716.

Knick, S.T., Dobkin, D.S., Rotenberry, J.T., Schroeder, M.A., Vander Haegen, W.M., & Van Riper III, C. (2003). Teetering on the edge or too late? Conservation and research issues for avifauna of sagebrush habitats. *The Condor, 105*, 611-634.

Kohonen, T. (1982). Self-organized formation of topologically corrected feature maps. *Biological Cybernetics, 43*, 59-69.

Kohonen, T. (1988). *Self organization and associative memory*. Berlin: Springer-Verlag.

Kohonen, T. (1990). The self-organizing map. *Proceeding of the IEEE, 78*(9), 1464-1480.

Kolesnikova, I. V., Potapov, S. V., Yurkin, M. A., Hoekstra, A. G., Maltsev, V. P. & Semyanov, K. A. (2006). Determination of volume, shape and refractive index of individual blood platelets. *Journal of Quantitative Spectroscopy & Radiative Transfer, 102*, 37-45.

Kosko, B. (1986). Fuzzy entropy and conditioning. *Information Science, 30*, 165-74.

Kotani, M., Ochi, M., Ozawa, S., & Akazawa, K. (2001). Evolutionary discriminant functions using genetic algorithms with variable-length chromosome. *IEEE Transactions Systems, Man, and Cybernetics, 31*, 761-766.

Kotsiantis, S., & Pintelas, P. (2004). Combining bagging and boosting. *International Journal of Computational Intelligence, 1*(4), 324-333.

Kotsiantis, S., Kanellopoulos, D., & Pintelas, P. (2006). Local boosting of decision stumps for regression and classification problems. *Journal of Computers (JCP), 4*(1), 30-37.

Kovacevic, R., & Zhang, Y. M. (1997). Neurofuzzy model-based weld fusion state estimation. *IEEE Control Systems Magazine, 17*(2), 30-42.

Kovalerchuk, B., & Vityaev, E. (2000). *Data mining in finance: Advances in relational and hybrid methods*. Dordrecht: Kluwer, Academic Publishers.

Kreinovich V., Lakeyev, A., Rohn, J., & Kahl, P. (1997). *Computational complexity and feasibility of data processing and interval computations*. Dordrecht: Kluwer.

Kreinovich, V., Longpre, L., Starks, S. A., Xiang, G., Beck, J., Kandathi, R., Nayak, A., Kreinovich, V., Xiang, G., Starks, S. A., Longpre, L., Ceberio, M., Araiza, R., Beck, J., Kandathi, R., Nayak, A., Torres, R., & Hajagos, J. (2006). Towards combining probabilistic and interval uncertainty in engineering calculations: Algorithms for computing statistics under interval uncertainty, and their computational complexity. *Reliable Computing, 12*(6), 471-501.

Kreiss, J.-P. (1992). Bootstrap procedures for AR(1)-processes. In K.H. Jöckel, G. Rothe, & W. Sender (Eds), *Bootstrapping and Related Techniques. Lecture Notes in Economics and Mathematical Systems 376*. Heidelberg: Springer.

Kuan C., & White, H. (1994). Artificial neural networks: An econometric perspective. *Econometric Review, 13*, 1–91.

Kubat, M., Holte, R., & Matwin S. (1998). Machine learning for the detection of oil spills in satellite radar images. *Machine Learning, 30*, 195-215.

Kulkarni, A. D. & Cavanaugh, C. D. (2000). Fuzzy neural network models for classification. *Applied Intelligence, 12*, 207-215.

Kulkarni, A. D. & McCaslin S. (2004). Knowledge discovery from multispectral satellite images. *IEEE Geoscience and Remote Sensing Letters, 1*(4), 246-250.

Kulkarni, A. D. & McCaslin S. (2006). Knowledge discovery from satellite images. *WSEAS Transactions on Signal Processing, 11*(2), 1523-1530.

Kulkarni, A. D. (2001). *Computer vision and fuzzy-neural systems*. Upper Saddle River, NJ: Prentice Hall PTR.

Kulkarni, A. D., Giridhar, G. B., & Coca, P. (1995). Neural network based fuzzy logic decision systems for multispectral image analysis. *Neural, Parallel, & Scientific Computations, 3*(2), 205-218.

Kulkarni, A.D. & Lulla, K. (1999). Fuzzy neural network models for supervised classification: Multispectral image analysis. *Geocarto International, 14*(4), 41-49.

Kulkarni, A.D. (1998). Neural fuzzy models for multispectral image analysis. *Applied Intelligence, 8,* 173-187.

Kumar, M., Moorthy, U., & Perraudin, W. (2003). Predicting emerging market currency crashes. *Journal of Empirical Finance, 10,* 427-454.

Kunsch, H.R. (1989). The jackknife and the bootstrap for general stationary observations. *The Annals of Statistics, 17,* 1217-1241.

La Rocca, M., & Perna C. (2005). Variable selection in neural network regression models with dependent data: A subsampling approach. *Computational Statistics and Data Analysis, 48,* 415-429.

La Rocca, M., & Perna C. (2005). Neural network modeling by subsampling. In J. Cabestany, A. Prieto, & F. Sandoval (Eds), *Computational intelligence and Bioinspired Systems, Lecture Notes in Computer Science 3512,* pp. 200-207. Springer.

Lahiri, S. N. (1999). Theoretical comparisons of block bootstrap methods. *The Annals of Statistics, 27,* 386-404.

Lawrence, R. A., Powell, B.S., &. Zambon, M. (2004). Classification of remotely sensed imagery using stochastic gradient boosting as a refinement of classification tree analysis. *Remote Sensing of Environment, 90,* 331-336.

Lazzeroni, L. & Owen, A. (2002). Plaid models for gene expression data. *Statistica Sinica, 12,* 61 – 86.

LeBaron, B. (1997). *An evolutionary bootstrap approach to neural network pruning and generalization.* Working paper, Dept. of Economics, University of Winsconsin, Madison.

LeBaron, B., & Weigend, A. S. (1998). A bootstrap evaluation of the effect of data splitting on financial time series. *IEEE Transactions on Neural Networks, 9,* 213–220.

Lee, D.S., Iyengar, S., Czanner, G., & Roscoe, J. (2005). *Bayesian wavelet representation of neuron signals via perfect sampling.* Paper presented at the 2nd IMS-ISBA Joint Meeting, Bormio, Italy.

Lee, H., & Tanaka, H. (1999). Upper and lower approximation models in interval regression using regression quantile techniques. *European Journal of Operational Research, 116,* 653-666.

Lee, J. I., & Rhee, S. (2000). Prediction of process parameters for gas metal arc welding by multiple regression analysis. *Proceedings of Institute of Mechanical Engineers Part. B, 214,* 443-449.

Lemmen, S. (2000). Building loyalty and minimising churn in telecoms. Presentation of Telfort's loyalty programme: http://www.pimonline.nl/activities/tshistory/2000/pim20001031Telfort-copyright.ppt

Levich R. M., Majnoni, G., & Reinhart C. (2002). *Ratings, rating agencies and the global financial system.* Boston: Kluwer Academic Publishers.

Lewis, D., & Catlett, J. (1994). Heterogeneous uncertainty sampling for supervised learning. Proceedings of 11th Conference on Machine Learning, 148-156.

Lewis, D.D. (1997). *Reuters-21578 Distribution 1.0.* Retrieved March 2007 from http://kdd.ics.uci.edu/databases/reuters21578/

Li, D.-C., & Lin, Y.-S. (2006). Using virtual sample generation to build up management knowledge in the early manufacturing stages. *European Journal of Operational Research, 175,* 413-434.

Li, D.-C., Chen, L.-S., & Lin, Y.-S. (2003). Using Functional Virtual Population as assistance to learn scheduling knowledge in dynamic manufacturing environments. *International Journal of Production Research, 17,* 4011–4024.

Li, S., Ogura, Y., & Kreinovich, V. (2002). *Limit theorems and applications of set valued and fuzzy valued random variables.* Dordrecht: Kluwer.

Li, X. (2006). Temporal Structure of Neuronal Population Oscillations with Empirical Mode Decomposition. *Physics Letters A, 356,* 237-241.

Li, X., Simpson, S. W., & Rados, M. (2000). Neural networks for online prediction of quality in gas metal arc welding. *Science and Technology of Welding and Joining, 5*(2), 71-79.

Lin, C. T. & Lee, George C. S. (1991). Neural network based fuzzy logic control and decision system. *IEEE Transactions on Computers, 40*, 1320-1336.

Lin, C-C., & Chen, A-P. (2002). Generalisation of Yang et al.'s method of fuzzy programming with piecewise linear membership functions. *Fuzzy sets and Systems, 132*, 346-352.

Lindvall, T. (2002). *Lectures on the coupling method.* Dover Publications.

Liu, J. & Wang, W. (2003). Op-cluster: Clustering by tendancy in high dimensional space. *Proceedings of the 3rd IEEE International Conference on Data Mining*, Melbourne, Florida, USA, 187 – 194, IEEE Computer Society Press.

Liu, X., Cheng, G., & Wu, J. X. (2002). Analyzing outliers cautiously. *IEEE Transactions on Knowledge and Data Engineering, 14*(2), 432-437.

Llew Mason, J.B., Bartlett, P., & Frean, M. (2000). Boosting algorithms as gradient descent. In S.A. Solla, T.K. Leen, & K.-R. Muller (Ed.), *Advances in Neural Information Processing Systems 12*, pp. 512-518. MIT Press.

Lo, K. L. (2004). The fuzzy decision tree application to a power system problem. *COMPEL, 23*(2), 436-451.

Lu, J. (2002). Predicting customer churn in the telecommunications industry - An application of survival analysis modeling using SAS°R. *SUGI 27 Proceedings.*

Lumer, E. D. & Faieta, B. (1994). Diversity and adaptation in populations of clustering ants. *Proceedings of 3rd International Conference on Simulation of Adaptive Behaviour*, August 8-12, Brighton, UK, MIT Press.

Machida, M. (2004). Perfect rejection sampling algorithm for simple mixture models. Preprint from http://www.math.tntech.edu/machida/

MacQueen, J.B. (1967). Some methods for classification and analysis of multivariate observations, *Proceedings of 5-th Berkeley Symposium on Mathematical Statistics and Probability*, Berkeley, 1, 281-297, University of California Press.

Maderia S. C. & Oliveira, A. L. (2004). Biclustering algorithms for biological data analysis: A survey. *IEEE Transactions on Computational Biology and Bioinformatics, 1*(1), 24-45.

Makretsov, N. A., Huntsman, D. G., Nielsen, T. O., Yorida, E., Peacock, M., Cheang, M. C. U., Dunn, S. E., Hayes, M., van de Rijn, M., Bajdik, C., & Gilks, C. B. (2004). Hierarchical clustering analysis of tissue microarray immunostaining data identifies prognostically significant groups of breast carcinoma. *Clinical Cancer Research, 18*(10), 6143 – 6151.

Maltsev, V. P. & Lopatin, V. N. (1997). Parametric solution of the inverse light-scattering problem for individual spherical particles. *Applied Optics, 36*, 6102-6108.

Mamdani, E. H. (1977). Applications of fuzzy logic to approximate reasoning using linguistic synthesis. *IEEE Transactions on Computers, 26*(12), 1182-1191.

Manly, B.F.J., McDonald, L.L., Thomas, D.L., McDonald, T.L., & Erickson W.P. (2002). *Resource selection by animals, statistical design and analysis for field studies. 2nd Edition.* Dordrecht: Kluwer Academic Publishers.

Marinari, E., & Parisi, G. (1992). Simulated tempering: A new Monte Carlo scheme. *Europhysics Letters, 19*, 451-458.

Marsden Jerrold E., & Hoffman, M.J. (1993). *Elementary classical analysis*, Second Edition. W. H. Freeman and Company.

Maslov, S., Sneppen, K., & Zaliznyak, A. (2004). Detection of topological patterns in complex networks: Correlation profile of the Internet. *Physica A, 333*, 529 – 540.

Matheron, G. (1975). *Random sets and integral geometry.* J. Wiley.

MATLAB (1998). *Fuzzy logic tool box: User's Guide.* Natick, MA: The Math Works Inc.

Medaglia, A. L., Fang, S-C., Nuttle, H. L. W., & Wilson, J. R. (2002). An efficient and flexible mechanism for constructing membership functions. *European Journal of Operational Research, 139*, 84-95.

Mengersen, K., & Tweedie, R. (1996). Rates of convergence of the Hastings and Metropolis algorithms. Annals of Statistics, *24*, 101-121.

Mengersen, K.L., Robert, C.P., & Guihenneuc-Jouyaux, C. (1999). MCMC convergence diagnostics: A review. In J. Berger, J. Bernardo, A. Dawid, D. Lindley, & A. Smith (Eds.), *Bayesian Statistics 6*, pp. 415-440. Oxford University Press.

Metropolis, N., Rosenbluth, A., Rosenbluth, M., Teller, A., & Teller, E. (1953). Equations of state calculations by fast computing machines. *Journal of Chemical Physics, 21*, 1087-1092.

Meyn, S.P., & Tweedie, R.L. (1993). *Markov chains and stochastic stability.* Springer.

Mikut, R., Jäkel, J., & Gröll, L. (2005). Interpretability issues in data-based learning of fuzzy systems, *Fuzzy Sets and Systems, 150*, 179-197.

Millenium Ecosystem Assessment. (2005). Ecosystems and Human Well-being: Biodiversity Synthesis. Retrieved August 6, 2007 from http://www.milenniumassessment.org

Milligan, G. W. & Cooper M. C. (1985). An examination of procedures for determining the number of clusters in a dataset. *Psychometrika, 50*, 159-179.

Millspaugh, J.J., & Marzluff, J.M. (Eds) (2001). *Radio tracking and animal populations.* Orlando, FL: Academic Press.

Mira, A., Moller, J., & Roberts, G. (2001). Perfect Slice Samplers. *Journal of the Royal Statistical Society Series B, 63*(3), 593-606.

Mitchell, M. (1996). *An introduction to genetic algorithms.* MIT Press.

Mitra S. & Acharya, T. (2003). *Data mining: Multimedia, soft computing, and bioinformatics.* Hoboken, NJ: Wiley-Interscience.

Mitra, S. & Hayashi, Y. (2000). Neuro-fuzzy rule generation: survey in soft computing framework. *IEEE Transactions on Neural Networks, 11*(3), 748-768.

Mitra, S. &. Pal, S. K. (1995). Fuzzy multi-layer perceptron inferencing and rule generation. *IEEE Transactions on Neural Networks, 6*(1), 51-63.

Mitra, S., De, R. K, & Pal, S. K. (1997). Knowledge-based fuzzy MLP for classification and rule generation. *IEEE Transactions on Neural Networks, 8*(6), 1338-1350.

Mitra, S., Pal, S. K. & Mitra, P. (2002). Data mining in a soft computing framework: A survey. *IEEE Transactions on Neural Networks, 13*(1), 3-14.

Mladenic, D., & Grobelnik, M. (1999). Feature selection for unbalanced class distribution and naive Bayes. 16th International Conference on Machine Learning, 258-267.

Moller, & Beer, M. (2004). *Fuzzy randomness: Uncertainty in Civil Engineering and Computational Mechanics.* Springer-Verlag.

Moller, J. (1999). Perfect simulation of conditionally specified models. *Journal of the Royal Statistical Society Series B, 61*(1), 251-264.

Moller, J. (2003). *Spatial statistics and computational methods.* Springer.

Moller, J., & Nicholls, G. (1999). Perfect simulation for sample-based inference. Preprint from http://www.math.auckland.ac.nz/~nicholls/linkfiles/papers.html

Moller, J., & Schladitz, K. (1999). Extension of Fill's algorithm for perfect simulation. *Journal of the Royal Statistical Society Series B, 61*, 955-969.

Moller, J., & Waagepetersen, R. (2003). *Statistical inference and simulation for spatial point processes.* Chapman & Hall/CRC.

Montgomery, D. C. (1997). *Design and analysis of experiments.* New York: Wiley.

Moody's (2006). Rating Definitions - Bank Financial Strength Ratings. Retrieved on June 26, 2006, from http://www.moodys.com.

Moon, H., & Na, S. J. (1996). A neuro-fuzzy approach to select welding conditions for welding quality improvement in horizontal fillet welding. *ASME Journal of Manufacturing Systems, 15*(6), 392-402.

Morales, J.M., Haydon, D.T., Friar, J., Holsinger, K.E., & Fryxell, J.M. (2004). Extracting more out of relocation data: Building movement models as mixtures of random walks. *Ecology, 85*, 2436-2445.

Morgan, M. (2003). Unearthing the customer: data mining is no longer the preserve of mathematical statisticians. Marketeers can also make a real, practical use of it (Revenue-Generating Networks). *Telecommunications International.*

Morik, K., & Kopcke, H. (2004). Analysing customer churn in insurance data - A case study. *Proceedings of the European Conf. on Principles and Practice of Knowledge Discovery in Databases*, Pisa, Italy, pp 325-336.

Mozer, M., Wolniewicz, R.H., Grimes, D.B., Johnson, E., & Kaushansky, H. (2000). Churn reduction in the wireless industry. *Advances in Neural Information Processing Systems, 12*, 935-941.

Murdoch, D.J., & Green, P.J. (1998). Exact sampling from a continuous state space. *Scandinavian Journal of Statistics, 25*, 483-502.

Murthy S. K. (1998). Automatic construction of decision trees from data: multi-disciplinary survey. *Data Mining and Knowledge Discovery, 2*, 345-389.

Murugan, N., & Parmer, R. S. (1994). Effect of MIG process parameters on the geometry of the bead in the automatic surfacing of stainless steel. *Journal of Material Processing Technology, 41*, 381-398.

Murugan, N., Parmer, R. S., & Sud, S. K. (1993). Effect of submerged arc process variables on dilution and bead geometry in single wire surfacing. *Journal of Materials Processing Technology, 37*, 767-780.

Nagesh, D. S., & Datta G. L., (2002). Prediction of weld bead geometry and penetration in shielded metal-arc welding using artificial neural networks. *Journal of Materials Processing Technology, 79*, 1–10.

Nascimento, C.A.O., Guardani, R. & Giulietti, M. (1997). Use of neural networks in the analysis of particle size distributions by laser diffraction. *Powder Technology, 90*, 89-94.

Nauck, D.D. (2003). Fuzzy data analysis with NEF-CLASS. *International Journal of Approximate Reasoning, 32*, 103-130.

Nauck, D.D. (2003). Measuring interpretability in rule-based classification systems. *Proceedings of the 2003 IEEE International Conference on Fuzzy Systems (FuzzIEEE2003), 1*, pp. 196-201. Saint Louis, MO: IEEE Press.

Nauck, D.D., Ruta, D., Spott, M., & Azvine, B. (2006) A tool for intelligent customer analytics. *Proceedings of the IEEE International Conference on Intelligent Systems*, pp. 518-521. London: IEEE Press.

Nauck, D.D., Spott, M., & Azvine, B. (2003). Spida – A novel data analysis tool. *BT Technology Journal, 21*(4), 104–112.

Neilson, W., & Stowe, J. (2002). A further examination of cumulative prospect theory parameterizations. *The Journal of Risk and Uncertainty, 24*(1), 31-46.

Neri, F., & Saitta, L. (1996). Exploring the power of genetic search in learning symbolic classifiers. *IEEE Transaction Pattern Analysis and Machine Intelligence*, 18, 11, 1135-1141.

Nguyen, H. T. & Tran, H. (2007). On a continuous lattice approach to modeling of coarse data in system analysis. *Journal of Uncertain Systems, 1*(1), 62-73.

Nguyen, H. T. (2006). *An introduction to random sets*. Chapman and Hall/CRC Press.

Nguyen, H. T., & Kreinovich, V. (1996). Nested intervals and sets: Concepts, relations to fuzzy sets, and applications. In R.B. Kearfott & V. Kreinovich (Eds.). *Applications of interval computations*, pp. 245-290. Dordrecht: Kluwer.

Nguyen, H. T., & Walker, E. A. (2006). *A first course in fuzzy logic* (3rd edition). Chapman and Hall/CRC Press.

Nguyen, H. T., Wang, Y., & Wei, G. (in press). On Choquet theorem for random upper semicontinuous functions. *International Journal of Approximate Reasoning*.

Nielsen, S.E., Boyce, Stenhouse, G.B., & Munro, R.H.M. (2002). Modeling grizzly bear habitats in the Yellowhead Ecosystem of Alberta: Taking autocorrelation seriously. *Ursus, 13*, 45-56.

Niyogi, P., Girosi, F., & Tomaso, P. (1998). Incorporating prior information in machine learning by creating virtual examples. *Proceeding of the IEEE, 86*(11), 275-298.

Noland, R. (2003). Traffic fatalities and injuries: the effect of changes in infrastructure and other trends. *Accident Analysis & Prevention, 35*, 599-611

Norris, J.R. (1997). *Markov chains*. Cambridge University Press.

Olaru, C., & Wehenkel, L. (2003). A complete fuzzy decision tree technique. *Fuzzy Sets and Systems, 138*, 221-254.

Olden, J.D., & Jackson, D.A. (2002). A comparison of statistical approaches for modeling fish species distributions. *Freshwater Biology, 47*, 1-20.

Onyeahialam, A., Huettmann, F., & Bertazzon, S. (2005). Modeling sage grouse: Progressive computational methods for linking a complex set of local biodiversity and habitat data towards global conservation statements and decision support systems. Lecture Notes In *Computer Science (LNCS) 3482, International Conference on Computational Science and its Applications (ICCSA) Proceedings Part III*, pp.152-161.

Pal, S. K. & Mitra, S. (1992). Multilayer perceptron, fuzzy sets, and classification. *IEEE Transactions on Neural Networks, 3*, 683-697.

Papadopoulos, G., Edwards, P. J., & Murray, A. F. (2000). Confidence estimation methods for neural networks: A practical comparison. *Proceedings of ESANN 2000*, Bruges (Belgium), April 26 – 28, 2000, D-facto public., 75-80.

Peng, Y. (2004). Intelligent condition monitoring using fuzzy inductive learning. *Journal of Intelligent Manufacturing, 15*, 373-380.

Philippe, A., & Robert, C. (2003). Perfect simulation of positive Gaussian distributions. *Statistics and Computing, 13*(2), 179-186.

Piney, C. (2003). Applying utility theory to risk management. *Project Management Journal, 34,*(3), 26-31.

Polikar, R. (2006). Ensemble based systems in decision making. A tutorial article on ensemble systems including pseudocode, block diagrams and implementation issues for AdaBoost and other ensemble learning algorithms. *IEEE Circuits and Systems Magazine, 6*(3), 21-45.

Politis, D. N., & Romano, J. P. (1992). A circular block-resampling procedure for stationary data. In C. Page & R. LePage (Eds.), *Exploring the limits of the bootstrap.* New York: Springer-Verlag.

Politis, D. N., & Romano, J. P. (1994). The stationary bootstrap. *JASA, 89*, 1303-1313.

Politis, D. N., J. P. Romano, & Wolf, M. (1999). *Subsampling.* Springer.

Poon W. P. H., Firth, M., & Fung, M. (1999). A multivariate analysis of the determinants of Moody's bank financial strength ratings. *Journal of International Financial Markets Institutions and Money, 9*, 267-283.

Popp, J., Neubauer, D., Paciulli, L.M., & Huettmann, F. (in press). Using TreeNet for identifying management thresholds of mantled howling monkeys' habitat preferences on Ometepe Island, Nicaragua, on a tree and home range scale. *Journal Scientific International.*

Prasad, A.M., Iverson, L.R., & Liaw, A. (2006). Newer classification and regression tree techniques: Bagging and random forests for ecological prediction. *Ecosystems, 9*, 181-199.

Prelec, D. (1998). The probability weighting function. *Econometrica, 66*(3), 497-527.

Primack, R. B. (1998). *Essentials of conservation biology.* Second Edition. New York: Sinauer Associates Publishers

Propp, J.G., & Wilson, D.B. (1996). Exact sampling with coupled Markov chains and applications to statistical mechanics. *Random Structures and Algorithms, 9*(1/2), 223-252.

Propp, J.G., & Wilson, D.B. (1998). How to get a perfectly random sample from a generic Markov chain and generate a random spanning tree of a directed graph. *Journal of Algorithms, 27*, 170-217.

Quakenbush, J. (2001). Computational analysis of microarray data. *Nature Review Genetics, 2*(6), 418 – 427.

Quilan J. R. (1986). Induction decision trees. *Machine Learning, 1*, 86-106.

Quilan J. R. (1993). C4.5: *Programs for machine learning.* San Mateo, CA: Morgan Kaufmann.

Quinlan, J.R. (1987). Simplifying decision trees. *International J. Man-Machine Studies*, 27, 221-234.

Rabinovich, S. (2005). *Measurement errors and uncertainties: Theory and practice.* New York: Springer-Verlag.

Ramos, V. & Merelo, J. (2002). Self-organized stigmergic document maps: Environment as a mechanism for context learning. *1st Spanish Conference on Evolutionary and Bio-Inspired Algorithms*, Merida, Spain.

Raser, J. M. & O' Shea E. K. (2005). Noise in gene expression data: Origins and control. *Science, 309*, 2010-2013.

Rasmussen, B., & Hines, J. W. (2004). Prediction interval estimation techniques for empirical modelling strategies and their applications to signal validation tasks. *Applied Computational Intelligence*, Proceedings of the 6th International FLINS Conference, Blankenberge, Belgium, September 1-3, 2004.

Refenes, A.P.N., & Zapranis, A.D. (1999). Neural model identification, variable selection and model adequacy. *Journal of Forecasting, 18*, 299-332

Reynolds, C. W. (1987). Flocks, herds, and schools: A distributed behavioral model. *Computer Graphics (ACM), 21*(4), 25-34.

Rinnooy-Kan, A. & Timmer, G. T. (1987). Stochastic global optimization methods. Part I: Clustering methods. *Mathematical Programming, 39*, 27-56.

Rinnooy-Kan, A. & Timmer, G. T. (1987). Stochastic global optimization methods. Part II: Multilevel methods. *Mathematical Programming, 39*, 57-78.

Ritter, J. (2007). *Wildlife habitat modeling in the Toklat basin study area of Denali National Park and Preserve, Alaska.* Unpublished M.Sc. Thesis. University of Alaska-Fairbanks.

Roa-Sepulveda, C. A., Herrera, M., Pavez-Lazo, B., Knight, U. G., & Coonick, A. H. (2003). Economic dispatch using fuzzy decision trees. *Electric Power Systems Research, 66*, 115-122.

Robert, C.P., & Casella, G. (2004). *Monte Carlo statistical methods (2nd ed.).* Springer.

Roberts, D. K., & Wells, A. A. (1954). Fusion welding of aluminium alloys. *British Welding Journal, 12*, 553-559.

Roberts, G., & Rosenthal, J. (1999). Convergence of slice sampler Markov chains. *Journal of the Royal Statistical Society Series B, 61*, 643-660.

Roberts, G.O. (1996). Markov chain concepts related to sampling algorithms. In W.R. Gilks, S. Richardson & D.J. Spiegelhalter (Eds.), *Markov chain Monte Carlo in practice,* pp. 45-57. Chapman & Hall.

Rockafellar, R. T., & West, J. B. (1984). Variational systems an introduction. In *Springer lecture notes in mathematics,* Vol. 1091, 1–54.

Rodriguez, I., Lawry, J., & Baldwin, J. (2002). A hierarchical linguistic clustering algorithm for prototype induction. *Ninth International Conference Information Processing and Management of Uncertainty in Knowledge-based Systems IPMU 2002*, Annecy, 195-202.

Rosenthal, D. (1941). Mathematical theory of heat distribution during welding and cutting. *Welding Journal, 20*(5), 220-234.

Ross, M. S. (1987). *Introduction to probability and statistics for engineers and scientists.* John Wiley & Sons, Inc.

Rowlands, H., & Antony, F. (2003). Application of design of experiments to a spot welding process. *Journal of Assembly Automation, 23*(3), 273-279.

Rumelhart, D. E. & Zipser, (1985). Feature discovery by competitive learning. *Cognitive Science, 9*, 75-112.

Rumelhart, D. E., McClelland, J. L., & PDP Group (1986). *Parallel distributed processing,* Vol I, Cambridge, MA: MIT Press.

Sachs, J.D., Tornell, A., & Velasco, A. (1996). *Financial crises in emerging markets: the lessons from 1996.* Brookings Papers on Economic Activity, 147-215.

Safranek, R. J., Gottschlich, S., & Kak, A. C. (1990). Evidence accumulation using binary frames of discernment for verification vision. *IEEE Transactions on Robotics and Automation, 6*, 405-417.

Salford Systems. (2002). *TreeNet version 1.0 data mining software documentation.* Retrieved on February 25, 2007, from http://www.salford-systems.com/. San Diego, CA.

Sander, J., Ester, M., Kriegel, K. P., & Xu, X. (1998). Density-based clustering in spatial databases: The algorithmic GDBSCAN and its applications. *Data Mining and Knowledge Discovery, 2*(2), 169 – 194.

Schneider, U., & Corcoran, J.N. (2004). Perfect sampling for Bayesian variable selection in a linear regression model. *Journal of Statistical Planning and Inference, 126*, 153-171.

Schulze, A. & Downward, J. Navigating gene expression using microarrays – A technology review. *Nature Cell Biology, 3*(8), E190 - 195.

Scott A. J. & Symons, M. J. (1971). Clustering methods based on likelihood ratio criteria. *Biometrics, 27*(2), 387-397.

Segal, E. Taskar, B., Gasch, A., Friedman, N., & Koller, D. (2003). Decomposing gene expression into cellular processes. *Proceedings of the Pacific Symposium on Biocomputing,* Lihue, Hawaii, USA, 89 – 100, World Scientific Press.

Semyanov, K. A., Tarasov, P. A., Soini, J. T., Petrov, A. K. & Maltsev, V. P. (2000). Calibration-free method to determine the size and hemoglobin concentration of individual red blood cells from light scattering. *Applied Optics, 39*, 5884-5889.

Setiono, R. & Leow, W. K. (2000). FERNN An algorithm for fast extraction of rules from neural networks. *Applied Intelligence, 12*, 15-25.

Shafer G., & Srivastava, R. (1990). The Bayesian and belief-function formalisms: A general perspective for auditing. In *Auditing: A Journal of Practice and Theory.* Reprinted in J. Pearl & G. Shafer (Eds.) *Readings in uncertain reasoning*, pp. 482-521. San Mateo, CA: Morgan Kaufmann.

Shafer, G. A. (1976). *Mathematical theory of evidence.* Princeton: Princeton University Press.

Shemer, J. (2004). Traffic Accidents - The National Killer. *Harefuah, 143*(2), 90-91.

Sheng, Q., Moreau, Y., & De Moor, B. (2003). Biclustering microarray data by Gibbs sampling. *Bioinformaics, 19*(Supp. 2), ii196 – ii205.

Shimizu, K. & Ishimaru, A. (1990). Differential Fourier-transform technique for the inverse scattering problem. *Applied Optics, 29*, 3428-3433.

Singleton, J. C., & Surkan, J. S. (1991). Modelling the judgement of bond rating agencies: Artificial intelligence applied to finance. *Journal of the Midwest Finance Association, 20*, 72-80.

Sinha, D. & Dougherty, E. (1993). Fuzzification of set inclusion: theory and applications. *Fuzzy Sets & Systems, 55*, 15–42.

Smets, P. (1991). Varieties of ignorance and the need for well-founded theories. *Information Sciences, 57-58*, 135-144.

Smith, S.F. (1983). Flexible learning of problem solving heuristics through adaptive search. *Proceedings Eight International Conference on Artificial Intelligence.* Karlsruhe, Germany: Morgan Kaufmann, 422-425.

Solymosi, T., & Dombi, J. (1986). A method for determining weights of criteria: The centralized weights. *European Journal of Operational Research, 26*, 35-41.

Spott, M. & Nauck, D.D. (2005). On choosing an appropriate data analysis algorithm. *Proceedings of the IEEE International Conference on Fuzzy Systems 2005*, Reno, NV: IEEE Press.

Spott, M. (1999). A theory of possibility distributions. *Fuzzy Sets and Systems, 102*, 135-155.

Spott, M. (2001). Combining fuzzy words. *Proceedings of IEEE International Conference on Fuzzy Systems 2001.* Melbourne, Australia: IEEE Press.

Spott, M. (2005). Efficient reasoning with fuzzy words. In S.K. Halgamuge & L.P. Wang (Eds.), *Computational intelligence for modelling and predictions,* pp. 117-128. Studies in Compuational Intelligence 2. Berlin: Springer Verlag.

Srivastava, R. P., & Liu, L. (2003). Applications of belief functions in business decisions: A review. *Information Systems Frontiers, 5*(4), 359-378.

Staehelin, J., Kegel, R. & Harris, N. R. P. (1997). Trend analysis of the homogenised total ozone series of AROSA (Switzerland), 1926 – 1996. *Journal of Geophysical Research.*

Steuer, E. R. (1986). *Multiple criteria optimization: Theory, computation and application.* John Wiley & Sons, Inc.

Storn, R., & Price, K. (1997). Differential evolution - A simple and efficient heuristic for global optimization over continuous spaces. *Journal of Global Optimisation, 11*(4), 41-359.

Sun, B., Wilcox, R.T., & Li, S. (2005). Cross-selling sequentially ordered products: an application to consumer banking services. Forthcoming, in *Journal of Marketing Research.*

Szmidt, E., & Kacprzyk, J. (2000). Distances between intuitionistic fuzzy sets. *Fuzzy Sets and Systems, 114*(3), 505-518.

Szmidt, E., & Kacprzyk, J. (2001). Entropy for intuitionistic fuzzy sets. *Fuzzy Sets and Systems, 118*(3), 467-477.

Szmidt, E., & Baldwin, J. (2003). New similarity measure for intuitionistic fuzzy set theory and mass assignment theory. *Notes on Intuitionistic Fuzzy Sets, 9*(3), 60-76.

Szmidt, E., & Baldwin, J. (2004). Entropy for intuitionistic fuzzy set theory and mass assignment theory. *Notes on Intuitionistic Fuzzy Sets, 10*(3), 15-28.

Szmidt, E., & Baldwin, J. (2005). Assigning the parameters for intuitionistic fuzzy sets. *Notes on Intuitionistic Fuzzy Sets, 11*(6), 1-12.

Szmidt, E., & Baldwin, J. (2006). Intuitionistic fuzzy set functions, mass assignment theory, possibility theory and histograms. *Proceedings of 2006 IEEE World Congress on Computational Intelligence*, Vancouver, Canada, 234-243, Omnipress (IEEE Catalog Number: 06CH37726D; ISBN: 0-7803-9489-5).

Szmidt, E., & Kacprzyk, J. (2005). A new concept of a similarity measure for intuitionistic fuzzy sets and its use in group decision making. In V. Torra, Y. Narukawa, & S. Miyamoto (Eds.), *Modelling decisions for artificial intelligence. Lecture notes on artificial intelligence, 3558*, 272-282. Springer-Verlag.

Szmidt, E., & Kacprzyk, J. (1998). Group decision making under intuitionistic fuzzy preference relations. *Seventh International Conference Information Processing and Management of Uncertainty in Knowledge-based Systems, 172*-178. Paris, La Sorbonne.

Szmidt, E., & Kacprzyk, J. (2002). Analysis of agreement in a group of experts via distances between intuitionistic fuzzy preferences. *Ninth International Conference Information Processing and Management of Uncertainty in Knowledge-based Systems IPMU 2002*, Annecy, 1859-1865. ESIA: Universite de Savoie, France.

Szmidt, E., & Kacprzyk, J. (2002). An intuitionistic fuzzy set based approach to intelligent data analysis (an application to medical diagnosis). In A. Abraham, L. Jain, & J.

Kacprzyk (Eds.), *Recent advances in intelligent paradigms and applications*, pp. 57-70. Springer-Verlag.

Szmidt, E., & Kacprzyk, J. (2004). A similarity measure for intuitionistic fuzzy sets and its application in supporting medical diagnostic reasoning. *Lecture Notes on Artificial Intelligence, 3070*, 388-393.

Szmidt, E., & Kacprzyk, J. (2004). A concept of similarity for intuitionistic fuzzy sets and its use in group decision making. *Proceedings 2004 IEEE International Conference on Fuzzy Systems*, Budapest, 1129-1134. FUZZY IEEE 2004 CD-ROM Conference Proceedings. IEEE Catalog Number: 04CH37542C, ISBN: 0-7803-8354-0.

Szmidt, E., & Kacprzyk, J. (2006). An application of intuitionistic fuzzy set similarity measures to a multi-criteria decision making problem. *Lecture Notes on Artificial Intelligence, 4029*, 314-323. Springer-Verlag.

Szmidt, E., & Kacprzyk, J. (2006). Distances between intuitionistic fuzzy sets: Straightforward approaches may not work. *3rd International IEEE Conference Intelligent Systems IS'06*, London, 716-721.

Szmidt, E., & Kacprzyk, J. (2006). A model of case based reasoning using intuitionistic fuzzy sets. *2006 IEEE World Congress on Computational Intelligence*, 8428-8453.

Szmidt, E., & Kacprzyk, J. (2007). Some problems with entropy measures for the Atamnassov intuitionistic fuzzy sets. *Applications of Fuzzy Sets Theory. Lecture Notes on Artificial Intelligence, 4578*, 291-297. Springer-Verlag.

Szmidt, E., & Kacprzyk, J. (2007). A new similarity measure for intuitionistic fuzzy sets: Straightforward approaches may not work. *2007 IEEE Conference on Fuzzy Sytems, 481*-486. IEEE Catalog Number: 07CH37904C, ISBN: 1-4244-1210-2.

Szmidt, E., & Kukier, M. (2006). Classification of imbalanced and overlapping classes using intuitionistic fuzzy sets. Third International IEEE Conference "Intelligent Systems", 722-727, University of Westminster. IEEE Catalog Number: 06EX1304C, ISBN: 1-4244-0196-8.

Taha, I. A. & Ghosh, J. (1999). Symbolic interpretation of artificial neural networks. *IEEE Transactions on Knowledge and Data Engineering, 11*(3), 448-463.

Tamayo, D. Slonim, J. Mesirov, Q. Zhu, S. Kitareewan, E. Dmitrovsky, E. S. Lan-der, & Golub, T. R. (1999). Interpreting patterns of gene expression with self-organizing maps: Methods and application to hematopoietic differentiation. *Proceedings of the National Academy of Sciences of the United States of America, 96*(6), 2907-2912.

Tanaka, H., Uejima, S., & Asai, K. (1982). Linear regression analysis with fuzzy model. *IEEE Transactions on Systems, Man, and Cybernetics, 12,* 903-907.

Tanay, A. Sharan, R., & Shamir, R. Discovering statistically significant biclusters in gene expression data. *Bioinformatics, 18*(1), S136-44.

Tarng, Y. S., & Yang, W. H. (1998). Optimization of the weld bead geometry in gas tungsten arc welding by the Taguchi method. *International Journal of Advanced Manufacturing Technology, 14,* 549–554.

Tarng, Y. S., Tsai, H. L., & Yeh, S. S. (1999). Modeling, optimization and classification of weld quality in tungsten inert gas welding. *International Journal of Machine Tools & Manufacturing, 39*(9), 1427-1438.

Tavazoie, S., Hughes, J. D., Campbell, M. J. Cho, R. J., & Church, G. M. (1999). Systematic determination of genetic network architecture. *Nature genetics, 22*(3), 281-285.

Thonnes, E. (2000). A primer in perfect simulation. In K.R. Mecke & D. Stoyan (Eds.), *Statistical Physics and Spatial Statistics,* pp. 349-378. Springer.

Thorisson, H. (2000). *Coupling, stationarity and regeneration.* Springer.

Tibshirani, R. (1996). A comparison of some error estimates for neural network models. *Neural Computation, 8,* 152-163.

Tibshirani, R., Walther, G., & Hastie, T. (2001). Estimating the number of clusters in a dataset via the gap statistic. *Journal of the Royal Statistical Society: Series B (Statistical Methodology), 63*(2), 411-423.

Tierney, L. (1996). Introduction to general state-space Markov chain theory. In W.R. Gilks, S. Richardson & D.J. Spiegelhalter (Eds.), *Markov chain Monte Carlo in practice,* pp. 59-74. Chapman & Hall.

Tkadlec, J., & Bruha, I. (2003). Formal aspects of a multiple-rule classifier. *International Journal of Pattern Recognition and Artificial Intelligence,* 17, 4, 581-600.

Toronen, P., Kolehmainen, M., Wong, G., & Castren, E. (1999). Analysis of gene expression data using self-organizing maps. *FEBS Letters, 451*(2), 142 – 146.

Traffic Safety Facts (2004). State Alcohol Estimates, www.nhtsa.dot.gov.

Troyanskaya, O., Cantor, M., Sherlock, G., Brown, P., Hastie, T., Tibshirani, R., Botstein, D., & Altman, R. B. (2001). Missing value estimation methods for DNA microarrays. *Bioinformatics, 17*(6), 520 – 525.

Tummala, V M R., & Burchett, J. F. (1999). Applying a risk management process (RMP) to manage cost risk for an EHV transmission line project. *International Journal of Project Management, 17*(4), 223-235.

Tummala, V. M. & Rao Leung, Y. H. (1996). A risk management model to assess safety and reliability risks. *International Journal of Quality & Reliability Management, 13*(8), 53-62.

Turney, P.D. (1995). Cost-sensitive classification: Empirical evaluation of a hybrid genetic decision tree induction algorithm. *J. Artificial Intelligence Research.*

Tversky, A., & Kahneman, D. (1992). Advanced in prospect theory: Cumulative representation of uncertainty. *Journal of Risk and Uncertainty, 5*(4), 297-323.

UCI Machine Learning Repository, http://www.ics.uci.edu/~mlearn/MLRepository.html

Ulanowski, Z. (1988). PhD thesis: *Investigations of microbial physiology and cell structure using laser diffractometry.* Hatfield: Hatfield Polytechnic.

Ulanowski, Z. & Ludlow, I. K. (1989). Water distribution, size, and wall thickness in Lycoperdon pyriforme spores. *Mycological Research, 93,* 28-32.

Ulanowski Z., Wang, Z., Kaye, P. H., & Ludlow, I. K. (1998). Application of neural networks to the inverse light scattering problem for spheres. *Applied Optics, 37,* 4027-4033.

Ulanowski, Z., Ludlow, I. K. & Waites, W. M. (1987). Water-content and size of spore components determined by laser diffractometry. *FEMS Microbiology Letters, 40*, 229-232.

University of California at Irvine (2007). UCI Machine Learning Repository. Accessed March, 26, 2007 at http://www.ics.uci.edu/~mlearn/MLRepository.html.

van der Laan, M. J. & Pollard, K. S. (2001). *Hybrid clustering of gene expression data with visualization and the bootstrap.* (Technical Report 93), *U.C. Berkeley Division of Biostatistics Working Paper Series, Berkeley, California, University of California, School of Public Health, Division of Biostatisitcs.*

Vannoorenberghe, P. (2004). On aggregating belief decision trees. *Information Fusion, 5*, 179-188.

Vapnik, V.N. (1995). *The nature of statistical learning theory.* New York: Springer.

Vargas-Ubera, J., Aguilar, J. F., & Gale, D. M. (2007). Reconstruction of particle-size distributions from light-scattering patterns using three inversion methods. *Applied Optics, 46*, 124-132.

Vincent, C., McConnell, B.J., Fedak, M.A., & Ridoux, V. (2002). Assessment of Argos location accuracy from satellite tags deployed on captive grey seals. *Marine Mammal Science, 18*, 301-322.

Visa S., & Ralescu A. (2004). Experiments in guided class rebalance based on class structure. *Proceedings of the 15ᵗʰ Midwest Artificial Intelligence and Cognitive Science Conference.* Dayton, USA, 8-14.

Von Neumann J., & Morgenstern, O. (2004). *Theory of games and economic behavior.* Princeton: Princeton University Press, New Work.

Wackerly, D. D., Mendenhall, W., & Scheaffer, R. L. (1996). *Mathematical statistics with applications*, Fifth Edition. Wadsworth Publishing Company.

Wang L. & Mendel, J. M. (1992). Generating fuzzy rules by learning from examples. *IEEE Transactions on Systems, Man, and Cybernetics, 22*(6), 414-1427.

Wang, J. & Beni, G. (1988). *Pattern generation in cellular robotic systems.* Arlington, VA/Piscataway, NJ: IEEE.

Wang, J. & Beni, G. (1989). *Cellular robotic system with stationary robots and its application to manufacturing lattices.* Albany, NY/Piscataway, NJ: IEEE.

Wang, J. & Beni, G. (1990). *Distributed computing problems in cellular robotic systems.* Ibaraki, Japan: IEEE.

Wang, X., Chen, B., Qian, G., & Ye, F. (2000). On the optimization of fuzzy decision trees. *Fuzzy Sets and Systems, 112*, 117-125.

Wang, X., Nauck, D. D., Spott, M., & Kruse, R. (2007). Intelligent data analysis with fuzzy decision trees. *Soft Computing, 11*, 439-457.

Washington, S., Metarko, J., Fomumung, I., Ross, R., Julian, F., & Moran, E. (1999). An inter-regional comparison: fatal crashes in the Southeastern and non-Southeastern United States: preliminary findings. *Accident Analysis & Prevention, 31*, 135-146.

Waters, K. M., Pounds, J. G. & Thrall B. D. (2006). Data merging for integrated microarray and proteomics analysis. Briefings in Functional Genomics and Proteomics, 5(4), 261 – 272.

Wei, G., & Wang, Y. (in press). On metrization of the hit-or-miss topology using Alexandroff compactification. *International Journal of Approximate Reasoning.*

Weigend, A. S., & LeBaron, B. (1994). Evaluating neural network predictors by bootstrapping. In *Proceedings of the International Conference on Neural Information Processing*, ICONIP'94, Seoul, Korea, 1207-1212.

Wen, X., Fuhrman, S., Michaels, G. S., Carr, D. B., Smith, S., Barker, J. L., & Somogyi, R. (1998). Large Scale temporal gene expression mapping of central nervous system development. *PNAS, 95*(1), 334-339.

White H., & Racine J.(2001). Statistical inference, the bootstrap and neural network modelling with application to foreign exchange rates. *IEEE Transaction on neural Networks, 12*, 657-673

White, H. (1989). Learning in artificial neural networks: A statistical perspective. *Neural Computation, 1*, 425-464.

Whittingham, M.J., Stephens, P.A., Bradbury, R.B., & Freckleton, R.P. (2006). Why do we still use stepwise modelling in ecology and behavior? *Journal of Animal Ecology, 75*, 1182-1189.

Wilson, D.B. (2000). How to couple from the past using a read-once source of randomness. *Random Structures and Algorithms, 16*(1), 85-113.

Wirth, R., Shearer, C., Grimmer, U., Reinartz, J., Schloesser, T.P., Breitner, C., Engels, R., & Lindner, G. (1997). Towards process-oriented tool support for knowledge discovery in databases. *Principles of Data Mining and Knowledge Discovery. First European Symposium, PKDD '97,* pp. 243–253. Lecture Notes in Computer Science 1263, Berlin: Springer-Verlag.

Witten, I.H. & Frank, E. (2000). *Data mining: Practical machine learning tools and techniques with JAVA implementations.* San Francisco: Morgan Kaufmann Publishers.

Wu, C. S., Polte, T., & Rehfeldt, D. (2001). A fuzzy logic system for process monitoring and quality evaluation in GMAW. *Welding Research Supplement, 2,* 33-38.

Wu, G., & Gonzalez, R. (1996). Curvature of the probability weighting function. *Management Science, 42,* 1676-1690

Wyatt, P.J. (1980). Some chemical, physical and optical properties of fly ash particles, *Applied Optics, 7,* 975-983.

Xiang, G. (2007). Interval uncertainty in bioinformatics. *Abstracts of the New Mexico Bioinformatics Symposium,* Santa Fe, Mexico, March 8–9, p. 25.

Yager, R.R. (1979). Level sets for membership evaluation of fuzzy subsets. Technical Report RRY-79-14, Iona Colledge, New York. Also in: R.Yager (Ed.), *Fuzzy set and possibility theory - Recent developments,* 1982, 90-97. Oxford: Pergamon Press.

Yamada, K. (2001). Probability-possibility transformation based on evidence theory. Proceedings. IFSA-NAFIPS'2001, 70-75.

Yan, L., Miller, D.J., Mozer, M.C., & Wolniewicz, R. (2001). Improving prediction of customer behaviour in non-stationary environments. *Proceedings of International Joint Conference on Neural Networks*, pp. 2258-2263.

Yang, J., Wang, H., Wang, W., & Yu, P. (2003). Enhanced biclustering on expression data. *Proceedings of the 3rd IEEE Symposium on BioInformatics and BioEngineering (*BIBE '03). IEEE Computer Society, 321 - 327.

Yang, W.X. (2004). An improved genetic algorithm adopting immigration operator. *Intelligent Data Analysis,* 8, 385-401.

Yen, P., Huettmann, F. & Cooke, F. (2004). Modelling abundance and distribution of Marbled Murrelets (*Brachyramphus marmoratus*) using GIS, marine data and advanced multivariate statistics. *Ecological Modelling, 171,* 395-413.

Yodhida, T. & Omatu, S. (1994). Neural network approach to land cover mapping. *IEEE Transactions on Geosciences and Remote Sensing, 32*(5), 1103-1109.

Yu, C-S., & Li, H-L. (2001). Method for solving quasi-concave and non-cave fuzzy multi-objective programming problems. *Fuzzy Sets and Systems, 122,* 205-227.

Yu, L., Lai, K.K., & Wang, S.Y. (2006). Currency crisis forecasting with general regression neural networks. *International Journal of Information Technology and Decision Making, 5*(3), 437-454

Yuan, Y., & Shaw, M. J. (1995). Induction of fuzzy decision trees. *Fuzzy Sets and Systems, 69,* 125-139.

Zadeh L. A. (1973). Outline of a new approach to the analysis of complex systems and decision processes. *IEEE Transactions on Systems, Man and Cybernetics-Part A: Systems and Humans, SMC-3,* 28-44.

Zadeh, L. A. (1965). Fuzzy sets. *Information and Control, 8*(3), 338-353.

Zadeh, L. A. (1973). Outline of a new approach to analysis of complex systems and decision processes. *IEEE Transactions on Systems, Man, and Cybernetics, 3,* 28-44.

Zadeh, L. A. (1994). Fuzzy logic, neural networks, and soft computing. *Communications of the ACM, 37,* 77-84.

Zadeh, L. A. (1999). Some reflections o the anniversary of Fuzzy Sets and Systems. *Fuzzy Sets and Systems, 100,* 1-3.

Zadeh, L. A. (2005). Toward a generalized theory of uncertainty (GTU) – An outline. *Information Sciences, 172,* 1-40.

Zadeh, L.A. (1978). Fuzzy sets as the basis for a theory of possibility. *Fuzzy Sets and Systems, 1,* 3 - 28.

Zakovic, S. (1997). PhD thesis: *Global optimization applied to an inverse light scattering problem.* Hatfield: University of Hertfordshire.

Zakovic, S., Ulanowski, Z. & Bartholomew-Biggs, M. C. (1998). Application of global optimization to particle identification using light scattering. *Inverse Problems, 14*, 1053-1067.

Zakri, A.H. (2003). *Millennium ecosystem assessment: Integrated assessment through the millennium ecosystem assessment.* United Nations University Institute for Advanced Studies. Retrieved August 6, 2007 from http://www.milenniumassessment.org

Zeeberg, B.R., Feng, W., Wang, Geoffrey, W., Wang, M. D., Fojo, A. T., Sunshine, M., Narasimhan, S., Kane, D. W., Reinhold, W. C., Lababidi, S., Bussey, K. J., Riss, J., Barrett, J. C., & Weinstein, J. N. (2003). GoMiner: A resource for biological interpretation of genomic and proteomics data. *Genome Biology, 4*, R28.

Zha, H., Ding, C., Gu, M., He, X., & Simon, H.D. (2002). Spectral relaxation for k-means clustering. *Proceedings Neural Information Processing Systems, 14*, 1057 – 1064.

Zhang, J. & Foody, G. M. (1998). A fuzzy classification of land cover from remotely sensed imagery. *International Journal of Remote Sensing, 19*(14), 2621-2738.

Zhang, J., & Mani, J. (2003). knn approach to unbalanced data distributions: A case study involving information extraction. *Proceedings of the ICML-2003 Workshop: Learning with Imbalanced Data Sets II*, 42-48.

Zlatoper, T. J. (1991). Determinants of motor vehicles deaths in the Unites States: A cross sectional analysis. *Accident Analysis and Prevention, 23*(5), 431-436.

Zobeck, T. S., Grant, B. F., Stinson, F. S., & Bettolucci, D. (1994). Alcohol involvement in fatal traffic crashes in the United States 1979–90. *Addiction, 89*, 227-231.

About the Contributors

Hsiao-Fan Wang is the Tsing Hua chair professor and the vice dean of the College of Engineering of National Tsing Hua University, Taiwan, Republic of China. She has been teaching at the Department of Industrial Engineering and Engineering Management at the same university, NTHU after she graduated from Cambridge University, UK in 1981. She used to be the head of the department of IEEM, NTHU, President of Chinese Fuzzy Systems Association, Vice President of International Fuzzy Systems Association and Erskine fellow of Canterbury University, NZ. Also, she has been awarded the Distinguished Research Award from National Science Council of Taiwan, ROC; Distinguished Contracted Research Fellow of NSC and Distinguished Teaching Award of Engineering College, NTHU. She used to be the editor-in-chief of the *Journal of Chinese Industrial Engineering Association*; also the *Journal of Chinese Fuzzy Set and Theories* and now is the area editor of several international journals. Her research interests are in multicriteria decision making, fuzzy set theory and operations research.

* * *

Christoph Adl received his MSc degree in computer science from Vienna University of Technology, Austria, in 2004. In his masters thesis, he developed an expert system for diagnosis of toxoplasmosis in pregnant woman using fuzzified automatons. After his graduation he started a six-month placement at BT in Adastral Park where he worked in the area of churn prediction. After the placement, he went back to Austria and started a job as junior researcher at the Austrian Research Centers GmbH - ARC. Currently, he is working on his PhD about machine learning in bioinformatics. His research interests include medical computer science, eHealth, expert systems, machine learning, data mining, and fuzzy set theory.

Michael Bartholomew-Biggs is a reader in computational mathematics at the University of Hertfordshire. Since 1968, he has worked with the Numerical Optimization Centre on the development and application of algorithms for constrained and unconstrained minimization. Many of these applications have been in the aerospace industry, but other recent projects have included route-planning, maintenance scheduling and portfolio selection.

Malcolm J. Beynon is a reader in Cardiff Business Cardiff at Cardiff University (UK). He gained his BSc and PhD in pure mathematics and computational mathematics, respectively, at Cardiff University. His research areas include the theoretical and application of uncertain reasoning methodologies, including Dempster-Shafer theory, fuzzy set theory, and rough set theory. Also the introduction and development of multi-criteria based decision making and classification techniques, including the Classification and Ranking Belief Simplex. He has published over 100 research articles. He is a member of the International Rough Set Society, International Operations Research Society, and the International Multi-Criteria Decision Making Society.

Ivan Bruha was born in Prague, Czechoslovakia. There he received the degree Dipl. Ing. (subject Technical Cybernetics) at Czech Technical University, Prague, Faculty of Electrical Engineering (1969), RNDr. (Theoretical Cybernetics) at Charles University, Faculty of Mathematics and Physics (1974), and PhD (Artificial Intelligence) at Czech Technical University (1973). He had been teaching at Czech Technical University for 12 years. In 1976-77, he visited Edinburgh University, Machine Intelligence Research (chair prof. D. Michie) for one year as a PostDoc. When he was 39, he emigrated with his family to Canada, and since 1986 he has been with McMaster University, Ontario. So far, he has written three monographs and more than 100 papers in peer-reviewed journals and proceedings; also, he has chaired several workshops. He is a member of several editorial and advisory committees of both journals and conferences.

Erica H. Craig is a certified wildlife biologist in Alaska applying interdisciplinary GIS research methods to examining conservation issues affecting golden eagles in the Western United States. She has been studying species at risk and the issues that affect their long-term population stability, such as environmental contamination and habitat alterations, since 1977.

Martin Crane received his BA BAI (mech. eng.) degrees from Trinity College Dublin in 1989 and his PhD from the same institution in 1993. He has worked in a variety of areas of computational science such as CFD, combustion modelling, financial data analysis and, more recently, systems biology. He currently is a senior lecturer at Dublin City University.

Xiaohui Cui is a research staff member at the Oak Ridge National Laboratory. He received a PhD degree in Computer Science and Engineering from University of Louisville in 2004. His research interests include swarm intelligence, intelligent agent design, agent based modeling and simulation, emergent behavior in complex system, information retrieval and knowledge discovering. He is a member of the North American Association for Computational Social and Organizational Sciences. His research works include large volume information stream analysis, collective intelligence of multi-agent systems, swarm based insurgency warfare simulation, adaptive agent cognitive modeling, and malicious insider detection in the cyber system.

Gráinne Kerr received her BA degree in Computer Science (2002) from Trinity College Dublin and in 2004 she received a MSc in Bioinformatics from Dublin City University. At the same institution and in affiliation with the National Institute of Cellular Biotechnology, she currently is researching for a PhD, studying methods of high-level analysis of gene expression data.

Jagadeesh P. Ganjigatti completed his graduation in industrial and production engineering from Basaveshwar Engineering College, Bagalkot, Karnataka University, India, in 1988. He obtained M. Tech. in production engineering and systems technology from Kuvempu University, India, in 1996.

He received his PhD from IIT Kharagpur, India, in 2006. He is working as a professor in Siddaganga Institute of Technology, Tumkur, India. He is working on modeling of manufacturing processes using soft computing.

Francesco Giordano is an associate professor of statistics at the University of Salerno. He has received a degree in economics from the University of Salerno in 1992 and the PhD in Statistics from the University of Bari (Italy) in 1997. He taught computational statistics and probability at the University of Sannio in Benevento (Italy) from 1996 to 2000. He is a member of the Italian Statistical Society. He has been associate professor of statistics at the University of Salerno since 2004. His research activity focuses on non parametric models for time series, artificial neural network models, resampling techniques, and bilinear models for time series. He published his own researches on several Italian and international scientific journals.

Fei-Chen Hsu is an industrial engineer at TSMC, Taiwan after she received her master's degree from the Department of Industrial Engineering and Engineering Management, National Tsing Hua University in 2005. Her research interests are on Fuzzy Set Theory and risk management.

Chun-Jung, Huang received double bachelor's degrees of management and business from National Cheng Kung University, and MBA from National Taiwan University of Science and Technology, Taiwan, R.O.C. Currently he is a PhD candidate in National Tsing Hua University, Taiwan, R.O.C. His research interests include soft computing, applied mathematics, and schizophrenia.

Falk Huettmann is a quantitative wildlife ecologist in Alaska applying interdisciplinary GIS research methods world-wide for progress with sustainability issues of the global village. His latest modeling applications explore and develop public marine, arctic online biodiversity databases, as well as data for Nicaragua and Papua New Guinea. Current address: EWHALE lab- Biology and Wildlife Dept., Institute of Arctic Biology, 419 Irving I, University of Alaska Fairbanks AK 99775-7000 USA. E-mail: fffh@uaf.edu, Phone: (907) 474-7882; Fax : (907) 474-6716.

Yu Jiao is a research staff member at the Oak Ridge National Laboratory. She received a BSc degree in Computer Science from the Civil Aviation Institute of China in 1997. She received her MSc and PhD degrees from The Pennsylvania State University, in 2002 and 2005, respectively, both in computer science. Her main research interests include software agents, pervasive computing, and secure global information system design.

Vladik Kreinovich received his PhD from the Institute of Mathematics, Soviet Academy of Sciences, Novosibirsk. In 1979, he worked on error estimation and intelligent information processing. In 1989, he was a visiting scholar at Stanford University. Since 1990, he has been with the University of Texas at El Paso. Also, he served as an invited professor in Paris, Hong Kong, St. Petersburg, Russia, and Brazil. His main interests are representation and processing of uncertainty, especially interval computations. He has published six books and more than 600 papers and is a member of the editorial board of the journals, *Reliable Computing, International Journal of Approximate Reasoning*, and several others.

Arun Kulkarni is a Professor of computer science at The University of Texas at Tyler. He has more than 60 refereed papers to his credit, and he has authored two books. His awards include the 2005-06 President's Scholarly Achievement award, 2001-2002 Chancellor's Council Outstanding Teaching award, 1999-2000 Alpha Chi Outstanding Faculty Member award, 1997 NASA/ASEE Summer Faculty Fellowship award, and 1984 Fulbright Fellowship award. He has been listed in Who's Who in America. He has successfully completed eight research grants during the past 10 years. Dr. Kulkarni obtained his PhD from the Indian Institute of Technology, Bombay, and was a post-doctoral fellow at Virginia Tech.

Marta Kukier is a PhD student with the Systems Research Institute, Polish Academy of Sciences. She is graduate of the Technical University of Łódz, Technical Physics, Comuter Science and Applied Mathematics Department. Since 2004, she has been with the Polish Academy of Sciences—as an assistant first, and mpw—PhD student. Her main research interests concern representation and processing of imperfect information.

K K Lai is the chair professor of management science at City University of Hong Kong, and he is also the associate dean of the faculty of business. Currently, he is also acting as the dean of college of business administration at Hunan University, China. Prior to his current post, he was a senior operational research analyst at Cathay Pacific Airways and the area manager on marketing information systems at Union Carbide Eastern. Professor Lai received his PhD at Michigan State University, USA. Professor Lai's main research interests include logistics and operations management, computational intelligence and business decision modeling.

C.L. Liu received his advanced degrees from the Massachusetts Institute of Technology. He taught at MIT, the University of Illinois at Urbana Champaign, and the National Tsing Hua University. From 1996 to 1998, he served as associate provost at UIUC. From 1988 to 2002, he was President of National Tsing Hua University (NTHU). Dr. Liu is a member of Academia Sinica, and also, fellow of IEEE and ACM. After his term as President of NTHU, Dr. Liu continues his teaching and research activities. He also serves as consultant to high tech companies, works for a charitable foundation in Hong Kong, and, in the last two years, hosts a weekly radio show on technology and humanities on the radio station IC975 in Hsinchu, Taiwan, ROC.

Dominic Savio Lee is a senior lecturer in the Department of Mathematics and Statistics at the University of Canterbury. His research interests are in computational, Bayesian and nonparametric statistics, with applications in medical research, bioinformatics, signal processing and image processing.

Sara E. McCaslin received the BS in mechanical engineering (2000) and the MS in computer science (2002) from the University of Texas at Tyler, where she now works as an adjunct senior lecturer for the computer science department. She is pursuing a PhD in mechanical engineering at the University of Texas at Arlington with a specialization in solid mechanics, and is actively working on her dissertation involving finite element analysis. Her research interests include artificial intelligence, fuzzy neural networks, and closed-form solutions for finite element applications

Detlef Nauck is a chief research scientist in BT's Intelligent Systems Research Centre where he is leading an international team of researchers in intelligent data analysis. Detlef holds a Master's degree in computer science (1990) and a PhD in computer science (1994) both from the University of Braunschweig. He also holds a Venia Legendi (Habilitation) in computer science from the Otto-von-Guericke University of Magdeburg (2000), where he is a visiting senior lecturer. He has published eight books and more than 110 papers on computational intelligence and related areas. For his industrial projects he has won two medals from the British Computer Society. Between 2002 and 2006 he served as an associate editor of the IEEE Transactions on Systems, Men and Cybernetics - Part B. Detlef's current research interests include the application of computational intelligence, intelligent data analysis and machine learning in different areas of Business Intelligence. His current projects include research in pro-active intelligent data exploration and platforms for real-time business intelligence and predictive analytics in customer relationship management.

Hung T. Nguyen received his BSc degree in Mathematics from the University of Paris XI (1967), MSc degree in Probability from the University of Paris VI (1968), and PhD in mathematics from the University of Lille, France (1975). He worked at the University of California, Berkeley, and at the University of Massachusetts, Amherst. Since 1981, he is with the New Mexico State University. He also held visiting positions with Harvard University, University of Southern California, Tokyo Institute of Technology, and many other institutions. His research interests include mathematical statistics, probability theory (especially foundations of random sets), and fuzzy logic for intelligent systems. He published 20 books and numerous journal articles. He is on the editorial board of several leading international journals.

Robert M. Patton is a research staff member at the Oak Ridge National Laboratory. He received his PhD degree in computer engineering from the University of Central Florida in 2002. His research interests include software agents, intelligent data analysis, and applications of computational intelligence to information fusion, text analysis, sampling, and event detection.

Cira Perna is a full professor of statistics at the University of Salerno. She has received a degree in mathematics from the University of Naples in 1983 and the M. Phil and in statistics from the CSREAM, University of Naples, in 1985. She had faculty positions, as associate professor, at the University of Calabria (1992-1994) and at the University of Salerno (1994-1999). She has been full professor of statistics at the University of Salerno since 2000. She has published over 50 technical papers in scientific journals and books. Her current research focuses on non linear time series analysis, artificial neural network models, resampling techniques. She is a member of the Italian Statistical Society and the IASC. She is also in the board of the ANSET (Italian Time Series Analysis Research Group).

Thomas E. Potok is the Applied Software Engineering Research group leader at the Oak Ridge National Laboratory. He received his PhD degree in computer engineering from North Carolina State University in 1996. He has published 50+ refereed papers, received four U.S. patents, currently serves on the Editorial Board of International Journal of Web Services Research and International Journal of Computational Intelligence Theory and Practice, and also conference organizing or program committees for IEEE Swarm Intelligence Symposium; 4th International Joint Conference on Autonomous Agents and Multiagent Conference; 9th International Conference on Knowledge-Based Intelligent Information & Engineering Systems, etc.

Dilip Kumar Pratihar (BE(Hons.), M. Tech., PhD) received his PhD from IIT Kanpur, India, in the year 2000. Besides several scholarships, he received a University Gold Medal for securing highest marks in the University in 1988, A.M. Das Memorial Medal in 1987, Institution of Engineers' Medal in 2002, and others. He completed his post-doctoral studies in Japan (six months) and Germany (one year) under the Alexander von Humboldt Fellowship Programme. He is working, at present, as an associate professor, in the Department of Mechanical Engineering, IIT Kharagpur, India. His research areas include robotics, soft computing, manufacturing science. He has published about 80 papers in different journals and conference proceedings.

Michele La Rocca graduated in economics cum laude from the University of Naples "Federico II" (Italy). He obtained his master diploma in statistics from the "Centro di Specializzazione e Ricerche di Portici" (Italy) and his PhD in statistics from the University of Bari (Italy). He was a visiting research associate at the Statistical Laboratory of the Department of Pure Mathematics and Mathematical Statistics, University of Cambridge (UK) and visiting fellow at the Institute for Statistics and Econometrics, Humboldt-University of Berlin (Germany) and the Department of Probability and Mathematical Statistics, Charles University, Prague (Czech Republic). He taught advanced courses in statistics in several Master and PhD programmes in statistics and economics. Currently he is full professor of statistics in the faculty of political sciences at the University of Salerno (Italy), where he is also member of the Department of Economics and Statistics and the Statlab. His research activity focuses on neural networks, non-linear time series, resampling, robust, and non-parametric inference. He published his own researches on several Italian and international scientific journals.

Heather J. Ruskin received her BSc degree in physics and MSc in medical statistics from London University (Kings/London School of Hygiene and Tropical Medicine) and her PhD in statistical and computational physics from Trinity College Dublin. She is currently a professor in the School of Computing and associate dean of research in engineering and computing in Dublin City University. Her research interests include computational models for complex systems; spatiotemporal processes and many-body problems in biosystems (cellular/macroscopic) and in socioeconomic systems (traffic and finance).

Dymitr Ruta received a MSc degree in computer science from Silesian Technical University, Poland (1999) and subsequently a PhD in pattern recognition from the University of Paisley, Scotland (2003). Having completed research studentship at the Nottingham Trent University he took up a PhD studentship challenge of developing high performance classifier fusion systems, successfully accomplished in 2003. During this time he held a Lecturer post at the University of Paisley where he was delivering a mixture of mathematical and computing modules to BSc and MSc students. He joined BT in 2004 where he now holds the post of senior research scientist at Intelligence Systems Research Centre. His research interests include data mining, knowledge discovery, supervised and unsupervised learning, information fusion, evolutionary computation, physics of information, probabilistic, and fuzzy reasoning. He published 30 papers, and he is a regular member of program committees for conferences in the areas of artificial intelligence and pattern recognition. He reviews publications for the reputable journals in these domains and actively participates in various research initiatives organized within BCS and NISIS organisations.

Martin Spott works as a principal research scientist in BT's Intelligent Systems Research Centre in the area of intelligent data analysis. Martin received a diploma (MSc) in Mathematics in 1995 from the University of Karlsruhe, Germany. Afterwards, he worked as a research assistant in the Innovative Computing Group of Prof. G. Goos at the University of Karlsruhe, where he finished his PhD in computer science in 2000. He joined BT in 2001 where current research interests include the automation of data analysis, rule-based reasoning, and generally the application of soft computing and machine learning methods to business problems. Applications include real-time business intelligence, risk management, and customer relationship management. He has published numerous papers in the areas of soft computing and machine learning, is a regular reviewer for renowned conferences and journals, and has been awarded two medals by the British Computer Society for his contributions to industrial projects.

Eulalia Szmidt is an associate professor in Systems Research Institute, Polish Academy of Sciences. She has a PhD in automatics control and informatics (from Warsaw University of Technology, Electronics Department), MBA in management and marketing (from University of Illinois at Urbana-Champaign), and D.Sc. in artificial intelligence (from Bulgarian Academy of Sciences). Her main interests concern soft computing, artificial intelligence, representation and processing of imperfect information, fuzzy sets, intuitionistic fuzzy sets, and decision making.

Zbigniew Jozef Ulanowski is a senior research fellow at the University of Hertfordshire. He obtained his PhD in 1988 on the topic "Investigations of Microbial Physiology and Cell Structure Using Laser Diffractometry." His main research interests are: light scattering with special emphasis on single particle characterization and atmospheric particles and micro-manipulation techniques, including both optical and electrodynamic trapping. His Web page is: http://strc.herts.ac.uk/ls.

Shouyang Wang received the PhD degree in operations research from Institute of Systems Science, Chinese Academy of Sciences (CAS), Beijing in 1986. He is currently a Bairen distinguished professor of Management Science at Academy of Mathematics and Systems Sciences of CAS and a Lotus chair professor of Hunan University, Changsha. He is the editor-in-chief or a co-editor of 12 journals. He has published 18 books and over 150 journal papers. His current research interests include financial engineering, e-auctions, knowledge management, and decision analysis.

Gang Xiang was born on February 16, 1979 in Hefei, Anhui Province, China. In June 2001, he received a Bachelor's degree in computer science from Zhejiang University, Hangzhou, Zhejiang Province, China. After graduation, he worked at China Telecom at Shenzhen, Guangdong Province, China. Since 2003, he is a graduate student with the Department of Computer Science, University of Texas at El Paso. He has defended his PhD dissertation in Fall 2007. His main research area is practically useful combinations of interval and probabilistic uncertainty. He published more than 20 papers, most of them in international journals and proceedings of international conferences.

Lean Yu received a PhD in management sciences and engineering from Institute of Systems Science, Academy of Mathematics and Systems Sciences, Chinese Academy of Sciences in 2005. He is currently a research fellow at Department of Management Sciences of City University of Hong Kong. He has published about 20 papers in journals including *IEEE Transactions on Knowledge and Data Engineering*, *Expert Systems with Applications*, *European Journal of Operational Research*, *International Journal of Intelligent Systems*, and *Computers & Operations Research*. His research interests include artificial neural networks, evolutionary computation, decision support systems, and financial forecasting.

Stanislav Zakovic graduated from University of Belgrade in 1991. He obtained his PhD in 1997, from University of Hertfordshire, for a thesis entitled "Global Optimisation Applied to an Inverse Light Scattering Problem." From 1998 to 2006 he worked as a research associate/fellow at Imperial College, London. His main areas of research include worst-case design, min-max algorithms, and its applications. Other interests include global optimization, nonlinear programming, and stochastic optimization. Currently he works at ABN AMRO Bank in Amsterdam, as a credit risk analyst.

Index